Guide to the Aria Repertoire

Indiana Repertoire Guides

Mark Ross Clark

Guide to the Aria Repertoire

Indiana University Press

Bloomington and Indianapolis

This book is a publication of

Indiana University Press
601 North Morton Street
Bloomington, IN 47404-3797 USA

http://iupress.indiana.edu

Telephone orders—800-842-6796
Fax orders—812-855-7931
Orders by e-mail—iuporder@indiana.edu

Library of Congress Cataloging-in-Publication Data

Clark, Mark Ross, date
   Guide to the aria repertoire / Mark Ross Clark.
       p.   cm. — (Indiana repertoire guides)
   Includes index.
   ISBN 978-0-253-34668-1 (cloth : alk. paper) — ISBN 978-0-253-21810-0
(pbk. : alk. paper)
  1. Operas—Excerpts—Bibliographies. I. Title.
   ML128.O4C53 2007
   016.7821'143—dc22

                                                              2006032174

1 2 3 4 5   12 11 10 09 08 07

As you get to know your voice and your body by thorough work and practice; as you study and develop your talents and your strengths; and as you recognize the areas in which you need more work at any given point, then you should consider the repertory listed here that is available to you—and choose carefully the aria(s) which will show your talent and your strengths off to best advantage. In addition, give yourself the challenge of working on those aspects of your auditions and performances that require more attention. But most important of all, use all these criteria intelligently to find yourself a list of arias that you really want to sing—chances are, if you want to sing it, and you do it well, people will want to hear it!

—Warren Jones, pianist and coach

Contents

Part IV. Baritone and Bass Arias

Acknowledgments

I would like to thank my research associates for their tireless efforts helping me compile the aria database that informed this book.

Doctoral students, Indiana University

David Sievers
Todd Wieczorek
Patricia Thompson
Rachel Holland
Jessica Riley

I would also like to thank the following professionals who generously contributed their time and expertise.

Contributors: Singers/vocal professors/conductors/directors

Martina Arroyo	Singer; Voice Professor, Indiana University
Costanza Cuccaro	Singer; Voice Professor, Indiana University
Patricia Wise	Singer; Voice Professor, Indiana University
Virginia Zeani	Singer; Distinguished Vocal Professor, Indiana University
Carol Vaness	Singer; Master Teacher
Sally Wolf	Singer; Voice Professor, Westminster Choir College
Benita Valente	Singer; Master Teacher
Hakån Hagegård	Singer; Master Teacher
Sherrill Milnes	Singer; Voice Professor, Northwestern University
Sandra Bernhard	Director; Professor of Opera, Cincinnati Conservatory of Music
Thor Steingraber	Director
Susanne Mentzer	Singer; Voice Professor, DePaul University
Michael Ehrman	Director; Professor of Opera Studies, Roosevelt University
James McDonald	Singer; Voice Professor, Indiana University
Vivica Genaux	Singer
Regina Resnik	Singer; Director; Master Teacher
Gino Quilico	Singer

George Shirley	Singer; Voice Professor, University of Michigan
Stanford Olsen	Singer; Voice Professor, Florida State University
Henry Price	Singer; Voice Professor and Director of Opera, Pepperdine University
Kevin Langan	Singer; Master Teacher
David Effron	Conductor; Professor of Conducting, Indiana University
William Bolcom	Composer; Professor of Composition, University of Michigan
Mark Adamo	Composer
Bright Sheng	Composer; Professor of Composition, University of Michigan
Kirke Mechem	Composer
Edwin Penhorwood	Composer
Richard Stilwell	Singer; Professor, Roosevelt University
Frederica von Stade	Singer; Master Teacher
Timothy Noble	Singer; Voice Professor, Indiana University
Giorgio Tozzi	Singer; Voice Professor, Indiana University
Kosta Popovich	Vocal coach, Metropolitan Opera
Dale Moore	Singer; Voice Professor, Indiana University
Michael Belnap	Singer, Voice Professor, Indiana University
Jerold Siena	Singer; Voice Professor, University of Illinois
Judith Christin	Singer; Master Teacher

Grateful acknowledgment is made to the following sources for permission to reprint selected aria plot notes and translations:

G. SCHIRMER AMERICAN ARIA ANTHOLOGY: BARITONE/BASS
Copyright © 2004 by G. Schirmer, Inc. (ASCAP)
International Copyright Secured. All Rights Reserved.
Reprinted by Permission.

G. SCHIRMER AMERICAN ARIA ANTHOLOGY: MEZZO-SOPRANO
Copyright © 1991 by G. Schirmer, Inc. (ASCAP)
International Copyright Secured. All Rights Reserved.
Reprinted by Permission.

G. SCHIRMER AMERICAN ARIA ANTHOLOGY: SOPRANO
Copyright © 1991 by G. Schirmer, Inc. (ASCAP)
International Copyright Secured. All Rights Reserved.
Reprinted by Permission.

Guide to the Aria Repertoire

Introduction

In recent years, the opera aria has become central to most classical vocal study. Not only does the aria allow the singer to celebrate and showcase the beauty of his or her instrument, but the aria is also a crucial part of a larger story. It is the synthesis of the composer and librettist's intent for a character—a highly charged dramatic or comic moment that can only be expressed musically. Although some arias are reflections, they are rarely muted contemplations. Instead, they deal with inner and outer conflict, obstacles of every kind, and deep-seated, passionate desires. And while the voice is of greatest importance in this musical expression, one must also examine what drives and inspires the character to sing. The goal should ultimately be that the singer understands the character and the music so thoroughly that the performance becomes real, honest, and interesting.

This book brings together different resources for performers to start their journey toward more powerful performances. First, we need to know what is available. Too often we take a scattershot approach to choosing arias—relying on well-known pieces that might not be right for us at the time, available material from anthologies, and pieces we have heard other people sing. Rarely do we take a systematic approach to aria selection.

Second, we need to know if an aria is right for us vocally. What is the range? What is the tessitura? Does it lie in the best part of our voice? Are the music and text interesting enough for extended study and performance? Although the arias in this resource book are categorized by *fach* and voice type, singers should not feel restricted to only one area of classification.

Third, we need to acquaint ourselves with the character and the operatic scene: is the character and his or her situation interesting and/or sympathetic? When an opera is set in another time, place, and/or culture, it is often difficult for us to empathize with a character. The more tools we have to help study a character and his or her times, the closer we come to understanding the intent and purpose of an aria.

How the Book Is Organized

The purpose of this book is to assist singers in identifying, choosing, and understanding arias for study and performance. Each entry presents a profile of a different aria. At the top of each entry is an overview of the basic aria information: range, composer, librettist, historical style, duration, range, and tessitura. Notes that describe the setting, the character, the aria's context in the opera, and the vocal demands of the aria follow the overview. When appropriate, a literal translation and/or notes from professionals in the field of opera are also included.

Some of the arias are well known, while others are lesser known but still worthy of study. Some are contemporary pieces, and some come from early opera. To help you in your search, the arias are indexed in several different ways: by aria title, by opera, by language, and by historical period. The entries are organized first by voice (i.e., soprano, mezzo-soprano, tenor, baritone and bass) and then by vocal fach (e.g., lyric coloratura, soubrette, lyric). It is important to recognize that assigning vocal *fach* to an aria or role is very subjective, and hotly debated. Don't limit yourself to the arias within one section—read entries that surround your chosen section and refer to the indexes. You will notice that several arias appear in more than one category.

The over four hundred arias listed in this book are by no means comprehensive; I have tried to provide a variety of styles for all voice types and dramatic weights. Although some would seem to be too challenging for the young singer, a number of the pieces are arias for future study and performance.

How to Use the Book

You can use the book in several ways. Singers can browse through the entries relating to their voice to identify arias for audition and competition packages. Teachers can use the book as a resource to help young singers choose repertoire for study (e.g., lessons, recitals, opera workshop classes).

The entries can also provide a basis of study for each aria—a place to begin the work. Once an aria is identified, the singer or teacher can easily locate the music (e.g., the piano/vocal score reference at the bottom of each entry) and use the notes as a reference as he or she examines the score for the first time.

As the singer goes on to learn the music and text and investigate the character through the libretto more completely, I encourage him or her to revisit the entry for greater insight. The description of the setting and the references to other characters in the scene can be used for blocking and focal points (focus shifts). The vocal analysis can inform the interpretation of musical phrases and highlight dynamic markings.

Conclusion

As you read through the entries, keep an open mind. Artistic Directors, who hear thousands of auditions each year for their young artist programs, often feel that a good audition package includes well-known pieces as well as obscure arias that the young singer has studied and sings well. Rather than limiting oneself to five or six steady pieces, the young artist will want to have at least 10–12 arias that they have studied intensely and can mix and match according to whom they are singing for.

Young voices in training are changing constantly. What is too heavy for a singer to sing at one point will be perfectly suited at a different time. In addition, the repertoire may be comfortable for the singer, but judges at competitions and Artistic Directors of young artist programs may deem the material unsuitable for the young singer at that particular time. Consider whether the aria reflects the vocal demands of the entire role. The teenage Marguerite in Gounod's *Faust* sings the "Jewel Song" lyrically and youthfully, but she must also to be able to sing above a heavy orchestra with Faust and Mephistopheles in the climactic final trio.

Don't be restricted by a vocal category. In many opera houses, creative casting is more the rule than the exception, especially in the Mozart roles, which were composed before many of the vocal delineations we now use. Thus, the casting of Dorabella in *Così fan tutte* can be with a dramatic mezzo-soprano or a full lyric soprano. The title role of Don Giovanni can be cast with a lyric baritone or a bass voice. We have mezzo-sopranos like Cecilia Bartoli singing Zerlina in *Don Giovanni* and Despina in *Così fan tutte*. These are two roles that are commonly cast with a soubrette soprano.

Next, identify the setting and purpose of the performance—is this an audition for a small opera house or a competition in a large hall? Finally, try to have variety without sacrificing your vocal identity. If your choices are extremely disparate in a *fach* ("Vissi d'arte" from *Tosca* and "Vedrai carino" from *Don Giovanni*), artistic directors building a young artist roster may be unable to adequately categorize you.

One point made by Artistic Directors regarding the choice of opera arias is extremely consistent—they want singers to choose pieces that the young singer can sing well now, not at some time in the unforeseeable future. The vocal technique has to be at the point that all of the coloratura is in place and all of the low and high notes are freely produced. Observing all of the markings in the score is a good place to start so that the performance is musical. Notice that I use the word "performance" rather than "audition." There needs to be an understanding of the character and situation that results in a powerful performance in which the singer has something to say. If the performer has chosen a longer aria, make sure that every moment of the aria is understood.

Each aria entry in this book is just a place to start—a stepping-off place toward greater understanding. As you read and reread sections of this book, ask yourself questions: What is the purpose of this aria? Exactly where does this aria fit into the scene and opera as a whole? Will there be a decision made in the aria? When is the decision made? What has the character learned within this aria? What is the musical and dramatic shape of the aria? What are the contrasts that give the aria interest? How is the *da capo,* or repeat of the first section, different the second time? If more than one verse is sung, how are the subsequent strophes different?

Keep in mind that there are not necessarily right or wrong answers to these questions, but it is important for the singing actor to continue to question the purpose and intent of an aria at all times. It is not about second-guessing oneself; it is about keeping the energy alive. The important thing is that the aria you choose should be sung well. The entire aria, with all of its coloratura and range demands, should be sung with beauty and technical control, while displaying no tension or vocal strain. The text should be enunciated and pronounced clearly and correctly, with the understanding of the text inspiring the production of the diction. The characterization should be thoughtful and clear, and the setting should be present in the performance. You should have something to say—and say it well.

Part I

Soprano Arias

No. 1

Voice: soprano
Aria Title: "Saper vorreste," Canzone (Oscar)
Opera Title: *Un ballo in maschera*
Composer: Giuseppe Verdi (1813–1901)
Historical Style: Italian Romantic (1859)
Range: D4 to B6

Fach: lyric coloratura
Librettist: Antonio Somma (1809–1864),
after Eugène Scribe's libretto *Gustave III* or
Le bal masqué (1833)
Aria Duration: 1:45
Tessitura: G4 to G5

Position: Act III, scene 3

Setting: A ballroom. Groups of guests have been promenading. Some are masked; others are in normal gala dress and unmasked. The guests are gaily trying to guess the identity of the masked dancers.

Riccardo is the Governor of Boston (although in the version set in Sweden he is the King). Sam and Tom are a part of an anti-Riccardo faction, and are joined in their assassination plans by Renato, Riccardo's secretary. Riccardo has fallen in love with Amelia, wife of Renato. Oscar, the romantic young male page of Governor Riccardo, recognizes Renato, and in turn Oscar is subsequently unmasked. Renato tricks Oscar into revealing that the Governor is present at the party, but Oscar will not tell Renato how he is disguised.

In the aria Oscar sings jokingly that Renato would of course like to know what Riccardo is wearing, but that's why he wants to be concealed. The first melody is legato, with clearly marked accents to show Oscar's self-confidence in his knowledge: "Oscar knows, but he won't tell," which is followed in the poco più mosso section by seven measures of "tra la la" in which he gleefully taunts Renato because while Oscar knows where the Governor is, Renato does not. Once again, there are seven measures of "tra-la" taunting up to a high B, the end of verse 1.

In the second verse young Oscar says, "Though full of love, my bounding heart is able to keep a secret. Not rank or beauty will ever steal it," followed once again by teasing "Tra-la-la" sections (poco più mosso) to the conclusion of the aria.

Piano/vocal score: p. 268 (Kalmus)

No. 2

Voice: soprano
Aria Title: "Volta la terrea," Ballata (Oscar)
Opera Title: *Un ballo in maschera*
Composer: Giuseppe Verdi (1813–1901)
Historical Style: Italian Romantic (1859)
Range: D4 to D6

Fach: lyric coloratura
Librettist: Antonio Somma (1809–1864), after Eugène Scribe's libretto *Gustave III* or *Le bal masqué* (1833)
Aria Duration: 1:45
Tessitura: F4 to G5

Position: Act I, scene 1

Setting: A hall in the Governor's house, Boston, late 17th century

Riccardo (the Governor of Boston, or King of Sweden in the version set in Sweden) has been given a judicial paper to sign that will exile the sorceress Ulrica for the charge of practicing witchcraft. Oscar, the young idealistic page to the Governor, speaks up in defense of the fortune teller. "She is a great fortune teller," Oscar tells the judge. Riccardo asks Oscar to elaborate.

"I wish to defend her," Oscar starts his aria (allegretto). He shows his youthful ardor, confidence, and flamboyance in the rhythms, accents, and intervallic leaps of the melodic line (F♯ octave leap in the melody). Dynamics and articulations, including grace notes, are very clearly marked in the score. He says that Ulrica's eyes sparkle when she foretells the happy or sad ending of her petitioners' loves. "What a protector!" Riccardo jokingly exclaims. "Whoever touches her bewitched skirt will learn from her his fortune to ease his doubting heart. With Lucifer she is always in agreement," Oscar sings, sarcastically. Because he is under the protection of the Governor, Oscar is able to joke with the magistrates and make fun of their accusations.

Piano/vocal score: p. 28 (Kalmus)

No. 3

Voice: soprano
Aria Title: "Eccomi in lieta vesta . . . Oh! Quante volte, Oh! Quante" (Giulietta)
Opera Title: *I Capuleti e i Montecchi*
Composer: Vincenzo Bellini (1801–1835)
Historical Style: Bel canto (1830)
Range: D4 to C6

Fach: lyric coloratura
Librettist: Felice Romani (1788–1865), after Matteo Bandello's 16th-century novella *Giulietta e Romeo* and Luigi Sceola's play of the same name (1818)
Aria Duration: 9:10
Tessitura: G4 to F5

Position: Act I

Setting: Giulietta's balcony in the Capulet palace, Verona, Italy, 15th century

Giulietta, daughter of Capellio, sadly prepares for her prearranged marriage to Tebaldo. However, she is in love with Romeo and waits with ardor for him to come. She wonders why he has not yet arrived. She wishes to see his silhouette in the light of the day and hear his sigh that reminds her of the breeze. For the unaccompanied recitative, take care to observe the diction, inflection, and marked accents:

Here I am, in joyous garments . . . here I am, adorned like a victim at the altar.
Oh, if I only could fall victim at the foot of the altar!
Oh, wedding torches so abhorrent to me, so inevitable,
May you be my funeral lamp.
I am burning up. A flame, a fire, all consumes me. (*She goes to the open window*)
A soothing coolness of the winds I ask in vain. Where are you, Romeo?
In what land are you wandering? Where shall I send you my sighs?

The aria is marked andante sostenuto in 4/4 meter:

Oh, how often have I wept to heaven for you!
With what ardor I await you and deceive my desire!
A ray of your countenance seems to me the light of day.
Ah! The air that wafts around me seems to me one of your sighs.

The language and vocal line are very important (observe the double-dotted rhythms). The coloratura comes from Giulietta's emotional intentions; it is not designed only to show off the singer's vocal technique. The high C is embedded in a 16th-note decorative passage, and it needs to be sung freely within the phrase.

(Translation by Nico Castel)

Piano/vocal score: Vol. 2, p. 108 (*G. Schirmer Opera Anthology: Arias for Soprano*)

No. 4

Voice: soprano
Aria Title: "Les oiseaux dans la charmille," No. 12, Couplets (Olympia)
Opera Title: *Les contes d'Hoffmann*
Composer: Jacques Offenbach (1819–1880)
Historical Style: French Romantic (1881)
Range: D♯4/E♭4 to D♯/E♭6

Fach: lyric coloratura
Librettists: Jules Barbier (1825–1901) and Michel Carré (1822–1872), based on their play (1851), based on tales by E. T. A. Hoffmann
Aria Duration: 4:41
Tessitura: G♯/A♭4 to A♯/B♭6

Position: Act I

Setting: The elegant parlor of Spalanzani the scientist, 19th century; candles illuminate the scene

Hoffmann is in love with a woman he thinks is the daughter of an inventor, Spalanzani. The inventor is afraid that Coppelius, who also specializes in gadgets (particularly eyes), will want a share of the profits from his latest invention, and offers to buy him out. The inventor introduces Olympia, the singing doll, to the public. Spalanzani winds Olympia up to sing for his guests. Spalanzani accompanies her on the harp with light arpeggiated figures. The aria is marked moderato and should not be too fast. The soprano must have the technical ability to sing rapid passages cleanly and detached, then sing roulades of connected 16th notes. The dynamics, too, alternate between a pattern sung forte, then piano. Although the aria does not call for any sustained tone above high G (except when the doll is winding down both verses on B♭), the voice touches frequently on tones above the staff, including a high G above high C (16th note).

The first verse talks of the birds, the star of daylight in the sky. Everything speaks to a young girl of love. Recommended are quick movements of the head and eye focus, the arms saying (but not constant movement), "This is a doll" without distractingly repeated gestures. Sustaining each "pose" is good. When the doll "runs down" it is traditional for the singer to sag and bend forward to be winded up in short movements by Spalanzani (this can be mimed). Right before running down, the "ah" in the coloratura is marked molto animato the second time.

The second verse can have some steps to intimate that Olympia is going a little out of control with her excited verse. "Everything that sings and sounds and sighs moves the heart, which trembles with love!" The doll is increasingly more animated in verse 2.

Piano/vocal score: p. 110 (G. Schirmer)

> Notes by singer and voice professor Patricia Wise: The trick to this aria is to keep the mechanical effect of the doll without tensing the upper body or neck, which could be detrimental to the clarity and accuracy of the staccato. When preparing for performance, the singer should improvise movements of all kinds, trying to find her own essence of a mechanical toy. This will make the rehearsals less stressful and will endear the singer to the director, who may have set ideas about how he wants the doll to move.

No. 5

Voice: soprano
Aria Title: "Quel guardo il cavaliere . . . So anch'io la virtù magica," No. 5, Cavatina (Norina)
Opera Title: *Don Pasquale*
Composer: Gaetano Donizetti (1797–1848)
Historical Style: Bel canto (1843)
Range: D4 to D♭6

Fach: lyric coloratura
Librettists: Giovanni Ruffini (1807–1881) and the composer, after Angelo Anelli's libretto for Stefano Pavesi's *Ser Marc' Antonio* (1810)
Aria Duration: 6:10
Tessitura: F4 to A6

Position: Act I, scene 2

Setting: Norina's house, Rome, early 19th century

Although Norina is a young woman, she has already been widowed—most likely by a husband who was much older and had money. Because she has been widowed she has social "permission" to act personally bolder than a young unmarried woman. This aria is the audience's introduction to Norina, and first glance tells us that she is like other young women: she is reading a romance novel, and it appears as if she is fully committed to the notion of the lovestruck knight "Riccardo." These lines are long, languid, with "frilly" decorative 16th- and 32nd-note figures. The lines do not reach above the staff, except for a passing high G ("non volgeria il pensier/he would not think of any other woman"). We are taken aback at the end of this section by Norina's sudden cynical laughter at the behavior of the knight. The allegretto begins with the orchestral introduction, which is light, bright, and coy.

Many of the lines begin with "I" and reveal this character's confidence—and playfulness. She shows her control in the way she handles the rubato and sudden changes in dynamics. The text is set syllabically to the vocal line. As she sings "I know the thousand means that love's frauds use," after repeating "conosco/I know" three times, her voice soars to a high B, then down to the bottom of the staff, and then again up to high C. She knows "the charms and arts used to seduce a heart."

The next section goes on to say how she also has other personality quirks: she has an odd mind, ready wit. She rarely remains calm if she gets angry. She repeats: "I have an odd mind, but an excellent heart." This section, with its multitude of syllables and fast rhythm, is like a patter song for soprano, but then added is a sustained, playful trilled F at the top of the staff sustained for seven measures to the next phrase, which then repeats the section from before ("So anch'io come si bruciano/I also know how hearts burn"). At the poco più marking Norina repeats "Ho testa bizzara/I have an odd mind." With "mi piace scherzar /I like to play" Norina sings the exclamation "Ah!" again in rapid 16th-note coloratura for six measures up to high C♭ with a flourish, ending with the repetition of the text "mi piace scherzar."

Piano/vocal score: p. 44 (Ricordi)

Notes by singer and voice professor Costanza Cuccaro: Norina is feisty, but never mean. She has a sense of humor and enjoys the fun of intrigue. She is quick of mind, wise, and very knowing. Norina has inner strength and determination. It is a mistake to play her tough and hard; Norina's happiness and joy of life should be apparent. The aria requires brilliance of voice, command of coloratura and articulation, dynamic variety, a wide range, and warmth and legato in the cavatina. Special care must be taken that the acciaccaturas are clearly delineated. An excellent resource for style and interpretation of the aria is provided in Ricci's *Variazioni-Cadenze Tradizioni,* Vol. I (*Voci Femminili*).

No. 6

Voice: soprano
Aria Title: "Chacun le sait," No. 3 (Marie)
Opera Title: *La fille du régiment*
Composer: Gaetano Donizetti (1797–1848)
Historical Style: Bel canto (1840)
Range: F4 to C6

Fach: lyric coloratura
Librettists: Jean François Bayard (1796–1853) and Jules-Henri Vernoy de Saint-Georges (1799–1875)
Aria Duration: 2:21
Tessitura: G4 to F5

Position: Act I

Setting: An army campsite in a valley in the Swiss Tyrolese Mountains, 1815

Marie was found as an infant on the battlefield and was raised by the regiment as their "daughter." Now grown up and beautiful, she has tumbled into the stalwart arms of Tonio, and he has fallen in love (she was picking flowers near a precipice and slipped and fell). Sulpice (the Sergeant) reminds her that she may marry only a member of the regiment. Tonio is found nearby and is captured as a spy. Marie tells the troops that he has saved her life, and he is released into Marie's care as her "prisoner."

The grenadiers from the 21st French Regiment call on Marie to sing the invigorating song of the regiment. This infectious tune with its dance rhythm comes right on the heels of her story of Tonio's saving her, and the soldiers toasting France. Marie has sung this song to the soldiers many times before, and they have encouraged her to sing it again for them. The men repeat the chorus. In this aria she describes the regiment: "the handsome twenty-first . . . everyone gives credit to them . . . It has won so many battles . . . It's feared by one sex and loved by the other."

Rhythms, articulations, and all accents are important as well as diction in the playful delivery of this aria. The range only extends to G and A above the staff, and the coloratura is limited to the cadential sections.

Piano/vocal score: p. 53 (Kalmus)

No. 7

Voice: soprano
Aria Title: "Piangerò la sorte mia" (Cleopatra)
Opera Title: *Giulio Cesare*
Composer: George Frideric Handel (1685–1759)
Historical Style: Italian Baroque (1724)
Range: E4 to A6

Fach: lyric coloratura
Librettist: Nicola Francesco Haym (1678–1729), after Giacomo Francesco Bussani's *Giulio Cesare in Egitto* set by Sartorio (1676) and a 1685 setting of the same libretto
Aria Duration: 7:19
Tessitura: G4 to G5

Position: Act III, scene 1

Setting: The woods near Alexandria, Egypt, 48 B.C.

Cleopatra's brother Tolomeo (Ptolemy) has ordered Cleopatra to prison for scheming with the now-apparently drowned Cesare (Caesar). Saddened by the turn of events, Cleopatra contemplates in the preceding recitative and aria the turn of events that fate has granted her. She talks about the loss of Cesare and the suffering of Sesto and Cornelia at the hands of her brother. The idea that when she is dead, she could come back and haunt her brother sustains her.

The beginning section is slower and sustained in 3/8 meter as she sings, "Piangerò la sorte mia/I will lament my fate, so cruel and brutal, as long as I have life in my body." The accompaniment is simple. In the intervals between vocal phrases a simple instrumental "echo" of the voice evokes the plaintive quality of Cleopatra. Some of the unstressed notes need a light attack at high F♯ and A above the staff, and there is a high A that is within an 8th-note phrase and should not "jump out" of the vocal line.

She concludes, "But later dead, when I am made a ghost, from all around I will haunt the tyrant night and day." This section is marked allegro and calls for coloratura with leaps to high A. The dotted rhythms need to be very clear and specific within the coloratura to demonstrate Cleopatra's strong personality and desires.

Piano/vocal score: p. 207 (Bärenreiter)

> Notes by conductor and conducting professor David Effron:
> "Piangerò" is a long aria and must be kept interesting throughout. It does show much in the voice and has the possibility of "holding the audience in your grasp" through vocal colors, ideas, and embellishments during the recapitulation. The coloratura must be planned and written for the young singer singing it, not just a repetition of what Beverly Sills sang on the recording, for instance.

No. 8

Voice: soprano
Aria Title: "V'adoro, pupille" (Cleopatra)
Opera Title: *Giulio Cesare*
Composer: George Frideric Handel (1685–1759)
Historical Style: Italian Baroque (1724)
Range: F4 to G5

Fach: lyric coloratura
Librettist: Nicola Francesco Haym, after Giacomo Francesco Bussani's *Giulio Cesare in Egitto* set by Sartorio (1676) and a 1685 setting of the same libretto
Aria Duration: 5:40
Tessitura: G4 to F5

Position: Act II, scene 1

Setting: Palace of the Goddess of Virtue, Alexandria, Egypt, 48 B.C.

Cleopatra (in disguise) has arranged an elaborate set piece for the seduction of Cesare (Caesar). He is promised a meeting with "Lidia," who will introduce him to Cleopatra. Marked largo, the beautiful melody features an intervallic leap from the middle A to high F♯. The vocal line needs to be even to the top, with strong rhythmic values, again emphasizing Cleopatra's strength of personality and desires.

> I adore you, eyes, arrows of love.
> By your sparks I am pierced in the heart.
> Pity from you begs my sad heart, that every hour calls you its dearly beloved.

This is a beautiful melody that can leave a haunting impression in an audition.

Piano/vocal score: p. 113 (Bärenreiter)

No. 9

Voice: soprano
Aria Title: "Sombre forêt," No. 9, Recitative and Romance (Mathilde)
Opera Title: *Guillaume Tell*
Composer: Gioacchino Rossini (1792–1868)
Historical Style: French Romantic (1819)
Range: D4 to A♭6

Fach: lyric coloratura (dramatic)
Librettists: Etienne de Jouy (1764–1846) and Hippolyte Louis-Florent Bis (1789–1855), after Johann Christoph Friedrich von Schiller's play *Wilhelm Tell* (1804)
Aria Duration: 8:00
Tessitura: E♭4 to F5

Position: Act II

Setting: A deep valley in Switzerland during the 13th century. In the distance, the village of Brunnen nestles at the foot of the towering mountains behind the Rütli plateau. The shore of Lake Lucerne is to one side; night is falling.

Managing to separate herself from the hunting party of which she is a part, Mathilde, an Austrian Princess of the House of Hapsburg, knows that her beloved Arnold follows her and will arrive soon. She trembles in anticipation of seeing the man to whom she has given her heart. She decides that she prefers the lonely forest to the pleasures of the palace because it is the only place that she can reveal her secret longings and desires. The recitative is largely unaccompanied, with orchestral intervals between phrases:

They are going, at last; I had hoped to see him among them; my heart hasn't deceived my eyes. He has followed my steps; he is near here. I tremble . . . if he were to appear! What is this feeling—profound, mysterious—for which I nourish this ardor that I cherish . . . perhaps? Arnold! Is it really you, simple dweller of these meadowlands, the hope, the pride of these mountains, who charms my thoughts and causes my fear. Ah, if I could at least admit it to myself! Arnold, it is you that I love; you did save my life, and my excuse for loving you is my gratitude for what you did.

The aria is rhythmically and melodically complex—the quarter-note value on beat 1 followed by 16th-note triplets and the many accidentals convey a sense of urgency and agitation. There is a challenging interval from F in the lower register to high A♭, sustained. At the end of both sections there are suggested decorative cadenzas. The second one rises to a sustained high B♭.

Shadowy forest, desert sad and savage, I prefer you to the splendors
of palaces.
It is in the mountains, in this region of storms,
That my heart is able to be born again and feels a sense of peace.
But the echo alone will learn of my secrets.
You are the gentle and shy moon of shepherds
That illuminates my path with your gentle light.
Ah! Also be my star and my guide!
Like the moon, your rays are discreet and the echo alone will tell my
secrets.

Piano/vocal score: p. 176 (Kalmus)

No. 10

Voice: soprano
Aria Title: "Où va la jeune Hindoue," Bell Song (Lakmé)
Opera Title: *Lakmé*
Composer: Léo Delibes (1836–1891)
Historical Style: French Romantic (1883)
Range: E4 to E6

Fach: lyric coloratura
Librettists: Edmond Gondinet (1829–?) and Philippe Gille (1831–1901)
Aria Duration: 7:50
Tessitura: B5 to B6

Position: Act II

Setting: A public square in a town in India, 19th century

The plot focuses on the fanatical hatred of the Brahmin priests in 19th-century India for the English invaders, who forbid them to practice their religion. Ordered by her father (the Brahmin priest), Lakmé sings the "Bell Song" so that the English intruder Gérard will be drawn to her and identify himself to her father, who has plans to eliminate the intruder. In "the Bell Song" Lakmé sings the legend of the pariah's daughter.

The aria is filled with decorative figures. The vocal line is descriptive of the text, as Lakmé sings about the light of the moonlight flickering on the trees (staccato 8th-note triplets up to high B). The first section ends with "E riant à la nuit/She smiles (*laughs*) at the night," ascending to a sustained high B. In the allegro moderato section, Lakmé tells of the lost traveler who "wanders bewildered. The wild beasts roar with pleasure, and go to pounce on their prey." The young girl saves him with a wand of magic bells (più animato). This section is filled with coloratura passages in describing the sound of the magic bells, mostly staccato, touching the B at the top, then sustaining high B at the end of the "bell" section.

Her story continues (a tempo), as the stranger, dazzled, looks at the young girl. He owes his life to her. He lulls her to sleep in a dream and transports her to heaven. "Your place is there. It was Vishnu, son of Brahma," explains Lakmé. After noting that sometimes the traveler may hear the faint sound of the magic wand, Lakmé repeats the bell-like refrain. This phrase is exotically drawn with triplets and enharmonic tones.

Piano/vocal score: p. 157 (International)

Notes by singer and voice professor Patricia Wise: To keep this aria from seeming like some boring and repetitive verses punctuated with squeaky dotted notes, the soprano needs to relate to the story she is telling with 100 percent commitment. That is, she must seem to truly tell the story. Experiment with tempo, rubato, and dynamics. Exaggerate the text, as if you are catching the attention of a group of very young children. The staccati should be sung as if they were on a line. This has the effect of bringing out the chord structure, and it makes the coloratura easier to sing.

No. 11

Voice: soprano
Aria Title: "Je suis Titania," No. 12, Polonaise (Philine)
Opera Title: *Mignon*
Composer: Ambroise Thomas (1811–1896)
Historical Style: French Romantic (1866)
Range: C4 to E♭6

Fach: lyric coloratura
Librettists: Michel Carré (1822–1872) and Jules Barbier (1825–1901), after Johann Wolfgang von Goethe's novel *Wilhelm Meisters Lehrjahre* (1796)
Aria Duration: 6:00
Tessitura: G♭4 to A6

Position: Act II, scene 2

Setting: A park in a German castle, late 1700s

Philine, a beautiful member of a troupe of actors, has finished her show, *A Midsummer Night's Dream,* and declares that she loves playing Titania, the fairy queen. The theatrical performance has just ended. Philine is still wearing her stage costume. She is elated by her success. She sings the brilliant polonaise "Je suis Titania/I am Titania" as the actors come out into the park. Her audience is the Prince, the Baron and Baroness, the other comedians, Frédéric, Ladies and Gentlemen, and servants bearing torches.

The many coloratura figures in the aria (sung on "Ah!") reflect the bravura, cleverness, youth, and vitality of Philine. The articulation markings leave an impression of her vivaciousness and flirtatiousness. The double-dotted rhythms augment her energy. The aria can showcase a singer's ability to sing the embellishments fluidly, and the staccato markings in a number of phrases call for articulated clarity of French diction. The trill on a sustained high A to B exemplifies the brilliance of the character. All in all this is a sparkling showpiece.

Piano/vocal score: p. 245 (G. Schirmer)

No. 12

Voice: soprano
Aria Title: "Nel sen mi palpita," No. 4 (Aspasia)
Opera Title: *Mitridate, re di Ponto*
Composer: Wolfgang Amadeus Mozart (1756–1791)
Historical Style: Classical (1770)
Range: D4 to A♭5

Fach: lyric coloratura
Librettist: Vittorio Amedeo Cigna-Santi (c. 1730–after 1795)
Aria Duration: 2:12
Tessitura: G4 to G5

Position: Act I

Setting: The temple of Venus in the land of Pontus, a Hellenic kingdom on the southern shores of the Black Sea. The opera is set in the port of Nymphaea in the Crimea and takes place after Mitridate's final defeat by the Roman general Pompey in 66 B.C.

While on campaign, Mitridate has left his young betrothed, the Greek princess Aspasia, in the care of his two sons, Sifare and Farnace. Aspasia repels Farnace's offer to make her his Queen, and when he threatens force, Sifare steps between them. A quarrel between the brothers is averted by Arbate's announcement that Mitridate is alive and about to arrive in the city. Aspasia finds herself torn between her duty toward Mitridate and her love for Sifare. She sings, allegro agitato, underscored by a constant 8th-note pulse in orchestra:

In my breast my heart throbs sadly; my grief calls me to weep;
I cannot resist. I cannot remain.
But my eyes are wet with tears.

Believe me, it is only your peril which is the cruel reason for my suffering.

(*She leaves, escorted by the priests*)

This piece has extremes in vocal range, exploring the bottom of the staff above middle C, and then skipping up to high G at the top of the staff. Finally, toward the end of the aria she touches on the high A♭ (dotted half note). Tied 8th notes with rests in between can convey a breathless quality or heartfelt emotion.

Piano/vocal score: p. 62 (Bärenreiter)

No. 13

Voice: soprano
Aria Title: "Qui la voce . . . Vien, diletto" (Elvira)
Opera Title: *I puritani*
Composer: Vincenzo Bellini (1801–1835)
Historical Style: Bel canto (1835)
Range: E♭4–D♭6

Fach: lyric coloratura
Librettist: Count Carlo Pepoli (1796–1881), after Jacques-Arsène Ancelot and Joseph-Xavier Boniface's play *Têtes Rondes et Cavaliers* (1833)
Aria Duration: 5:03
Tessitura: A♭4–A♭5

Position: Part II (The Fortress)

Setting: A hall in the castle near Plymouth, England, during the English Civil War (1649). The hall has an outlook over the English camp.

Elvira is the daughter of the Puritan Governor-General Sir Gualtiero Valton. Elvira loves Arturo, a Cavalier, though her father wants her to marry someone else. Earlier in the opera, Elvira has demonstrated characteristics of a darkened (slightly unstable) mind. Before the aria in Act II, Giorgio (Elvira's good-hearted uncle) describes Elvira's ravings. Riccardo (Colonel in the Puritan army who loves Elvira) brings news that Parliament has condemned Arturo to the scaffold. The mad Elvira enters, still dreaming of her lost love.

In the aria "Vien, diletto," the almost delirious Elvira (con abbandono) wants her beloved to come: "The moon is in the sky. Everything is quiet around us; until day breaks in the sky, come and alight upon my heart! Hurry, Arturo!" In a rapidly ascending scalelike passage, Elvira sings to a sustained high A♭. The orchestra is marked pianissimo, sotto voce, with carefully marked accents and fermatas. The cascading 16th-note descending scales start at the top of the staff (F, G, A♭, B♭, and finally high D♭). At the end of the verse is sung a chilling descent from a high B♭ in chromatic descent by half steps on 32nd notes. Elvira will sing the piece twice, with added embellishments the second time.

In the context of the opera, Elvira will sing the last section with both Giorgio and Riccardo (in the bass clef) singing about her true heart, with Elvira singing up to a sustained high C, B♭, and A♭. In the last section there are measures of descending chromatically 32nd-note passages, accents, intervallic leaps, and contrasting staccato/legato articulation.

(Translation by Nico Castel)

Piano/vocal score: p. 195 (Ruder)

> Notes by singer and voice professor Virginia Zeani: Although Bellini is Italian, there is a plaintive quality in his melodies that is sad. It may be shown mostly in the abundant chromaticism used by the composer. The character is languishing in long plaintive legato lines. "Dolorosa" is Elvira's quality of sadness that comes to mind. Elvira is mad and "sees him" and "hears his voice."

No. 14

Voice: soprano
Aria Title: "Je veux vivre dans ce rêve,"
No. 3, Arietta (Juliette)
Opera Title: *Roméo et Juliette*
Composer: Charles-François Gounod (1818–1893)
Historical Style: French Romantic (1867)
Range: C4 to D6

Fach: lyric coloratura
Librettists: Jules Barbier (1825–1901) and Michel Carré (1822–1872), based on the tragedy by William Shakespeare (1596)
Aria Duration: 4:00
Tessitura: E4 to A6

Position: Act I

Setting: The Capulets' ballroom, Verona, Italy, 14th century; it is the Capulets' ball

Tybalt and Paris are introduced (Paris would like to be Juliette's intended), and Capulet introduces his daughter, Juliette. When Gertrude, the nurse, speaks of marriage to her, Juliette sings that she would like to live inside "this intoxicating dream" where it is "eternally spring." When she sings "Ah!" with her accompanying coloratura, it is a reflection of her youthful energy and her desire to feel free when others would arrange her life and love for her. As she sings, "Je veux vivre/I want to live," it is sung piano, almost breathless in its excitement, as the two quarter notes are separated. When she sings "dans mon âme comme un trésor!/in my soul like a treasure" she soars to a high A with crescendo, followed by a diminuendo back to a repetition of the beginning phrase of music and text. "This day still, sweet flame I keep you in my soul like a treasure!" Double-dotted rhythms give her more energy as the line descends. "This intoxication of youth lasts one day! Then comes the hour when one weeps," which is an echoed phrase, written as two 8th notes to a half-note pattern, followed by a chromatic ascending scale to high A, and then the descent transitioning once again into the opening melody and text of "je veux vivre."

The last section (un poco meno allegro, ma poco) has a languid feel to it, as she sings quarter-note and half-note values to the following text: "Far from the morose winter let me slumber and inhale the rose before plucking its petals." At tempo 1, a pattern of scale figures ascend to high A, then a pattern of repeated descending scales begin on high A three times before the sustained high A with a trill. Once again the words "sweet flame!"

"Stay in my soul like a sweet treasure for a long time still/longtemps encore," followed by a cadenza-like 8th-note coloratura up to high D before one last accompanied phrase: "longtemps encore!"

The aria calls for a vocal line consisting of many embellishments and coloratura sung with youthful abandon. It has energy that is not "held" in the body. The singer must let go but must not lose focus. Whom are you addressing? Be aware of foreshadowing in this piece. "The intoxication lasts one day, then comes the hour when one weeps. Far from the morose winter let me slumber and inhale the rose before plucking its petals." At this early point in the opera she does not want to get married. She wants to hold onto her youth.

Piano/vocal score: p. 49 (G. Schirmer)

No. 15

Voice: soprano

Aria Title: "In uomini, in soldati" (Despina)

Opera Title: *Così fan tutte*

Composer: Wolfgang Amadeus Mozart (1756–1791)

Historical Style: Classical (1790)

Range: C4 to A6

Fach: soubrette

Librettist: Lorenzo da Ponte (1749–1838)

Aria Duration: 4:59 (with recitative)

Tessitura: F4 to F5

Position: Act I, scene 3

Setting: The living room of Dorabella and Fiordiligi's home, Naples, 18th century

After Dorabella declares that because of her grief she cannot live while Ferrando is gone, Despina tells her mistresses that one cannot expect men, especially soldiers, to be faithful and stable. She goes on to describe men as creatures that use women for pleasure and can change at any moment. Despina states that, therefore, women should only be faithful to their own self.

The aria (allegretto) is brightly and knowingly sung in 2/4 meter. The phrases are short, and the text is set syllabically into the music. The rhythms, accidentals, and trills must be "thrown off" with confidence and a brash-ness that is important in the character of Despina.

The allegretto second section is a dancelike 6/8 that features octave repe-titions of the C down to middle C. "They are windblown branches, change-able breezes," she declares. As the aria continues, Despina goes from a laughing tone to a more condemning and pointed voice: "False tears, sus-picious glances, deceiving voices, lying vices are their main qualities. They only love us when it suits their delight. Then they deny us affection. It's useless to ask them for pity" (to high A♭, fermata). Finally, Despina swings into a condemnation of men: "Let's pay them back, this accursed race. Let's love for *our* convenience and vanity!" she sings, followed by a "la ra la" with short trills that is almost a taunting figure to all men. Remember that Despina's audience is two women who are trying to ignore her, and De-spina delights in shocking them as much as possible.

Piano/vocal score: p. 84 (G. Schirmer)

> Notes by singer and master teacher Judith Christin: When I fondly look at this creature that lives in a chaotic household supporting two overly neurotic and hormonal females, I am reminded of the wonderful British director John Copley's words that Despina knows the gritty details of these ladies as well as serves tea. Despina can be the mirror to Alfonso's jaded views of young love. In this aria, Despina uses tricks to woo each lady according to their personalities.

No. 16

Voice: soprano
Aria Title: "Una donna a quindici anni"
(Despina)
Opera Title: *Così fan tutte*
Composer: Wolfgang Amadeus Mozart
(1756–1791)
Historical Style: Classical (1790)
Range: D4 to B6

Fach: soubrette
Librettist: Lorenzo da Ponte (1749–1838)
Aria Duration: 3:07 (with recitative)
Tessitura: D4 to G5

Position: Act II, scene 1

Setting: The dressing room of Dorabella and Fiordiligi, Naples, 18th century

After encouraging the sisters to have the "Albanians" back to their house, Despina sings this aria, saying that a girl of 15 should know how to flirt successfully. To be successful she should be able to lead on any man and lie when needed.

The aria is a reaction to the long recitative between Fiordiligi, Dorabella, and Despina that precedes it. Despina, their chambermaid, boldly suggests that the women entertain the new young men while also waiting for their betrothed to come back from battle, in other words—"buttering their bread on both sides." Despina reminds the young women that the Albanian men (Guglielmo and Ferrendo in disguise) had the courage to "die" for their sake in the previous act. Fiordiligi does not want them to become the object of gossip, and she does not want them to betray their lovers—even though they are far away. When Fiordiligi questions Despina about the Albanian men's behavior, Despina tells them it is the effects of the poison they took. Despina tells the ladies that the men are actually polished, modest, and decent.

Despina launches into the aria (andante), which is sung in a dancelike 6/8 meter: "A woman who is fifteen needs a complete education . . . She must know the methods, where the devil keeps his tail, what's good and bad. She must know the little indiscretions that enamor lovers."

The aria calls for a simple, honest delivery. Despina is a member of the servant class and is direct and straightforward, though she might cajole a little when met with resistance. Musically, the aria has simple grace through the vocal embellishments and energetic dotted rhythms. She sings repeated unaccented high G's at the end of a number of phrases ("finger riso, finger pianti/to feign laughter, to feign tears"), which call for good vocal control.

The second section is allegretto and suggests an even more playful and suggestive approach. A woman must give "hope to all, be they handsome or ugly. They must know how to lie without blushing." The melody and text of the allegretto section is repeated. Fiordiligi and Dorabella are pretending to not listen to Despina's homily. They continue to turn away, and Despina must repeat, and enhance, the message to get their attention. "This queen can make them obey," sings Despina as she realizes the young ladies have finally listened to, and agreed with, her message. "Long live Despina, who knows how to serve!" Despina boasts. The vital dotted rhythms, G's sung above the staff, passing high B's—all lend a confidence and a brash quality to Despina.

Piano/vocal score: p. 205 (G. Schirmer)

> Notes by singer and master teacher Judith Christin: In this aria Despina uses tricks to woo each lady according to their personalities. Ornaments and appoggiaturas can be debated and remain for the specific occasion. Remember to serve the action when they are employed. The ending needs simplicity and a sense that Despina has left the sisters to think that all her ideas she planted are their own.

No. 17

Voice: soprano
Aria Title: "Batti, batti," no. 8 (Zerlina)
Opera Title: *Don Giovanni*
Composer: Wolfgang Amadeus Mozart (1756–1791)
Historical Style: Classical (1787)
Range: C4–B♭6

Fach: soubrette
Librettist: Lorenzo da Ponte (1749–1838), after Giovanni Bertati and Giuseppe Gazzinga's opera *Don Giovanni Tenorio, o sia Il convitato di pietra* (1787)
Aria Duration: 3:16
Tessitura: F4 to F5

Position: Act I, scene 4

Setting: A garden in Seville. Don Giovanni's palace is in the background. Zerlina, Masetto, and chorus of villagers are already onstage.

We have not seen Masetto and Zerlina since Masetto's jealous aria "Ho capito/I understand" and Zerlina's duet with Giovanni "La cì darem la mano/Give me your hand," after which, Masetto believes, she goes off with the Don. Masetto is now walking with friends, ignoring Zerlina. She touches him. "Don't touch me," he says, "Why should I tolerate the touch of a faithless hand?" Masetto is extremely angry. Zerlina claims that the Don "never touched even my fingertips." She also tells Masetto that she was tricked. Denying his accusations and blaming Don Giovanni for the circumstances does not calm Masetto down. She disarms him in an unexpected way that "twists him around her finger," as he later claims. She was in the wrong, and she expects to be scolded. She knows he will be unable to do so: "Strike me, handsome Masetto."

Although the aria has a very simple and straightforward melody in 2/4 meter, the rhythms are not predictable and must be sung precisely to capture Zerlina's strength and character. She is not going to give up until the brooding Masetto smiles. She tries to make eye contact to make him smile in any way she can. By the 6/8 section she is back in control: "Let us enjoy our days and nights." Although this aria presents no insurmountable obstacles, it takes a solid and confident technique to sing the coloratura well (16th notes up to high A and Bb two times). There is also very little time to rest and catch the breath—Zerlina keeps the pressure on Masetto until the very last note.

(Translation by Camila Argolo Freitas Batista)

Piano/vocal score: p. 113 (Boosey & Hawkes)

> Notes by singer and voice professor Patricia Wise: It's a good tried-and-true beginner's piece for soprano: it presents no hurdles and shows right away what the voice will be capable of. Also, it's fun to sing.

No. 18

Voice: soprano
Aria Title: "Vedrai carino," no. 19 (Zerlina)
Opera Title: *Don Giovanni*
Composer: Wolfgang Amadeus Mozart
(1756–1791)
Historical Style: Classical (1787)
Range: G4 to G5

Fach: soubrette
Librettist: Lorenzo da Ponte (1749–1838),
after Giovanni Bertati and Giuseppe
Gazzinga's opera *Don Giovanni Tenorio, o
sia Il convitato di pietra* (1787)
Aria Duration: 3:40
Tessitura: G4 to F5

Position: Act II, scene 1

Setting: Seville; night on the street outside Donna Elvira's house, with a balcony

After all that the peasants Zerlina and Masetto have been through, this scene brings the couple together again. Masetto has been tricked by Don Giovanni when the Don struck him on the back of the head with Masetto's own weapon as he was trying to hunt down the Don. As Masetto lies there in pain, his masculine ego the major casualty of the beating, Zerlina comes to comfort him and assuage his pain.

The aria is in two parts. In the first part she draws him in immediately in a playful, teasing fashion, treating him like a young boy. She tells him that "if he is good" she has a remedy for him from his "injuries." The apothecary cannot fix it; it is her own balm: "Shall I tell you where I keep it?" Mozart provides the space for the question (fermata) and her prepared response. The second musical section is a repeated low C series of 16th notes in the bass that connote the beating of her heart. "Feel it beating," she says as she puts his hand over her heart. "Touch me here." Masetto feels better instantly. The dotted rhythms need to have energy here to bring the phrases forward with momentum. There are many short rhythms, and the composer sets the text syllabically at the top of the staff, so there is the chance that the singing can become "chirpy" unless the singing is connected to the breath support. Zerlina needs to be confident and sure here; Masetto is the one who is now excited.

This is an excellent piece for the young soprano. Although Zerlina sings a simple melody that is lightly decorative, phrasing is important. The melody line does not extend above the staff except for the last phrase, which extends to an 8th-note G.

(Translation by Camila Argolo Freitas Batista)

Piano/vocal score: p. 200 (Boosey & Hawkes)

No. 19

Voice: soprano
Aria Title: "Della crudel Isotta," Cavatina (Adina)
Opera Title: *L'elisir d'amore*
Composer: Gaetano Donizetti (1797–1848)
Historical Style: Bel canto (1832)
Range: D♯4 to B6

Fach: soubrette
Librettist: Felice Romani (1788–1865), after Eugène Scribe's libretto for Daniel-François Auber's *Le philtre* (1831)
Aria Duration: 3:50
Tessitura: E4 to G♯5

Position: Act I, scene 1

Setting: An Italian village, 19th century; lawn of Adina's farm

Adina is the most popular girl in the village. She is pretty and confident, and she owns the family farm. As the peasants rest from their labors, Adina is quietly reading a story. She laughs aloud at the absurd story she is reading, and the others crowd 'round to discover why she is laughing. She says that it is the story of Iseult (Isolde) and of the magician who gave Tristan such a powerful love potion that Iseult never left him again, adding that she wished she knew the recipe for such an elixir.

The aria is in the form of verses with choral refrain as she sings about "such an elixir." The varied verses are sung simply; there are a number of repeated pitches and phrasing to emphasize the important words of each line.

The cavatina is mostly in the middle range, with a dotted half note on the high G and a phrase (unaccompanied) down to middle C ("Per sempre benedì"). Adina is ridiculing the story, so part of the aria can be sung with exaggerated passion. She thinks that the story is ridiculous, but those listening (including Nemorino) do not. The aria could be sung in a matter-of-fact way until she realizes that the peasants are caught up in the story.

Piano/vocal score: p. 16 (Ricordi)

No. 20

Voice: soprano
Aria Title: "Prendi; prendi, per mei sei libero" (Adina)
Opera Title: *L'elisir d'amore*
Composer: Gaetano Donizetti (1797–1848)
Historical Style: Bel canto (1832)
Range: C4 to C6

Fach: soubrette
Librettist: Felice Romani (1788–1865), after Eugène Scribe's libretto for Daniel-François Auber's *Le philtre* (1831)
Aria Duration: 3:36
Tessitura: F4 to A6

Position: Act II, scene 2

Setting: The interior of Adina's house in an Italian village, 19th century

Adina is a young farm owner. She is the most popular girl in town as she has looks and personality, and her family has wealth. Belcore, a self-important dandy in the Army, is wooing her. Nemorino, a simple village peasant, is infatuated with Adina and wants desperately to be taken seriously as a suitor. He thinks he has no chance until he meets the "quack" Dr. Dulcamara, who sells him the "elixir of love." Nemorino wants to drink more, and to purchase another supply he joins the Army for a small stipend to pay for the miracle potion. Adina has purchased Nemorino's enlistment papers back from the Army. She has realized that she loves him and doesn't want him to enlist. She advises Nemorino that he should stay at home where everyone loves him.

This aria in the second act comes after Nemorino's aria "Una furtiva lagrima." Nemorino has been so confident of the elixir's power that he has played hard to get. Even then, he is overwhelmed with the possibility that she cares for him. The opening phrases of her aria are "Take it (*the enlistment papers*), because of me you're free. Stay on your native soil. There is not destiny for you so bitter that will not change one day." The melody is decorative with appoggiaturas and mordents. It is set high on the staff and is sung softly, intimately. "Here, everyone respects and loves you. No need to be unhappy. You will not always feel this way." More decorative figures and cadenza follow in a cascade of 32nd notes. She does not realize that he is unhappy only because he has seen a tear in her eye, and that affects him enough to sing "Una furtiva lagrima." Later in their duet she will tell him of her love.

Piano/vocal score: p. 234 (Ricordi)

No. 21

Voice: soprano
Aria Title: "Welche Wonne, welche Lust,"
No. 12 (Blonde)
Opera Title: *Die Entführung aus dem Serail*
Composer: Wolfgang Amadeus Mozart
(1756–1791)
Historical Style: Singspiel (1782)
Range: D4 to A6

Fach: soubrette
Librettist: Gottlieb Stephanie the younger
(1741–1800), after Christoph Friedrich Brentzer's *Bellmont und Constanze, oder Die Entführung aus dem Serail* set by Johann André
(1781)
Aria Duration: 4:20
Tessitura: G4 to G5

Position: Act II

Setting: The gardens of Pasha Selim's country house, the coast of Turkey

The servant Pedrillo tells Konstanze's English servant Blonde that Belmonte (Konstanze's loved one), a Spanish nobleman, has arrived—posing
in disguise as an architect. The Pasha has also accepted him as a potential
employee. Belmonte has a ship ready to take them all away to safety.
Pedrillo will give Osmin, their overseer, a sleeping potion, and they will
escape. Blonde sings of her joy and promises to tell Konstanze right away.

This aria comes right after Konstanze sings "Marten aller Arten," in
which she vows to the Pasha that she will never be untrue to Belmonte.
Blonde, on the other hand, remarks that some of the Turkish men are very
attractive. If she didn't have Pedrillo around to console her, there is no telling what "agreements" she might come to. And shouldn't women sometimes enjoy themselves, too? Blonde is excited and sings (allegro) syllabically, always ascending in her excitement up to high A. The tessitura stays
at the top of the staff. Blonde is especially excited to think that this news
would cure Konstanze's sick heart. She repeats the first section of the text
and melody: "what bliss, what rapture now reigns in my breast!" She exits
to tell to Konstanze the news.

Piano/vocal score: p. 93 (Peters)

No. 22

Voice: soprano
Aria Title: "Sul fil d'un soffio etesio"
(Nannetta)
Opera Title: *Falstaff*
Composer: Giuseppe Verdi (1813–1901)
Historical Style: Italian Romantic (1893)
Range: D♯/E♭4 to A6

Fach: soubrette
Librettist: Arrigo Boito (1842–1918), after
the comedy *The Merry Wives of Windsor* by
William Shakespeare (1597) and incorporat-
ing material from Shakespeare's histories
Henry IV Parts I and *II* (1597/1598)
Aria Duration: 1:50
Tessitura: E4 to F5

Position: Act III, scene 2

Setting: The country village of Windsor, Herne's Oak in the park; midnight on a moonlight night during the reign of Henry IV

Nannetta, the young daughter of Alice and Mr. Ford, sings this aria. Nannetta is in love with Fenton, who is the first to enter in this scene, singing poetically of the nature of love. Nannetta answers his musical phrases offstage.

The stage is now set for the ruse to teach John Falstaff a lesson. After Falstaff has entered the scene and is thoroughly frightened, Nannetta sings from offstage, calling the nymphs, elves, sylphs, dryads, and sirens. All are children dressed up as part of the plot. She begins "sul fil d'un soffio etesio/borne on the fresh breeze," leading them and instructing them as she brings them onstage for the game. Nannetta must sing from E at the bottom of the staff to the octave above, then to touch a high A at the end of phrase. There are a number of sustained F♯'s at the top of the staff. Falstaff is now prone in paralyzed fright, and by now the children are enjoying the game, commenting in unison about the atmosphere of the park.

As Nannetta sings the next verse, she is more confident in her disguise and in her role as fairy princess with "fairy folk":

> Aria translation by Martha Gerhart, from the *G. Schirmer Opera Anthology: Arias for Soprano,* edited by Robert L. Larsen (used by permission):
> "Let us wander beneath the moon, choosing flower by flower; each crown of petals in its heart brings its good fortune. With the lilies and the violets, let us write secret names; from our enchanted hands may words blossom."

The last line ascends up to high sustained A, which diminuendos (marked morendo).

Piano/vocal score: p. 354 (G. Schirmer)

> Notes by conductor and conducting professor David Effron: The beginning of this piece can be problematic for the singer, for we have a "two against three" in the rhythm. It is tricky. In this aria Nannetta must retain a freshness and transparency in the voice at the end of the opera after singing in many ensembles. Here she is exposed, with the melody lying in the *passaggio* of the vocal line. It must also be sung in a style that is almost like singing an art song, since it is so exposed, with intimate personal reflection. The last notes have a tricky diminuendo on high A, and it is important to pace this. Do not get too "little" too early, or it will dissipate too soon.

No. 23

Voice: soprano
Aria Title: "Mein Herr Marquis," no. 8, Couplets (Adele)
Opera Title: *Die Fledermaus*
Composer: Johann Strauss, Jr. (1825–1899)
Historical Style: Viennese Operetta (1874)
Range: D4 to D6

Fach: soubrette
Librettists: Carl Haffner (1804–1874) and Richard Genée (1823–1895)
Aria Duration: 3:42
Tessitura: D4 to D5

Position: Act II

Setting: A party in Prince Orlofsky's house, Vienna, 1870

Adele has run into her mistress's husband, Gabriel von Eisenstein, at a grand party. He believes that he recognizes her as his wife's chambermaid, but she convinces him that a chambermaid would never be found at a party such as this one. It should also be pointed out that Eisenstein is also not supposed to be at the party (he is supposed to be going to jail!), and is there without the knowledge of his wife, Roselinda.

In this aria Adele has the party guests watching and listening. She addresses the "Marquis" in front of the guests. This is a highly charged atmosphere because she is trying to pull off a disguise, and she knows *he* is not supposed to be there. That's why, perhaps, she acts playfully with the "Marquis." She is trying to diffuse his accusations by laughing it off and making fun of his claims.

It is also important to realize that Adele has enlisted the help of the guests before she sings the aria (which is in verses). Before the aria, Eisenstein has stated, "I could have sworn it was she." Adele demures, "He's [*Eisenstein*] trying to be funny, ha, ha, ha!" The guests comment, "How impolite . . . " The phrases in the aria are short and sung curtly—as if she is offended by his claim that she is a chambermaid. The series of "ah, ah, ahs," that Adele sings at the end of phrases should be thrown off (up to high A, G), almost as if she is tossing the notes into his face. This aria takes control above the staff, articulating high A and B staccato, like a laugh. But there is also some singing in the lower range: "What chambermaid you know could have so much to show?" she asks on a D below the staff.

The section that has more continuous laughter, "It's too funny, ha ha ha, please excuse me," can be seen as Adele's attempts to share this silliness with the party and stay away from the inquisitive gaze of Eisenstein, who (despite some party imbibing) is pretty sure that this soprano is his chambermaid. The final cadenza has a trill on high G, then goes up to high B to touch the D above before spiraling down to the D below the staff and leaping up to an extended high C (as the chorus catches up for the last laugh). If there is a difference in text between verses 1 and 2, it is that Adele is increasingly more confident; she is emboldened enough to ask for an apology from the accusing gentleman in verse 2.

Piano/vocal score: p. 69 (G. Schirmer)

No. 24

Voice: soprano
Aria Title: "Giunse alfin il momento . . . Deh vieni, non tardar," No. 27 (Susanna)
Opera Title: *Le nozze di Figaro*
Composer: Wolfgang Amadeus Mozart (1756–1791)
Historical Style: Classical (1786)
Range: A4 to A6

Fach: soubrette
Librettist: Lorenzo da Ponte (1749–1838), after Pierre-Augustin Caron de Beaumarchais's play *La folle journée, ou Le mariage de Figaro* (1784)
Aria Duration: 2:45
Tessitura: D4 to F5

Position: Act IV

Setting: Gardens of the Count Almaviva, three leagues from Seville, 18th century, night

In the last act of the opera, Susanna enters the gardens to entrap her lecherous master. Her fiancé, Figaro, sees her and misunderstands the situation. He hides, but she knows he is there. Although this aria is sung by many young sopranos, it has a depth of feeling that often belies the youth of the singer. It important for young singers to consider the circumstances, context, and environment of the aria. What is Susanna's intent? Let us take a moment to think through a possible staging of this aria.

Susanna enters the garden with the Countess in the recitative before Susanna's aria. It is clear in the recitative with the Countess that Susanna knows at this point that this is a charade, so she begins the recitative "giunse alfin il momento/the moment finally arrives" as an "actor" urging the imaginary Count to come quickly to her. Half of the fun is seeing Figaro's reaction to her words, so this could be part of her focus shift. Mozart provides the spaces for the shifts of her thoughts and eyes to occur. However, Susanna is in the gardens on a beautiful night, and it is possible that in the body of the aria she could "let go" of her game as she realizes that these gardens have been the place where she has met many times with her Figaro. The text indicates this emotion when Susanna speaks of "the river murmuring and the playing of light that restores the heart." It is possible that by the sustained, repeated words "vieni, vieni!/come, come!" Susanna has stopped playing her "role" and is now appealing to Figaro himself. "Let us stop the game and run to each other's arms!" could be her subtext. These possibilities shift this aria from "acting" to a sincere, simple expression of love and affection.

Vocally, the aria calls for an even line that has an interval up to the top of the staff (F) in the line but must not abruptly "pop" out. The aria sits mostly within the staff, but the singer must sing down to a low B♭ (on an accented syllable) to A. At the top, the aria touches only a high A, but it must be effortless and within the vocal line. Of utmost importance is that Susanna understands every word and "sees" her environment. She must also know specifically in her imagination what the gardens look like when she sings the aria out of context of the opera.

Piano/vocal score: p. 415 (G. Schirmer)

No. 25

Voice: soprano
Aria Title: "Fair Robin I love" (Dorine)
Opera Title: *Tartuffe*
Composer and Librettist: Kirke Mechem
(b. 1925), after the play by Molière (1664)
Historical Style: 20th-century American (1980)
Range: E to High C (A optional)

Fach: soubrette (lyric coloratura)
Aria Duration: 3:00
Tessitura: A to F

Position: Act I

Setting: Paris, 17th century; the house of Orgon, a wealthy aristocrat

> Opera plot note from the *G. Schirmer American Aria Anthology: Soprano,* edited by Richard Walters (used by permission):
> Moliere's classic comedy is about how Tartuffe, a religious hypocrite, finagles his way into a wealthy, middle-class Parisian home and nearly brings the family to ruin before the king intervenes. In this aria the audacious maid Dorine has overheard Orgon's intent to go back on his word regarding a promise to allow his daughter Mariane to marry Valère. When the two are alone on the stage, Mariane teasingly asks Dorine how she herself can bear to be separated from her love, Robin. Dorine gives a light-hearted reply. The stylized words of her aria are from "Amphitryon" (1690) by John Dryden. Dorine, the saucy maid to Orgon's daughter Mariane, sings a song to her mistress, attempting to educate her on the lighter side of romance. In Dryden's original poem, the name "Robin" was "Iris."

A delightful piece for the young soprano, this aria offers many opportunities for the singer to project strength of personality through energized rhythms and rubati. Personality and temperament are also shown off in its frequent madrigal-like "fa-la-la" passages at the end of each section. The aria needs an easy high A (C optional) at the top, and in the entire piece there is little "rest" time, underlining the youthful energy of the character.

Piano/vocal score: p. 47 (*G. Schirmer American Aria Anthology: Soprano*)

> Notes by composer Kirke Mechem: The singer should play to the hilt the teasing, pert aspect of the words and Dorine's character. Her first line, for instance, "Fair Robin I love and hourly I die," should be sung with mock sentimentality, followed by the opposite (pragmatism) in the next line, "But not for a lip nor a languishing eye." Remember that Dorine is wise in the ways of love, and she is making fun of Mariane's swooning kind of adolescent foolishness as she gives her this "lesson for today." By the same token, the word "fickle" should be emphasized (as it is in the staccato woodwind accompaniment), and the fa la la's are further expressions of Dorine's blasé, devil-may-care nonchalance.

No. 26

Voice: soprano
Aria Title: "Ma quando tornerai" (Alcina)
Opera Title: *Alcina*
Composer: George Frideric Handel (1685–1759)
Historical Style: Italian Baroque (1735)
Range: F4 to A6

Fach: lyric
Librettist: Antonio Marchi (fl. 1692–1725), based on Antonio Fanzaglia's *L'isola d'Alcina* set by Broschi (1728), after cantos VI–VIII of Lodovico Ariosto's epic poem *Orlando furioso* (1516)
Aria Duration: 4:31
Tessitura: G4 to G5

Position: Act III, scene 2

Setting: Alcina's enchanted island, the exquisite entrance hall of Alcina's palace

Alcina is an enchantress who attracts men to her magic island, where they are transformed into rocks, streams, trees, and wild beasts. But for the first time she has fallen in love with someone, Ruggiero, and Alcina has cast a spell over him. Ruggiero's former tutor, Melisso, breaks this spell, and Alcina finds out that Ruggiero has betrayed her and is planning to escape. In vain the enchantress attempts to prevent his departure. Alcina confronts Ruggiero: she vows vengeance, but will forgive him if he returns to her. Ruggiero makes plans for his escape.

In the recitative that precedes the aria, Alcina tells Ruggiero that she loves him. He says that time is no more, and she calls him ungrateful. Honor and glory urge him to go. "Go, you have insulted me enough. Go, traitor!" she demands.

The aria begins with an allegro in which Alcina tells him that when he returns, "with your feet in bonds, expect from me then only harshness and cruelty." The rhythms are crisp and defined. She is confident, proud, and rather formal. There are a number of challenges for the singer: some intervals call for the voice to leap up to the high G and F, which should be without strain. A number of trills are composed and 16th-note coloratura patterns over two measures.

The largo section in the key of Ab has more feeling: "And yet because I have loved you, I still feel compassion. You still have time to placate me. My love, do you not wish to?" she asks. This is sung with directness to Ruggiero, without embellishments or decorations, and is not sung dramatically above the staff. Finally, she sings, "Leave me, traitor, and go!" and repeats the allegro section with embellishments.

Piano/vocal score: p. 162 (Bärenreiter)

No. 27

Voice: soprano
Aria Title: "While I waste these precious hours," Romanza (Amelia)
Opera Title: *Amelia Goes to the Ball* (*Amelia al ballo*)
Composer and Librettist: Gian Carlo Menotti (b. 1911)
Historical Style: 20th-century American/Italian (1937)
Range: D4 to B♭6

Fach: lyric
Aria Duration: 3:30
Tessitura: G4 to G5

Position: One-act opera

Setting: Amelia's opulent apartment in a "grand city" of Europe

Amelia speaks with her lover. Her husband is on his way to the apartment, and Amelia is ushering the lover out in anticipation of his arrival. Amelia's one desire is to go to the ball. With a sigh, Amelia regards the city and the white phantom of the cathedral, bathed in moonlight. The bells strike (heard in the music), and she becomes pensive.

> While I waste these precious hours, hear a woman's prayer, O ye heav'nly Powers!
> You must know woman wants but little here below.
> Many may pray for lands and oceans, woman holds more modest notions.
> But alas! Why do men get all the best of things,
> While we women must be thankful for the rest?
> Not for glory I pray, nor pow'r, just for a ball, an innocent ball.
> You whose finger moves the stars, make them linger, stay the hours, hold back the moon.
> O Heaven, halt all time's flight so that I may go to the ball,
> That I may go to the ball tonight.
> To the ball! (*pianissimo, sustained high A*)

Up to this point in the opera, Amelia has seemed to be a shallow, superficial character, but this piece reveals the depth of her character and her ability to reflect deeply. In this aria the text is of great importance, and singers should have the ability to convey text in the high range of the voice in softer dynamic ranges. The aria is consistent with a restless characteristic that is important in her role.

Piano/vocal score: p. 67 (G. Ricordi)

No. 28

Voice: soprano
Aria Title: "Son pochi fiori" (Suzel)
Opera Title: *L'amico Fritz*
Composer: Pietro Mascagni (1863–1945)
Historical Style: Verismo (1891)
Range: D4 to G5

Fach: lyric
Librettist: P. Suardon (Nicola Daspuro) (1853–1941)
Aria Duration: 3:30
Tessitura: E♭4 to E♭5

Position: Act I

Setting: The dining room of Fritz's house, Alsace, late 19th century

The prosperous landowner Fritz Kobus, a confirmed bachelor, leads a contented life until he meets Suzel. She is the attractive daughter of the steward of Fritz's estate. As Suzel gives Fritz flowers as a present, she sings him an aria about her gift. "Just a few flowers, humble violets, they are the breath of April with their tender fragrance; and for you I have snatched them from the sunshine" is sung very simply with chordal accompaniment. Some of the words are written in faster rhythmic values (16th notes), almost as if Suzel were a little nervous in the presentation.

The second section, "If they could speak you would hear them say," leads to a more active orchestration (andante sostenuto): "We are timid and shy daughters of spring. We are your friends; we shall die this evening, but we are happy to wish you, who love the unfortunate: may heaven grant you all the good things that it is possible to hope for."

With a key change she adds a blessing, "And in my heart adds a modest but sincere word: May your life which brings comfort to others be eternal spring . . . Ah, desire to accept all that I can offer!" The vocal line is written simply, syllabically, and has very few sustained tones. The melody is largely limited to the middle voice, with one unaccented, unforced, high G. The piece is charming, straightforward, and a good aria for young voices.

Piano/vocal score: p. 18 (Casa Musicale Sonzogno-Milano)

No. 29

Voice: soprano
Aria Title: "Always through the changing" (Baby Doe)
Opera Title: *The Ballad of Baby Doe*
Composer: Douglas Moore (1893–1969)
Historical Style: 20th-century American (1956)
Range: D♯4 to B6

Fach: lyric
Librettist: John Latouche (1914–1956), based on the life of Elizabeth "Baby Doe" Tabor
Aria Duration: 4:15
Tessitura: F♯4 to F♯5

Position: Act II, scene 5

Setting: Colorado, 1899–c. 1930s; the Matchless Mine

The final scene of the opera shows Horace Tabor's demise and death, and Baby Doe's faithfulness to him and his favorite silver mine, the Matchless Mine. Halfway through this aria, which concludes the opera, she pulls back a hood to reveal her white hair. The theatrical effect symbolizes the more than 30 years that Baby Doe spent as a recluse at the mine, ending with her death in 1935. She was found frozen to death.

Although the piece is simply sung, like a hymn, there are several challenges. At the end of the phrase ("changing") the soprano will need to sing a high F♯ on the unstressed syllable. In the musical/dramatic climaxes, she must sing a sustained high G♯, A, and B.

Piano/vocal score: p. 246 (Chappell Music)

> Notes by director and opera professor Michael Ehrman: This is not a song of mourning, but a hymn to the power of love. One must be careful not to overindulge in the sad, tragic quality; if Baby fo-

cuses too much on the death of Horace, it will be near impossible
to get through the aria without crying. Many sopranos in rehears-
al have not been able to make it through until they focused on the
more positive aspects of the aria. It is at first a lullaby, a song of
comfort (sung as to a child in a mother's arms), and then grows
into a declaration of strength and passion. Rather than thinking of
the loss, think of the joy of the great love you have shared with
this man . . . By the end of the aria, as she stands in the falling
snow by the Matchless Mine and the years go by, Baby has found
a sense of inner peace and calm as she guards and honors her
promise to Horace and patiently waits.

No. 30

Voice: soprano
Aria Title: "Dearest Mama" (Baby Doe)
Opera Title: *The Ballad of Baby Doe*
Composer: Douglas Moore (1893–1969)
Historical Style: 20th-century American
(1956)
Range: E4 to C#6

Fach: lyric
Librettist: John Latouche (1914–1956),
based on the life of Elizabeth "Baby Doe"
Tabor
Aria Duration: 3:25
Tessitura: E4 to A6

Position: Act I, scene 4

Setting: Lobby of the Clarendon Hotel, Leadville, Colorado, 1880
   The Ballad of Baby Doe is based on the true rags-to-riches-to-rags story of
Elizabeth "Baby Doe" Tabor, second wife of silver magnate and U.S. Senator
Horace Tabor. At this point in the opera, Baby Doe has ensnared Horace
Tabor, and they are having an affair. Horace's wife Augusta finds a gift intended for Baby Doe while sorting through her husband's desk. When confronted, Tabor is unrepentant, and Augusta threatens to create a scandal
by publicizing the affair unless he sends Baby Doe away. As she prepares
to leave Leadville, Baby Doe writes a letter to her mother.
   This aria has a beautiful, poignant melody that needs to be delivered
simply. The middle section, however, begins piano and shows more tem-

perament in its fast rhythms and intervallic leaps to high C♯, before returning to the original melody. The closing section needs a full, sustained
high A.

Piano/vocal score: p. 75 (Chappell Music)

> Notes by director and opera professor Michael Ehrman: This aria
> reveals several conflicting sides of Baby's character. She is genu-
> inely torn between her feelings for Horace and her sense of what is
> morally proper. In her words to her mother, she reveals her genu-
> ine feeling for Horace, as well as her ambitions and dreams of
> glory and power. By the end of the aria she has convinced herself
> that, painfully, she must end the relationship.

No. 31

Voice: soprano
Aria Title: "The Silver Aria" (Baby Doe)
Opera Title: *The Ballad of Baby Doe*
Composer: Douglas Moore (1893–1969)
Historical Style: 20th-century American
(1956)
Range: E4 to C♯6

Fach: lyric
Librettist: John Latouche (1914–1956),
based on the life of Elizabeth "Baby Doe"
Tabor
Aria Duration: 3:10 and 4:15
Tessitura: F♯4 to A6

Position: Act I, scene 6

Setting: A suite in the Willard Hotel, Washington, D.C., 1883

Senator Horace Tabor and Baby Doe have divorced their spouses and just
been married. At their elaborate wedding reception, political dandies have
stated that the silver standard is soon to be obsolete, replaced by the gold
standard. Horace, a silver magnate, is angry, but Baby Doe temporarily
calms him and the other men with an ode to silver. The challenges for the
singer are the intervallic leaps to high A, melismatic figures, and finally a
high C♯ that is sustained. Much of the aria is marked piano.

Piano/vocal score: p. 123 (Chappell Music)

> Notes by director and opera professor Michael Ehrman: This is Baby's public declaration of love for the man she has just married. "Silver" and "Horace" are interchangeable. She is defending her husband to a quartet of snobby Washington dandies. Rather than "attack" them with anger, she uses her charm to calm the argument. Some of the phrases are directed to the men; others are meant for Horace and should be sung to him. It is really her love song to the man she adores and must be sung with great warmth, charm, and simplicity.

No. 32

Voice: soprano
Aria Title: "Willow Song" (Baby Doe)
Opera Title: *The Ballad of Baby Doe*
Composer: Douglas Moore (1893–1969)
Historical Style: 20th-century American (1956)
Range: F4 to D6

Fach: lyric
Librettist: John Latouche (1914–1956), based on the life of Elizabeth "Baby Doe" Tabor
Aria Duration: 3:00
Tessitura: F4 to F5

Position: Act I, scene 2

Setting: Lobby of the Clarendon Hotel, Leadville, Colorado, 1880

This opera is based on the true rags-to-riches-to-rags story of Elizabeth "Baby Doe" Tabor, second wife of silver magnate and U.S. Senator Horace Tabor. Baby Doe, newly arrived in town, has caught Horace's eye. He overhears two saloon girls gossiping about her and learns that she has a husband in Central City and was given her nickname by the miners. As Baby Doe sits at a piano in the hotel lobby, playing and singing, Tabor is hopelessly smitten.

Baby Doe begins the aria languidly on an "Ah," sung freely over her notes, which leads into the "Willow Song." It is a simple melody, pulled perhaps from her reminiscing. It is marked piano, and she needs a high B♭ (fermata), sung without strain. The last verse will call for a high D (to make sure Horace will notice her?). At the end of the aria, there is a more extended "Ah" that sweeps up higher, and with more flamboyance than at the beginning. Although the aria has a languid feel (legato), the rhythms are marked specifically.

Piano/vocal score: p. 38 (Chappell Music)

> Notes by director and opera professor Michael Ehrman: Interpretation of this aria depends upon how "innocent" one believes Baby Doe to be. Historical research has led me to believe that Baby Doe came to Leadville with hopes of meeting the famous, fabulous Horace Tabor. She had left her husband Harvey and, according to several sources, had other "gentlemen friends" before meeting Horace. When she first approaches him in scene 1, her opening line is "I beg your pardon, can you direct me to the Clarendon Hotel?" As the hotel façade forms the major part of the set, with large letters saying "Clarendon Hotel," it seems unlikely that she is approaching him without ulterior motive. After he leaves, she turns and says (to herself), "I'm sure we'll meet again, Horace Tabor, indeed we'll meet again" in music that is determined and triumphant. Her next appearance is for the "Willow Song," which I believe she sings knowing very well that Horace is outside, listening. The song alternates between moments of coquettishness, seductiveness, and several pangs of melancholy, but it is not a weepy, self-pitying dirge or a tragic aria. If the Baby Doe is charming (and she must be!), and is not played as too calculating, she can use this aria as a means of drawing Horace to her.

No. 33

Voice: soprano
Aria Title: "Ah, my darling, we could grow together like a single vine" (Mařenka)
Opera Title: *The Bartered Bride* (*Prodaná nevěsta*)
Composer: Bedřich Smetana (1824–1884)
Historical Style: Czech Nationalist (1869)
Range: C4 to A♭5

Fach: lyric
Librettist: Karel Sabina (1813–1877)
Aria Duration: 3:50
Tessitura: G4 to E♭5

Position: Act I, scene 2

Setting: A village square, gaily decorated for the celebration of the spring festival

All the villagers are in a festive mood except Mařenka, who is unhappy. She tells Jeník, her sweetheart, that in spite of her love for him, her parents have arranged her marriage to the son of Mícha, a wealthy landowner. Trusting in true love, the two pledge themselves to one another. Mařenka begins the aria simply, singing the melody to Jeník to see if he will respond to her words. "You seem almost indifferent," she says in the proceeding recitative. "Oh, tell me that you love me!" she demands.

"If we should have to part," she passionately sings above the staff (with sforzando and accents). The next section connects to a repetition of the first melody. "Since the glowing day" is repeated with the same text, intervals, and rhythm, but at a different pitch level (one step below). As she sings, "If your heart remains my own, oh, how can my heart forget you if our hearts are one?" Mařenka draws out the words, as if for greater emphasis. Finally, she concludes with a question: "Darling, if our hearts are one?"

Piano/vocal score: p. 34 (G. Schirmer)

No. 34

Voice: soprano
Aria Title: "Donde lieta" (Mimì)
Opera Title: *La bohème*
Composer: Giacomo Puccini (1858–1924)
Historical Style: Verismo (1896)
Range: D♭4 to B♭5

Fach: lyric
Librettists: Giuseppe Giacosa (1847–1906) and Luigi Illica (1857–1919), based on Henry Mürger's novel *Scènes de la vie de bohème* (1845–9) and his play (with Théodore Barrière) *La vie de bohème* (1849)
Aria Duration: 3:45
Tessitura: E♭4 to E♭5

Position: Act III

Setting: The Barrière d'Enfer, on the outskirts of Paris. It is dawn's first light at the end of February with snow everywhere. There is a tavern and a toll-gate. Although early it is busy: street sweepers and peasants coming with goods to sell in the city. Custom officers are onsite, having a drink in the tavern.

At this point in the opera, Mimì has been separated from Rodolfo for some months. She has come, desperately, to this location to speak with Rodolfo's friend Marcello. "I hoped to find you here," she says. Marcello awkwardly engages her in small talk. Bursting into tears, she tells Marcello that she needs help and does not know what to do. Rodolfo has run away from her and is madly jealous about everything she does. Marcello, who has jealousy control issues of his own, is even more uncomfortable as this conversation continues. As Rodolfo wakes in the tavern and comes outside to talk with Marcello, Mimì hides after telling Marcello she will go home, and overhears the dialogue between Marcello and Rodolfo. He tells Marcello that he can no longer be with Mimì. Rodolfo reveals that what torments him is the fact that Mimì is dying. He is afraid and frightened of seeing her die. The hiding Mimì realizes how much Rodolfo loves her and feels that he cannot provide for her, ultimately proving to be responsible for her death. No longer able to control her coughing, Mimì is discovered hiding. Rodolfo realizes that she has heard everything and tries to minimize the weight of his previous comments. She is now face-to-face with Rodolfo. "If we are to part," she sings, "let it be without rancor."

Although the farewell is an emotional one for both of them, she is very clear and straightforward in what she wants him to do. A drawer in his apartment contains some of her belongings. As she begins to leave she asks him to "Gather my things from the drawer," and she will send someone to pick them up. But she has something else to say, another request that keeps him near her for a little longer. On the pillow she has left a pink cuffietta (bonnet) that he can keep as a memory of her. This is the strongest emotion in the aria, as Mimì crescendos to a high B♭ on "ricordo d'amor/memory of love," sung on high A♭. Then she closes with, again, "goodbye without regret." Rhythms and text are important in this aria; the range extends to D♭ at the bottom of the staff two times. She sings a moving lyric line, and, of course, the situation is highly charged, but she does not need to emote or indicate tragic sadness. In fact, although Mimì is dying, Rodolfo is the one who needs comfort and strength in this situation. He needs to decide that they will stay together (until the spring) and that he will remain strong for her.

Piano/vocal score: p. 217 (G. Schirmer)

Notes by director and opera professor Sandra Bernhard: It is important that Mimì realizes that in this aria she is repeating music and text from Act I. What did she experience with Rodolfo before this? We see so little of it onstage, but there was so much that she relives during this aria. Beyond a sad, distant memory, this is a reexperiencing of their intimacy. Mimì's decision—that she needs to go—was made before the aria begins, and it is only as the aria unfolds that Mimì realizes the impact of her decision.

No. 35

Voice: soprano
Aria Title: "Mi chiamano Mimì" (Mimì)
Opera Title: *La bohème*
Composer: Giacomo Puccini (1858–1924)
Historical Style: Verismo (1896)
Range: D4 to A5

Fach: lyric
Librettists: Giuseppe Giacosa (1847–1906) and Luigi Illica (1857–1919), based on Henry Mürger's novel *Scènes de la vie de bohème* (1845–49) and his play (with Théodore Barrière) *La vie de bohème* (1849)
Aria Duration: 4:29
Tessitura: F♯4 to F♯5

Position: Act I

Setting: Christmas Eve, French Quarter in Paris. An attic room where Rodolfo, a poet, lives, with a large window, a stove, a small bookcase, an easel, a bed, some books, two candlesticks, and two doors.

Mimì's aria begins in response to Rodolfo's question, "Speak of yourself. Who are you? Will you tell me?" She is shy and hesitant to answer, but he has already broken the ice with his aria. Rodolfo is an ebullient mood after horseplay with his friends. Mimì, on the other hand, has been alone and sick for a long time. She has had no one to talk to, and she longs for contact with someone. She begins her story in a recitative-like fashion with little melodic shape. She says that the story is brief, that she "embroiders in tranquility." She enjoys making roses and lilies. Rodolfo is listening intently, wanting her to continue. He believes that her humility and simplicity is endearing.

She begins to sing melodically with "mi piaccion quelle cose/I like these things" in the middle of the voice about her passions: about all things that have gentle magic, that speak of love and spring. She recalls that spring is the best time of the year for her, as it brings to her the rebirth of flowers and the sunshine that allow her to breathe without wracking coughs. To Mimì, spring symbolizes life and health. For the first time in the aria she sings above the staff with the words "di primavera/of spring." She likes dreams, illusions, and everything that is called poetry (Rodolfo is a poet). "Do you understand?" she asks him. They look at each other.

As she begins the aria again, she is shy, but then describes the way she lives. She lives alone in a small room looking out over the roofs and sky. She focuses on the sun, the "first kiss of April." She is like a flower in the sun that unfolds its pedals in the sunshine and blossoms. These phrases are sustained, as if she is getting her health back again. Finally, with "così gentil il profumo d'un fior!/that gentle perfume of a flower!" she smells the perfume of the flower, and she can breathe! But regretfully, "the flowers that she makes are not real"; she ends in a parlando. She is once again the shy and humble girl who does not know what to say about herself.

(Translation by Robert Glaubitz)

Piano/vocal score: p. 73 (G. Schirmer)

> Notes by director and opera professor Sandra Bernhard: This aria underlines Mimì's tenderness, simplicity, and sweetness (espressivo, dolcemente). Look to the text of the piece to notice that

Mimì uses the word "sola/alone" a lot to underline the fact that she is alone ("vivo sola," a capella, "sola, mi fo il pranzo da mi stessa/alone, I make myself lunch"). She has been listening to Rodolfo intently, for she tries to use his words to describe her life, how she lives, what she does.

No. 36

Voice: soprano
Aria Title: "Quando m'en vo'," Musetta's Waltz (Musetta)
Opera Title: *La bohème*
Composer: Giacomo Puccini (1858–1924)
Historical Style: Verismo (1896)
Range: E4 to B6

Fach: lyric
Librettists: Giuseppe Giacosa (1847–1906) and Luigi Illica (1857–1919), based on Henry Mürger's novel *Scènes de la vie de bohème* (1845–9) and his play (with Théodore Barrière) *La vie de bohème* (1849)
Aria Duration: 2:18
Tessitura: E4 to E5

Position: Act II

Setting: The Café Momus on Christmas Eve night, with a milling crowd: townspeople, soldiers, children and their parents, vendors

Musetta is flirtatious and flamboyant. She likes finery and attention. Now estranged from her boyfriend, Marcello, she is with a "man of means"; he has paid for her shopping trip, and he is now carrying the gifts she has bought herself with his money. Musetta is the catalyst for the action in this scene. After the scene is established and Mimì cuddles with Rodolfo at the table with his friends, Marcello, Schaunard, and Colline, Musetta sees them all and decides to make a "scene." Everyone at the café is aware of Musetta's dramatic entrance except Marcello, who is pretending not to be interested in her. Musetta sings "Quando m'en vo/When I walk" with much elegance, assurance, and joy in the attention she is getting ("felice me fa/it makes me happy"). She basks in the attention.

Vocally, the aria is sung with control and legato phrasing. The passing high B♭ in the phrase "tutta ricerca in me/look to me" should not "pop" out and distort the vocal line. As she sings "ed asssa poro allor la bramosia sotti/and then I taste the slight yearning" she could begin to flirt with others at the tables to arouse Marcello's ire. "But still he pretends not to care!" she sings. Musetta goes on to the final section, a recapitulation of the opening melody, "E tu che sai/And you—while knowing," as she is addressing Marcello directly while he still pretends not to notice. She knows he is dying to run to her, but he continues to show no emotion. She is frustrated and could even be angry about his lack of "interest." Her final phrase is a cadential figure that is dramatic and pointed. She sings up to a high B strongly ("senti/you feel"), then diminuendos to a nonchalant "ti morir/that you are dying." Marcello would like to leave and run from the spell she has cast, but he cannot resist.

Musetta shows temperament with her accents and attitude with the staccato markings. Her quickly changed dynamics show a person who is unpredictable. Her moods are mercurial, as she can sing beguilingly in a lovely lyric legato and then sing with anger and disdain.

Piano/vocal score: p. 139 (G. Schirmer)

No. 37

Voice: soprano
Aria Title: "Je dis que rien ne m'épouvante," No. 21 (Micaela)
Opera Title: *Carmen*
Composer: Georges Bizet (1838–1875)
Historical Style: French Romantic (1875)
Range: E♭4 to B6

Fach: lyric
Librettists: Henri Meilhac (1813–1897) and Ludovic Halévy (1834–1908), after the novella by Prosper Mérimée (1845, rev. 1846)
Aria Duration: 4:52
Tessitura: E4 to G5

Position: Act III

Setting: The camp of the gypsies and smugglers set in a wild place among rocks near Seville in Spain. It is late at night with total darkness.

We have already met Micaela, a pretty country girl, at the beginning of the opera, when she is looking for José. At that time, she resists the advances of the soldiers, finally finding Don José after he has first had contact with Carmen. Micaela has brought him money and greetings from his home. She has also brought a letter and a kiss from his mother, who has raised Micaela as an orphan. His mother has written that she expects José to return home soon and marry Micaela. Much happens by Act III. José goes to jail for Carmen, who is now attracted to Escamillo, the bullfighter. José follows Carmen into the mountains, where she assists outlaws in smuggling goods.

Micaela, accompanied to the forbidding place by a guide, comes in search of José, whom, with God's help, she hopes to save. She will stay until she is able to talk with him. As Micaela comes into the scene, the guide tells her to be careful—one of the smugglers will be acting as a lookout. He observes that Micaela is courageous, and she tells him that she is not afraid. The guide is anxious to leave and wait for her at the inn at the foot of the mountain. He leaves, hoping that all the saints in heaven will aid Micaela in her endeavor.

Alone, she softly sings in the middle of her range a beautiful, lyric melody saying that although she tries to tell herself that she is courageous, deep down she is afraid (as she crescendos up to high G, then a sudden diminuendo to the middle voice, as if she is afraid that her sudden crying out will be heard). Alone in this savage place she is afraid. But she's wrong to be frightened, she says, as her voice more confidently rises to a sustained high G with more assurance. "You will give me courage and protect me, O Lord," she says as she sings with strength above the staff.

In the next section, marked allegro molto moderato, she sings about Carmen: she will see who this woman is who has led the man she "used to love" to dishonor (rising to high Bb). Carmen is beautiful and dangerous. Micaela will not be afraid and will speak up before her. She will tell José that his mother is dying. "Ah!" she exclaims on a high B: "The Lord will protect me." She now repeats the first section, with new confidence and assurance as the piece becomes more prayer-like. Micaela is a sweet, young girl, but filled with inner fortitude. Although this aria is lyric in nature, it is also at times a dramatic expression that is accompanied throughout by strings and winds, including French horns.

Piano/vocal score: p. 299 (G. Schirmer)

No. 38

Voice: soprano
Aria Title: "Elle a fui, la tourterelle," No. 25, Romance (Antonia)
Opera Title: *Les contes d'Hoffmann*
Composer: Jacques Offenbach (1818–1890)
Historical Style: French Romantic (1881)
Range: D4 to A6

Fach: lyric
Librettists: Jules Barbier (1825–1901) and Michel Carré (1852–1872), based on their play (1851), based on tales by E. T. A. Hoffmann
Aria Duration: 4:37
Tessitura: G4 to F♯/G♭5

Position: Act III, scene 1

Setting: A room in Crespel's house, Munich, 19th century, sunset. The room is oddly furnished. At the right is a clavichord, at the left is a sofa and armchair. On the walls hang violins; at back, two doors set at an angle; in the foreground, a bay window opening on a balcony. At the back, between the two doors, a large portrait of a woman (Crespel's dead wife, Antonia's mother) hangs on the wall.

Antonia is seriously ill and is hidden away by her father, Crespel, to prevent her from exerting herself. He is afraid that she has inherited her mother's fatal respiratory ailments. Although her father has forbidden her to sing, she sings this poignant song at the beginning of Act III, accompanying herself. She sings of her sorrow over a lost lover. She wishes that he would return to her. "The turtledove has fled." Then she continues in accompanied recitative: "Alas, Memory too sweet, image too cruel. On my knees I hear and see him."

The melody does not take too much of her strength to sing, but she is in distress as she continues: "But she (*the turtledove*) is always faithful and keeps her vow" "My beloved, my voice calls you." These phrases ascend with a crescendo to F♯ at the top of the staff, then finally to high A as she sings, "My heart is yours." Then the text is repeated softly on the lower F♯ at the bottom of the staff. The first haunting melody is repeated to complete the section. In the repetition of the melody she is seeking an answer to the question "Does he still live?" and makes the plea "Let your heart come to me" as she once again crescendos on the high F♯ to a sustained A, then repeats the text piano an octave lower (F♯), finally finishing the piece the way she has started. At the end of the aria, she is spent from the emotional exertion.

Piano/vocal score: p. 219 (G. Schirmer)

No. 39

Voice: soprano

Aria Title: "O wär' ich schon mit dir vereint," No. 2 (Marzelline)

Opera Title: *Fidelio*

Composer: Ludwig van Beethoven (1770–1827)

Historical Style: German Romantic (1814)

Range: G4 to A6

Fach: lyric (soubrette)

Librettist: Joseph Sonnleithner (1766–1835), with revisions by Stephan von Breuning (1774–1827) and Georg Friedrich Treitschke (1776–1842), after Jean-Nicholas Bouilly's libretto *Léonore, ou L'amour conjugal* (1789)

Aria Duration: 3:25

Tessitura: G4 to G5

Position: Act I, scene 2

Setting: The courtyard of a state prison close to Seville, 18th century

Marzelline is a young girl who is the daughter of the jailer, Rocco. She has fallen in love with her father's assistant (Fidelio), who is really a woman (Leonora). She is in disguise in order to gain entry to the prison, where she believes her husband is a political prisoner. The aria "O wär' ich schon mit dir vereint" follows a playful duet Marzelline sings with Jaquino, the young prison turnkey who is infatuated with her. After Jaquino exits the stage, Marzelline has the following words to say: "Poor Jaquino makes me almost sorry. I used to like him well enough; then Fidelio came to our house, and since that time everything in me and around me is changed."

There is a two-measure instrumental interlude played by three flutes (andante con moto). She sings about how things would be if she were united with Fidelio as husband, when "nothing on earth could disturb us" (she sighs and lays her hand on her breast). Hope and delight are in her breast (but the melody is written in the minor key). She dreams, "When we awake in the morning we will greet each other tenderly. We will rest from our troubles each blessed night when work is done." She repeats the melody and text "hope already is in my breast with inexpressible sweet delight" poco più allegro, as she ascends to a high sustained G, followed by a fermata rest. "How happy I shall be," she repeats.

An excellent aria for young soprano, the aria expresses Marzelline's feelings for Fidelio (Leonora) with youthful enthusiastic idealism. The aria does not extend too high into the soprano range, nor does it ask for climactic crescendi. The phrases are rather short, so the text and rhythmic precision are important to show the character's vitality and strength of purpose.

Piano/vocal score: p. 19 (Boosey & Hawkes)

No. 40

Voice: soprano
Aria Title: "O mio babbino caro" (Lauretta)
Opera Title: *Gianni Schicchi*
Composer: Giacomo Puccini (1858–1924)
Historical Style: 20th-century Italian (1918)
Range: D♯/E♭4 to G♯/A♭5

Fach: lyric
Librettist: Giovacchino Forzano (1884–1970), based on an episode in Dante's *Inferno* (c. 1307–21)
Aria Duration: 2:03
Tessitura: F4 to G♯/A♭5

Position: One-act opera

Setting: The bedroom of Buoso Donati, Florence, 1299

In the midst of mass confusion as the family of the dead man bickers, the composer provides this lyrical oasis: Lauretta, the young daughter of Gianni Schicchi, pleads for her father to give his blessing to her union with Rinuccio. Buoso Donati has died; his relatives have found his will and discovered that he has left all of his money to the church. Furious, they do not know what to do. Rinuccio, who is in love with Lauretta but is forbidden to marry her unless he was left some of the inheritance, sends for Schicchi to see if he can help the family sort this out. When the relatives find this out, they are furious and argue with Schicchi. Fed up, he starts to leave, but Lauretta stops him with this aria, singing that she loves Rinuccio, and if Schicchi does not help them, she will throw herself in the river Arno and die.

Her aria consists of a simple, straightforward melody that is very well known through its use in movies and advertisements. Although Lauretta is young and well meaning, the soprano who sings this aria must keep a number of things in mind: first of all, she has the strength of will to stop the "madness" and make these demands. It takes fortitude to say, "I want to go to Porta Rossa and buy the ring!" There is desperation and some youthful melodrama involved in threatening to jump into the river if she doesn't get what she wants. Think of the stakes involved here and the short time she has to plead her case to give this aria some urgency and meaning. That being said, although many young sopranos sing this aria, it is not that easy to sing well.

There are a number of intervallic leaps from the middle-voice A♭ to the high A♭ above the staff, and the phrases are extended. Observe the clearly marked crescendi and diminuendi. You can imagine the father (Gianni Schicchi) looking away during the aria as Lauretta is asking, pleading, and finally, begging.

Piano/vocal score: p. 71 (Ricordi)

No. 41

Voice: soprano
Aria Title: "Der kleine Taumann heiss' ich"
(Dew Fairy)
Opera Title: *Hänsel und Gretel*
Composer: Engelbert Humperdinck (1814–1921)
Historical Style: German Romantic (1893)
Range: F4 to A6

Fach: lyric (soubrette)
Librettist: Adelheid Wette (1858–1916), after the tale by the Brothers Grimm
Aria Duration: 1:40
Tessitura: A5 to F#5

Position: Act III, scene 1

Setting: The witch's house. The background is hidden in mist, which gradually rises and falls. Morning is breaking.

The Dew Fairy steps forward and shakes dewdrops from a bluebell over the sleeping children. The phrases are relatively short and simply sung, accompanied by the harp. There are many accidentals in the vocal line, and intonation is important. The Dew Fairy sings "Ding! Dong! Ding!" (as she drops of dewdrops onto the children) on the high G, and then sings a number of high A's, one sustained. The piece is through composed and continues to unfold. The only unifying element is the dotted quarter followed by the 8th note.

I am named the little dewman (*dawn fairy*), and with the sun I wake; from east to west I know who is lazy and who is not. I sound the waking tones. I come with the gold of sunshine, and the beams shine into your eyes to wake with the soft light whoever has been sleeping. Then you wake up, to find courage in the morning hours. Wake up, sleepy head! The light of day shines. Wake up.

The children begin to stir as the Dew Fairy hurries off singing a sustained, yet soft, D.

Piano/vocal score: p. 103 (G. Schirmer)

No. 42

Voice: soprano
Aria Title: "Tandis qu'il sommeille," No. 13 (Eudoxie)
Opera Title: *La Juive*
Composer: Jacques Halévy (1799–1862)
Historical Style: French Romantic (1835)
Range: D4 to Bb6

Fach: lyric
Librettist: Eugène Scribe (1791–1861)
Aria Duration: 5:55
Tessitura: F4 to F5

Position: Act III, scene 1

Setting: Eudoxie's apartment in the Emperor's palace, Constance, Switzerland, 1414

At a sumptuous fête, Éléazar, a Jewish goldsmith, and his daughter Rachel deliver a gold chain which the Princess Eudoxie has ordered for her husband and find that the husband, Prince Leopold, is none other than Samuel. "Samuel" has been working in Éléazar's workshop. At the beginning of Act III, scene 1, Eudoxie is alone in her apartment. She sings a recitative that has periodic interjections of chords and allegro arpeggiated figures (forte):

Long enough fear and sadness inhabits the walls of this palace! Let rapture and pleasure reign from now on. While he sleeps and without awakening him, may his ears in a happy dream hear my songs and remind him of the features of she who lies awake here thinking of him!

The vocal line is supported by the accompaniment throughout the aria, with chords lightly played on some of the beats, mostly on beat 1 of each measure. At "Qu'un songe heureux/May a happy dream," the phrase is repeated three times. The opening melody and text are then repeated at the close of the first section of the aria.

The next section (allegro non troppo) begins with an instrumental interlude of 10 measures. As her excitement grows there is more embellishment in the vocal line. "I did see him again and was able to tell him of my torments and my love." This section has decorative patterns and many dotted rhythms. It extends to high G at the top of the staff, without climactic phrases that call for a crescendo of the line.

"Oh sweet joy, happy rapture, with you everything is as it was before!" As the text is repeated the melodic range is expanded to reach the top of the staff. "What importance of the past unhappiness, in one single day they all were wiped out!" The "Ah" that is sung after this phrase begins at the high A and descends chromatically in a 16th-note passage. The same chromatically descending melodic passages from the high A and G are repeated with the words "je l'ai revu/I did see him again." Finally, there is a cadenza (a piacere) reflecting Eudoxie's hopes and excitement.

Piano/vocal score: p. 211 (Brandus & Co.)

No. 43

Voice: soprano
Aria Title: "Es lebt' eine Vilja, ein Waldmäg-delein," Vilja's Lied (Hanna Glawari)
Opera Title: *Die lustige Witwe*
Composer: Franz Lehár (1870–1948)
Historical Style: Viennese Operetta (1905)
Range: D4 to B6

Fach: lyric (full lyric)
Librettists: Victor Léon (1858–1940) and Leo Stein (1861–1920 or 1921)
Aria Duration: 6:00
Tessitura: G4 to G5

Position: Act II

Setting: Grounds of Hanna Glawari's house near Paris, turn of the 19th century

Hanna Glawari has recently been widowed, and she is now fabulously wealthy. In Act II she throws a party with everyone in their Pontevedrian costumes. The act opens with the chorus singing and dancing a piece from their mythical Eastern European country. Hanna tells her guests a story about a vilja, a "witch of the woods."

The melody is charming and should be sung simply and in a straightforward manner. There are a number of octave leaps to the top of the staff that are challenging and call for vocal control. In the chorus the dynamic marking is pianissimo as the soprano sings up to the G again, and there is an optional high B on the last note of the song.

There are two verses about the vilja. The spell of her beauty enchanted a hunter. She kissed him as no mortal could! He lay at her feet, and she vanished into the woods. "He called her vainly till his dying day." As Hanna sings these words to her guests, there is an intended connection between this mythical story and how Hanna feels about Danillo at the beginning of Act II. Their relationship is based on a playful baiting of each other's true feelings for each other.

Piano/vocal score: p. 82 (Dover)

No. 44

Voice: soprano
Fach: lyric
Aria Title: "Adieu, notre petite table" (Manon)
Opera Title: *Manon*
Composer: Jules Massenet (1842–1912)
Historical Style: French Romantic (1884)
Range: D4 to F5

Fach: lyric (full lyric)
Librettists: Henri Meilhac (1831–1897) and Philippe Gille (1831–1901), based on the Abbé Antoine-François Prévost's novel *L'histoire du chevalier des Grieux et de Manon Lescaut* (1731)
Aria Duration: 4:30
Tessitura: G4 to F5

Position: Act II

Setting: The apartment of the Chevalier des Grieux, Paris, France, 18th century

A nobleman has just told Manon that her love Des Grieux will soon be kidnapped by his father's men to get him away from her. She knows that the happy days they have spent in Des Grieux's apartment will soon be at an end and takes the opportunity to bid adieu to the setting in which they spent happy time together. Des Grieux is at that moment posting a letter to his father, which he optimistically feels will change his father's feelings toward the couple. He will be back soon.

Let's go . . . it is necessary! For his sake!
My poor knight! Oh, yes, it's him that I love.
Yet, I hesitate today! No! No! I am no longer worthy of him!
I hear that voice that captivates me against my will:

Manon, you will be queen, queen by your beauty!
I am nothing but weakness and fragility!
Ah! in spite of myself, I feel the flowing of my tears.
Before these obliterated dreams!
Will the future have the charms of those beautiful days?
Goodbye, our little table at which we met so often!
Goodbye, our little table, yet so large for us!
One thinks that it's unimaginable,
So small a space when we're embracing.
Goodbye, our little table!
The same glass was ours, there searched one set of lips for the other.
Ah! Poor friend that loved me!
Adieu, notre petite table/Goodbye, our little table.

There are many marking in the score reflecting changes in dynamics, tempo, meter and mood (espressivo). The range is not too demanding, but the aria has subtle changes that require a solid vocal technique.

An important focal point for Manon during the aria is a window on to the street. Des Grieux has gone to mail the letter; she wonders if he will be back soon. There is a sense of urgency in her glance. She also imagines the two of them seated at the table—these are lovely memories, not sad. Finally, she takes in the whole of the room and "takes a memory snapshot" of everything in it.

(Translation by Robert Glaubitz)

Piano/vocal score: p. 157 (G. Schirmer)

No. 45

Voice: soprano
Aria Title: "Monica's Waltz" (Monica)
Opera Title: *The Medium*
Composer and Librettist: Gian Carlo
Menotti (b. 1911)
Historical Style: 20th-century American
(1946)
Range: D4 to B♭6

Fach: lyric
Aria Duration: 5:45
Tessitura: G4 to G5

Position: Act II

Setting: The outskirts of a large city, 1940s; the shabby parlor of Madame Flora's flat

The young Monica lives with her mother, Madame Flora (an alcoholic), and Toby, a mute boy found on the streets. Madame Flora (also known as Baba) performs séances at her home so that her clients can have contact with the dead, who are often dear, departed family members. Flora plans "events" with the assistance of Monica and Toby so that the clients are tricked into believing the spirits are present. It is a strange atmosphere for the teenage girl.

Monica and Toby have had many fantasy-based games in the past. But now, for Toby, childhood friendship is becoming love. Monica is observing an imagined puppet performance, while Toby is the puppet master. At the opening of the piece (allegro) Monica applauds Toby as he comes out to acknowledge her applause. The "waltz" melody of the aria is written in a 12/8 meter, giving it a dancelike lilt. It is playful, as Toby becomes the puppet and Monica controls his actions. The first section is not extraordinarily challenging for the singer. The rhythms and melody are rather predictable; only a G at the top of the staff is called for, without dramatic intensity. The second section, beginning after "I'm flying with you," becomes more challenging: the melody sounds more difficult to find, as the accompaniment is more harmonically disjunct with the vocal line. The "follow me" now extends up to a high A.

The next section is Toby's confession of love for her, which Monica continues to think is still Toby playing their game. It builds to "You haunt the mirror of my sleep, you are my night. You are my light and the jailer of my day." The "play" continues as Monica sings the climactic passage of the fantasy: "Monica, Monica, fold me in your satin gown. Give me your mouth, fall in my arms," culminating in a high, sustained, B♭. She has taken the game too far. However, it is her only escape from the harsh reality of her existence to play with Toby's affections, for he does love her. She realizes that he has been crying, and she says, "I want you to know that you have the most beautiful voice in the world!"

Piano/vocal score: p. 63 (G. Schirmer)

No. 46

Voice: soprano
Aria Title: "The Black Swan" (Monica)
Opera Title: *The Medium*
Composer and Librettist: Gian Carlo Menotti (b. 1911)
Historical Style: 20th-century American (1946)
Range: D4 to G5

Fach: lyric
Aria Duration: 3:25
Tessitura: F4 to F5

Position: Act I

Setting: The outskirts of a large city, 1940s; the shabby parlor of Madame Flora's flat

The teenage Monica lives with her mother Madame Flora (an alcoholic) and Toby, a mute boy found on the streets. Madame Flora (also known as Baba) performs séances at her home so that her clients can have contact with the dead, who are often dear, departed family members. Flora plans the "events" with the assistance of Monica and Toby so that the clients are tricked into believing the spirits are present.

As Baba holds a séance for several customers, the phony medium feels a hand at her throat. Blaming the mute boy Toby, she beats him to confess that he was actually the one who touched her. Monica pulls her terrified and deranged mother away from Toby, and rests Baba's head on her lap.

The wistful tune "Oh Black Swan," is sung by Monica to soothe her distraught mother. The gypsy-like, haunting melody connotes a special connection between mother and daughter. Perhaps Flora has sung the song to Monica when she was growing up.

The vocal line begins pianissimo in the lower part of the soprano voice lending the melody a mysterious quality. In contrast to the low-range melodic phrases, "Where, oh, where is my lover gone" is a repeated cry at the top of the staff. In the middle section, Monica tries to chromatically find her way back to the original melody. She finally reclaims the melody through a rhythm from the first section (dotted 8th followed by a 16th-note rhythm, two 8th notes, half note). "The spools unravel and the needles break," repeats the opening melody. "Oh, black wave, take me away with you" is foreboding in its tone, but it is followed by "I will share with you my golden hair, and my bridal gown."

The last eight measures are the most challenging, as Monica sings an octave interval leap to high G, sustained with a fermata ("Oh, take me down with you"). Remaining at the top of the staff, Monica ends with a sustained high G, "With my child unborn."

Piano/vocal score: p. 51 (G. Schirmer)

No. 47

Voice: soprano
Aria Title: "Steal me, sweet thief" (Laetitia)
Opera Title: *Old Maid and the Thief*
Composer and Librettist: Gian Carlo Menotti (b. 1911)
Historical Style: 20th-century American (1939)
Range: C4 to B6

Fach: lyric
Aria Duration: 4:15
Tessitura: G4 to F5

Position: One-act opera, scene 6

Setting: A small New England town, 1939; the kitchen of Miss Todd's house

Opera plot note from the *G. Schirmer American Aria Anthology: Soprano*, edited by Richard Walters (used by permission):

Miss Todd, an aging old maid desperate for male company, takes in a beggar who turns out to be a thief. She won't let him leave, going so far as to steal liquor (to avoid the shame of being seen buying it) to keep him happy. Alone in the kitchen, the unmarried Laetitia, Miss Todd's maid, romantically daydreams about Bob the beggar while mending and pressing his trousers.

Laetitia is irritated as she does the ironing: "What a curse for a woman is a timid man." He has been there an entire week, but he hasn't made any "advances," though he has had plenty of chances. Miss Todd gives him money, and he takes it, with a charming smile. "He eats, sleeps, talks of sports, but that is all." She ties the piece together dramatically with the same words from the beginning of her monologue: "What a curse for a woman is a timid man!" Many of the lines from the first section begin at the bottom of the staff and descend. In the first section Laetitia experiences a number of emotions: irritability, helplessness, disappointment, impatience, astonishment, surprise, wistfulness, misery, and cynicism.

As she irons, she sings, "Steal me, sweet thief" plaintively. She wants to be taken away from this small town, from working for this "old maid," Miss Todd. She is young now but does not want to end up like Miss Todd. She sings longingly at first as she pleads, then she sings desperately, "Oh, sweet thief, make me die (*to high B*) before dark death steals her prey." There is a diminuendo to the next phrase, as she softly sings, "steal my lips, my heart, my cheeks, my breath, my heart." This plea is followed by a climactic phrase, "Oh, steal my breath and make me die." Finally, hopefully, desperately, she sings, "Oh, steal me" on a high B♭. The final phrase, "for time's flight is stealing my youth," diminuendos in the middle range, as she wistfully returns to ironing his clothes.

Piano/vocal score: p. 91 (Ricordi)

No. 48

Voice: soprano
Aria Title: "Qual fiamma avea nel guardo!"
(Nedda)
Opera Title: *I Pagliacci*
Composer and Librettist: Ruggiero Leon-
cavallo (1857–1919)
Historical Style: Verismo (1892)
Range: D4 to A6

Fach: lyric
Aria Duration: 2:45
Tessitura: E4 to F#5

Position: Act I, scene 2

Setting: The entrance to a village, Calabria, Italy, 1860s. It is the Feast Day of the Assumption.

Nedda is the young wife of Canio, the aging leader of a traveling commedia dell'arte performing company. The company arrives at a village square, announcing a performance that evening at 9 o'clock. Canio watches jealously over Nedda, whom he found as an orphan in the streets. Amid the joyous announcement of the show that night, there is an underlying sense of danger when a bystander makes a jokingly teasing reference to the desirability of his wife and Canio overreacts. After everyone leaves, Nedda is left to muse (in the lower voice) about Canio's dangerous eyes. He may discover her secret. "How brutal he would be if he found out. Enough! I will not have these fearful dreams overcome me," she sings in the recitative. She reacts to the sound of a sequence of chords: "Now the sun is beautiful, and I am full of life. I am restless."

She looks to the sky, as the orchestra imitates the sound of the wings of birds. "Oh!" she exclaims to the birds, "As my mother told me, you have your own language. If I were only as free as a bird." She soars up to G#, and the aria builds to a final high A (con anima e passione). The tessitura is high, but the piece also descends to a low C# in the middle of a phrase. The melody should be sung legato, while the accompaniment is arpeggiated.

Piano/vocal score: p. 68 (G. Schirmer)

Notes by singer and voice professor Virginia Zeani: Nedda is a full-blooded, temperamental, fiery, passionate woman of the verismo style. Each word that she sings is filled with passionate meaning.

No. 49

Voice: soprano
Aria Title: "Caro nome" (Gilda)
Opera Title: *Rigoletto*
Composer: Giuseppe Verdi (1813–1901)
Historical Style: Italian Romantic (1851)
Range: B4 to C♯6

Fach: lyric (coloratura)
Librettist: Francesco Maria Piave (1810–1876), after Victor Hugo's tragedy *Le roi s'amuse* (1832)
Aria Duration: 6:20
Tessitura: F♯4 to A6

Position: Act I, scene 2

Setting: Mantua, Italy, 16th century; courtyard of Rigoletto's house, night

After the Duke of Mantua in the guise of a poor student (Gualtier Maldè) has seduced her, the young Gilda sings of her newfound love. Flute arpeggios accompany the opening of the introduction to the aria, when she dreamily sings the student's name (repeated at the end of the aria). A solo flute plays the melody of "Caro nome/Sweet name" before the aria begins. "Sweet name, you who made my heart throb for the first time." The throbbing of the young heart is here delicately reflected in the halting rhythms of the vocal line. "You will always remind me of the pleasures of love" completes the first melodic section of the piece.

A focus shift occurs with the orchestra interlude and a birdlike figure from the solo flute, as she sings, "My desire will fly to you on the wings of thought." "Volerà/will fly" is an octave leap from the F♯ above middle C to the top of the staff, as the words are more and more embellished. "A te/to you," a repeated pattern of the interval of the 6th, must be precisely sung, off the beat, but is marked dolce. Variety of articulation markings is important, and since the text is so often repeated, different emotions that are clarified by the singer can give the voice different colors. Gilda is young and in love, but more specifically, she is in turn giddy, determined, in awe of her own awakened feelings, playful, enraptured, and for the first time she feels as if her spirit has been set free (she has been almost a prisoner in her father's house).

The aria closes with cadenzas that ascend to a high C♯, and a simple repetition of the "Caro nome" melody heard in the beginning of the aria. She finally sings his name: "Gualtier Maldè!" two times on an E at the top of the staff, the second time with an added sustained trill for two measures.

Piano/vocal score: p. 136 (Ricordi)

Notes by conductor and conducting professor David Effron: Gilda must not be too naïve in this aria. She is falling in love, and is more womanly—like a flower blooming. It should not be sung as simply a vocal tour de force. The characterization is important, and the coloratura must be meaningful, not only a vocal exercise. She is "getting into love" in this coloratura.

No. 50

Voice: soprano
Aria Title: "Chi il bel sogno di Doretta" (Magda)
Opera Title: *La rondine*
Composer: Giacomo Puccini (1858–1924)
Historical Style: Verismo (1917)
Range: C4 to C6

Fach: lyric
Librettist: Giuseppe Adami (1878–1946)
Aria Duration: 3:40
Tessitura: F4 to F5

Position: Act I

Setting: Magda's house in Paris in the time of the Second Empire (1860–1880). The scene is set in an elegant salon in the house. In the right corner, there is a Winter Garden with large windows, through which can be seen a portion of the Tuileries in the fading daylight. The entrance door is a little to the left, in back, and is quite large and hung with rich draperies. A smaller door leads to the boudoir. Around the scene are chairs, couches, small tables, a screen. A grand piano sits near the middle of the room with a vase of red roses on it. There are small lamps on the tables, diffusing a muted and intimate light.

When the curtain rises, the red reflections of the sunset are fading away. Magda's friends are gathered in the salon engaged in lively conversation. Prunier, a writer and poet, is getting the most attention, as he says that in Paris "romance is now in fashion," while some of the other guests think that he's merely being sentimental. Magda, the hostess of the gathering, encourages him to continue, while the others continue to mock his philosophy. Prunier talks about his new fictional character who has developed an addiction to this "strange affliction: love." Magda asks him to continue, and Prunier, at the piano, accompanies himself as he sings of the story of "sweet Doretta," who gave up a king's ransom for love.

Prunier sings the first verse, but he cannot continue. He cannot find a "finale." He surrenders the piano to Magda, who sits down and begins the same tune and text. In the second line of text she elaborates, bringing more "shocking passion" into the story for her guests. She goes on, singing "ardent rapture . . . burning kisses!" on A and G above the staff. The soprano will also need the low (middle) C for the ends of two phrases at the beginning of the song. She embellishes further at her "finale," as she sings "Ah! Mio sogno!/Ah! My dream" to the high C on "Ah!" She now continues (poco allargando) with the "moral" of the story: "What matters if one has no riches, if happiness can flourish and if love can live! O dream of joy (*high B♭*) to find a love like this." The two double-dotted quarter notes give the last phrase a sense of vibrancy. Prunier, bowing to Magda, speaks in mocked response: "At your feet all the riches of springtime!"

Piano/vocal score: p. 19 (Universal)

No. 51

Voice: soprano
Aria Title: "Ah, sweet Jesus, spare me this agony" (Annina)
Opera Title: *The Saint of Bleecker Street*
Composer and Librettist: Gian Carlo Menotti (b. 1911)
Historical Style: 20th-century American (1954)
Range: D4 to C6

Fach: lyric
Aria Duration: 5:55
Tessitura: F4 to F5

Position: Act I, scene 1

Setting: A cold-water flat in the tenements of Bleecker Street. Upstage is the entrance from the hallway; right is a door leading to Annina's bedroom; next to it a small, heavily adorned altar displaying a monochrome picture of the Virgin.

Annina is a deeply religious girl who has been having visions and performing miracles. These acts have a debilitating effect on her, leaving her drained and weak. In this aria Annina is in the throes of a vision and the painful appearance of stigmata, surrounded by onlookers. She sings with her eyes closed and a tormented expression on her face (as if fighting a fearful force): "Ah, sweet Jesus, spare me this agony. Too great a pain is this for one so weak. Ah, my aching heart, must you again withstand the trial?" She looks at the neighbors gathered around her, "Where am I? Who are these people?" she asks. "When have I seen this road before, when this barren hill? What is this drunken crowd waiting for?" Unaccompanied, she adds, "Ah, dreadful presentiment!" She moves through the kneeling neighbors: "Eager and loud, they push and sway under the festival sun. What do they want? What are they waiting for?" Finally, she understands, "I see now, oh blinding sight! Oh, pain! Oh, love!"

The con moto section is Annina's delirious narration of the crucifixion of Christ. She talks about the wailing women behind the crowd, "swaying like reeds as they slowly move." Annina asks of Mary, "Why did you come? Oh, women, take her home. It is her very flesh that will be torn by spear and nail. Take her." This section leads to the climactic phrases "The whole world (*sung on high A*) can see the son of God, sweet Jesus, lying there. His palm is now held open. Those hands that gave us all, by us are to be pierced. Soldier, soldier, have mercy on Him, for he alone is your savior. The nail is held in place. The huge hammer is raised. Ah!" She ends on a high C that descends, portamento, as she falls back on the pillows.

Piano/vocal score: p. 35 (G. Schirmer)

No. 52

Voice: soprano
Aria Title: "Someday I'm sure to marry you" (Jenny MacDougald)
Opera Title: *The Sojourner and Mollie Sinclair*
Composer and Librettist: Carlisle Floyd (b. 1926)
Historical Style: 20th-century American (1963)
Range: D4 to Bb6

Fach: lyric
Aria Duration: 2:25
Tessitura: G4 to G5

Position: Act I, scene 1

Setting: A plantation on the Cape Fear River in colonial North Carolina, mid-18th century. The exterior and front yard of a large, rambling frame house. In the yard are tree stumps and shrubs. In the distance, to the rear and sides of the house, are acres of cultivated land, and on the horizon, woods. On the porch sit two rocking chairs. In spite of the rough-hewn character of the property there is an unmistakable feeling of grandeur about it; this is the home of a country squire.

Lachlan Sinclair wants Jenny MacDougald to marry him, and they have a playful scene before the aria "Someday I'm sure to marry you." They argue a little about their respective families, and how the families do not get along. Lachlan then makes a serious profession of love for Jenny and asks when she will be his bride. She sings, "Someday I'm sure to marry you," but her heart tells her to wait "'til it is no longer shy of you" (high G, mezza voce).

Next, she poses some difficult questions: "Would you love me all my life when the color fades from my eyes, the sheen is gone from my hair? When my body has thickened and sagged from bringing children into the world, when I am old? Will you love me then?" Before he can answer she says (più intenso), "I could spend my life adoring you and when the years had stiffened your limbs and age had creased your face, I would love you all the more" (high A). She ascend to a high, sustained Bb: "Will you love me then as I will love you—all my life?" After three silent measures she relents: "Aye, aye, Lachlan Sinclair. Someday I will marry you."

Piano/vocal score: p. 11 (Boosey & Hawkes)

No. 53

Voice: soprano
Aria Title: "Ain't it a pretty night?"
(Susannah)
Opera Title: *Susannah*
Composer and Librettist: Carlisle Floyd
(b. 1926), after the story in the Apocrypha
Historical Style: 20th-century American
(1956)
Range: Bb4 to Bb6

Fach: lyric
Aria Duration: 6:00
Tessitura: Eb4 to F#5

Position: Act I, scene 2

Setting: New Hope Valley, Tennessee, the front porch of the Polk house after the church square dance at which Susannah has met the Reverend Blitch

The youthful Susannah has just come back with Little Bat to the primitive, remote Polk farm ranch after the square dance. She is "radiant with excitement." She hears the jealous talk of the women behind her back, but tonight she has forgotten all of her problems. She has been the attractive object of attention by many, including the worldly Reverend Blitch, new to the town.

Susannah is enthusiastic and happy as she looks up into the sky and sings the first words of the aria, "Ain't it a pretty night" without accompaniment. Her focus is the stars in the sky, and she is also talking with the emotionally immature Little Bat, who worships Susannah but is full of fear and worry about what the townspeople say and think. Susannah sings "ain't it a pretty night" once again, now accompanied.

Susannah wonders what lies beyond the mountains that surround her home and dreams of visiting the outside world. At ancora più mosso she reveals her hopes and dreams of leaving the valley to see what lies outside, including "the tall buildin's and all the street lights an' to be one o' them folks myself" (which carries the phrase to the high sustained A#). She is excited, hopeful, determined, and even fearful. At the poco ritardando, her focus shifts back to New Hope Valley, and she wonders if she would be lonesome for the valley if she left. This passage is very low for the young soprano, extending down to low Bb. The following climactic phrases (con moto) inspires her to once again think of leaving, and coming back just to visit if she is homesick, "when I've seen what's beyond them mountains" (high sustained Bb, accompanied by agitated double-dotted rhythms.

Abruptly, there is silence, and Susannah once again sings the unaccompanied phrase "Ain't it a pretty night." Her simple, limpid embellishments also color the final phrases, which extend to a top A (fermata), and a portamento from the top A down the octave, to finish quietly and peacefully on the low D♭.

Piano/vocal score: p. 25 (Boosey & Hawkes)

No. 54

Voice: soprano
Aria Title: "The trees on the mountain are cold and bare" (Susannah)
Opera Title: *Susannah*
Composer and Librettist: Carlisle Floyd (b. 1926), after the story in the Apocrypha
Historical Style: 20th-century American (1956)
Range: D♭4 to B♭6

Fach: lyric
Aria Duration: 5:30
Tessitura: G4 to G5

Position: Act II, scene 3

Setting: New Hope Valley, Tennessee, the front porch of the Polk house

At home Susannah compares her new life as an outcast from the town to the winter descending on the mountains. The mood of Susannah in this scene is a marked contrast from her optimistic mood in the Act I aria after the square dance ("Ain't it a pretty night?").

She is no longer a happy-go-lucky innocent young girl. Instead, she has been seduced and betrayed by the Reverend Blitch, and the town has ostracized her. Her brother Sam, with whom she is close, is out hunting and drinking. She is by herself and consoles herself the only way she knows—with music (even though her song is a sad one). It is a folk song that she sings to herself. It is sad, but not lethargic (andante piangendo). There are dotted note values in the vocal phrase that give the line vitality. The song is probably familiar to her, like the "Jaybird Song" that she sings earlier with Sam. Perhaps the song is one from her memory sung to her by her mother.

After an eight-measure introduction of homophonic chordal strumming, the accompaniment moves underneath the melody like a stream. With the words "Come back, O summer, come back, blue flame" Susannah sings an octave up to high G, which is a more dramatic outburst, and then leaps up to high B♭ with "Come back, o lover, if jes' fer a day," which is all above the staff, fortissimo. It is difficult to establish clarity of diction while singing the words above the staff.

The aria then goes into a more somber middle section, changing its tonality. The melody continues to look for a new tonal center and finally finds its way with "like a falsehearted lover," repeated, followed by the climactic repetition of "Come back, O summer" and "Come back, O lover." The last measures (meno mosso) are also marked sotto voce, with the same strummed chords underneath. Susannah sings once again, "Come back, O lover" on the high B♭, this time marked pianissimo. Her last words ("come back") are octave intervals that ascend to high G with fermatas. Each "come back" can be sung in a different way, even though they have the same dynamic (pianissimo): one can be urgent, one can focus on the imagined lover, one can be determined, and so forth.

Piano/vocal score: p. 93 (Boosey & Hawkes)

No. 55

Voice: soprano
Aria Title: "Hello, hello? Oh, Margaret, it's you" (Lucy)
Opera Title: *The Telephone*
Composer and Librettist: Gian Carlo Menotti (b. 1911)
Historical Style: 20th-century American (1947)
Range: D4 to D6

Fach: lyric
Aria Duration: 3:30
Tessitura: E4 to F5

Position: One-act opera

Setting: Lucy's apartment

   In the exchange between Lucy and Ben before the aria as the curtain goes up, Lucy is busily opening a gift—a piece of abstract sculpture—that Ben has just given her. He then tells her that he is going away, and that his train leaves in an hour. He is trying to tell her that when he returns he would like her to consider marrying him, but he does not complete the question, as the telephone rings and Lucy answers it. She continues the conversation with animation and joy while Ben waits. The articulation, phrasing, and accidentals give the "one-sided" conversation life and interest. The next section, established by the exclamations "Ha, ha!" and "Ah!" needs specific emotions attached to the vocal expressions (e.g., joy, amazement, and the emotions displayed in turn will color the voice).

   Finally there is a trill on high A to high D followed by a chromatic descent. It is important for the soprano in all cases to imagine a clear dialogue with the imaginary "Margaret" on the line. Lucy finally is saying goodbye (imagine Ben's impatience) when Margaret tells her one more story that is more hysterical than the others (allegro con brio), and Lucy here has reactive "Ha, ha!" and "Ah's" that trill in arpeggiated staccato figures of cascading laughter, followed by two glissandi from E to high A. The meno mosso (p. 15) that is sometimes cut in audition settings (to "goodbye") is marked legato and is more caring in tone. It must drive Ben crazy as she continues the endless phone conversation: "How is the pussycat, how is the dog?" Finally, "goodbye," but Lucy cannot get Margaret off the phone until Lucy sings a sustained high C, then an accompanied casual but abrupt, "So long!"

Piano/vocal score: p. 7 (G. Schirmer)

> Notes by singer and voice professor Patricia Wise: I recommend this aria to young (18–21-year-old) sopranos. It has a good range, is showy but not too difficult, and there is a lot of text, so it's good for diction training. It is also a fun aria to sing and act.

No. 56

Voice: soprano
Aria Title: "Signore, ascolta" (Liù)
Opera Title: *Turandot*
Composer: Giacomo Puccini (1858–1924)
Historical Style: 20th-century Italian (1926)
Range: D♭4 to B♭6

Fach: lyric
Librettists: Giuseppe Adami (1878–1946)
and Renato Simoni (1875–1952), loosely
based on the play by Carlo Gozzi (1762)
Aria Duration: 2:45
Tessitura: D♭4 to A♭5

Position: Act III

Setting: The gardens before the walls of Peking (Beijing) in fabled times

Liù, a young slave girl, is a good and gentle spirit. She has been the traveling companion to Timur, who is the dethroned Tartar King and the father to Calaf. After Liù is captured and tortured because she knows Calaf's name, she is asked by Turandot why she resists the torture so well. Liù replies that her love for the "Unknown Prince" keeps her from telling his name. The crowd calls for her execution. The people need for Liù to be silenced, for an agitated Princess will certainly punish everyone.

With great courage, Liù speaks directly to Turandot. Liù knows that she has lost Calaf to Turandot, as Liù will also lose her own life. Liù calls out for the Princess to hear her. "You who is girdled with ice and vanquished by fire. You will love him, too," she says, "Before the break of day I shall close my tired eyes that he may win yet again . . . never to see him once more." She snatches a dagger from a soldier and stabs herself before the crowd can force her to reveal his name.

The aria is sung legato (con dolorosa espressione). It is sung with a calmness that comes from inner strength, and from a decision already made—to take her own life. Much of the aria is in the middle voice, with climactic sections ascending to high A♭ and finally high B♭ ("not to see him again!").

Piano/vocal score: p. 115 (Ricordi)

No. 57

Voice: soprano
Aria Title: "Tu che di gel sei cinta" (Liù)
Opera Title: *Turandot*
Composer: Giacomo Puccini (1858–1924)
Historical Style: 20th-century Italian (1926)
Range: E♭4 to B♭6

Fach: lyric
Librettists: Giuseppe Adami (1878–1946) and Renato Simoni (1875–1952), loosely based on the play by Carlo Gozzi (1762)
Aria Duration: 3:05
Tessitura: E♭4 to F5

Position: Act III

Setting: The gardens before the walls of Peking (Beijing) in fabled times

Liù, a young slave girl, is a good and gentle spirit. She has been the traveling companion to Timur, who is the deposed Tartar King and the father to Calaf. Liù, Calaf, and Timur are in the midst of a processional to the execution of the Prince of Persia, who attempted to win the Princess Turandot by answering three riddles. If he had given the correct answers, he would have married the Princess, but the price for incorrectly answering them is death.

During the processional, Calaf catches a glimpse of Turandot, falls in love with her immediately, and decides to attempt to answer the three riddles. Timur begs his son not to leave him alone in the world at his old age: "Are there no words which can touch your cruel heart?" "My Lord, hear me!" begs Liù. "Liù can bear no more. Her heart is breaking!" She has walked many miles with his name in her heart, his name on her lips! "But if your fate tomorrow be decided we shall die on the path of exile." She pleads with Calaf that Timur will lose a son.

The aria is brief, but has a variety of dynamics, rhythms, and the range is wide—from low D♭ at the bottom of the staff to the climactic "pietà!/mercy!" at the end of the piece on high B♭ (after which she after which she "falls to the ground, sobbing and spent," as directed in the score). The text should be enunciated clearly even within the legato vocal line.

Piano/vocal score: p. 340 (Ricordi)

No. 58

Voice: soprano
Aria Title: "Ach, ich fühl's" (Pamina)
Opera Title: *Die Zauberflöte*
Composer: Wolfgang Amadeus Mozart (1745–1791)
Historical Style: Singspiel (1791)
Range: D4 to A♯/B♭6

Fach: lyric
Librettist: Emanuel Schikaneder (1751–1812)
Aria Duration: 4:25
Tessitura: F3/G♭4 to G5

Position: Act II

Setting: Described as "a short hallway"

It should be noted that Pamina has not yet seen Tamino in this act. The second act focuses on the trials for Tamino, Papageno, and Pamina. The spirits instruct Tamino and Papageno before Pamina's entrance that they must not speak. While Papageno ignores their admonitions, Tamino obeys the rules. They also tell Tamino that he will triumph but must remain silent. After the spirits exit, Pamina excitedly enters, having heard the sound of Tamino's flute—thinking that he is signaling her. He is sad that he cannot speak to her and motions for her to leave. She understands this to mean that he does not care for her anymore. In stunned grief, she begins the aria:

> Forever gone love's happiness!
> Nevermore will come the hour of bliss
> Back to my heart!
> See, Tamino, these tears,
> Flowing, beloved, for you alone!
> If you don't feel the longing of love,
> Then there will be peace in death!

As her feelings unfold, the aria is through composed, without repeated phrases. The accompaniment of repeated chords is heard underneath the voice in a rhythmic pattern of two 8th notes, 8th rest. The aria cannot be sung too slowly, for some of the phrases cannot be completed on one breath without momentum and must be sung as marked (andante—not adagio). Challenges are the long phrases, a light accompaniment that leaves the soprano "walking a virtual tightrope," and a floating and freely sung high B♭ that can be very touching. Some of the high notes are marked legato, and some are delineated by a little marked separation as she sings the word "Ruh/peace" on high G.

Although Pamina is an innocent and vulnerable young woman, and this aria represents a plea for Tamino to speak to her, she is also a strong character and would be frustrated when Tamino does not respond. She tries to elicit help from Papageno, but he usually has food in his mouth, or feels so sorry for her that he cannot speak. When Pamina sings, "Sieh, Tamino/see, Tamino," she can demand that he acknowledge her. When he does not and she has no one to turn to (not Sarastro, the Queen, Tamino, or Papageno), she will decide at some point to end her own life. This decision must be clear in Pamina's mind and be conveyed to the audience when she finally sings, "So wird Ruh' im Tode sein/Then there will be peace in death."

Piano/vocal score: p. 108 (G. Schirmer)

> Notes by singer and master teacher Benita Valente: The young singer should first look to the text, the story. How do the words make you feel? Speak the words the way you feel them. Find the center of how it makes you feel. Do *not* look at the tempo markings initially; find the tempo through the weight of your voice—both spoken and sung—and the strength of your convictions. This is not an easy piece to sing technically, but it is not made easier by a singer's focus on technique when performing (Although technique is your tool in freedom of expression). Focus on the emotions of Pamina's pleas for help; her disappointment, suffering, and anguish; and, finally, her resignation.

No. 59

Voice: soprano
Aria Title: "Allor che i forti corrono," Cavatina (Odabella)
Opera Title: *Attila*
Composer: Giuseppe Verdi (1813–1901)
Historical Style: Italian Romantic (1846)
Range: B4 to C6

Fach: dramatic coloratura
Librettist: Temistocle Solera (1815–1878)
Aria Duration: 7:10
Tessitura: E4 to G5

Position: Prologue

Setting: The main square of Aquileia, a Roman city, 426; Attila, the "scourge of God," is on his way to besiege Rome

After being overrun by the Huns, the surviving Aquileians are rounded up and brought before Attila, leader of the Huns. Odabella is the daughter of the Lord of Aquileia. After Attila questions why some women have been spared against his orders, he is told that the Aquileian women fight beside their men and thus had been spared. Odabella then steps out to criticize the women in Attila's tribe for staying in their tents during the battle instead of taking part in it.

She declaims in "Allor che i forti corrono/While your warriors run" that the women of Italy will always be in the thick of the fight. The legato line is important, but she also has clear accents within the line, and while there are decorative touches, the performance indication is "grandioso e fiero." The range is wide, from some of the phrases lingering at the bottom of the staff to the high B when she sings "sulfumido terreno sempre vedrai pugnar/the women fighting on the smoldering battlefield," with the phrase "sempre vedrai pugnar" repeated in descent, staccato, to the low B below the staff. The last part of this aria with its repetition of text is set very high, with beginnings of phrases on the high G, and the word "sempre" soars up in a 32nd-note flourish to high C before the final cadenza.

Odabella asks that her sword be returned to her, and Attila gives Odabella his own sword. Odabella bursts out in a cabaletta of savage joy: "Da te questo or m'e concesso/You give me this (*sword*)." With the sword, symbol of divine justice, she will be revenged upon her country's foe. She has lost her father and her fiancée. The cabaletta is marked by its brilliance, force, and wide melodic range (high B down two octaves in a 16th-note scale passage: "coll'acciar dell'oppressor/with the sword of the oppressed." The dotted rhythms in the voice also reinforce the determination of the character. The accompaniment is the typical (8th note, two 16th notes, followed by four 8th notes) rhythm for the cabaletta. "The hour of vengeance has come," she says. "The Lord has given a sign."

(Translation by Nico Castel)

Piano/vocal score: p. 13 (G. Ricordi)

No. 60

Voice: soprano
Aria Title: "Oh! Nel fuggente nuvolo,"
Romanza (Odabella)
Opera Title: *Attila*
Composer: Giuseppe Verdi (1813–1901)
Historical Style: Italian Romantic (1846)
Range: F4 to C6

Fach: dramatic coloratura
Librettist: Temistocle Solera (1815–1878)
Aria Duration: 3:30
Tessitura: F4 to G5

Position: Act I, scene 1

Setting: A forest near Attila's camp near Rome, 426, night

Odabella is alone and mourning her dead father and her love Foresto, whom she also believes is dead. All strings play the mournful, beautiful prelude. In the accompanied recitative she slowly sings, "Weep freely now, oh heart, do not curb yourself. In this quiet hour even the tiger rests. Only I rush from place to place. And yet I have been praying for this hour."

The sound of the solo flute is heard ascending, other solo instruments, the harp. Her ascending line and the solo instruments are very descriptive of the text: "Oh! Is this not your likeness, my father, in that fleeting cloud? Heavens! The likeness has changed! It is my Foresto!" (sempre sotto voce). "Stop the flow of the brook, the whisper of the breeze. Let me hear the adored voice of these souls," she sings in a beautiful vocal line that is delicately embellished. It must float to the high B, con dolcezza, and when she sings "amati spiriti/loving souls," there is a lovely chromatic descent, and a trill on "possa la voce udir/adored voice," accompanied by the orchestra with harp and solo flute.

Piano/vocal score: p. 63 (G. Ricordi)

No. 61

Voice: soprano
Aria Title: "Non più di fiori," No. 23, Rondo (Vitellia)
Opera Title: *La clemenza di Tito*
Composer: Wolfgang Amadeus Mozart (1756–1791)
Historical Style: Classical (1791)
Range: G3 to A6

Fach: dramatic coloratura
Librettist: Pietro Metastasio (1698–1782)
Aria Duration: 9:00
Tessitura: F4 to F5

Position: Act II

Setting: The imperial garden, Rome, 80 A.D.

Vitellia, daughter of the deposed Emperor Vitellius, is in love with Emperor Titus. He loves another, so she persuades Sextus, friend of the Emperor who is in love with her, to murder him. Sextus does not succeed, but is accused, and she realizes that she must confess before the Emperor that she asked him to commit the crime, as Sextus is prepared to die for her if she does not. She realizes that she must abandon her hopes for the throne and marriage to Titus by telling the truth:

This is the time, oh Vitellia, to examine your steadfastness. Will you have the necessary strength to look upon your bloody and loyal Sextus again? Sextus, who loves you more than his own life? Who, because of guilt, became a criminal? Who obeyed you, cruel one; who adored you, the unjust one? Who in the face of death maintains such great loyalty to you? And you, in the meantime, cognizant of it all, will go in all tranquility to the Emperor's nuptial bed? Ah, I always see Sextus around me. And I would fear that the breezes and the stones might speak and reveal me to Titus. I must go prostrate myself before him and tell him all. Thus if one cannot excuse Sextus's crime, his guilt will be lessened by my wrong. Farewell to empires and to hopes of matrimony.

Much of the recitative is unaccompanied, with the orchestra punctuating and emphasizing important syllabic inflections. "Ah, I always see Sextus" builds to a G♭ half note at the top of the staff, which is the highest pitch in the recitative.

No more will Hymen (*the god of marriage*) descend to entwine lovely chains of flowers.

Bound in barbarous, harsh chains, I see death drawing near.
Unhappy me! What horror! Ah, about me what will they say?
Whoever could see my suffering would take pity on me.

The aria is melodic, but has extremely florid decorative 32nd-note patterns and 16th-note triplet figures weaving in and out of the melody. The range is extreme, exploring the area below the staff down to low A and G, while singing a fermata on high A♭ and A. The text is repeated in the allegro section with the same rhythm at different pitch levels

Piano/vocal score: p. 168 (International)

No. 62

Voice: soprano
Aria Title: "Come scoglio" (Fiordiligi)
Opera Title: *Così fan tutte*
Composer: Wolfgang Amadeus Mozart (1756–1791)
Historical Style: Classical (1790)
Range: A4 to C6

Fach: dramatic coloratura
Librettist: Lorenzo da Ponte (1749–1838)
Aria Duration: 4:30
Tessitura: F4 to G5

Position: Act I, scene 3

Setting: The living room of Dorabella and Fiordiligi's house, Naples, 18th century

Two mysterious "Albanians" (Guglielmo and Ferrando in disguise) have shown up at the sisters' door accompanied by Don Alfonso. The two men attempt to woo them. Fiordiligi will have nothing to do with them, though, and in this aria declares her loyalty to Guglielmo and asks the strangers to stop attempting to win them.

The aria is sung with great solemnity in a section of the opera that is still comic in tone. Although this aria is a difficult piece to sing technically, and the soprano must concentrate on vocal technique to sing it successfully, there are comic elements to keep in mind. First of all, the aria is intended to give Fiordiligi a classic opera seria aria, an aria that would historically give the singer an "exit aria" that would allow the soprano to leave the stage. However, Fiordiligi is blocked by these two strange Albanians, who have appeared on the same day that their betrothed have left for war, and the audacious pair of men have gained entrance to the women's living room and are blocking her exit. Also mimicking the classic opera seria text, Fiordiligi compares her loyalty and devotion to being solid as a fortress against the storm (sending the soprano to a high sustained B after singing an A below the staff while invoking cosmic symbols to make her point). Among the many challenges in this piece include accidentals that need to be finely tuned, 16th-note rhythmic passages, tremendous leaps of intervals, and long phrases: in the last section (più allegro), the word "speranza/hope" will be extended through six measures of triplet patterns. In the final cadences the soprano needs to sing two high B♭'s.

The aria is not sung in a vacuum: it is addressed to the two outlandish outsiders who have penetrated her fortress. It is also possible that the men are amused at her serious response to their lighthearted play at wooing them, and that Dorabella, Fiordiligi's flamboyant sister, could be interested in and flirting with Guglielmo, giving the aria more of a point and an urgency.

Piano/vocal score: p. 115 (G. Schirmer)

No. 63

Voice: soprano
Aria Title: "Per pietà," No. 25 (Fiordiligi)
Opera Title: *Così fan tutte*
Composer: Wolfgang Amadeus Mozart
(1756–1791)
Historical Style: Classical (1790)
Range: A4 to B6

Fach: dramatic coloratura
Librettist: Lorenzo da Ponte (1749–1838)
Aria Duration: 6:53
Tessitura: B4 to G5

Position: Act II, scene 2

Setting: The living room of Dorabella and Fiordiligi's house, Naples, 18th century

After having begun to feel passion for one of the "Albanians," Fiordiligi apologizes to the absent Guglielmo, her love. She sings that her feelings have betrayed him and that she will hide this terrible incident from him.

This recitative and aria fall right in middle of the second act, a placement that emphasizes their importance. All of the events take place in one day's time, and so her loved one has left for the "war" that very day, and she finds herself having feelings for another man (an "Albanian," who is Ferrando— the tenor—in disguise). Ferrando has just sung an ardent aria in which he claims that if she does not return his affections, she will condemn him to die. The game has gone too far, and Fiordiligi is conflicted, not wanting to hurt Ferrando *or* Guglielmo.

The recitative that precedes the aria sets up the conflict in Fiordiligi. She first blames herself for succumbing to feelings for the tenor. Mozart provides the spaces between phrases to have different thoughts that she articulates, driving the final phrase of the expression to a high G and the cadence to a low unstressed B below the staff ("perfidia, e tradimento!/deceit and betrayal!").

The aria (adagio) is surprisingly tranquil after such a display of emotion, but it is sung with a longing and regret to the absent Guglielmo. It calls for an even singing between the low B below the staff and the high G, and a difficult intervallic descent between the high G and low C sharp. The text gives Fiordiligi an opportunity to focus outside of herself: "Fra quest' ombre, e queste piante sempre ascoso, oh Dio, sarà/among these shadows and these groves, oh God, (*my error*) will always be hidden."

The second section of the aria (allegro moderato) she addresses directly to the absent Guglielmo: "A chi mai manco di fede questo vano, ingrato cor?/To whom did this vain, ungrateful heart fail in loyalty? You were owed better, my dearest, for your purity." Here "caro bene/my dearest" is sustained on a middle B over eight beats. "Perdona/forgive" is in the lowest part of the range at the bottom of the staff. It is not all dark: she has hopes that her courage and constancy will erase the memory of horror that makes her feel "shame and horror" (descending to a low A as she sings "vergogna e orror mi fà/fills me with shame and horror"). Although the aria increasingly adds more coloratura in 16th-note passages and triplets, and the range becomes more extended, Fiordiligi has not become agitated in this section. The aria will finally cadence with trills to a high sustained G♯, and an 8th-note passing high B. She continues to display the qualities of love and devotion, nobility, tenderness tinged with regret, and sorrow.

Piano/vocal score: p. 250 (G. Schirmer)

No. 64

Voice: soprano
Aria Title: "Non mi dir" (Donna Anna)
Opera Title: *Don Giovanni*
Composer: Wolfgang Amadeus Mozart
(1756–1791)
Historical Style: Classical (1787)
Range: E4 to B♭6

Fach: dramatic coloratura
Librettist: Lorenzo da Ponte (1749–1838),
after Giovanni Bertati and Giuseppe
Gazzinga's opera *Don Giovanni Tenorio, o
sia Il convitato di pietra* (1787)
Aria Duration: 4:25
Tessitura: G4 to B♭6

Position: Act II, scene 4

Setting: A darkened room in Donna Anna's house in Spain, 18th century

This scene occurs after Don Giovanni and Leporello are in the cemetery after the statue of the Commendatore accepts Giovanni's invitation to dinner. Don Ottavio asks Donna Anna to calm herself, that Giovanni will soon be punished and they will be avenged. "Submit to the will of heaven," he says. He is asking her to accept his heart, hand, and tender love. Donna Anna is shocked by his words, and her sharp response causes him to call her "cruel." In the recitative before her aria, she says that it grieves her to "postpone their happiness," but she is worried about what people would say—"ma il mondo/but the world." It is sufficient that he has said that he loves her—"abbastanza per te mi parla amore/which already pleads your loving cause," she sings, piano, with a top B♭ in the phrase. In the body of the aria she wants him to know that she does love him, and her word is firm. By this point in the opera Ottavio feels frustrated and powerless. He has not been able to bring Don Giovanni, a fellow nobleman, to justice. He has lost Donna Anna to sorrow about her father and guilt that she feels, for her father died to defend her honor. The aria is in two parts. The first part, larghetto, is sung simply with some rapid figures (32nd notes) and embellishments. The phrases are long and calmly sung as she tries to placate him. The tessitura lies in the upper middle of the staff. There are many enharmonic notes in the melody, as if she is still searching for the melody she can sing to best express her feelings so that Don Ottavio will understand.

Toward the end of this first section, as she sings the interval of C to high A♭, she is asking him to not put so much pressure on her that her grief is multiplied when he is demanding of her at this time. The last section, allegretto moderato, cannot be sung at too fast a tempo because of the coloratura that predominates. In this section Donna Anna is hopeful for the sake of their relationship: "Forse un giorno il cielo ancora sentira pieta di me/perhaps one day heaven will again have mercy on me." Although these thoughts excite her, the coloratura still be controlled and carefully articulated. The range extends up to high B♭ but is not sustained at that tessitura. She is singing to Don Ottavio, but also reassures herself to build her inner fortitude.

Piano/vocal score: p. 253 (Boosey & Hawkes)

Notes by singer and master teacher Carol Vaness: "Non mi dir" is a very high aria which requires a calm that the character needs but is often hard to do late at night. The best way to portray this is with the accompanied opening recitative. I believe the best Mozart style is to keep in your head the beat exactly as it appears on the page. The music should never go out of time. Even if the appearance of repeated notes seem free, they should not be treated as if they really are. It may seem at first artificial, but when sung with full rich voice and expression, it is what causes the slowness of certain lines to be poignant. It is also vocally and musically more secure and comforting. This is true throughout the entire recitative right up until the "mi parla amore." The high B♭ should not be held an extraordinarily long time, as it is *not* the point; the point is the warmth of the vocal sound as Anna reassures her lover (or nonlover as the case may be), and the desperate emotion of "O Dio" when she is overwhelmed by everything that has happened to her that dreadful night of her father's murder. Another important point is to express through the clean vocal line while still keeping the emotions viable. That is the tricky part. There should be no crying in Mozart, but a feeling of being about to cry can give you a little bit extra to hold onto at the ends of the long beautiful phrases. The small coloratura bit is to be sung lyrically and even slightly slower than the pace of the aria. The musical moments determine the emotional state in which we find Donna Anna. Her first recitative preceding the Act I aria blows up with stress and worry but then she proceeds to run the show. She knows what she lost with her father, and she knows why it was her fault. "Non mi dir" should be sung with a type of love to fit the individual interpretation. The coloratura/cabaletta should be sung within the comfortable range of the individual facility of each soprano: accuracy is imperative in this final section.

No. 65

Voice: soprano
Aria Title: "Ach, ich liebte" (Konstanze)
Opera Title: *Die Entführung aus dem Serail*
Composer: Wolfgang Amadeus Mozart
(1756–1791)
Historical Style: Singspiel (1782)
Range: F4 to D6

Fach: dramatic coloratura
Librettist: Gottlieb Stephanie the younger
(1741–1800), after Christoph Friedrich Brentzer's *Bellmont und Constanze, oder Die Entführung aus dem Serail* set by Johann André
(1781)
Aria Duration: 5:47
Tessitura: A♯/B♭5 to A6

Position: Act I

Setting: The seaside country house of Pasha Selim on the coast of Turkey

The aria marks Konstanze's first entrance in the opera. She has been kidnapped by pirates and sold to Pasha Selim. He has a harem, but is especially enamored with Konstanze. She is sad in this aria, but she also reflects on her memories of happiness. The dialogue before the aria between Konstanze and Selim is important to know before singing the aria. The Pasha does not want her to be downcast. He could command her to be his, but tells her that she must give him her heart of her own free will. She calls him a "generous man." He will treat her as "his only treasure." She asks for forgiveness as she divulges the reason why she cannot love Pasha Selim: "She was in love and so happy, she knew nothing of love's pain."

The opening of the aria quickly demands control of the voice at the top of the staff with stressed and unstressed syllables (*"gluck*-lich, *Treu*-e"). The phrases are short, with a more extended last cadential phrase up to a high B♭ down to the inflected word (*"ganzes Herz"*). When she sings "Kummer ruht in meinem Schoss/sorrow rests in my breast," Konstanze must sing in the higher register up to high B♭ in passing tones on "in" toward "Schoss." The second time the phrase is sung she begins a coloratura passage to high D above high C in repeated short 8th notes in a legato then short rhythmic pattern. Then once again, she sings an extended coloratura passage on the same text. This demands range, control, and attention to articulation. After a short interlude the same text is repeated with different melodic figures. Once again, when she sings "kummer ruht in meinem Schoss," she sings up to high D above high C. Konstanze sings the word "kum-mer" with the second syllable on the higher notes, calling for vocal control. Each passage can be colored with a different dramatic intent, changing the colors of the voice (e.g., resistance, holding onto sweet memories, reflecting on her lonely situation). Although she is a prisoner of the Pasha, we should not forget that he is treating her like a "treasure," and is in love with his prisoner.

Piano/vocal score: p. 47 (Peters)

> Notes by singer and voice professor Costanza Cuccaro: Konstanze is steadfast and true. She is noble—but not cold—multifaceted, warm, and caring. She has depth and strength of character; willing to sacrifice her life for her love. The contrast between the lyric and coloratura sections should be stressed. The role of Konstanze is technically challenging and requires great stamina. This aria requires an easy high, excellent coloratura, clean articulation, and endurance in the high tessitura. Also necessary are warmth of voice, beautiful legato, evenness of registers, and dynamic control.

No. 66

Voice: soprano
Aria Title: "Ernani, Ernani involami" (Elvira)
Opera Title: *Ernani*
Composer: Giuseppe Verdi (1813–1901)
Historical Style: Italian Romantic (1844)
Range: B♭4 to B6

Fach: dramatic coloratura
Librettist: Francesco Maria Piave (1810–1976), after Victor Hugo's tragedy *Hernani* (1830)
Aria Duration: 6:22
Tessitura: B♭5 to A5

Position: Act I (The Bandit), scene 2

Setting: Elvira's richly furnished apartment in Don Ruy Gomez de Silva's castle, Spain, 1519, night

Elvira is in love with Ernani, a "mountaineer and bandit," but is betrothed to her uncle Silva, who is her guardian. "The night has fallen, and Silva has not returned," she sings, unaccompanied. "Oh, that he would never return." She descends into the low range as she sings, "The more this loathsome old man pursues me like some foul ghost . . . with talk of love the more Ernani is fixed in my heart."

The cavatina begins with a lilting tempo: "Ernani, take me away from his hateful embrace . . . let us run off . . . and if love will let me live with you, I shall follow you through caverns, across barren plains. And those caverns will be a paradise for me." The final section repeats the melody to a final cadenza. The demands of range (to high C) are considerable, with delicate embellishments at the top of the range. Elvira's ladies enter, carrying extravagant wedding presents. "How many young women would envy you, my lady," sing the ladies. "Silva adores you. With these sparkling jewels you will look like a queen. Tomorrow all will joyfully greet you as a bride."

Elvira replies that she is charmed by her simple wishes from their hearts. The cabaletta begins as Elvira vents her scorn. "No jewel can change hatred into love. Hurry, time, to the happy moment of my escape! Waiting is a torture to a loving heart." The melody feels spontaneous and is repeated with more coloratura.

(Translation by Nico Castel)

Piano/vocal score: p. 32 (Kalmus)

No. 67

Voice: soprano
Aria Title: "Il dolce suono mi colpì di sua voce," Mad Scene (Lucia)
Opera Title: *Lucia di Lammermoor*
Composer: Gaetano Donizetti (1797–1848)
Historical Style: Bel canto (1835)
Range: E♭4 to E♭6

Fach: dramatic coloratura
Librettist: Salvatore Cammarano (1801–1852), after Sir Walter Scott's novel *The Bride of Lammermoor* (1819)
Aria Duration: 15:30
Tessitura: E♭4 to E♭5

Position: Act III

Setting: Scotland, end of the 16th century; a hall in Ravenswood Castle, belonging to Sir Henry Ashton

Lucia of Lammermoor is in love with Edgardo, who is a hated rival of her family. Her brother Enrico has forged a letter from Edgardo to convince Lucia of Edgardo's infidelity. Enrico also tells her of his desperate political position and that only her marrying Arturo can save him. The chaplain Raimondo further weakens Lucia by reminding her of her obligations to her family. Pressure is put on her to marry Arturo, and she does so, but Edgardo unexpectedly appears and curses Lucia for signing the contract to marry Arturo.

The wedding festivities are interrupted by Raimondo's disclosure that Lucia has murdered Arturo, and she appears in front of the wedding guests, dazed, crazed by the horror of the act. After killing Arturo, Lucia begins the "mad scene" by switching back and forth between joy and horror. In addition to hallucinating that Edgardo is there, she also sees the ghost that foretold the bloody end of her romance with Edgardo.

Il dolce suono/The sweet sound descends into my heart. Edgardo, I surrender to you! (A chill creeps into my breast!) Sit a while with me next to the fountain (*of Act I scene 2*). A terrible phantom arises and separates us. Let us take refuge by the foot of the altar, strewn with roses. A harmony celestial, do you not hear? It plays the marriage hymn! The ceremony for us draws near! Happiness! The joy that one feels and does not speak of! The incense burns. Brilliant are the sacred, shining torches. Here is the minister! Give me your right hand! O joyous day! At last I am yours and you are mine.

There are rapid tempo changes from section to section: andante, allegretto, and allegro vivace. The recitative "qui ricovriamo, Edgardo" has unaccompanied passages. There are rapid changes between legato, sustained passages, and 32nd-note coloratura, which reflect Lucia's crazed state.

Piano/vocal score: p. 190 (G. Schirmer)

No. 68

Voice: soprano
Aria Title: "Regnava nel silenzio" (Lucia)
Opera Title: *Lucia di Lammermoor*
Composer: Gaetano Donizetti (1797–1848)
Historical Style: Bel canto (1835)
Range: C4 to C6

Fach: dramatic coloratura
Librettist: Salvatore Cammarano (1801–1852), after Sir Walter Scott's novel *The Bride of Lammermoor* (1819)
Aria Duration: 9:20
Tessitura: G4 to F#5

Position: Act I, scene 2

Setting: Scotland, end of the 16th century. The entrance of a park on the grounds near the Castle of Ravenswood. At the back is a gateway; toward the front is a fountain.

Lucia is at the fountain where an ancestor hid the corpse of a "Lammermoor lass." The ancestor had slain the girl in a jealous rage. Lucia is frightened because she has recently seen the girl's ghost. She describes the episode vividly to Alisa, her maid, mentioning that the water had turned blood-red. Her vocal line is accompanied by arpeggiated harp:

Regnava nel silenzio (*larghetto*)/The night, deep and dark, reigned in the silence . . . a pale ray from the gloomy moon shone on the fountain . . . then a low sigh was heard throughout the air; and there (*crescendo*) on the fountain's edge the shadow appeared to me.

The composer uses the vocal ornaments for dramatic ends; the embellishments vividly convey Lucia's unstable state. Lucia is waiting secretly for a clandestine meeting with Edgardo, a hated rival of her family. She knows that her brother Enrico with his furious temper must not find out.

The next verse is the same melody and continues the story:

Her lips moved as if speaking, and with her lifeless hand she seemed to call me. She stood there, motionless, and she suddenly disappeared and the water, earlier so limpid, became as red as the blood.

This verse has increasingly more embellishments in the vocal line.

Alisa declares that Lucia's love for Edgardo is beset with difficulties and urges her to discard him. However, Lucia believes in him. The cabaletta is marked moderato, in which Alise joins her in the last phrase:

Quando rapito in estasi/When enraptured in ecstasy by the most burning love, and with the language of the heart, he swears to me eternal faith. I forget my troubles, tears become joy. It seems to me that near him heaven opens for me.

The cabaletta has staccato passages as well as legato coloratura passages, chromatic 16th-note scales, wide intervallic leaps, to the sustained high A, B, and C.

Piano/vocal score: p. 32 (G. Schirmer)

No. 69

Voice: soprano
Aria Title: "Anch'io dischiuso un giorno" (Abigaille)
Opera Title: *Nabucco*
Composer: Giuseppe Verdi (1813–1901)
Historical Style: Italian Romantic (1842)
Range: D4 to C6

Fach: dramatic coloratura
Librettist: Temistocle Solera (1815–1878)
Aria Duration: 3:45
Tessitura: D4 to A6

Position: Part II (L'Empio/The Wicked Man), scene 1

Setting: An apartment in the royal palace of Nabucco (Nebuchadnezzar) in Babylon, 6th century B.C.
   Abigaille has found the document that proves that she was not Nabucco's daughter but, rather, the daughter of a slave and one of Nabucco's wives who have both been put to death for her birth. In the recitative preceding the aria, Abigaille describes her deep desire for revenge, but then, as she begins the aria, she changes the mood to talk about the love she feels for Ismaele. As Abigaille enters hastily, holding a parchment in her hand, she sings:

Happily I found you, o fatal document! Carelessly, in his bosom, the king hid this document that would prove my shame! Abigaille a daughter of slaves! Well, then, let her be such! (Allegro) What am I here? Even though the Assyrians believe me to be Nabucco's daughter, I am worse than a slave! The throne the king confides to the younger Fenena, while he sets his mind to exterminate Judea with his weapons! Me, the amorous doings of others, he sends from the battlefield to watch here! Oh, wicked all (sung on high B♭ on the -u- vowel), and more deluded still! You know little of Abigaille's heart! You will see my fury fall upon everyone! Ah, yes, let Fenena, my pretended father, and the realm all fall! And my ruin befall me, oh fatal slander! Each phrase of this accompanied recitative is delineated to underline her strong will.

Cantabile:
I too once opened my heart to happiness.
Around me I heard everything speak to me of holy love;
I wept at other's tears, I suffered of others the pain;
Ah! Who can give back to me only one day of that lost enchantment?

Observe strong rhythmic patterns, accents, chromatic 32nd-note figures, and a high C "Ah!" in the final cadenza.

Piano/vocal score: p. 151 (Ricordi)

No. 70

Voice: soprano
Aria Title: "No word from Tom . . . I go to him" (Anne Trulove)
Opera Title: *The Rake's Progress*
Composer: Igor Stravinsky (1882–1971)
Historical Style: 20th-century English (1951)
Range: B4 to C6

Fach: dramatic coloratura
Librettists: W. H. Auden (1907–1973) and Chester Kallman (1921–1975), after William Hogarth's cycle of paintings of the same name (1735)
Aria Duration: 7:20
Tessitura: F4 to G5

Position: Act I, scene 3

Setting: Autumn night, full moon. Anne enters from a house in the country in traveling clothes.

Anne Trulove is worried about Tom. He has left the country and her side for London, where he hopes to make his fortune. He is young, naïve, and idealistic, and Anne is worried about him. A mysterious stranger named Nick Shadow (the devil in disguise) has made a pact to serve him. "No word from Tom," she begins, and the cavatina should not begin too slowly. It needs some urgency. The text is poetic, with rich images, so diction is of supreme importance in the recitative: "Has love no voice?" she asks. "Fades it as the rose cut for a rich display? He needs my help. Love hears, Love knows, Love answers him across the silent miles, and goes." The intervals in the vocal line are not predictable, and the notes are "all over the staff." Thought processes during the introduction are important: "What am I thinking about right now?" is a question the singer should ask oneself.

She asks the moon to guide her as the aria begins. Although the notes are written out, the music has an air of improvisational embellishments with mordent-like figures. The primo tempo and cabaletta call for flexibility of voice, with 32nd-note patterns ("It cannot be thou art") from the high B down to the low B below the staff ("upon a colder heart"). Anne hears her father's voice and has to decide in the recitative whether or not she will leave him to follow Tom to London, even though she comes out of the house already in traveling clothes. "No," her father has "strength of purpose, while "Tom is weak and needs my helping hand." She asks God to "protect dear Tom, support my father, and strengthen my resolve." She bows her head, then rises and comes forward with great decisiveness. "I go to him," the cabaletta, is very fast, with wide intervallic leaps from the bottom of the staff to the top and is difficult for the accompanist to play. Much of it is written at the top of the staff in her resolve as she sings through the *passaggio* and up to sustained A♭, with a final note on high C sustained for two measures: "Time cannot alter a loving heart, an ever loving heart!"

Piano/vocal score: p. 60 (Boosey & Hawkes)

No. 71

Voice: soprano
Aria Title: "Mercè, dilette amiche," Sicilienne (Helen)
Opera Title: *I vespri siciliani* (Italian version)
Composer: Giuseppe Verdi (1813–1901)
Historical Style: Italian Romantic (1855)
Range: A4 to C#6

Fach: dramatic coloratura
Librettists: Eugène Scribe (1791–1861) and Charles Duveyrier (1803–1866)
Aria Duration: 4:30
Tessitura: E4 to G#5

Position: Act V

Setting: The gardens of the palace of Monfort, Palermo, Sicily, 1282

Arrigo has found out that his loathed enemy is his father, Monfort. Elena is one of the conspirators who are planning to assassinate Monfort, but Arrigo intervenes and Monfort is saved. The conspirators are jailed, except for Arrigo. Monfort will kill Elena unless Arrigo agrees to call him "father." Arrigo agrees, and Monfort releases all of the conspirators and allows Elena and Arrigo to be married—to seal the peace between the opposing factions. Elena knows that a ship laden with arms for the uprising is at the moment of the wedding lying in wait in the harbor. The fanatical Procida informs Elena that when the wedding bells ring to announce the wedding, the armed Sicilians will fall upon the French and slaughter them all. This is a highly charged atmosphere.

After the marriage ceremony, Elena sings of her great joy in a dancelike fashion that is more akin to a Spanish bolero than a siciliana. She comes down the steps of the palace. The maidens move toward her, offering her flowers.

> Thank you, beloved friends, for those pretty flowers;
> The beloved gift is the image of your lovely innocence!
> Oh, lucky the bond that love prepares for me!
> If you bring happy wishes to my heart as assistants before my wedding,
> Thanks for the gift, ah yes!
> Oh beloved dream, oh sweet intoxication!
> With unknown love leaps my heart!
> Heavenly an air already I breathe, that all my senses became intoxicated!

(Translation by Nico Castel)

Piano/vocal score: p. 371 (Lucie Galland)

No. 72

Voice: soprano
Aria Title: "Der Hölle Rache kocht in meinem Herzen," No. 14 (Queen of the Night)
Opera Title: *Die Zauberflöte*
Composer: Wolfgang Amadeus Mozart (1756–1791)
Historical Style: German Singspiel (1791)
Range: F4 to F6

Fach: dramatic coloratura
Librettist: Emanuel Schikaneder (1751–1812)
Aria Duration: 3:03
Tessitura: A5 to C6

Position: Act II, scene 3

Setting: Pamina's room in ancient Egypt

Act II in *Die Zauberflöte* is devoted to the trials—not only for Tamino and Papageno, but also for Pamina. The evil Monostatos finds Pamina asleep in her room, and he burns with desire for her. He sings about his desires as he sneaks up to her while she is asleep. She awakes, and the Queen appears suddenly, accompanied by thunder and lightning. Pamina is saved and falls into her mother's arms. The Queen produces a dagger that has been sharpened to kill Sarastro, who has been like a father to Pamina. "You will kill him," she tells Pamina. The Queen launches into the aria, marked allegro assai. "Hell's revenge cooks in my heart. Death and despair flame about me!" she sings, up to a high, and sustained, B♭. "If Sarastro is not killed by you, you will no longer be my daughter," she says. "Nevermore," with the last syllable ascending to a repeated, staccato high C. The vocal line extends up to the high F above high C.

After this section one can imagine in the interval poor Pamina going to her mother and pleading, with the Queen stopping her to continue her tirade: "disowned you will be forever" (from F at the top of the staff to the octave below). These are unaccented syllables and need not be punched in the chest voice. The burden to accomplish this murder of Sarastro is on Pamina: "If not," the Queen says, "Destroyed be forever all the bonds of nature." This phrase is repeated on triplet 8th-note figures before ascending once again to a cackling staccato on high F. Finally, the Queen cries out (with an extended high B♭) to the "gods of revenge to hear a mother's oath."

Piano/vocal score: p. 99 (G. Schirmer)

Notes by singer and voice professor Sally Wolf: In the second-act aria the Queen of the Night shows her "true colors" to Pamina (and the audience) when, in "Der Hölle Rache," she says that if Pamina does not kill Sarastro and bring her the "sevenfold shield of the sun," she will disown and abandon her. I found that in this aria I had to keep my wits about me not only technically for the demanding tessitura and coloratura accuracy, but also emotionally— not to let the anger of the aria get the better of me. The coloratura in this aria is the Queen's "mad scene"; she is over the top with anger and desperation.

No. 73

Voice: soprano
Aria Title: "O zittre nicht . . . Zum Leiden bin ich auserkoren," No. 4 (Queen of the Night)
Opera Title: *Die Zauberflöte*
Composer: Wolfgang Amadeus Mozart (1756–1791)
Historical Style: Singspiel (1791)
Range: D4 to F6

Fach: dramatic coloratura
Librettist: Emanuel Schikaneder (1751– 1812)
Aria Duration: 5:03
Tessitura: G4 to E♭5

Position: Act I, scene 1

Setting: A magical forest in ancient Egypt

Tamino, the Prince, has just been given a portrait of Pamina and has sung about her beauty ("Dies Bildniss ist bezaubernd schön"). He wants the three ladies to lead him to Pamina, so that he can save her. Amid thunder and lightning, the Queen of the Night makes a dramatic appearance. She sings to Tamino. In the opening measures she sings of Tamino's innocence, piety, and wisdom. As such a youth he must do his best to comfort "this deeply troubled mother's heart." She obviously wants something from him.

She sings of her own suffering, as her daughter has been taken away from her.

She loses her intended calm when she talks about "her fortune being lost by an evil one." The rhythms become more pointed, the voice goes above the staff, and the orchestral accompaniment is forte. She goes on: "I still see her trembling" (ascending to a high A♭). Then she brings to life her memory of the cries of Pamina, "Ach, hilft!/Oh, help!" (again, ascending to a high A♭). She ends the first section with the realization "My help was too weak."

She turns her attention from Pamina's plight and her own weakness in helping her to Tamino in the allegro moderato section. "You will go to set her free," she demands. She has shifted from playing the bereaved mother to ordering Tamino to action. She does not ask or plead, she orders him to be her savior. Only then will Pamina be his.

The well-known coloratura passages show two sides of the character—lovely, but evil; lyric, but dramatic. The Queen needs to be in command and technically in control. The coloratura goes to the high F above high C. There are three or four measures at a time of connected 16th notes in sequential patterns. There are also connected 16th notes and articulated staccato. The soprano must have a dramatic delivery, but she cannot sing with a heavy production to be able to negotiate the coloratura. In the higher staccato passages it is helpful after technical vocal mastery to think of cackling laughter from the character's emotions rather than concentration on vocal technique.

Piano/vocal score: p. 28 (G. Schirmer)

> Notes by singer and voice professor Sally Wolf: I think that "O zittre nicht" is the more difficult of the two Queen of the Night arias. It is difficult technically because of the varied tessitura. In the first aria there is the gorgeous legato singing and the wonderful character of deception and different colors of the text. The Queen must convince Tamino (and the audience) that she represents good and Sarastro is evil. She must make him believe that she is heartbroken and devastated at losing her daughter. All she truly wants is to get the power from Sarastro, no matter what the cost! She then entices Tamino with the brilliant second half of the aria. I like to think of it as a hypnotic device—very manipulative—to try to get him to help her.

No. 74

Voice: soprano
Aria Title: "To this we've come," Paper Aria
(Magda)
Opera Title: *The Consul*
Composer and Librettist: Gian Carlo
Menotti (b. 1911)
Historical Style: 20th-century American
(1949)
Range: B4 to B♭6

Fach: full lyric
Aria Duration: 7:50
Tessitura: F4 to F5

Position: Act II, scene 2

Setting: The waiting room of a consulate in a large anonymous European city in a totalitarian European country after World War II

John Sorel is a freedom fighter, but he is hiding from the police. He tries to flee the country. His wife, Magda, repeatedly goes to the consulate for a visa, but the Consul does not appear. At this point in the opera, Magda is hounded by the police, her baby has died, and she does not know where her husband is. After a bitter argument with the Secretary, Magda's frustration culminates in the words "To this we've come . . . that men withhold the world from men. No ship nor shore for him who drowns at sea. No home nor grave for him who dies on land." The rhythm of her speech is mirrored in the changes in meter between 2/4, 4/4, and 3/4. The words flow naturally. "That he be hunted without the hope of refuge" is sung forte, at the top of the staff. "Tell me, secretary, who are these men? Who (*sustained high A*) are these dark archangels?" is sung without accompaniment. "Have you ever seen the Consul?" she desperately pleads (with almost a touch of madness in her voice). "Have you ever spoken with him?" (She breaks down and turns away to control herself). The others in the waiting room ask the Secretary the same question.

Magda turns her attention to the papers on the desk: "Papers! Papers! Don't you understand? (*andante mosso*) My child is dead . . . John's mother is dying, my own life is in danger. I ask you for help, and all you give me is . . . papers" (unaccompanied). She repeats the impersonal litany of the consulate questions: "name, age, color of eyes and hair." She then becomes completely crazed, picks up the papers on the desk, and throws them as she cries "Papers!" over and over again. "Look at my eyes, they are afraid to sleep," is sung at the top of the staff. "Look at my hands, at these old woman's hands." With mounting anguish, she poses the question again and again: "What is your name?" She answers, "My name is woman, my age is still young, my color of hair is gray. Color of eyes: the color of tears. Occupation: Waiting, waiting," she sings over and over. "Oh! The day will come, I know, when our hearts aflame will burn your paper chains. Warn the Consul. That day neither ink nor seal shall cage our souls. That day will come." She ends on a triumphal high A♭. The composer uses repetition and unaccompanied sections to emphasize the text. He also uses silence to emphasize tension. This aria is the turning point for Magda; at the end of the opera she will take her own life.

Piano/vocal score: p. 198 (G. Schirmer)

No. 75

Voice: soprano
Aria Title: "Ruskai pogibnu," Letter Scene (Tatiana)
Opera Title: *Eugene Onegin*
Composer: Pyotr Ilyich Tchaikovsky (1840–1893)
Historical Style: Russian Romantic (1877)
Range: D4 to B♭6

Fach: full lyric
Librettists: The composer and Konstantin Shilovsky (1849–1893), based on Aleksandr Pushkin's verse novel *Eugene Onegin* (1831)
Aria Duration: 12:50
Tessitura: G4 to F5

Position: Act I, scene 2

Setting: Tatiana's bedroom in Madame Larina's house in the country, St. Petersburg, Russia, 1820s. Tatiana's room is very simply furnished with old-fashioned white chairs covered with chintz, and window curtains of the same material. There is a bed, a bookshelf, a chest of drawers covered with a cloth, and on it a mirror on a stand and vases of flowers. At the window there is a table with writing materials.

Tatiana has a rich fantasy life, demonstrated at the beginning of the opera when she is seen dreamily reading a romance novel. When Tatiana meets the worldly Onegin in Act I, she sees in him the man fate has chosen for her, even though his first comments to her are patronizing.

As the curtain rises in scene 2, Tatiana, in a white nightdress, is sitting before her mirror, lost in thought. The nurse is standing near her and tells her that it's late and she must be up in time for church in the morning. Tatiana says she can't sleep—it's too hot. She asks the nurse to open the window. Restless, she asks the nurse to tell her of the past. The nurse demurs, "My mind grows weaker every day." Tatiana wants the nurse to tell her about her first love, but the nurse resists, simply stating that her parents arranged her marriage when she was 13 years old. Tatiana confides how unhappy she is. The nurse says she must be ill. "I'm in love," Tatiana tells the nurse before she leaves. Tatiana remains onstage lost in thought, but then she rises agitatedly with an expression of resolute determination. Tatiana decides that the only way to express her love for Onegin is to write him a letter in which she explains her feelings toward him. She has difficulty starting the letter; as she writes she pauses, rereading what she has written. As she writes, she plumbs the depth and strength of her love for him.

In this aria enunciation is especially important; even the lyric passages are set syllabically. The numerous changes in tempo markings (allegro non troppo, andante, moderato assai quasi andante, adagio, moderato) reflect Tatiana's changes of emotion. As she finishes the letter she becomes even more agitated (più mosso/with increasing intensity): "I fear my reason will desert me; to find release I'd gladly die! I long for you!" She descends to D♭ at the bottom of the staff as she articulates her fears: "To leave me desolate and wretched." Still, she is hopeful at the end of the scene: "But since his honor is my pledge, I boldly trust he will not fail me" (to high A♭). Although much of the aria is sung in the middle voice, with full high notes above the staff in climactic passages, many of the lyric phrases begin at the top of the staff.

Piano/vocal score: p. 76 (Schauer–London)

No. 76

Voice: soprano
Aria Title: "Ah, je ris de me voir," 2nd part
of No. 9, Jewel Song (Marguerite)
Opera Title: *Faust*
Composer: Charles Gounod (1818–1893)
Historical Style: French Romantic (1859)
Range: C♯/D♭4 to A6

Fach: full lyric (coloratura)
Librettists: Jules Barbier (1825–1901) and
Michel Carré (1822–1872), after Part I of
Johann Wolfgang von Goethe's play *Faust*
(1808)
Aria Duration: 4:49
Tessitura: F♯/G♭4 to G5

Position: Act III

Setting: The garden of Marguerite in a German city, 16th century. There is a wall at back, with a little door, a bower at left, and a house at right, with a window toward the audience. Trees and shrubs dot the scene.

Marguerite is very young, innocent, and has a rich imagination (given the text of this aria). At the end of the preceding act Marguerite has modestly rejected Faust's advances. He is at this point a stranger, an unknown "handsome man." At the beginning of Act III, Siebel, who is infatuated with Marguerite, leaves a bouquet of flowers for her. Faust, playing the romantic idealist, "blesses" her home and its place in nature. Mephisto positions a jewel box near the bouquet. Marguerite enters, singing a ballad tinged with modal inflections about the King of Thule. She discovers both the bouquet and jewel box and erupts in a buoyant cabaletta, trying on earrings and a necklace. She is on the stage with her guardian, Marthe, who is very impressed with the gifts.

In the recitative when Marguerite sees the gifts she is at first suspicious and reluctant to open the jewel case. The young girl has never seen such riches. She puts on the earrings, and the aria begins with a sustained trill as she looks at herself in a mirror found in the case. The high A as she exclaims "Ah!" should not be overvocalized, it is representational of a cry of delight. She is speaking to herself in the mirror: "Is it you? Marguerite?" The soprano needs to sing easily up to F and sustained G at the top, also with a number of important words and notes at the bottom of the staff: "d'un roi/of a king" to E. Before the repetition of the melody and text beginning the same way (with a sustained trill on B), Marguerite becomes emboldened and puts on a bracelet and a string of pearls: "God! It's like a hand which is placed on my arm!" (remember that these gifts actually come from Mephisto). The second time the melody is sung, then, it becomes more flamboyant, daring, urgent, to a short phrase that includes a sustained trill on F♯ at the top of the staff going up to high B (fermata) to finish on an unaccented E.

Piano/vocal score: p. 127 (G. Schirmer)

> Notes by singer and voice professor Virginia Zeani: The "Jewel Song" calls for a lyric voice that is not too light. It is a role that needs dramatic intensity and power by the end of the evening singing the role. Although written in French, it has an elegant Italian style to it, calling for an agile voice with facility on the higher pitches. Marguerite is young, delicate, and innocent—but the role calls for fervent intensity in the voice and character.

No. 77

Voice: soprano
Aria Title: "Klänge der Heimat," No. 10, Czàrdàs (Roselinda)
Opera Title: *Die Fledermaus*
Composer: Johann Strauss, Jr. (1825–1899)
Historical Style: Viennese Operetta (1874)
Range: C♯/B♭4 to D6

Fach: full lyric
Librettists: Carl Haffner (1804–1874) and Richard Genée (1823–1895)
Aria Duration: 4:37
Tessitura: D4 to A6

Position: Act II

Setting: A party in Prince Orlofsky's house, Vienna, 1870

The chorus sings happily at the Act II party scene. The host, Prince Orlovsky, welcomes the guests, and Eisenstein claims that one of the dressed-up guests is his chambermaid, Adele. In "My dear Marquis," she ridicules his accusations and demands an apology, virtually laughing in his face.

He sees a mysterious, exotic woman, who actually is Roselinda, his wife, in disguise. They sing a duet as he tries to unmask her, and she pockets his watch as a souvenir as she "counts the beat of his heart." He still wants to know more about this mysterious stranger, and Roselinda sings the Czàrdàs, a melody of her "homeland," to tell all about herself. The first section is marked langsam (slow). Remember that Roselinda is making this all up as she goes along. It has the flourishes and embellishments that she feels are necessary to show her "feelings" for her homeland, wherever that may be. It begins lower in her range, and rapidly rises to the top of the staff ("I'm lonely for you, my native skies") to F♯ at the top of the staff. This section has a rubato that you would associate with a gypsy-like style for this mysterious and exotic creature. "Wherever I may wander" is sung without accompaniment, strongly, up to high A with a flourish on A, and then goes on to say "to you (*homeland*) my thoughts will fly" (up from middle B to high B descending chromatically/exotically down the scale). At this point, Roselinda has engaged Eisenstein's attention fully. He would like her to be as passionate about him as she is about her "homeland." She is more confident now, having fun as she launches into the fast section (Friszka). Roselinda needs a tambourine to accent her call to "lift your glasses, pass the bottles, drown your sorrow, 'til tomorrow." Her range is above the staff, but she must also sing "hear the Csàrdàs sound" down to D below the staff. The last section (più allegro) is pure energy, all sung on "La" with a sustained trill on high A sung for four measures, and then the final tag is high B, A, and finally a thrown-off high D (8th note) with flair.

Piano/vocal score: p. 85 (G. Schirmer)

No. 78

Voice: soprano
Aria Title: "Il est doux, il est bon" (Salomé)
Opera Title: *Hérodiade*
Composer: Jules Massenet (1842–1912)
Historical Style: French Romantic (1881)
Range: E♭4 to B♭6

Fach: full lyric
Librettists: Paul Milliet and Henri Grémont (Georges Hartmann [1842–1900])
Aria Duration: 5:10
Tessitura: F4 to F5

Position: Act I

Setting: The courtyard of Hérode's (Herod's) palace, Jerusalem, during the reign of King Herod Antipas, 30 A.D.

Salomé is looking for her mother. She was abandoned at birth and does not know that she is actually the daughter of the King's wife, Hérodiade (Herodias). She tells Phanuel of her determination to find her mother and then continues, telling him that the only one who understands her is the prophet Jean (John the Baptist).

The beginning of the melody is fragmented, separated by pauses: "He is beautiful as the sky . . . his voice is melody." A piano high G begins the line: "If he speaks everyone keeps silent—a sigh is not heard as far as the bird flies. He speaks." The voice begins at the top of the staff (con ardore) as she pleads, "Ah, when will he return? When will he understand who I am? I am suffering alone on earth and have peace from you—I hear your accented tone, melodious and pure. I have peace from you!" She sings a powerful forte: "Beautiful angel, shall I live if you fail my heart?" and then relents with a rallentando: "Return to me, who does not know life without you."

The melody of the piece is beautiful, but clarity of articulated diction is important. There is also rhythmic variety in the vocal line, including 8th-note triplet figures.

Piano/vocal score: p. 31 (Ricordi)

No. 79

Voice: soprano
Aria Title: "Lo vidi e 'l primo palpito," Cavatina (Luisa)
Opera Title: *Luisa Miller*
Composer: Giuseppe Verdi (1813–1901)
Historical Style: Italian Romantic (1849)
Range: F♯4 to C6

Fach: full lyric
Librettist: Salvatore Cammarano (1801–1852), after Johann Christoph Friedrich von Schiller's "bourgeois tragedy" *Kabale und Liebe* (1784)
Aria Duration: 3:31
Tessitura: G4 to B6

Position: Act I (Love), scene 1

Setting: Early 17th century; a pleasant village: on one side is Miller's humble dwelling, on the other side is a little country church. In the distance, through the trees, rise the towers of Count Walter's castle. A crystal-clear spring day is dawning on the horizon.

The villagers are gathered to celebrate Luisa's birthday. Miller and his daughter come out of the cottage and exchange greetings with the villagers. Laura, Luisa's friend, suggests that they all go to the church and invoke God's blessing. Miller thanks them all, but Luisa is clearly looking for someone who should be there and is not. Although Miller is uneasy and tells her that this new young man Carlo could be dangerous, Luisa is convinced that Carlo has a noble heart and loves her as she loves him.

"Love at first sight" is the theme of her cavatina. The piece is simple and has a purpose: Luisa is an artless village maiden whose joyous, trusting nature is perfectly expressed in this aria. The villagers present Luisa with flowers, and there is a sudden pause as she recognizes a young huntsman who comes to offer a flower. "Lo vidi, e 'l primo palpito/I saw him, and the first palpitation" has a light, bright, and energetic tone to it. "I saw him, and my heart felt its first thrill of love; as soon as he saw me, the heart sprang up. On meeting here on earth our souls recognized each other; God created them in heaven (*a triplet pattern to high C*) to love each other!" The melody is repeated with more embellishments, including a trilled high G for two measures on the word "ciel/heaven" followed by once more a triplet pattern, staccato, from high C descending, then ascending again to the high C.

Piano/vocal score: p. 26 (Kalmus)

No. 80

Voice: soprano
Aria Title: "Tu puniscimi, o signore" (cavatina), "A brani, a brani o perfido" (cabaletta) (Luisa)
Opera Title: *Luisa Miller*
Composer: Giuseppe Verdi (1813–1901)
Historical Style: Italian Romantic (1849)
Range: C♯4 to B6

Fach: full lyric
Librettist: Salvatore Cammarano (1801–1852), after Johann Christoph Friedrich von Schiller's "bourgeois tragedy" *Kabale und Liebe* (1784)
Aria Duration: 2:51
Tessitura: E4 to A6

Position: Act II (Intrigue), scene 1

Setting: A room in Miller's cottage in the Tyrolean Mountains, early 17th century. Two doors on either side of the stage, one leading to Miller's room, the other to Luisa's. By the first hang a sword and an old military uniform. At the back are the front door and window, through which part of the church can be seen.

Led by Laura, Luisa's friends come pouring into the cottage in great agitation. They have seen Miller being marched off the prison in chains by the Count's guards, all because Luisa and Rodolfo, the Count's son, are in love. Wurm, the Count's secretary, tells Luisa the only way to save her father is to write a letter saying that she loves Wurm and that she never loved Rodolfo. She writes it, and then before signing she breaks into an andante aria:

Tu puniscimi, O Signore/Punish me, O Lord, if I offended you and I am content, but do not abandon me, Lord, to the fury of those cruel villains. To save me from fate of death an innocent father, they demand, I shudder to say it, they demand his daughter's dishonor.

This section is sung in the grand manner, the village maiden becoming nearly engulfed by the prima donna: wide intervallic leaps and range from low C♯ to high B, striding rhythm, major tonality, patterned accompaniment—all contribute to this effect. Unfortunately, Wurm is not moved, and Luisa signs the letter. Wurm is not finished. Luisa must swear by her father's head that she wrote the letter of her own free will and must come to the castle and declare before all that she loves Wurm himself. Luisa agrees, and a diabolical smile springs to Wurm's lips.

Luisa's cabaletta ("a brani, a brani o perfido/in pieces (*my heart*), wicked man"), with its typical accompanying rhythms, is written with a minor/major tonal design in two parts. A touch of chromaticism in the first part produces a momentary tonal ambiguity, emphasized by the clarinet. The beginning is higher, brighter, and has many accents: "O perfidious wretch, you have torn my heart to shreds! At least hasten to restore my unfortunate father to me." The second part of the cabaletta is pianissimo, legato: "The violent shudder of death now invades my whole body. Let my father's hand at least close my eyes!" Wurm sings that he cherishes the hope of clasping her hand before she repeats the cabaletta.

(Translation by Nico Castel)

Piano/vocal score: p. 171 (Kalmus)

No. 81

Voice: soprano
Aria Title: "E Susanna non vien! . . . Dove sono" (Countess)
Opera Title: *Le nozze di Figaro*
Composer: Wolfgang Amadeus Mozart (1756–1791)
Historical Style: Classical (1784)
Range: D4 to A6

Fach: full lyric
Librettist: Lorenzo da Ponte (1749–1838), after Pierre-Augustin Caron de Beaumarchais's play *La folle journée, ou Le mariage de Figaro* (1784)
Aria Duration: 4:50
Tessitura: G4 to G5

Position: Act III

Setting: A richly decorated hall prepared for a wedding festivity, with two thrones; Count Almaviva's castle, about three leagues from Seville, 18th century

The Countess sings of her wish that her marriage was happy like it once was. At the beginning of Act III, the Countess is emboldened to tell Susanna that she should offer to meet the Count in the garden, so that he will be caught with her. The Countess is then absent during the Count's duet with Susanna and his subsequent aria, and the comic recitative and sextet that uncovers the parentage of Figaro. The Countess enters and is understandably agitated, not knowing where Susannah is and what is happening. She knows that the plot is very daring and dangerous. She comes to terms with her husband's infidelities and betrayal of her. This sets up the lovely plaintive melody of the aria: "Dove sono," she asks, "where have the moments of sweetness and pleasure gone?"

The aria, begun piano, emerges seamlessly from the recitative, without orchestral prelude. The phrases are very long, and thus the aria should not be sung too slowly. Phrasing is important, with the inflected syllables of importance emphasized. The extremely important dotted rhythmic values (quarter, 8th, 16th) give the vocal line an energy and vitality. There are many accidentals in the vocal line, almost as if the Countess is walking a tightrope.

The allegro section is sparked by her own faithfulness and hope, "which still loves amidst its suffering." She still hopes that she could "hope to change that ungrateful heart." It is telling that she should repeat "l'ingrato cor/that ungrateful heart" five times after the high A. By the end of the aria the Countess is anxious to exit and find Susanna.

Piano/vocal score: p. 331 (G. Schirmer)

> Notes by director Thor Steingraber: In the recitative and aria "Susanna non vien . . . Dove sono," the Countess renews the courage of her convictions and finds the words to clearly express all that she has suffered and how she will persevere. It is only her plan that changes between Acts II and III; the true aspects of her character do not. When approaching the aria and recitative, one must divide the piece into distinct sections and decide how and when the Countess's hope is restored. In doing so, one must also structure the sections so that the repeat of "Dove sono" means something altogether different from the first time it is sung.

No. 82

Voice: soprano
Aria Title: "Porgi amor, qualche ristoro," Cavatina, No. 10 (Countess)
Opera Title: *Le nozze di Figaro*
Composer: Wolfgang Amadeus Mozart (1756–1791)
Historical Style: Classical (1784)
Range: D4 to A♭5

Fach: full lyric
Librettist: Lorenzo da Ponte (1749–1838), after Pierre-Augustin Caron de Beaumarchais's play *La folle journée, ou Le mariage de Figaro* (1784)
Aria Duration: 4:20
Tessitura: G4 to G5

Position: Act II, scene 1

Setting: The Countess's bedroom; a luxurious room, with an alcove and three doors in the castle of Count Almaviva, about three leagues from Seville, 18th century

The opening of Act II introduces the audience to the Countess. We have met the Count in Act I and are aware of his personal characteristics and his interest in Susanna. This gives us an idea already as to the Countess's plight. The brief aria has only four lines of text: "O love, give me some remedy for my sorrow and my sighs. Either give me back my treasure (*love*), or at least let me die."

The aria (larghetto) should not be sung too slow, or with only the quality of sorrow. Each line needs momentum toward the word "morir/die." The Countess is still young, and she does hope for love again to be restored in her life. And she must certainly remember the love that once was, the memories. The challenges in the aria are to keep the momentum in the lines to the end of each phrase; three of the lines enter on F at the top of the staff, so the aria is not sung too heavily. The range is not great, but the tessitura is mostly the upper part of the staff. There is one climactic phrase to a fermata on the high A♭.

Piano/vocal score: p. 125 (G. Schirmer)

Notes by director Thor Steingraber: We first meet Mozart's Rosina in her aria that opens Act II, "Porgi amor." Yet her character is one we know so well. Rossini's portrait of her leaves a lasting impression of determination, good humor, and radiant beauty, the kind of beauty that inspired the Count to fight so hard to have her and make her his Countess. One is certain that Mozart's Rosina is the same woman by the constant references to her made in Act I of *Figaro* by the other characters, not least of all Cherubino. The Countess is still young and beautiful. Perhaps only her idealism has faded. That the Count is cheating on her is less a reflection of her than of him and his indulgence in his "feudal rights." "Porgi amor" is a quiet, private moment. The Countess is alone in her room. It's the beginning of an act that will end in a rowdy romp. The aria is honest and simple. When I direct *Figaro*, I always warn the singer against indulging in self-pity. The text does allow that possibility, but that's not the Rosina we already know and admire, and it's no way to start an act. The text also allows for hope and that special brand of Rosina determination. Those are the qualities that sustain an alluring character.

No. 83

Voice: soprano
Aria Title: "Ave Maria" (Desdemona)
Opera Title: *Otello*
Composer: Giuseppe Verdi (1813–1901)
Historical Style: Italian Romantic (1887)
Range: E♭4 to A♭5

Fach: full lyric
Librettist: Arrigo Boito (1842–1918), after
the tragedy by William Shakespeare (1604)
Aria Duration: 5:00
Tessitura: E♭4 to E♭5

Position: Act IV

Setting: Cyprus, late 15th century; Desdemona's bedroom, late at night. There is a bed, table, looking glass, and chairs. A burning lamp is suspended in front of the image of the Madonna, above the bed. There is a door to the left, and a lit candle is on the table.

This aria follows the Willow Song (see next entry). Emilia, Desdemona's maid and the wife of Iago, has just left Desdemona in her bedroom. Desdemona is filled with foreboding as she awaits her husband, Otello.

Desdemona begins to sing the traditional prayer to the Virgin (in Italian), Ave Maria (sotto voce on the E♭ at the bottom of the staff), and ends with "blessed be the fruit, oh blessed one, of thy womb, Jesus." She continues, cantabile, with a personal prayer that asks for mercy "for the sinner and for the one who is innocent; for the oppressed and for the mighty; for the one who bows his head under injustice and under misfortune, in the hour of our death." She then returns to the text of the Ave Maria.

The piece is marked dolce with carefully marked dynamics and articulations. The first prayer requests lie melodically at the top of the staff. "Prega per noi, prega/pray for us, pray" ends on a pianissimo E♭ at the top of the staff, before descending again to the E♭ at the bottom of the staff as in the beginning. She ends with "nell ora della morte/in the hour of our death" before a last "Ave!/hail" that ascends to a high A♭, dolcissimo, and then drops to a final "Amen" on a low E♭.

Piano/vocal score: p. 338 (G. Schirmer)

No. 84

Voice: soprano
Aria Title: "Mia madre aveva una povera ancella," Willow Song (Desdemona)
Opera Title: *Otello*
Composer: Giuseppe Verdi (1813–1901)
Historical Style: Italian Romantic (1887)
Range: C♯4 to A♯6

Fach: full lyric
Librettist: Arrigo Boito (1842–1918), after the tragedy by William Shakespeare (1604)
Aria Duration: 8:25
Tessitura: F♯4 to F♯5

Position: Act IV

Setting: Cyprus, late 15th century; Desdemona's bedroom, late at night. There is a bed, table, looking glass, and chairs. A burning lamp is suspended in front of the image of the Madonna, above the bed. There is a door to the left, and a lit candle is on the table.

At this point in the opera, Desdemona's husband Otello is in a state of uncrontrollable jealously. Desdemona is alone with Emilia, her maid, whose husband Iago has conspired against her and Otello. Emilia asks Desdemona if Otello was calm the last time she saw him. Desdemona says yes; he told her to await him in her bedchamber. Desdemona asks Emilia to lay her wedding night sheets on the bed. And if she should die before Emilia, Desdemona would have as her death shroud the same sheet. "I am sad always," Desdemona says. She sits down mechanically on the bed and looks into the looking glass before relating a reminiscence: "My mother had a poor maid who was beautiful and in love. Her name was Barbara. She loved a man who abandoned her and she sang a song, the song of the willow." She asks Emilia to undo her hair. She cannot get the song out of her head, which leads to andante mosso, the introduction to the "Willow Song."

The articulation is clearly marked in this simple melody. The poor young girl, weeping and unaccompanied, sings "salce, salce, salce/willow, willow, willow," in repeated descending minor 3rds. The haunting phrase is repeated with a *portando la voce* to the repetition of the "salce." "Hurry," Desdemona whispers to Emilia, who is combing her hair. "Otello will be coming in a little while."

The next verse, with a descriptive orchestral accompaniment of flowing 16th notes, describes the flowing brook and the girl's grief, followed again by "salce," and the refrain "cantiamo/let us sing." The last verse tells of birds that fly down from the branches toward the sweet singing, as the

113

orchestra echoes the words with delicate grace note figures. She concludes, "Her eyes wept so much that the rocks pitied her."

Desdemona then takes the wedding ring from her finger and gives it to Emilia. "Here, take this ring," Desdemona says. Her mind goes back to poor Barbara, and she sings, "He was born for glory, I for love." The end of the piece is a quick farewell to Emilia, with a final cry, *con passione,* on a high A♯: "Ah!" Up to this point the aria is marked (for the most part) piano, dolcissimo.

(Translation by Nico Castel)

Piano/vocal score: p. 327 (G. Schirmer)

No. 85

Voice: soprano
Aria Title: "I want magic!" (Blanche DuBois)
Opera Title: *A Streetcar Named Desire*
Composer: André Previn (b. 1929)
Historical Style: 20th-century American (1998)
Range: E4 to B5

Fach: full lyric
Fach: full lyric
Librettist: Philip Littell, based on the 1947 play by Tennessee Williams
Aria Duration: 2:30
Tessitura: G4 to E♭5

Position: Act III, scene 2

Setting: A bedroom in Stanley and Stella's apartment in the French Quarter of New Orleans, during the restless years following World War II

> Opera plot note from the *G. Schirmer American Aria Anthology: Soprano,* edited by Richard Walters (used by permission):
>
> Blanche DuBois, whose life came crashing down around her in her native Mississippi town, has fled to her sister Stella in New Orleans. Stella's husband Stanley is unsympathetic to the fragile Blanche's plight, and is intolerant of her eccentricities and what he sees as her deluded, fake sophistication. Stanley's friend Mitch has become Blanche's suitor. Mitch has become suspicious of Blanche for various reasons. He moves to turn on the lights, saying, "I've never had a real good look at you, and that's a fact." Blanche is extremely sensitive about her age and appearance. He says he is being realistic. She asks, "Real! Who wants real?"

The delivery of the text is very important in this aria. In fact, the opening of the aria is marked "half spoken," and there is a spoken phrase. Vocally, the singer will need to make large intervallic leaps in the piece up the high A, as well as sing a high G♯, sustained on the -oo- vowel ("truth") and then diminuendo. There is a climactic high B, sustained for two beats. It is not a long aria, but it gives the soprano a chance to show range of voice and acting ability.

Piano/vocal score: p. 211 (*G. Schirmer American Aria Anthology: Soprano*)

No. 86

Voice: soprano
Aria Title: "Madame Pompous's Audition" (Madame Pompous)
Opera Title: *Too Many Sopranos*
Composer: Edwin Penhorwood (b. 1939)
Historical Style: 20th-century American (1997)
Range: A2 to B4

Fach: full lyric (spinto)
Librettist: Miki L. Thompson
Aria Duration: 4:00
Tessitura: F4 to D5

Position: Act I

Setting: The parlor of Heaven

Four Divas arrive in heaven to learn there is not enough room for all of them in the Heavenly Chorus. Because too many tenors and basses are in Hell, only one of the sopranos will be allowed into the chorus. The sopranos are appalled that they must audition, but they submit.

Madame Pompous's aria demonstrates character's flamboyance and strength of will. All of the many tempo changes, ritardandos, key changes, and extremes of range with strong dotted rhythms have a sense that they come from Madame's formidable overwhelming personality. This aria demands a strong high A, and the final note of the piece is a sustained high B, sung fortissimo. The following section should be sung semirecitative:

When you look upon myself and see this famous face,
You're sure to recognize me for I'm known in every place.
I have sung for kings and popes, and even presidents,
So I do not hesitate without reticence.
I have sung for the biggies, I have sung for the great.
I have dined with prime ministers and embraced heads of state.
If you saw my résumé you would melt for despair for you simply
can't match it.
Just try, if you dare.
Applause is my fanfare and I've heard—a lot—
I cannot leave the stage without encores
   . . . Cannot!!

This aria is, by nature, a showy piece. The singer will need a strong high
A and B as well as a sustained D at the bottom of the staff. There are a
number of key changes as the character switches tactics to gain admittance
to the Heavenly Chorus. The text is humorous and should be clearly enunciated at all times.

Piano/vocal score: p. 50 (T. I. S. Music Publishing)

Notes by composer Edwin Penhorwood: Diva attitude is all-
important in this aria. This audition aria should be presented with
plenty of confidence and self-importance, yet with plenty of charm
so as to not turn off the audience. This diva can sing anything, but
Wagner and Strauss are her specialties. A full lyric, spinto, or dramatic soprano is best suited to this aria. Special care should be
taken to make the words understood.

No. 87

Voice: soprano
Aria Title: "Tacea la notte" (Leonora)
Opera Title: *Il trovatore*
Composer: Giuseppe Verdi (1813–1901)
Historical Style: Italian Romantic (1853)
Range: E♭4 to D♭6

Fach: full lyric
Librettist: Salvatore Cammarano (1801–1852) and completed by Leone Emanuele Bardare (1820–1874), after Antonio García Gutiérrez's play *El trovador* (1836)
Aria Duration: 5:00
Tessitura: E♭4 to F5

Position: Part I (The Duel), scene 2

Setting: The provinces of Arragon and Biscay, in Northern Spain, during a border war, 15th century. The scene is set in the gardens of a palace. On the right is a marble staircase leading to the apartments. It is the middle of the night; thick clouds pass and cover the moon.

Leonora, a lady-in-waiting, and her confidante, Ines, are in the gardens of the palace. Leonora has been waiting to catch sight of the mysterious serenader. The exchange between Leonora and Ines is important to know before studying the aria. Ines is wondering why Leonora lingers outside so late at night. The Queen wants to see Leonora. "Take heed of her," Ines says to Leonora, who admits to Ines that she is in love with the troubadour whom she first saw at a jousting tournament before the civil war broke out. "He was a momentary vision in a fleeting dream. And then . . . " Ines wants to know what happened, which sets up the aria. "Listen," says Leonora, and she begins to describe the night she last heard the troubadour. The solo melody in the orchestra is mysterious, exotic, foreboding.

The first beautiful phrases need a full lower middle range as Leonora describes the night: peaceful and moonlit with the sweet sad sounds of a lute. She sings a phrase up to the F at the top of the staff. The next phrase rises up to high B♭ as she sings of the melancholy song that affects her so greatly. "It was a humble prayer," she sings, "like a prayer to heaven," repeating the opening melody. She then says that she hears her own name spoken by the troubadour. Eagerly she runs to the balcony. She felt such great joy that "only angels know." To her heart, earth seemed heaven itself. This is all a repetition of the first melody, with the climactic phrase (high B♭ and cadenza to high D♭) at the text "earth seemed to be heaven." Ines is alarmed by what Leonora has told her. She is afraid. Ines suggests that Leonora forget him. Leonora orders her to be silent. Ines cannot understand Leonora's feelings.

The cabaletta (allegro giusto) is carefully marked with specific articulations, including accents, legato/short markings, and short rhythmic patterns that paint the picture of breathlessness. To sing the cabaletta takes great vocal control and an even tone throughout the range. There are an abundance of trills, and coloratura up to high B♭ and C down to low A♭ below middle C (optional is the octave higher) as Leonora sings, "My heart is aflame with such love that words can scarce express it, a love I alone know. Only by his side can I fulfill my destiny . . . if I cannot live for him, then I will die." After Ines remarks that she hopes Leonora will never have cause to regret it, Leonora sings the cabaletta again, this time with more assurance and flourishes. Ines joins Lenora in the final lines of the cabaletta, cautioning Leonora to take care.

Piano/vocal score: p. 22 (G. Schirmer)

> Notes by singer and voice professor Martina Arroyo: The young spinto soprano should not undertake this aria too soon or sing the entire role until she is prepared both technically and dramatically. She must be able to execute the crescendi, decresendi, and coloratura demanded to perform this role. The singer should not lose herself in the drama to the detriment of the voice. She must maintain the quality of the voice at all times, making sure to have proper breath support for the tone and to "spin" the voice at all times, so that the voice does not harden, and still present the passion and involvement of the character. This should be true of any role, but the Verdi soprano is just as exposed technically as the Mozart singer. The soprano must choose each moment in which to sing dramatically, making sure not to lose control.

Of course, for every aria and role, the text is paramount. The lyrics must be translated, and each word must be understood. The text tells the story and gives life to the character and the music. Without the words, there is no opera.

No. 88

Voice: soprano
Aria Title: "Pace, pace mio Dio!" (Leonora)
Opera Title: *La forza del destino*
Composer: Giuseppe Verdi (1813–1901)
Historical Style: Italian Romantic (1862)
Range: C#4 to Bb6

Fach: spinto
Librettist: Francesca Maria Piave (1810–1876)
Aria Duration: 6:00
Tessitura: F4 to F5

Position: Act IV, scene 2

Setting: Spain and Italy, the end of the 18th century. It is outside the cave where Leonora has come to live out her remaining days in repentance, in a valley among inaccessible rocks, traversed by a stream. At the right is the entrance to a grotto, above it a bell that can be rung from within. It is sunset; the scene darkens gradually, and a full moon appears.

At the beginning of the opera, Don Alvaro, a Peruvian of Inca blood, is in love with Leonora di Vargas. She has accepted his offer of marriage, but her father—the Marquis of Calatrava—is against the marriage. He catches them as they are eloping. Accepting the blame for the elopement, Alvaro throws his pistol to the ground to disarm himself. It goes off, mortally wounding the Marquis, who curses his daughter as he dies. After five years have passed Don Alvaro is now Padre Raphael, known for his kindness toward those who suffer. We have not seen Leonora since the end of Act II, when she departed to a mountain retreat under the protection of the monastery.

In Act IV, scene 2, Leonora, pale and worn, emerges from her cavern to pray. She is still tormented by memories of her ill-fated love. She calls for peace from God on her tortured soul. She still loves Alvaro after all these years and the unfortunate events in the past. She calls on God to end her suffering.

The prelude to the aria is the well-known agitated theme of the overture. Leonora sings the first phrase accompanied only by harp. She sings, "Pace, pace mio Dio/Peace, peace, my Lord," starting on F at the top of the staff, sung piano, as she emerges from the grotto. She talks of her bitter misfortune, sung in the middle voice, and followed by the same "Pace, pace mio Dio" melodic phrases as before. She still loves Alvaro and cannot help it, but it is fate (repeated on a high G, forte, then piano in the octave below two times) that is the curse of this tragedy. "I love you, Alvaro," she says, "but it is the decree of heaven that I shall not see you again." The agitated overture theme is heard again as she sings, distraught, "Oh, God, let me die . . . In vain my soul seeks rest."

Next, she sings, accompanied by the harp, "Invan la pace quest'alma/in vain this soul of mine seeks peace," as she leaps up an octave to high B♭, pianissimo, on the word "pace." During the orchestral interval she crosses to a rock where there is some food left by Padre Guardiano. "Miserable food . . . this will only prolong my wretched life," she says. She hears someone approaching (allegro): "Who profanes this sacred place? It is the curse/ maledizione!" she exclaims. The last syllable is sung on high B♭ as she darts back into the cave.

Piano/vocal score: p. 346 (Ricordi)

No. 89

Voice: soprano
Aria Title: "In quelle trine morbide" (Manon)
Opera Title: *Manon Lescaut*
Composer: Giacomo Puccini (1848–1924)
Historical Style: Verismo (1893)
Range: D♭4 to B♭6

Fach: spinto
Librettists: Marco Praga, Domenico Oliva, Giulio Ricordi (1840–1912), Luigi Illica (1857–1919) and Giuseppe Giacosa (1847–1906), after the Abbé Antoine-François Prévost's novel *L'histoire du chevalier des Grieux et de Manon Lescaut* (1731)
Aria Duration: 2:31
Tessitura: F4 to F5

Position: Act II

Setting: An elegant salon in Geronte's house, Paris, 18th century

At the beginning of the opera, the young girl Manon Lescaut is on the way to the convent with her brother and an elderly wealthy gentleman, Geronte. Geronte would like to tempt Manon away from her appointment with the convent, as would Des Grieux, who offers her love but no riches or security. Sure enough, she tires of love without financial stability, and so in Act II she is living with the wealthy Geronte.

At the beginning of Act II Manon is seen sitting at a dressing table, wrapped in a large, white hairdresser's cape. A hairdresser and apprentices bustle around her, trying to please her. She is no longer the unspoiled young maid. Her young brother Lescaut enters to speak with her. He understands why she has left Des Grieux, who has no talent for money.

Manon longs for news of him, and she does not do a good job of disguising her feelings for him. She left him "without a farewell or kiss," she argues. She looks around, focusing on the alcove. "In those soft hangings . . . of the gilded alcove there is a mortal chill and a silence."

The aria begins piano (moderato con moto), doubled by the strings, in a descending vocal line. The accompaniment is chordal and off the beat. "And I, who had grown accustomed to a fond caress, now do not have passion." Manon Lescaut finishes her vocal line at the bottom of the staff. "O my humble little dwelling, you return before me happy, secluded, innocent like a gentle dream of peace and love."

The piece starts very straightforward and simply, but by the end has more little decorative embellishments, almost as if she is remembering the life she has chosen. Important directions to be observed are specific articulation markings, directions for dynamics, and rhythmic detail—as well as word inflection. The singer will need a strong high B♭ as well as strength at the bottom of the staff.

Piano/vocal score: p. 113 (International)

No. 90

Voice: soprano
Aria Title: "Senza mamma" (Suor Angelica)
Opera Title: *Suor Angelica*
Composer: Giacomo Puccini (1858–1924)
Historical Style: Verismo (1918)
Range: D4 to A6

Fach: spinto
Librettist: Giovacchino Forzano (1884–1970)
Aria Duration: 4:50
Tessitura: E4 to E5

Position: One-act opera of the three-opera *Il trittico*

Setting: The cloisters of a nunnery near Florence, 17th century. In the background is the cemetery; beyond the left-hand arcade is the vegetable garden.

The sisters of the convent are joyfully going about their business, while

Sister Angelica tries unsuccessfully to hide her unhappiness; in the seven years she has been in the convent, she has not heard any news from her family. Soon her elderly aunt, a Princess, comes to visit. From their conversation we learn that Angelica's family has put her in the convent as a punishment for having an illegitimate child. Her aunt callously informs her that the child is now dead. The Princess leaves Angelica alone to weep, desiring only to end her sorrows and join her child in heaven. She kneels and sings with a mournful voice (molto sostenuto):

Without your mother, oh my baby, you die!
Without my kisses your lips grow pale and cold.
Close your pretty eyes.
I cannot caress you
And you are dead without knowing how loved you were by your mother!
Now you are an angel in heaven.
You can see your mother, you can descend and let your essence linger around me.
Tell me, when will I see you in heaven?
When will I be able to kiss you?
Oh sweet end to all my sorrows, when I greet you in heaven, when will I greet death?
Tell your mother, beautiful creature, with a sparkle of the stars.
Speak to me, my loved one!

Piano/vocal score: p. 76 (Ricordi)

> Notes by conductor and conducting professor David Effron: Don't sing this piece too dramatically! Other parts of the opera are more dramatic for this character. This aria is more personal and internal. It is a personalization of her thoughts, and the text is very important. It must be sung pianissimo, and it is written at a range level that is not problematic for the soprano. When these directions are followed the effect of the piece is much more emotional for the audience than a showing of the dramatic voice.

No. 91

Voice: soprano
Aria Title: "Vissi d'arte" (Tosca)
Opera Title: *Tosca*
Composer: Giacomo Puccini (1848–1924)
Historical Style: Verismo (1900)
Range: E♭4 to B♭6

Fach: spinto
Librettists: Giuseppe Giacosa (1847–1906)
and Luigi Illica (1857–1919), based on
Victorien Sardou's play *La Tosca* (1887)
Aria Duration: 3:05
Tessitura: G♭4 to E♭5

Position: Act II

Setting: The office of Baron Scarpia, head of the police. Scarpia has been torturing Tosca's lover, Cavaradossi, in a downstairs chamber.

Tosca has heard her lover Cavaradossi's cries of pain. By this point in the scene the crafty Baron Scarpia has brought Cavaradossi into his office hoping that Tosca will persuade him to divulge information as to the whereabouts of the political dissident Angelotti. Tosca is a famous singer in Rome, a celebrity, and Scarpia enjoys the power he feels over her—a powerful, independent woman. He also lusts after her, and if he can conquer her through a bargain he makes with her, he will still have Cavaradossi executed.

At the time of this aria, Scarpia has been chasing Tosca around his office, and she has experienced all of Cavaradossi's pain. Scarpia demands that she choose between torture and death for her lover or giving herself to Scarpia. Her spirit is broken, and although the aria begins on an E♭ at the top of the staff, it must be sung piano. "I lived for my art, I lived for love, I never did harm to a living soul!" she says, ironically. She has an octave leap to high A♭ within the line "con man furtive quante miserie connobbi, aiutai/with a secret hand I relieved as many misfortunes as I knew of."

Always with true faith my prayer rose to the holy shrines.
Always with true faith I gave flowers to the altar.
In the hour of grief, why, O Lord, why do you reward me thus?
I gave jewels for the Madonna's mantle,
And I gave my song to the stars, to heaven, which smiled with more beauty.
In the hour of grief why, O Lord, why do you reward me thus?

At the end of the aria, her spirit is crushed; she is begging at his feet for mercy. Tosca does not play the victim well, and after she agrees to Scarpia's "proposal," she will murder him before going through with the bargain.

Tosca's character is tremendously complex, even contradictory. It is passionate and religious, commanding and playful, superstitious and spontaneous.

Piano/vocal score: p. 222 (G. Schirmer)

Notes by singer and master teacher Carol Vaness: One of the most important things about this aria is to begin in the most natural fashion for the individual singer—never loud, but with emotion and direction. The *language* in this aria is of utmost importance, and the Italian needs to be movingly free and perfect; each word should feel like delicious chocolate to savor, hence there can be a danger of too slow a tempo. This aria is *not* slow, it is like an ABA form: the first section (A) until "diedi fiori al gli'altar/I gave flowers to the altar," middle (B) "nell l'or del dolore/in the hour of grief," final (A) return to "diedi giolleli." This form will move the aria to the climax (which is the "Ah! Ah!" not the B♭ "Signor"). Young singers can hold the B♭ as long as possible or as long as *comfortable,* but remember that the "ah, ah" on the A♭–G is very difficult and immensely important as an expression of pain—the animalistic pain that ultimately causes Tosca to murder Scarpia. If these two notes are truly emotional, not just sung piano, then the aria will be successful. Also, Tosca must not neglect the final utterance; to finish well with a beautiful "così" is to carry on the action stopped by Tosca's pain. She must carry this on even in an audition. There will always be a feeling of great *suspension* when the singer attempts this. It is better not to be too soft until the technique to do so is achieved, but always, always not sung as a closure—but rather leading to the inevitable giving in.

No. 92

Voice: soprano
Aria Title: "Dich such' ich Bild!" (Marietta)
Opera Title: *Die tote Stadt*
Composer: Erich Korngold (1897–1957)
Historical Style: 20th-century German (1920)
Range: D4 to B♭6

Fach: spinto
Librettist: Paul Schott (pseudonym of Eric and Julius Korngold [1860–1945]), after Georges Rodenbach's novel *Bruges-la-morte* (1892)
Aria Duration: 3:22
Tessitura: G4 to G5

Position: Act III, scene 1

Setting: Bruges, late 19th century; a bleak morning; Paul's room, which is devoted to his dead wife, Marie. It is a "temple of memories," including a braid of her hair and photos.

After spending the night with Paul, Marietta—a young dancer who bears an uncanny resemblance to Paul's dead wife, Marie—tells the portrait of Paul's dead wife that Marie has died again since now Paul loves Marietta and not his dead wife.

Marietta regales the portrait with stories of her night of love, soaring to a sustained high B. Paul and Marietta, not Marie, are alive. They breathe and live. The melody accelerates and climbs in range and dynamics.

So there you are! It's you I want to talk to.
You, like me, had beauty—but where is it now?
Where is your power?
You died once more, proud one,
A second time through me, the living one,
Who gave him her love.
You, who are dead and buried, rest in peaceful slumber.
Don't haunt the living, who feel joy in taking and giving!
Leave us, those living and breathing, to our sorrow and happiness,
Leave us to revel in madness, in joy, and in pleasure.

This aria needs flexibility of voice and rhythm (observe the portamento marking). The piece calls for high, sustained G, B, and B♭, and then concludes on the low C♯ of "Liebe/love."

Piano/vocal score: p. 150 (Schott)

No. 93

Voice: soprano
Aria Title: "Glück, das mir verblieb,"
Marietta's Lied (Marietta)
Opera Title: *Die tote Stadt*
Composer: Erich Korngold (1897–1957)
Historical Style: 20th-century German
(1920)
Range: F4 to B♭5

Fach: spinto
Librettist: Paul Schott (pseudonym of Eric
and Julius Korngold [1860–1945]), after
Georges Rodenbach's novel *Bruges-la-morte*
(1892)
Aria Duration: 6:00
Tessitura: B♭4 to G

Position: Act I

Setting: Paul's room, which is devoted to his dead wife, Marie; Bruges, late 19th century

Although Paul is gloomily obsessed with the memory of his dead wife Marie (he preserves a room full of her affects, a "temple of memories"), he has met the vivacious Marietta and impetuously asks her to visit him. Marietta, a dancer, bears a striking resemblance to his deceased wife.

She sings a verse of a song for him, "Glück, das mir verblieb/Joy that near to me remains," marked sehr langsam, with the characteristic Korngold rhythmic flexibility. The melody soars to a sustained high B♭, piano. Paul knows the "sad song, the song of true love that must die." He heard it often in younger, better days. (Marietta can sing this in a solo version.) "It has another verse," Paul says. "Does he know it still?" They sing the melody together: "Though sorrow becomes dark, come to me, my true love. Lean to me your pale face. Death will not separate us. If you must leave me one day, believe, there is an afterlife," they sing in unison, the first interval to a sustained high B♭, sung piano. It is all marked langsam and is sung broadly (breit). Once again, there is characteristic flexibility of rhythm, and a change of meter. The final line of their duet is sung in thirds:

Come to me, my true love.
Lean (*to me*) your pale face.
Death will not separate us.
If you must leave me one day, believe, there is an afterlife.

She so arouses Paul's passions that he tries to embrace her. As she pulls away from him, she uncovers what should be a picture of Marie. Instead, she is surprised to see what appears to be her face on the canvas.

Piano/vocal score: p. 37 (Schott)

No. 94

Voice: soprano
Aria Title: "Do not utter a word" (Vanessa)
Opera Title: *Vanessa*
Composer: Samuel Barber (1910–1981)
Historical Style: 20th-century American
(1957)
Range: B4 to B6

Fach: spinto
Librettist: Gian Carlo Menotti (b. 1911)
Aria Duration: 4:45
Tessitura: F4 to A6

Position: Act I, scene 1

Setting: A night in early winter in Vanessa's luxurious drawing room. All the mirrors in the room and one large painting over the mantelpiece are covered with cloth. The fireplace is lit. There is a snowstorm outside.

Vanessa, a woman in her late 30s, her mother, the Baroness, and her niece, Erika, are waiting for the return of Vanessa's lover, Anatol, who left 20 years ago. When he arrives he turns out to be the son of her lover, and is also named Anatol; his father is dead. In the scene preceding the aria there is great anticipation as sleigh bells are heard announcing an arrival. "He has come!" Vanessa cries out. "Call the servants!" Vanessa grabs Erika: "Let me be alone with him," she says. She is tempted to uncover the mirror to look at herself, but she resists the impulse. In great agitation Vanessa paces up and down the room.

Suddenly, the door is thrown open. In the semidarkness, the figure of Anatol is seen standing silhouetted in the lighted doorway. "Do not utter a word," sings Vanessa, with restrained emotion, and without looking or moving toward him. At first the phrases are short, separated by awkward silence. Finally, the emotions spill out. The intervals are not predictable. There is a climactic musical/dramatic passage as she sings, "I have scarcely breathed so that life should not leave its trace and that nothing might change in me—that you loved (*to high A, forte, followed by a languid descent on the word "loved"*) alone" (intervallic leap from E at the bottom of the staff to high G♯, diminuendo, with another descent as the one before). Anatol slowly approaches her and gradually takes her hand. She rises suddenly, always with her back to him, and sings quickly and agitatedly, "Oh, how dark, how desperate, how blind." She modulates between forte to piano: "To let the days go by unmarked, unheeded."

There is a great amount of rhythmic variety in the final lines. "How end-less, how lonely, how wrong to rob a beating heart of time and space!" She sings a climactic phrase to high A♭, then B♭ back to A♭ ("Beauty is the hardest gift to shelter, harder than death to stay") and accents the rhythms of "All this I have done for you," as Anatol approaches her from behind and grasps her outstretched hand.

Piano/vocal score: p. 28 (G. Schirmer)

No. 95

Voice: soprano
Aria Title: "Ebben! Ne andrò lontana"
(Wally)
Opera Title: *La Wally*
Composer: Alfredo Catalani (1854–1893)
Historical Style: Verismo (1892)
Range: E4 to B6

Fach: spinto
Librettist: Luigi Illica (1857–1919)
Aria Duration: 4:45
Tessitura: E4 to G5

Position: Act I

Setting: The main square of Hochstoff, Switzerland, in the Tyrolean Alps, 19th century

The vulnerable Wally is involved in a love triangle with Gellner (whom her father wants her to marry), and Hagenbach, whom she loves. At her father's 70th birthday, Wally rejects Gellner, and her father turns her out, all in full view of the party guests.

"Well then! I shall go far away like the echo of the pious church bell goes away," she sings, with repeated, bell-like, notes. "There somewhere in the white snow; there amongst the clouds of gold, there where hope, hope (*to high G*) is regret and sorrow," descending to E at the bottom of the staff. "From my mother's cheerful house (*piano, dolcissimo con espressione*) La Wally is to go away from you (*pianissimo*), to perhaps (*to high sustained A*) never again to return. I will go away alone and far (*climactic passage, sung to high sustained B*), somewhere in the white snow, amongst the clouds of gold," as the aria ends at the bottom of the staff.

While she sings, Wally is aware that there are guests on stage, which affect her focal points and her emotional state at the beginning of the aria. She guards her emotions at first, but she breaks down by the end of the piece (morendo).

Piano/vocal score: p. 55 (Ricordi)

No. 96

Voice: soprano
Aria Title: "O patria mia" (Aida)
Opera Title: *Aida*
Composer: Giuseppe Verdi (1813–1901)
Historical Style: Italian Romantic (1871)
Range: C4 to C6

Fach: dramatic
Librettist: Antonio Ghislanzoni (1824–1893)
Aria Duration: 4:30
Tessitura: F4 to F5

Position: Act III

Setting: Shores of the Nile, granite rocks overgrown with palm trees. On the summit of the rocks, a temple dedicated to Isis, half hidden in foliage. It is night with stars and a bright moon.

The male priests are heard singing offstage in the temple. The high Priestess and Ramphis lead the prayers, sung in an exotically shaped melody. Amneris (daughter of the Pharaoh) is with Ramphis. Aida enters onstage cautiously, veiled, to a tentative melodic figure played by the violins. She is the servant of Amneris, and it is not known that Aida is the daughter of the Ethiopian King, Amonasro, enemy of the Pharaoh. She awaits her lover Radames, the general who has captured her father and conquered her homeland: "Radames will be here soon . . . what will he say to me? I tremble." The recitative is piano and lies at the bottom of the staff. The vocal line ascends briefly ("If he comes to say farewell, the dark whirlpool of the Nile will give me a tomb") and then descends down to a pianissimo middle C ("and give me peace, perhaps, and oblivion").

Aida sings, unaccompanied, "o patria mia/oh, my country I'll never see again." The melody is heard again, and Aida repeats "mai più/never again." Accompanied by shimmering strings in the orchestra, she reminisces about the blue skies and soft breezes of her country. Aida continues to repeat that she will see her country "mai più." The melody line weaves its way up chromatically with carefully marked articulation, finally reaching a sustained high C (on a -u- vowel) before descending. This is a difficult phrase to manage, as it begins softly (pianissimo) before descending to the bottom of the staff. The words "O patria mia" begin again (pianissimo) on the high A and descend to the low middle C, tying the aria together with a final "mai più" before ascending, smorzando, to high A.

(Translation by Rebecca Burstein)

Piano/vocal score: p. 209. (G. Schirmer)

No. 97

Voice: soprano
Aria Title: "Ritorna vincitor" (Aida)
Opera Title: *Aida*
Composer: Giuseppe Verdi (1813–1901)
Historical Style: Italian Romantic (1871)
Range: D♯4 to B♭6

Fach: dramatic
Librettist: Antonio Ghislanzoni (1824–1893)
Aria Duration: 6:50
Tessitura: E4 to G5

Position: Act I

Setting: A hall in the Palace of the King (Pharaoh) at Memphis. To the right and left are colonnades with statues and flowering shrubs. At the back is a grand gate from which may be seen the temples and palaces of Memphis and the pyramids.

The slave girl, Aida, is a servant to the Pharaoh's daughter, Amneris. At this point in the opera it is not known that Aida is herself a Princess of Ethiopia and the daughter of King Amonasro, Egypt's worst enemy. In the first act Radames, Captain of the Guard, is hoping to be appointed general to lead the Egyptians into battle. He privately expresses his love for Aida. They are interrupted by Amneris, who covets Radames. Amneris suspects that they are lovers and is seized by a fit of jealousy. Surrounded by the Egyptian crowd, the Pharaoh announces the choice of a commander to lead the army, Radames. Everyone pays homage to him and wishes for his victorious return. The eager general and the crowd exit as Aida, alone, finds herself repeating the words of the crowd: "Ritorna vincitor/Return victorious!" But she realizes in her recitative that a victorious Radames in battle will mean victory over her father and her country. Many of the lines are declamatory, with only the F♯ at the top of staff ("trionfar nel plauso/triumphant in the applause") sustained.

Next, she imagines her father, the Ethiopian King, conquered, as he is led in behind Ramades's chariot, in a passage sung with increasing dramatic intensity ascending with two quarter notes to the top G followed by a fermata/rest that is extremely effective in its silence after the outburst. She now asks the gods to forget her previous words (sung pianissimo in a long ascending sweeping line that moves quickly in cut time più mosso) and requests to be returned to her father, struggling (repeated whole notes on high G) against the oppressor, as the word is accented on each syllable. "Ah!" she now cries out on a high, and sustained, B♭.

She realizes her condition as she goes into the next section of the aria (andante poco più lento). "How can I forget my ardent love?" she asks. "Even though I am a slave, my love has made me happy here." In this section her emotional turbulence is transmitted through the wandering, chromatic melodic line, the rhythms, and the rising and falling of the dynamic level. "Ah! No heart has ever suffered so much anguish!" she sings as she begins the line on a high A♭, then descends to the bottom of the staff. Another melody unfolds in the next section (allegro giusto poco agitato) as she realizes her plight: for whom should she pray? The text here is very important, set to active rhythms, accents, and accidentals in the melodic line. The tessitura remains at the top of the staff. In the final section (cantabile), "Gods, have mercy on my suffering" is her prayer, sung pianissimo. "There's no hope," she sings, and yet she continues to pray and ask for mercy. "Ah! Pietà/Have mercy!" sung on the high A♭ is the only sustained strong dynamic expression. Triplets connect the line. The final phrase, "pietà, pietà—del mio soffrir/have pity on my suffering," is separated by quarter rests and is marked pianissimo. She can hardly bear to go on. She is carrying an enormous emotional weight on her shoulders.

(Translation by Christie Turner)

Piano/vocal score: p. 52 (G. Schirmer)

No. 98

Voice: soprano

Aria Title: "Es gibt ein Reich" (Ariadne)

Opera Title: *Ariadne auf Naxos*

Composer: Richard Strauss (1864–1949)

Historical Style: 20th-century German (1916)

Range: A♭3 to B♭6

Fach: dramatic

Librettist: Hugo von Hofmannsthal (1874–1929)

Aria Duration: 5:51

Tessitura: E4 to G5

Position: One-act opera and Prologue. The performance of this opera is a "play within a play."

Setting: The house of the richest man in Vienna, 18th century; a sumptuous banquet

The owner of the house is a generous patron of the arts and has ordered both comic and serious entertainment for after the banquet. However, because a firework display is also planned for the guests, time is short, and the two entertainments are "thrown" together, with the composer revising the work and worrying over the result.

The revised *Ariadne* performance begins with Ariadne, prostate on the ground before the mouth of a cave. The story is based on the Greek legend in which the kingdom of Crete exacted an annual payment of tribute in the form of a number of young men and maidens who were sacrificed to the Minotaur (a monster who was half-bull, half-man). One year Theseus (son of the King of Athens) came to the island, determined to slay the monster. He was able to find his way out of the Minotaur's labyrinth with the aid of a ball of wool given him by Ariadne, the daughter of Pasiphae, who had fallen in love with him. Theseus promised to marry Ariadne, but when they took a brief rest on the island of Naxos, he abandoned her while she slept.

Understandably, Ariadne is anguished as she lies at the mouth of this cave and speaks of the "Totenreich/realm of death," a realm in which all is pure. Here she rises: "Here nothing is pure," she says. "All is finished here," she says as she pulls her robe close around her. She now describes Hermes, who guides all souls to the underworld. "O beautiful, serene god! See! Ariadne awaits you!" She wants her heart to be cleansed of all wild grief. "Then your presence will call me, your footsteps will approach my cave, darkness will cover my eyes. The silent cave will be my tomb, but my soul will follow its new lord, as a light leaf in the wind flutters downward, gladly falling."

Darkness will cover my eyes and fill my heart.
This body will remain, richly adorned and all alone.
You will set me free.
This burdensome life, take it from me.
I will lose myself entirely in you, with you Ariadne will abide.

Piano/vocal score: p. 117 (Boosey & Hawkes)

No. 99

Voice: soprano
Aria Title: "Abscheulicher! Wo eilst du hin? . . . Komm, Hoffnung" (Leonora)
Opera Title: *Fidelio*
Composer: Ludwig van Beethoven (1770–1827)
Historical Style: German Romantic (1814)
Range: B4 to B6

Fach: dramatic
Librettist: Joseph Sonnleithner (1766–1835), with revisions by Stephan von Breuning (1774–1827) and Georg Friedrich Treitschke (1776–1842), after Jean-Nicholas Bouilly's French libretto *Léonore, ou L'amour conjugal*
Aria Duration: 7:05
Tessitura: E4 to F♯5

Position: Act I, scene 6

Setting: The courtyard of a state prison close to Seville, 18th century
Leonora is disguised as a man, Fidelio, in order to gain entry to a prison where she believes her husband is a political prisoner. Leonora's disguise is good enough that Rocco's daughter, Marzelline, is attracted to him (her). Leonora overhears Don Pizarro, governor of the prison, talking to Rocco, the jailer, about killing a prisoner she thinks is her husband. The good-natured Rocco is horrified at the governor's suggestion, but Pizarro tells him that he will kill the prisoner himself and orders Rocco to go dig the grave in the dungeon. In a state of growing anxiety, Leonora enters,

and with growing alarm watches the departure of Pizarro and Rocco: "Abscheulicher!/Monster!" she calls Pizarro. In a different tone, she sings, "des Mitleids Ruf/the call of pity, the voice of humanity," and then concedes that hatred and rage storm in Pizarro's soul. "In me there shines a rainbow," she sings, calmly and softly. The range does not extend above the staff. The aria begins (adagio): "Komm, Hoffnung/Come, hope, let the last star not forsake the weary."

The sound of two French horns is present throughout the aria. Consonants are extremely important. The voice ascends diatonically to a high B. The melody is driven and developed by the hopefulness of the text. Leonora describes her goal: Love will reach it. She sustains the word "Liebe/love" at the top of the staff. The second section (allegro con brio) describes Leonora's inner strength. This is her duty of faithful married love. It is her commitment (demonstrated by wide intervallic leaps) to find the place where evil has thrown her love in chains. She will not falter. She will offer him sweet comfort (sung pianissimo). Finally, her strength of spirit carries her up the scale on 8th notes to a sustained high B.

Piano/vocal score: p. 69 (Boosey & Hawkes)

No. 100

Voice: soprano
Aria Title: "Suicidio!" (La Gioconda)
Opera Title: *La Gioconda*
Composer: Amilcare Ponchielli (1834–1886)
Historical Style: Italian Romantic (1876)
Range: C♯4 to B6

Fach: dramatic
Librettist: Arrigo Boito (1842–1918) (under the pseudonym Tobia Gorrio), based on Victor Hugo's play *Angelo, tyran de Padoue* (1835)
Aria Duration: 4:12
Tessitura: F♯4 to F♯5

Position: Act IV

Setting: A room in a ruined palace on the Giudecca Island, Venice, 17th century

La Gioconda is a street singer. Her poor mother, La Cieca, is blind. Gioconda is in love with Enzo, who is really a Genoese nobleman in disguise. Enzo is in love with a noble woman, Laura, who is married to Alvise. Enzo loved Laura before her marriage. When Alvise learns of Laura's relationship with Enzo, he intends on poisoning her, but Gioconda substitutes sleeping potion for the poison. Enzo, thinking that Laura is dead, tries to kill Alvise and is arrested. In order to save Enzo, Gioconda offers herself to the evil spy Barnaba, who wants to posses her. Gioconda, whose mother has disappeared, now contemplates suicide, hoping that it will release her from the pain that she feels.

She holds the vial of poison. "Suicide! You alone remain to me, tempt me." Two dramatic phrases are sung in sequence up to sustained E and G at the top of the staff. "Last voice of my destiny (*piano*), last cross of my journey," followed by the orchestra interlude with a repeated melodic/rhythmic motif.

Once upon a time the hours happily flew by,
Lost now is my mother and my love.
I overcame the fever of jealousy,
Now I sink exhausted in the dark.
I am reaching the end . . . I only ask heaven to sleep quietly within
the grave.

The aria calls for passion, control, legato, and even vocal production and a powerful, sustained fortissimo at the top of the staff. The singer will also need a strong low C♯. The dynamic markings call for extreme contrasts throughout the range.

Piano/vocal score: p. 317 (Ricordi)

No. 101

Voice: soprano
Aria Title: "Una macchia è qui tuttora!"
(Lady Macbeth)
Opera Title: *Macbeth*
Composer: Giuseppe Verdi (1813–1901)
Historical Style: Italian Romantic (1847)
Range: B4 to B♭6

Fach: dramatic (mezzo-soprano)
Librettist: Francesco Maria Piave (1810–1876) with additions by Andrea Maffei (1798–1885), after the tragedy by William Shakespeare (1605)
Aria Duration: 6:50
Tessitura: F4 to G♯5

Position: Act IV, scene 2

Setting: A hall in Macbeth's castle, Scotland, Medieval times

In the same setting as her aria in Act I, scene 2 ("Vieni t'affretta . . . Or tutti, sorgete"), Lady Macbeth is sleepwalking, with a doctor and her maid looking on, and tries to "wash" off her hands the blood of those murdered in her husband's rise to the throne through her encouragement ("Out, damned spot!").

This is the penultimate scene of the opera. At this point it is clear that Macbeth's brief reign is crumbling. When Lady Macbeth talks about the "blood on her hands" and madly tries to get it off, she is "talking" to Macbeth. "You tremble?" she says to an imaginary Macbeth. She sarcastically berates him for being afraid. She sings (con forza) "these hands will never be clean" at the top of the staff. She laments that she "bears the smell of human blood. All the perfumes of Arabia cannot cleanse my hand. Banquo is dead, and the dead have never risen from the grave."

Finally, she chides the imaginary Macbeth: "To bed. Come, Macbeth, do not let your pallor betray you." As she begins to exit, she ascends to the high B♭. With the last "andiam/come," she sings high F up to A♭ to high D♭ and sleepwalks off stage. Lady Macbeth will be found dead in her bedroom.

Piano/vocal score: p. 266 (Ricordi)

No. 102

Voice: soprano
Aria Title: "Vieni! T'affretta . . . Or tutti, sorgete" (Lady Macbeth)
Opera Title: *Macbeth*
Composer: Giuseppe Verdi (1813–1901)
Historical Style: Italian Romantic (1847)
Range: B4 to C6

Fach: dramatic (mezzo-soprano)
Librettist: Francesco Maria Piave (1810–1876) with additions by Andrea Maffei (1798–1885), after the tragedy by William Shakespeare (1605)
Aria Duration: 4:40
Tessitura: F4 to G♯5

Position: Act I, scene 2

Setting: A hall in Macbeth's castle, Scotland, medieval times

Lady Macbeth has just read aloud a letter from Macbeth saying that he has been appointed Thane of Cawdor. Right before he was appointed Thane, a group of witches prophesized that soon he would be both Thane and King. Lady Macbeth is excited about this prospect. "Come! Hasten," she demands. She is anxious to get started, to encourage Macbeth when he arrives and give him courage to complete the bold task (of murdering the King). "The throne of Scotland is promised. Why delay? Accept the gift, and reign. "Che tardi?/Why is he late?" Ascend the throne," she repeats. The wide range, sudden interval leaps, accents, unprepared shifts in dynamics from forte to pianissimo, short rhythms, accents and trills—all portray her emotional imbalance. The bravura presented by the ascending lines to sustained pitches above the staff underlines her ambitious nature. When she suddenly sings, "che tardi, che tardi" with its short, fast rhythms, it shows her impatience.

A servant announcing that at nightfall King Duncan will be coming to the castle to stay the night interrupts her reverie (allegro). In the cabaletta, with its accompanying rhythm, Lady Macbeth summons the "ministers of hell." She sings piano, then suddenly fortissimo, legato, then staccato 16th notes (ascending to high B). She calls for the night to "enshroud them with thick darkness" (pianissimo). She finally talks about the dagger striking the breast. She is almost gleeful in her anticipation. Observed in this section are many accents, as the line ascends to a sustained high G, then B. The cabaletta can be cut here to the end of the aria with accented quarter notes up to a sustained high B to conclude, or it can be repeated as written.

Piano/vocal score: p. 37 (Ricordi)

No. 103

Voice: soprano

Aria Title: "Casta diva" (Norma)

Opera Title: *Norma*

Composer: Vincenzo Bellini (1801–1835)

Historical Style: Bel canto (1831

Range: F4 to C6

Fach: dramatic

Librettist: Felice Romani (1788–1865)

Aria Duration: 6:30

Tessitura: G4 to B6

Position: Act I

Setting: Night in the Druids' sacred forest, Gaul, around 50 B.C.

The sacred bronze instrument calls the people to the temple, and the priest and priestesses approach the altar. Norma, the high priestess, ascends the steps. Norma is in love with the Roman Proconsul, Pollione, and she has broken her vows of chastity to have two children with him. No one suspects her of intimacy with the Roman enemy. The Druids (the heathen priests and priestesses) and the people want to revolt against their Roman oppressors, but Norma convinces them that it is not yet the right time. "Rome will be defeated by her own failings," she says. She seeks to avert the danger that would threaten Pollione should Gaul rise against the Romans.

Norma, the priestess, invokes the moon and prays for peace. The opening melody of "Casta diva," invoking the "silver goddess," is a long legato line in the middle of the voice, with embellishments that come from Norma's intent to invoke the spirits more than to decorate the vocal line. Even though the line is marked legato, there is a pointed energy that comes from the rhythms within the vocal phrase. As Norma sings "a noi volgi il bel sembiante/asking the goddess to turn her face to us, unclouded and unveiled," the melody turns upward to a repeated high A accented off the beat, sempre crescendo, up to a dotted 8th note on the high B♭ before finally descending.

The next section is the repeated text "senza vel/unveiled" in a vocal line that is highly decorated on 32nd notes and has a chromatically exotic flavor. The chorus is simultaneously singing underneath the "casta diva" text in the opera. The melody now repeats in the next section with new text: "tempra, O Diva, tempra tu de cori ardenti/temper, oh Goddess, the brave zeal of the ardent spirits. Scatter on the earth the peace thou make reign in the sky," and there is a cadenza (a piacere) as the section ends.

The allegro section begins as the offstage *banda* is heard. This section has the quality of an accompanied recitative and is very important. The voice rises to a high B♭ with the text "dal druidico delubro la mia voce/my voice will thunder from the Druidic temple." The chorus once again joins her vocal line. She sings, aside: "He will fall. I can punish him, but my heart is unable to do so." As the cabaletta begins, Norma worries that the hatred for the Romans must also translate to hatred for Pollione. She asks to be returned to her first true love. There are intervallic leaps to high A, high B♭, and C. There are also many off-the-beat accented figures, specific articulating marks, and mellismatic passages. After the chorus and Oroveso sing, Norma repeats the section. The più mosso section has even more accents, more rhythmic variety, and intricate chromaticism.

Piano/vocal score: p. 61 (Schirmer)

Notes by singer and master teacher Carol Vaness: For the young singer "Casta diva" is a bit of a vocal exercise; it is dangerous to just throw oneself into this treacherous aria full of emotion until the recitative is sorted out, both technically and histrionically and with full command of the Italian diction. If you choose *not* to sing the recitative, then it is simply a beautiful song. An even line and tone must be achieved, and the melismas (notice I do *not* say coloratura) must be sung slightly ahead of the beat to fit with the piano or orchestra. To do this is an experienced singer's forte and a younger singer's duty to try. They must *never* drag. The cabaletta is straightforward and even (top notes should be full and pinging and the scales fully learned). I do *not* recommend this aria for a singer with just a big voice. It is confining in its preciseness. Attention to every detail of musical markings will give the impression of involvement without causing the singer undue vocal distress.

No. 104

Voice: soprano
Aria Title: "Dich teure Halle" (Elisabeth)
Opera Title: *Tannhäuser*
Composer and Librettist: Richard Wagner
(1813–1883), after medieval German history
and mythology
Historical Style: German Romantic (1845)
Range: D♯4 to A6 (B6)

Fach: dramatic
Aria Duration: 4:45
Tessitura: G4 to E5

Position: Act II

Setting: Thuringia and the Wartburg at the beginning of the 13th century, the hall of minstrels in the Wartburg. At the back is an open prospect of the valley.

It is the tournament of song; the theme of the contest is to be the nature and praise of love. The prize of the victor is the hand of Elisabeth, whom Tannhäuser loves, and by whom he is beloved. Elisabeth enters into the empty hall in joyous emotion. Although the hall is empty, there is much to focus upon. She greets the hall as a familiar, friendly space, in which she will soon see Tannhäuser.

In the opening phrase, she greets the hall and sings directly up a 4th to a sustained high G, without accompaniment. The first two pages are declarative, and without an active accompaniment. "In you (*the hall*) awaken his (*Tannhäuser's*) song," she says. "Wie jetzt mein Busen hoch sich hebet/ That now lifts high my heart," she continues, describing the lifting of her spirits. As the orchestra plays a countermelody, the vocal lines extend up to F♯, G, and A. With the repetition of "sei mir gegrüsst/to me his greeting" the orchestra has written repeated 8th-note chords that create excitement and momentum. "Dich teure Halle" is sung with an extended six beats on high G, repeated two times, and finally "sei mir gegrüsst," with the final syllable sung on a high G.

The aria calls for a large soprano voice, because even though much of the music is above the staff, and there are unaccompanied phrases, other sections in the aria have heavy instrumental accompaniment. All extended notes above the staff must be sung with strength and sufficient power to crescendo in the vocal line, and not "run out of steam."

Elisabeth is a strong character: the minstrels come close to destroying Tannhäuser in the second act but for the sudden intercession of Elisabeth.

Tannhäuser, who sees too late that an illusion has blinded him, despairingly joins a pilgrimage to Rome, while Elisabeth, whose love and life are blighted by the discovery of his unworthiness, begs him to repent.

Piano/vocal score: p. 99 (G. Schirmer)

No. 105

Voice: soprano
Aria Title: "In questa reggia" (Turandot)
Opera Title: *Turandot*
Composer: Giacomo Puccini (1858–1924)
Historical Style: 20th-century Italian (1926)
Range: C#4 to B6

Fach: dramatic
Librettists: Giuseppe Adami (1878–1946) and Renato Simoni (1875–1952), after the play by Carlo Gozzi (1762)
Aria Duration: 5:45
Tessitura: F#4 to A6

Position: Act II, scene 2

Setting: The big square in front of the palace in Peking (Beijing). In the center of the scene is an enormous marble staircase, which ends at the top under a triple arch. The staircase has three big landings. At the head of the staircase, seated on a big ivory throne, is the Emperor Altoum. As the scene opens, numerous servants place variously colored lanterns everywhere. The crowd gradually fills the square.

Prince Calaf will be beheaded if he fails to answer Turandot's three riddles. He is warned by the Emperor, who is weary of his rule being stained by the horror of the beheading of so many men who cannot answer the riddles.

Princess Turandot takes her place at the foot of the throne. Beautiful, impassive, she gives the Prince a cold glance and begins the aria solemnly. She begins a long narrative that describes the history of Princess Lo-u-Ling, Turandot's ancestress. She defied the harsh domination of men. "Today you live in me," Turandot says. Characteristics of this piece include a large amount of text, many dynamic shadings specifically marked, and rhythmic complexity. "War broke out, the kingdom was conquered, Lo-u-Ling was dragged away by a man like you, a stranger, and she was murdered."

She goes on to describe the terror in the kingdom, the roar of arms.

"Quel grido e quella morte!/that cry and that death," she sings at high A and B (fermata). "No man will ever possess me," Turandot declares at the top of her range (high A, sustained B). "Stranger, do not tempt fortune," she sings on F♯ at the top of the staff. "The riddles are three, death is one!" The riddle scene follows and continues to be highly charged and dramatic for the soprano. The scene is heavily orchestrated with brass and percussion.

Piano/vocal score: p. 231 (Ricordi)

No. 106

Voice: soprano	**Fach:** dramatic
Aria Title: "Du bist der Lenz" (Sieglinde)	**Aria Duration:** 2:03
Opera Title: *Die Walküre,* the second of the four operas in Wagner's *Der Ring des Nibelungen*	**Tessitura:** A♭4 to E5
Composer and Librettist: Richard Wagner (1813–1883), after German mythology	
Historical Style: German Romantic (1870)	
Range: C4 to G♯/A♭5	

Position: Act I, scene 3

Setting: The interior of Hunding's house, German forests during mythical times. At the center rises the trunk of a huge ash tree.

Sieglinde, the wife of Hunding (she is the daughter of the god Wotan and a mortal woman) sees a stranger (Siegmund) stagger into her house during a storm. The man is being pursued. She gives him water and begs him to stay. They are attracted to each other. She sees something familiar and heroic in his eyes. She drugs her husband, Hunding, with a sleeping potion and shows Siegmund a sword that has been thrust into a tree, explaining that no one has had the strength to draw it out. The door blows opens and—magically—it is a spring night. The stranger sings in praise of the spring ("Winterstürme/winter storms"). Like a brother, spring has freed love, its sister, from the storms of winter. The metaphor soon turns into reality. She answers with "du bist der Lenz/you are the spring for which I longed in the wintertime." Sieglinde is Siegmund's twin sister. She was terrified when she first saw him. She had only seen strangers, and her surroundings were friendless. "When my eyes saw you, you belonged to me, when in frosty lonely strangeness I saw my friend."

The lower passages are lightly accompanied. It all should be sung simply, directly, without forcing the voice or oversinging. A momentum of excitement is important, because the vocal lines are long. The phrase "Wie tönender Schall/Like a resounding echo" is composed in the high range with a repeated ascending phrase at the end of the aria. It is the climax of the piece and must be sung strongly and full of passion.

Piano/vocal score: p. 58 (G. Schirmer)

Part II
Mezzo-Soprano Arias

No. 1

Voice: mezzo-soprano
Aria Title: "Di te mi rido" (Ruggiero)
Opera Title: *Alcina*
Composer: George Fridrich Handel
(1685–1759)
Historical Style: Italian Baroque (1735)
Range: D4 to A5

Fach: lyric coloratura
Librettist: Antonio Marchi (fl. 1692–1725),
based on Antonio Fanzaglia's *L'isola d'Alcina*
set by Broschi (1728), after cantos VI–VIII of
Lodovico Ariosto's epic poem *Orlando furioso* (1516)
Aria Duration: 4:08
Tessitura: G4 to D5

Position: Act I

Setting: The exquisite palace of the enchantress Alcina on her island
   The enchantress Alcina has fallen in love with Ruggiero. This aria is sung by Ruggiero, a knight betrothed to Bradamante, looking all around him: "Why does Alcina not come?" He directs his next remarks to Bradamante and Melisso. "You annoy me," he sings. The aria has a two-measure orchestral introduction. To Bradamante, he sings, "I scorn you, you foolish simpleton." Directing his next line to Melisso, he sings, "I serve Cupid, I adore a lovely face, and would never be untrue." Once again, he sings to Bradamante the text repeated to a cadence (adagio), at which time Bradamente and Melisso exit.

   My beloved who fills me with love, where can she be?
   Why has she still not come back?
   What is she doing? Where is she?

This is a da capo aria, meaning the first section is repeated.
   This aria asks for melismatic flexibility of voice, such as singing triplet patterns for five measures on one syllable. There are also repeated dotted rhythms that energize the emotional Ruggiero, dressed for battle. The highest tone sung is an 8th-note G, and an F at the top of the staff, sustained by a fermata.

Piano/vocal score: p. 31 (Bärenreiter)

No. 2

Voice: mezzo-soprano
Aria Title: "Stà nell'Ircana pietrosa tana" (Ruggiero)
Opera Title: *Alcina*
Composer: George Frideric Handel (1685–1759)
Historical Style: Italian Baroque (1735)
Range: B4 to G5

Fach: lyric coloratura
Librettist: Antonio Marchi (fl. 1692–1725), based on Antonio Fanzaglia's *L'isola d'Alcina* set by Broschi (1728), after cantos VI–VIII of Lodovico Ariosto's epic poem *Orlando furioso* (1516)
Aria Duration: 5:47
Tessitura: D4 to E5

Position: Act III, scene 1

Setting: Atrium of the palace on Alcina's enchanted island. Alcina is a sorceress who attracts men to her deserted island, loves them, and transforms them into animals, stones, trees, or waves.

Ruggiero is a knight, betrothed to Bradamante. Alcina tries once more to cast a spell on Ruggiero (caught in an emotional tug of war between Alcina and Bradamante) to make him love her. However, his spell fails, and Ruggiero declares his triumph.

Bradamante and Melisso (Bradamante's Governor) enter in scene 3 and tell Ruggiero that the island is surrounded by armed ships and bewitched monsters. Ruggiero says that he will fight, but Melisso says that human strength is not enough. Ruggiero tells Bradamante that to leave her will grieve his soul.

There are 14 measures of orchestral introduction. The first section of the aria is marked allegro. Ruggiero tells of a tigress in her stony lair, uncertain whether to flee or await the hunter. The range extends between low D and high G, with a good number of coloratura patterns and sequences of 16th notes.

"She longs to save herself from the arrow's thrust," he sings in the A section, "but this would leave her offspring undefended."

The B section is a little slower as he continues: "She shudders and is assailed both by lust for blood and fear for her young; but love triumphs." This section is followed by a cadenza.

The A section is repeated with embellishments, followed by another cadenza. Ruggiero exits. Ruggiero is a character who projects strength, but the aria cannot be sung heavily and must have a forward momentum to sustain the spirit of the piece.

Piano/vocal score: p. 167 (Bärenreiter)

No. 3

Voice: mezzo-soprano
Aria Title: "Verdi prati e selve amene"
(Ruggiero)
Opera Title: *Alcina*
Composer: George Frideric Handel (1685–1759)
Historical Style: Italian Baroque (1735)
Range: C♯4 to E5

Fach: lyric coloratura
Librettist: Antonio Marchi (fl. 1692–1725), based on Antonio Fanzaglia's *L'isola d'Alcina* set by Broschi (1728), after cantos VI–VIII of Lodovico Ariosto's epic poem *Orlando furioso* (1516)
Aria Duration: 4:16
Tessitura: E4 to C♯5

Position: Act II

Setting: A rich and stately chamber (a subterranean apartment) in the enchanted palace of Alcina

Bradamante, the knight Ruggiero's betrothed, arrives at an enchanted island in an attempt to rescue him. Alcina has fallen in love with the knight and has detained him on the island. Morgana, Alcina's sister, discovers Ruggiero and Bradamante together in Act II, as Ruggiero is singing "Verdi prati." Alcina will try to use her powers to detain Ruggiero, but Ruggiero is protected by a magic ring, given to him by Bradamante's guardian Melisso.

> You green meadows and charming woods, you will lose your beauty.
> Lovely flowers, running streams, your charm, your beauty will soon be changed.
> You green meadows and charming woods, you will lose your beauty.
> And everything of beauty will be transformed, and you will all return to the horror of your former state.
> You green meadows and charming woods, you will lose your beauty.

This is a beautiful, sustained melody that is not too demanding in range for the mezzo-soprano. With its repetitions there are opportunities of embellishments for the inspired Ruggiero.

Piano/vocal score: p. 130 (Bärenreiter)

No. 4

Voice: mezzo-soprano
Aria Title: "Per questa fiamma indomita"
(Jane Seymour)
Opera Title: *Anna Bolena*
Composer: Gaetano Donizetti (1797–1848)
Historical Style: Bel canto (1830)

Range: B4 to A6
Fach: lyric coloratura
Librettist: Felice Romani (1788–1865)
Aria Duration: 2:36
Tessitura: G#5 to E5

Position: Act II, scene 2

Setting: The antechamber that leads into the hall where the Council of Peers is meeting in the early 16th century, London. The double doors are closed and guarded.

Jane Seymour (Anne Boleyn's lady-in-waiting) is ravaged by remorse. She cannot endure the thought that she has contributed to Anne's fate: execution. Therefore she has come to bid King Henry a final farewell. Henry reminds her that he is more than her king, he is her lover. Soon they will be married. Jane swears she longs only to go far away. Her attitude, Henry says, only makes him hate Anne more, if she has caused Jane to stop loving him. Despairing, Jane confesses that she is still consumed by love and begs in the name of this love that Henry grant her wish not to be the cause of Anne's death.

The aria is marked cantabile set to 3/4 meter. The accompaniment is classic bel canto, supporting the melody. There are florid 16th-note passages that touch on the high A, as well as from sustained high F# down to D# at the bottom of the staff.

Most of the piece is sung in the middle of the voice and does not call for a dramatic building and crescendos to the highest pitches. There is a florid cadenza at the end of the aria.

> Ah! It is not extinguished . . . It devours my heart!
> For this mastering flame that takes precedence over virtue . . .
> For those bitter pangs, for the weeping they cost me . . . hear my prayer . . .
> Do not let Anna die because of me, before heaven and men do not make me guiltier.

Piano/vocal score: p. 250 (Ricordi)

No. 5

Voice: mezzo-soprano
Aria Title: "Non più mesta" (Cinderella)
Opera Title: *La Cenerentola*
Composer: Gioacchino Rossini (1792–1868)
Historical Style: Bel canto (1817)
Range: A4 to B6

Fach: lyric coloratura
Librettist: Giacomo Ferretti (1784–1852), after Charles Perrault's story *Cendrillon* (1697), Charles-Guillaume Étienne's libretto *Cendrillon* (1810), and Francesco Fiorini's libretto *Agatina* for Stefano Pavesi (1814)
Aria Duration: 3:16
Tessitura: E4 to E5

Position: Act II, finale

Setting: The throne room in Don Ramiro's palace; present are Ramiro, Cenerentola (Cinderella), Dandini, Courtiers, Magnifico, Alidoro, Clorinda, and Tisbe (stepsisters)

Before the scene changes to the palace, Cinderella falls in love with a "servant" who is really Prince Ramiro, unbeknownst to Cinderella. Ramiro does not know that Cinderella is a maid. He leaves behind a bracelet that she will wear if she agrees to marry him. Revealing that he is really the prince, Ramiro sees that she wears the bracelet and announces to the horror of the family that Cinderella will be his bride. Ramiro is about to punish the family for their cruelty, but at that point Cinderella falls at his feet, telling him that in her mind the past has vanished. "I ascend the throne and wish to be greater than the throne," she says.

As the chorus hails her, Cinderella tells her stepfather and sisters that her revenge will be their pardon. After a nine-measure instrumental introduction marked andante, Cinderella explains, quietly and simply, that she was "born to sorrow and tears and suffered with a silent heart." The word "heart" is sung on a cadential embellishment. "*But . . .* "—and here the line becomes increasingly more florid—"by some sweet enchantment in youth, swiftly, my fortune has changed, swift as a flash of lighting." She sings rapid 64th-note patterns to high B, then descends to low A below the staff. To Don Magnifico and the sisters she says, "No, no, no, no, dry your tears. (*allegro*) Why do you tremble? Fly to me, embrace me!" The orchestra plays a 10-measure interlude (meno allegro).

The singing of "Non più mesta," the aria with chorus that closes the opera, is characteristic of the transformation of Cenerentola herself. No longer will she sing her song by the fireside. The melody of the aria begins very simply, humbly, piano. It then grows more confident as she adds embellishments and the self-assurance necessary to sing the decorative patterns. "The long years of heartache were but a streak of lightning, a game." Two times she sings from high A, descending rapidly on 16th notes, to low G. Later she ascends on this text to high, sustained B. Her long sadness was a dream that is over, and she discards the memories happily. The chorus joins her song as they sing: "Everything changes, little by little, cease sighing."

Piano/vocal score: p. 346 (Ricordi)

> Notes by singer Vivica Genaux: "Non più mesta" now is one of my favorite arias, but I don't think I ever used it in competition or as an audition piece. For me, it is much easier to sing in the context of the opera where everything builds up to this final moment when Angelina realizes that her dream of being rescued by Prince Charming has actually come true. I remember seeing an interview with Frederica von Stade in the La Scala production available on video, where they asked her if this wasn't one of the most difficult arias to sing. She replied that at that moment in the opera it was actually quite easy for her because it was the only thing you really wanted to do at that point, feeling the joy of your character after all the suffering Angelina has been through. The pyrotechnics in the ornamentation are technically difficult and need to be very clean and well executed, but they are also a cathartic release, expressing Angelina's overwhelming happiness.

No. 6

Voice: mezzo-soprano
Aria Title: "Deh per questo istante solo," No. 17, Rondo (Sextus)
Opera Title: *La clemenza di Tito*
Composer: Wolfgang Amadeus Mozart (1756–1791)
Historical Style: Classical (1791)
Range: C4 to G5

Fach: lyric coloratura
Librettist: Pietro Metastasio (1698–1782)
Aria Duration: 6:28
Tessitura: A4 to E5

Position: Act II

Setting: A pleasant apartment in the imperial palace on the Palatine, A.D. 79

Sextus has been manipulated by Vitellia into betraying his friend, the Emperor Titus, in a plot to kill him, but the plot goes awry. Sextus's guilt is admitted to Titus, and Sextus requests the penalty of death. He is trying to shield Vitellia from blame because he loves her, but Titus takes his attitude as arrogance, and angrily the Emperor confirms the death sentence. Sextus repeats his admission of remorse and insists on his resolve to atone for his treachery by death.

In the aria "Deh per questo istante solo," Sextus reminds Titus of how Sextus used to love him and how it is torturing Sextus that he betrayed him.

The aria is marked adagio composed in 4/4 meter, and is sung piano. It should be sung with restraint, a quiet control that has the singer sing between low C at the bottom of the staff and repeatedly to the F at the top of the staff, sometimes with an intervallic leap of the 10th. Although the piece is marked adagio in the first section, the aria is very active rhythmically and requires flexibility to be sung successfully.

"Ah, for this single moment remember our former love, for your anger, your severity, makes me die of grief," Sextus sings to Titus. The text is now repeated. "Unworthy of pity, it is true, I ought only to inspire horror," he says. "Yet you would be less harsh if you could read my heart."

The last section is marked allegro: "In despair I go to death, but dying does not affright me. The thought that I was a traitor to you tortures me! A heart can suffer such anguish and yet not die of sorrow! Sextus repeats the text (dolce) "unworthy of pity . . . " to the end of the aria. At the repetition of "In despair . . . " più allegro is indicated.

Piano/vocal score: p. 144 (International)

No. 7

Voice: mezzo-soprano
Aria Title: "Parto, parto," No. 8a (Sextus)
Opera Title: *La clemenza di Tito*
Composer: Wolfgang Amadeus Mozart
(1756–1791)
Historical Style: Classical (1791)
Range: D4 to B♭5

Fach: lyric coloratura
Librettist: Pietro Metastasio (1698–1782)
Aria Duration: 5:50
Tessitura: F4 to E♭5

Position: Act I

Setting: The Imperial garden in Rome, A.D. 79

The aria is sung by Sextus (Sesto), friend of Titus (the Roman Emperor), who is the lover of Vitellia (daughter of the emperor Vitellius). Vitellius has been dethroned and murdered. Vitellia hopes to mount the throne as wife of Titus, but sees that her plans are about to be thwarted by Titus, who is about to marry Berenice, daughter of the King of Judea. Vitellia conspires to murder Titus and has involved Sextus to implement her plans. Sextus is torn by conflict. He loves Vitellia but is also a friend of Titus's. After Servilia orders Sextus to kill Titus and set fire to Rome, Sextus meekly acquiesces and sings that he will do anything for her beauty and love. Skillfully fanning the flames of Sextus's passion and jealousy, she urges that their plan be carried out at once: the Capitol must be set on fire and Titus must die.

Vitellia sings,

Did you not hear the new affronts to me? . . . That he prevents you from winning my heart; that if he remains alive I may relent; that I could perhaps love him again. Now go: if you are unmoved by desire for glory, ambition, love, if you can tolerate a rival who stole my affections, now opposes them and could steal them from you, I will say that you are the most despicable of men.

Sextus replies:

You assail me from every side! Enough, enough, no more: your fury, Vitellia, has already inspired me. You shall soon see the Capitol aflame and this dagger in Titus's breast. (*Vitellia:*) And what are you thinking now? Then hurry: Why do you not go?

Sextus sings the aria (in three sections), which begins (adagio) in 3/4 meter:

Parto/I go, but, my dearest
(*an unaccompanied triad to the high F at the top of the staff*)
Make peace with me again.
I will be what you would most have me be,
Do whatever you wish.
(*The second section [allegro] is in 4/4 meter, with the orchestra playing a six-measure introduction.*)
Look at me, and I will forget all
And fly to avenge you.
(*Sextus sings with a determined and forceful attitude.*)
I will think only of that glance at me.
Ah, ye gods, what power you have given beauty.

He sings rapid triplet figures of 8th-note coloratura patterns that ascend to a high B♭. Sextus exits.

Energy is infused into the vocal line through the dotted rhythms. The mournful sound of the countermelody in the solo clarinet contributes to the mood.

Piano/vocal score: p. 65 (International)

No. 8

Voice: mezzo-soprano
Aria Title: "Amici, in ogni evento . . . Pensa alla patria," Recitative and Rondo (Isabella)
Opera Title: *L'italiana in Algeri*
Composer: Gioacchino Rossini (1792–1868)
Historical Style: Bel canto (1813)
Range: A4 to B6

Fach: lyric coloratura
Librettist: Angelo Anelli (1761–1820), first set by Luigi Mosca (1808)
Aria Duration: 9:40
Tessitura: E4 to E5

Position: Act II, scene 3, Algiers, near the seaside palace of the mighty Bey Mustafa. The plot is placed in a fictitious sultanate.

Mustafa, Bey of Algiers, has gone overboard for Isabella. Her love, Lindoro, is also in the palace, and Isabella would like to escape with him and all of the other Italian slaves. The Italian girl Isabella at this point is playing with Mustafa and promotes a sham ceremony in which the Italian slaves will all take part. She hopes to instill courage in them and Lindoro, reminding them that their time for going home is approaching.

In the recitative "Amici, in ogni evento" she tells them all that she relies on them, and very soon she hopes to "bring her plan to fruition." She addresses Lindoro directly, noticing that he has turned pale. "Remember," she sings, "that you are Italian. Allow a woman to teach you to be strong." "Think of your country," she sings, beginning on a sustained E at the top of the staff. "Fearlessly do your duty (*a piacere*). Look and see throughout Italy examples of bravery and courage." The aria is characterized by energized dotted rhythms and decorative 32nd-note patterns, and it lies low in the vocal range.

Piano/vocal score: p. 305 (G. Schirmer)

> Notes by singer Vivica Genaux: Isabella is trying to bolster the morale of her fellow Italians, trying to convince them that her plan of escape will work. Probably the biggest challenge expressively is to build a story line through the aria, as it's quite long. After the chorus and Taddeo pretty much reject her first recitative about how together they are sure to triumph, Isabella has to find ways of convincing Lindoro, Taddeo, and the chorus of her plan. For example, one can think of "Pensa alla patria" as directed at the chorus, one strophe of the "Qual piacer" as directed to Lindoro, and the final one partially to Taddeo and partially to everyone on stage and in the audience, who should now be on her side. As with every aria, you have to be sure in your mind whom you're singing to at any particular time, and what your character hopes to accomplish by saying what they do.

No. 9

Voice: mezzo-soprano
Aria Title: "Cruda sorte," No. 4 (Isabella)
Opera Title: *L'italiana in Algeri*
Composer: Gioacchino Rossini (1792–1868)
Historical Style: Bel canto (1813)
Range: B4 to F5

Fach: lyric coloratura
Librettist: Angelo Anelli (1761–1820), first
set by Luigi Mosca (1808)
Aria Duration: 4:47
Tessitura: C4 to C5

Position: Act I, scene 2

Setting: The seashore of Algeria, early 19th century

A tempest has driven a ship onto the rocks. Its mast is broken by the storm that is gradually subsiding. Isabella, an Italian lady, disembarks. She is looking to find her fiancé, Lindoro. She is surrounded by pirates. Initially she is frightened. The male chorus of pirates observe that she will make a "dainty morsel" for Mustafa, the Bey of Algiers. Isabella's first focus is on her cruel fate, and as she sings the words "amor tiranno!/cruel love!" she cadences the phrase to the middle C. "Is this a reward for her devotion and love?" is decorated with rising 32nd notes. "No horror or anguish exists compares to that which I suffer," again completing the phrase on the C.

Next is the focus on her lost fiancé, Lindoro: "For you, Lindoro, I find myself in such peril. From whom, O God, can I hope for counsel? Who will give me comfort?" Once again the vocal line is decorated with patterns of 16th notes, and the cadence is again on middle C. After the pirates remark that she will be a perfect catch for their master, Isabella realizes she must pull herself together and put her woman's wiles to good use. "No more terror, now is the time for courage," she remarks. "Now they'll see who I am!" she declares.

This melody is sung deliberately with determined dotted rhythms and 8th notes. The orchestra punctuates with its own dotted 8th notes in support. In the next section the orchestra sets the tone with repeated 8th-note chords that provide excitement for Isabella's next comments. She tells herself that "from experience" she knows how to tame men, confidently punctuating her thoughts with "si, si, si, si/yes, yes, yes, yes." The last "si" is triumphantly sung on the F at the top of the staff, which follows an ascending pattern of decorative 16th notes. She looks over the men now, no longer afraid of them. Isabella is more confident and begins the next lines with three repeated, determined quarter notes. She even flirts with the men with her eyes; she sings, "Be they gentle or rough, cool or ardent, they're all more or less alike" in repetition of her earlier melodic material. She continues, "They all long for happiness from a pretty woman." The tempo marking of the final section is poco più, and the aria builds momentum to the end. Isabella sings in the lower range of the staff, embellished by quickly moving 16th notes that ascend to the top of the staff and then descend. The orchestra accompanies on the off beat of the measures, also providing momentum to the vocal line. The ending is decorative, feminine, but also persistent and always determined and confident.

Piano/vocal score: p. 62 (G. Schirmer)

> Notes by singer Vivica Genaux: In less than four minutes I could show the different colors of the voice in the first part of the aria, really show off the fast coloratura at the end, and know that I had done something that made me stand out from the other singers. It is a fine example of an aria that was extremely easy for me to sing, but gave the impression of being very difficult to those listening. Probably the most important thing I learned from competitions especially is that if a singer brings in a terribly complicated piece of music but the judges/audience don't *realize* that it's so incredibly difficult, the singer is not going to impress very many people. Judges in competitions, and for that matter many general or artistic directors who are casting a season for their company, do not always know what's difficult and what's not. In my experience it's better to do something one can really show off with rather than be intellectually smug about.

No. 10

Voice: mezzo-soprano
Aria Title: "Per lui che adoro," No. 11, Cavatina (Isabella)
Opera Title: *L'italiana in Algeri*
Composer: Gioacchino Rossini (1792–1868)
Historical Style: Bel canto (1813)
Range: A4 to B6

Fach: lyric coloratura
Librettist: Angelo Anelli (1761–1820), first set by Luigi Mosca (1808)
Aria Duration: 5:14
Tessitura: E4 to E5

Position: Act II, scene 2

Setting: A magnificent apartment on the ground floor with, in the background, a delightful balcony overlooking the sea; Algeria, 19th century. On the right, the entrance to various rooms. Isabella, in front of a large portable mirror, is finishing dressing in Turkish style.

The instrumental introduction has a plaintive quality with a solo, embellished flute. "For him whom I adore, who is my treasure, make me more beautiful, Mother of Love," sings Isabella. The vocal line lies in the middle of the staff and is marked piano. It is a lyric melody delicately embellished with 32nd notes, and the last phrase is repeated with more embellishments. The singer needs to keep momentum here, continuing to move the long line forward. The melody continues in the lower range of the voice, with embellishments: "You know how I love him, how I long to please him," she sings, followed by a fermata rest; then (allegro) she exclaims, "Ye Graces, lend me charms and splendor!"

The next section is set syllabically on 16th-note values. Aside, Isabella sings, "Look, look; wait, wait. . . . You don't yet know who I am."

The hidden Lindoro, Mustafa, and Taddeo observe and comment: Mustafa speaks about her beauty, and Lindoro and Taddeo remark that she is a traitor, thinking that she is making herself beautiful for Mustafa.

Isabella then primps further, commenting on the placement of veil and feathers, with the help of the servants. She has short conversational phrases (with instrumental interruptions) for brief observation and comment. She then reprises the opening section. The final section (marked più mosso) is almost sung in a patter style, as Isabella continues to make asides: "My dear Turk, you're already there: a mere tap, and you're bound to fall." Mustafa, Lindoro, and Taddeo also make asides with chordal ensemble support: "Oh what a woman she is! She'd make any man crazy."

Piano/vocal score: p. 229 (G. Schirmer)

No. 11

Voice: mezzo-soprano
Aria Title: "Io seguo sol fiero" (Rosmira)
Opera Title: *Partenope*
Composer: George Frideric Handel (1685–1759)
Historical Style: Italian Baroque (1730)

Range: C4 to E5
Fach: lyric coloratura
Librettist: after Silvio Stampiglia's *La Partenope* set by Luigi Manza (1699)
Aria Duration: 4:32
Tessitura: C4 to C5

Position: Act II

Setting: A royal apartment in the palace of Partenope, first century B.C.

Rosmira, Princess of Cyprus and the fiancée of Arsaces but disguised as a soldier, has followed Armindo (one of Queen Partenope's three suitors) to Partenope's court in Naples. Rosmira, disguised as the Armenian Prince Eurimene, challenges Arsaces, a suitor to Partenope and favored by the Queen, to a duel, wanting to teach him a lesson.

Rosmira is singing to Armindo. Recitative:

My heat is all devoted to another. I fly with caution from the wilds
of love
And to Diana dedicate my vows.

Aria:

My genius leads me to the glades, the lonely lawns, and silent shades
To see my swift unerring spear overtake the fearful flying deer.
The fatal paths of love I fly, and wisely know the reason why,
For Cupid's unrelenting mind is ever cruel to our kind;
But at my feet my conquered prize the humble wounded savage dies.

Brightly sung in two, this piece has a dancelike feel that is joyful and calls for flexibility and many intervallic leaps. The aria exploits the lower and upper regions of the mezzo voice.

Piano/vocal score: p. 46 (Breitkopf)

No. 12

Voice: mezzo-soprano
Aria Title: "Quel volto mi piace" (Rosmira)
Opera Title: *Partenope*
Composer: George Frideric Handel (1685–1759)
Historical Style: Italian Baroque (1730)

Range: B4 to E5
Fach: lyric coloratura
Librettist: after Silvio Stampiglia's *La Partenope* set by Luigi Manza (1699)
Aria Duration: 4:00
Tessitura: F4 to C5

Position: Act III, scene 4

Setting: Naples, first century B.C.

Partenope (64 B.C.–A.D.19), the daughter of King Eumelius, founded the city of Partenope, now known as Naples. She has three suitors and is at war with one of them. She favors the Corinthian Prince Arsaces, not knowing that he has abandoned his fiancée, Rosmira. Rosmira, Princess of Cyprus and disguised as a soldier, has followed Armindo to Partenope's court. Rosmira (disguised as the Armenian Eurimene) is challenged to a duel by Arsaces, which is to be bare-chested. Rosmira (Eurimene) decides to reveal her identity without revealing anything else.

> His lovely fame my fancy charms
> But ah! His heart my fear alarms
> His fickle, faithless heart I fear,
> That lately cause my soul so dear.
>
> I feel my love, that ne'er can cease,
> Importunately plead for peace
> But then disdain and glowing rage
> 'Tis not so easy to assuage.

This aria, in A–B–A, form moves with a lilt sung in the triple meter and requires the voice to move gracefully and produce a tone that allows flexibility in the vocal line. It is a good piece to show an even tone with many phrases ascending in sequential patterns. Much of the vocal line is doubled in the violin.

Piano/vocal score: p. 101 (German Händel Society)

No. 13

Voice: mezzo-soprano

Aria Title: "Cara sposa" (Rinaldo)

Opera Title: *Rinaldo*

Composer: George Frideric Handel (1685–1759)

Historical Style: Italian Baroque (1711)

Range: B4 to E5

Fach: lyric coloratura

Librettist: Giacomo Rossi (fl. 1710–1731), to a scenario by Aaron Hill, after Torquato Tasso's *Gerusalemme liberate* (1575)

Aria Duration: 10:24

Tessitura: E4 to D5

Position: Act I, scene 7

Setting: The action takes place in Outremer in the Middle East during the First Crusade (1096–1099)

Christian forces led by Goffredo are laying siege to the city of Jerusalem, which is defended by its King, Argante. Argante's ally and lover is Armida, a formidable sorceress. With Goffredo are his brother and daughter Almirena, who loves and is loved by the Christian knight Rinaldo. Her hand is promised to him if the Christians are victorious. Argante is fearful of defeat and requests a three-day truce, which Goffredo agrees to. Armida descends from the skies in a chariot drawn by dragons. She vows to deprive the Christian forces of Rinaldo's support, and she will undertake this task.

In a beautiful garden with singing birds Almirena and Rinaldo exchange endearments until suddenly Armida tries to abduct Almirena. Armida and Rinaldo both draw their swords and prepare to fight, but as they are ready to engage a black cloud descends, filled with horrible monsters, emitting flames and smoke and bellowing. It covers Almirena and Armida and carries them off into the sky, leaving in their place two hideous furies who, after mocking Rinaldo, sink below the ground, leaving Rinaldo horrified and distraught.

Rinaldo alone (andante, larghetto, piano): "My dear betrothed, my dear love," he sings. "Where are you? Come back at my tears!" His melody ascends to E at the top of the staff before descending to B below middle C. Most of the tones are sustained, and many of the phrases begin with a three- or four-beat sustained crescendo as the melody unfolds.

The next section (allegro, non tanto, piano) is composed in 4/4 meter: "Evil spirits, I defy you with the fire of my wrath on your infernal altar." The text here is set syllabically, with 16th-note values, marked staccato in the accompaniment.

In the da capo section, the singer can add some simple embellishments.

It is more movingly heartfelt after the lashing out of the B section to sing the return of the beginning section softer and a little slower.

Piano/vocal score: p. 76 (Bärenreiter)

No. 14

Voice: mezzo-soprano
Aria Title: "Venti, turbini, prestate" (Rinaldo)
Opera Title: *Rinaldo*
Composer: George Frideric Handel (1685–1759)
Historical Style: Italian Baroque (1711)
Range: D4 to E5

Fach: lyric coloratura
Librettist: Giacomo Rossi (fl. 1710–1731), to a scenario by Aaron Hill, after Torquato Tasso's *Gerusalemme liberate* (1575)
Aria Duration: 3:40
Tessitura: D4 to E5

Position: Act I, scene 9 (finale)

Setting: The action takes place in Outremer in the Middle East during the First Crusade (1096–1099)

Rinaldo is a celebrated Christian hero. Christian forces led by Goffredo are laying siege to the city of Jerusalem, which is defended by its king, Argante. Argante's ally and lover is Armida, a formidable sorceress. With Goffredo are his brother and daughter Almirena, who loves and is loved by Rinaldo. Her hand is promised to him if the Christians are victorious. Argante is fearful of defeat and requests a three-day truce, which Goffredo agrees to. Armida descends from the skies in a chariot drawn by dragons. She vows to deprive the Christian forces of Rinaldo's support, and she will undertake this task.

In a beautiful garden with singing birds Almirena and Rinaldo exchange endearments until suddenly Armida tries to abduct Almirena. Armida and Rinaldo both draw their swords and prepare to fight, but as they are ready to engage in combat a black cloud descends, filled with horrible monsters, emitting flames and smoke and bellowing. It covers Almirena and Armida and carries them off into the sky, leaving in their place two hideous furies who, after mocking Rinaldo, sink below the ground, leaving Rinaldo horrified and distraught. It is in this dramatic context that he sings the aria "Cara sposa." Rinaldo tells Almirena's father Goffredo what has happened, and he and his brother Eustazio suggest that he seek help from a Christian sorcerer. Rinaldo is encouraged and calls on the winds and the heaven to second his revenge.

Rinaldo (alone):

Let a ray of hope once more shine down
On my bewildered heart; yes my beloved!
I run to attack those who deceived me;
Cupid, be merciful, give me your wings! (*allegro*)
Winds, whirlwinds, lend your wings to my feet.
Heavens, gods, strengthen my arm
Against those who have caused me sorrow.

Piano/vocal score: p. 89 (Bärenreiter)

No. 15

Voice: mezzo-soprano
Aria Title: "Bel raggio lusinghier," No. 7 (Semiramide)
Opera Title: *Semiramide*
Composer: Gioacchino Rossini (1792–1868)
Historical Style: Bel canto (1823)
Range: C♯4 to A5

Fach: lyric coloratura
Librettist: Gaetano Rossi (1774–1855), after the play *Sémiramis* by Voltaire (1748)
Aria Duration: 7:00
Tessitura: E4 to E5

Position: Act I

Setting: The hanging gardens of Babylon. Semiramide is seated in a flowery arbor as young minstrels and maidens in various groups are trying to distract her.

The action of the opera takes place in Babylon after the death of King Nino and the disappearance of his son Ninia, which took place under mysterious circumstances 15 years before. Babylon has been governed by Queen Semiramide, Nino's widow and Ninia's mother. The city is laboring under the fierce displeasure of the gods.

In the hanging gardens Semiramide is resting with her ladies-in-waiting. She is sure she will find peace of mind now that Arsace has returned. However, Arsace loves the Princess Azema. Semiramide thinks that she will marry Arsace, and the gods will be appeased.

The beginning is marked andante grazioso, and is composed in 6/8 meter. The music is florid, with 32nd notes and other complex groupings of embellishments to high A at the top. The accompaniment punctuates the melody line:

Lovely ray of enchanting hope and pleasure at last for me shines.
Arsace has returned, yes, and to me he will come. (*The Chorus repeats the text.*)
My soul, which till now grieved, feared, languished . . .
Oh how it can breathe again!
Every one of my cares has vanished from my heart,
My thoughts, has vanished the fear, yes.
The calm to my heart Arsace will bring.

Now there is a new section, distinguished by off-beat accents. There are longer florid 32nd-note patterns of four-measure length in the vocal line ascending to high A. The chorus joins for the repeat and strengthens the cadence at the end of the piece.

Sweet thoughts of that moment, at you will smile that loving heart.
Yes.
How much dearer after the torment is the lovely moment of joy and love.

Piano/vocal score: p. 123 (Kalmus)

No. 16

Voice: mezzo-soprano
Aria Title: "In si barbara," No. 13 (Arsace)
Opera Title: *Semiramide*
Composer: Gioacchino Rossini (1792–1868)
Historical Style: Bel canto (1823)

Range: G3 to G5
Fach: lyric coloratura
Librettist: Gaetano Rossi (1774–1855), after the play *Sémiramis* by Voltaire (1748)
Aria Duration: 2:49
Tessitura: C4 to D5

Position: Act II

Setting: The action of the opera takes place in Babylon, 1200 B.C.

After the death of King Nino and the disappearance of his son Ninia, which took place under mysterious circumstances 15 years previously, Babylon has been governed by Semiramide, Nino's widow and Ninia's mother. The city is laboring under the displeasure of the gods. Semiramide thinks she can rely on Arsace, the army commander, to punish Assur (Prince of the line of Baal) for the murder of King Nino, while Assur declares his desire to take revenge on Semiramide, however high the price.

Oroe, the High Priest of Baal, reveals that Arsace is Ninia, the son of King Nino. Arsace is horrified to learn that he is engaged to marry his own mother, Semiramide. Then Oroe reads Nino's last words: "I die, poisoned. Let Ninia, my son, someday avenge me. Assur is the traitor," as Arsace collapses into Oroe's arms at this news.

The nine measures of orchestral introduction are marked andante sostenuto, fortissimo and piano, and staccato. Arsace talks to Oroe about "such barbarous misfortune. Open your arms to me at least. Let me pour out my bitter woe and weep upon your breast." The vocal line is extremely florid, with 16th-note triplet figures, dotted rhythms, and accidentals. Although the vocal line is important, it has an agitated quality. The range, rapidly negotiated, is G below the staff to E♭ at the top. It lies in the low middle range of the voice.

In the opera Oroe and Magi respond, "Rouse yourself, remember who you are. Serve heaven, obey your father and wield his sword. He asks for vengeance for his son. Go, hasten to strike and avenge." Their first entrance is accompanied by horns in the orchestra. Arsace sings (allegro, forte), "Yes, vengeance! Give it to me!"

Oroe gives Nino's sword to Arsace. "Sacred weapon of my father, you awaken my courage," he says. "I already feel myself a worthier man." Once again, the tessitura is low, and remains on middle C. Oroe and Magi hear the demands that Assur must perish. "Yes, he shall perish!" commands Arsace. There is now a change of focus, sung dolce, piano, as it moves to the minor key. "Ah, she is my mother! Seeing me weep, perhaps my father will be pleased to pardon her." This next section, allegro, vivace, con brio, is sung by Oroe and the chorus of Magi. "Yes, my father avenged, the traitor slain for him, my spirit may hope for peace. My heart will beat contentedly once more with happiness and love." Again, this vocal line is florid and lies low. There are accents and defined dotted rhythms to observe. Finally, as Arsace sings that happiness in his heart "ritornerà/will return," the word is excitedly repeated 11 times in scale passages and arpeggios, two times ascending to a sustained high G.

Piano/vocal score: p. 276 (Kalmus)

No. 17

Voice: mezzo-soprano
Aria Title: "Quel mesto gemito" (Semiramide)
Opera Title: *Semiramide*
Composer: Gioacchino Rossini (1792–1868)
Historical Style: Bel canto (1823)
Range: B♭4 to F♭5

Fach: lyric coloratura
Librettist: Gaetano Rossi (1774–1855), after Voltaire's play *Sémiramis* (1748)
Aria Duration: 4:45
Tessitura: E♭4 to C♭5

Position: Act I, scene 13

Setting: Babylon, around 1200 B.C.. A magnificent throne room in the palace overlooking Babylon with a throne on one side and an antechamber on the other containing the magnificent tomb of King Nino. At the beginning of the scene is the procession of the royal party, accompanied by ladies and slaves. The people gather at the back and between the columns.

The action takes place in Babylon after the death of King Nino and the disappearance of his son Ninia, which took place under mysterious circumstances 15 years before. Babylon has been governed by Queen Semiramide, Nino's widow and Ninia's mother. The city is laboring under the fierce displeasure of the gods. Semiramide is infatuated with Arsace, the young commander of the Babylonian army. He is in love with Azema, Princess of the line of Baal, but Semiramide believes the young man is devoted to her. At the end of Act I, Semiramide announces to all assembled that she has chosen a king—Arsace, who tries to extricate himself from the embarrassing situation. Suddenly, Nino's ghost appears, saying that Arsace will be king, but he must first descend into Nino's burial vault and offer up a sacrificial victim there.

The piece is marked andante, sotto voce:

What melancholy groaning from that tomb. What shout of doom darkly resounds, falls heavily on my heart! My blood freezes from vein to vein. Atrocious throbbing oppresses my soul, I breathe barely in my terror.

Even though sung sotto voce, with the vocal line unaccompanied while the orchestra rhythmically punctuates, the rhythms of the vocal line are energized, with double-dotted rhythms and marked accents. The melody and text is repeated, and within the context of the opera Idreno, the Indian Prince, will be singing with Semiramide after she sings the initial melody.

Piano/vocal score: p. 191 (Kalmus)

No. 18

Voice: mezzo-soprano
Aria Title: "Oh patria! Dolce, e ingrate patria! . . . tu que accendi questo core" (Tancredi)
Opera Title: *Tancredi*
Composer: Gioacchino Rossini (1792–1868)
Historical Style: Bel canto (1812)
Range: A♭3 to F5

Fach: lyric coloratura
Librettist: Gaetano Rossi (1774–1855) after Voltaire's play *Sémiramis* (1748)
Aria Duration: 8:10
Tessitura: F4 to D5

Position: Act I, scene 2

Setting: The action takes place at Syracuse in the year 1005; a pleasant garden of the palace of Argirio, leader of the Senate

Tancredi, a military leader, has been exiled but is in love with Argirio's daughter, Amenaide. She expresses anxiety about the absence of her beloved Tancredi, and she has secretly invited him to return to her. Argirio tells Amenaide that he has promised her hand in marriage to Orbazzano, one of the other leaders of Syracuse.

The garden adjoins the shore and the sea, and a ship approaches, from which Tancredi and his followers disembark. He has not received Armenaide's message but is resolved to defend his native city against the enemy and to see again his beloved. He greets his native land: "O my country, dear thankless country."

His thoughts turn to Amenaide: "You who set aflame this heart," and he begs for her forgiveness for the pain he has caused her. "After such beating of the heart, such torment," now at last he will see her again.

Piano/vocal score: p. 47 (Belwin Mills)

No. 19

Voice: mezzo-soprano
Aria Title: "Acerba voluttà" (Principessa di Bouillon)
Opera Title: *Adriana Lecouvreur*
Composer: Francesco Cilea (1866–1950)
Historical Style: Verismo (1902)
Range: C4 to A6

Fach: lyric
Librettist: Arturo Colautti (1851–1914), after Eugène Scribe and Ernest Legouvé's play *Adrienne Lecouvreur* (1849)
Aria Duration: 4:18
Tessitura: F4 to C5

Position: Act II

Setting: Paris, 1730, Mlle. Duclos's villa by the Seine

The Princesse de Bouillon is competing with Adriana Lecouvreur, the star of the Comédie Française, for the love of Maurizio. In the opening of Act II, in a fever of jealous anticipation, the Princess anxiously awaits the arrival of Maurizio, who, unknown to her, is the Comte de Saxe and pretender to the throne of Poland. The Princess is obsessed with the idea that he loves another woman.

There are five measures of allegro introduction. Demonstrating the extremes of range and temperament, the Princess sings in the opening phrase an unstressed high A♭ ("acerba/waiting") and the low middle C ("offesa/offense"). The dynamics also change abruptly from forte to piano. The singer also needs to observe precise, energized dotted rhythms and accent markings:

> Aria translation by Martha Gerhart from the *G. Schirmer Opera Anthology: Arias for Mezzo-Soprano,* edited by Robert L. Larsen (used by permission):
>
> Waiting brings back intense pleasure, sweet torment, enduring pain, quick offense, fire, ice, trembling, rage and fear to my loving breast!

There are three measures of 6/4 meter marked largo, then the tempo is agitato:

> Every echo, every shadow in the incandescent night conspires against my impatient soul: Completely suspended between doubt and desire, it measures eternity in the moment.

The Princess sings a high G on the -oo- vowel of "misura/measures."
The next section (con moto) has a fragmented quality:

> Will he come? Has he forgotten me? Is he hurrying? Or perhaps he is changing his mind? There, he's coming! No, it's the sound of the stream, mingled with the sigh of a sleeping tree. [*The final section is marked sostenuto in 3/4 meter.*] Oh, vagrant star of the east, do not wane; smile at the universe and, if he is not lying, guide my love!

In the final section the singer must ascend from sustained phrases in the lower middle of the voice to high A♭'s at the end of the phrase.

Piano/vocal score: p. 79 (Casa Musicale Sonzogno di Piero Ostali)

No. 20

Voice: mezzo-soprano
Aria Title: "Temer? Perchè?" (Bersi)
Opera Title: *Andrea Chénier*
Composer: Umberto Giordano (1867–1948)
Historical Style: Verismo (1896)
Range: F4 to G5

Fach: lyric
Librettist: Luigi Illica (1857–1919), based
on the life of André Chénier
Aria Duration: 1:30
Tessitura: G4 to E5

Position: Act II

Setting: Café Hottot, Paris, the time of the French Revolution; to one side there is a bust of Revolutionary leader and martyr Marat; behind is the Perronet Bridge, which spans the river Seine and leads to the palace of the Five Hundred

Several years have passed since Act I. The Bastille has been taken, and the Revolution rules everything. At the opening of Act II Chénier is seated alone at a table. Bersi, the mulatto maid who formerly was Maddalena's servant, is now dressed as a *merveilleuse,* an elegantly dressed streetwalker at the time. She is now pretending to be a jolly revolutionary and is speaking with a man called simply Incredibile, a spy in the service of Gérard. In devil-may-care fashion Bersi announces that happiness is being a revolutionary, but she doesn't quite convince the spy.

Before the aria begins, Bersi asks Incredibile if Robespierre is training spies. "I don't know, nor can I know it! Have you something to fear?" asks Incredibile.

The aria is marked a piacere:

Fear? Why? Why should I be afraid? Am I not, like you, a true child of the Revolution? I love living like this, (*allegro brillante*) living in haste in this feverish gaiety of brief, pointed, and thoughtless pleasure!

Here play and pleasure . . . there, death! Here the sound of coins and the lottery! There the cannon and the roll of drums! Here the intoxication of wine, there the intoxication of blood!

(*She points to the Palace of the Five Hundred.*)

Here laughter and love, there they think and they hate! Here like the *merveilleuse* who toasts with champagne; the vendors and there the fish-wives and the cart of Sanson (*name of the public executioner*).

She raises a glass of champagne toward the cart bearing the condemned to the guillotine.

The aria calls for a freedom of expression that is indicated in the makeup of the character, and solid sustained tones (G) at the top of the staff. The piece lies high in the voice.

Piano/vocal score: p. 74 (International)

No. 21

Voice: mezzo-soprano
Aria Title: "Il vecchiotto cerca moglie" (Berta)
Opera Title: *Il barbiere di Siviglia*
Composer: Gioacchino Rossini (1792–1868)
Historical Style: Bel canto (1815)
Range: C#4 to A5

Fach: lyric
Librettist: Cesare Sterbini (1784–1831), after Pierre-Augustin Caron de Beaumarchais's play *Le barbier de Séville* (1775) and Giuseppe Petrosellini's libretto for Giovanni Paisiello (1782)
Aria Duration: 2:25
Tessitura: F#4 to E5

Position: Act II

Setting: Seville, 18th century; the home of Dr. Bartolo

After Figaro and the Count have been so emphatically booted by Dr. Bartolo from his house after the shaving scene and Rosina banished upstairs to her room, Bartolo tells the servant Ambrosius to run and find Don Basilio. "Tell him I must see him immediately," Dr. Bartolo says. "You, Berta, guard the door," he orders. "No, I cannot trust her," he says as he leaves the room. "My old master suspects everything," she replies. "I once found him good, but now I can't stand him! It's always bedlam here, shouts, riots, tears, threats, quarrels. They argue, they cry they threaten! What a house! What a house in confusion!"

The aria (allegro) is written in A major, but it can be sung transposed into G major as well. There are 25 measures of introduction, composed in 2/4 meter. The simple melody is introduced in the accompaniment (staccato, piano). Berta can be actively dusting here to show her frustration.

The old man wants a wife, the girl wants a husband, they're both raving mad. Si! Si! (*high F♯, E quarter notes*) They're both raving mad! But what is this love that makes one delirious? It's an unusual sickness, a craze, a tickle, a torment. I feel it, too, alas. And I don't know how it will end.

The text is syllabically set on the repeated E at the top of the staff, followed by three measures of interlude in the accompaniment.

Verse 2 begins as she goes to the mirror, as can be imagined before she sings the following text:

Oh, the sadness of old age. Nobody knows. Nobody cares. I'm despised by everyone. I shall die unwanted, a desperate old maid. I might as well die.

The text is repeated, più mosso. At the cadence of the piece, Berta sings a variety of articulations in her vocal phrase between staccato and legato triplet patterns in melancholic pain. Contrasts of articulation are necessary to sustain interest in the piece and to deliver the text.

Piano/vocal score: p. 259 (G. Schirmer)

> Notes by singer and master teacher Judith Christin: Because it sits in the *passaggio,* by the time one arrives at the end of the aria the larynx can be climbing to a fevered pitch, which can sacrifice the final high note. It is also a lesson in doing staccato phrases in a style that maintains a charming sense of Berta's overworked condition and not a hammered old unsupported sound that makes the audience wish the piece had been cut. Also, singing the triplets with legato and yet rhythmical accuracy shapes the contrast to the beleaguered scale-like phrases. In the section which starts "Elgli un male universale, una smania un pizzicore, un soletico, un tormento/It's a universal epidemic, a frenzied itch, a tickle, a torment," the singer needs to employ different colors for each meaning of the feelings Berta is expressing. Performing comprimario roles requires many vocal colors, but the artist needs to always return to a legitimate quality whenever she can. We can coax the voice to many areas, but the core must be ready at the drop of a hat to remind the vocal mechanism it is in play at all times.

No. 22

Voice: mezzo-soprano
Aria Title: "Una voce poco fa," Cavatina (Rosina)
Opera Title: *Il barbiere di Siviglia*
Composer: Gioacchino Rossini (1792–1868)
Historical Style: Bel canto (1816)
Range: A4 to C6

Fach: lyric (coloratura)
Librettist: Cesare Sterbini (1784–1831), after Pierre-Augustin Caron de Beaumarchais's play *Le barbier de Séville* (1775) and Giuseppe Petrosellini's libretto for Giovanni Paisiello (1782)
Aria Duration: 5:28
Tessitura: A4 to E5

Position: Act I, scene 2

Setting: A room in Dr. Bartolo's house, Seville, 1775

The young Rosina is a ward of Dr. Bartolo and is completely under his thumb, virtually a prisoner. In scene 1 she has been secretly serenaded by the "student" Lindoro, who has been chased away by Bartolo. Lindoro is really the Count Almaviva, coached by Figaro. The Count wants a woman to fall in love with him for himself, not his title. He has been able to pass a letter to Rosina. At the opening of scene 2, Rosina has been reading the letter, which sparks all kinds of hopes and dreams in the girl. "A voice has just echoed here into my heart. My heart is wounded, and it is Lindoro who shot." It begins in the low, middle voice. The vocal line is connected, but the dotted rhythms and short-note values are energized and vital, excited. The accompaniment is chordal and delicate, on beats 1 and 3 for light support and momentum.

Although Rosina is youthful and feminine, she is also decisive—and it is at this point she desperately needs to be released from Bartolo's bonds, but on her terms. She sings, "Yes! Lindoro will be mine!" as her melody leaps up to E at the top of the staff and descends, decoratively. All of her coloratura comes from excitement, determination, femininity, joy, decisiveness, and control.

The next section is reflection, almost sung parlando, as Rosina thinks through the situation, saying that most certainly Bartolo will refuse permission, but she will "sharpen her mind" and will triumph, repeating her bravura coloratura.

In the next section, after 12 measures of orchestral interlude, Rosina plays the obedient child, saying that she can be gentle, sweet, loving, but if she is crossed she can be a viper (her vocal line descends to low G♯) and set a hundred traps, as she sings excitedly 16th-note patterns descending from high G♯, F♯, E, D♯ before the cadence, which can ascend to a high B if desired.

Piano/vocal score: p. 75 (G. Schirmer)

> Notes by singer Vivica Genaux: I have found that this aria can be one of the most important ones a young coloratura mezzo or soprano can prepare. As far as a competition piece, it shows a bit of everything in the voice, a good legato as well as showing off the coloratura, ornamentation, and some good high notes. For mezzos and sopranos at the young professional level, Rosina is a role that is often used by opera companies to try out new singers. As the opera's success does not necessarily hinge on the character of Rosina, they can afford to take a chance on an unknown singer, which is not the case with many other bel canto leading roles. In my own experience, I have made several company debuts with Rosina, leading to further contracts.

No. 23

Voice: mezzo-soprano
Aria Title: "Smanie implacabili" (Dorabella)
Opera Title: *Così fan tutte*
Composer: Wolfgang Amadeus Mozart (1756–1791)
Historical Style: Classical (1790)
Range: D4 to G5

Fach: lyric
Librettist: Lorenzo da Ponte (1749–1838)
Aria Duration: 4:03
Tessitura: F4 to G5

Position: Act I, scene 3

Setting: The living room of Dorabella and Fiordiligi's house, Naples, 18th century

After her fiancé has gone off to war, Dorabella grieves his leaving and overreacts somewhat to the point where she is hysterical. In this mock-heroic aria, she is singing that her grief is too much to bear, and thus she should die. This aria represents the dramatic entrance of Dorabella in scene 3. The servant Despina is trying to present the ladies' breakfast, while Dorabella melodramatically brushes Despina (and the breakfast) aside, for she might do something desperate. "Shut the curtains!" she orders Despina. "I hate the light, the air I breathe, myself!" Despina has seen this behavior before, and she laughs. "Who laughs at my pain? Who will console me? Away! (*directed to Despina*) Flee! Leave me alone!"

The aria begins (allegro agitato) as the rolling figure of the orchestra in its constant motion throughout the piece represents the rolling motion of the water, where Dorabella cannot get solid footing. She hardly has a chance to catch her breath in the piece, and the opening phrase is separated by rests, almost as if she is hyperventilating. She is tormented by "implacable pangs" and will not subside until the anguish brings her death. "If I remain alive I will furnish the Furies with a wretched example of tragic love, with the dreadful sound (*to the high, sustained G♭*) of my sighs." Then the phrase repeats for emphasis interspersed with 8th rests to connote turbulent emotions. The text and rhythm are repeated on a different pitch level, creating a melodic shape not unlike the opening. At "col suono orribile/with the dreadful sound" the voice reaches up from high G♭ to G and finally an A♭ at the top, with more "sighing" figures to close.

Piano/vocal score: p. 74 (G. Schirmer)

No. 24

Voice: mezzo-soprano
Aria Title: "Now may there be a blessing" (Mary Stone)
Opera Title: *The Devil and Daniel Webster*
Composer: Douglas Moore (1893–1969)
Historical Style: American Folk Opera (1939)
Range: C4 to F5

Fach: lyric
Librettist: Stephen Vincent Benét (1898–1943)
Aria Duration: 2:19
Tessitura: F4 to D5

Position: One-act opera

Setting: New Hampshire, 1940s

The opera begins with a country festival celebrating the marriage of Jabez and Mary Stone. The Stones were always poor, but Jabez has prospered, and there's talk of him running for Governor. A Boston lawyer appears, who terrifies Jabez and the town. Jabez has sold his soul to the devil. Now appearing is another guest, the famous folk hero Daniel Webster.

Webster exhorts Mary Stone to deliver "the prayers of the innocent" to help her husband. It is a simple, straightforward plea, calmly sung (piano).

Now may there be a blessing and a light betwixt thee and me, forever. For as Ruth unto Naomi, so do I cleave unto thee. Set me as a seal upon thy heart, as a seal upon thine arm, for love is strong as death. Many waters cannot quench love, neither can the floods drown it. As Ruth unto Naomi, so do I cleave unto thee.

Recitative:

The Lord watch between thee and me when we are absent, one from another. Amen. (*The singer sings a piano high E, to D, then a sustained high F.*) Amen.

The vocal line crescendos to a sustained D, then to a high, sustained F. The singer is also required to sing a decrescendo on the sustained D.

Piano/vocal score: p. 54 (Boosey & Hawkes)

No. 25

Voice: mezzo-soprano
Aria Title: "Ne pensons qu'au plaisir d'aimer" (Dulcinée)
Opera Title: *Don Quichotte*
Composer: Jules Massenet (1842–1912)
Historical Style: French Romantic (1910)
Range: B4 to G5

Fach: lyric
Librettist: Henri Cain (1859–1937), after Jacques le Lorrain's verse play *Le chevalier de la longue figure* (1906)
Aria Duration: 1:52
Tessitura: F4 to C5

Position: Act IV

Setting: Soirée in the garden of Dulcinée's house

La belle Dulcinée is a capricious small-town tart. Surrounded by her admirers, Dulcinée longs for some new sensation to satisfy her hungry flesh. She then chases away her melancholy mood with a flamboyant song to her own guitar accompaniment.

She begins the song fortissimo, with fire: "Alza!" on sustained high E, then again "Alza!" ascending from low E in a scalelike flourish of 16th notes to high G♯ and down again. The aria is accompanied by guitar with dancelike rhythms. The rhythms include exotically set flourishes of 16th notes, and portamenti. The tone of the aria is playful, sensual, confident, deliberate.

Think only of the pleasures of love, the feverish, fleeting hours when we feel our hearts swooning at the touch of the lips we kiss! (*Verse 2 is marked pianissimo.*) Let eyes gaze into eyes, desires run wild; you that are young, remember that love favors the brave. Anda! Think only of the fleeting moments when the soul swoons in an ecstasy of adoration and the touch of a lover's lips! (*She dances.*)

The aria needs a warm, sensual tone on the middle C, with a sudden sustained fortissimo high E ("Olé!").

Piano/vocal score: p. 172 (Heugel)

No. 26

Voice: mezzo-soprano
Aria Title: "Oh, don't you see that lonesome dove?" (Jennie Parson)
Opera Title: *Down in the Valley*
Composer: Kurt Weill (1900–1950)
Historical Style: Folk Opera (1948)
Range: C4 to F5

Fach: lyric/soprano
Librettist: Arnold Sundgaard (b. 1911)
Aria Duration: 2:20
Tessitura: F4 to C5

Position: One-act opera

Setting: A small community on the American frontier; outside the Parsons' family home; night

Jennie's lover Brack Weaver has been held in jail. He is convicted of killing Bouché (in self-defense). Brack has broken out of jail to see Jennie once more, but it is inevitable that he will be caught and eventually hanged. He runs to the field next to her home. They embrace, and Brack says they are searching for him, but he had to find her to "learn her mind." She is afraid. Her father wouldn't let her write, and that's why he has not heard from her.

Jennie sings two verses of this simple folk song, which needs to be sung in a simple fashion, without the addition of emoting or "drama." Many of the phrases begin on middle C, but it is sung as a pickup to the phrase. The singer will need a freely sung high E and F. Jennie is trying to create a fantasy and an oasis here, where they can block out the reality of their situation: this is the last time they will be together. The meaning is especially poignant when she sings, "You are the darling of my heart until my dying day." Obviously there is urgency because of Brock's imminent capture. Their "oasis" creates the need for flashback, so that in the opera we now find out about the events leading up to Brock's first arrest.

Piano/vocal score: p. 31 (G. Schirmer)

No. 27

Voice: mezzo-soprano
Aria Title: "Faites-lui mes aveux," No. 7 (Siebel)
Opera Title: *Faust*
Composer: Charles Gounod (1818–1893)
Historical Style: French Romantic (1859)
Range: D4 to G5

Fach: lyric
Librettists: Jules Barbier (1825–1901) and Michel Carré (1819–1872), after Part I of Johann Wolfgang von Goethe's play *Faust* (1808)
Aria Duration: 3:03
Tessitura: G4 to E5

Position: Act II, scene 1

Setting: The garden of Marguerite in a German city, 16th century. A wall at back, with a little door. A bower at left, a house at right, with a window toward the audience. Trees and shrubs dot the scene.

The curtain rises, and Siebel, a young man in love with Marguerite, enters. He has vowed to protect her while her brother Valentin is away at war. Siebel stops by a bed of roses and lilies. The music (allegro agitato) features incessant 2nds, the F against G played in the accompaniment in repeated 8th notes. The vocal phrases are short, breathless, and excited, the text syllabically set to the music, but there is also opportunity for the singer to sustain the E, F♯, and G at the top of the staff to show the youth's ardent feelings as each phrase ascends.

Siebel gathers flowers to give to Marguerite. He hopes that they will convey his love to her, and talks directly to the flowers with this desire. He plucks a flower, but the flowers die as soon as he plucks them (Mephistopheles is at work), and we have an accompanied recitative section (andante). He dips his hand in holy water in a little font attached to the wall. "It's here that Marguerite prays each evening," he remarks. "Let's see (*allegro*) now—will the flowers now wilt if I try again? No! Satan, I laugh at you," he sings as the piece moves into a return of the opening melody once more, this time with a more confident Siebel singing the melody (without the incessantly repeated 2nds in the accompaniment), and with a different text: he hopes that the flowers he now kisses, she will later hold near her mouth, and will carry his kiss to her. Siebel will remain in the garden after the aria.

Piano/vocal score: p. 103 (G. Schirmer)

No. 28

Voice: mezzo-soprano
Aria Title: "Ich lade gern mir Gäste ein,"
No. 7, Couplets (Prince Orlofsky)
Opera Title: *Die Fledermaus*
Composer: Johann Strauss, Jr. (1825–1899)
Historical Style: Viennese Operetta (1874)
Range: C4 to G♯/A♭

Fach: lyric
Librettist: Carl Haffner (1804–1874) and
Richard Genée (1823–1895)
Aria Duration: 2:48
Tessitura: D♯/E♭4 to D♯/E♭5

Position: Act II

Setting: A party in Prince Orlofsky's house, Vienna, 1870

As Act II opens, all the guests feel fortunate to be invited and are impressed by the opulent surroundings and their host. Prince Orlofsky is enjoying the party he has thrown and tells everyone that they must enjoy the party in their own way: "Chacun à son goût." This "request" comes in the form of his couplet, which is charming yet forceful, as delivered by someone used to getting his way at his own party. His wit is dry, his accent is usually thickly Russian. In the first verse he is the perfect host. He also wants his guests to enjoy themselves, but "don't get in my way," he warns. At the end of verse 1 he says, "We Russians have a motto: Chacun à son goût," which, of course, is the saying of only the rich, aristocratic Russians who have the privilege of knowing the French culture. In verse 2 Orlofsky talks about himself: "There's not a place he has not been, nor a price or sum he cannot afford." But he is still bored.

The last section is addressed bluntly, directly to the audience, as he tells them he does not care for music, even that of Johann Strauss. And the operetta he hates most is called *Fledermaus,* repeated for emphasis. "If you don't like it either, you know what you can do—get up and leave the theater!" he orders.

Each verse is in two sections: the first phrases repeat with the higher note (D♭) for the "pick-up," as if Orlofsky is grabbing your attention, then the following two phrases begin with the "pick-up" of a high A♭ 8th note, like a hiccup. The accompaniment in section 1 is a repeated quarter-note rhythm, with three-beat chords followed by a quarter rest. The second section (poco meno) of both verses looks to be more connected note-to-note, but it is also marked marcato in the voice and orchestra. This means that the line stays away from a sentimental tone that the legato delivery can produce. There are grace notes in this section of the music, but Orlovsky's delivery is still forceful and straightforward, without affectation.

Piano/vocal score: p. 65 (G. Schirmer)

No. 29

Voice: mezzo-soprano
Aria Title: "Al suon del tamburo" (Preziosilla)
Opera Title: *La forza del destino*
Composer: Giuseppe Verdi (1813–1901)
Historical Style: Italian Romantic (1862)
Range: B4 to G5

Fach: lyric
Librettist: Francesco Maria Piave (1810–1876)
Aria Duration: 3:12
Tessitura: D5 to C5

Position: Act II, scene 1

Setting: An inn in the village of Hornachuelos, Spain, mid-18th century

In the large ground floor kitchen of the inn is a cupboard with dishes and other artifacts and tables with bottles and glasses on them; the fireplace in the background has several pots boiling. The host and hostess are preparing dinner; the muleteers are near their pack saddles; peasants and other families are sitting and standing about.

Preziosilla, a lively young gypsy, enters and announces that war has just broken out and that all men should not lose time in going off to Italy to fight the Germans. She begins to tell fortunes, and after Don Carlo (brother of Leonora and traveling under the assumed name Pereda) finishes his story, she lets him know that she hasn't believed one single word of it.

> Hurrah for War! (*The students repeat the cheer.*)
> Run then to Italy and fight against the Germans,
> And I will be there with you. Viva!

The aria is marked allegro and is sung piano; it is composed in the low range requiring a B below middle C, then ascending to E with careful rhythmic patterns and accents, finally rising to G♯ at the end of the first section.

> At the sound of the drum, at the mettle of the steed,
> At the blue cloud of the cannon warring;
> At the noise of the battlefields our souls are inflamed!
> The war is beautiful! Hurrah for war!

The students cheer. During the next section there is a development of the first melody with a repeat of "evviva!" at the end of the section:

> He alone is forgotten who dies a coward.
> The reward of glory and honor is reserved for the brave soldier of true valor . . .

If you come, brother, you'll be a corporal,
And you a colonel, and you a general.

This is marked pianissimo, leggerissimo; the next section is another variation of the original melody with "evviva!" again at the end of the section.

The roguish god with the immortal bow (*Cupid*)
Will pay homage to the brave officer by making him lucky in love.

Piano/vocal score: p. 58 (Ricordi)

No. 30

Voice: mezzo-soprano
Aria Title: "Nobles seigneurs, salut!"
(Urbain)
Opera Title: *Les Huguenots*
Composer: Giacomo Meyerbeer (1781–1864)
Historical Style: French Romantic (1836)
Range: F/G3 to B♭5

Fach: lyric
Librettists: Eugène Scribe (1791–1861) and Emile Deschamps (1791–1871), based on historical events
Aria Duration: 4:02
Tessitura: E♭4 to E♭5

Position: Act I

Setting: France, 1570s; a large hall in the castle of the Count de Nevers, an important Catholic leader

> Aria plot notes from the *G. Schirmer Opera Anthology: Arias for Mezzo-Soprano*, edited by Robert L. Larsen (used by permission):
> The Protestant nobleman, Raoul de Nangis, has been invited by the Count de Nevers to his home to meet his Catholic friends and to attempt a reconciliation between their two parties. The young page of Marguerite de Valois, Urbain, the page of Marguerite de Valois, appears and greets the assembled nobles. His purpose is to escort Raoul, the Protestant nobleman, to an unspecified destination. The atmosphere is extremely tense.

"Noble lords, greetings!" is marked by an arpeggio leap to the sustained high F, unaccompanied; then the figure is repeated to high G, followed by a cadenza that ascends to high A in the opening.

The aria continues, marked cantabile, in a lilting 9/8 meter:

> Aria translation by Martha Gerhart, from the *G. Schirmer Opera Anthology: Arias for Mezzo-Soprano,* edited by Robert L. Larsen (used by permission):
>
> A noble and virtuous lady, of whom kings should be envious, has entrusted me with this message for one of you, chevaliers, without my naming her;
> Honor here to the gentleman whom she has chosen!
> [*dolce*] You can believe that no lord has ever had so much glory or good fortune—no, never! Do not fear a lie or a trap, chevaliers, in my speech!
> Now farewell! May God protect your battles, your loves!

The nature of the shape of Urbain's melody shows a flair and flamboyance, and a self-importance, which also defines the strong rhythmic values. Look for the embellishments that have unexpected off-the-beat accents. Looking into the text, there is a possibility for sarcasm and forced charm that is also the result of the tension in the room.

Piano/vocal score: p. 86 (Kalmus)

No. 31

Voice: mezzo-soprano
Aria Title: "Blow ye the trumpet" (Annie Brown)
Opera Title: *John Brown*
Composer and Librettist: Kirke Mechem (b. 1925)
Historical Style: 20th-century English (1993)
Range: C4 to G5

Fach: lyric
Aria Duration: 1:20
Tessitura: G4 to E5

Position: Act II

Setting: The plains of Kansas, May 1856

Aria plot notes from the *G. Schirmer American Aria Anthology: Mezzo-Soprano,* edited by Richard Walters (used by permission):

The opera concerns the struggles in Kansas in the aftermath of the 1854 Kansas-Nebraska Act passed by Congress, which dictated that the question of slavery in those territories was to be decided by their residents in elections.

Kansas became a bloody political battleground for North and South. John Brown (1800–1859) was an antislavery activist who was executed for his attempts to end slavery by violence. In Act II the struggles over slavery have consumed Kansans.

This brief piece will show range in the voice, for it requires a solid high G and F, and a solid middle voice as well. The lowest tone required is a sustained middle C.

Piano/vocal score: p. 88 (*G. Schirmer American Aria Anthology: Mezzo-Soprano*)

Notes by composer Kirke Mechem: In a scene that shows the resolve of the abolitionists, Annie, Brown's daughter, describes her father's strength and tenderness to them as children, and how he sang his favorite hymn, "Blow Ye the Trumpet." Her family and friends respond in chorus. In the choral versions of this piece (SATB, TTBB, and SSAA), a number of different hymn tunes and verses have this same title; as I have been unable to discover which version Brown knew, I have chosen the text I found most beautiful and appropriate—indeed, prophetic—for his life and death. It seems to prophesy both the day of jubilee and the martyr's death which Brown knew would hasten the destruction of slavery. None of the existing hymn tunes used these words, so I gave them a new melody in the style of early American folk music. The singer should be mindful of the importance of this text and try to perform with both simplicity and deep feeling. There is a great contrast between the first section and the Poco più animato (measure 11), which becomes exalted and joyful. The old meaning of the word "start" here means "to be startled."

No. 32

Voice: mezzo-soprano

Aria Title: "Things change, Jo" (Meg March)

Opera Title: *Little Women*

Composer and Librettist: Mark Adamo
(b. 1962), after Louisa May Alcott's novel
Little Women (1869)

Historical Style: 20th-century American (2001)

Range: G3 to G♯5

Fach: lyric

Aria Duration: 3:16

Tessitura: D4 to D5

Position: Act I, scene 2

Setting: A small New England town, mid-1800s; the March family attic; this scene takes place two years before the Prologue

> Aria plot notes from the *G. Schirmer American Aria Anthology: Mezzo-Soprano,* edited by Richard Walters (used by permission):
> Brooke has just proposed to Meg. Although Jo had tried to convince her sister to reject him, Meg has accepted his proposal. Jo feels betrayed by her decision.

This aria is demanding for the young singer and has the ability to show the singer's range, intonation, ability to deliver text while singing the legato line, and changing thought focuses. The singer is asked to sing a high G pianissimo at the top of the staff after more than an octave leap from D below the staff.

Piano/vocal score: p. 162 (G. Schirmer)

> Notes by composer Mark Adamo: Surprised by Jo's interpreting Meg's love for Brooke as an abandonment, Meg impetuously blurts out, "Things end." As Jo, devastated, looks on in judgment, Meg, needing both to console her devastated sister and to confide to her all the billowing new feelings of first love, tries to convince Jo that one day she too will have this same change of heart, and that it will be a beginning, not an end.

No. 33

Voice: mezzo-soprano
Aria Title: "What am I forbidden?" (Lizzie Borden)
Opera Title: *Lizzie Borden*
Composer: Jack Beeson (b. 1921)
Historical Style: 20th-century American (1966)
Range: B4 to G♯5

Fach: lyric (dramatic)
Librettist: Kenward Elmslie (b. 1929), based on a scenario by Richard Plant
Tessitura: B4 to G♯5

Position: Act II

Setting: Fall River, Massachusetts, in the 1880s, a summer evening after supper; the large living room of Andrew Borden's dark, imposing Victorian house; a standing desk for Mr. Borden, a successful self-made businessman; a weapons collection owned by Mr. Borden

Lizzie Borden, about 30 years of age, lives with her younger sister, Margret, her father, Andrew, and their stepmother, Abigail. Lizzie's sainted mother died many years ago. Lizzie, dark and intense, teaches Sunday school but harbors a deep anger and resentment of her father and stepmother. In the scene before this aria, Lizzie watches her father drive away Margret's love interest, never to return. Furthermore, Andrew Borden humiliates Lizzie by offering her to Captain Jason McFarlaine instead of Margret, who has been secretly seeing Jason for two years. Andrew Borden then makes it clear to Lizzie that she is forbidden to see the Reverend, the Sunday school children's choir, the Captain, or even mention McFarlaine's name. Lizzie is left alone as Andrew goes upstairs.

In the aria she finds herself acting out pent-up emotions. This energy is released with complex rhythms and intervals. She is in an "embattled" mood. She sits at his desk and pretends to do his accounts after his death. She sees "two old ladies in a childless house: Miss Lizzie and Miss Margret. The house all to ourselves." She unlocks the front door and throws it open. "No one will guard this house. No one will sit at his desk. Trespassers will be welcomed and men of the sea with violent eyes," sings Lizzie. Her voice ascends up to high, sustained A. "All these walls." She then hears the sound of a foghorn, and she gains control of herself as her voice calms somewhat. She sings in her lower-middle voice. She imagines the parlor game they played before with their guests. She then turns violently on her dead mother's portrait. "You are no longer mother," she angrily sings, mimicking her father's voice. "Abigail is mother," all in descending figures to the low B♭, fortissimo. Finally, she focuses on her stepmother and father in increasingly fragmented phrases that embellish her own fragile emotional deterioration, and the aria suddenly breaks off after she sings, "Lizzie must be dead," breaking off on the final high sustained G♯.

Piano/vocal score: p. 159 (Boosey & Hawkes)

No. 34

Voice: mezzo-soprano
Aria Title: "Yes! I am she!" (Madame Mao)
Opera Title: *Madame Mao*
Composer: Bright Sheng (b. 1955)
Historical Style: 20th-century American (2003)
Range: B♭4 to A5

Fach: lyric (dramatic)
Librettist: Colin Graham (b. 1931)
Aria Duration: 3:17
Tessitura: B♭4 to A5

Position: Act I

Setting: 20th-century China

Aria plot notes from the *G. Schirmer American Aria Anthology: Mezzo-Soprano,* edited by Richard Walters (used by permission):

The opera is about Jiang Ching [Madame Mao], the powerful wife of Chinese Communist leader Mao Tse-Tung. The role is divided between two singers: a soprano sings the young Jiang Ching; a mezzo-soprano sings the more mature woman.

In Act I time goes backwards from the death of Madame Mao and the trial that preceded it, to her first meeting with Mao as a young actress and her existence as a chattel of men.

Act II moves forward from her youth until her death, including her sexual ascendancy over Mao, her revenge against her enemies in the Cultural Revolution, the death of Mao, her unsuccessful attempt to succeed him, and the fiasco of her trial. "Yes! I am she!" begins the opera.

The aria is challenging for a young mezzo-soprano and demands high, sustained F$\sharp$, G, and A above the staff—and a fortissimo extended low B and low B$\flat$ (after a drop from high A for effect) below middle C. The piece is rhythmically interesting and never static.

Piano/vocal score: p. 136 (*G. Schirmer American Aria Anthology: Mezzo-Soprano*)

Notes by composer Bright Sheng: The challenge in this aria is to sing evenly and equally powerfully in both the highest and lowest registers.

No. 35

Voice: mezzo-soprano
Aria Title: "Adieu, forêts" (Jeanne)
Opera Title: *The Maid of Orleans*
Composer and Librettist: Pyotr Ilyich Tchaikovsky (1840–1893), after Johann Christoph Friedrich von Schiller's tragedy translated by Vasily Andreyevich Zhukovsky, Jules Barbier's *Jeanne d'Arc,* and Auguste Mermet's libretto for his own opera, after Barbier (1876), with various details adapted from Henri Wallon's biography of Joan of Arc
Historical Style: Russian Romantic (1881)
Range: D$\flat$4 to A5

Fach: lyric
Aria Duration: 4:40
Tessitura: F$\sharp$4 to E$\flat$5

Position: Act I

Setting: A forest near Domrémy

Maidens are celebrating a villa festival. A peasant enters and warns the villagers that an English attack in imminent. Joan reassures the crowd with a prophecy, which is soon proven true. Joan is acclaimed a seer. Obedient to her calling, she sings a farewell to her native land, as she sets out to save France.

The aria is marked andantino, cut time (alla breve) with many accidentals. The piece calls for many sustained F's at the top of the staff. At "Seigneur/ Lord" there is a high A (half note), and another high A (fermata) at "Ah! Recevez mon eternal adieu!/Receive my final farewell" at the last phrase of the aria. Some of the climaxes have a heavy accompaniment, but the singer should be careful not to push the voice. Remember that Jeanne is still a very young, idealistic character, and not too dramatic or "mannered."

It is the Lord's will. I must obey His orders, and obey the wishes of the Saints. Why do I have such a feeling in my heart? Why am I afraid? Why do I tremble?

(*andantino, piano*) Goodbye forests, goodbye flowers, the country, the valley, adieu! Today Jeanne will speak the last farewell. Yes, forever. Goodbye! my precious flowers, my dark forests, your flowers—are now for others. Goodbye forests, your purity from heaven: I will depart, Jeanne will depart, yes, and never return.

Oh, sweet valley that I knew, my lambs in the green hills. (*più mosso*) I must show honor and must be brave for this victory. I hear the voice of the saints and of God, you know of my love, I am fearful, and I am sorrowful, you see me tremble.

There is repetition of text and musical phrases to the end.

The aria requires a strong sustained F at the top of the staff with climactic high A's. The piece is poignant and is a call for courage and action.

Piano/vocal score: p. 112 (*Operatic Anthology: Celebrated Arias Selected from Operas by Old and Modern Composers*, vol. 2 [G. Schirmer])

No. 36

Voice: mezzo-soprano
Aria Title: "Nimmermehr wird mein Herze
sich grämen," No. 14 (Nancy)
Opera Title: *Martha*
Composer: Friedrich von Flotow (1812–
1883)
Historical Style: German Romantic (1847)
Range: C4 to A5

Fach: lyric
Librettist: Friedrich Wilhelm Riese (1805–
1879)
Aria Duration: 1:35
Tessitura: F4 to C5

Position: Act III

Setting: England during the reign of Queen Anne, c. 1710, a wood

Lady Harriet, maid of honor to the Queen, is bored with court life and longs to escape the advances of her elderly foppish cousin. Her maid, Nancy, suggests diversions, and they end up on their way to Richmond, where they end up at the hiring fair, where they pose as maids and are hired by two young farmers. "Martha–Lady Harriet" and "Julia–Nancy" find it difficult to adapt to life as working girls. They are rescued by the foppish cousin. In Act III, on a hunting party with the Queen, the two women are recognized by the two young farmers.

The aria is marked andante and composed in 9/8 meter.

No more will my heart suffer, no more will it be sad; I do not know what these sighs mean, I am so young—why I should I groan? But I hear a voice in my heart, what can it be? Love alone! Yes, the sighs mean that I am in love! Yes! One could sigh for love! Happy is the heart, when Love calls. Life is the flowers and love the scent! . . . Sighs truly mean love!

The text and melody are repeated, becoming more ornate as it ascends to high A♭, sustained for three beats. The piece also calls for the low A♭.

In this version Nancy's folk song couplets is interpolated within the appendix aria as the huntresses return: "Huntress fair . . . " The song is set in the middle of the voice, between middle C and the octave above. The notes are composed in short rhythmic values on the beat in 2/4 meter, allegro non troppo.

Her song is followed by a B section to the aria, describing Cupid as the hunter. This melody is very ornate, and it extends to a high sustained F♯, and an alternate high B♭, if desired, with the huntresses singing over a chordal accompaniment.

Piano/vocal score: p. 166 (G. Schirmer)

No. 37

Voice: mezzo-soprano
Aria Title: "Kiss me not goodbye" (Merry)
Opera Title: *The Mighty Casey*
Composer: William Schuman (1910–1992)
Historical Style: 20th-century American (1953)
Range: C♯4 to G5

Fach: lyric (soprano)
Librettist: Jeremy Gury (1913–1995), based on Ernest L. Thayer's poem *Casey at the Bat* (1888)
Aria Duration: 2:45
Tessitura: A4 to E5

Position: One-act opera, scene 1

Setting: Late 19th century, Mudville, USA (believed to be Stockton, California); the day of the all-important baseball game against Centerville

Casey comes up to bat, but strikes out. Merry, Casey's girlfriend, asserts that Casey wouldn't want to play anywhere but Mudville, but the watchman tells her that a man ought to take every chance he can get. She sings this piece, marked moderato in 3/4 meter, legato, in reply. In a strong tone set in a lyrical melody, Merry states:

Never leave me, don't go away. Love me enough to stay. Never say you're missing me. Just kiss me instead. But kiss me not goodbye.

This piece should be simply sung, without emoting. Although it is set in a straightforward manner without rhythmic complexity, there are many enharmonic tones and challenging intervals in the piece. Mary needs a strong high F♯ and G, both sustained at the end of phrases with crescendo. Also important are the pitches at the bottom of the staff.

Piano/vocal score: p. 34 (G. Schirmer)

No. 38

Voice: mezzo-soprano

Aria Title: "Connais-tu le pays?" Romance (Mignon)

Opera Title: *Mignon*

Composer: Ambroise Thomas (1811–1896)

Historical Style: French Romantic (1866)

Range: Db4 to F5

Fach: lyric

Librettists: Michel Carré (1819–1872) and Jules Barbier (1825–1901), based on Johann Wolfgang von Goethe's novel *Wilhelm Meisters Lehrjahre* (1796)

Aria Duration: 5:35

Tessitura: F4 to C5

Position: Act I

Setting: The courtyard of an inn, Germany, late 18th century

Townsfolk and travelers enjoy the hospitality of the inn. Philine and Laertes, members of a theatrical troupe, watch from a balcony. Gypsies arrive, and the leader orders one of the gypsy girls, Mignon, to dance. The girl, showing her strength of character, refuses to perform. "I defy your threats!" she says. "At last I am weary of obeying you." The leader takes a stick and is about to strike her for her disobedience when Lothario, an elderly man, and Wilhelm, a student, come to her aid. Philine and Laertes also defend her. Mignon offers flowers to her defenders and (aside) a prayer to the Virgin of thanks.

All exit as Mignon finds herself alone with Wilhelm. She is tremendously thankful for his kindness in protecting her, and he is curious about her background, asking her many questions: "What is your name? How old are you?" She doesn't know. Her mother "sleeps," she says, and "the great devil is dead"—her first master. Wilhelm wants to know more: "Let me know all about your past! What, why are you silent?" "Alas," she says. "Of all my childhood only one memory remains," and proceeds to tell him of her abduction when she was a child. Wilhelm pleads with her to remember something about her youth—and memory that is retained." If you were free, where would you go? Where is your homeland?"

The aria is marked andantino, dolce, and is sung piano.

Do you know the land where the orange tree blooms?/Kennst du das Land, wo die Zitronen bluhn? (*text after Goethe*) The land of golden fruit and red roses. (*The melody is repeated, pianissimo.*) Where the breeze is gentler and the bird lighter, where in every season the bees forage. Where shines and smiles like a gift from God an eternal spring. Under an ever blue sky! Alas! That I may not follow you toward that happy land from which Fate drove me. It is there (*piano, then the phrase is repeated forte to the F at the top of the staff*) that I wish to live, love, and die! Yes, it is there!

After a 10-measure interlude, Mignon sings a second verse, asking Wilhelm whether he knows the house that she dreams of:

The hall with golden furnishings, where marble statues call me in the night and hold out their arms to me! And the courtyard where one dances in the shade of a great tree, and the clear lake. (*The accompaniment becomes descriptive here and more active.*) On whose waters glide a thousand light boats just like birds. Alas, that I may not follow you toward that happy land from which Fate drove me. It is there that I wish to live, to love, and to die. Yes, it is there!

The simple melody has a delicate transparent accompaniment. This aria calls for warm, dolce singing at the bottom of the staff, as well as a strong F at the top. Observe the rhythmic variety in the melody, as well as the marked contrasts between forte and piano.

Piano/vocal score: p. 94 (G. Schirmer)

No. 39

Voice: mezzo-soprano
Aria Title: "Me voici dans son boudoir,"
Gavotte (Frédéric)
Opera Title: *Mignon*
Composer: Ambroise Thomas (1811–1896)
Historical Style: French Romantic (1866)
Range: Bb4 to F5

Fach: lyric
Librettists: Michel Carré (1819–1872) and Jules Barbier (1825–1901), based on Johann Wolfgang von Goethe's novel *Wilhelm Meisters Lehrjahre* (1796)
Aria Duration: 3:05
Tessitura: Eb4 to C5

Position: Act II, scene 1

Setting: A boudoir in the castle of Baron Rosenberg, Germany, late 18th century

At the conclusion of the preceding act, Mignon the gypsy begs the student Wilhelm to allow her to become his servant and escape the gypsies. He refuses, but the elderly Lothario suggests that Mignon accompany him, and Wilhelm promises to protect her. Philine, the lighthearted actress, is present at the castle with her friend Laertes. Philine ridicules Mignon, mostly out of jealousy. Alone, Mignon applies makeup and admires herself and dons a gown. Frédéric, a young nobleman, enters and sings about Philine. He is upset because Philine has been placed in his aunt's room, while Mignon is primping in the dressing room of Philine. He awaits the hour to see Philine again, and he revels in drinking in the atmosphere of the room that she occupied. He feels his heart beating with hope and awaits the hour to see her again. He sings forte: "I must touch the heart of the unfaithful one! I wish to be loved and I hope in turn to be happy! So much the worse for her other lovers!" The first section is then repeated.

Almost all of the youthful, energetic Frédéric's lines are punctuated by an exclamation mark. Much of the charming melody is text set syllabically, marked staccato, with double-dotted rhythms, delicate trills, and some accents. There are no demands to sing above the staff, but there is an interval leap of the F at the bottom of the staff to the F at the top, sustained on the top pitch. Wilhelm returns to argue with Frédéric.

Piano/vocal score: p. 350 interpolated into Act II, p. 201 (sometimes cut) (G. Schirmer)

No. 40

Voice: mezzo-soprano
Aria Title: "Non so più cosa son, cosa faccio," No. 6 (Cherubino)
Opera Title: Le nozze di Figaro
Composer: Wolfgang Amadeus Mozart (1756–1791)
Historical Style: Classical (1786)
Range: D♯/E♭4 to G5

Fach: lyric
Librettist: Lorenzo da Ponte (1749–1838), after Pierre-Augustin Caron de Beaumarchais's play La folle journée, ou Le mariage de Figaro (1784)
Aria Duration: 2:52
Tessitura: F4 to G5

Position: Act I

Setting: A room in Count Almaviva's castle, about three leagues from Seville, 18th century

After being dismissed from his position as the Count's page for being discovered alone with the gardener's daughter, Cherubino tells Susanna that, suddenly, every woman excites him to no end. Cherubino is extremely young, headstrong, and tries to make excuses for always showing up in compromising situations.

> I don't know any more what I am, what I'm doing, Now I'm fire, now I'm ice,
> Any woman makes me change color, Any woman makes me quiver.
> At just the names of love, of pleasure, My breast is stirred up and changed,
> And a desire I can't explain, Forces me to speak of love.
> I speak of love while awake, I speak of love while dreaming,
> To the water, the shade, the hills, The flowers, the grass, the fountains,
> The echo, the air, and the winds, Which carry away with them
> The sound of my vain words. And if there's nobody to hear me, I speak of love to myself.

Piano/vocal score: p. 68 (G. Schirmer)

> Notes by singer and voice professor Susanne Mentzer: "Non so più" is very spontaneous. It needs to be sung like you have been shot out of a cannon or are a horse just out of the starting gate. It needs constant momentum. It also needs for the words to be very clear but also painted. It should have a blend of ecstasy and frustration. Think about the guys in junior high and high school. Cherubino is awkward but also cannot help himself. If it were modern day he would watch only the cheerleaders at the sports events, not the athletes. He also has trouble staying still, so think of this aria a bit like Cherubino with A.D.D. Musically it is very important to observe tempo markings and dynamics, at the "ogni donna/every woman" with a subito piano on "donna" and particularly after the ascending and high "via con se/away with them." Go right back to tempo on the next "portano via con se/carry away with them." Also, observe the fermata on the first syllable of "ven-ti/winds" each time. The first is commonly and mistakenly sung on the "ven-." It should not be so. The second time it comes, you do lin-

ger on "ven-." Finally, leading into the last section with the suspended "se" before "e se non ho chi moda/and if there's no one to
hear me," hold the "se" as long as possible and let the accompaniment leave you there all by your lonesome. "E se non ho chi
moda" comes two times in a row. Most conductors will let you be
free here, but I rather like doing it in strict rhythm until the final
"moda." "Parlo d'amor con me, con me, parlo d'amor con me/I
speak of love to myself": the first is fast, a tempo, the second slow
with a forte "con" and a pianissimo at "me." The last statement
should be fast and adamant. This is a wonderful audition aria as it
shows immediate energy.

No. 41

Voice: mezzo-soprano
Aria Title: "Voi che sapete," No. 11, Arietta
(Cherubino)
Opera Title: *Le nozze di Figaro*
Composer: Wolfgang Amadeus Mozart
(1756–1791)
Historical Style: Classical (1786)
Range: C4 to F5

Fach: lyric
Librettist: Lorenzo da Ponte (1749–1838),
after Pierre-Augustin Caron de Beaumarchais's play *La folle journée, ou Le mariage
de Figaro* (1784)
Aria Duration: 2:42
Tessitura: F4 to F5

Position: Act II

Setting: The Countess Almaviva's bedroom, about three leagues from Seville, 18th century

Act II opens with an expression of the Countess's grief ("Porgi, Amor/
Give, Love") followed by the entrance of her servants Susanna and then
Figaro. They offer the Countess comfort and hope in the form of proactive
steps that will "distract" the Count. Figaro exits, and the teenaged Cherubino
enters, infatuated with the Countess. Susanna goads him into singing his
latest love poem (inspired by the Countess), as Susanna accompanies him
on the guitar.

You ladies, who know what love is, See if I have it in my heart!
I'll tell you what I'm going through, It's new to me; I can't under-
stand it.
I feel a liking full of desire, That now is pleasure, now is agony.
I freeze, and then feel my soul burning, And in another moment go
back to freezing.
I look for a good outside myself, I don't know who has it, I don't
know what it is.
I sigh and groan without wanting to, I quiver and tremble without
knowing it,
I find no peace night or day, And yet I like suffering this way!

Piano/vocal score: p. 140 (G. Schirmer)

Notes by singer and voice professor Susanne Mentzer: "Voi che
sapete" is one of the hardest arias for the mezzo because of where
it lies—mostly in the upper middle range. By the time the reprise
comes, most of us are pretty tired, and our voices don't want to
settle. All the more reason to really be grounded when singing the
reprise.

Read the rhyme scheme a few times. It is incredibly simple and
young, as if a boy did write it. This was brilliant and deliberate on
Da Ponte's part. The aria should be sung as honestly as possible
and with much legato. He should be a bit nervous and embar-
rassed at the start, but really start to speak from the heart and be
focused only on the Countess. For auditioning, just keep the focus
simple and explain the feelings simply and not overact. Boys keep
their bodies much more relaxed and less posed. A suggestion is to
let your arms be expressive and stay loose.

Personally, the Cherubino arias were my lucky audition arias,
and the role was often my debut role with opera companies. You
might get tired of them and have a hard time keeping them fresh,
but if done well, they can be enormously successful.

No. 42

Voice: mezzo-soprano
Aria Title: "Che farò senza Euridice?"
(Orfeo)
Opera Title: *Orfeo ed Euridice*
Composer: Christoph Willibald von Gluck
(1714–1787)
Historical Style: Italian Baroque (1762)
Range: C4 to G5

Fach: lyric
Librettist: Raniero de' Calzabigi (1714–1795), based on Greek mythology
Aria Duration: 5:08
Tessitura: E4 to C5

Position: Act III

Setting: Mythological times, a region between the Elysian Fields and the surface of the earth

At the beginning of the opera Orfeo mourns his wife Euridice's death. He cries out her name plaintively. Orfeo resolves to recover Euridice from the dead, and the God of Love encourages him. As Orpheus approaches the banks of the river Cocytus in Act II, the furies' wrath is aroused. His singing grows so eloquent that they allow him passage. Finally, in Act III, scene 1, at a dark, twisted path in a repellent landscape leading away from Hades, Euridice is released. But Orfeo, overjoyed at her release, has to let go of her hand and must not look at her, to fulfill conditions imposed by the God of Love in Act I. She reproaches him for his apparent coldness and articulates her suspicions of his behavior. "Why does he no longer love me? Has he been unfaithful to me?" Finally, she feels that death is preferable to his lack of affection and the possibility that he may have betrayed her. Orfeo can bear her scorn no longer, and as he turns to look at her, she dies again. His grief is fully realized in the aria "Che farò," and he readies himself for a self-inflicted death.

Recitative:

Alas, where have I traveled? Where has the delirium of love taken me? Wife! Euridice! Partner! Ah, she no longer lives! I call her in vain. (*His exclamations are punctuated by chords in the accompaniment.*) Miserable me, I lose her once again, forever! Oh law of the gods! Oh death! Cruel memory! I have no help; counsel is not with me! I see only . . . fiery sight! The unhappy aspect of my horrid state. Be satisfied, horrid fortune. I am desperate!

The aria is marked allegretto, piano. The melody is heard in the accompaniment of the prelude to the piece, as Orfeo would accompany himself:

What will I do without Euridice? Where will I go without my beloved? What will I do? Where will I go? What will I do without my beloved? (*The poet who used to be confident can now only ask questions that are undirected.*) Euridice! Oh, God! Answer! I am still your *faithful* one. Ah, no more help, no more hope for me comes forth from earth, nor from heaven!

There is much repetition in the piece, so it is important that the Orfeo discovers different ways (emotions) to repeat the text, which brings different colors into the voice (loving, pleading, guilt, bitterness, deliberateness). The singer will need to sing an easy high E in passing, and in the climactic phrase the high F (two times), as the vocal line remains at the top of the staff in the last section of the aria.

Piano/vocal score: p. 162 (Bärenreiter)

No. 43

Voice: mezzo-soprano
Aria Title: "Ah, quel dîner" ("I've dined so well"), Tipsy Waltz (La Périchole)
Opera Title: *La Périchole*
Composer: Jacques Offenbach (1819–1880)
Historical Style: French Operetta (1868)
Range: C4 to E5

Fach: lyric
Librettists: Henri Meilhac (1831–1897) and Ludovic Halévy (1834–1908)
Aria Duration: 2:10
Tessitura: G4 to C5

Position: Act I

Setting: A public square in the capital of a mythical kingdom called Peru, in the mythical period called the nineteenth century. Several streets open into this square, which is adorned with a fountain, statue, and palm tree, all surrounded by a grass plot and benches. Downstage left is the terrace of the Café of the Three Cousins. Tables and chairs are set out on the sidewalk in front of it. Opposite of the café is an elegant hotel. The total effect is semitropical.

Périchole is a street singer much in love with Piquillo, also a street singer. They are too poor even for a wedding license. Don Andres, the Viceroy, is so taken by her beauty that he would like her to move into his palace as the lady-in-waiting. However, to arrange this officially, she must be a married woman—so the logical idea is to have Périchole marry Piquillo without their knowledge of the plan. Unfortunately, Piquillo has just received a despairing letter from Périchole, and they are so drunk by the time of the wedding that they do not recognize each other.

Ah, what a glorious supper I have just eaten! And what a simply fabulous wine! I drank so much of it . . . so very, very much, that I am afraid it has made me slightly tipsy . . . Hush, though, no one must know it! Hush! If my speech is somewhat slurred, if I sway right and left as I walk, and if there's a naughty look in my eye, it's not to be wondered at, since I am slightly tipsy . . . hush though, no one must know it! Hush!

Although the role of Périchole is listed as a piece for soprano, this particular song in two brief verses is sung commonly by the mezzo voice. The top pitch is E♭ (not sustained) at the top of the staff. The "tipsy" is in the music: the short phrases, clearly marked articulations. It should not be overdone physically in its delivery. Those who are tipsy are trying to not appear inebriated. She is trying hard to articulate her words and keep her balance, and this is humorous. Her audience on stage is Don Andres and the rest of the cast present for the "wedding."

Piano/vocal score: p. 60 (Boosey & Hawkes)

No. 44

Voice: mezzo-soprano
Aria Title: "Do you wish we had wed?"
Waltz (Regina Giddens)
Opera Title: *Regina*
Composer and Librettist: Marc Blitzstein
(1905–1964), based on Lillian Hellman's
play *The Little Foxes* (1939)
Historical Style: 20th-century American
(1949)
Range: C4 to A5

Fach: lyric
Aria Duration: 4:25
Tessitura: F4 to C5

Position: Act II, scene 2

Setting: Bowden, Alabama, 1900; ballroom and veranda of the Giddens' house; night

Regina Giddens is middle aged and is the mother of Alexandra. To realize her dream of fleeing small-town Alabama for Chicago's high society, Regina double-crosses her brothers for a larger stake in a business deal that will ensure her future even as it destroys her family.

A ball is underway, hosted by Regina in honor of her husband Horace's return, and also to celebrate a key deal with business guest William Marshall from Chicago. She runs into an old beau, John Bagtry. Musicians hired for the party play a waltz, and Regina begins to sing the melody of this aria over their onstage accompaniment. The melody is full of enharmonic tones and complex rhythms.

Dialogue between Regina and Horace that proceeds her aria:

Regina (sees Bagtry): John Bagtry, my old beau! (*goes to him*) You look so distinguished!
Bagtry: Regina, Regina, lovelier than ever.
Regina: Come close, John.

The piece is marked allegretto lusingando tempo di Valse, un poco rubato; it is set in 3/4 meter.

Do you wish we had wed years ago? You remember I said we might marry then, and then you went away. Do you wish we had wed that day? If you could, would you care for me now? Would you sing a sad song, with a soulful art, to all my heart requires? Do you dream what my heart desires?

(*poco meno*) Hail the haggard swain, complete with courtliness and grace. No one would divine the wispy weakness of your face, or note the slight shine in your sighs. (*A portamento in the melody descends from E♭ at the top of the staff to F.*) Is my beauty still warm in your eyes? Have my cheeks any charm of enduring you, for your sweet tooth to crave? Did you wander on wind and wave, still ever my love-sick slave? Decrepit and brave, my soldier slave.

(*The next section is marked l'istesso, risoluto.*) Youth was one thing, wonderful yearning, burning a burning feverish brew. But childhood is childhood and done with! Sense a new century, too. If I'm restless, restless for something, sorry, that something, burning anew, is not you! You're a wretched reply to my fires. Now hark to my heart's desires: there are diamonds that sparkle and shine. There are fineries, furs, and a thousand things. I count those things for mine. (*This text is sung brightly.*) I'm no simpering saint with wings, to whom vacuous Virtue clings. I don't mind handling money, handfuls of money. Money means things. And—the things I can do with things! For the half poor are poorer than poor, unhappy, unloved, unsure; more feeble by far than the meek and the weak are the noble, the nibbling, the Not Quite Poor. I'm in love with things. You've a thousand rivals— things.

The aria requires low sustained tones, sung fortissimo, on the middle C♯, D, and E♭ at the bottom of the staff. The singer will also need a sustained high F and A, sustained by a fermata.

Piano/vocal score: p. 152 (Chappell)

No. 45

Voice: mezzo-soprano
Aria Title: "Gerechter Gott" (Adriano)
Opera Title: *Rienzi*
Composer and Librettist: Richard Wagner
(1813–1883), after Edward Bulwer-Lytton's
novel *Rienzi, the Last of the Roman Tribunes*
(1834)
Historical Style: German Romantic (1842)
Range: C4 to A5

Fach: lyric (dramatic)
Aria Duration: 4:15
Tessitura: G4 to G5

Position: Act III

Setting: Rome in the mid-14th century; a city square with ruined columns
and broken capitals; bells are ringing, sounds of alarm, cries of battle

The Pope has fled to Avignon. His departure has fanned the flames of a
feud between the noble houses of Orsini and Colonna. Anarchy prevails.
Paolo Orsini and his followers try to abduct Irene, the sister of Rienzi. Adriano, the son of Steffano Colonna (a nobleman), frees Irene.

In Act III the nobles are gathering their forces for a march against Rienzi.
Adriano is torn between his allegiance to Rienzi (and the common people)
and loyalty to his father, Stefano Colonna. In this aria Adriano expresses
the hope that the two will be reconciled.

"Almighty powers, long their swords will clash." The aria includes
monologue-like expressions with many accidentals, beautiful melodic passages: "In seiner Bluthe bleicht mein Leben/My life is fading in full bloom"—
embellishments, florid 16th-note passages, contrasted markings of tempi,
and articulations. There are many Eb's, F's, and G's (and a climactic sustained high Ab) at the top of the staff.

Adriano enters on the high G. The aria lies high, with the lowest note a
D above middle C, though not sustained. Although much of the aria is declamatory, there are also simple decorative embellishments in the vocal line
and florid passages.

The final section of the aria calls for the young man to kneel (maestoso)
in prayer. After seven measures the piece is marked vivace, in cut time.
"Celestial spirit, now descend and make their hearts be together as one!"

Piano/vocal score: p. 217 (Schott)

No. 46

Voice: mezzo-soprano
Aria Title: "Illustratevi, o cieli" (Penelope)
Opera Title: *Il ritorno di Ulisse in patria*
Composer: Claudio Monteverdi (1567–1643)
Historical Style: Italian Baroque (1640)
Range: C4 to C5

Fach: lyric
Librettist: Giacomo Badoaro (1602–1654), after Homer's *Odyssey*
Aria Duration: 2:12
Tessitura: E4 to C5

Position: Act III

Setting: Penelope's palace in Ithaca, where she awaits the return of her husband Ulysses (Odysseus) from the Trojan War

Ulysses is changed into an old man by the goddess Minerva (Athena) so that he can outwit in his palace three suitors who have insinuated themselves into the offices of state and are seeking his wife Penelope's hand. Penelope is urged to forget Ulysses and love another, but she remains steadfast. In Act III Penelope cannot be convinced that the old beggar that she has seen is really her long-lost husband, Ulysses. Even when he enters in his true form she fears a trick. Penelope is finally convinced only when Ulysses correctly describes the embroidered quilt on their nuptial bed. After "Illustratevi, o cieli," they are rejoined in a blissful love duet.

The aria is marked animato, con grandezza, dancelike:

Illustratevi, o cieli/Shine brightly, oh heavens!
Blossom forth o meadows!

Rejoice, breezes, rejoice!
Little singing birds, murmuring brooks
Be merry again!

3rd verse:
Verdant grass and those rippling waters
Be now consoled.
(*recitando*)
Already from Trojan ashes my Phoenix has risen.

The aria has much text painting, with the murmuring brooks, for example, in the flowing 8th-note coloratura. It is a very good piece for the young singer learning to move the voice, declaim the Italian text, and discover the different colors of the voice that result from the text coloring.

Piano/vocal score: p. 211 (Universal Edition, vol. 12)

No. 47

Voice: mezzo-soprano
Aria Title: "Que fais-tu, blanche tour-terelle?" Chanson (Stéphano)
Opera Title: *Roméo et Juliette*
Composer: Charles Gounod (1818–1893)
Historical Style: French Romantic (1867)
Range: F4 to C6

Fach: lyric
Librettists: Jules Barbier (1825–1901) and Michel Carré (1822–1872), after the tragedy by William Shakespeare (1597)
Aria Duration: 4:10
Tessitura: A5 to F5

Position: Act III, scene 2

Setting: The square in front of the Capulets' palace; Mantua, early 14th century

Roméo's page, Stéphano, sings a mock serenade to Juliette, intending to sarcastically provoke an incident. Grégorio engages in a duel with him. He begins alone as he sings, "since yesterday I've looked for my master in vain!" (looking at the balcony at the Capulets). "Is he still at your house, my lords Capulets?" (arrogantly) "Let's see if your *worthy* servants reappear when they hear my voice this morning." (He pretends to strum a guitar with his sword.) Stéphano's energy is underlined by the rhythmic variety in the vocal line. The grace notes that he sings are sung in a condescending manner, sarcastically.

What are you doing, white turtledove, in this nest of vultures? Someday, spreading your wings, you will fly after love! For vultures, thy must fight, to strike, cut and thrust, their beaks are sharpened! Leave the birds of prey there, Turtledove who finds your joy in loving kisses! Guard the beauty well! Who lives shall see! Your turtledove will escape you!

A wood-dove, far from forests green, drawn away by love to the edge of this savage nest gave a sigh, I believe! The vultures go after their quarry; their songs scare off the love-goddess, making their grand racket! But, in their sweet intoxication, our lovers confide their affection to every star in the night! Guard the beauty well! Who lives shall see! Your turtledove will escape you!

This aria calls for a lyric mezzo voice that has the vocal control to sing unaccented syllables at the top (A) of her range. Other vocal challenges are the attacks of some phrases on high F without bringing weight into the voice, and moving the vocal line rapidly in the 16th-note triplet passages and the grand, bold flourish of 32nd notes ascending and descending at the end of the aria. Shown in this piece are a young man's vitality, sassiness, boldness, and pointed insinuations in rhythm and text while singing a seemingly harmless charming melody. The variety in the two verses is the change in meter between 2/4 and 3/4, the subtle changes in tempo between andantino, poco animando, allegretto, and poco meno mosso.

Piano/vocal score: p. 136 (G. Schirmer)

No. 48

Voice: mezzo-soprano
Aria Title: "Ombra mai fu" (Serse)
Opera Title: *Serse* (*Xerxes*)
Composer: George Frideric Handel (1685–1759)
Historical Style: Italian Baroque (1738)
Range: C4 to F5

Fach: lyric
Librettist: Giovanni Bononcini (1670–1747)
Aria Duration: 3:03
Tessitura: F4 to F5

Position: Act I

Setting: In a garden in King Serse's (Xerxes') palace, Persia, 5th century B.C.

The historical background is derived from Herodotus's account of the Greco-Persian wars. The title role represents the Persian king Xerxes I (reigned 485–465 B.C.), and the action supposedly takes place at the time of his expedition against Greece, about 470 B.C. Reference is made to Xerxes' attempt to bridge the Hellespont with boats and to his reverence for a plane tree, seen in the garden.

Serse, King of Persia, enjoys the shade provided by the plane tree. He enters the scene at the beginning of the opera. He is alone, and it is possible that he remembers this tree from childhood. He is a king and a general, but the tree is something that represents not only beauty, but stability—and it is venerable.

Recitative:

Tender and beautiful fronds of my beloved plane tree,
Let Fate smile upon you.
May thunder, lightning, and storms never bother your dear peace,
Nor may your blowing winds be profaned.

The introduction here is stately and noble, with repeated quarter-note values in the accompaniment as Serse looks closely at the tree. It is a short aria that is very sustained. It takes control for the singer to sing, as the first note is sustained over four measures, and the high F sung on the text "so-ave più" (more gentle) must be sung softly.

Aria (3/4 meter, allegretto, not largo, as it is often labeled):

Never was made a vegetable (*a plant*)
More dear and loving or gentle.

> Notes by singer and master teacher Frederica von Stade: "Ombra mai fu" is quite another type of aria representing the somewhat self-centered concerns of a young king; Xerxes is most preoccupied with his day and how it will develop. It is one of the loveliest melodies in the world.

No. 49

Voice: mezzo-soprano
Aria Title: "Hold on a moment, dear" (Elmire)
Opera Title: *Tartuffe*
Composer and Librettist: Kirke Mechem (b. 1925), based on the play by Molière (1664)
Historical Style: 20th-century American (1980)
Range: D4 to F5

Fach: lyric
Aria Duration: 1:23
Tessitura: A4 to D5

Position: Act II

Setting: Paris, the 17th century; a well-furnished apartment in a house owned by the well-to-do Orgon

Elmire, on her way to see Orgon, sings this to Tartuffe. This is a brief, delightful piece, but it shows much in the voice: the syllabically set text must be enunciated clearly; many of the sustained pitches have crescendi/decrescendi; there are many changes of tempo markings, rhythmic variety, and change of meter. Finally, many of the entrances begin on the high F, on unaccented syllables.

Piano/vocal score: p. 198 (*G. Schirmer American Aria Anthology: Mezzo-Soprano*)

Notes by composer Kirke Mechem: Molière's classic comedy is about how Tartuffe, a religious hypocrite, finagles his way into a wealthy, middle-class Parisian home and nearly brings the family to ruin. This is true in the play, not in the opera. In this aria Damis has told his father, Orgon, of Tartuffe's duplicity. But his father believes in Tartuffe's sincerity and casts Damis out of the house. Elmire, Orgon's wife, sings this aria in response. Elmire represents the voice of reason in this opera. She sings this aria without histrionics, but tries to make both her husband and Tartuffe act reasonably.

No. 50

Voice: mezzo-soprano
Aria Title: "Dry those eyes" (Ariel)
Opera Title: *The Tempest*
Composer: Henry Purcell (1659–1695)
Historical Style: English Baroque (1674)
Range: A4 to F5

Fach: lyric
Librettist: John Dryden (1631–1700), after the play by William Shakespeare (1611)
Aria Duration: 5:37
Tessitura: A5 to D5

Position: Act II

Setting: A deserted island, legendary times

The piece is composed in triple meter; the first section of the piece is repeated twice. This aria needs a flexible range to the high, sustained E and F. There are six and seven measures of florid patterns to sing, and some tones lie low (A below middle C).

The spirit Ariel sings these words:

Dry those eyes which are o'erflowing, All your storms are over blowing.
While you in this isle are biding, you shall feast with out providing.
(*The text is repeated.*)
Every dainty you can think of, every wine that you can drink of,
Shall be yours and want shall shun you. Ceres' blessing too is on you.

Piano/vocal score: p. 136 (Novello)

No. 51

Voice: mezzo-soprano
Aria Title: "Must the winter come so soon?" (Erika)
Opera Title: *Vanessa*
Composer: Samuel Barber (1910–1981)
Historical Style: 20th-century American (1958)
Range: E♭4 to F5

Fach: lyric
Librettist: Gian Carlo Menotti (b. 1911)
Aria Duration: 2:15
Tessitura: G4 to E♭5

Position: Act I

Setting: Vanessa's country house in an unspecified northern country, c. 1905. The first act takes place in Vanessa's luxurious drawing room. There is a fireplace stage left, and a small table is set for supper, stage right.

All the mirrors in the room and one large painting over the mantelpiece are covered over with cloth. Vanessa is uncomfortable with the passing of time since her lover Anatol left her 20 years ago. Since then, Vanessa is living under the delusion that Anatol will return. She has received a message that Anatol is coming to the house after a winter storm, leaving at dawn to arrive that night, and the house is in a flurry to prepare for his arrival. The snow is deep, and there is a delay in his arrival. It is clear from the conversation that Vanessa's niece Erika is a caretaker for Vanessa and watches over her. Erika reads to Vanessa (from *Oedipus Rex*) as they wait.

Erika is a young girl of 20. Also living in the house with Vanessa and Erika is the elderly Baroness, and they are attended to by servants. It is still snowing as it grows late. Vanessa thinks she sees lanterns outside, but Erika tells her that no, it is dark.

No one is there. She tells Vanessa to go up to bed. Erika's intent, after looking out the window one more time, is to put out the candles and go up to her bedroom. She sings the poignant, plaintive aria "Must the winter come so soon?" It begins piano, tranquil and sustained, lyrically, almost mournfully. The mezzo needs enough vocal control and technique to attack the E♭–F at the top of the staff a number of times in the piano dynamic, followed by a slight crescendo. Vocal line and phrasing is important, but the rhythms also need to be articulated with energy. The final phrase is the most challenging, beginning piano and ascending to high F on the extended word "soon," crescendo to forte, almost in a controlled "wail" without too much sliding in its shape.

Erika is only 20 years old and is devoted to Vanessa. She is the age that Vanessa was when she met Anatol. Vanessa's house is remote. She sees only the dour Baroness, Vanessa, and the family Doctor. Erika refuses to accept the bitter truth that the composer states in the score: "Life offers no solution except its own inherent struggle."

Piano/vocal score: p. 20 (G. Schirmer)

No. 52

Voice: mezzo-soprano
Aria Title: "Va! Laisse couler mes larmes" (Charlotte)
Opera Title: *Werther*
Composer: Jules Massenet (1842–1912)
Historical Style: French Romantic (1892)
Range: D4 to F5

Fach: lyric
Librettists: Edouard Blau (1836–1906), Paul Milliet, and Georges Hartmann (1843–1900), after Johann Wolfgang von Goethe's novel *Die Leiden des jungen Werthers* (1774)
Aria Duration: 2:10
Tessitura: F4 to D4

Position: Act III

Setting: December 24th, 5:00 in the evening in the drawing room of Albert's house in Wetzlar, near Frankfurt, toward the end of the 18th century. Stage right, the door of Albert's room; stage left, the door of Charlotte's room; in the foreground a desk, a sofa stage right; a lit lamp on the table.

Charlotte is the eldest daughter of the magistrate, a widower. She has a number of younger brothers and sisters, one of whom is Sophie. Charlotte has promised to marry Albert, and she does marry him, even though Werther loves her. Werther knows that he can never be hers and tells Sophie that he is going away forever. In Act III Charlotte rereads Werther's letters. Sophie enters and notices that Charlotte begins to weep at the mention of Werther's name. She orders Sophie to leave as all of her emotions burst forth. Alone, Charlotte will pray for strength to withstand her love for a man who is not her husband.

Sophie sings, "Let's laugh, laugh again as in other times! Yes, laughter's a gift, so quick, so light, so joyous!" Sophie leads Charlotte to the chair and slips down to her knees to sing: "Listen. I am old enough to know when people hide their feelings. Yes, all the faces here have grown so long and gloomy . . . ever since Werther ran away. But could he not have sent some message . . . to those who have remained so loyal? You're crying? Please forgive me. Yes, I should not have mentioned it at all."

Charlotte can contain her emotions no longer as the aria begins, forte:

Go! Let my tears flow freely. This will do me good, my own darling. The bitter tears we cannot shed seem to sink back again within us, and there, relentless and unceasing, they pound on the sick, weary heart. Its strength exhausted, it fights no longer. The heart grows weak, its beat grows faint. So great a wound cannot be healed, So great a sorrow soon will break it, soon will break it!

The clarity of diction and inflection (while singing F at the top of the staff) is extremely important, as well as following the exact rhythmic markings, helping to sustain emotional intensity in the situation (double-dotted rhythms) When the dynamics are piano and the vocal line low in the vocal range, the support must remain strong with the "core" remaining in the voice.

Piano/vocal score: p. 158 (Heugel)

No. 53

Voice: mezzo-soprano
Aria Title: "Werther, Werther," Letter Aria (Charlotte)
Opera Title: *Werther*
Composer: Jules Massenet (1842–1912)
Historical Style: French Romantic (1892)
Range: C4 to G♭5

Fach: lyric
Librettists: Edouard Blau (1836–1906), Paul Milliet, and Georges Hartmann (1843–1900), after Johann Wolfgang von Goethe's novel *Die Leiden des jungen Werthers* (1774)
Aria Duration: 6:54
Tessitura: F4 to E♭5

Position: Act III

Setting: December 24th, 5:00 in the evening in the drawing room of Albert's house in Wetzlar, near Frankfurt, toward the end of the 18th century. Stage right, door of Albert's room; stage left, door of Charlotte's room; in the foreground a desk, a sofa stage right; a lit lamp on the table.

Charlotte is the eldest daughter of the magistrate, a widower. She has a number of younger brothers and sisters, one of whom is Sophie. Charlotte has promised to marry Albert and marries him, even though Werther, a young poet, loves her. Werther knows that she can never be his and tells Sophie that he is going away forever. In Act III Charlotte rereads Werther's letters. Sophie enters and notices that Charlotte begins to weep at the mention of Werther's name. She orders Sophie to leave as all of her emotions burst forth. Alone, Charlotte will pray for strength to withstand her love for a man who is not her husband.

Werther! . . . Ah, Werther! Could anyone have told me the place he'd hold in my heart to this time? Yet since he went away, I am weary of life. (*She lets her work fall.*) And my soul lives only for him. (*Slowly she gets up as if drawn toward the writing desk, which she opens.*) These letters, these letters! Ah, how often I have read them. How they enthrall me and yet fill me with such sadness! I know I should destroy them. But I cannot. (*She has come back near the table, her eyes fixed on the letter she is reading.*) Here in my room I'm writing you this letter. Overhead the skies of December, heavy and gray, hang like a shroud. And I'm alone. All alone. Ah, alone and no one near! No companion to share his lonely life or speak a kindly word. God, how could I have found the desperate courage to decree such an exile far from all his friends?

After a time she has taken another letter and opens it. There are six measures of piano orchestral interlude. The vocal line ascends to a sustained E and F at the top of the staff as her excitement increases. Reading:

The children's happy cries float through my garret window. Such happy cries! And I think of those joyous times when round us in your home the children played and sang. Perhaps they will forget me? (*stops reading*) No, ah no, you will always have your own special place in their hearts, and when at last you come . . . yes, but ought you to come? (*fearfully*) Ah, this last letter chills my heart with fateful terror! Wait 'til Christmas, you said, and I cried out—no more! We both will know quite soon now who was right, you or I. And if on the day that you spoke of I do not come back again, then do not condemn, but forgive.

She repeats the text in terror, afraid of understanding: "Then do not condemn, but forgive." She continues her reading: "When with those eyes that so enchant me you read my letters once again, then your tears will fall and bedew them. Oh Charlotte, then you'll be afraid" (to high Gb) She repeats the phrase two times.

The singer must emphasize the delivery of the text, and bring out the surges of passion that are connected to the variety of dynamics, colors, and emotions.

Piano/vocal score: p. 141 (Heugel)

No. 54

Voice: mezzo-soprano
Aria Title: "We've always known each other" (Kate)
Opera Title: *The Wings of the Dove*
Composer: Douglas Moore (1893–1969)
Historical Style: 20th-century American (1961)
Range: D4 to F5

Fach: lyric
Librettist: Ethan Ayer (?–1987), based on the novel by Henry James (1902)
Aria Duration: 2:20
Tessitura: G4 to D5

Position: Act I, Scene 3

Setting: London, 1900; a room in the National Gallery of Art with a Turner sunset, *Hope* by Frederick Watts, and *The Blessed Damozel* by Rossetti. A lecturer is explaining Turner to the crowd.

This morality tale finds Milly, a young American heiress, dying from a mysterious disease and utterly alone. Her new European friends, Kate and Miles, hope to convince her that one of them loves her, thereby acquiring Milly's fortune upon her death. Kate tells Milly she would be better off without her group of London friends, but Milly discerns that Kate is really warning her away from Miles. She asks if Kate and Miles are engaged.

Kate is a handsome, spirited young woman compelled by circumstances to live with her rich aunt. "I think he loves you," Milly says. Kate turns away in agitation, but regains her composure and goes on.

The aria is marked più calmo, andante, piano. The text is set syllabically to the music, and the explanation of Kate's story is extremely important. She explains that she's always known Miles. They met abroad traveling with their fathers, and they thought they might marry:

He may care for me, but he'll get over it. I told him I don't love him anymore. Maybe *you* [Milly] could help him to forget me. Ask him to come to Venice . . . (*Miles enters.*)

There are rapid changes in meter and accompaniment, and there are a number of difficult intervals and sudden switching of vocal registers. There is also a sustained E♭, E, and F (dotted quarter note) at the top of the staff, and the sustained E diminuendos to a F quarter note in the following phrase, sung piano.

Piano/vocal score: p. 78 (G. Schirmer)

No. 55

Voice: mezzo-soprano
Aria Title: "All that gold" (Mother)
Opera Title: *Amahl and the Night Visitors*
Composer and Librettist: Gian Carlo
Menotti (b. 1911)
Historical Style: 20th-century American
(1951)
Range: B♭4 to G5

Fach: dramatic
Aria Duration: 2:30
Tessitura: E♭4 to E♭5

Position: One-act opera

Setting: Poor dwelling of the Mother and her son, Amahl, a crippled boy, somewhere in the Middle East at the time of the birth of Jesus

In the opera Amahl, a poor crippled boy with a vivid imagination, wakes his mother to tell her that there are three kings at the door. As the woman lives a hopeless existence, she is angry with the boy and does not believe him. To her surprise, there really are three kings at the door who look for a place to rest while on their journey to take gifts of gold, frankincense, and myrrh to the child they seek. In a discussion with the kings, the mother is briefly hopeful that the child they seek could be Amahl, but he is not, say the kings, in an emotional but brief quartet. While the kings and Amahl sleep, the mother is wakeful and desperate as she sees the gold in front of the sleeping kings. Just a little of that gold could help sustain her and her son, and save them from their poor existence.

The aria begins extremely quietly at the lower range of the voice, as, of course, she does not want to wake anyone. Very quickly, however, her focus goes from the gold and her own misery to the kings with a sweeping vocal line: "Do they know how a child could be fed? Do rich people know?" She continues the questions with the words "Do rich people know?" which descend to a strong low B♭. The meter changes frequently, the accompaniment becomes more and more active. The dynamics are echoed forte/piano at "Do they know? Do they know?" as if she is afraid that she will be heard and the kings will awake. She unleashes all of her desperation now, fortissimo, as she sings "All that gold! All that gold!" to the high sustained G, as if it is an internal scream. Then, suddenly, she sings, "Oh, what I could do for my child (*high E♭*) with that gold," that is again all text and then becomes more a part of the scene and action, hushed: "Why should it go to a child they don't even know?" she asks. "They are asleep," she observes.

Fermata pause. "Do I dare? If I take some they'll never miss it," she whispers, pianissimo (here she crawls toward the gold). "For my child . . . for my child . . . for my child . . . " she sings (parlando) in a hushed whisper on the low D, before the Page awakes.

Piano/vocal score: p. 50 (G. Schirmer)

No. 56

Voice: mezzo-soprano
Aria Title: "Augusta! How can you turn away?" (Augusta Tabor)
Opera Title: *The Ballad of Baby Doe*
Composer: Douglas Moore (1893–1969)
Historical Style: 20th-century American (1956)
Range: B4 to G♯/A♭5

Fach: dramatic
Librettist: John Latouche (1914–1956)
Aria Duration: 4:06
Tessitura: F4 to F5

Position: Act II, scene 4

Setting: Augusta Tabor's parlor, Denver, Colorado, 1896

When the curtain rises Augusta is standing at the window of her room looking out, listening to the newsboys cry out the news of William Jennings Bryan's defeat. Mama McCourt (mother of Baby Doe) enters, on a "sad errand": "Tabor is penniless. They're taking everything from him. I thought you'd want to help him . . . on account of the children. He can't work as a laborer at his age." Augusta is moved by this information. "Did he ask you to come?" "No, he is too proud." "Horace told me to leave him in peace," Augusta continues, and then quotes his words, which are engraved on her heart. "Will you forgive him?" asks Mama. "He has been punished enough. He has been humbled," says Mama. "If he's so humble then let him come here and ask me himself," Augusta says. "If I was to do that," says Mama, "he'd lose the last thing that keeps him going, Lizzie's [Baby Doe's] respect." Augusta then proceeds to tell Mama that nothing can be done. She closed the door when she left Colorado on all that had been. "I can't help him." Mama points out that by leaving, Augusta "holds on to your dollars, dollars that Tabor gave you too." "Leave him in peace. That's what he said," says Augusta. At the allegro agitato, Mama moves toward the exit. "I can see I was a fool to come," says Mama. The music is marked andante doloroso as Augusta speaks the following words to herself: "Augusta, Augusta! How can you turn away? He was so dear to you when you promised always to cherish him." The aria proper begins:

Augusta sings in halting phrases in crisp rhythmic values. She sings, forte: "What can have happened? Can this be you, Augusta? Do you not know Horace Tabor? Is he less than a stranger?" Augusta questions, fortissimo. "Go to him now, Augusta," she tells herself. "Hold out your hand to him," she sings, più mosso. "Forget your pride; he is in trouble. Now your place is there beside him." "Alas the years have twisted you," Augusta sings, allegro appassionata. "You are sick and old. Be kindly and be merciful, before it is too late," sung to the high G, dotted quarter note. "Augusta—Augusta!" she sings, andante doloroso, piano. "This is your failure too! You bear his name. Although he has grieved you, he is still a part of you," sung piano. It is more lyrically melodic here: "All of the memories, joys you had together be uprooted now. They are twined inside you," sung pianissimo in the lower range. "The years of bitterness, years of emptiness and heartbreak." As her emotions build she crescendos to forte: "All these must pass," she sings, in determined repeated quarter notes, "forgotten now. Now he needs you, Augusta." With a forte outburst, marked appassionata, Augusta sings "Tabor, my husband! Tabor, my dear one! Why, did you ever leave me? Now at last, now that Tabor needs Augusta, I should go but I am afraid." These phrases are sung in shorter, brittle rhythms. She crescendos: "Tabor once loved me. Once again I hear him call, calling on Augusta . . . " she sings on a high sustained A♭, marked with a molto ritardando, allargando molto. "But—" she pauses, then continues piano, deliberately. "I cannot go!" she exclaims in the lower range.

The curtain falls. This aria is extremely important in the opera and to the development of Augusta's character. It takes place 15 years after Tabor has left her. Augusta describes the parting and what Horace told her at their parting before the separation—a scene that is not revealed earlier in the opera. Augusta hardly pauses in this monologue. Many of her feelings spill out after so many years.

Piano/vocal score: p. 213 (Chappell)

No. 57

Voice: mezzo-soprano
Aria Title: "Have you seen her, Samantha?"
(Augusta Tabor)
Opera Title: *The Ballad of Baby Doe*
Composer: Douglas Moore (1893–1969)
Historical Style: 20th-century American (1956)
Range: C4 to G♭5

Fach: dramatic
Librettist: John Latouche (1914–1956)
Aria Duration: 2:05
Tessitura: E4 to E5

Position: Act I, scene 3

Setting: The large, ornate living room of Augusta and Horace Tabor's hotel apartment, Leadville, Colorado, 1892, deepening twilight outside. Samantha, an impassive middle-aged maid, has lit the lamps in the apartment.

Augusta Tabor has been married to Horace for almost 27 years. With her help, Horace has become an extremely successful businessman and aspiring politician. They have built their fortune from nothing, and Augusta considers Horace a risk-taking, extravagant personality. He has fallen for the extremely young and glamorous Elizabeth Doe (Baby Doe), and in this scene Augusta has just intercepted a love poem from Horace to Baby Doe. Augusta initially responds with rage, then asks Samantha if she has seen the girl: "I suppose she's young and pretty, giddy, and frivolous, to have such slender hands," she remarks, for she has also found a gift of gloves Horace intends for Baby Doe. "Look at my hands!" she plaintively sings, fortissimo. "They're old and twisted. On them is written, in ev'ry aging wrinkle, the record of the bitter years—these hands have worked to help him." The music is marked più mosso, piano, allegro pesante, in 4/4 meter. "Hands rough with working, cooking, scrubbing, mending—hands that even held an ax and lifted rocks to build a home. Digging fields and tending kids, hands that are twisted by winters in the wilderness." Her voice crescendos to forte: "working side by side with him to build a life together. No, they're not pretty hands! Not like hers!" she sings. The vocal line (piano) lies at the bottom of the staff. "Not like hers!" she bitterly sings.

This excerpt captures the moment in which Augusta realizes Horace's unfaithfulness. Perhaps she suspected it before, but this time she possesses evidence and a real rival in the young, glamorous Baby Doe. Augusta has the opportunity to explore a great range of emotions in the piece, including rage, disappointment, bitterness, jealousy, and self-righteousness.

Piano/vocal score: p. 58 (Chappell)

No. 58

Voice: mezzo-soprano
Aria Title: "Re dell'abisso, affrettati," Invocation Aria (Ulrica)
Opera Title: *Un ballo in maschera*
Composer: Giuseppe Verdi (1813–1901)
Historical Style: Italian Romantic (1859)
Range: C4 to G5

Fach: dramatic
Librettist: Antonio Somma (1809–1864), after Eugène Scribe's libretto *Gustave III, ou Le bal masqué* (1833)
Aria Duration: 3:56
Tessitura: C4 to C5

Position: Act I, scene 2

Setting: Boston, near the close of the 17th century (or Stockholm in the Swedish version); Ulrica's dwelling; on the left a fire, over it the magic cauldron suspended from a tripod; cabalistic emblems hang from the ceiling and on the walls

In Act I Ulrica, a sorceress, is to be declared a menace to the town and banished. Riccardo, Governor of Boston (King of Sweden in the version set in Sweden), believes in her predictions and reprieves her. The Governor, in disguise, decides to pay a surprise visit to her dwelling to draw his own conclusions from what she tells him. He is followed by Sam and Tom, leaders of an opposing faction.

Women and Children: "Quiet! Do not break the spell; Satan himself is about to speak to her." Ulrica (as in a trance):

King of the abyss, make haste, plunge through the air,
Without unleashing your thunderbolts enter my dwelling.
Three times now the owl from high above has sighed;
The fire-spitting salamander three times has hissed,
And a moan from the graves three times to me has spoken.

The piece lies low, but builds to a high, sustained G on "tre volte a me parlo/Three times to me has spoken." The vocal line is lyric and sustained, but it energized by double-dotted rhythms. Enharmonic tones lend this aria an exotic feeling.

Piano/vocal score: p. 48 (G. Schirmer)

No. 59

Voice: mezzo-soprano
Aria Title: "Skuchno Marine, akh kak skuchno-to!" (Marina)
Opera Title: *Boris Godunov*
Composer and Librettist: Modest Musorgsky (1839–1881), based on Alexander Pushkin's historical drama and Nikolai Karamzin's *History of the Russian State* (1824)
Historical Style: Russian Nationalist (1874)
Range: A3 to G#5

Fach: dramatic
Aria Duration: 3:20
Tessitura: E4 to E5

Position: Act III, scene 1

Setting: A castle in Poland, 1598; the boudoir of Marina Mnichek, a Polish aristocrat, in Sandmierz Castle. Marina is seated at her dressing table; young girls have been entertaining her with songs.

The beginning of the piece is marked alla Mazurka, piano, in the key of E minor with a transition to E major.

In the final section of E major (tempo 1) the upper voice is explored, including G#, all quarter notes, none sustained. Otherwise, the piece lies in the upper-middle voice, needing to repeat a number of E half notes. Most of the text in the aria is set syllabically.

All of the attendants leave. The markings are moderato non troppo allegro e sempre cariccioso.

Marina is bored. "How tediously and slowly the days drag by, one after another. Empty, so stupid and fruitless. A whole throng of princes and counts and grandees will not dispel this hellish boredom."

There has been a repetition of phrases to underline Marina's boredom.

"Only there, in the misty distance has a bright dawn lit up the horizon; it was there Marina was attracted by the rogue of Moscow. My Dimitri, merciless avenger (*poco più mosso*).

"God's judgment and punishment for the Tsar. The little boy, the victim of insatiable power, the victim of the greed and malice of the evil Godunov: I shall bathe you in tears of burning passion, the entreaty of youth." The lords' banal speeches are too boring for Marina. Marina wants power, glory: "I shall take my place on the throne and shall shine like the sun in my purple robe. And with my sumptuous beauty I shall slay the dull-witted Muscovites, and I shall force the herds of haughty boyars to obey me. (*accelerando poco a poco*) They will glorify me in their stories, tales and fables."

Marina bursts out into laughter, walks toward the door, and pauses by the mirror, admiring herself and adjusting her crown.

Piano/vocal score: p. 151 (Breitkopf)

No. 60

Voice: mezzo-soprano
Aria Title: "En vain pour éviter," Card Aria (Carmen)
Opera Title: *Carmen*
Composer: Georges Bizet (1838–1875)
Historical Style: French Romantic (1875)
Duration: 3:20
Range: B4 to F5

Fach: dramatic
Librettists: Henri Meilhac (1831–1897) and Ludovic Halévy (1834–1908), after the novella by Prosper Mérimée (1845, rev. 1846)
Tessitura: B4 to D5

Position: Act III

Setting: Near Seville, 1820; a mountain pass, wild rocky place; complete solitude, dark night

This scene follows Carmen's duet with Don José in the mountains. He has followed Carmen and confronts her: "Then you don't love me any longer?" he asks. "What I want is to be free and do what I like," Carmen replies. "You're a devil, Carmen," sings José. "If you speak again to me of separating . . . " he threatens. "You'd kill me, perhaps?" Carmen teases. Her friends Frasquita and Mercedes deal the cards to tell their future. Carmen turns up her cards. "Diamonds. Spades! It's death," Carmen says. "First me, then him." The music is marked allegro molto moderato, pianissimo. Carmen's vocal line begins in the lower range, and begins to weave its way carefully, chromatically, to the top of the staff. The text is set syllabically to the music on the crescendo to the sustained F at the top of the staff: "You can reshuffle twenty times, the card repeats: Death!" she cries. She turns up the cards again—"Again, death! Again, always death!" Frasquita and Mercedes repeat their opening music as an emotional/musical counterpoint to Carmen's musing on the imminent death that the cards predict. Carmen repeats the words: "always death, death!"

Piano/vocal score: p. 272 (G. Schirmer)

No. 61

Voice: mezzo-soprano
Aria Title: "L'amour est un oiseau," Habañera (Carmen)
Opera Title: *Carmen*
Composer: Georges Bizet (1838–1875)
Historical Style: French Romantic (1875)
Range: D4 to F#/Gb5

Fach: dramatic
Librettists: Henri Meilhac (1831–1897) and Ludovic Halévy (1834–1908), after the novella by Prosper Mérimée (1845, rev. 1846)
Aria Duration: 4:13
Tessitura: D4 to D5

Position: Act I

Setting: A square in Seville, 1820; left, the door of the tobacco factory; right, the guardhouse

The soldiers have entered the scene, and all gather to see the cigarette factory girls returning to work at the factory. Their reputation precedes them. They are "loose women" who are not only smoking cigarettes: they offer flirtatious looks. The most infamous of the girls is "Carmencita." When she enters, young men surround her. "Tell us which day you will love us!" they say. "When I'll love you?" she responds. "I've no idea! Perhaps never, perhaps tomorrow [Don José, Corporal of Dragoons, enters], but not today, that's certain!"

Carmen seductively sings an exotic melody about love and its unpredictable actions. Her vocal line starts at the D, sung pianissimo, and descends gradually by half steps to the warmth of the low range, only to sweep up in an octave portamento to repeat the melody again two times in the same fashion. "Love is a rebellious bird that nobody can tame, and it's all in vain to call it if it chooses to refuse. Nothing helps, not threats nor prayers; one man is smooth-tongued, another's silent, and he's the one I prefer: he says nothing, but he pleases me." Carmen sings teasingly, seductively, languidly. She pulls all into her web, but there is one who does not seem to be interested in her, the serious corporal Don José. She needs to conquer him, too. The next section of the seductive melody is "Love, love, Love is a gypsy child who has never known a law" (as the chorus of cigarette girls, young men, and working men sing underneath her melody). The many dynamics and rhythms in her melody are unpredictable, surprising, elusive. "Though you don't love me, I love you, and if I love you, then beware!" she sings at the high F♯ unaccompanied cadence, with flamboyance and flair. The entire first melodic section is now repeated with the following text: "The bird you thought you'd caught spread its wings and flew off . . . Love stays away and you must wait for it, then when you don't expect it, there it is . . . All around you, quickly it comes and goes and then returns. You think you hold it, it escapes you, you try to escape it, it holds you fast." The same flamboyant cadence is now sung to conclude the aria with a high F♯ to the tonic.

Piano/vocal score: p. 44 (G. Schirmer)

> Notes by singer, master teacher, and director Regina Resnik:
> Carmen is not a tart or a whore. She is a gypsy, and that means that she is meant to be free and not to be a "caged bird." All the men are attracted to her in this scene, except for Don José—who is different from the other men. She makes it her goal to conquer him in the scene.

No. 62

Voice: mezzo-soprano
Aria Title: "Les tringles des sistres tin-taient," Chanson bohémienne (Carmen)
Opera Title: *Carmen*
Composer: Georges Bizet (1838–1875)
Historical Style: French Romantic (1875)
Range: B4 to G♯5

Fach: dramatic
Librettists: Henri Meilhac (1831–1897) and Ludovic Halévy (1834–1908), after the novella by Prosper Mérimée (1845, rev. 1846)
Aria Duration: 5:29
Tessitura: E4 to E5

Position: Act II, scene 1

Setting: The inn of Lillas Pastia, Seville, 1820

Carmen is with her friends Frasquita and Mercedes. Zuniga, Andres, and other officers are watching. Some gypsy girls are dancing. It is a highly charged atmosphere. It's late, close to closing, and the crowd has been eating and drinking all evening. Carmen sings a wild gypsy song about dancing and seduction to the joyous tavern crowd.

Carmen narrates the story of the gypsy girls dancing to the frenzied guitars and percussive sistrum bars, playing the same refrain. The text is set syllabically and articulated in a variety of short and legato articulation markings. The accompaniment is marked staccato, piano. The refrain, sung on "Tra-la-la, la," is marked pianissimo but contains strong rhythmic pulses on E at the top of the staff, with accompanying tambourine. The refrain, sung with Mercedes and Frasquita, ends on the sustained high E. The dance ceases as the second verse begins: "Copper and silver rings gleamed on swarthy skins; fabrics striped in orange or red fluttered in the breeze. Dance was married to song, tentative and timid at first, then ever livelier and faster still it grew!" The frenzied refrain is repeated: "Tra-la-la-la . . . " almost out of control to the conclusion of the song. There is a third verse (forte): "Vigorously the gypsies drove their instruments wild, and this dazzling din held the gypsy women spellbound. Under the rhythm of the song, ardent, wild, feverish, intoxicated, they let themselves be carried away by the whirlwind dance! Tra-la-la-la . . . " Mercedes, Frasquita, and Carmen join in the dance.

Piano/vocal score: p. 115 (G. Schirmer)

No. 63

Voice: mezzo-soprano
Aria Title: "Près des remparts de Séville,"
Seguidilla (Carmen)
Opera Title: *Carmen*
Composer: Georges Bizet (1838–1875)
Historical Style: French Romantic (1875)
Range: B4 to B6

Fach: dramatic
Librettists: Henri Meilhac (1831–1897) and
Ludovic Halévy (1834–1908), after the no-
vella by Prosper Mérimée (1845, rev. 1846)
Aria Duration: 4:30 with duet
Tessitura: D4 to E5

Position: Act I

Setting: A square in Seville, 1820; left, the door of the tobacco factory; right, the guardhouse

After Carmen is arrested for fighting another girl in the cigarette factory. Zuniga tries to question the gypsy, but, self-assured and impudent, all she does is hum to herself. Corporal Don José is assigned to watch her. She sings that she wants to go to her friend Lillas Pastia's inn and promises José a rendezvous at the tavern.

Here is the dialogue before the aria:

Carmen (softly): Let me escape.
Don José: We're not here to talk nonsense . . . You have to go to prison.
Carmen: You'll do what I ask you . . . you'll do it because you're in love with me . . .
Don José: What, me?
Carmen: Yes, you love me . . .
Don José: Stop talking to me, do you hear? I forbid you to speak to me.
Carmen: You forbid me to speak. Very well, I won't say any more.

And she begins her song, allegretto, with deliberate meaning, and throwing frequent glances at Don José, who gradually comes nearer and nearer.

Pianissimo, she sings a melody that is marked leggiero, but energized by dotted rhythm on the word "Sé-vil-le." She speaks about the tavern, and tells José what she will do there: drink manzanilla and dance the seguidilla. The new section of text is set syllabically. She will be bored there all alone, so she hopes to take her lover (unnamed) along. She laughs, "My lover! He's disappeared. I left him yesterday," as she crescendos to the E at the top of the staff. She confides to José, marked pianissimo, that she has many lovers, but they are not to her taste, she teases. She sings a portamento to the lower range of the staff: "Who wants my heart? It's there.

Who wants to love me?" she asks. Carmen then launches into a repeat of the first melody, playfully singing (marked staccato). Then in the score is written a fermata—rest, pause—followed by Carmen resolutely declaring, "Yes, I am going to Lillas Pastia's!" In the opera there is a further exchange here between Carmen and José, quasi recitative. Once again, José forbids her to talk. "I do not talk to you, I sing for my own pleasure," taunts Carmen, and she teases him further about his rank and continues to draw him toward a rendezvous at the tavern. He unties her hands, and Carmen triumphantly sings one more chorus of her song, completing it with pointed and playful "tra-la-la"s to the final high B as she runs off. When singing the aria alone, this last verse is substituted for the pianissimo "Près des remparts de Séville" on p. 99 (G. Schirmer).

Piano/vocal score: p. 95 (G. Schirmer)

No. 64

Voice: mezzo-soprano
Aria Title: "Voi lo sapete, o mamma" (Santuzza)
Opera Title: *Cavalleria rusticana*
Composer: Pietro Mascagni (1863–1945)
Historical Style: Verismo (1890)
Range: B4 to A6

Fach: dramatic
Librettists: Gioanni Targioni-Tozzetti (1863–1934) and Guido Menisci (1867–1925), after the play by Giovannai Verga (1883)
Aria Duration: 3:15
Tessitura: B5 to F♯5

Position: One-act opera

Setting: A village square in front of a church in a small town in Sicily; Easter morning

> Opera plot notes from the *G. Schirmer Opera Anthology: Arias for Mezzo-Soprano*, edited by Robert L. Larsen (used by permission):
> Townsfolk have entered the church for Easter Sunday services. Mamma Lucia, keeper of a wine shop, and Santuzza, a village girl, are left alone in the piazza. Santuzza tells Lucia of her desperate passion for the woman's son, Turiddu, who has thrown her aside for his old love, Lola, wife of Alfio.

The beginning is marked largo and sostenuto in 2/4 meter, piano, mestamente con semplicità. "You know what happened, Mamma: before he went as a soldier Turiddu swore to Lola a vow of undying faith," Santuzza sings, with attention to the vocal line and with meaning. The rhythms (8th-note triplet patterns) and accents as well as the rests are all meaningful in the expressive aria.

"He swore to Lola a vow of undying faith. Returning, he found her married; and with another love he hoped to quench the fire that burned within his heart."

The next phrases are more fragmented with rests in between the phrases, representing a greater emotional weight, as if she cannot go on. "He loved me, I loved him, ah!" sung on the high A, fermata, fortissimo, con grande passione. "I loved him!" Santuzza confesses.

The rhythm of the chords played by the orchestra underneath the melody are off the beat, carried over the bar lines, giving the piece momentum. There is very little repetition—only of the triplet rhythm in the melody.

She sings, pianissimo: "That woman, envious of my every joy, forgetful of her newly wedded husband, was consumed, consumed with jealousy," as she ascends to high G. "She stole him from me! Despoiled of my honor, despoiled, I am left," as she crescendos ed animando to high A. "Lola and Turiddu are lovers, and I must weep, weep, weep!" In the final phrase Santuzza sings, "I am left, dishonored: Lola and Turiddu love each other, and I weep." The words "io piano/I weep" is repeated three times. The final expression begins on the low B below middle C. This aria occurs in the opera almost exactly half way through the score, demonstrating the strategic importance of the aria in the opera. The emotional temperature of the drama begins its ascent to its ultimate tragedy beginning with this aria.

Piano/vocal score: p. 74 (Kalmus)

No. 65

Voice: mezzo-soprano
Aria Title: "I do not judge you, John"
(Elizabeth Proctor)
Opera Title: *The Crucible*
Composer: Robert Ward (1917–1994)
Historical Style: 20th-century American (1961)
Range: C4 to A♭5

Fach: dramatic
Librettist: Bernard Stambler (1910–1994),
based on Arthur Miller's play *The Crucible*
(1953)
Aria Duration: 3:36
Tessitura: E♭4 to E♭5

Position: Act I

Setting: Salem, Massachusetts; spring of 1692; the kitchen of John Proctor's farmhouse; appropriate furnishings; doors upstage center and left; fireplace, right; mantel somewhat cluttered but with a rag puppet visible; a musket above the mantel

Elizabeth Proctor is the wife of John, a farmer. The entire town has been whispering about witchcraft, since Betty, the daughter of Reverend Parris, went under a "spell" after being seen dancing in the woods the night before with her cousin, Abigail. Others have been stricken, and accusations have been made as to responsibility.

At the beginning of Act II John returns from a day's planting to find Elizabeth listless and moody, while he is in an ebullient mood. In her mind the witch trials have become a part of her own struggles at home. Abigail has been helping her in the house, and she does not trust the girl, believing that Abby's claims of witchcraft spells are fraudulent, only an attempt by the girl to gain attention. Abigail has admitted to John in private as much, and Elizabeth wants to know why he will not reveal her fraudulence. John is reluctant to expose the girl but is unable to explain to Elizabeth the reason why: this would also reveal the fact that John has had an illicit affair with the young girl. By the end of their dialogue, John has become very defensive and argumentative: "I have not moved from here to there without I think . . . and try to please you and still an everlastin' fun'ral marches round your heart. I cannot speak but I am doubted, every movement judged for lies as tho' I come into a court when I come into this house," he says. It's not easy to prove fraud, he has no hard evidence, she'll strike back. "Do not judge me. Judge me not," pleads John, singing a high sustained F.

Elizabeth finally answers, beginning mezzo-piano in the middle of her voice. She gradually sings poco a poco più forte e agitato: "I do not judge you, John. The court that judges you sits in your own heart." The middle of this vocal line is a half note F at the top of the staff. "I never thought you but a good man. A good man though perhaps (*she sings an E♭ half note at the top of the staff*) a little bewildered. That's all . . . " marked stenato mesto a tempo ma lusingando in a new section. "But oh, the dreams I had for our proud young love, a love that would never turn or falter. But now," as the aria crescendos and ascends to the top of the staff, "it's shattered, lost and gone. And an icy hand closes round my heart. How could it be you turned from me to one like Abigail? How could it be, John? How could it be?" she sings on the high F, marked forte, with accents. Elizabeth goes on, in the middle of her voice, to ask him to think about his sons, and of those who are in jail, victims of the fraudulent claims of others. Elizabeth asks John (singing to the high A♭) to go to Abigail, so that she might confess her wrongdoings, that "she may dream no more" to the authorities. Elizabeth is afraid of Abby. "You must tear yourself free of her, you must," Elizabeth sings, sustaining an E to a climactic high G♯ in the next phrase at the top of the staff, to conclude on the high F♯. "You will!" she exclaims, "for know that I will be your only wife, or no wife at all!"

Piano/vocal score: p. 127 (Highgate/Galaxy Press)

No. 66

Voice: mezzo-soprano
Aria Title: "Nel giardin del bello," Veil Song (Princess Eboli)
Opera Title: *Don Carlo* (Italian version)
Composer: Giuseppe Verdi (1813–1901)
Historical Style: Italian Romantic (1867)
Range: E4 to A5

Fach: dramatic
Librettists: François Joseph Méry (1798–1865) and Camille du Locle (1832–1903), based on Johann Christoph Friedrich von Schiller's play *Don Carlos, Infant von Spanien* (1787) and on Eugène Cormon's play *Philippe II, roi d'Espagne* (1846) for the original five-act French version. The revised Italian four-act version was adapted by Antonio Ghislanzoni.
Aria Duration: 4:52
Tessitura: A4 to E5

Position: Act I

Setting: Spain, the 16th century; a delightful spot outside the Saint-Just Monastery gates; a fountain, grassy banks, clusters of orange trees, pines; the blue mountains on the horizon; at the back the monastery gate, with steps leading up to it

Outside the monastery gates the court ladies wait for their Queen. Princess Eboli entertains them with the "Song of the Veil."

Eboli sings, accompanied by Theobald, Elizabeth's page.

In the gardens of the fine Moorish palace,
Amid the scent, the cool shade of the laurels and the flowers,
A lovely almah hidden in her veil seemed to be gazing at a star in
the sky.
Mohammed, the Moorish king, goes out into the garden and says to her:
"I adore you, O tender beauty!"
(*The next phrase is marked parlato.*)
"Come, the King invites you to reign with him: I no longer desire
the Queen. Ah!"
(*The refrain is sung with Theobald and the women's chorus.*)

The song, composed in 6/8 meter with accents (marcate), is sung with bravura and flourish. It also has an exotic feel to it with its embellishments, triplet patterns, and chromatic inflected melody. There are sudden "echo-like" dynamic effects to the song.

Piano/vocal score: p. 38 (G. Schirmer)

No. 67

Voice: mezzo-soprano
Aria Title: "O don fatale" (Princess Eboli)
Opera Title: *Don Carlo* (Italian version)
Composer: Giuseppe Verdi (1813–1901)
Historical Style: Italian Romantic (1867)
Range: B4 to B6

Fach: dramatic
Librettists: François Joseph Méry (1798–1865) and Camille du Locle (1832–1903), based on Johann Christoph Friedrich von Schiller's play *Don Carlos, Infant von Spanien* (1787) and on Eugène Cormon's play *Philippe II, roi d'Espagne* (1846) for the original five-act French version. The revised Italian four-act version was adapted by Antonio Ghislanzoni.
Aria Duration: 4:45
Tessitura: D#/E♭4 to G#/A♭5

Position: Act III, scene 1 of the four-act version

Setting: The King's study, Madrid, 1559, early morning; a table strewn with papers; two candles are burnt down; a window

Princess Eboli is the lady-in-waiting to the Queen of Spain, Elizabeth. At the beginning of the act King Philip II (Filippo) has been up all night, despairing over the burdens of ruling the kingdom and his personal trials. His reverie is interrupted by the entrance of the Grand Inquisitor, representing the church, all-powerful and invasive.

The King is warned of the danger in his personal affairs. After the Inquisitor exits, the Queen enters, agitated, and the King confronts her as to her relationship with Carlo, the King's son (by an earlier wife). She confesses her love for Carlo, and Eboli and Rodrigo (a friend of Carlo's) enter at the sound of the Queen's distress. Eboli has betrayed her Queen and friend to the King because her advances to Carlo have been rejected. In retaliation, Elizabeth gives her the choice of being exiled or becoming a nun. After she leaves, Eboli curses the gift of beauty that she has been given, saying that it has been the cause of all her problems. She swears to save Carlo from the imprisonment that has resulted from her betrayal.

Before beginning the aria proper, Eboli exclaims that she will never see the Queen again: "O terrible gift, o cruel gift that an irate heaven made me!" The lines are separated by a fermata rest. The melody descends through the middle of the voice. There are accents and flourishes. Eboli is proud and determined. The melody is repeated in the first phrase, then develops further. The accompaniment rhythmically punctuates unaccompanied phrases.

"You make us so vain and proud, I curse you, o beauty!" she says to herself.

"I can only shed my tears "she sings, più mosso, with repeated rhythmic/ melodic figures in the accompaniment. "I've no hope, I can only suffer! My crime is so horrible that it will never fade! I curse you, o beauty." There is a sustained "Ah!" sung on a high C♭, descending to the low C♭ at the bottom of the staff. She now begins to sing a new section (molto meno, cantabile). This part of the aria is sung lyrically, piano. At the beginning the voice is muted in the lower part of the staff, and soon rises. "O, my Queen, I sacrificed you to the crazed passion of my heart. Ah!" She sings a high B♭, sustained by a fermata. "Only in a cloister can I now hide my suffering from the world!"

Here her phrases are halting, almost breathless. "Alas! O, my Queen, O God! Carlos! Tomorrow he will die, o great God! Tomorrow I'll see him die!" She enters on a high G♭, then high B♭, with an expression that is decisive, hopeful, determined. "Ah! I've one day more, there is hope, ah, heaven be blessed! I'll save him! One more day, ah, heaven be blessed! I'll save him!" she sings. The aria is extremely demanding vocally and dramatically. It is important to find the piano passages, the reflective passages, and to focus the highly charged emotional passages.

Piano/vocal score: p. 237 (G. Schirmer)

No. 68

Voice: mezzo-soprano
Aria Title: "Ich habe keine gute Nächte" (Klytemnästra)
Opera Title: *Elektra*
Composer: Richard Strauss (1864–1949)
Historical Style: 20th-century German (1909)
Range: A♭3 to G5

Position: One-act opera

Fach: dramatic
Librettist: Hugo von Hofmannsthal (1872–1929), after the tragedy by Sophocles (410 B.C.)
Aria Duration: 5:55
Tessitura: E♯4 to D♯5

Setting: Antiquity, a decade after the end of the Trojan War; the inner court of the palace of Agamemnon (murdered soon after his return) in Mycenae, Greece; at the back the palace can be seen

Klytemnästra is the widow of Agamemnon, whom she and her lover murdered in his bath on his return from the Trojan War; her daughter is Elektra. The widow is bloated and decayed, and sleepless nights have left her looking haggard; she walks with the aid of a stick. She breathes laboriously and flies into a rage easily. She hates and fears her daughter and is tormented by dreams. Does Elektra know any remedies for them? Is there not some sacrifice she can make to the gods to alleviate the tortures she suffers?

The music is marked piano and is written low in the range at the beginning, sung misterioso.

"I have no good nights," she says. "Know you no remedy for dreams?" "Do you dream, mother?" asks Elektra. "Whoever grows older dreams. But they can be chased away. There are rituals. There must be a proper ritual for everything." "That is why I wear precious stones, because there resides in each one a power," Klytemnästra sings as she ascends to a sustained D toward the top of the staff.

"One must know how to make use of them. If you only wanted to, you could tell me something that would help me," sings Klytemnästra. "I, mother, I?" asks Elektra. "Yes, you! Because you are clever. In your head is everything firm," she sings—to high sustained F, then quickly descends and remains low and below the staff. "You could tell me a great deal that would help me. Even if a word has no significance! What is then a breath? And yet, between night and day, as I lie with my eyes open, something crawls over me. It is not a word, it is not a pain, it doesn't weigh on me, it doesn't choke me. It is nothing, not even a nightmare." Here the tempo is marked etwas breiter/broadened, "and yet, it is so frightful that my soul wishes to be hanged, and every limb in me screams for death," sung on the E and F at the top of the staff, "and with all of that I live and am not even sick: You see me, don't you? Do I look like a sick woman? Can one then pass away, living, like a rotten carcass? Can one decay when one is not even sick? Decay with an alert mind, like a dress eaten away by the moths?" There is a five-measure interval played by the orchestra, marked accelerando, più mosso." And when I sleep, and dream . . . dream, that the marrow in my bones is dissolving, and stagger up again, and not even a tenth part of the hour glass has run through." Klytemnästra is at the top of the staff, the tempo poco a poco più mosso, "and what under the curtain grins is not yet the pale morning?" she asks, at the high F♯ for four beats. "No, always still the torch in front of the door, which horribly twitches like a living thing and spies on my sleep. These dreams must come to an end. Whoever sends these dreams to us, whatever demon it may be will leave us alone, as long as the right blood is spilled." The mezzo must sing a high sustained G for seven beats on the -oo- vowel at this climactic phrase. There are many fragmented phrases, with a very active orchestration. Carefully tuned intervals must be negotiated with multiple accidentals in the vocal line. There are also much rhythmic variety and many changes of tempo markings and meter.

This piece is extremely challenging for the young singer, and the role should only be undertaken by a mature singer secure in her technique and who is careful not to cross dramatic boundaries that would sacrifice the health of her voice. The aria is included for study purposes and may be sung in auditions under special circumstances.

Piano/vocal score: p. 71 (Boosey & Hawkes)

No. 69

Voice: mezzo-soprano
Aria Title: "O mio Fernando!" (Leonora)
Opera Title: *La favorita* (Italian version)
Composer: Gaetano Donizetti (1797–1848)
Historical Style: Bel canto (1840)
Range: B4 to A6

Fach: dramatic
Librettists: Alphonse Royer (1803–1875), Gustave Vaez (1812–1862), and Eugène Scribe (1791–1861), after Baculard d'Arnaud's play *Le comte de Comminge* (1764), based on the story by Leonora de Guzman
Aria Duration: 2:55
Tessitura: E4 to E5

Position: Act III

Setting: A great hall, palace of Alcazar, 14th-century Spain

Alphonse, King of Castile, intends to divorce his wife and make his mistress, Leonora, his Queen. Leonora begs him to release her from what is a humiliating position. Covered with honor for defeating the Moors, Fernando comes to meet with the King. Fernando asks for Leonora's hand, for he has long loved her. The King agrees to grant his request. Leonora loves his sincerity, but does not feel worthy of him.

The recitative (allegro agitato) shows a confused Leonora. The phrases are short and rather extreme in range: F at the top of the staff, middle C at the bottom.

Is it then true . . . ? O heaven! He, Fernando, Leonora's bridegroom! Ah! Everything tells me it is so. (*lento*) But still I hesitate to believe such unexpected joy! I? To marry him? O my deep, deep shame! Must I take, as dowry, dishonor to the hero? (*allegro*) No! Never! Even should he curse me and desert me, He must know who she is, The woman he loves so much!

There is an instrumental introduction of 11 measures before the aria begins (andante cantabile):

Oh, my Fernando, were I the empress of the world,
My heart the throne would yield to call you mine!
But my love, though purer than forgiveness, is doomed, alas, to horror unconfined!
For when the truth is known, your deep disdain will be the greatest punishment to bear.
Ah! If your scorn should then be less, my God, then let me die!
Ah! If your scorn should then be less, ah, great God, then let me die!
Come tormentors! Who will stop you? Heaven itself decreed my grief!
Come, attend the celebration, strew the altar cloth with flowers!
At my feet the grave has opened, covered with a sable veil.
May she be, unhappy bride, who, an outcast, cannot hope for pardon from on high,
Cursed is she, and cannot hope for pardon from on high. No, not for her!
Cursed is she, and may not hope for heaven. No, not for her

Although the aria lies low, there are a number of accented leaps to F at the top of the staff.

(Translation by Nico Castel)

Piano/vocal score: p. 209 (Ricordi)

No. 70

Voice: mezzo-soprano
Aria Title: "Stella del marinar," Romanza (Laura)
Opera Title: *La Gioconda*
Composer: Amilcare Ponchielli (1834–1886)
Historical Style: Italian Romantic (1876)
Range: C#4 to A5

Fach: dramatic
Librettist: Arrigo Boito (1842–1918) (under the pseudonym Tobia Gorrio), based on Victor Hugo's play *Angélo, tyran de Padoue* (1835)
Aria Duration: 2:11
Tessitura: G4 to E♭5

Position: Act II (The Rosary in the Waters of Fusina)

Setting: Venice, 17th century, night; Enzo Grimaldo's ship, *The Hecate,* seen from the side

Enzo, who is a nobleman disguised as a sailor, awaits his beloved Laura (who is married to the nobleman Alvise) and sings the well-known aria "Cielo e mar." The ship lies anchored by an uninhabited island in the Fusina lagoon. To one side is an altar to the Virgin with a red oil lamp burning. Barnaba, who is a spy of the Inquisition, appears near Enzo's ship and views the situation. He sends Isepo to inform Alvise and his men, who are waiting in the lagoon. Barnaba's boat appears and draws alongside. Enzo sees that the boat carries Laura. Barnaba leaves while the two lovers are united. They will sail away once the moon has set when they can leave undetected. Enzo has to make the final preparations and goes below deck as Laura prays to the Blessed Virgin.

The aria is marked allegro, with six measures of orchestral introduction, as the strings play off the beat. "My heart is full of tears" she sings, pianissimo, sotto voce. "What is that light? . . . Ah, a Madonna!" While Laura prays, Gioconda (who is in love with Enzo), emerges from a hiding place.

The marking is now Andantino agitato, pianissimo, con passione, in 3/4 meter, with a key change to a minor key. "Star of the mariner! Blessed Virgin!" she sings, with repeatedly accented high E's, with a constant, relentless rhythmic ostinato in accompaniment. "Protect me in this supreme hour. You see what passion drew me to such a daring step!" The vocal line leaps up to E, then ascends to a passing high G before descending. "Under your veil that covers the wretched, shelter me as I pray and tremble." The music here is marked meno, dolcissimo, and there is a key change to A major. "With this fervent prayer, Mother of Pardon, may a blessing descend on my head," she sings at the top of her range, with a passing high A. The text is repeated, with accents on the B in the middle of the staff and the third higher.

The music is now marked più accelerato, crescendo agitato, repeating the text in a cadenza-like ending as she sings, "O Virgin, to me let there descend a blessing, your blessing, your blessing," rallentando molto to the high sustained A for the climactic phrases.

To sing this aria successfully, it will necessitate vocal control, a sustained vocal line, and attention to rhythmic accuracy, as well as to the articulation and dynamic markings.

Piano/vocal score: p. 168 (International)

No. 71

Voice: mezzo-soprano
Aria Title: "Stranger and darker" (Hannah)
Opera Title: *The Ice Break*
Composer and Librettist: Michael Tippett
(1905–1998)
Historical Style: 20th-century English
(1977)
Range: B♭4 to A♭5

Fach: dramatic
Aria Duration: 4:39
Tessitura: B♭4 to A♭5

Position: Act II, scene 5

Setting: Contemporary, surrealistic setting in the United States

Hannah, a nurse, is introduced in a U.S. airport lounge as she awaits the arrival of her celebrity-sportsman boyfriend. Nadia is at the airport waiting for her husband Lev, a Soviet dissident, to arrive. He has served a 20-year sentence in a Russian prison.

Intimate scenes in Act II, within the tensions of the relationships, are set against scenes of a violent race riot.

Hannah's extended aria, in the middle of the opera, tests the singer on many levels. The intervallic skips are challenging, and there is much rhythmic complexity. The aria paints poetic images with the voice, sustaining syllables and words over many measures. She touches high A♭ at the top of her voice, but most of the sustained higher pitches are E♭ and F at the top of the staff. The piece has a stream-of-consciousness style.

"Stranger and darker, deeper into my self. Blue night of my soul," she sings on a sustained low C♯. "Blue black within this city's night I scrabble." The aria here is more agitated with vigorous rhythms. "For unformed letters that might make a word to speak sense to the blue night of my soul, blue black within this night."

The following section is marked allegro agitato: "But no, no, no time, no time is as yet for sense. Alone . . . " (the word is repeated three times over two pages of melismatic passages of varied colors). "Deep in the body: dark in the soul an incommunicable voice murmuring: Not that, only not that!"

Piano/vocal score: p. 159 (Schott)

No. 72

Voice: mezzo-soprano
Aria Title: "Now I am no more afraid"
(Thea)
Opera Title: *The Knot Garden*
Composer and Librettist: Michael Tippett
(1905–1998)
Historical Style: 20th-century English (1970)
Range: B3 to A♭5

Fach: dramatic
Aria Duration: 2:38
Tessitura: B♭4 to F5

Position: Act III (Charade)

Setting: Present time, in a rose garden

Thea is a gardener, and is married to Faber, a civil engineer. She is in her mid-30s.

Characteristic of Tippett's style, this piece is challenging to the singer for its difficult intervals and rhythmic patters. The words are poetic, reflective, and each syllable is set to patterns of melodic sequences. Great vocal control is needed to enter the phrase on the F at the top of the staff marked piano.

Also needed is a high F♯ with diminuendo. She is also required to sing a phrase at the B-below-middle C level.

Mangus (an analyst), Faber, and Thea finish putting away the chess set. The men exit. Thea is alone:

> I am no more afraid.
> So we swing full circle back towards the sanctuary of marriage.
> Oh, strange enigma!
> This morning my garden seemed a sanctuary from where I hated him and fought all day.
> Now I know Nature is us.
> Oh, strange enigma! Now I am no more afraid.

Piano/vocal score: p. 257 (Schott)

No. 73

Voice: mezzo-soprano
Aria Title: "Entweihte Götter!" (Ortrud)
Opera Title: *Lohengrin*
Composer and Librettist: Richard Wagner (1813–1883), after German legends
Historical Style: German Romantic (1850)
Range: F♯4 to A♯6

Fach: dramatic
Aria Duration: 4:00
Tessitura: A5 to F♯5

Position: Act II

Setting: Antwerp, in the first half of the 10th century. Ortrud and Count Friedrich, both in disguise, dressed in dark garments, are seated on the steps of the cathedral. Ortrud is gazing fixedly at the windows of the palace, which is brightly illuminated; Frederick is musing gloomily.

King Henry I has come to Brabant to call the men as an army to fight against the Hungarians, and he can see that they have no leader. The former leader, before his death, assigned his two children to the care of Count Friedrich, and the girl (Elsa) was given the opportunity to have the Count's hand in marriage, but she spurned him. Her brother was supposedly murdered. The Count married Ortrud, who is from a line of heathen princes who ruled before Christianity. A champion (Lohengrin) has come to fight for Elsa and defend her against charges that she murdered her brother. He fights the Count and fells him, sparing his life, and there is rejoicing by the spectators. In Act II the dejected Count and Ortrud blame each other for his defeat, but Ortrud means to wrest the secret of the mysterious knight by using cunning or force that will rob him of his powers. Together, they swear a pact of revenge. The balcony opens, and Elsa appears and sings about the mysterious knight, not seeing the two villains below her. Ortrud tells Friedrich to leave while she hatches a plot against Elsa. Ortrud makes her presence known and preys on Elsa's propensity for sympathy. Elsa is coming down to let Ortrud in, at which time Ortrud launches into this monologue.

The piece is marked molto allegro, in the key of F♯ minor; the first line ascends to high G♯:

Ye gods profaned! Help me now in my revenge!
Punish the ignominy that you have suffered here!
Strengthen me in the service of your holy cause!
Destroy the vile delusions of the apostate!
Woden! I call on you, O god of strength!
Freyja! Hear me, O exalted one!

These exclamations enter on high F♯. "Bless my deceit and hypocrisy, that I may be successful in my revenge!" she sings, to the high A♯, sustained by a fermata.

There are many effects in the orchestra that are sudden for dramatic effect, including the marking fp, and 16th-note pickups over arpeggiated chords in the orchestra. The aria is sustained, with many whole and half notes, but there is a sense of urgency, as Elsa is on her way downstairs.

Piano/vocal score: p. 142 (G. Schirmer)

No. 74

Voice: mezzo-soprano
Aria Title: "La luce langue" (Lady Macbeth)
Opera Title: *Macbeth*
Composer: Giuseppe Verdi (1813–1901)
Historical Style: 19th-century Italian
Romantic (1847)
Range: B4 to B6

Fach: dramatic
Librettist: Francesco Maria Piave (1810–
1876) with additions by Andrea Maffei
(1798–1885), after the tragedy by William
Shakespeare (1605)
Aria Duration: 3:55
Tessitura: E4 to F♯5

Position: Act II, scene 1

Setting: A private room in Macbeth's castle in Scotland, medieval times

At the beginning of Act II, Macbeth is deep in thought, having just murdered King Duncan. Macbeth is now king of Scotland. Lady Macbeth confronts him, asking him why he's always deep in thought. Why does he brood over the murder? "What's done is done," she says. "The son of Duncan has fled to England, leaving the throne vacant for Macbeth," the ambitious Lady Macbeth states. But Macbeth argues that the witches have prophesized that Banquo is next in line. "Is it necessary for more blood to be spilled?" Macbeth asks. His wife drives him forward to be steadfast in purpose to do what he needs to gain the throne, and Macbeth exits, strong in purpose. This fuels Lady Macbeth's excited expectations, that Banquo will be the next to fall.

With a gentle, bubbling accompaniment, Lady Macbeth sings an eerie melody that features wide intervals from the lower range to high F♯ and descends to low B. She observes that "the light fades, the eternal beacon from heaven dies. Longed-for night, providently veil the guilty hand poised to strike." Now the melody is in the orchestra, with Lady Macbeth, almost speaking, musing: "Another crime! . . . Another crime!" sung piano. Two accented quarter-note chords, marked fortissimo, ascend to high F: "It must be done! It must be accomplished!" The next section (andante, pianissimo) has a change of key to E major, written in the low range of the voice with the following text: "The departed have no wish to rule—for them a requiem and eternity." Now the music is marked vivo, and it crescendos from piano to forte as the accompaniment ascends to Lady Macbeth's ecstatic next vocal entrance: "Oh! Lust for the throne!" The ambitious Lady Macbeth can almost taste it. "O scepter, finally you are mine!" Quarter notes ascend to high G, fortissimo—"Every mortal desire is silenced and satisfied in you!" sung to the high B. There are eerie figures in orchestra, punctuated by the following fragmented vocal phrases: "soon . . . this evening." Then the music is sustained with double-dotted rhythms on E to E♯ to a sustained F♯ to the top of the staff: "He who was predicted King (*to high A*) will fall" as the line descends, then leaps up to E again: "will fall" she repeats. The music is filled with fragmented thoughts and double-dotted rhythms.

Piano/vocal score: p. 115 (G. Schirmer)

No. 75

Voice: mezzo-soprano
Aria Title: "We cannot retrace our steps"
(Susan B. Anthony)
Opera Title: *The Mother of Us All*
Composer: Virgil Thomson (1896–1989)
Historical Style: 20th-century American (1947)
Range: D4 to G5

Fach: dramatic
Librettist: Gertrude Stein (1874–1946), after a scenario by Maurice Grosser
Aria Duration: 5:40
Tessitura: G4 to E5

Position: Act II, scene 3

Setting: 19th-century America, the Congressional Hall

In the final scene (epilogue) there is an unveiling ceremony for a statue of Susan B. Anthony (1820–1906), who was in the forefront of activities to gain American women the right to vote. The scene takes place some years after the death of Anthony, and her ghost haunts the scene, wondering if the struggle was worth it.

The festivities for the unveiling ceremony get out of hand, but finally the statue is unveiled. Susan B. herself, regally dressed, is on the pedestal. The guests leave, and she reflects on her long life in semidarkness to an empty stage.

"We cannot retrace our steps going forward may be the same as going backwards." Thomson repeats key phrases here, "we cannot retrace our steps," and cleverly begins with an interval of an ascending 4th, repeating the interval of "retrace our steps" while reversing the interval (4th down) for the word "backwards."

There is a dramatic validity to the reflection as Susan brings thoughts to the surface in fragments, to be in the moment of monologue thought, and not a thoroughly thought-through articulate speech. It begins piano and calls for an even vocal production through E♭ and F at the top of the staff in the softer dynamics.

"We do not retrace our steps—but. But we do not retrace our steps, all my long life, and here, here we are here, in marble and gold, did I say gold, yes I said gold," she sings, fortissimo.

After an instrumental 19-measure orchestral interval (molto espressivo), she continues, "Where is where—in my long life of effort and strife, dear life, life is strife, in my long life, it will not come and go, I tell you so, it will stay it will pay but." There is a quarter rest, written in 3/2 meter, pianissimo. "But do we want what we have got, has it not gone, what made it lie, because now it is had, in my long life in my long life," sung fortissimo. "Life is strife, I was a martyr all my life not to what I won but to what was done." She echoes this phrase, pianissimo. "Do you know because I tell you so, or do you know, do you know?" she sings pianissimo, with a high sustained G above the staff. "My long life, my long life."

The melody is hymnlike, but with reflective, sustained notes, balanced with a moving 8th-note triplet motive and more complex rhythmic combinations.

Piano/vocal score: p. 153 (Music Press)

No. 76

Voice: mezzo-soprano
Aria Title: "Sgombra è la sacra selva . . . Deh! Proteggimi, O Dio!" (Adalgisa)
Opera Title: *Norma*
Composer: Vincenzo Bellini (1801–1835)
Historical Style: Bel canto (1831)
Range: A♯/B♭4 to F♯/G♭5

Fach: dramatic
Librettist: Felice Romani (1788–1865)
Aria Duration: 4:40
Tessitura: F4 to E♭5

Position: Act I

Setting: Night in the Druids' sacred forest, Gaul; around 50 B.C., during the Roman occupation

At moonrise the Druids expect the Druid princess, Norma, to signal a revolt against the Romans. Adalgisa, a young priestess of Irminsul, goes into the sacred wood to meet Pollione, the Roman Proconsol. Pollione's love for Norma has been quenched by a new passion for Adalgisa. After the Gauls assemble, Norma sings "Casta diva," invoking the moon. She still longs to win back Pollione's love. Left alone, Adalgisa prays for relief from the emotions that torment her, and she prays to her god to protect her from her love.

Recitativo (andante):

Cleared is the sacred forest, finished the rite.

Adalgisa sings in a determined tone. Her vocal line is rhythmically active and descends to low B♭.

To crave the sight, at last I can, here . . . where for the first time the fatal Roman offered himself to me . . . that makes me a traitor to the temple, to the god. (*con forza appassionato*) If only it had been the last time! Vain desire!

Irresistible force here me drags (*tremolo is heard in the strings*) and on that dear face the heart feeds itself . . . And of his dear voice the breeze that blows to me repeats the sound.

Largo:

Protect me, oh God! (*The vocal line is sustained, and is characterized by triplet figures.*) Protect me, protect me, oh God, protect me. Lost I am, great God, protect me.

Some of the phrases are unaccompanied. The vocal line is sustained and is characterized by triplet figures. The singer will need to begin some phrases at the top of the staff, and the final cadenza requires a sustained high F followed by G♭.

Piano/vocal score: p. 52 (Belwin Mills)

No. 77

Voice: mezzo-soprano/contralto
Aria Title: "Ah! Mon fils, sois béni" (Fidès)
Opera Title: *Le prophète*
Composer: Giacomo Meyerbeer (1791–1864)
Historical Style: French Romantic (1849)
Range: B#4 to A#6

Fach: dramatic
Librettist: Eugène Scribe (1791–1861)
Aria Duration: 4:26
Tessitura: C#4 to C#5

Position: Act II

Setting: Jean's Inn, Leyden, Holland, 15th century. The stage depicts the inn of Jean and his mother on the outskirts of Leyden; doors in the rear and a casement open onto a countryside.

Fidès is the mother of Jean and has earlier come from Leyden to take her son's betrothed home with her, but Berthe cannot leave without the Count's consent. The Count refuses and has both Berthe and Fidès arrested. Jean has to choose between his mother, whose life is threatened, and Berthe. He sacrifices his betrothed, and his mother calls upon God to bless her son for his suffering. Meyerbeer in this aria begins with short phrases, which he will then expand. The aria (andante espressivo) is sustained and heartfelt. It is in 3/4 meter in the key of F# minor.

"Ah, my son, be blessed! Your poor mother dearer to you than your Berthe, than your love!" Again she sings, "Ah, my son!" to link to the beginning of the aria. "You have just given for your mother, alas! More than your life in giving your happiness!" now is sung in shorter rhythmic values with 16th rests to give this a breathless quality, and then "Ah! My son" is sung once again. "Toward heaven may my prayer rise," she sings, as the vocal line ascends with rhythmic energy, and the key changes to the major as the melody ascends to "ciel/heaven," to the high F#. "And may you be blessed in the Lord, my son, be blessed—be blessed in the Lord" is repeated in different dynamic markings, forte and piano. The phrases are again fragmented at the end of aria in the lower range. There also is a cadenza that repeats the text "sois beni dans le Seigneur!/Be blessed in the Lord!"

Piano/vocal score: p. 83 (Kalmus)

No. 78

Voice: mezzo-soprano
Aria Title: "Donnez, donnez" (Fidès)
Opera Title: *Le prophète*
Composer: Giacomo Meyerbeer (1791–1864)
Historical Style: French Romantic (1849)
Range: B4 to G5

Fach: dramatic
Librettist: Eugène Scribe (1791–1861)
Aria Duration: 4:46
Tessitura: E4 to E5

Position: Act IV

Setting: The stage depicts a square in the city of Munster, Germany; several streets meet in the square. At right is the door of the City Hall; several steps lead up to it.

The square is now occupied by the Anabaptists. The rich burghers are forced to surrender their treasures and to curry the rebels' favor. Fidès (mother of the false prophet Jean) arrives, now a beggar. She believes her son to be dead. Fidès is a matriarch equal in nobility and pathos to the great father figures of the Verdi operas. Her music is distinguished by its urgency and vitality, following the changing passions in the text.

In the scene Fidès is seen seated on a stone at the rear of the stage. "What are you doing here?" they ask the woman. Some of the citizens lead the woman downstage. In a plaintive voice, she begs for alms, haltingly at first (andantino quasi allegretto) in 3/4 meter, with a 10-measure orchestral introduction. "Give for a poor soul," she begs, her phrase broke by 16th, 8th, and quarter rests, in the key of B minor. She begins piano, then crescendos, as she sings, "Open paradise to him" (who gives me alms). "Donnez, donnez/Give, give," she pleads again. "Noble Lords, give, for pity's sake," she sings, unaccompanied with accents to emphasize her need. There is a key change to E major, marked a tempo, pianissimo. "Have mercy, rich lord! Give to say a mass, alas, for my lost child. Ah!" she cries out, ascending to the high F♯, forte, then lyrically, pianissimo, repeating "my poor lost child."

Some citizens give alms to Fidès and leave. Others arrive and gather round her to listen to her. The key signature changes again to the key of G. She is cold, she says, and hungry. "No matter," she sings as her vocal line ascends, forte, to the high G—then suddenly descends to low B–middle C: "The grave is colder still," she sings. "Who will then pray for his fate?" she asks. She then sings lyrically as the key changes back again to E major, repeating the earlier melody: "Amid your wealth," she sings, "have mercy, rich lord. Give to say a mass," she repeats. "for my lost child. Ah! Alas!" Weeping, she receives alms from the citizens.

Piano/vocal score: p. 237 (Kalmus)

No. 79

Voice: mezzo-soprano
Aria Title: "Scorned! Abused! Neglected!" (Baba the Turk)
Opera Title: *The Rake's Progress*
Composer: Igor Stravinsky (1882–1971)
Historical Style: 20th-century English (1951)
Range: A4 to A6

Fach: dramatic
Librettists: W. H. Auden (1907–1973) and Chester Kallman (1921–1975), after William Hogarth's cycle of paintings of the same name (1735)
Aria Duration: 1:45
Tessitura: C4 to D#/E♭5

Position: Act II, scene 3

Setting: The morning room of Tom Rakewell's London house, which is filled with statues, stuffed animals, and other knick-knacks; 18th century

Baba the Turk, a bearded lady, had been telling Tom all about her collection of knick-knacks that fills the morning room. However, he isn't particularly interested, and Baba gets very angry. She rushes about the room, smashing items of her collection while she accuses Tom of still being in love with Anne. In truth, Tom *is* still in love with Anne and hates himself for marrying Baba. He ends her rampage by taking off his wig and putting it over her face. Baba suddenly comes to a halt and remains in that frozen position for the rest of the scene.

"Scorned! Abused! Neglected! Baited!" At the end of each of these exclamations that are notes sung at the top of the staff to the octave below, Baba picks up some object and smashes it. Although this is not done, of course, when the aria is sung out of the context of the opera, the violent intent is there and can be seen in the eyes, the intensity in the delivery of the diction, and the body language. "Wretched me!" Baba exclaims, with sequenced patterns of 16th notes. "Why is this? Why is this?" she asks, singing with accents at the top of the staff and descending to the octaves below.

This melodic pattern continues, with the ornate patterns of rapidly sung 16th notes to the top of the staff, then the octave intervals up and down. "I know who is your bliss, your love, your life," she sings, to the high, sustained A.

The same melody material is repeated with the same active accompaniment marked più mosso, with new text, sarcastically extolling the virtues of Tom's love. She finally declares, "For she your wife shall never be, oh no!" singing an increasingly ornate melismatic vocal line, before Tom suddenly seizes his wig and plumps it down over her face, which cuts off her melisma off before she can finish. (Later in the opera, as Tom's belongings are being auctioned off, the auctioneer takes the wig off Baba, and she resumes in mid-melisma where she left off.)

Piano/vocal score: p. 119 (Boosey & Hawkes)

No. 80

Voice: mezzo-soprano/contralto
Aria Title: "Give him this orchid" (Lucretia)
Opera Title: *The Rape of Lucretia*
Composer: Benjamin Britten (1913–1976)
Historical Style: 20th-century English (1946)
Range: G3 to A6

Fach: dramatic
Librettist: Ronald Duncan, (1914–1982), based on André Obey's play *Le viol de Lucrèce* (1931)
Aria Duration: 6:55
Tessitura: F4 to E5

Position: Act II, scene 2

Setting: Lucretia's home, Rome, 500 B.C.

At the opening of the opera (a military camp outside Rome), the Male and Female Choruses recount how the Etruscan upstart Tarquinius Superbus seized power in Rome and how his son Tarquinius Sextus has become a warrior leader and "treats the proud city as if it were his whore." Collatinus, one of the important generals of Rome, boasts to Tarquinius and the other generals that his wife, Lucretia, is virtuous. Tarquinius rides at night to Rome to her home to prove Collatinus wrong. On his arrival in the middle of the night, Lucretia offers him a guest bed for the night. Drawing his sword, he rapes her. The next morning Lucretia's maids Bianca and Lucia extol the beauty of the morning and flowers. Lucretia enters in a trancelike state. "Give him this orchid" has a forceful entrance, fortissimo, at the top of the staff. Enunciation of the text over busy strings (though the orchestra numbers only 12) is important.

Lucretia says she hates the flowers and gives an orchid to Lucia for a messenger to take to her husband Collatinus with a message—that a Roman harlot has sent it, as her voice ascends to the high G. "Tell the messenger to tell my husband to come home. Go!" she repeatedly orders Lucia. "No!" she exclaims on a sustained high A, crescendo to forte. In hysteria, she laughs out loud. "Wait—tell the messenger to take my love—to the stable boy, the coachman," she rants. "Hurry!" She sings, fortissimo, furioso on the middle C. "For all men love the chaste Lucretia!" she sarcastically declares, to the low G. She makes a wreath from the remaining orchids. "Flowers bring to every year the same perfection," she sings. The vocal line is marked by repeated 8th notes and evokes a hypnotic, trancelike state. "Women bring to ev'ry man the same defection, Even their love's debauched by vanity, or flattery," she sings, to the top of the staff, accented. "Flowers alone are chaste"—this is a phrase that is set apart, pianissimo. "Let their pureness show my grief to hide my shame, and be my wreath" is sung ad lib below the staff.

She eventually tells Collatinus what happened. He forgives her, but she stabs herself to death.

Piano/vocal score: p. 177 (Boosey & Hawkes)

No. 81

Voice: mezzo-soprano
Aria Title: "Wie Du warst!" (Octavian)
Opera Title: *Der Rosenkavalier*
Composer: Richard Strauss (1864–1949)
Historical Style: 20th-century German (1911)
Range: C#/Db4 to G5

Fach: dramatic
Librettist: Hugo von Hofmannsthal (1874–1929)
Aria Duration: 8:00
Tessitura: C#/Db4 to G5

Position: Act I

Setting: The boudoir of the Marschallin, Vienna, mid-18th century, the first years of Maria Theresa's reign

Count Octavian Rofrano is a young nobleman, 17 years old. The Marschallin is 32.

Octavian is most likely only one in a series of lovers the Marschallin takes while her husband is away. After making love to the married Marschallin, Octavian speaks with her, saying that he feels a great attraction to her that is beyond words.

"How you are—how you have been! This (*he ascends to high F♯*) no one knows except me." The Marschallin has a line here: "Beklagt Er sich über das, Quinquin? Möcht' Er, dass viele das wüssten?/You're complaining about it, Quinquin? Would you like it if many others knew?"

Octavian continues in a fiery response: "Angel! No! Blessed am I that am the only one who knows who you are." He continues in a more peaceful manner: "You. You. You!" he sings passionately to high F♯. Octavian now philosophizes in a parlando style: "What is it about the words 'you' and 'I?' They are only words. But nevertheless, there is something . . . a dizziness, a pull, a craving and pressing, languishing and burning."

"Now my hand to your hand comes, this wanting and clinging, (*accelerando*) this is I that wants you . . . But this I is lost in this you . . . I am your boy, but when then my hearing and sight is lost, where is then your boy?" he concludes, peacefully.

The meter changes constantly between 4/4 and 3/4 according to text inflection. This is a lyric parlando style, with variance in the text between youthful passion and musing philosophy. Enharmonic steps and intervals are interspersed throughout the piece. The aria encompasses a wide range for the mezzo voice, lying at the bottom of the staff at times, then soaring to the top. Attention to diction and rhythm is extremely important.

Orchestral score: p. 9 (Boosey & Hawkes)

> Notes by singer and master teacher Frederica von Stade: This is the opening line of Octavian's in *Der Rosenkavalier* and is the musical representation of a passionate declaration of love by a young lover for his more senior partner. It is full of the ardor and desire of this "hot" situation and is expressed in a long phrase, the first sung music in the opera after a most passionate orchestral opening.

No. 82

Voice: mezzo-soprano
Aria Title: "Ah, Michele, don't you know?"
(Desideria)
Opera Title: *The Saint of Bleecker Street*
Composer and Librettist: Gian Carlo
Menotti (b. 1911)
Historical Style: 20th-century American (1954)
Range: B4 to A6

Fach: dramatic
Aria Duration: 2:09
Tessitura: E4 to E5

Position: Act II

Setting: An Italian neighborhood in New York City, 1954; scene of a wedding reception in an Italian restaurant in the basement of a house on Bleecker Street

Desideria is the girlfriend of the brother of Annina, a passionate religious mystic who experiences stigmata, the bleeding of the hands that represent the crucifixion of Christ. Desideria objects to Michele's obsession with his saintly sister, and when she accuses him of being in love with Annina, Michele stabs Desideria.

The scene begins with a wedding reception at an Italian restaurant and is festive in contrast with the turn of events and tragic conclusion. Michele, Annina's brother, is a very dangerous character and has an explosive temper. Desideria is also temperamental.

As Michele and Desideria approach the restaurant from the outside, Desideria asks Michele (with cruel persistence), "Will you take me in with you?" Michele is silent. "Answer me," she insists. The next section is marked andante. "Ah, Michele, don't you know that love can turn to hate at the sound of one word, if the word is said too late? Love can never heal its wounds unless the cry is answered, unless the scar is seen." At the end of the vocal line a passionately sung sustained F and passing high A♭ are called for.

At the beginning of the piece the text is set syllabically, and care must be taken to still connect the notes so that there is not too much of an adverse affect on the voice. The melody has many accidentals and must be carefully tuned.

"All the tears one weeps alone do not unlock the pounding gates of the heart. Like stars they fall in deathly stillness—but leave a poisoned trail," sung on a sustained high F. The next section is marked piano, dolcissimo:

"Only he, whose tears are mirrored, can bear the secret pain of living—those of us, who find our love on earth, must celebrate—our fleeting triumph; who welcomes in silence or hides it like a crime shall soon run to the wastelands to escape its blinding vengeance." The octave-apart two 8th notes to the B, repeatedly played, heighten the dramatic intensity here. After four measures (rallentando), she sings, "Ah, Michele, don't forget that love is a pitiless hunter when allied with death," as she crescendos to the sustained high G♯.

Although the aria is expressive and passionate, there is an underlying sense of foreshadowing danger with enharmonic tones in the vocal line, and repeated 8th-note octaves in the accompaniment. We must remember that Desideria knows Michele and his volatile personality well. The articulation is extremely important, and the rhythmic variety is wedded to the text.

Piano/vocal score: p. 176 (G. Schirmer)

No. 83

Voice: mezzo-soprano
Aria Title: "Amour! Viens aider ma faiblesse!" (Dalila)
Opera Title: *Samson et Dalila*
Composer: Camille Saint-Saëns (1835–1921)
Historical Style: French Romantic (1877)
Range: G♯/A♭3 to G5

Fach: dramatic
Librettist: Ferdinand Lemaire (fl. 1860–1870), after the story in the Bible
Aria Duration: 4:55
Tessitura: D♯/E♭4 to C5

Position: Act II

Setting: The valley of Soreck, ancient Palestine in Old Testament times. To the left, Dalila's dwelling, fronted by a delicate porch and surrounded by Asian plants and luxuriously growing lianas. It is dusk and becomes gradually darker through the act.

The curtain rises to disclose Dalila, decked out in finery, and seated on a rock near the porch of her house. She is thoughtful. Dalila knows that

Samson is entranced with her and will come to her instead of leading the revolution against the Philistines. She sings seductively of the powers of love to ensnare Samson.

Recitative, marked animato: "Samson, seeking me again, is bound to come here this evening. This is the hour of vengeance which must satisfy our gods!"

The next section is marked moderato, and there is a lyric orchestral introduction to the aria: "Love, come to aid me in my weakness! Pour the poison into his breast! See to it that, overcome by my wiles, Samson lies in fetters tomorrow!" There is a focus shift here: "In vain would he like to be able to drive me out, to banish me from his heart! Could he extinguish the flame which memory sustains?" she sings piano. "He is mine, he is my slave! My brothers fear his wrath." There is an accelerando here: "I, alone among all, do dare him and keep him at my knees!" In the vocal line is written a sustained E♭ for two measures to high G before a cascading descending scale of 32nd notes to the low B♭. "Love, come to aid me in my weakness." Dalila then repeats the opening of the aria.

The last section (dolce) lies in the middle/lower region of the voice: "Against love his strength is useless; and he, the strongest among the strong, he who burst a nation's bonds, will succumb to my endeavors."

Piano/vocal score: p. 104 (A. Durand)

No. 84

Voice: mezzo-soprano
Aria Title: "Mon coeur s'ouvre à ta voix" (Dalila)
Opera Title: *Samson et Dalila*
Composer: Camille Saint-Saëns (1835–1921)
Historical Style: French Romantic (1877)
Range: A♯/B♭4 to G5

Fach: dramatic
Librettist: Ferdinand Lemaire (fl. 1860–1970), after the story in the Bible
Aria Duration: 5:59
Tessitura: D♯/E♭4 to D♯/E♭5

Position: Act II, scene 3

Setting: The valley of Soreck, ancient Palestine in Old Testament times. To the left, Dalila's dwelling, fronted by a delicate porch and surrounded by Asian plants and luxuriously growing lianas. It is dusk, and the night is gradually darkening. There is lightning in the distance.

In an attempt to close the trap which she has set for Samson, Dalila tells Samson seductively that she is completely his if he wants her. She begs him to respond to her caresses, hoping that he will finally let go of all other things and concentrate completely on her, allowing the High Priest of Dagon to capture him. Their dialogue before her aria is important to the understanding of her aria. Samson curses his love, yet still loves . . . he cannot listen to her entreaties of love without shame or remorse. She was always dear to his heart. "Has love lost its delights for you?" she asks him. "This must be our last farewell," he says, ordained by the Lord. "A god greater than yours speaks through my mouth, the god of love," she says.

The well-known melody with its flowery poetry begins, dolcissimo e cantabile, "My heart opens to your voice as the flowers open to dawn's kisses." Although the melody is legato, through the voice observe the dotted rhythms within the line, for they provide for energy and vitality of delivery.

"But, o my beloved, the better to dry my tears, let your voice speak once more! Tell me that you are coming back to Dalila forever! Reminding me once again of the promises of past days, those promises I loved!" The phrases build to an extended "Ah" that is sustained on the middle C that calls for a controlled diminuendo, with ritartando, connecting it to the next melody, which is somewhat slower: "Answer my tenderness! Fill me with ecstasy!" Although the melody is marked pianissimo, it needs intensity as it descends to the lower ranges of the staff to the end of the phrase, and then repeats. The melody, repeating the same text, now crescendos and builds to the high G♭. "Dalila, I love you!" responds Samson.

Dalila now sings a second verse, with more motion and momentum. "Like ears of corn rippling in the gentle breeze so flutters my heart, ready to take comfort from your beloved voice! The arrow is less swift in carrying death than is your lover in flying into your arms! In flying into your arms!" The refrain ("Answer my tenderness . . . ") is sung in duet with Samson within the context of the opera, so that the voices weave together. Samson closes the piece in the opera, while Dalila will sing the closing phrase: "Samson, Samson, je t'aime!/Samson, I love you!" when singing the aria alone (to the high, sustained B♭).

Piano/vocal score: p. 155 (A. Durand)

Note by director and opera professor Sandra Bernhard: Dalila during the first verse is seducing Samson for the purpose of trapping him, but in verse 2 she herself is seduced. There is something between them she has never experienced. Important is the music after the aria, which is accompanied by nature's reaction: storm, lightning, and destruction.

No. 85

Voice: mezzo-soprano
Aria Title: "Printemps qui commence" (Dalila)
Opera Title: *Samson et Dalila*
Composer: Camille Saint-Saëns (1835–1921)
Historical Style: French Romantic (1877)
Range: B4 to E5

Fach: dramatic
Librettist: Ferdinand Lemaire (fl. 1860–1870), after the story in the Bible
Aria Duration: 6:17
Tessitura: E4 to C♯/D♭5

Position: Act I

Setting: The public square of Gaza, ancient Palestine in Old Testament times
    Dalila is the Philistine Princess of Dagon. At the opening of the opera the Hebrew warrior Samson has refused to share the despondency of the Hebrews and incites his people to rebellion against the Philistines.
    In an attempt to seduce Samson away from his leadership of the Israelite uprising, Dalila and a group of girls dance for him, and Dalila sings of how spring blossoms all around her.
    The maidens accompanying Dalila wave their garlands as they dance and seem to provoke the Hebrew warriors accompanying Samson. Profoundly agitated, he vainly seeks to avoid Dalila's glances; in spite of himself, Samson's eyes follow her every movement. She remains among the Philistine girls, joining in their voluptuous poses and dances before she sings.
    "Printemps qui commence" is a very simple piece in melodic repetition in the middle range of the voice, not exceeding the E at the top of the staff. It begins dolce, seductively, accompanied by a repeated, sustained B in the cello, until the section marked poco animato. "En vain je suis belle!/

unavailing my beauty," she says, accompanied by a crescendo as she sings, "My heart full of love, weeping for the unfaithful one, awaits his return! Living in hope, my disconsolate heart treasures the memory of past happiness." She now addresses Samson directly with the same melody in verse 2 as the opening: "At nightfall, a sad lover, I shall go and sit down by the stream to await him in tears!" At this point in the vocal line there are no rests written in the score to the conclusion of the piece. Dalila does not allow an interruption from Samson or the Old Hebrew. "Casting off my sadness (*crescendo*) . . . should he come back one day, for him my tenderness and the sweet rapture that a burning love (*accelerando*) saves for his return!"

Much of the melody lies in the lower middle of the voice, bringing out the seductive warm colors of the voice.

Piano/vocal score: p. 94 (A. Durand)

No. 86

Voice: mezzo-soprano
Aria Title: "Condotta ell'era in ceppi" (Azucena)
Opera Title: *Il trovatore*
Composer: Giuseppe Verdi (1813–1901)
Historical Style: 19th-century Italian Romantic (1853)
Range: A4 to B♭6

Fach: dramatic
Librettists: Salvatore Cammarano (1801–1852) and Leone Emanuele Bardare (1820–1874), after the play *El trovador* by Antonio García Gutiérrez (1836)
Aria Duration: 4:45
Tessitura: E4 to E5

Position: Act I (The Gypsy), scene 1

Setting: Beginning of the 15th century, Spain; a broken-down hovel on the side of a mountain in Biscay. At the back, practically in the open, burns a large fire; it is early dawn, and a group of gypsies are scattered around.

Gypsies are encamped at the foot of a mountain in Biscay. With them is Manrico (a member of the faction opposed to the King) and his mother, Azucena. As dawn breaks the gypsies begin work at their anvils, and

Azucana sings a ballad about the burning of the old gypsy woman. When the others have left to search for food, Manrico asks his mother for the truth behind the ballad. She tells him the whole story of how her mother was executed and how, when she cried out for vengeance, Azucena kidnapped the Count of Luna's brother. After the gypsies leave, Azucena tells Manrico of his grandmother, whom the Count accused of witchcraft, asserting that she had cast a spell on his infant son. She was brought to the stake, where she was burned to death.

The piece begins andante mosso, the two measures piano, sung sotto voce: "In chains they led her to her terrible fate." The first vocal phrase is legato, but the accompanying bass line is repeated staccato 8th notes, and there are a number of very short rhythmic values, accents, and sudden changes of dynamics that all contribute to the dramatic intensity. "With a child in my arms (*the voice crescendos in ascent to E*) I followed her, but they would not let me through. In vain the poor woman (*again the voice ascends to E*) tried to stop and give me her blessing! For with obscene oaths striking her with their lances, the vile guards dragged her to the stake" (the music is filled with dramatic repeated accents, dotted rhythms, and is sung forte). "Then half choking, she cried, Avenge me!—Her words echo forever in my heart." Manrico asks, "Did you avenge her?" ascending to F at the top of the staff with repeated accents. "I stole the Count's child and brought it her with me . . . the flames were burning," sings Azucena. "The flames? Oh, horrors! What did you do?" he asks. "The child was crying out," she related. "My own heart was racked with pain" (as she ascends to high G and descends with 8th-note accents).

The following section (allegretto) is written in 3/8 meter, sotto voce e declamato: "Then suddenly to my afflicted heart, as in a dream, appeared the dreadful image of grim ghosts! The guards . . . the stake . . . my mother with ashen face, barefoot and disheveled . . . her cry . . . I heard that familiar cry—Avenge me!" she sings, with a sustained high A (allegro agitato). "Trembling, I stretched out my hand, seized the victim, and threw him into the fire . . . my fatal delirium passed, and the dreadful scene vanished. Only the flames were roaring, consuming their new prey. Yet when I looked round, there before me I saw the wicked Count's child still lying." "What are you saying?" Manrico asks. "It was my own child!" she exclaims, sung on high E, with accents. "It was my own child that I had burned. Ah!" she cries out on high B♭, then sings the repeated text, accompanied by quarter accents on F at the top of the staff. After an eight-measure interlude, diminuendo, during which time Manrico digests the horrific story, Azucena sings the final lines in her lower range in sustained note values, below the staff: "I still feel my hair standing on end."

Piano/vocal score: p. 63 (G. Schirmer)

No. 87

Voice: mezzo-soprano
Aria Title: "Stride la vampa" (Alzucena)
Opera Title: *Il trovatore*
Composer: Giuseppe Verdi (1813–1901)
Historical Style: Italian Romantic (1853)
Range: B4 to G5

Fach: dramatic
Librettists: Salvatore Cammarano (1801–1852) and Leone Emanuele Bardare (1820–1874), after Antonio García Gutiérrez's play *El trovador* (1836)
Aria Duration: 5:15
Tessitura: B5 to E5

Position: Act II (The Gypsy), scene 1

Setting: A broken-down hovel on the side of a mountain in Biscay, 1409; at the back, practically in the open, burns a large fire; it is early dawn

As dawn breaks the gypsies begin work at their anvils, and Azucena sings a ballad about the burning of an old gypsy woman. She sings the story to Manrico, her son, and the crowd of gypsies. While Azucena sings, the gypsies gather around her. The accompaniment is purely supportive, and we have two measures (a dancelike, 3/8 meter, E minor) of staccato, chordal introduction. Although it is marked piano, the vocal line has distinct accented attacks and is exotic with its trills and dotted rhythms at the end of the phrase:

Stride la vampa!/The flames are roaring!
A wild crowd, mad for excitement, surges towards the fire.
Shouts of joy echo around.
Surrounded by guards, a woman comes forward.
On their hateful faces shines the lurid glow
From the flames leaping up to heaven.

The melodic phrase develops to a sustained trill on "ciel/heaven" in the middle of the staff up to the high G. Second verse:

The flames are roaring!
They near the victim clad in black disheveled and barefoot.
Savage howls for death are raised,
Repeated by the echo from cliff to cliff.
On their hateful faces shines the lurid glow
From the flames leaping up to heaven!

Azucena, the master storyteller, is telling a true story in lurid detail. Her mother was burned at the stake for being a witch while the ones who falsely convicted her laughed and enjoyed themselves. It is important for her son, Manrico, to know that vengeance must be sought. The energy found in the vigorous rhythms of the vocal line must be brought out. The tessitura is in the middle of the staff, but the line does descend to low B (on the unaccented syllable). The measures of cadence at the conclusion of both verses going up to high G continue through the vocal line to "ciel/ heaven," resting on high E at the top of the staff. The voice is then unaccompanied on the high G, exposed, and the vocal line gains momentum to the final note, not straining or becoming shrill on the high G to the tonic E.

Piano/vocal score: p. 56 (G. Schirmer)

No. 88

Voice: mezzo-soprano
Aria Title: "Avancez! Reculez!" (Madame de la Haltière)
Opera Title: *Cendrillon*
Composer: Jules Massenet (1842–1912)
Historical Style: French Romantic (1899)
Duration: 5:09
Range: C4 to F♯5

Fach: contralto
Librettist: Henri Cain (1859–1937), after Charles Perrault's story *Cendrillon* (1697)
Tessitura: E4 to C5

Position: Act IV

Setting: The terrace of Cendrillon's home, France, 17th century

Madame de la Haltière enters with the news of a grand assembly of princesses to try on the missing slipper. Cendrillon shows interest in Madame's announcement, because it means that her dream was true.

The beginning is very animated in the introduction, with strong 16th-note patterns in the accompaniment. "Advance!" Madame sings, at once leaping to a sustained E. "Recede!" sung piano, with attention to rhythm. "You must know that this day an order of the King convokes a fine array of princesses" she excitedly recites, unaccompanied, in the middle range of the voice (A) "who at his call have flown from regions that are well, or very little known."

Some have come from Japan, some from Spain and from Tyre,
Some from the banks of Thames, and from the land of Eire,
Some from Cambodia, and others who are Norwegian,
And very soon, past here, they will march in procession. (*changing her tone*)
Then, as the clear blue sky appears when storms are o'er,
(*rallentando, with melismatic 8th-note triplets*)
And breezes gently murmur when winds have ceased to roar
(*she sings mysteriously, in the low range near middle C*)
With a fine noble air, there will come, toward the last
Like a bright vision fair, moving forward sedately,
Three women of poise most demur, yet most stately.
And then, as you shall hear, a tremor will run past,
For all the crowd will cry: "Behold these three unknown,
Who, because of the prince, from the sky have come down!"
And they never will dream 'tis my daughters and I,
On our way to the court, to salute his Majesty!
(*16th-note pickups add an energetic and energetic quality to the phrases.*)
Behold! 'Tis we, 'tis I! We greet his Majesty! (*with grand reverence*)

Piano/vocal score: p. 329 (Heugel)

No. 89

Voice: mezzo-soprano
Aria Title: "Lorsqu'on a plus de vingt quar-
tiers" (Madame de la Haltière)
Opera Title: *Cendrillon*
Composer: Jules Massenet (1842–1912)
Historical Style: French Romantic (1899)
Range: D4 to F♯5

Fach: contralto
Librettist: Henri Cain (1859–1937), after
Charles Perrault's story *Cendrillon* (1697)
Aria Duration: 4:49
Tessitura: A4 to E5

Position: Act III, scene 1

Setting: Home of Madame de la Haltière, France, 18th century

After the ball at which Cinderella captivates all present (including the prince), Madame de la Haltière and her daughters upbraid Pandolfe (her hen-pecked husband) for his bad behavior at the ball. She is defensive because she has not received the attention she feels that she deserves.

Madame de la Haltière lists her family tree connections to show how important she is (not counting all the rest):

(*animated*)
Four Chief Justices, mortar-boards, a Doge, among one's cousins:
And priests and bishops by dozens,
An admiral, a cardinal, six abbesses and many a nun,
Two or three king's mistresses,
Who all of them may, more or less, be ranked as having worn the crown:
Not mentioning the small fry like princes, be they ne'er so high,
One should press onward through the masses
Like some great ship that proudly passes,
Serene and self-contained and grand,
Disdaining tempests and their noises.
(*She sings a sustained E at the top of the staff, fortissimo.*)
One really ought, you understand, when upon the top one poises,
To hold up one's head and one's eyes, And leave meek airs to your people of naught!

The variety of articulation and dynamic markings help to define Madame de la Haltière's traits: proud, defensive, cackling-like, self-importance. Each phrase has specific markings that contribute to her character. As stated, there are a number of sustained high E's, but only one higher note higher: an emphatic F♯ quarter note.

Piano/vocal score: p. 233 (Heugel)

No. 90

Voice: mezzo-soprano
Aria Title: "I shall find for you," Lullaby (Magda's Mother)
Opera Title: *The Consul*
Composer and Librettist: Gian Carlo Menotti (b. 1911)
Historical Style: 20th-Century American (1950)
Range: (A)F3 to E♭5

Fach: contralto
Aria Duration: 3:29
Tessitura: C4 to D♭5

Position: Act II, scene 1

Setting: A large city in a police state, somewhere in Europe, post–World War II; a small, shabby apartment shared by John and Magda Sorel, their baby, and John's mother; evening

The mother is singing to her sickly grandchild lying in a primitive cradle in the poor apartment. The lullaby is in contrast with the tense atmosphere. The police are watching the apartment, and Magda can look down to the street where the police agents can be seen.

The lullaby begins with two measures of lilting 6/8, andantino, piano.

"I shall find for you shells and stars," as the piece dips to low A, "I shall swim for you river and sea. Sleep, my love," the Mother sings to E♭ at the top of the staff. "Sleep for me. My sleep is old. I shall feed for you lamb and dove. I shall buy for you sugar and bread. Sleep, my love, sleep for me. My sleep is dead," she says, descending to sustained middle C. Sung movendo: "Rain will fall but Baby won't know. He laughs alone in orchards of gold. Tears will fall but Baby won't know. His laughter is blind," she exclaims, forte, to the E♭ at the top of the staff. Sung subito piano: "Sleep, my love, for sleep is kind. Sleep is kind when sleep is young. Sleep for me, sleep for me." Tempo 1: "I shall build for you planes and boats. I shall catch for you cricket and bee. Let the old ones watch your sleep. Only death will watch the old. Sleep . . . " The word "sleep" is repeated in the lower range of the voice, descending to an optional low F below middle C. As befitting the lullaby, repeated rhythmic motives in the melody are composed of a quarter note followed by an 8th note. The subito piano can be the dramatic "beat" of the fear the baby is waking. The chromaticism in the piece and some of the text underscore the underlying feeling of danger in the room.

Piano/vocal score: p. 115 (G. Schirmer)

No. 91

Voice: mezzo-soprano
Aria Title: "When I am laid in earth," No. 31, Dido's Lament (Dido)
Opera Title: *Dido and Aeneas*
Composer: Henry Purcell (1659–1695)
Historical Style: English Baroque (1689)
Range: G4 to G5

Fach: contralto
Librettist: Nahum Tate (1652–1715), after Virgil's *Aeneid*
Aria Duration: 3:18
Tessitura: G4 to D5

Position: Act III

Setting: Dido's palace, ancient Carthage, soon after the fall of Troy
     Prince Aeneas has escaped the sack of Troy. He sails for Italy, where he is destined to found a new Troy (i.e., Rome), but is blown off course to Carthage, where he is welcomed by Queen Dido, who is burdened by affairs of state and unspoken grief. She falls in love with Aeneas. A sorceress who plots the Queen's downfall tricks Aeneas into recognizing his destiny in Italy, and he realizes he must comply. The Queen hears of his decision to leave and bitterly confronts a cowardly Aeneas, who says he will stay—but then departs. Dido realizes that she cannot live without him. Inconsolable,

she sings a great lament in the presence of Belinda, her confidant, and the Queen dies.

The aria has a heavy sadness that comes from the "ground bass," which is a bass-line pattern that repeats throughout the aria. The vocal line is connected, but has a desperation that is hardly unaffected. The climactic phrase is "Remember me," which is sung on the high G. As the singer sings, "But ah! Forget my fate," the "ah!" feels like a wail of mourning. The "Remember me" is oft-repeated, so variety is important in the delivery of each phrase. Are some of the phrases sung out, calling Aeneas, already on his way to Rome? Are some of the phrases sung reflectively to herself? These are questions Dido should ask herself in the resultant dynamic choices, so that the dynamics are connected to the drama.

When I am laid in earth, may my wrongs create no trouble in thy breast. (*repeat*)
Remember me! But ah! Forget my fate!

Piano/vocal score: p. 78 (Oxford)

No. 92

Voice: mezzo-soprano
Aria Title: "Ja nye sposobna k grusti tomnoy" (Olga)
Opera Title: *Eugene Onegin*
Composer: Pyotr Ilyich Tchaikovsky (1840–1893)
Historical Style: Russian Romantic (1879)
Range: A4 to E5

Fach: contralto
Librettists: The composer and Konstantin Shilovsky (1849–1893), based on Aleksandr Pushkin's verse novel *Eugene Onegin* (1831)
Aria Duration: 3:20
Tessitura: C4 to C5

Position: Act I, scene 1

Setting: Twilight in the garden on Madame Larina's estate, St. Petersburg, Russia, late 1700s

Olga is the daughter of Madame Larina and sister of Tatiana. She is very young and carefree. Tatiana and Olga are now on the terrace of the house. Tatiana has her book in hand and remarks that she loves to hear people singing, and music makes her lose herself in endless yearning for something far away, which stimulates Olga's teasing—Tatiana's a daydreamer. The music here is marked poco più animato. Olga is not like Tatiana at all, she sings. The songs she hears make her dance. Olga dances and embraces her mother.

"In a cottage by the water lived a miller with his daughter." She sings this little light melody while dancing. "I'm not the sort to sit in silence," she confides in a more sustained vocal line of repeated notes with a 5th interval at the end of each line. "Or sigh, and sigh," she sings, descending to low A below the staff, "as if my heart would break." Olga does not linger here as she throws off the melancholy mood, leaping up to the top of the staff for the next phrases: "So why be sad? Behave as I do and lead a life that's always gay; for when you're cheerful and fond of laughter the heart grows younger ev'ry day. Never give way to sorrow or despair; each morning calls a new to pleasure." Each phrase begins at the top of the staff and quickly descends.

The next section is marked poco più animato once again. "My love of life is past all measure, that's why my heart is free from care!" she subsequently repeats, with a similar melodic phrase as earlier (andante mosso). Then she repeats the following text: "I'm not the sort to sit in silence; at night I never stay awake." During these repetitions the accompaniment is much more active underneath, with 16th-note chord outlines. The last melodic phrases are low and warm, again confiding in tone.

Piano/vocal score: p. 35 (Boosey & Hawkes)

> Notes by Metropolitan Opera coach Kosta Popovich: Olga's first lines depict her scorn for Tatiana's yearning—"you are always daydreaming." She continues in the same manner once the andante mosso has begun: "I am not capable of being melancholic, to dream in quiet, on the balcony, during the dark night to sigh from the bottom of my heart." All of these actions are, as I said before, so Russian/Tatiana's, and Olga is making fun of it. I always have the singer sing this "to sigh" (since it's repeated three times) every time more obnoxiously in order to really portray her contempt and disdain for her sister's feelings. From measure 26, middle of reh. J (all of these markings are from the Russian piano-vocal score, State Music Publishing, Moscow, 1964), Tchaikovsky masterfully

wrote Olga's explanation of her life philosophy. "Zatchem vzdyhat'" begins in E♭ minor, modulates to A major, and ends up on E♭ major (reh. K, measure 34), where the climax of the aria is located. Singers should start this section with a somber, darker sound, since it's in a minor key and still refers to Tatiana's sighing, but gradually brighten the voice and deliver the climax in a very convinced, declamatory, and optimistic intonation. The fact that Olga is only, let's say, 16 years old and already knows that her entire life is going to be one of joy and carefree happiness is in such a contrast to Tatiana's Russian brooding and thoughtful and emotional persona. Another important vocal point I try to make is that low passages in this aria shouldn't be sung in only chest voice, because the resulting sound will inevitably contradict Olga's age (plus, we have the Nurse, who's supposed to sing in chest voice as a sign of her uneducated, simple but caring personality). Olga (the singer) should be able to use the right amount of mixed head and chest voice in those places—the orchestra is not overpowering in these sections, and the singer should not worry about not being heard.

No. 93

Voice: mezzo-soprano
Aria Title: "Voce di donna o d'angelo" (La Cieca)
Opera Title: *La Gioconda*
Composer: Amilcare Ponchielli (1834–1886)
Historical Style: Italian Romantic (1876)
Range: A3 to F5

Fach: contralto
Librettist: Arrigo Boito (1842–1918) (under the pseudonym Tobia Gorrio), based on Victor Hugo's play *Angélo, tyran de Padoue* (1835)
Aria Duration: 5:05
Tessitura: G4 to E♭5

Position: Act I (The Lion's Mouth)

Setting: 17th-century Venice; the courtyard of the Ducal Palace, decorated for a holiday; a spring afternoon

Barnaba is a spy of the Inquisition and keeps his eye on everyone, entrapping anyone who is a threat to the state. Gioconda, a singer, leads in her blind mother, La Cieca, on their way to church. The regatta begins on the water, and the crowd exits to watch the race. Gioconda is in love with Enzo Grimaldo, a Genoese nobleman who has been banned from Venice but is nevertheless in the city in disguise. Barnaba bars Gioconda's way and declares his love, but he is rebuffed. She escapes Barnaba, leaving her blind mother on the steps of the church. Barnaba sees an opportunity to use the old woman as a means to obtain her daughter's love. The crowd returns, cheering the winner of the regatta. Barnaba convinces the loser that his boat was bewitched by La Cieca, and the crowd falls on her. She is saved by the nobleman Alvise, one of the heads of state, and his wife Laura. He demands that she should be fed. In thanks, the religious La Cieca gives Laura her rosary in thanks.

Cieca (to Laura who has released her; andante sostenuto, dolcissimo, espressivo, piano):

O voice of woman or angel who had freed me of my chains, my blindness forbids me
The sight of your saintly face. Still you cannot leave me without a pious offering.
I offer you this rosary. (*more sustained here, accompaniment staccato, pianissimo*)
Pray, accept it. With my prayers added it will bring you luck.

The highest note written is F at the top of the staff (in passing) to low B♭.

Although largely a sustained expression of long phrases, there are many varied shorter note values, and a variety of rhythmic figures. Important elements in the aria are its chromaticism and clarity of text, and although there are some repetitions of melodic phrases, it is largely through composed.

Piano/vocal score: p. 119 (G. Schirmer, Operatic Anthology, vol. 2)

No. 94

Voice: mezzo-soprano
Aria Title: "Priva son d'ogni conforto" (Cornelia)
Opera Title: *Giulio Cesare*
Composer: George Frideric Handel (1685–1959)
Historical Style: Italian Baroque (1724)
Range: B4 to D5

Fach: contralto
Librettist: Nicola Francesco Haym (1678–1729)
Aria Duration: 6:43
Tessitura: D4 to C5

Position: Act I, scene 1

Setting: The bridge over the Nile entering Alexandria, Egypt, 48 B.C.

Cornelia's husband, Pompeo (Pompey), has been killed by the Egyptians (and his head is displayed to prove that he is dead) to show their loyalty to Cesare (Caesar).

After unsuccessfully attempting suicide, she sings of her unhappiness and her loneliness.

The aria is marked largo, and is composed in 3/8 meter. Sustained tones across the measure are characteristic of this piece, with moving chords in the accompaniment. Eighth notes sung on beats 2 and 3 create a "sighing" effect. The aria lies in the lower middle of the voice.

Simple embellishments are heard in the form of rapid connecting passing tones.

Bereft of all comfort
And even the hope to die
Is prohibited me, woeful wretch.

My heart,
Laden with grief,
Is already weary of suffering,
And to die is denied me.

Piano/vocal score: p. 30 (Bärenreiter)

No. 95

Voice: mezzo-soprano
Aria Title: "Il segreto per esser felici,"
Ballata (Maffio)
Opera Title: *Lucrezia Borgia*
Composer: Gaetano Donizetti (1797–1848)
Historical Style: Bel canto (1833)
Range: C4 to F5

Fach: contralto
Librettist: Felice Romani (1788–1865), after
Victor Hugo's play *Lucrèce Borgia* (1832)
Aria Duration: 1:45
Tessitura: G4 to E5

Position: Act II, scene 2

Setting: A spacious room in the Negroni Palace, illuminated and prepared for the Princess Negroni's festive supper party

The festivities are at their height when Giubetta, to give the ladies an opportunity to retire, creates a diversion by mocking Orsini, who is about to sing a drinking song he has composed. Orsini is a friend of Gennaro's, and Orsini fears and hates Lucrezia Borgia. A key to his self-centered character in this drinking song is the ever-present *I* and *my* in the text.

The beginning is marked allegretto, written in 6/8 meter. The melody is light-hearted, marked staccato, with light embellishments. It is also interspersed with occasional accents. The piece is written in the middle voice, not extending above the E at the top of the staff, nor below middle C.

To happiness I have the key, I have proved it, my friends, you'll agree,
For whether the sky be blue or gray, hot or freezing cold the day,
I joke and I drink, and the madmen who think of tomorrow I scorn.
I joke and I drink. Tomorrow who knows what may happen,
Enjoy life today while you can.

Orsini is interrupted here, and if sung for an audition, the singer can put the two verses together. Verse 2:

While we're young we should live our lives fully,
And pleasure will help time pass slowly.
If pallid old age should appear at my shoulder, inviting to fear,
Then I jest and I drink, and the madmen who think of tomorrow I scorn.
(*The text "tomorrow who knows what may happen" is repeated.*)

Piano/vocal score: p. 193 (Ricordi)

Notes by singer Vivica Genaux: This is a great party piece! In the opera the setting is, of course, recklessly jolly but with a sense of darkness underneath as Orsini and his pals finally become aware of their own mortality. To me the "Carpe diem" theme is similar to that made familiar to many of my generation by the movie *Dead Poets Society*. The feeling of the aria is one of brashness and youth, tempered by the disconcerting suspicion that the uncertainty of tomorrow may be more imminent than you'd like to believe.

No. 96

Voice: mezzo-soprano
Aria Title: "Nella fatal di Rimini," Romanza (Maffio)
Opera Title: *Lucrezia Borgia*
Composer: Gaetano Donizetti (1797–1848)
Historical Style: Bel canto (1833)
Range: B♭4 to F♯5

Fach: contralto
Librettist: Felice Romani (1788–1865), after Victor Hugo's play *Lucrèce Borgia* (1832)
Aria Duration: 3:53
Tessitura: F♯4 to D5

Position: Prologue

Setting: The canals of Venice outside the Palace Grimani, which is splendidly illuminated for an evening party with partygoers in masks; gondolas occasionally pass by; in the distance Venice by moonlight

Gennaro and his friends enjoy the hospitality of the host, the orator Grimani, whom they plan to escort to Ferrara. There is mention of the name of Lucrezia Borgia, and they shiver at the mention. Maffio Orsini, also a friend of Gennaro, recalls an event: near death after having been saved in a battle by Gennaro and subsequently swearing eternal friendship, Orsini was visited by a mysterious presence who foretold that the two friends would meet their end together. They should fear La Borgia, for "where Lucrezia is, there is death."

The Romanza begins with two measures of repeated B minor chords, staccato and piano.

"Nella fatal di Rimini/During the battle of Rimini" he sings, on repeated F♯'s in the middle range, accented, mysteriously sung, as the story is told, "I lay on the ground. Gennaro aided me, carried me to safety in a lonely wood." Orsini uses some accents and intervallic skips to keep the attention and intensify the story. On the final word "salvo/saved" the singer leaps up to a sustained high F♯, crescendo, and descends in 16th- and 8th-note coloratura, repeating the text: "he carried me to safety." His companions remark that they are aware of Gennaro's virtue and compassion.

In the second verse, Orsini speaks of their pact of oath as friends, that they will "live and die together." A mysterious old man appeared and said, "Together you shall die." "Flee from the Borgias, the old man intones," Orsini continues. "Where Lucrezia is, is Death. Thus saying, he vanished. And the winds echoed three times the name I detest." Orsini then proceeds to sing this phrase three times. The last words of the verse are embellished. The highest note of the Romanza is F♯ at the top of the staff (sustained), and the lowest note is B♭ below the staff.

Piano/vocal score: p. 10 (Ricordi)

> Notes by singer Vivica Genaux: This aria shows the dramatic capabilities of the singer well, as Orsini tells of the unnerving encounter he and Gennaro have just had with a dark figure warning them of Lucrezia Borgia. The first "verse" is more buoyant and cavalier, as Orsini recounts the battle and his being saved by Gennaro, while the second "verse" spirals down into the sense of foreboding and dread that underlies the entire opera. The singer really has to paint a picture for the audience with this aria, and it is a great opportunity to show off various colors in the voice.

No. 97

Voice: mezzo-soprano
Aria Title: "I know a bank where the wild thyme grows" (Oberon)
Opera Title: *A Midsummer Night's Dream*
Composer: Benjamin Britten (1913–1976)
Historical Style: 20th-century English (1960)
Range: G3–C5

Fach: contralto
Librettists: The composer with Peter Pears (1910–1986), after the comedy by William Shakespeare (1593)
Aria Duration: 4:15
Tessitura: C4–A5

Position: Act I

Setting: An enchanted wood, deepening twilight, legendary times

Oberon, king of the fairies, has quarreled with his wife, Tytania, because she has an attendant stolen from an Indian king, and Oberon wants him. Tytania defies him, and Oberon plans his revenge, which will be juice of an herb sprinkled on the eyelids of someone who sleeps, making Tytania lose her feelings for the attendant that Oberon covets. She will instead love the first person she sees upon awaking. Oberon sends Puck for the herb. Meanwhile Oberon overhears a heated conversation in the woods between Helena and Demetrius. She loves Demetrius, but he wants nothing to do with her. Instead, he loves Hermia, who does not love him. Oberon decides that the herb will also serve to help Helena. If the juice is applied to the sleeping Demetrius's eyes, then if Helena wakes him, he will fall in love with her.

Puck returns with the magic herb. He gives Oberon the flower and lies at his feet.

The piece is marked quietly, tranquillo. Oberon speaks of the bank on which Tytania sleeps. Her eyes will be "streaked" with the juice of the herb. He also tells Puck to take some of it to anoint Demetrius while sleeping and make sure that the first person he sees upon awaking is Helena. He makes sure that Puck understands that he knows that Demetrius is identified by the Athenian garments that he wears.

This excerpt is an excellent example of descriptive, poetic text set to music. The language inspires the descriptive music and its articulation markings, which are very specific. The variety, then, comes from the articulation markings, tempo changes (tranquillo, gently flowing, more animated than before, flowing, and finally lento), and dynamics.

Although the role is often sung by a countertenor and was created by

273

Alfred Deller, a young contralto can sing this piece and learn from the application of English text to music. It lies very low (the top note is the C in the upper middle of the range), but since it lies a lot in the *passaggio,* the young singer will have to learn how to negotiate the shift in registers while articulating the language. The voice also has to be flexible, for there are many flourishes that mirror the harp figures in the accompaniment.

Piano/vocal score: p. 40 (Boosey & Hawkes)

No. 98

Voice: mezzo-soprano
Aria Title: "Do I not draw tears from your eyes" (Dame Doleful)
Opera Title: *Too Many Sopranos*
Composer: Edwin Penhorwood (b. 1939)
Historical Style: 20th-century American (1998)
Range: Bb2 to A5

Fach: contralto
Librettist: Miki Lynn Thompson
Aria Duration: 3:10
Tessitura: F4 to D5

Position: Act I

Setting: The parlor of heaven, the present

Four Divas arrive in heaven, only to learn there is not enough room for all of them in the Heavenly Chorus. Because too many tenors and basses are in Hell, only one of the sopranos will be allowed into the chorus. The sopranos are appalled that they must audition, but submit. Dame Doleful is the first Diva to sing.

She begins with the following spoken words: "All great operas have music sublime. Each has a story of once upon a time." Sung: "But the most important part is the maid who rends your heart, giving soul, giving soul to the rhythm and rhyme." The vocal line ascends by quarter notes to the sustained F♯ at the top of the staff.

The aria begins with five flats and is marked espressivo, piano. Although the piece is tonal, there are many enharmonic tones and challenging intervals. Dame Doleful needs to sing to the top of the staff with clear diction, and the rhythms need to come from the character's energy. She will also need a high A and sustained high A♭ (optional) as well as a B♭ below middle C. It is a fun piece to sing, a character that is "over the top," which shows off the voice throughout the range.

Do I not draw tears from your eyes and make you cry? If you do not start to feel sick at heart—I can't begin to think why. I weep for the lonely maiden whose lover has gone away. I warble and croon, and howl to the moon. So sad, so sad is the part I play.

Do I not draw the tears from your eyes. Are you not truly moved? I sing with heart and voice That is too painful to be soothed. To express all these deep emotions I tremble and moan. (*sung to a high A quarter note, followed by a glissando descending to F at the top of the staff*) I moan and sigh. I tremble, I moan, I moan and sigh. (*There is a six-measure interlude.*) So answer me— in all honesty—Do I not make you cry? (*ending the aria on middle C*)

Piano/vocal score: p. 28 (T. I. S. Music)

Notes by composer Edwin Penhorwood: This audition aria for a mezzo-soprano or soprano with a good low voice should be done with exaggerated expression—nearly over the top. The singer can use plenty of impassioned rubato and special emphasis on expressive words (tears, cry, weep, warble, croon, howl, painful, etc.). Dame Doleful believes she is the most expressive artist alive or dead and has no idea how ridiculous she is.

No. 99

Voice: mezzo-soprano
Aria Title: "Wo in Bergen du dich birgst"
(Fricka)
Opera Title: *Die Walküre*
Composer and Librettist: Richard Wagner
(1813–1883), after German mythology
Historical Style: German Romantic (1862)
Range: D♭4 to G♯5

Fach: contralto
Aria Duration: 6:30
Tessitura: E4 to E5

Position: Act II

Setting: The mountains, central Germany, mythological times

Siegmund and Sieglinde have discovered each other and realized that they are twins. Sieglinde is married to Hunding, who gives Siegmund sanctuary for the night but tells him he will kill him the next day to avenge his murdered kinsmen. In Act II Siegmund and Sieglinde have fled into the mountains to escape him. Wotan orders his favorite daughter, the Valkyrie Brünnhilde, to help Siegmund kill Hunding. Fricka, Wotan's consort, now approaches. As the guardian of marriage, she demands the death of Siegmund, who is guilty of both adultery and incest. When Wotan refuses to abandon Siegmund, Fricka lays bare his deception: Siegmund's fate has been preordained by Wotan. Wotan, as guardian of oaths, is compelled to punish Siegmund and must leave him to his fate without any protection.

This excerpt takes place at the beginning of the second act. Wotan is speaking with his daughter Brünnhilde. He is telling her to bridle her horse to charge into battle, for Siegmund must win. Brünnhilde warns him that Fricka, his wife, approaches: "A golden whip cracks in her hand. Animals bleat with terror. The wheels clatter furiously, she's coming to pick a quarrel. I am glad to leave you in the lurch." "The old storm, the old trouble. But I must make a stand," Wotan resolves.

Fricka enters. "In the mountains, where you hide yourself to escape your wife's notice, here all alone I have sought you out since you must promise me help." The request is strongly worded, but the emotions are reigned in at the beginning. He asks her to freely state what her request is. She has observed Hunding's distress, and she was called to avenge him (as the guardian of marriage). Fricka has promised to punish the pair who have wronged the husband, Hunding. These statements become much stronger in the voice, ascending to F at the top of the staff. In the opera Wotan here

asks what wrongs the two committed, since they are in love. Fricka becomes more confrontational: "How stupid and deaf you pretend to be, as if
you did not really know that it is about marriage, a holy vow." She then
sings "Ich klage/I am complaining," on two strong quarter notes at the top
of the staff. Wotan considers the union unholy without love. Fricka's response is to say Wotan cannot compare respectability to adultery. It is incest between siblings, she states. "My brain reels, my heart stops beating,"
she says in intensely sung rhythms ascending once again to the top of the
staff.

We now come to the climax of the piece emotionally. It is sung at the
top of her range with the strongest rhythms, fortissimo. "Is it the end, then,
of the gods? You think nothing of your noble family, and you reject everything you used to value," she sings. The next passage is more lyrical, connected, in the vocal line: "Why do I protest about marriage and vows since
you were the first to break them? Unceasingly you have cuckolded your
faithful wife. Everywhere you've looked with lecherous eye. You mock and
wound me to the heart. I had to bear it. You have abased yourself to the
dregs of disgrace, and a vulgar human being has bore you twins—now you
would sacrifice your wife to the she-wolf's litter. Do it. Trample on the wife
you have cheated." Here, at the height of her rage, she sings a sustained
G♯.

Piano/vocal score: p. 82 (Schott)

Part III

Tenor Arias

No. 1

Voice: tenor
Aria Title: "Albert the Good!/Heaven helps those who help themselves!" (Albert)
Opera Title: *Albert Herring*
Composer: Benjamin Britten (1913–1976)
Historical Style: 20th-Century English (1947)
Range: A♭2 to B♭5

Fach: leggiero
Librettist: Eric Crozier (1914–1994), after Guy de Maupassant's short story "Le rosier de Madame Husson" (1888)
Aria Duration: 6:30
Tessitura: E3 to G4

Position: Act III

Setting: April 10, 1900; a grocery in a provincial small English town; dusk streams through the window from the street

A disheveled Albert Herring enters the grocery. Albert is a simple young man who lives with his mother and works in their grocery. The "upright" members of the town, led by Lady Billows, have chosen Albert to be the May King because he is so pure and untouched by scandal. However, after the ceremony (in which his drink is spiked by Sid) he has "adventures" and spends all of his award money for "secular" needs.

He comes into the grocery disheveled and tipsy. He is not the timid Albert: he enters "gaily" and punctuates his song by banging the shop door and ringing the bell. He is off balance and is giggling and alternately angry in how he is perceived by his mother. The articulation of the vocal line, use of language, and choice of instrumentation bring this piece to life. Chromaticism, accents, poco a poco accelerando, exaggerate accents, sforzandi, and tremolo in the orchestra all contribute to the energy of the piece. It is characteristic for Albert to speak to himself in this state. At the beginning of the piece he begins by looking for his mother: "It's little Albert, your sugar plum of a prodigal son." The second part of the piece, after he looks for Mum and tries to light the furnace, is to recount his most recent experiences: "Golly! What a party! What a party!"

The critical dramatic moment in the piece is when Albert loosens his belt and begins to sing about what he ate. When he comes to the beverage, he describes about how good the lemonade was, and wonders what is in it. He then comments that Nancy would know the recipe. This moment transitions perfectly to the third section, which describes Nancy and his love life, and moves into a higher range. Britten does not give the singer a sustained tone on top, except for a G above the staff (half note).

Piano/vocal score: p. 247 (Boosey & Hawkes)

No. 2

Voice: tenor

Aria Title: "This is my box" (Kaspar)

Opera Title: *Amahl and the Night Visitors*

Composer and Librettist: Gian Carlo
Menotti (b. 1911)

Historical Style: 20th-century American
(1951)

Range: C♯3 to A♭4

Fach: leggiero

Aria Duration: 1:30

Tessitura: A4 to E4

Position: one-act opera

Setting: Biblical times, a peasant's hut

The opera imagines the journey of the Three Kings (Magi) following the Christmas star. They are bringing gifts for the Christ child, but they stop at the house of Amahl, a young crippled boy, and his mother for shelter. Although the surroundings are poor and primitive, the kings are glad for a place to rest from their journey.

Kaspar is the oldest King and is hard of hearing. He is playful in this little character aria. The aria is addressed to Amahl; the curious boy is impatient and wants to see what is in the box. The text is set syllabically, but there are a few opportunities to sing lyric passages. It is difficult to perform this aria without the requisite props that he is describing, but it can be effectively mimed. The aria is not demanding in range, but diction and characterization are very important. Kaspar is very proud of the jewels that he will present to the newborn King and should display them with a flourish.

Piano/vocal score: p. 25 (G. Schirmer)

No. 3

Voice: tenor
Aria Title: "Scherza infida" (Ariodante)
Opera Title: *Ariodante*
Composer: George Frideric Handel (1685–1759)
Historical Style: Italian Baroque (1735)
Range: D4 to G5

Fach: leggiero
Librettist: Handel after Antonio Salvi (1664–1724), after Ariosto's *Orlando furioso* (1516)
Aria Duration: 8:46
Tessitura: F4 to F5

Position: Act II

Setting: Night, with moonlight. It is a place of ancient ruins, in their midst a view of the secret door in the royal garden of the palace of the King of Scotland. The secret door corresponds with Ginevra.

Polinesso tries to convince Ariodante that Ginevra does not favor Ariodante; instead, Polinesso says, Ginevra is in love with him, but Ariodante doesn't believe him. However, then Ariodante sees Ginevra coming out of the private apartments of Polinesso (Dalinda in disguise). Ariodante, in despair, attempts suicide but is stopped by Lurcanio, his brother. Ariodante sings of his despair:

Scherza infida in grembo al drudo/The unfaithful woman frolics on the bosom of her lover. Io tradito a morte in braccio. Per tua colpa ora men vo/Betrayed, I go off into the arms of death, and it is your fault.

The aria captures Ariodante's state of mind at this particular moment and demonstrates his capacity for many emotions. He is not simply a serene lover; he has a fiery side, showing athletic coloratura in the cadenzas. He displays dejection over his fate, yet also displays a melodic confidence (except for the "scherzo" section). On the word "scherzo/frolic" the harmony is dissonant with suspensions and unstable rhythms in the vocal line.

The aria does not demand an extended range, but the orchestral textures are thick. The singer who created the role (Carestini) had a strong voice. The cadential figures at the end of the aria take the singer up to G above the staff and down to D above middle C. This is a long aria (8:46) and may need cuts if used for audition purposes.

Piano/vocal score: p. 70 (Kalmus full score)

No. 4

Voice: tenor
Aria Title: "Ecco ridente in cielo" (Count Almaviva)
Opera Title: *Il barbiere di Siviglia*
Composer: Gioacchino Rossini (1792–1868)
Historical Style: Bel canto (1816)
Range: F♯3 to B5 (C5)

Fach: leggiero
Librettist: Cesare Sterbini (1784–1831), after Pierre-Augustin Caron de Beaumarchais's play *Le barbier de Séville* (1775) and Giuseppe Petrosellini's libretto for Giovanni Paisiello (1782)
Aria Duration: 5:10
Tessitura: G3 to G4

Position: Act I

Setting: An open square in Seville, nearly dawn, 18th century. At the left, the house of Don Bartolo, with windows having bars and closed blinds that can be unlocked and locked.

Figaro, lantern in hand, ushers in a number of musicians who are carrying instruments. Count Almaviva, wrapped in a cloak, then enters. He wants to attract Rosina with a serenade, so that she will come to her window. The men accompany his serenade, "Ecco ridente." The song is lightly accompanied with strings and guitar. The Count sings lyrically with florid embellishments that come from the poetic use of flowery words. "Are you awake, my dearest?" he asks. The lines are sustained through the tenor's *passaggio*. At the end of the phrases, all beginning on G in the middle of the staff and ascending, she has still not come to the window.

As the band moves into a faster section (allegro), the vocal lines become more florid, faster moving, and the Count is more insistent here, perhaps even impatient. As he sings "quest'anima amante ottenne pieta/mercy is granted to my loving soul," the line becomes increasingly chromatically florid and must be cleanly sung. There are a number of repeats, and a cut from page 17 (second line/third measure) to page 18 (first line/second measure) in the Schirmer score is traditional. The tenor can sing a high C on the last note of "che egual non ha!/that has no equal!" if it can be sung freely.

Piano/vocal score: p. 13 (G. Schirmer)

No. 5

Voice: tenor
Aria Title: "Sì, ritrovarla io giuro" (Don Ramiro)
Opera Title: *La Cenerentola*
Composer: Gioacchino Rossini (1792–1868)
Historical Style: Bel canto (1817)
Range: D3 to C5

Fach: leggiero
Librettist: Giacomo (Jacopo) Ferretti (1784–1852), after Charles Perrault's story *Cendrillon* (1697), Charles-Guillaume Étienne's libretto *Cendrillon* (1810), and Francesco Fiorini's libretto *Agatina* for Stefano Pavesi (1814)
Aria Duration: 6:00
Tessitura: G3 to G4

Position: Act II, scene 1

Setting: A room in the palace of Don Ramiro, the Prince of Solerno

Cenerentola has given Don Ramiro (who is in disguise as the Prince's squire) a bracelet and told him that when he finds the match, she will be his. Then she exits. Alidoro (philosopher and tutor) encourages Ramiro to go after her, and he does. He says he'll no longer be in disguise and sings that he swears that he will find her. He is guided by love, and once he finds her she will never leave him. The opening is extremely florid with his commitment. He leaps up excitedly to a high C. The bracelet she has given him sparkles brightly, but the light in her eyes is far more brilliant.

The next section is lyric and sustained, with embellishments, as he begins to look at the bracelet. The men's chorus gently supports his melody. In the final section (allegro) Ramiro sings that he will press her to his lips and to his heart with syllabic anticipation. With the chorus he says that he will hasten and inquire, seek and find. The vocal line becomes more florid: "Sweet hope and cold fear within my heart are struggling. Love, you must guide me." The singer must be confident in his upper register—there are several high C's in the aria.

Piano/vocal score: p. 244 (Ricordi)

No. 6

Voice: tenor
Aria Title: "Oh, what a lovely ballroom this is!" (Magician/Nika Magadoff)
Opera Title: *The Consul*
Composer and Librettist: Gian Carlo Menotti (b. 1911)
Historical Style: 20th-century American (1950)
Range: F3 to A5

Fach: leggiero
Aria Duration: 2:00
Tessitura: G3 to F4

Position: Act II, scene 2

Setting: The consulate's waiting room in a large anonymous city in a totalitarian European country after World War II

The waiting room at the Consul's office is a cheerless, coldly lit room, furnished with benches and wall desks. In the corner of the room is the desk of the Secretary. A heavy wooden railing separates her from the applicants. Behind her is the door leading to the office of the Consul.

In the consulate's waiting room, Nika Magadoff sits next to Vera Bolonel. At the beginning of the scene, Anna Gomez, exhausted and frantic, is at the railing. Now it is time for the Magician (who has been introduced earlier in the opera) to take his place at the railing. Magda rushes in and bumps into him, trying to reach the desk. The police know that she is trying to secure an exit visa. Magadoff attempts to hold her back. He resents her pushing to the railing ahead of him while he has been waiting patiently.

The aria begins as the Magician produces a bouquet out of midair and presents it to the Secretary. He introduces himself to Magda in crisp rhythms (on middle G) with staccato accompaniment: He is an illusionist, hypnotist, ventriloquist, electrolevitator . . . Next, he produces a white dove. For purposes of singing this excerpt as an aria, you can cut from the last measure of p. 160 to p. 161, second system, second measure. At this point the Magician produces water from the air to fill the flower vase on the Secretary's desk.

The aria calls for precise pitches and rhythm and crisp diction. It alternates between different meters. Many enharmonic pitches that are not diatonic are written. The tenor must sing a high A♭ above the staff on the last word of "I have performed for . . . all the greatest people in the world."

Again for purposes of singing this piece as a solo aria out of context, you can cut from p. 164, last measure, to the top of 168 and pick up "But really!" at the top of the page. At the end of the piece there is a little cadenza to the high A♭ and a passing B♭, as befits the flourish of a magician. "Don't you know? Art is the artist's only passport. I shall prove it to you," he comically boasts. "Prestidigitation!"

Piano/vocal score: p.159 (G. Schirmer)

No. 7

Voice: tenor
Aria Title: "Un' aura amorosa," No. 17 (Ferrando)
Opera Title: *Così fan tutte*
Composer: Wolfgang Amadeus Mozart (1756–1791)
Historical Style: Classical (1790)
Range: D3 to A5

Fach: leggiero
Librettist: Lorenzo da Ponte (1749–1838)
Aria Duration: 4:30
Tessitura: A4 to A5

Position: Act I

Setting: Naples, 18th century

This aria is one of the first serious moments in the opera, after the young men in disguise "meet" the ladies. It is all fun until then. The aria is preceded by horseplay with the young men wanting to collect their bet from Don Alfonso, since the ladies have proven to be steadfast up to this point. Don Alfonso cautions that the "innocent little boys" are premature in celebrating their "victory." The "less sensitive" Guglielmo speaks of his hunger at this point, while the tenor longs for "other nourishment," foreshadowing differences in the young men's personalities that will be more noticeable in the second act.

The poetic Ferrando sings lyrically about his true love, Dorabella. It can be stimulated by seeing and smelling the flower that she could have thrown to the floor in her entrance outburst at the beginning of the scene before she sings "Smanie implacabili." The aria "Un' aura amorosa" shows lyricism and control and takes an effortless high A above the staff, which is sung repeatedly and must not "pop out" but should be sung within the sung line.

> A loving breath from our sweethearts,
> A sweet refreshment will bring to our hearts.
> The heart that is nourished by hope, by love, has no need of better food.

Piano/vocal score: p. 134 (G. Schirmer)

> Notes by singer and voice professor Stanford Olsen: Seamless legato and graceful phrasing are essential in this difficult aria! Keep the breath moving through each note, regardless of duration, and sing all the way to the end of each gorgeous phrase. A slight più mosso at "al cor che nudrito/the heart that is nourished" will help the aria from becoming too broad leading into the recapitulation; and a good understanding of the orchestration helps the singer to use appropriate phrasing and colors. As for those last four or five challenging phrases? They're the reason this has been a yardstick for lyric tenors for over 200 years!

No. 8

Voice: tenor
Aria Title: "Dalla sua pace," No. 11 (Don Ottavio)
Opera Title: *Don Giovanni*
Composer: Wolfgang Amadeus Mozart (1756–1791)
Historical Style: Classical (1787)
Range: D3 to G4

Fach: leggiero
Librettist: Lorenzo da Ponte (1749–1838), after Giovanni Bertati's opera *Don Giovanni Tenorio, o sia Il convitato di pietra* (1787)
Aria Duration: 4:00
Tessitura: G3 to G4

Position: Act I

Setting: Seville, 18th century; open country near Don Giovanni's palace

This aria follows Donna Anna's aria. She asks Don Ottavio (after recounting the murder of her father in clear detail) to take up his sword in vengeance against her father's murderer, now recognized by her to be Don Giovanni. Although Don Ottavio feels for Donna Anna and her pain, he remarks in his recitative before "Dalla sua pace" that he is skeptical of believing that Don Giovanni is capable of committing such "a black crime," for he is "a gentleman."

"Dalla sua pace" was not performed in the premiere of the opera, but was composed for the tenor Morella (who could not sing "Il mio tesoro"), so this aria was inserted in its place, and now usually both arias are sung in productions of the opera. The aria demonstrates the ability to sing limpid phrases lyrically, and musicianship and sensitivity above all. The opening vocal line is extremely exposed, as the accompaniment is simple sustained triads in the low range, played piano, while the singer is singing softly in his upper range.

> Peace of the heart depends on her; Her desires are the breath of life
> to me
> Her grief stabs me to the heart and will bring me death.
> I share her sighs, her anger, her tears. There is no joy for me when
> sadness is within her.

The young singer should not sing the second syllable of "death/morte" with emphasis, even though it is an ascending interval to G above the staff. Repeat the last line at a softer dynamic

Piano/vocal score: p. 100 (Boosey & Hawkes)

> Notes by singer and voice professor George Shirley: The first thing I focus upon is the fact that this monologue is a strong expression of compassion that is in no way the utterance of a weakling! The depth of feeling Don Ottavio holds for Donna Anna must generate the controlled passion that characterizes both this moment and his nature. The Don Ottavio encountered in the opera is a conservative, mature knight who does not under any circumstance act precipitously; he gives due thought to the issue at hand before deciding to pursue a course of action. He does not lose control easily, but when he makes up his mind, he acts. Whatever is sung must be imbued with strength. Proper cooperation between modal and

head registers, in addition to the ability to perform the *messa di voce* securely between D4 and G4, must be mastered if the student is to fully meet the challenge of realizing the expressive goals that constitute this aria. The ability to tinge the reiterations of the word "morte" with either anger or pain and to generate an expressive decrescendo on the G4 at the end of the first iteration of "s'ella non l'ha/if she does not have it" depends entirely upon ownership of the *messa di voce*. Performing the monologue lacking an effective *messa di voce*–head voice is not impossible, but it does severely narrow the interpretative range available to the singer.

No. 9

Voice: tenor
Aria Title: "Il mio tesoro" (Don Ottavio)
Opera Title: *Don Giovanni*
Composer: Wolfgang Amadeus Mozart (1756–1791)
Historical Style: Classical (1787)
Range: D3 to A5

Fach: leggiero
Librettist: Lorenzo da Ponte (1749–1838), after Giovanni Bertati's opera *Don Giovanni Tenorio, ossia Il convitato di pietra* (1787)
Aria Duration: 4:00
Tessitura: B♭4 to F4

Position: Act II

Setting: Seville, 18th century; a dark courtyard in Donna Anna's palace
    This is a more proactive aria for the nobleman Don Ottavio than "Della sua pace." It occurs immediately after Leporello's escape from Donna Elvira, Masetto, Zerlina, and Donna Anna. Don Ottavio's passion emerges in this aria, but the piece needs precise control. It takes enormous breath control to sustain F's near the *passaggio* for over two measures each time. It also shows the ability to sing florid passages. He cares again about Donna Anna and wants her tears to be dried, and he now goes to seek vengeance.
    Beginning with a sustained F for three measures followed by a florid passage of 16th notes to the end of the phrase, he sings, "My treasure, now come and console, and from her beautiful eyes seek to dry her tears." He then ascends to a high A (quarter note) at "Tell her that I have gone to seek

vengeance and only at that time will I return." The text is then repeated with a more complex florid passage, complete with chromaticism before the recapitulation of the melody.

Piano/vocal score: p. 230 (Boosey & Hawkes)

Notes by singer and voice professor George Shirley: This is Don Ottavio's vengeance aria, the only time in which he allows himself to lose control of his temper. The magnificent, long fioritura passage that ends the statement "nunzio voglio tornar!/(as) ambassador I wish to return!" embodies and encompasses the unleashing of his fury, the apex of his rage, and its gradual restraint. The great Irish tenor John McCormack set the mark for all would-be interpreters of this great aria with his phenomenal one-breath intoning of this melismatic vow of vengeance.

Attempting to gain ownership of the level of breath management necessary to spin the long phrase at "tornar/return" in one unbroken line is a wonderful exercise that will pay dividends even if the ultimate goal is never reached. I often purloin passages from Mozart arias and use them as vocalizes, making therapeutic use of the rigorous technical challenges they pose for the singer. Mozart will give you a thorough, healthy workout; Puccini, on the other hand, can kill you!

Again, ease and flexibility in the *passaggio* are requisite for mastery of this aria. Exercising the *messa di voce* up through G♯4 or higher, a most frustrating task for many of us, will strengthen the ability of the voice to function with increased malleability in this zone. Training oneself to think each pitch of the fioritura passages a split second before they are uttered will heighten the ability of the vocal mechanism to respond instantaneously and accurately to the changes in pitch. It is a fact that we cannot sing any passage faster than we can think it. This thought process is subconscious, but if we strive to wed the conscious to it, we can only enhance our control over the final product.

No. 10

Voice: tenor
Aria Title: "Quanto è bella," Cavatina (Nemorino)
Opera Title: *L'elisir d'amore*
Composer: Gaetano Donizetti (1797–1848)
Historical Style: Bel canto (1832)
Range: E3 to G5

Fach: leggiero
Librettist: Felice Romani (1788–1865), after Eugène Scribe's libretto for Daniel-François Auber's *Le philtre* (1831)
Aria Duration: 2:25
Tessitura: G3 to E4

Position: Act I, scene 1

Setting: Rural northern Italy, a small village, early 19th century

At the beginning of the opera the chorus of young ladies establishes the atmosphere of the piece. The lonely Nemorino (a young peasant) is pining over Adina: "How beautiful and dear she is." He also tells us in this aria his lack of confidence and hope: "I'm not capable of inspiring her. I'm always an idiot. I don't know but to sigh." The important energy in this aria comes from his two questions at the end of the aria. He asks, "Who will clear my mind? Who will teach me make myself beloved," and sets himself (and the audience) up for the later entrance of Dulcamara—the salesman of the magic elixir.

Nemorino's lack of confidence is demonstrated musically by rather large intervallic skips and the accidentals in the vocal line. When he sings that his heart is not capable of inspiring Adina, there are accents on almost every syllable, almost like he is pounding his breast as he sings. However, most of the aria is very lyric and "humbly" sung. The women's chorus then joins in as Nemorino repeats, "Who will clear my mind? Who will teach me to make myself beloved?"

The singer will need to keep an even line without reaching during the large intervallic skips to the top of the staff throughout the aria. The top pitch in the piece that is sustained is a G (quarter note)

Piano/vocal score: p. 8 (Ricordi); p. 13 (G. Schirmer)

No. 11

Voice: tenor
Aria Title: "Una furtiva lagrima," Romanza (Nemorino)
Opera Title: *L'elisir d'amore*
Composer: Gaetano Donizetti (1797–1848)
Historical Style: Bel canto (1832)
Range: F3 to A♭4

Fach: leggiero
Librettist: Felice Romani (1788–1865), after Eugène Scribe's libretto for Daniel-François Auber's *Le philtre* (1831)
Aria Duration: 3:45
Tessitura: B♭3 to A♭4

Position: Act II, scene 2

Setting: Rural northern Italy, a small village, early 19th century

Earlier in the act Nemorino (a young peasant) believes that the magic elixir that he has drunk is working, and that Adina now loves him. He has turned the tables on her so that she would know how it feels. "Love takes revenge on me . . . and Nemorino rejects me now," she says. All of the girls are now infatuated with him. He doesn't realize that this is because Gianetta and the girls have discovered that the formerly penniless Nemorino is the heir to a rich uncle who has died. Nemorino attributes this to the magic elixir.

With the words "una furtiva lagrima," Nemorino describes how he noticed one furtive tear in Adina's eye. The vocal line begins on the F and G at the top of the staff. "She seemed to envy those girls. What more do I want?" Nemorino sings. At the end of the first verse comes the realization "M'ami/She loves me." Although the aria, with the English horn introduction and the harp accompaniment, sounds plaintive, it is not a sad aria. On the contrary, it represents a recognition that "she loves me" at the center of the piece. And at the end of the aria he sings, "Oh heaven, I shall expire; I can't ask for more."

The aria is isolated dramatically, coming after the light Dulcamara-Adina duet. Nemorino's aria is the only time the harp is used in the entire opera, on the words "Cielo, si puo morir/Heavens, I then could die!" After this, the tone changes to a more "optimistic" major key, leading to a rapidly sung cadenza. There is a sense that this melody seems to wander until it finds the key words "M'ami" and "Cielo, si puo morir." The embellishments are important. They are not vocal decorations but are heartfelt, arising from the turbulent emotions of Nemorino.

Piano/vocal score: p. 229 (Ricordi); p. 349 (G. Schirmer)

No. 12

Voice: tenor

Aria Title: "O wie ängstlich" (Belmonte)

Opera Title: *Die Entführung aus dem Serail*

Composer: Wolfgang Amadeus Mozart (1756–1791)

Historical Style: Singspiel (1782)

Range: E3 to A5

Fach: leggiero

Librettist: Gottlieb Stephanie the younger (1741–1800), after Christoph Friedrich Brentzer's *Bellmont und Constanze, oder Die Entführung aus dem Serail* set by Johann André (1781)

Aria Duration: 5:00

Tessitura: A4 to F♯4

Position: Act I

Setting: The seaside country estate of Pasha Selim, Turkish coast; the middle of the 16th century

Belmonte is a Spanish nobleman who comes to save his beloved Konstanze, who has been kidnapped by pirates and sold to Pasha Selim. The trail has led to the Pasha's villa on the seashore of Turkey. At this point in the first act he has met the dangerous overseer Osmin, and the aria follows the dialogue with his sevant Pedrillo, who was with Konstanze when she was abducted. Pedrillo reveals that Konstanze is alive, and the aria is Belmonte's reaction to the news. He also learns that she is now with the Pasha. "What are you saying?" wonders Belmonte. He is eager to see her; his heart beats again as he trembles and falters:

Oh how anxiously, how passionately beats my love-filled heart! And tears at our reunion will be the reward for the pain of separation. Already I tremble, waver, hesitate and falter; my chest heaves. Is that her whispering? It makes me uneasy. Was that her sighing? My cheeks are hot, flushed. Does love deceive me? Is this a dream?

The aria is lyric and florid, but it also has much text, and the diction is extremely important. At the beginning of the aria the phrases are almost chopped as to be breathless (with contributing repeated rhythmic patterns in the accompaniment), but then are passionately florid (32nd notes) at "liebevolles Herz!/Heart filled with love." He is excited, but the aria cannot be too declamatory because of where he is and what is at stake. Many thoughts and emotions spill out, but especially at the beginning, the aria has a stately quality that befits Belmonte's noble station. When sung in German, with many words and important consonants, the vocal line is still important. In the middle section of the aria he works through his hopes to the point where he asks whether it is a dream that he has found her, entering on high A above the staff (ritardando) as he sings, "War es ein Traum?/Was it a dream?" There are no other sustained higher pitches or climactic phrases. The notes above the staff are in passing.

Piano/vocal score: p. 47 (Peters)

> Notes by singer and voice professor Stanford Olsen: The successful interpreter of this virtuosic aria will insist on a tempo quick enough to negotiate the long, extended phrase in one breath, yet not so quick that the "anxious" coloratura becomes frantic. Scrupulous observation of Mozart's phrasing and dynamic markings will guarantee an elegant execution of this compelling minidrama.

No. 13

Voice: tenor
Aria Title: "Dal labbro il canto" (Fenton)
Opera Title: *Falstaff*
Composer: Giuseppe Verdi (1813–1901)
Historical Style: Italian Romantic (1893)
Range: F3 to B♭5

Fach: leggiero
Librettist: Arrigo Boito (1842–1918), after William Shakespeare's comedy *The Merry Wives of Windsor* (1600–1601) and incorporating material from his histories *Henry IV,* Parts I and II (1597–1598)
Aria Duration: 3:00
Tessitura: A♭3 to G♭4

Position: Act III, scene 2

Setting: Windsor Forest, shortly before midnight, early 15th century in the reign of Henry IV. There is a "delicate atmosphere."

Shortly before midnight a masquerade is planned to confound Sir John Falstaff. Fenton arrives disguised as Oberon, the fairy king, and sings a serenade that ends as his sweetheart, Nanetta, answers his "call." Fenton should listen to the "orchestra" introduction to the aria. It is descriptive and sets up the atmosphere before he begins to sing.

From lips the rapturous song flies through the nocturnal silences and goes far off.

And finally it finds other human lips which respond to it with their word.

Then the note, which is not longer alone, vibrates with joy in a secret harmony

And, charming the antelucan air with another voice, flies back to its origin.

There it takes on tone again, but its interest always aims at uniting whoever divides it.

Thus did I kiss the mouth of desire!

A kissed mouth doesn't forfeit good luck.

But the song dies in the kiss that touches it.

Quiet, dolcissimo, and the lyric romantic quality of this aria and Nannetta's to follow are important in establishing a contrast to the ribald comedy of the joke on Falstaff. It is a lyric and quiet aria with gentle articulative separations. It must not break the calm of the scene. But the aria also exhibits a quality of youthful ardor, expectation and urgency, and hope. It is best, when singing the aria out of context (in an audition), for the piece to end on Fenton's line "ma il canto muor nel bacio che lo tocca/but the song dies in the kiss that touches it," showing the climactic B♭ in the piece. The voice in the passage "Con altra voce al suo fonte rivola/With the other voice it comes home again" must ascend to the G♯ without crescendo.

Piano/vocal score: p. 331 (G. Schirmer)

No. 14

Voice: tenor
Aria Title: "Ah, come il cor di giubilo" (Lindoro)
Opera Title: L'italiana in Algeri
Composer: Gioacchino Rossini (1792–1868)
Historical Style: Bel canto (1813)
Range: G3 to B5

Fach: leggiero
Librettist: Angelo Anelli (1761–1820), first set by Luigi Mosca (1808)
Aria Duration: 2:15
Tessitura: G3 to A5

Position: Act II

Setting: A small room between the apartments of the Bey of Algiers and those of his wife. There is a sofa in the middle of the room.

This aria follows a meeting between Isabella and Lindoro. Thinking that he is about to marry Elvira, she accuses him of being faithless, but he persuades her that she is mistaken. They come up with a plot to escape and plan to meet in the grove; however, for the moment they will separate. The cavatina "Oh, come il cor di giubilo/Oh, how the heart rejoices" finds Lindoro exulting with joy: "She sustains feelings of happiness in him." The cavatina (allegro) is extremely florid. The excitement of the piece is found in the off-the-beat accents, dotted rhythms, and appoggiaturas. The singer needs to go up to high A frequently in half-note values.

How the heart rejoices, exults in this moment!
To find an irate lover, and then placate her cruelty.
With this, love, your gifts are these delights.
You sustain the affections of my happiness.

Piano/vocal score: p. 209 (G. Schirmer)

No. 15

Voice: tenor
Aria Title: "Fantaisie aux divins mensonges" (Gérald)
Opera Title: *Lakmé*
Composer: Léo Delibes (1836–1891)
Historical Style: French Romantic (1883)
Range: F3 to A5

Fach: leggiero
Librettists: Edmond Gondinet (1828–1888) and Philippe Gille (1831–1901), after Pierre Loti's novel *Le mariage de Loti* (1882)
Aria Duration: 6:00
Tessitura: A♭3 to A♭4

Position: Act I

Setting: 19th-century India, a sacred grove

Gérard, a young officer in the British Army, is engaged to Ellen, the daughter of the governor. Ellen comes upon the stockade and is curious about what lies beyond, and who these people are. The governess warns her to not be curious. Gérard comes upon the scene with his friend, Frédéric, and receives information about the Indian Brahmin and his daughter, an enchantress (Lakmé).

Gérard, a young man who does not seem to be serious about anything, is suddenly interested in the "young, pretty princess." They venture beyond the barrier and see jewels in a shrine. Gérard is left alone and decides to sketch the jewels so that a copy can be made for Ellen to wear on their wedding day. In solitude as he begins to sketch the jewels, he realizes a "foolish fear" among the peaceful scene. Seeing the jewels that have adorned the princess, he begins to think of her and struggles with the exotic power that the jewels seem to have. There is dialogue in the opera, leading into the aria:

> Fantasy of divine illusions, you return to lead me astray once more.
> Go, return to the country of dreams, phantom of golden wings
> This bangle must have adorned the heathen's arm.
> I might clasp in mine the hand that slipped it on.
> The golden circlet has followed the errant steps
> Of a little foot that only treads on moss or flowers.
> And this necklace, still smelling sweet of her redolent person yet,
> The necklace has felt her faithful heart beating all aflutter
> At hearing her loved one's name!
> Be gone! Fly, visions, ephemeral dreams that trouble my reason,
> Fantasy of divine illusions.

The repeat is sung softly, with a line that sweeps up to high, sustained Ab. "O fantaisie/Oh, fantasy" and the phrases that follow start the phrase on a high Ab and are marked piano. The final phrase "aux ailes d'or!/on wings of gold!" ends on a sustained pianissimo high Ab.

(Translation by Nico Castel)

Piano/vocal score: p. 61 (International)

No. 16

Voice: tenor
Aria Title: "Quando le sere al placido"
(Rodolfo)
Opera Title: *Luisa Miller*
Composer: Giuseppe Verdi (1813–1901)
Historical Style: Italian Romantic (1849)
Range: D3 to A♭4

Fach: leggiero
Librettist: Salvatore Cammarano (1801–
1852), after Johann Christoph Friedrich von
Schiller's "bourgeois tragedy" *Kabale und
Liebe* (1784)
Aria Duration: 5:30
Tessitura: G3 to F4

Position: Act II, scene 3

Setting: The hanging gardens in the castle of Count Walter, a small village in the Tyrolese area ruled by the Count

Rodolfo, Count Walter's son, is a brash young man. He is unknown to the village and is using a false name. He is enamored of Luisa, a village girl. His father, the Count, believes his son is "raving mad, that his reason is blinded by his lack of wisdom."

Before the aria, Luisa writes a letter under duress to Rodolfo to say she never loved him in order to save her father. Rodolfo hurries in from his apartment with Luisa's letter in his hand. He summons Wurm (who has been earlier promised to Luisa, who wants nothing to do with him). It is an accompanied recitative with many unaccompanied passages. The text is very important:

If only I could deny trust in my very eyes.
If heaven and earth, mortals and angels were to reassure me that she is not guilty.
This is her writing! Such treachery! So black, so false.
But what of hopes, joy, tears, anguish? All is falsehood, betrayal, deception.

The orchestra plays a sobbing figure (strings chromatically descending) as Rodolfo sings, "When at eventide, the tranquil glimmer of a starry sky with me." At first, the aria seems eerily tranquil after such an agitated recitative, with only double-dotted rhythms to betray Rodolfo's agitation. With the words "she gazed lovingly and I felt this hand pressed by hers," he crescendos up to high G and A♭ and cries out passionately, "Ah, she betrayed me!" Again, with a pulsing downward pattern of dotted 16th-32nd rhythms, he repeats softly in the middle range, "Ah! Mi tradia/Ah! She betrayed me!"

He relents in the next section: "Then I, silent, ecstatic, would hang on to every one of her words when she in angelic tones said I love you/amo." As the aria ends, Rodolfo repeats "She betrayed me" on a fortissimo high Ab with a pianissimo immediately on the F (fermata), as if he cannot believe the betrayal. A cadenza is usually added to the aria. Rodolfo will later poison himself and Luisa and kill Wurm. The aria is dramatic but has many lyric moments.

(Translation by Nico Castel)

Piano/vocal score: p. 219 (Ricordi)

No. 17

Voice: tenor
Aria Title: "Già di pietà mi spoglio" (Mitridate)
Opera Title: *Mitridate, re di Ponto*
Composer: Wolfgang Amadeus Mozart (1756–1791)
Historical Style: Classical (1770)
Range: D3 to A5 (C5)

Fach: leggiero
Librettist: Vittorio Amedeo Cigna-Santi (c. 1730–after 1795), after Jean Racine's tragedy *Mithridate* (1673)
Aria Duration: 2:15
Tessitura: A4 to G4

Position: Act II

Setting: Apartments in the Macedonian port of Nymphaeum, first century B.C.

Mitridate comes to the realization that both sons are plotting against him separately. He will have revenge upon both of them, he says in the recitative that proceeds the aria: Sifare, on orders from Mitridate, is hiding as Aspasia enters. She implicates Sifare, while he cannot stop her from speaking the truth. Sifare comes out of hiding, and Mitridate tells them both that he will go to the palace and await them to "exact a famous revenge" with the slaughter of his sons and his bride. As would be expected, the aria is sung strongly, deliberately, with repeated quarter notes, syllabically set. The opening phrase of quarter, two 8th notes, to dotted quarter, is very decisive. The aria calls for high, sustained G's, with an opportunity in the final cadenza to show a sustained high C.

The aria also calls for the repetitions of phrases, some of the vocal lines doubled in the orchestra. The only chance for relief from the strident expression of the vocal line is in the middle section, when Mitridate is singing twice in the middle voice "Padre ed amante offeso/An outraged father and lover," marked fp on beats 1 and 3 of each measure. Then, the first time he sings "e voglio vendetta/and I want revenge," it is marked piano in the orchestra, almost as if Mitridate is reluctant to voice his decision out loud. It is too terrible to admit.

Piano/vocal score: p. 252 (Bärenreiter)

No. 18

Voice: tenor
Aria Title: "Quel ribelle e quell'ingrato" (Mitridate)
Opera Title: *Mitridate, re di Ponto*
Composer: Wolfgang Amadeus Mozart (1756–1791)
Historical Style: Classical (1770)
Range: C3 to A5

Fach: leggiero
Librettist: Vittorio Amedeo Cigna-Santi (c. 1730–after 1795), after Jean Racine's tragedy *Mithridate* (1673)
Aria Duration: 4:45
Tessitura: G3 to G4

Position: Act I

Setting: A square in the Macedonian port of Nymphaeum, first century B.C.

Mitradate finds out from Arbate, Governor of Nymphaeum, that his son Farnace conspires to take Mitridate's betrothed and his kingdom. Mitridate would like to see Farnace dead. This recitative and aria conclude Act I. The royal guards are in formation when Mitridate hears the news and sings the aria. In the accompanied recitative Mitridate speaks first as he addresses his own heart, but finds that his jealous rage is too strong. "For him I will forget that I am his father." I want him to fall lifeless at my feet . . . In his blood I avenge more than one offense" (his son and his betrothed).

The aria has a militaristic quality, with trumpets in the accompaniment. The brutality of his feelings are brought out by the opening phrases. "Quel ribelle e quel'ingrato/that rebel and that ungrateful son" is delineated by 8th rests, but the singer must still phrase to "l'ingrato/ungrateful (*son*)" and "sangue/blood" without accenting the 8th notes too heavily. Intervallic leaps between middle C and high A are sung on the word "più/more," while softer phrases like "più d'un fallo/shall I avenge" provide contrast as Mitridate tries to compose himself in front of the troops, or confides to Arbate in a conspiratorial tone. At the end of the aria, Mitridate departs for the city as Act I concludes.

Piano/vocal score: p. 137 (Bärenreiter)

No. 19

Voice: tenor
Aria Title: "Se di lauri" (Mitridate)
Opera Title: *Mitridate, re di Ponto*
Composer: Wolfgang Amadeus Mozart
(1756–1791)
Historical Style: Classical (1770)
Range: C3 to C5

Fach: leggiero
Librettist: Vittorio Amedeo Cigna-Santi
(c. 1730–after 1795), after Jean Racine's
tragedy *Mithridate* (1673)
Aria Duration: 4:45
Tessitura: G3 to G4

Position: Act I, scene 10

Setting: A Macedonian seaport with two fleets anchored on opposite sides of the harbor; in the distance lies the city of Nymphaea; first century B.C..

The story of the opera is built around the historical character of Mithridates VI (132–63 B.C.), King of Pontus. He spent much of his reign fighting the growing power of Rome in Asia Minor. The opera takes place after Mitridate's final defeat by the Roman general Pompey in 66 B.C.. While on campaign, Mitridate has left his young betrothed, the Greek princess Aspasia, in the care of his two sons, Sifare and Farnace. This scene is Mitridate's entrance at the end of the first act.

Arbate, the Governor, receives Mitridate and the royal guard on the beach. The aria "Se di lauri/Fruitful shores" is preceded by a march as a fleet of vessels sail in. Upon his entrance to the city, Mitridate states that while he lost the battle, he has not lost his courage. He sings, "even defeated and oppressed I do not return in shame. And I bring to you as ever a great heart in my breast."

In the recitative that follows the aria, Mitridate reveals that he is relieved to return from his long military campaign, but is bitter about his defeat at the hand of Pompey. All of his efforts have been swept away during a "single night" of battle. "You will no longer see the happy Mitridate of the past," he sings.

"Faithful shores, if I do not return to you" is a sustained aria. It has the requisite Mozart intervallic leaps in the second section of middle C to high A above the staff, and a leap from G in the middle of the staff to high B. The second part of the aria (same text and frame of the melody with different connected pitches and embellishments) benefits from a lyric approach, but the aria still has sustained pitches that should be sung with a rich tone. This aria also shows a wide range, with tones that descend to middle D, and a passing high C with sustained high A and B. The phrases do not build to a climax that represents carrying the weight of the voice to the top of the range.

Piano/vocal score: p. 100 (Bärenreiter)

No. 20

Voice: tenor
Aria Title: "Rosa del ciel" (Orfeo)
Opera Title: *L'Orfeo*
Composer: Claudio Monteverdi (1567–1643)
Historical Style: Italian Baroque (1607)
Range: D3 to F4

Fach: leggiero
Librettist: Alessandro Striggio (c.1573–1630), after *Euridice* by Ottavio Rinuccini (1600)
Aria Duration: 2:00
Tessitura: D3 to D4

Position: Act I

Setting: The fields of Thrace, mythological times

Orfeo, the great poet and singer, is to be married to Eurydice. He sings this hymn to his beloved. Nymphs and shepherds rejoice in song and dance. The mood of celebration built up during this act is extremely important for the events to follow to have impact (Eurydice's death from a snake bite). The aria is written in a recitative style and has a light accompaniment:

Rose of the heavens, life of the world, and noble offspring of him who rules the universe, O Sun, who encompasses and sees all from amongst the celestial orbits, tell me, did you ever see a happier and more fortunate lover than I? It was indeed a happy day, my beloved, when first I saw you, and happier still the hour when I sighed for you, since, when I sighed, you too sighed; but most happy of all, the moment when you gave me your fair hand in pledge of pure devotion. Had I as many hearts as eternal Heaven has eyes, or as these pleasant hills have leaves in verdant May, all would be brimful and overflowing with such joy as today makes me content.

This is a good piece for a young male voice that has not settled into the tenor/ lyric baritone voice. There is only one high F in passing, otherwise a sustained E♭ and D only. Attention to correct rhythm with diction is important. Singers must understand and inflect properly the text. The melody is driven by the text.

Piano/vocal score: p. 20 (Carisch, Milan)

No. 21

Voice: tenor
Aria Title: "O paradis sorti de l'onde" (Vasco da Gama)
Opera Title: *L'Africaine*
Composer: Giacomo Meyerbeer (1791–1864)
Historical Style: French Romantic (1865)
Range: F3 to B♭5

Fach: lyric
Librettist: Eugène Scribe (1791–1861), completed by François-Joseph Fétis (1784–1871)
Aria Duration: 3:30
Tessitura: B♭4 to G♭4

Position: Act IV

Setting: 15th century. Vasco da Gama, a naval officer, has sailed for the West Indies, but a storm drives his ships to the coast of India. The scene is outside a Brahmin temple. On stage left is the entrance of the temple; on the right is a palace. Priestesses, priests, Amazons, jugglers, and warriors enter.

Da Gama is the sole Portuguese male survivor of his ship. He first appears, accompanied by a rapturous clarinet melody beneath flute tremolo, a musical translation of his bedazzlement by the lush surroundings. He takes up the clarinet tune in the slow section of a grand air ("O paradis/Oh paradise"); his ecstatic music about the discovery of a new land is interrupted by shouts for his blood, and in the cabaletta he begs the warriors for mercy. Just as he is about to be beheaded, Sélika (a slave in Portugal but Queen in her native land) appears and orders her subjects to stop. She and da Gama later marry.

In the aria "O paradis," da Gama sings about the beauty of the island and the sparkling blue sky. He proclaims that this "new world belongs to me," which he will offer to his country (Portugal). The vocal line is legato and florid, with range needed within the vocal line to high B♭. After the initial melody and chorus reaction, there is a recitative section: "They call for my death? No!" In the next section (allegro agitato con moto), he asks "to be released to go home and tell his homeland, or let them learn that the victorious Vasco lost his life on this shore for immortal honor." The chorus continues to demand da Gama's death. Understandably, da Gama is agitated to think that he could lose his life and his honor. Finally, he asks for "God to receive him in his inmost heart." The high note is a B♭, but the tessitura is mostly within the staff but sung dramatically.

Piano/vocal score: p. 331 (Brandus & Dufour)

No. 22

Voice: tenor

Aria Title: "Che non avrebbe il misero" (Foresto)

Opera Title: *Attila*

Composer: Giuseppe Verdi (1813–1901)

Historical Style: Italian Romantic (1846)

Range: G3 to A5

Fach: lyric

Librettist: Temistocle Solera (1815–1878) with alterations by Francesco Maria Piave, after Zacharias Werner's tragedy *Attila, König der Hunnen* (1808)

Aria Duration: 3:35

Tessitura: G3 to A5

Position: Act III

Setting: In a forest between Attila's camp and Ezio's (Romans)

Foresto is waiting in the forest for the wedding feast of Odabella and Attila to take place; his heart is full of bitterness, and he is deeply troubled at what he supposes is the girl's infidelity. The orchestral introduction of Act III is moving in its chordal progression. "This is the meeting place where I will learn the hour of the wedding (of Attila and Odabella)." He describes how he will be a "thunderbolt" in his response. The wedding procession is on the way, says Uldine. Foresto tells Uldine to go to Ezio and the Roman troops and wait for the signal to attack Attila. This attack will also kill Odabella. "You will see how Foresto turns to you," he says with venom (up to G above the staff, forte). The chords before the aria begins are surprisingly quiet in contrast. Much of the recitative is without accompaniment, and punctuated only with instrumental "comments."

The aria begins andantino, con dolore. Foresto proclaims that he would have offered anything for Odabella. Ascending to a high G and Ab, he asks heaven for pardon. The aria calls for tremendous control, once again, with a crescendo up to G above the staff sustaining the note through the measure with crescendo and then diminuendo ("Heaven, why do you treat as an equal to angels one whose soul is so evil?"). He repeats this question four times, beginning each time with "perché/why." Each time the arching phrases ascend, beginning piano, to a forte high Ab. After the aria, Odabella escapes the wedding and asks for Foresto's forgiveness. He refuses. Odabella will mortally stab Attila as the Romans approach to fight him.

(Translation by Nico Castel)

Piano/vocal score: p. 176 (Ricordi)

No. 23

Voice: tenor
Aria Title: "Soon now my dearest" (Jeník)
Opera Title: *The Bartered Bride* (*Prodaná nevěsta*)
Composer: Bedřich Smetana (1824–1884)
Historical Style: Czech Nationalist (1866)
Range: E3 to A5

Fach: lyric
Librettist: Karel Sabina (1813–1877)
Aria Duration: 3:30
Tessitura: G3 to G4

Position: Act II

Setting: Inside a country inn

In spite of the love between Jeník and Mařenka, her parents have arranged her marriage to the son of a wealthy landowner. Kecal has brokered the arranged wedding. In Act II Mařenka tries to trick the proposed groom, and Jeník does the same. Kecal wants to broker Jeník's marriage to a wealthy girl if he will forsake Mařenka. To everyone's shock, Jeník agrees, but he has a plot in mind so that he and Mařenka will be united.

In the aria "Soon now my dearest," Jeník is trying to reassure Mařenka that they will be together. The piece starts on E (piano) and goes up to sustained high G and A: "Just one more hour and the trouble is past. Joy follows sorrow, sun follows rain." Throughout the aria, Jeník tries to comfort and reassure Mařenka. There are many dynamic changes, accents, and a playful staccato. Good vocal control is necessary to sing "joy follows sorrow," with the second unaccented syllable of sor-*row* on the high A, which should not be forced.

Piano/vocal score: p. 143 (G. Schirmer)

No. 24

Voice: tenor
Aria Title: "God o' mercy" (Captain Vere)
Opera Title: *Billy Budd*
Composer: Benjamin Britten (1913–1976)
Historical Style: 20th-century English (1951)
Range: C3 to A♭4

Fach: lyric
Librettists: E. M. Forster (1879–1970) and Eric Crozier (b. 1914), adapted from Herman Melville's story *Billy Budd, Foretopman* (1891)
Aria Duration: 2:10
Tessitura: E3 to F4

Position: Act II, scene 2

Setting: The captain's cabin on the berth deck of *H.M.S. Indomitable,* 1797, during the French wars

Claggart, the master-at-arms, tells Vere that Billy Budd (whom Claggart dislikes) poses a threat of mutiny. Vere does not believe him and sends for Billy Budd so that Claggart may confront him. Billy's stammer prevents him from responding to Claggart's false accusation, and in frustration Billy's right fist shoots out, striking Claggart on the forehead. Claggart falls and, after a couple of gasps, lies motionless as Vere sings, "God o' mercy," kneeling by Claggart's corpse.

Vere claims responsibility at the end of the monologue: "It is I whom the devil awaits." The piece has varied forms of expression: "O terror, what do I see?" is set dramatically, with a sustained high G♯ above the staff. Dynamics range from pianissimo to forte. Vere wants to save Billy, but he cannot. By the same token, he cannot condemn him because Vere is responsible as the Captain of the ship.

Piano/vocal score: p. 271 (Boosey & Hawkes)

No. 25

Voice: tenor
Aria Title: "I accept their verdict" (Captain
Vere)
Opera Title: *Billy Budd*
Composer: Benjamin Britten (1913–1976)
Historical Style: 20th-century English (1951)
Range: D♭3 to A♭4

Fach: lyric
Librettists: E. M. Forster (1879–1970) and
Eric Crozier (b. 1914), adapted from Herman
Melville's story *Billy Budd, Foretopman*
(1891)
Aria Duration: 2:50
Tessitura: F3 to F4

Position: Act II, scene 2

Setting: The captain's cabin on the berth deck of *H.M.S. Indomitable,* 1797,
during the French wars

The officers have prepared the cabin for the court. Before the court con-
venes, they carry the body of Claggart, master-at-arms, into another small
stateroom while Captain Vere stands rigidly at the side. Vere tells the court
exactly what has happened. As Billy Budd has killed Claggart, Vere and
the court must obey the articles of war, even though Billy is a loyal sailor
and earlier was unjustly accused by Claggart. Captain Vere tells the court
only exactly what he has seen, nothing more, and will not save Billy. The
penalty is hanging until death from the yardarm. "I accept the verdict,"
Vere tells the three officers who have pronounced sentence. Vere coldly accepts the verdict and (outwardly) remarks that Claggart will be buried with
full naval honors. "All hands will witness punishment in the morning."
Inwardly he is torn between duty and feelings for Billy's unfair situation.

The officers salute and exit, leaving Vere alone. He repeats the words to
himself ("I accept their verdict"), and remarks, "Death is the penalty for
those who break the laws of earth." He is the leader of "this fragment of
floating earth," and therefore is responsible for its order. He sings in short
melodic motivic fragments. There is much variety in the dynamics, rhythmic patterns, and articulation. When he sings, "I, Edward Fairfax Vere,
Captain of the Indomitable . . . Lost with all hands on the infinite sea," he
sings fortissimo on the F at the top of the staff, finally descending at "on
the infinite sea." At the end of the aria, Vere sings "The messenger of death"
to high G♭ ending on F at the top of the staff with accents, and goes into
Billy's cabin to convey the verdict to him.

Piano/vocal score: p. 303 (Boosey & Hawkes)

No. 26

Voice: tenor
Aria Title: "I am an old man" (Captain Vere)
Opera Title: *Billy Budd*
Composer: Benjamin Britten (1913–1976)
Historical Style: 20th-century English
(1951)
Range: D3 to A5

Fach: lyric
Librettists: E. M. Forster (1879–1970) and
Eric Crozier (b. 1914), adapted from Herman
Melville's story *Billy Budd, Foretopman*
(1891)
Aria Duration: 4:45
Tessitura: F3 to F♯4

Position: Prologue

Setting: Vere reflects on events that took place on board the battleship *H. M. S. Indomitable,* 1797, during the French wars

Captain Edward Fairfax Vere reflects on his life. He is now an old man and retired from the Navy. He ponders the nature of goodness and concludes that "all is tinged with imperfection." Obviously, the choice and color of language are of utmost importance, set off by variety of rhythms, dynamics, and articulation markings. Much of the text in this first excerpt is on a repeated tone, but there are some intervallic skips that are challenging, especially since the orchestra helps dramatically but does not support the singer harmonically.

When Vere sings, "There is always some stammer in the divine speech" (referring to Billy Budd's stammer that played a role in his striking and killing the master-at-arms, Claggart), the vocal line extends to a sustained high A♭ to G. He focuses on his own command of the *Indomitable* during the French wars and is tormented by his questionable leadership and judgment. When he says, "but I have been lost on the infinite sea," Britten colors this text with enharmonic intervals on the first syllable of the word "infinite," while the strings evoke the atmosphere of the sea. The words "Who has blessed me? Who saved me?" are chilling in the way they are set simply, with a transparent orchestra underneath.

Piano/vocal score: p. 1 (Boosey & Hawkes)

No. 27

Voice: tenor
Aria Title: "We committed his body to the deep" (Captain Vere)
Opera Title: *Billy Budd*
Composer: Benjamin Britten (1913–1976)
Historical Style: 20th-century English (1951)
Range: D3 to A♭4

Fach: lyric
Librettists: E. M. Forster (1879–1970) and Eric Crozier (b. 1914), adapted from Herman Melville's story *Billy Budd, Foretopman* (1891)
Aria Duration: 4:30
Tessitura: G3 to F4

Position: Epilogue

Setting: The quarterdeck of *H.M.S. Indomitable,* 1797, during the French wars. The light grows on Vere as an old man, as in the Prologue.

Captain Vere begins firmly, shamefully aware that he has been blessed and saved by the man (Billy Budd) whom he himself failed to save. "I could have saved him." He knew it, even his shipmates knew it, though "earthly laws silenced them." The monologue is alternately peaceful and dramatic. "O what have I done," Vere cries out on high F♯. "But he has saved and blessed me."

The next section is sung very quietly, molto tranquillo: "I was lost on the infinite sea." This section builds to a high, sustained G above the staff, forte with accents: "I've seen sighted a sail in the storm . . . there's a land where she'll anchor for ever." By the time Vere sings, "I am an old man now, and my mind can go back in peace" he has rediscovered his genuine, consummate goodness and is now at peace with himself. The opera ends quietly, morendo, with a slow curtain.

Piano/vocal score: p. 343 (Boosey & Hawkes)

No. 28

Voice: tenor
Aria Title: "Che gelida manina" (Rodolfo)
Opera Title: *La bohème*
Composer: Giacomo Puccini (1858–1924)
Historical Style: Verismo (1896)
Range: E♭3 to C5

Fach: lyric
Librettists: Giuseppe Giacosa (1847–1906)
and Luigi Illica (1857–1919), based on
Henry Mürger's novel *Scènes de la vie de
bohème* (1845–1849) and his play (with
Théodore Barrière) *La vie de bohème* (1849)
Aria Duration: 4:00
Tessitura: A♭3 to A♭4

Position: Act I

Setting: Puccini is very specific and clear about the setting of this apartment. It is Christmas Eve in Paris (1854). There is a window, a stove, a bed, table used by Rodolfo to write, and an artist's easel for Marcello, the painter. Books lie scattered around, and there are two candles. Rodolfo has briefly warmed the apartment (he used one of his plays for fuel in the stove), but the apartment is cold once again. There is the smell of paint and painter's supplies.

Mimì, living alone and suffering from coughing fits, hears Rodolfo's friends loudly leave the apartment. She shyly knocks on his door. Her candle has gone out, she needs it lit, but she also is most likely in need of companionship. Dropping her key (perhaps on purpose), she and Rodolfo look for it in the dark.

Rodolfo uses this opportunity to take her hand while she is looking for the key and comforts her by simply noticing that her hand is very cold as the aria begins. He changes the subject, talking about the beauty of the moon. Perhaps she feels uncomfortable and moves to leave. Entering a man's apartment alone in the 1800s, she is understandingly shy and reluctant to reveal too much about herself. Rodolfo asks her to stay ("aspetta, signorina/wait, miss"); he just wants to tell her about his life as a poet. He is inspired. Puccini uses the sweeping melody in the orchestra to emphasize text ("in poverta mia lietascialo da gran signore/I'm poor but I live like a lord").

The aria has a high tessitura, but it has lyrical sections that highlight the softer side of the character: Rodolfo is sensitive, he is charmed by Mimì's shyness, he reveals his dreams, but he doesn't want to scare her away. Rodolfo expands when he talks about "his dreams of the past stolen away, but the theft does not dismay him because hope has replaced it." Just before the conclusion of the aria, there is an optional high C ("la dolce speranza/sweet hope"). The aria is through composed without repetitions. Rodolfo's aria inspires Mimì to talk, and she opens up in her aria ("mi chiamano Mimì"). By the end of the scene, they are deeply in love with each other.

(Translation by Peter J. Nasau)

Piano/vocal score: p. 68 (Schirmer)

Notes by director and opera professor Sandra Bernhard: It is important for the tenor here to see the important effect on their hands touching in the sustained single note in the orchestra before the aria begins. This is not melodic vocalization at the beginning, but a tender observation about the coldness of her hands, and that is his focus.

No. 29

Voice: tenor
Aria Title: "It must be so" (Candide)
Opera Title: *Candide*
Composer: Leonard Bernstein (1918–1990)
Historical Style: 20th-century American (1956)
Range: G3 to E4

Fach: lyric
Librettist: Lillian Hellman (1905–1984) (rev. versions by Hugh Wheeler), based on the novel by Voltaire (1756); lyrics by Richard Wilbur; additional lyrics by John Latouche, Dorothy Parker, Hellman, Bernstein, and (in revised versions) Stephen Sondheim
Aria Duration: 2:00
Tessitura: G3 to E4

Position: Act I, scene 2

Setting: Westphalia, the castle of the Baron

The author Voltaire introduces the characters: Candide is a young man who is determined to follow his instructor's creed of mindless optimism. Even after being banished from his homeland, captured by Bulgarians, beaten and left for dead by the Spanish Inquisition, robbed of everything he owns, and torn repeatedly from the woman he loves, Candide still clings to the philosophy that everything is for the best in this, "The best of all possible worlds."

The aria "It must be so" follows Candide's spirited duet with Cunegonde, "O happy we." Cunegonde receives an elaborate and impromptu lecture from Dr. Pangloss on the specific gravitational forces by arranging themselves in a particular position. Intrigued by this new curriculum, Cunegonde rushes off to find Candide and put this new bit of knowledge to the test, and happily, the two of them agree that it is indeed a pleasant bit of philosophy! Unfortunately, feeling no shame and having made no attempt to hide themselves from view, the young couple are interrupted in their carnal experiment by the squeals of young Maximilian, who has spied on them through a window. The entire family quickly descends upon the innocent lovers, and a startled Candide finds himself forever banished from Westphalia. As he trudges off, never to return home, Candide sings of his loyalty to Dr. Pangloss's philosophy. There must be a very good reason, after all, for his banishment, for as the doctor has taught him: "Everything is for the best in this, the best of all possible worlds."

Candide's simple, straightforward piece is subtitled "Candide's first meditation." Harp and strings in chordal patterns accompany the two verses of the aria. The only challenging part of the song is the E at the top of the staff sung on the unaccented syllable and pianissimo. Clarity of text is very important. The singer should employ a tone and stance that is earnest, innocent, wide-eyed, and idealistic.

Piano/vocal score: p. 97 (Boosey & Hawkes)

No. 30

Voice: tenor
Aria Title: "Ah, se fosse intorno al trono,"
No. 8 (Tito)
Opera Title: *La clemenza di Tito*
Composer: Wolfgang Amadeus Mozart
(1756–1791)
Historical Style: Classical (1791)
Range: F♯3 to A5

Fach: lyric
Librettist: Caterino Tommaso Mazzola
(1745–1806), after Pietro Metastasio (1734)
Aria Duration: 2:00
Tessitura: A4 to F♯4

Position: Act I

Setting: The imperial garden, Rome, 79–81 A.D.

Tito addresses the Romans to tell them that Vesuvius has erupted and people are fleeing. He asks for a temple to be built for him. After Sevilia throws herself upon Titus's mercy, begging him to let her marry Annius, Titus agrees and says that if all were so honest, ruling would be easier: "If you, Sevilia, wish to fully show me your gratitude, to others inspire your gratitude. Try to let it be known to all that I am more pleased by truth though it may offend me, than by flattering lies."

In the recitative before the aria it is revealed that Sevilia refuses the throne to be faithful to Annius: "Ah, if about a throne every heart were so sincere, a vast empire would be not a torment but bliss. Rulers should not have to suffer such deep anxiety to distinguish hidden truth from deception."

The aria is a decisive expression, with some lovely legato phrases, including "ma saria felicita/not a torment but bliss" and "un vasto impero/a vast empire" on decisive half notes and two quarter notes. No notes are sustained above the staff. A dotted quarter rhythm is sung on the -i- vowel on the high A.

Piano/vocal score: p. 56 (International)

No. 31

Voice: tenor
Aria Title: "Del più sublime soglio," No. 6 (Tito)
Opera Title: *La clemenza di Tito*
Composer: Wolfgang Amadeus Mozart (1756–1791)
Historical Style: Classical (1791)
Range: E3 to A5

Fach: lyric
Librettist: Caterino Tommaso Mazzola (1745–1806), after Pietro Metastasio (1734)
Aria Duration: 2:45
Tessitura: G3 to G4

Position: Act I, scene 4

Setting: The Forum in Rome, adorned with arches, obelisks, and trophies; in the foreground the exterior of the Capitol and a magnificent street leading up to it; 79–81 A.D.

Senators and envoys from the provinces are present to pay the Senate their annual tribute. Titus and the Praetorian Guard, surrounded by a large crowd, come down from the Capitol. The orchestra plays a march. Annius and Publius hail Titus and his choice of bride. Titus announces that he will marry Sextus's sister, Servilia, because Rome will be pleased with the choice. He sings that the real advantages of being a ruler are being able to reward faithful subjects like Servilia with favors—like this marriage (even though she is in love with Annius).

The aria (andante) starts very slowly and uses a long, fluid, legato line. "This is the only reward of the highest office. The rest of it is torment and slavery." The vocal line at "che avrei/what should I have, were I also to lose the only happy hours I have in helping those in distress" is more florid with dotted rhythms and shows active passionate expression. The G at the top of the staff is the only sustained high tone (half note), and is sung on the -u- vowel in "servitù: "nel sllevar gli amici/for comforting friends, for dispensing treasures and richly rewarding the virtuous." This is an excellent Mozart aria for a young, lyric tenor.

Piano/vocal score: p. 43 (International)

No. 32

Voice: tenor
Aria Title: "Il était une fois à la cour d'Eisenach" (Hoffmann)
Opera Title: *Les contes d'Hoffmann*
Composer: Jacques Offenbach (1819–1880)
Historical Style: French Romantic (1881)
Range: E3 to A5

Fach: lyric
Librettists: Jules Barbier (1825–1901) and Michel Carré (1819–1872), based on their play (1851), based on tales by E. T. A. Hoffmann
Aria Duration: 5:00
Tessitura: E3 to A5

Position: Prologue

Setting: Luther's tavern, Nuremberg, 19th century

During the intermission of Stella's opera, a group of rowdy students are drinking in the tavern. The poet Hoffmann enters with Nicklaus (who is singing Leporello's opening "Notte giorno mal dormire" from Mozart's *Don Giovanni*); Hoffmann is moody and irritable. The poet has been tortured by a dream. The students want a story, and Hoffmann, throwing off his dark mood, calls for wine and tells the students the legend of Kleinzach, an incredibly ugly dwarf.

The narrative of this story is lightly and brightly told, like a ghost story, and brings the audience in to listen. It is syllabic, and the descriptive French text is important. Hoffmann must then sing up to an A above the staff on a sustained fermata with ringing high notes.

In the narrative he describes Kleinzach's legs, his hump, his head, but as Hoffmann begins to describe the features of the dwarf's face, he pauses and shifts (andante) to the subject of the face of his beloved. This section is difficult to sing, as it climbs stepwise through the *passaggio* from E to F, F♯ at the top of the staff, forte, then has a piano lyric expression as he sings tenderly about her eyes. The voice does not move above the staff, but stays in the transition area (E, F, F♯) as he sings of her vibrant, sweet voice. Nathaniel pulls him out of his reverie. The students want to hear about the dwarf. Hoffmann comically ends the story of Kleinzach, whose coat flops when he drinks too much.

Piano/vocal score: p. 37 (G. Schirmer)

No. 33

Voice: tenor
Aria Title: "Ah lo veggio quell'anima bella"
(Ferrando)
Opera Title: *Così fan tutte*
Composer: Wolfgang Amadeus Mozart
(1756–1791)
Historical Style: Classical (1790)
Range: F3 to B♭5

Fach: lyric
Librettist: Lorenzo da Ponte (1749–1838)
Aria Duration: 4:00
Tessitura: B♭4 to A♭5

Position: Act II, scene 2

Setting: Naples, 18th century, woods

The two couples are walking in the woods. The men are in disguise and are enjoying the "game," as the two women do not know who the men really are. Guglielmo has gone off with Dorabella (Ferrando's beloved), and Ferrando is with Guglielmo's love, Fiordiligi. Guglielmo and Dorabella have just sung a duet, and Guglielmo has been successful in wooing her. Before Ferrando's aria he cries out to Fiordiligi: "Barbara! Perché fuggi?/ Barbarous one! Why are you torturing me by fleeing?" Fiordiligi sees the darkness in this turn of events. She wants to be left alone in peace. All Ferrando wants is one glance to him, but she wants him to leave her alone and shouts for him to leave. "Oh heavens, look at me," he cries.

Ferrando begins to sing the aria to Fiordiligi: "Ah lo veggio quell'anima bello/I see that beautiful soul doesn't know to resist my weeping." The aria begins softly, as if he wants to caress her with his voice and not disturb her peace. However, he does want her to look at him and see his suffering. He knows that she will have pity on him if she will just look.

The aria is in two sections: in the first part (allegretto) Ferrando sings persuasively. It is marked legato with many connected 8th-note patterns in the phrases that extend the range to high A and B♭ within the phrase. The interval at "rubella/rebellious" where there is an interval of C in the middle range to high A above the staff to the unstressed final syllable (la), also on high A, is difficult. Toward the end of this section, there are sustained F's at the top of the staff for five beats that are repeated. She is still silent.

In the second section (allegro), Ferrando tries another choice of words to gain her attention. He sings, "Ah, cessate speranze fallaci, la crudel mi condanna morir/Ah, stop, wrong hope, the cruel one condemns me to die."

This section is especially challenging as Ferrando sings the phrase "condanna morir" on a phrase that keeps ascending to a passing high B♭ on the -i- vowel of "morir" three times in succession, with little chance to breathe in between the phrases. This aria is very demanding and is sometime cut in productions of the opera, since the tenor has two arias in Act II, while other principals have only one aria in the act.

Piano/vocal score: p. 243 (G. Schirmer)

No. 34

Voice: tenor
Aria Title: "Tradito, schernito" (Ferrando)
Opera Title: *Così fan tutte*
Composer: Wolfgang Amadeus Mozart (1756–1791)
Historical Style: Classical (1790)
Range: G3 to A5

Fach: lyric
Librettist: Lorenzo da Ponte (1749–1838)
Aria Duration: 3:30
Tessitura: G3 to A5

Position: Act II, scene 2

Setting: Naples, outdoors, in nature, when played in a four-scene configuration

Guglielmo has seduced Dorabella (Ferrando's lover) in their previous duet. Guglielmo with Ferrando has a wager that their beloved women will be true and constant. Since Guglielmo has seduced Ferrando's woman, his own Fiordiligi remains true, and he satisfies his own male ego in seducing a woman. He tries to calm Ferrando by singing "Donna mie/My ladies" to the women of the world, saying that even though man defends their honor with the sword, if necessary, women are in return deceitful.

After Guglielmo leaves the stage, Ferrando muses over the events of the day and the conflicts that he feels. He is the more sensitive of the two men and feels everything strongly. He feels that Don Alfonso is laughing at him. He wants to avenge himself, and his anger is now directed toward Dorabella, whom he would like to "erase from his heart."

The accompanied recitative takes him to the cavatina, which begins with fragmented, angry expressions separated by rests with fermatas. He feels scorned by her faithless heart. Then, with a beautiful, arching long phrase, Ferrando shows the breadth of his feelings with an intervallic jump from middle B♭ to high A♭ in a beautiful vocal phrase, which then repeats with some simple appoggiatura figures. He becomes more active and passionate as the phrase expands with "Io sento per essa le voci d'amor/I feel for her the pleadings of love." He repeats "d'amor" to F at the top of the staff twice, then to high A♭ sustained for two beats. The phrase "le voci d'amor" is sung again more passionately with an extended G above the staff for eight beats with an 8th-note flourish. Ferrando repeats the words "le voci" to a high A♭ on a half note before a final "le voci d'amor."

In the last section there is hardly time for a breath. Ferrando's ardent realization gives his emotions momentum toward the final phrase. Even though all of these phrases are passionate, they must be varied dynamically and sung with vocal control within the passion. By the end of the aria Guglielmo and Don Alfonso have walked in upstage to listen in the background.

Piano/vocal score: p. 274 (G. Schirmer)

No. 35

Voice: tenor
Aria Title: "Com'è gentil la notte" (Ernesto)
Opera Title: *Don Pasquale*
Composer: Gaetano Donizetti (1797–1848)
Historical Style: Bel canto (1843)
Range: G♯3 to A5

Fach: lyric
Librettists: Giovanni Ruffini (1807–1881) and the composer, after Angelo Anelli's libretto for Stefano Pavesi's *Ser Marc' Antonio* (1810)
Aria Duration: 4:00
Tessitura: A4 to A5

Position: Act III

Setting: A small grove in Don Pasquale's garden, late at night. On the left, steps leading to the house; on the right, a summerhouse; at the rear, a gate.

This serenade follows a duet by Pasquale and Malatesta in which a sputtering Pasquale vows revenge for Norina's walking all over him. Ernesto's aria, found almost at the end of the opera, brings back the melody first heard in the overture. Even though there are mean-spirited aspects of the plot, it is all in the name of love, this melody tells us. In this serenade, accompanied by guitar and the chorus, Ernesto (nephew of Don Pasquale) is trying to coax Norina from the summerhouse. Poetic images are invoked in the serenade: "How gentle is the night in April, blue the sky, the moon is without a veil. All is peace, mystery, love. Accented with breezes of love. When I will die, I will weep."

The song has the sweetness and simplicity of an Italian folk song. The challenge is for the tenor to sing easily and lyrically at the top of the staff through the *passaggio*. The vocal line is important with light embellishments, clear articulation, and energized rhythm. The aria should be lyrically sung, and never pushed.

Piano/vocal score: p. 206 (Ricordi)

No. 36

Voice: tenor
Aria Title: "And where is the one who will mourn me" (Brack Weaver)
Opera Title: *Down in the Valley*
Composer: Kurt Weill (1900–1950)
Historical Style: American Folk Opera (1948)
Range: E3 to F♯4

Fach: lyric
Librettist: Arnold Sundgaard (b. 1911)
Aria Duration: 1:45
Tessitura: G3 to F4

Position: One-act opera

Setting: A small-town jail on the edge of the American frontier; the night before Brack Weaver is to be executed for murder

Aria plot notes from the *G. Schirmer American Aria Anthology: Tenor,* edited by Richard Walters (used by permission):

In the words of the composer, this folk opera was "mainly conceived for production by nonprofessional groups" and requires minimal staging.(It was written at the urging of G. Schirmer editorial director Hans Heinsheimer.) The plot expands on the American folk song "Down in the Valley," in which two young men fight over a young woman, and one dies in the struggle. The survivor, Brack Weaver, is arrested and condemned to death for murder. Brack sits in his jail cell on the night before his execution, asking the guard if a letter has come from his beloved Jennie. It has not. There will be no more mail before the execution. Brack asks to be left alone.

The piece is folklike, with its simple, straightforward melody and verses. There are opportunities for artistic, sensitive singing by singing it softly with great feeling. The range stays between the staff (with an optional high A, piano), but the final pitch, an extended high F♯, calls for a diminuendo.

Piano/vocal score: p. 41 (*G. Schirmer American Aria Anthology: Tenor*)

No. 37

Voice: tenor
Aria Title: "Wenn der Freude Tränen fliessen" (Belmonte)
Opera Title: *Die Entführung aus dem Serail*
Composer: Wolfgang Amadeus Mozart (1756–1791)
Historical Style: Classical (1782)
Range: C3 to A♭4

Fach: leggiero
Librettist: Gottlieb Stephanie the younger (1741–1800), after Christoph Friedrich Brentzer's *Bellmont und Constanze, oder die entführung aus dem Serail* set by Johann André (1781)
Aria Duration: 4:15
Tessitura: F3 to G4

Position: Act II

Setting: The garden of Pasha Selim's country house, the coast of Turkey; middle of the 16th century

Finally, after almost two entire acts of the opera, Belmonte and Konstanze are united. Belmonte is a wealthy Spanish nobleman. He says that to see his beloved is worth more than all riches. They are finally able to meet after Pedrillo gets Osmin (Pasha's overseer) drunk and on his way to sleep it off. Although the aria has long, flowing lyric phrases, within its lyricism there are dotted values that must be energetic. Once again Belmonte demonstrates his enthusiasm by leaping intervals of D above middle C up to sustained high A♭ above the staff, and then middle C to high G.

The aria is in two parts: part 1 (adagio) is in cut time, and part 2 (allegretto) is in 3/4 time. As Belmonte talks about the pain that separation causes ("Dass wir uns niemals wiederfinden/that we never find again") he notes that it is his first experience with "the pain of separation."

When tears of joy are flowing, love smiles sweetly on lovers;
To kiss them from her cheeks is love's happiest, greatest reward.
Ah Konstanze, to see you, and in rapture and bliss,
To hold you close to my faithful heart is a prize no royal crown could match!
Ah, this blissful discovery made me first experience the pain of separation.

Part I (adagio) takes careful intonation. Control is important. There are places for cadential figures at the end of some phrases. The highest note is A♭ above the staff. This aria is followed by a quartet (double duet, actually), in which Belmonte confesses to harboring doubts about Konstanze's fidelity, as does Pedrillo about his own sweetheart, Blonde.

Piano/vocal score: p. 108 (Peters)

No. 38

Voice: tenor
Aria Title: "Frisch zum Kampfe!" No. 13 (Pedrillo)
Opera Title: *Die Entführung aus dem Serail*
Composer: Wolfgang Amadeus Mozart (1756–1791)
Historical Style: Singspiel (1782)
Range: D3 to B5

Fach: lyric
Librettist: Gottlieb Stephanie the younger (1741–1800), after Christoph Friedrich Brentzer's *Bellmont und Constanze, oder Die Entführung aus dem Serail* set by Johann André (1781)
Aria Duration: 2:45
Tessitura: F♯3 to A5

Position: Act II

Setting: The seaside country estate of Pasha Selim, Turkish coast; middle of the 16th century

Pedrillo is a servant and Blonde's lover. Osmin, who works for Pasha Selim, also loves Blonde, who is Konstanze's servant. Pedrillo confides to Blonde that he has a plot to put Osmin to sleep while they all escape. She is overjoyed and sings an aria that shows her joy for herself and Konstanze. Pedrillo is inspired to sing "Frisch zum Kampfe/Forward into battle" to show Blonde that he has decided to take charge and be the hero, even though he himself is probably more a lover than a fighter. "Only faint hearts are afraid," he says, encouraging himself to bolster his own nerves: "Should I tremble? Should I hesitate?"

The aria is declamatory, with half and quarter notes, then dotted-quarter/ 8th notes. The orchestra alternates quickly between forte and piano. The singer who is interested in exploring character in this piece will discover the humor between the strong declamatory "decisions" contrasted by the tentative nature of some of the questions and light staccato in the accompaniment. Pedrillo is excited for much of the piece, and the aria is pitched high. He has sustained high A's above the staff over nine beats, and one of the chordal outlines goes to high B. Beginning on "Nein, ach nein, es sei gewagt/No, let it (*my life*) be wagered," he decides to be resolute (after a fermata rest, which signifies the conclusion of the first part of the aria). As he makes the decision to show strength, Pedrillo then sings chordal outlines in the melody, like a military bugle call.

Piano/vocal score: p. 98 (Peters); p. 94 (Boosey & Hawkes)

Notes by singer and voice professor Jerold Siena: The aria shows two aspects of Pedrillo's character: the attempt to be daring and heroic, alternating with the fearful and frightened. It's a little like Papageno when he approaches the dead dragon in *Die Zauberflöte*. I remember quite clearly Leinsdorf's insistence on these two qualities in the aria when we did it with the Boston Symphony. Of course, in an audition the singer must show absolute security in the top A's, interspersed with self-doubt and fear, but also try to make Pedrillo charming and loveable, as he is in the rest of the opera.

No. 39

Voice: tenor
Aria Title: "Kuda, kuda, kuda, vy udalilis" (Lensky)
Opera Title: *Eugene Onegin*
Composer: Pyotr Ilyich Tchaikovsky (1840–1893)
Historical Style: Russian Romantic (1879)
Range: E3 to G#4

Fach: lyric
Librettists: The composer and Konstantin Shilovsky (1849–1893), based on Aleksandr Pushkin's verse novel *Eugene Onegin* (1831)
Aria Duration: 5:50
Tessitura: F3 to G4

Position: Act II, scene 2

Setting: A rustic mill on the banks of a wooded stream. Early morning; the sun has barely risen; winter in St. Petersburg, Russia, late 18th century.

After Onegin's makes advances toward Lensky's fiancée, Olga, Lensky challenges Onegin to a duel. In the moments before the duel, Lensky reminisces about his happy youth as he awaits Onegin's party. He believes he will die, and he doesn't really care, because he has already lost Olga. His greatest loss in death would be that he would never again see Olga's face. Lensky is with his friend Zaretsky, who is impatient. In the exchange before the aria, Zaretsky asks, "Where is he? Is he coming?" Zaretsky is nervous, but Lensky sits and meditates about "his golden days of spring." He is philosophical: "Blessed is a day of simple tasks and blessed is the day of troubles."

In the aria each phrase begins higher in the voice, and the lines descend. The vocal line is lyrical as he muses about the past. The middle section (più mosso) is more active as Lensky observes that the world will go on as before even as his life ends. The world will forget him. As the melody returns, Lensky whispers to the vision of Olga: "Will you, Olga, shed a tear?" His outcry, "Ah, Olga, I did love you!" is fortissimo on A♭ above the staff followed by a dotted quarter note/8th note on "Come, I am your husband!" He ends in the lower/middle voices with "how far away you seem now, happy days."

Piano/vocal score: p. 176 (Richard Schauer, London)

No. 40

Voice: tenor
Aria Title: "Salut! Demeure chaste et pure" (Faust)
Opera Title: *Faust*
Composer: Charles Gounod (1818–1893)
Historical Style: French Romantic (1859)
Range: E♭3 to C5

Fach: lyric
Librettists: Jules Barbier (1825–1901) and Michel Carré (1819–1872), after Part I of Johann Wolfgang von Goethe's play *Faust* (1808)
Aria Duration: 5:50
Tessitura: G3 to G4

Position: Act II

Setting: The garden of Marguerite in a German village, 16th century. There is a wall at back with a little door and a bower at left, a house at right, with a window toward the audience. There are trees and shrubs.

In the original play, Faust makes a pact with the devil because as an old man he despairs because there is so little time left to read, study, and learn the secrets of the world. In the opera by Gounod, the devil entices the old man to make the pact through the vision of the lovely, youthful Marguerite.

In Act II Mephisto leads Faust to the outside of Marguerite's house. The aria begins with Faust's observation that he feels himself taken hold of his very being by love. He has been an old man, and now he has newfound youth again. He "greets" her home as the retreat of her soul. He salutes nature as the source of her beauty. The aria is lyric as it unfolds, becoming stronger at the poco più mosso: "O nature, c'est la que tu la fissi belle!/Oh, nature, it's here you've made her so beautiful!" The orchestral accompaniment is a cascade of 16th notes that signify the blood flowing in him now has more "youthful" energy. There is a crescendo to the high A at "Tu fis avec amour/You (*nature*) made, with love, the woman blossom," but it is passing and not sustained. The recapitulation of the first melody ("Salut demeure") asks the tenor to leap from E♭ to a high C on a fermata; it must be connected, not pushed or accented, and always within the line.

This aria can show a lyric tenor voice at its best. It is reverent, never wanting to alarm Marguerite inside, and never wanting to disturb nature. Faust is in awe of all he observes around him. At the same time, he again feels the energy of youth that flows through his body. There is the expectation of meeting Marguerite for the first time. She is still idealized to him.

Piano/vocal score: p. 114 (G. Schirmer)

No. 41

Voice: tenor
Aria Title: "Spirto gentil" (Fernando)
Opera Title: *La favorita* (Italian version)
Composer: Gaetano Donizetti (1797–1848)
Historical Style: Bel canto (1840)
Range: G3 to C5

Fach: lyric
Librettists: Alphonse Royer (1803–1875), Gustave Vaëz (1812–1862), and Eugène Scribe (1791–1861), after Baculard d'Arnaud's play *Le comte de Comminge* (1764), based on the story by Leonora de Guzman
Aria Duration: 4:00
Tessitura: B4 to G4

Position: Act IV

Setting: The monastery of St. James of Compostella, Castile, Spain, c. 1340; here and there are tombs and wooden crosses. The dawning day illuminates only the uncovered part of the cloister.

Fernando is a young novice at the monastery of Saint James of Compostela. Not knowing that Leonore is the "favorite" of the King, Fernando asks the King for her hand in marriage and receives it because he has led Castile to victory in a battle over the Moors. Thinking that his bride is pure, he prepares to marry her. However, before she appears, he finds out that she has been the lover of the King. Heartbroken, he returns to the monastery and mourns for the betrayal and loss of his love: "The mistress of the King . . . into an abyss hollow under an infernal trap my glory has been swallowed, and from my sad heart all hope is gone."

> Angel so pure, who in a dream I believed to have found—you, whom I loved!
> Along with hope, sad lie! Fly away forever.
> For the love of a woman my love for God had weakened; have pity!
> I have given Thee my soul, pity, Lord, let me forget.
> Forgetfulness . . .

The aria has a long, plaintive vocal line. The above English translation is of the original French version ("Ange si pur"), but the aria is also often sung in Italian.

Piano/vocal score: p. 322 (Ricordi)

No. 42

Voice: tenor
Aria Title: "Ah, mes amis . . . Pour mon âme" (Tonio)
Opera Title: *La fille du régiment*
Composer: Gaetano Donizetti (1797–1848)
Historical Style: Bel canto (1840)
Range: G3 to C5

Fach: lyric
Librettists: Jean François Bayard (1796–1853) and Jules-Henri Vernoy de Saint-Georges (1799–1875)
Aria Duration: 4:00
Tessitura: G3 to C5

Position: Act I

Setting: A rustic scene in the Tyrol: an army campsite in a valley in the Swiss Tyrolese Mountains, 1815

Tonio is a Tyrolese peasant in love with the *vivandiere* Marie. He saved her life when she nearly fell off a precipice. Tonio has been lurking around the military encampment hoping to talk to Marie. Seized as a spy, he is claimed by Marie as her personal prisoner. Hoping to marry her, Tonio is surprised to learn that her future husband must be a member of the regiment. Tonio promptly enlists. After Tonio has been made a member of the French grenadiers, he approaches some of the members and explains that he has joined the regiment because he loves the regiment's "daughter," Marie.

The aria is spirited (allegro vivace), and is accompanied by strings, clarinets, horns, trumpets, and kettledrums. "I shall march under your flags": Tonio ascends to an extended high G. "Love, which has turned my head, is making me into a hero." He continues on staccato 16th notes, "si, si, si, si/yes, she for whom I live and breathe has deigned to smile upon my vows. And this sweet hope of happiness has shaken my mind and my heart." He ends the aria on an optional high B♭.

After the chorus sings, Tonio continues with the cabaletta "Pour mon âme/For my soul." Although it is at a fast tempo, the line is more sustained to the octave high C intervallic leaps that this piece is known for.

Piano/vocal score: p. 92 (Belwin Mills)

No. 43

Voice: tenor
Aria Title: "I thought I heard a distant bird" (Donald)
Opera Title: *Gallantry*
Composer: Douglas Moore (1893–1969)
Historical Style: 20th-century American (1958)
Range: E3 to G♯4

Fach: lyric
Librettist: Arnold Sundgaard (b. 1911)
Aria Duration: 2:15
Tessitura: F♯3 to F♯4

Position: One-act chamber opera

Setting: A television studio

The style of the piece is TV soap opera—complete with announcer. Donald is a patient in a hospital who needs his appendix removed. He immediately recognizes Lola, the anesthetist, and he professes his love for her. They sing a duet. The operating surgeon, Dr. Gregg, has also wooed Lola, but she is annoyed that he did not tell her that he was married. The surgery begins as the two argue. "One kiss to save your darling," the doctor says. Agitated, Lola threatens to expose the doctor. "He has gone too far."

Meanwhile, Donald is left abandoned on the operating table as Lola rushes off and the doctor follows. Dazed, Donald softly sings, "I thought I heard a distant bird." To show his disorientation there are many accidentals and awkward wandering intervals. "Who'll seek her woodland shelter" begins with the same tritone interval, but otherwise the piece is through composed. Demands at the top of the range include (forte) high G♯ and F♯. Donald is delirious at the end of the piece and quite obviously in pain.

Piano/vocal score: p. 52 (G. Schirmer)

No. 44

Voice: tenor
Aria Title: "Oh, the Lion May Roar," Aria of the Worm (Bégearss)
Opera Title: *The Ghosts of Versailles*
Composer: John Corigliano (b. 1938)
Historical Style: 20th-century English (1991)
Range: C♯3 to B5

Fach: lyric
Librettist: William M. Hoffman (1928), the text suggested by Arrigo Boito's epic poem *Il re orso* and Pierre-Augustin Caron de Beaumarchais's play *Le mère coupable* (1792)
Aria Duration: 4:15
Tessitura: G3 to A5

Position: Act I, scene 1

Setting: Present day in the palace of Versailles; the ghosts of the court of Louis XVI have been haunting the palace since their demise during the French Revolution

In the first scene of Act I, we learn that Patrick Honoré Bégearss, Count Almaviva's best friend and confidant, has been pretending and, in reality, is his worst enemy. Bégearss plans to steal the jewels the Count is planning to sell at a reception of the Turkish embassy. Driven by overwhelming jealousy and greed, Bégearss, who is covertly an agent of the Revolution, tells us the secret of his ability to thrive and survive.

The aria is a showy piece, allowing the villain Bégearss to sing conspiratorial piano phrases ("Oh, the lion may roar, and the eagle may soar, and man my sail the darkest sea") that swell to a forte ("But the worm lives on eternally") and back again to a subito piano ("Long live the worm"). In the aria Bégearss has opportunities to display many colors in his voice: mysterious, hateful, bitter, joyful, triumphant, and many others. It is not too often that the tenor gets to sing the art of the villain with such exciting music. Bégearss continues to revel in the story of the worm: "Cut him in two, each part'll renew. Slice him to bits, the worm persists. He still crawls on, scales walls on sheer will and burrows burning sand."

As the melody continues in the orchestra, Bégearss speaks over the orchestra, in a *Sprechstimme* style: "The wind whistles and the storm bristles, and mud—covers the ground." Bégearss extols the lasting qualities of the worm, repeating a variation of the A section, but this time with a quasi cadenza and "maniacal laughter" before the final triumphant phrase: "But the worm lives on eternally." It is followed once more with a conspiratorial whisper, "Long—live—the worm."

Piano/vocal score: The score for *The Ghosts of Versailles* has not been released for general publication. One copy does exist in the U.S. Library of Congress. "The Aria of the Worm" can be purchased individually through Hal Leonard Publishing, and is available in the *G. Schirmer American Aria Anthology: Tenor.*

No. 45

Voice: tenor

Aria Title: "Firenze è come un albero fiorito" (Rinuccio)

Opera Title: *Gianni Schicchi*

Composer: Giacomo Puccini (1858–1924)

Historical Style: 20th-century Italian (1918)

Range: F3 to B♭5

Fach: lyric

Librettist: Giovacchino Forzano (1884–1970), based on an episode in Dante's *Inferno* (c. 1307–21)

Aria Duration: 2:50

Tessitura: B♭3 to A♭4

Position: One-act opera (part three of *Il Trittico*)

Setting: The bedchamber of Buoso Donati, Florence, 1299

As his family quarrels over the fact that the deceased Buoso Donati has left virtually nothing of value to the family in his will, Rinuccio tries to tell them that Gianni Schicchi (father of his beloved Lauretta) will solve the problem. Rinuccio asks and answers the questions that concern the family over the involvement of Schicchi. He then sings an ode to their great home-town, Florence, hailing it as home to the painter Giotto and the Medici (e.g., men who built the city). He goes on to name their true successor: Gianni Schicchi; to emphasize his point, he sustains the last -i- vowel of Schicchi on a high B♭. The aria is argumentative but lyric and has momentum. Rinuccio does not allow the relatives to raise any objections, or interrupt the flow of the aria. This aria demonstrates the character's youth, energy, and passion.

> You're wrong! He's refined! Astute . . .
> Every trick of laws and codes he knows and knows intimately.
> A jokester! A prankster! Is there a new and rare joke to be played?
> It's Gianni Schicchi who prepares it!
> His cunning eyes light up with laughter.
> His strange face [is] shaded by that great nose of his which seems like a huge, isolated tower!
> He comes from the countryside? Well? What does that mean?
> Enough of these narrow-minded and petty prejudices!
> Florence is like a blossoming tree which has its trunk and branches in the Piazza dei Signori;
> But the roots bring forth new vitalities from the fertile valleys!
> And Florence grows; and staunch palaces and slender towers rise up to all the stars!

The Arno River, before running to its mouth sings, kissing the Piazza Santa Croce;
And its song is so sweet and so sonorous that the little brooks have run down to it in chorus!
Likewise, may experts in arts and sciences descend here to make Florence richer and more splendid!
And down from the castles of the Val d'Elsa may Arnolfo be welcomed here to make the beautiful tower!
And may Giotto come from the wooded Mugello, and Medici, the courageous merchant!
Away with narrow-minded hatreds and with grudges!
Long live the newcomers . . . and Gianni Schicchi.

Piano/vocal score: p. 49 (Ricordi)

No. 46

Voice: tenor
Aria Title: "L'angue offeso" (Sextus)
Opera Title: *Giulio Cesare*
Composer: George Frideric Handel (1685–1759)
Historical Style: Italian Baroque (1724)
Range: C3 to G4

Fach: lyric
Librettist: Nicola Francesco Haym (1678–1729), after Giacomo Francesco Bussani's *Giulio Cesare in Egitto* set by Antonio Sartoio (1677)
Aria Duration: 4:50
Tessitura: F3 to F4

Position: Act II, scene 2

Setting: The garden of the king's harem; surrounded by an enclosure where wild beasts are kept, Alexandria, Egypt, 48 B.C.

Tolomeo (Ptolemy)—who lusts for Cornelia—and his general, Achilla, have just accosted her. After they leave, Cornelia prepares to throw herself to the tigers that guard the seraglio. Sextus, her son, enters after having escaped from imprisonment. Sextus likens the revenge he plans to take against Tolomeo to a striking serpent.

Recitative: "There is not a son who is not concerned with avenging his father's murder." Sextus imagines he is speaking directly to Tolomeo: "Up then, prepare yourself for revenge."

The aria is marked andante, but moves rather quickly (ma appassionato). Terraced dynamics of fortissimo to piano 16th-note rhythmic passages mark the introduction. The two-part aria lies low for the tenor, but the singer must enter the phrase "se il veleno/if the venom" a number of times on an unaccented G above the staff, and then again in the same fashion at "dentro il sangue all offensor/Wounded, the serpent never rests. His venom spreads its anguish through the body of his foe." On the word "spande/anguish" the vocal line is four measures of 16th notes that move quickly. Once again, with the word "sangue/blood," Sextus sings three measures of florid 16th-note passages.

The larghetto section begins more sustained: "così l'alma mia/thus my soul." Vocally, nothing extends above the staff, but an F at the top of the staff is called for three times, with the opportunity (optional) in the cadenza to sing to a high A and B♭ in passing tones.

Piano/vocal score: p. 97 (Peters)

No. 47

Voice: tenor
Aria Title: "Svegliatevi nel core" (Sextus)
Opera Title: *Giulio Cesare*
Composer: George Frideric Handel (1685–1759)
Historical Style: Italian Baroque (1724)
Range: C3 to G4

Fach: lyric
Librettist: Nicola Francesco Haym (1678–1729), after Giacomo Francesco Bussani's *Giulio Cesare in Egitto* set by Antonio Sartoio (1677)
Aria Duration: 4:40
Tessitura: F3 to F4

Position: Act I, scene 1

Setting: Open country in Egypt with an ancient bridge over a branch of the Nile entering Alexandria, Egypt, 48 B.C.

Cesare (Caesar) agrees to peace requested by Cornelia and her young son, Sextus. The severed head of Pompeo (Pompey) is presented to his widow, Cornelia, by Tolomeo's (Ptolemy's) general, Achilla, as a sign of "friendship" for Cesare. In her grief Cornelia tries to kill herself, but her son prevents her from this. He then assures her he will avenge his father's death.

He says "there is no time for lamenting: it's time to vindicate my father." No fear affects him before launching into "Svegliatevi/Come, rouse yourself to vengeance—furies with hatred fire me," in the first section of the aria.

The aria is marked allegro energico and lies in the middle voice, doubled in the orchestra by the violin. Although sung with conviction and declamatory in style, the aria should not be sung too dramatically. Sextus sings "svegliatemi/rouse yourself" two times on the octave C down to middle C; this may be difficult for some tenors to manage. But diction, conviction, and anger played out in the dotted-8th rhythm pattern are more important than heavy vocal production on the middle C. Much of the first section is set syllabically, which has the effect of greater bitter anger with energized diction.

The largo section revives the shadow (memory) of Sextus's father. His father tells Sextus that his death must be avenged, returning Sextus to tempo 1 for a short recapitulation of the beginning section. With the text "a far d'un traditor/upon a traitor" the vocal line goes to F at the top of the staff for a half note, then into a final cadenza with a sustained G above the staff up to a high B♭ if desired. A less florid option is offered in the Peters Edition. This aria does not extend the singer very much over the staff, moves the voice, offers contrasting emotion possibilities starting with the accompanied recitative, and demonstrates the importance of Italian diction with conviction.

Piano/vocal score: p. 21 (Peters)

No. 48

Voice: tenor

Aria Title: "Ne m'abandonne point . . . Asile héréditaire," No. 19 (Arnold)

Opera Title: *Guillaume Tell*

Composer: Gioacchino Rossini (1792–1868)

Historical Style: French Romantic (1829)

Range: F3 to C5 (E♭5)

Fach: lyric

Librettists: Étienne de Jouy (1764–1846) and Hippolyte-Louis-Florent Bis (1789–1855), after Johann Christoph Friedrich von Schiller's play *Wilhelm Tell* (1804)

Aria Duration: 6:30

Tessitura: G3 to B♭5

Position: Act IV

Setting: The ruined house of Melcthal, Altdorf, Switzerland, 13th century

At this point in the opera, William Tell is imprisoned. Arnold is a Swiss patriot, and all that detains him now is a hope of vengeance. "My soul is impatient. I will go on! Here my father died," he sings. The orchestral introduction begins with strings and a horn. The aria has a beautiful vocal line to high G in the middle of the vocal line. The second phrase ascends to high B♭, as Arnold speaks of the land of his ancestors. It is often a challenge for young tenors to sing repeated high F♯'s to high G and A and crescendo. Arnold repeats the melody with some textual alteration as he sings of "this dwelling where my eyes first saw the light of day."

In the allegro section the male chorus calls him to action, "to vengeance!" Arnold leads the others to action in a cabaletta-like section. His vocal line contains accents and stepwise singing up to high C's above the chorus, calling them to arms and inspiring them to save William Tell. At the end of the opera Arnold and his forces have captured the castle of Altdorf.

Piano/vocal score: p. 369 (Kalmus)

No. 49

Voice: tenor
Aria Title: "Languir per una bella" (Lindoro)
Opera Title: *L'italiana in Algeri*
Composer: Gioacchino Rossini (1792–1868)
Historical Style: Bel canto (1813)
Range: F3 to C5

Fach: lyric
Librettist: Angelo Anelli (1761–1820), first set by Luigi Mosca (1808)
Aria Duration: 6:00
Tessitura: B♭4 to B♭5

Position: Act I, scene 2

Setting: A small room in the palace of Mustafa, Bey of Algiers. The room is between the apartments of the Bey and those of his wife, Elvira. In the middle is a sofa.

Mustafa, tired of his wife Elvira, gives orders for Elvira to marry the young Italian slave, Lindoro (his favorite prisoner). Meanwhile, the pirates are to capture a new, and livelier, Italian wife for Mustafa; he and the Captain exit. Lindoro enters, alone. After three months in Algiers, the young Italian prisoner is bitterly missing the woman he loves and longs with passion for the day when he can return home.

The introduction calls for the melody to be played by a solo horn. Lindoro enters and sings that he "languishes for a beauty who is far away. To be far away is the cruelest torment." The vocal line is decorative, but all embellishments come from his emotional state, rather than a vocal demonstration of technique. The singer will need to go up frequently to a high G, A♭, and B♭. Flexibility is also important, with florid 16th- and 32nd-note passages. The melody is repeated twice.

Next, Lindoro notes that "Perhaps the moment will come, but he cannot hope for it yet." As he sings "forse verra/perhaps it will come," he shows some frustration and anxiety by singing the words on 16th notes twice very quickly, unaccompanied. The melody comes back and closes with cadential figures, as he repeats the text "e star lontan da quella/far away from her." The allegro section has a florid 16th-note passage that takes the singer above the staff to the high C. Lindoro says that his soul "is content amidst its woes, finding peace only in thinking of his loved one."

The "frame" of this melody is between the B♭ in the middle of the staff and the octave above it. Toward the end of the aria Lindoro becomes much more excited, singing accented quarter notes followed by 8th-note triplets.

He has five measures of 16th-note passages and an extended high B♭, and climbs by half steps to high C.

Piano/vocal score: p. 39 (G. Schirmer)

No. 50

Voice: tenor
Aria Title: "Rachel, quand du Seigneur" (Éléazar)
Opera Title: *La Juive*
Composer: Jacques-François-Fromental Halévy (1799–1862)
Historical Style: French Romantic (1835)
Range: E♭3 to B5

Fach: lyric
Librettist: Eugène Scribe (1791–1861)
Aria Duration: 4:20
Tessitura: F3 to A♭4

Position: Act IV

Setting: The Emperor's palace, Constance, Switzerland, 1414

Éléazar is a Jewish goldsmith and father of Rachel. Rachel has been condemned to death by Cardinal de Brogni for consorting with the Christian prince Leopold. However, Brogni does not realize that Rachel is actually his own daughter, saved from a fire in Rome years ago and raised as Éléazar's own daughter. Éléazar knows he can save her life by revealing this, but he's unable to reconcile his Jewish faith with forcing his daughter to change her faith.

The aria begins lyrically, with a vocal line that is long and sustained: "When the Lord's saving grace into my trembling hands committed your cradle, I made your happiness my entire goal of my life." It soars from C up to high A♭ on "Et c'est moi qui te livre au bourreau/And it is I who sends you to your execution." The orchestra plays a plaintive melody for four measures before Éléazar continues: "But I hear a voice cry out to me: Save me from death which awaits me. I am young and cling to life (*up to high A♭ in the phrase*). Oh, my father, spare your child" (repeated to a high, sustained B♭). Now the opening melody and text are repeated, with the closing text "Rachel, je te livre au bourreau!/Rachel, I send you to your execution!" repeated, and "Rachel" sustained from an F at the top of the staff to the high A♭ (fermata). And then "c'est moi/it is I" comes on repeated quarter notes in the lower middle voice before Éléazar cries out, once again to the high A♭: "c'est moi que te libre au bourreau!/it is I who rescues you from death!"

The allegro section is declamatory and similar to an accompanied recitative: "And by a word which will stop the sentence . . . I can rescue you from death! I will give up my vengeance forever. You shall not die!" There are no notes above the G in this section, but it is sustained with intensity at the top of the staff at the singer's *passaggio*.

Piano/vocal score: p. 344 (Choudens)

No. 51

Voice: tenor
Aria Title: "Dein ist mein ganzes Herz" (Sou-Chong)
Opera Title: *Das Land des Lächelns*
Composer: Franz Lehár (1870–1948)
Historical Style: Viennese Operetta (1929)
Range: E♭3 to A♭4

Fach: lyric
Librettists: Ludwig Herzer (1872–1939) and Fritz Beda-Löhner (1883–1942), after Viktor Léon's libretto to *Die gelbe Jacke* (1923)
Aria Duration: 3:35
Tessitura: F3 to A♭4

Position: Act II

Setting: A reception hall in Prince Sou-Chong's Palace, 1912

An aristocratic Viennese girl, Lisa, falls in love with the Chinese Prince Sou-Chong in 1912 Vienna, but is unable to adapt to the demands made on her in the Prince's own country, where all passions are concealed behind enigmatic, disciplined smiles.

The aria "Dein ist mein ganzes Herz" follows a heated exchange between Prince Sou-Chang and his uncle, Tschang. The latter maintains that the Prince has to follow his duty in China of marrying the four Manchu maidens without delay. The Prince maintains that he is already married, but the uncle scoffs at that: "According to the laws of our country, she is not your wife." Sou-Chong says that the laws are outmoded, and the people must adapt themselves to his new decrees, but the Prince is interrupted by his uncle, who tells Sou-Chong to "heed my warning, and fear the gods!" before exiting.

Alone, the Prince asks the gods if he has done wrong. His heart belongs to Lisa, and although she is not in the room, he sings the piece to her vision.

> Yours is my heart alone, and in you lies happiness!
> So must the flower fade if denied the sun's caress.
> Yours is the song I sing for it was born of my love for you,
> Oh, let me hear you say, "I love but you!"
> No matter where I go, dear, you're there with me, you know.
> Far from you, I feel you near me, the dream of you is there to uplift me.
> You, you alone! How wondrous fair is your beautiful hair,
> Radiant as summer skies is your eyes!
> How my heart does rejoice with the sound of your voice,
> Which is music to me.

The A section of music and text is repeated, with a final high A♭, sustained. The aria calls for a delivery that is youthful, ardent, and energized. A vocal line with attention to rhythmic impulse is important with a strong high A♭.

Piano/vocal score: p. 57 (Glocken-Verlag)

No. 52

Voice: tenor
Aria Title: "Tombe degl' avi miei . . . Fra poco a me ricovero" (Edgardo)
Opera Title: *Lucia di Lammermoor*
Composer: Gaetano Donizetti (1797–1848)
Historical Style: Bel canto (1835)
Range: F3 to A5 (B♭5)

Fach: lyric
Librettist: Salvatore Cammarano (1801–1852), after Sir Walter Scott's novel *The Bride of Lammermoor* (1819)
Aria Duration: 7:13
Tessitura: A3 to F♯4

Position: Act III, scene 2

Setting: A place outside the Castle of Wolf's-Crag, the tombs of the Ravenswoods. There is a practicable gateway; an illuminated hall is seen in the distance; night.

Sir Edgardo di Ravenswood comes to his family tombs to meet Enrico, the brother of Lucia. From the beginning of the opera, it is clear that Edgardo is Enrico's hated rival. Waiting, he thinks he no longer wants to live since Lucia has betrayed him. The beginning of the recitative "Tombe degl'avi miei/Tombs of my ancestors" is a capella interspersed with accompanied recitative. Differing tempo markings, from maestoso to allegro to larghetto, are also interspersed. Specific rhythmic values and diction are extremely important. There is an optional cadenza (to high B♭) before the aria introduction begins in 3/4 meter (larghetto).

The aria is Edgardo's farewell to earth ("Fra poco ame ricovero/Soon a neglected grave") and is legato with important rhythmic variety and some accents that must be carefully observed. The well-known melody has challenging intervals from A in the middle up to F♯ and G at the top of the staff. At "rispetta almen le ceneri/respect the ashes" the melody is repeated to a high A, sustained. At "Mai non passarvi/But do not come this way" (poco più) Edgardo becomes more agitated, focusing his anger on the presumably faithless Lucia. The tenor must climb twice to F♯ and G through the *passaggio* before the conclusion of the aria as he sings, "Io moro per te/I die for you." Edgardo now knows that Lucia is dead. He looks forward to their reunion in heaven ("tu che a Dio spiegasti l'ali/you who have spread your wings to God") and stabs himself.

Piano/vocal score: p. 220 (G. Schirmer)

No. 53

Voice: tenor
Aria Title: "Horch, die Lerche singt im Hain!" (Fenton)
Opera Title: *Die lustigen Weiber von Windsor*
Composer: Otto Nicolai (1810–1849)
Historical Style: German Romantic (1849)
Range: G3 to G♯4

Fach: lyric
Librettist: Salomon Hermann von Mosenthal (1821–1877), after the comedy by William Shakespeare (1600–1601)
Aria Duration: 5:20
Tessitura: B4 to E4

Position: Act II, scene V

Setting: Windsor, England, c. 1600; the garden of Mr. Page's house. There are groups of trees and bushes. The house is seen in the background.

Anne's two unwanted suitors, Slender and Cajus, unknown to each other, plan to meet her during her daily walk in the garden. When Fenton (Anne's true love) arrives, they are forced to hide. Fenton sings a Romance outside the house, singing of larks singing high (G♯) above early in the day. He wants Anne to open her windows to listen to what the larks say.

> The birds speak of love: Hark, the lark sings in the grove!
> Listen, sweetheart, quietly.
> Open gently your little window; hear what it desires.
> Clear is the tone of the song; whoever loves here will understand it!
> Hear the tender sound, sweetheart, rises up to you.
> Do not question what the song, dear one, longingly strives for.

To inspire the object of his affection, Fenton sings repeated high notes (G and G♯ above the staff), appoggiaturas, and mordents. His singing is energized with precise rhythms and clear diction.

Piano/vocal score: p. 129 (G. Schirmer)

No. 54

Voice: tenor
Aria Title: "Ah, la paterna mano" (Macduff)
Opera Title: *Macbeth*
Composer: Giuseppe Verdi (1813–1901)
Historical Style: Italian Romantic (1847)
Range: F3 to B♭♭5

Fach: lyric
Librettist: Francesco Maria Piave (1810–1876) with additions by Andrea Maffei (1798–1885), after the tragedy by William Shakespeare (1606)
Aria Duration: 3:20
Tessitura: A♭3 to A♭4

Position: Act IV, scene 1

Setting: A deserted place on the border of Scotland and England; in the distance Birnam Wood

The broken Scottish refugees slowly stagger onto the stage and commiserate the state of the people under Macbeth's rule. Macduff, noble Scott, is heartbroken to learn of the deaths of his wife and children. As he addresses the refugees in recitative, "Children, my children!" he must be thinking about his own loss.

The plaintive quality of this aria mourns the loss of his family and articulates the guilt he feels over the state of ruin that rules the people: "I was not there to shield you." The first section of the aria needs to have a sweetness and suffering to it. The articulation markings are extremely specific and detailed and heartfelt. At the words "Trammi al tiranno in faccia/ Bring me face to face with this tyrant," Macduff is proactive: "Bring me face to face with the tyrant, O Lord, and if he escapes me then extend to him thine arms in pardon." The singer does not sing forte until "possa a colui le braccia/extend to him thine arms" (an ascending phrase that crescendos to a high A♭). The phrase is repeated in a cadenza to an A. It is clear that Macduff is suffering his loss more deeply as he looks into the eyes of the poor refugees.

Piano/vocal score: p. 249 (Ricordi)

No. 55

Voice: tenor
Aria Title: "Ah! Fuyez douce image"
(Des Grieux)
Opera Title: *Manon*
Composer: Jules Massenet (1842–1912)
Historical Style: French Romantic (1884)
Range: F3 to B♭5

Fach: lyric
Librettists: Henri Meilhac (1831–1897) and
Philippe Gille (1831–1901), after the Abbé
Antoine-François Prévost's novel *L'histoire
du Chevalier des Grieux et de Manon Les-
caut* (1731)
Aria Duration: 4:10
Tessitura: B♭4 to G4

Position: Act III, scene 2

Setting: The seminary at St.-Sulpice

Des Grieux has been abducted and taken to the seminary. He has just been preaching. His father is proud of him, but Des Grieux is full of bitterness. He is determined to take his vows, but left alone he confesses that the image of Manon still haunts him ("Ah! fuyez, douce image/Ah! Fly, sweet image"). He wants the "sweet image" of her in his mind to "fly away."

This is a very demanding aria that begins pianissimo on high G and stays in a high tessitura at the beginning of the aria. Des Grieux is asking for his soul to be calmed, but his bitterness and temperament comes through at the beginning of each phrase with a double-dotted quarter-note value. As he struggles with his thoughts of Manon (in the recitative), the sound of the organ in the distance tells him that the service is starting.

This prayer is sung in the *passaggio* and is not easy for most tenors to sing in tune. With a crescendo to tempo 1 and the support of the full orchestra, Des Grieux asks once again that Manon's sweet image fly from his mind, "loin de moi/far from me."

Piano/vocal score: p. 258 (G. Schirmer)

> Notes by singer, voice professor, and director Henry Price: The opening line of "Ah, fuyez" need not be a silvery pianissimo unless that particular effect is a strength of the singer. An ease of production combined with a sound that reflects Des Grieux's intense personal pain is what is necessary. Only a tenor who is extremely secure in the passaggio and revels in his B♭'s should attempt this aria or this role.

No. 56

Voice: tenor
Aria Title: "En fermant les yeux," Le Rêve (Des Grieux)
Opera Title: *Manon*
Composer: Jules Massenet (1842–1912)
Historical Style: French Romantic (1884)
Range: E3 to A5

Fach: lyric
Librettists: Henri Meilhac (1831–1897) and Philippe Gille (1831–1901), after the Abbé Antoine-François Prévost's novel *L'histoire du chevalier des Grieux et de Manon Lescaut* (1731)
Aria Duration: 3:00
Tessitura: A4 to F4

Position: Act II

Setting: Paris, 1721; an apartment in the rue Vivienne, Paris, where Des Grieux and Manon are now living

Earlier in the act, Des Grieux has written a letter to his father to explain his relationship with Manon. While Des Grieux is out posting the letter, Manon is tempted to abandon him for a glamorous life of riches with the wealthy Brétigny. This is an offer she cannot resist. When he returns he finds her in tears. He describes a daydream that he has had in which all is paradise—but she is not in the dream.

It's true . . . my mind is raving! But happiness is temporary,
And heaven has made it so fleet that one is always afraid it will fly away!
To the table! Enchanting moment when apprehension is suspended—
When we two are alone! Listen, Manon: while walking, I've just had a dream.
Closing my eyes, I see over there a humble retreat—
A cottage all white in the depth of the woods!
In its tranquil shade the clear and joyful brooks,
In which the foliage is mirrored, sing with the birds!
It is paradise!
Oh, no! Everything there is sad and gloomy, for there is one thing missing:
It still needs Manon!
Come! There our life will be, if you wish it. Oh, Manon!

Manon interrupts the aria to say that his words represent just a crazy dream, but he continues. The aria is sung slowly, intimately, lyrically, softly, and articulation of text is important. There is lyric singing at the top of the staff with articulated text. There is only one forte phrase: "Car il y manque une chose: Il y faut encor Manon/For there is one thing missing: It still needs Manon!" The dreamlike state of the aria is mirrored in the accompaniment by a hypnotic ostinato.

Piano/vocal score: p. 161 (G. Schirmer)

> Notes by singer, voice professor, and director Henry Price: "Le Rêve" is one of those arias that lies right in the *passaggio*. A tenor with an easily supported silvery *messa di voce* will find no terrors here. Some tenors are better when they sustain a fuller sound in this aria, keeping in mind that a piano marking indicates an ease of production and a sensitivity to the character's feelings, not necessarily a low decibel level. Be careful not to set too slow a tempo. (You will die!) The support of a sensitive conductor/accompanist (à la Julius Rudel) can be your best friend here.

No. 57

Voice: tenor
Aria Title: "Ach, so fromm" ("M'apparì tutt'amor") (Lionel)
Opera Title: *Martha*
Composer: Friedrich von Flotow (1812–1883)
Historical Style: German Romantic (1847)
Range: F3 to B♭5

Fach: lyric
Librettist: Friedrich Wilhelm Riese (1805?–1879), after Jules Henri Vernoy de Saint-Georges's ballet-pantomime *Lady Henriette, ou La Servante de Greenwich* (1844)
Aria Duration: 2:45
Tessitura: A4 to G4

Position: Act III

Setting: Outside a rustic inn in the hunting park in Richmond Forest, England; 18th century during the reign of Queen Anne

Lionel is Plunkett's foster brother and is a farmer by trade. After meeting Lady Harriet (a maid of honor to Queen Anne) the night before disguised as "Martha," Lionel sees her again with the ladies-in-waiting for Queen Anne. Wandering alone, he is struck again by her beauty and grieves that he will probably never be with her again. He holds in his hand a rose that she has given to him, singing of his love and despair. This aria is one of the most famous melodies in the tenor repertoire.

Ah, so innocent, so dear. My eyes have beheld her.
Ah, so gently and purely her image penetrated my heart.
Sad dejection, before she came, clouded the future for me.
But with her a new sense of being bloomed joyfully in me.
Woe, it vanished—what I had found.
Ah, I scarcely glimpsed my happiness—I awoke, and the night robbed me of the sweet dream.
Martha, Martha! You vanished, and you took my happiness with you.
Restore to me what you found, or share it with me.
Yes, with me!

The aria should be sung lyrically, but the dotted rhythms add energy to the vocal line. Much of the accompaniment is a simple broken chord–arpeggiated pattern. The melody carries the voice through the *passaggio* (F, G, and A♭ at the top of the staff). At the conclusion, Lionel calls out Martha's name as it continues with momentum toward the "Gib mir wieder, was du fandest/restore to me what you found" to a high A sustained on the word "Ja! Theile es mit mir/Yes! Share it with me!" and then "Ja, mit mir!/Yes, with me!" An unaccompanied "Ja" on high B resolves to the tonic F ("mit mir!").

Piano/vocal score: p. 174 (G. Schirmer)

No. 58

Voice: tenor

Aria Title: "Adieu, Mignon!" No. 11 (Wilhelm)

Opera Title: *Mignon*

Composer: Ambroise Thomas (1811–1896)

Historical Style: French Romantic (1866)

Range: F3 to A5

Fach: lyric

Librettists: Michel Carré (1819–1872) and Jules Barbier (1825–1901), after Johann Wolfgang von Goethe's novel *Wilhelm Meisters Lehrjahre* (1796)

Aria Duration: 2:30

Tessitura: G3 to F♯4

Position: Act II, scene 1

Setting: Filina's dressing room in a German castle, late 1700s

Mignon has been following Wilhelm around for a long time. Wilhelm decides that he must tell her that he isn't interested in her. He tries to do this in a kind way, telling her that he must leave her. "Goodbye, Mignon. Courage!" he softly sings, "God will console you." As the melody plays in the orchestra, he tries to comfort her: "Do not weep. I leave you with tender regret, and my tender soul shares your pain."

The second verse refers to her youth; he begs her forgiveness: "Sorrows are forgotten at your early age. Do not accuse my heart of cold indifference. Do not reproach me from following a foolish love! In saying goodbye to you I keep the hope to see you again one day."

To encompass both the sweet lyricism and the stronger vocal expression necessary for the aria, good vocal control is essential. The singer also needs to be careful regarding diction and the enharmonic tones.

Piano/vocal score: p. 210 (G. Schirmer)

No. 59

Voice: tenor
Aria Title: "Inkslinger's Song" (Johnny Inkslinger)
Opera Title: *Paul Bunyan*
Composer: Benjamin Britten (1913–1976)
Historical Style: 20th-century English (1941)
Range: D3 to A5

Fach: lyric
Librettist: W. H. Auden (1907–1973)
Aria Duration: 4:45
Tessitura: B♭4 to F4

Position: Act I, scene 2

Setting: The mythical American northern frontier, 19th century; a logging camp; night

Paul Bunyan is described as an operetta in two acts. The origin of the opera is documentary film music the composer, Benjamin Britten, wrote in the mid-1930s. The opera was premiered in 1941, not to be produced again until 1976. The character, Johnny Inkslinger, is an intellectual book-keeper and Paul Bunyan's aide-de-camp. He grudgingly becomes a book-keeper in the camp to ensure getting regular meals. The librettist, W. H. Auden, describes him as "a man of speculative and critical intelligence, whose temptation is to despise those who do the manual work that makes the life of thought possible." Britten was inspired by the "dazzling complexity" of Auden's text.

The melody itself is simple, reminiscent of Kurt Weill's style. The many triplet rhythms highlight the text. It is a quasi-recitativo style with very little melodic repetition. There are many enharmonic tones. The range extends from the D above middle C all the way up to A above the staff (but it is not sustained). The "Inkslinger's Song" is the story of the character's life as told to his dog, Fido.

"May I tell you the story of my life?" the Inkslinger asks the dog. It is a witty narrative, telling the dog that it "was out in the sticks that the fire of my existence began." He learned his prose style from "the preacher and the facts of life from the hens."

He fell in love with his teacher and dreamed of writing a novel, "but I guess that a guy gotta eat" and he "can think of much nicer professions than keeping a ledger correct." He goes on to tell Fido all the things he would like to do, "but I guess that a guy gotta eat."

The lumberjacks don't understand him, he says. The camp is a prison; he's tired of looking at trees. "Where is the beautiful place," he asks, "where the joy shines out of men's faces, and all get sufficient to eat?"

Piano/vocal score: p. 78 (Faber)

No. 60

Voice: tenor
Aria Title: "Je crois entendre encore" (Nadir)
Opera Title: *Les pêcheurs de perles*
Composer: Georges Bizet (1838–1875)
Historical Style: French Romantic (1863)
Range: F3 to B5

Fach: lyric
Librettists: Eugène Cormon (1810–1903) and Michel Carré (1819–1872)
Aria Duration: 3:20
Tessitura: A4 to G4

Position: Act I

Setting: A wild beach on a rocky coast in Ceylon, tribal era, sunset

The pearl fishers are preparing for the fishing season. Nadir is a hunter and friend to Zurga. Both have fallen in love with a beautiful young woman and have taken a vow not to pursue her—or their friendship could be affected. Despite his oath to his friend, Nadir alone admits that he remembers the magic of the experience of seeing Leila and being recognized by her.

Before he falls asleep, he sings the aria. It is lullaby-like, hypnotic, lyric, floating, plaintive, and poignant. The harmonic changes are beautiful. It cannot be sung full voice for the proper effect. The tenor starts on the E at the top of the staff, and he will need to sing up to a sustained, pianissimo, high B.

Concealed beneath the palm trees,
I think I hear once more her voice tender and resonant, like a song of wood pigeons.
Oh, enchanting night—heavenly rapture . . .
Oh, charming memory—foolish intoxication, sweet dream!

In the light of the stars I think I see her once more opening her long
veils a little
To the tepid breezes of the evening.
Charming memory!

Piano/vocal score: p. 64 (Kalmus)

No. 61

Voice: tenor
Aria Title: "Here I stand . . . Since it is not
by merit" (Tom Rakewell)
Opera Title: *The Rake's Progress*
Composer: Igor Stravinsky (1882–1971)
Historical Style: 20th-century English
(1951)
Range: E3 to A5

Fach: lyric
Librettists: W. H. Auden (1907–1973) and
Chester Kallman (1921–1975), after William
Hogarth's cycle of paintings of the same
name (1735)
Aria Duration: 2:45
Tessitura: G3 to F4

Position: Act I, scene 1

Setting: 18th-century England, the garden of Trulove's home in the country
Tom is in love with Anne, Trulove's daughter. The opera opens with Tom
and Anne in nature singing a duet. Trulove suggests that Tom get a job,
but Tom has other plans. He sings, "Here I stand" and "Since it is not by
merit" in response to the concerns of Trulove (whom he calls "the old
fool").

"Here I stand" begins with an accompanied recitative in which he is asking himself questions: "I submit to the drudge's yoke? I slave through a
lifetime to enrich others, and then be thrown away like a gnawed bone?"
and then answers, "Not I!" The piece demands difficult intervallic adjust-
ments. While Tom ponders the questions there is a weaving quality to the
melody. There are some G's and A's above the staff and a few sustained
tones. Diction is very important and reflects the conviction with which
young Tom sings. He is young, naïve, bold, brash, and about to roll the
dice—so to speak—on his future.

The aria proper (slightly faster than the recitative) answers the questions posed during the recitative: "Since it is not by merit we rise or we fall, but the favour of fortune that governs us all." There is an important rhythmic motive in the vocal and accompaniment line (two 16th notes tied to an 8th). Before the last section of the aria, Tom makes the decision that since the world is vast, "This beggar shall ride." He repeats the phrase with an energy that continues into his spoken words: "I wish I had money!" His wish is granted.

Piano/vocal score: p. 11 (Boosey & Hawkes)

No. 62

Voice: tenor
Aria Title: "Love, too frequently betrayed" (Tom Rakewell)
Opera Title: *The Rake's Progress*
Composer: Igor Stravinsky (1882–1971)
Historical Style: 20th-century English (1951)
Range: E♯3 to G♯4

Fach: lyric
Librettists: W. H. Auden (1907–1973) and Chester Kallman (1921–1975), after William Hogarth's cycle of paintings of the same name (1735)
Aria Duration: 2:30/3:15
Tessitura: G♯3 to F♯4

Position: Act I, scene 2

Setting: Mother Goose's brothel, London
    Tom has left Anne in the country to go to London as advised by Nick Shadow (the devil in disguise), who introduces Tom before the cavatina. Tom's downfall comes from his denial of nature.
    Tom's cavatina in the brothel describes his regret at betraying true love (to the whores' delight). Entrances of phrases are never on beat 1 of the measure; this contributes to the sense of Tom's regret and lack of the sureness that he displays in his first aria.
    This piece has a lot less bravura than "Vary the song, O London, change," but still offers glimpses of Tom's youthful ardor with the rhythmic flourishes of 32nd notes. There are no sustained high tones, and the final note is G♯ in the middle of the range. There is only one display of great emotion

when he pleads, "Goddess, O forget me not. Lest I perish, O forget me not." The singer must carefully negotiate intervals and the grouped 32nd-note passages. The aria shows musicianship, coloring of text, and vocal control.

Piano/vocal score: p. 50 (Boosey & Hawkes)

No. 63

Voice: tenor
Aria Title: "Vary the song, O London, change" (Tom Rakewell)
Opera Title: *The Rake's Progress*
Composer: Igor Stravinsky (1882–1971)
Historical Style: 20th-century English (1951)
Range: D♯3 to A♭4

Fach: lyric
Librettists: W. H. Auden (1907–1973) and Chester Kallman (1921–1975), after William Hogarth's cycle of paintings of the same name (1735)
Aria Duration: 3:15
Tessitura: G3 to F4

Position: Act II, scene 1

Setting: Tom Rakewell's house in London

Tom, who is young and idealistic, has left Anne in the country to go to London as advised by Nick Shadow (the devil in disguise). Tom is bored with the fashionable life of those more fortunate than he. This piece has a three-part construction that uses short phrases and short note values to show the character's disdain for the city, and his distaste and anger.

The recitative follows as he questions leaving the country. In the last section there is much rhythmic variety, again entrances off the beats. There is also a key change. Tom is only sure of one thing: "Who's honest, chaste and kind? One, only one" (Anne).

The stage direction ("He rises") shows a Tom who recognizes nature as being of supreme importance. Tom's words are delineated in a declamatory fashion; they are all sung on quarter notes to a high A♭. This piece needs the ability to sing florid passages while declaiming important text and carefully negotiating intervals.

Piano/vocal score: p. 71 (Boosey & Hawkes)

No. 64

Voice: tenor
Aria Title: "Tarquinius does not wait" (Male Chorus)
Opera Title: *The Rape of Lucretia*
Composer: Benjamin Britten (1913–1976)
Historical Style: 20th-century English (1946)
Range: E♭3 to B♭5

Fach: lyric
Librettist: Ronald Duncan (1914–1982), based on André Obey's play *Le viol de Lucrèce* (1931)
Aria Duration: 3:05
Tessitura: G3 to G4

Position: Act I

Setting: Narrative

The Rape of Lucretia is a chamber opera with 12 accompanying instruments in the orchestra and piano. Two of the most important roles are those of the Male and Female Chorus, who are not in costume, but act as narrators of the action. In this excerpt from Act I, the Male Chorus begins his descriptive narrative as Tarquinius goes off with sudden resolution to Rome. Speaking of Tarquinius (the Etruscan Prince), the Male Chorus sings (allegro con fuoco, energico, forte), "He snatches a bridle and forcing the iron bit through the beast's bared white teeth, runs him out of the stable, mounts without curb or stable, the stallion's short straight back." The Male Chorus "sees" the action as he relates it to the audience.

The piece is not melodic, but instead is declamatory. At the words "Now who rides? Who's ridden?" the vocal line becomes more florid with 16th-note passages as the Male Chorus depicts Tarquinius's furious ride to Rome to ravish Lucretia. The accompaniment describes the murmuring of the river as he comes to the Tiber. The horse will not cross, but Tarquinius forces it to. The Male Chorus sings (pianissimo), "Now stallion and rider wake the sleep of water disturbing its cool dream . . . with hot flank and shoulder." Ascending to B♭ he sings, "He's heading here!" He hauntingly sings a descending passage to end fortissimo, "Lucretia!"

There are no sustained notes above the staff or ascending long climactic phrases. The music sustains tension and builds, using language, dynamics, and the colors of the voice. The excerpt is challenging sing in a declamatory style as it lies at the E/F pitch level above the staff (in the *passaggio*).

Piano/vocal score: p. 53 (Boosey & Hawkes)

No. 65

Voice: tenor
Aria Title: "Ella mi fu rapita . . . Parmi veder le lagrime" (Duke of Mantua)
Opera Title: *Rigoletto*
Composer: Giuseppe Verdi (1813–1901)
Historical Style: Italian Romantic (1851)
Range: D3 to B♭♭5

Fach: lyric
Librettist: Francesco Maria Piave (1810–1876), after Victor Hugo's tragedy *La roi s'amuse* (1832)
Aria Duration: 5:30
Tessitura: B4 to G4

Position: Act II, scene 1

Setting: A reception room in the Duke's palace. There are two side doors and a large folding door at the back, on either side of which—left and right, respectively—hang full-length portraits of the Duke and his wife. A large armchair stands near a table covered with velvet; other furniture.

The Duke of Mantua enters in extreme agitation. He fears he has lost Gilda; when he returned to her house shortly after their parting he had found it deserted. Although he is a hedonistic womanizer, it may be possible that the Duke has true feelings for this girl. In "Ella mi fu rapita!/She's been taken from me" he reviews what has happened, finding the door ajar and the "dear angel" taken away from him. "He will take revenge," he vows.

Much of the opening recitative is not accompanied. With "E dove ora sara quell'angiol caro?/Where is the dear angel now?" the vocal line is gently accompanied by the strings. The Duke admits that she is the only one who has kindled these feelings in him. He repeats the words "Ella mi fu rapita!" ascending quickly with accents to high A♭ this time. He is more agitated, and more heroic (con forza), singing at high A♭, G♭ above the staff.

There are three measures of introduction before the aria begins on G♭: "Parmi veder le lagrime/I can almost see her tears." The specific rhythms, articulations, rubato, and text are important in this aria. The melodic line takes vocal control; it carries the singer up to notes above the staff on unaccented syllables. The melody ascends as the Duke remarks that he "does not envy the angels in heaven when she is near."

> Notes by singer and voice professor Michael Belnap: This aria sung by the Duke in Act II of *Rigoletto* will show if a tenor "has the stuff." It is not overly heavy or dramatic, but demands just about everything that an aria can demand from a tenor.

Piano/vocal score: p. 165 (Ricordi)

No. 66

Voice: tenor
Aria Title: "La donna è mobile" (Duke of Mantua)
Opera Title: *Rigoletto*
Composer: Giuseppe Verdi (1813–1901)
Historical Style: Italian Romantic (1851)
Range: F#3 to B5

Fach: lyric
Librettist: Francesco Maria Piave (1810–1876), after Victor Hugo's tragedy *Le roi s'amuse* (1832)
Aria Duration: 2:10
Tessitura: B4 to F#4

Position: Act III, scene 1

Setting: An inn next to a river, Mantua, 16th century

The Duke enters the inn wearing the uniform of a minor cavalry officer. He sits down and demands a room and some wine—at once. He drinks wine and sings to himself, "La donna è mobile/Woman is fickle, changing constantly." It is an active and bright aria sung in two verses.

> She changes the tone of her voice, and her thoughts.
> Always a sweet, pretty face, in tears or in laughter she is always lying.
> Woman is fickle, changing constantly.
> She changes the tone of her voice, and her thoughts.
> He is always miserable who trusts and confides in her, his unwary heart!
> Yet nobody feels happy fully who does not drink love.
> Woman is fickle,
> She changes the tone of her voice, and her thoughts.

The aria employs a range of dynamics, from pianissimo to forte, very specifically for effect. Articulation is clearly marked and must be observed. Like the Duke's opening aria, the piece has a "bravura" quality, but this aria also has a darker side ("she is always lying"). At the end of each verse there is a sustained F# with a crescendo that in the second verse can have a final flourish with a sustained high B.

Piano/vocal score: p. 254 (Ricordi)

No. 67

Voice: tenor
Aria Title: "Possente amor mi chiama"
(Duke of Mantua)
Opera Title: *Rigoletto*
Composer: Giuseppe Verdi (1813–1901)
Historical Style: Italian Romantic (1851)
Range: F♯3 to A5 (D5)

Fach: lyric
Librettist: Francesco Maria Piave (1810–
1876), after Victor Hugo's tragedy *La roi
s'amuse* (1832)
Aria Duration: 2:00
Tessitura: A4 to F♯4

Position: Act II

Setting: A salon in the Ducal palace. There are two side doors and a large folding door at the back, on either side of which—left and right, respectively —hang full-length portraits of the Duke and his wife. A large armchair stands near a table covered with velvet.

The Duke enters in agitation at the beginning of Act II. At this point in the opera, he reviews the abduction of Gilda and does not know who her abductors are. He sings in the cavatina tenderly about her purity. The courtiers enter hastily and tell the Duke that they are responsible for taking Gilda. They thought the girl was Rigoletto's mistress, and as a joke they have gone into his house to kidnap the girl. The Duke hides his feelings for the girl, but wants to know where they have taken her. To his surprise, they tell him that the girl is now in the palace.

The cabaletta, which follows "Ella mi fu rapita" (No. 50), should be sung as an internal monologue; the Duke does not want to reveal his emotions to the courtiers. The piece (allegro) has accents and dotted rhythms that mark the Duke's excitement; though sung as an aside (piano in voice and orchestra), he sings that a great love beckons and he must rush to her. The Duke admits to himself that he would give up his crown to cheer up her sad heart: "Let her know at last who loves her. She shall know who I am, she will see that Love is master even over the powerful." The Duke crescendos to high A with the last line, "apprenda ch'anco in trono/she will see that Love is master even over the powerful." The cabaletta is repeated after the chorus sings, "What can he be thinking?" But this time the Duke declares his love out loud; the repeat is marked forte, con forzo and deciso.

Piano/vocal score: p. 189 (Ricordi)

No. 68

Voice: tenor
Aria Title: "Questa o quella" (Duke of Mantua)
Opera Title: *Rigoletto*
Composer: Giuseppe Verdi (1813–1901)
Historical Style: Italian Romantic (1851)
Range: E♭3 to B♭5

Fach: lyric
Librettist: Francesco Maria Piave (1810–1876), after Victor Hugo's tragedy *Le roi s'amuse* (1832)
Aria Duration: 1:50
Tessitura: A♭3 to A♭4

Position: Act I, scene 1

Setting: Mantua, 16th century, a sumptuous hall in the palace of the Duke of Mantua

This aria is the audience's introduction to the Duke. It should be elegantly sung (after all, he *is* the Duke), but with an imperious quality that shows that he doesn't really romantically invest himself in his adventures of love. He is sarcastic and boastful, but the aria is also sung *con eleganza*.

> This girl, that girl are the same to me,
> To all the others I won't give away my heart to this or that beauty.
> Their charm is a gift given by destiny to embellish their lives.
> If today I love this one, I'll probably love someone else tomorrow.

The phrase is repeated, which includes the ascending phrase to a sustained high A♭ at the end of verse 1.

> We detest constancy, the tyrant of the heart as if it were a cruel plague.
> Let those who want to be faithful keep their fidelity alive,
> There is no love without freedom.
> The rage of jealous husbands and lovers' woes I despise,
> I can defy Argo's hundred eyes if I want a beautiful girl.

The aria is set in a bawdy party atmosphere. The Duke could just as well be in the locker room bragging to his male friends about his exploits. The articulation marks in this early Verdi opera are extremely specific and important to the singing of the aria. Two verses are sung, and specific knowledge of all of the text is essential. A solid, sustained, A♭ is also important.

Piano/vocal score: p. 9 (Ricordi)

No. 69

Voice: tenor
Aria Title: "Vainement, ma bien-aimée"
(Mylio)
Opera Title: *Le roi d'Ys*
Composer: Edouard Lalo (1823–1892)
Historical Style: French Romantic (1888)
Range: E♭3 to A5

Fach: lyric
Librettist: Edouard Blau (1836–1906), after
a Breton legend
Aria Duration: 3:15
Tessitura: A4 to E4

Position: Act III

Setting: Legendary times; a gallery in the palace of the king of Ys

It is the wedding day of Rozenn, the King's daughter, and Mylio. In observance of Breton custom, female attendants guard the bride's door against entry by the groom's men. Before the procession by the bride, Mylio sings this charming Aubade, accompanied by the women's chorus.

Since one cannot sway those jealous protectresses,
Ah, let me tell my sorrows and my feelings!
In vain, my beloved, they think they're making me desperate;
Near your closed door I still wish to dwell!
The suns will die out, the nights replace the days,
Before I reproach you and before I complain.
There I will remain, forever!
I know your soul is sweet,
The hour will soon arrive when the hand that spurns me will
Reach out toward mine!
Do not be too late in letting your heart soften!
If Rozenn doesn't come soon, alas, I'm going to die!

The aria is good for young singers because it is strophic and can be approached lyrically (see notes below).

Piano/vocal score: p. 162 (Heugel)

Notes by singer and voice professor James McDonald: This is
a good piece for the young singer for the following reasons:
(1) There are two simple verses, with not a whole lot of French.
(2) The singer is forced to work on the all-important *passaggio*

without the piece lying in the *passaggio.* (3) The aria is not long. (4) If the singer does not yet have a developed high voice, he can still effectively perform the aria by utilizing a mixed voice or falsetto for the top. (5) The music is simple, singable, and agreeable. (6) The aria does not require a "dramatic" approach to be successful—something important for almost all young tenors.

No. 70

Voice: tenor
Aria Title: "Ah, lève-toi, soleil!" (Roméo)
Opera Title: *Roméo et Juliette*
Composer: Charles Gounod (1818–1893)
Historical Style: French Romantic (1867)
Range: F3 to B♭5

Fach: lyric
Librettists: Jules Barbier (1825–1901) and Michel Carré (1819–1872), after the tragedy by William Shakespeare (1596)
Aria Duration: 3:55
Tessitura: G3 to G4

Position: Act II, scene 1

Setting: Juliette's balcony at the Capulet estate, Verona, 14th century

Roméo has left his drinking companions in search of Juliette's room. He sees her on her balcony. It is important to realize that at this point in the opera, the young man has only exchanged a few words with the girl. This is the first time he will be alone with her.

The text of the piece is very similar to Shakespeare's play: "What is that sudden light that dazzles at that window?" The fading star metaphor in the text is reflected in the chromatic descent of the melody and accompaniment in the outer sections of the piece. The phrases are not long in the aria. Roméo is excited, almost breathless. Gounod gives Roméo time in the accompanied recitative to look for, and find, the balcony of Juliette. He sees her at a distance in the darkness: "Her radiant beauty is the sun, that makes pale the stars." The intervals are not predictable, and both tuning and intonation are important. The aria also calls for language and diction nuance.

The aria begins in earnest as Roméo declaims, "Ah! Lève-toi! Parais!/ Ah! Arise! Appear!" It is risky for him to cry out like that in the night, but the exclamations reflect his youthful excitement. He is not careful or mannered. The aria concludes on a high B♭ ("Parais!/appear!"), but the aria does not cause the singer to lift up the weight of the voice. The accompaniment is transparent, and there is a beautiful instrumental obbligato that begins while he is observing her on the balcony from afar. The instrumental line represents his impressions of her dreaming ("Elle rêve/She dreams").

Piano/vocal score: p. 82 (G. Schirmer)

> Notes by singer and voice professor Dale Moore: In dealing with "Ah, lève-toi," the first thing one must realize is that the operatic anthologies present it a half step lower than it is in the opera. What is most noteworthy is that the tenors I have work on it have found that it sings more easily in B major than in B♭ major.

No. 71

Voice: tenor
Aria Title: "I know that you all hate me" (Michele)
Opera Title: *The Saint of Bleecker Street*
Composer and Librettist: Gian Carlo Menotti (b. 1911)
Historical Style: 20th-century American (1954)
Range: D3 to C5

Fach: lyric
Aria Duration: 3:30
Tessitura: G3 to E♭4

Position: Act II

Setting: The action takes place in the section of New York known as Little Italy; an Italian restaurant in the basement of a house on Bleecker Street; the wedding of Carmela, a good friend of Annina's. Stage right, there is a door with a sign "Banquet Room"; stage left, there is another door leading to the kitchen.

The story centers on the conflict between a religious mystic, the sickly

Annina, and her agnostic brother Michele. The wedding is marred by an argument between Michele and his mistress, who has not been invited. He drinks too much. Annina tries to make peace, but Michele pushes her away. He raises his hand to strike the priest and is told to leave the party. He defiantly faces the hostile crowd to sing, "I know that you all hate me."

The aria is set syllabically, and diction is important. The rhythm is varied and reflects his agitated state of mind. The meter changes between 2/4, 3/4, and 4/4. "What right have you to judge me? Look at yourselves!" he sings. "Although you made this land your home, you live like strangers. You are ashamed to say 'I was Italian.' And for such little gain you sold your noble, ancient dreams."

Throughout the aria, varied, precise rhythm is very important. Michele ascends to a sustained high C with "Perhaps if I could see just once that sad, sweet country, I would be proud to say 'I am Italian' and would forget your eyes." He grabs a glass of wine and sings, "Take your wine," on a high G before he throws the wine in their faces. He collapses on a chair by a table and buries his head in his arms. Annina makes excuses for him, and as the crowd leaves the restaurant his mistress accuses Michele of being in love with his sister. Michele responds by fatally stabbing his mistress.

Piano/vocal score: p. 189 (G. Schirmer)

No. 72

Voice: tenor
Aria Title: "Light of my soul" (Majnun)
Opera Title: *The Song of Majnun*
Composer: Bright Sheng (b. 1955)
Range: Eb3 to Bb4
Historical Style: 20th-century American (1992)

Fach: lyric
Librettist: Andrew Porter (b. 1928)
Tessitura: Ab3 to G4
Aria Duration: 4:50

Position: Scene 2

Setting: Ancient Persia; a small village

Aria plot notes from the *G. Schirmer American Aria Anthology: Tenor,* edited by Richard Walters (used by permission):

The opera is a stylized tale of unrequited love and its tragic consequences. Young Majnun has fallen in love with Layla, but her parents separate them. Majnun's father goes to Layla's parents to arrange a marriage between the girl and his son. When her parents refuse, Majnun goes mad. Once he has sung "Light of my soul," it [the song] is passed from villager to villager, until it eventually becomes famous throughout the land.

This piece is a very interesting piece to study and perform. It is varied in almost every phrase rhythmically, with difficult intervals and many accidentals. All markings are extremely specific involving articulation, dynamics, and tempo changes. It may be difficult for the young singer to articulate all syllables in an internal passage above the staff, but the composer has provided an option at a lower level.

Piano/vocal score: p. 129 (*G. Schirmer American Aria Anthology: Tenor*)

Notes by composer Bright Sheng: "Light of my Soul" is a tenor aria that appears in scene 2 of the opera, which is based on a Persian "Romeo and Juliet" legend. "Majnun" in Arabic literally means a "madman." Here Majnun (tenor) expresses his longing for Layla (soprano), and the torment of his ill-fated love. The music strives to show Majnun's anguish and suffering—he is on the verge of becoming insane.

No. 73

Voice: tenor
Aria Title: "Lonely House" (Sam Kaplan)
Opera Title: *Street Scene*
Composer: Kurt Weill (1900–1950)
Historical Style: 20th-century American (1946)
Range: F3 to B♭5

Fach: lyric
Librettist: book by Elmer Rice (1892–1967); lyrics by Langston Hughes (1902–1967), based on the play by Rice (1929)
Aria Duration: 3:35
Tessitura: G3 to E♭4

Position: Act I

Setting: The action takes place on a sidewalk in New York City. It is the exterior of a walk-up apartment in a "mean quarter" of New York; an evening in June. "Awful heat" is how the weather is described at the beginning of the play.

Sam Kaplan is a poet in love with Rose. He lives downstairs in the house in the floor below the Maurrants. He has a Yiddish accent and reads extensively. Rose's mother describes him as "such a nice boy. So quiet and gentle." Rose says he's just about the brightest boy she ever met and that she's sure "some day he'll . . . " Rose's father is the abusive Maurrant, and Sam tries, unsuccessfully, to talk with him about his abusive drunkenness. Maurannt's reaction is to sing, "Let things be like they always was," in response to Sam's enlightened ideas about society. We hear a school song in the background as graduating high school students celebrate their graduation and dreams of the future.

As Sam walks toward the house, he sings "Lonely House." He is talking specifically about the building where he and the Maurrants live and the neighborhood overall. It is ironic that with so many people in New York it is a lonely place. Sam's poetic nature comes out as he sings, "the night for me is not romantic, unhook the stars and take them down." This section is sung with bitterness, forte, and the highest note is G♭ above the staff (dotted 16th note). But then poignantly, sadly, and softly, Sam sings a high B♭, A♭, G ("lonely house"). As Sam walks into the house, Rose comes home from a date with Mr. Easter, who is Rose's boss and is trying to pressure her into a different sort of life. The text of the aria is melancholy; the mood, varied dynamics, and tuning are all important components in singing this aria successfully.

Piano/vocal score: p. 115 (Chappell & Co.)

No. 74

Voice: tenor
Aria Title: "It's about the way people is made" (Sam)
Opera Title: *Susannah*
Composer and Librettist: Carlisle Floyd (b. 1926), after the story in the Apocrypha
Historical Style: 20th-century American (1956)
Range: E3 to A5

Fach: lyric
Aria Duration: 2:00
Tessitura: F♯3 to F♯4

Position: Act I, scene 5

Setting: The Polks' rundown farmhouse in the remote mountain village of New Hope Valley, Tennessee, 1950s

Sam, the brother of the 19-year-old Susannah, has brought her up after the death of their parents. Because of their poverty Sam and Susannah are held in contempt by the villagers, who view Sam as a drunkard and Susannah as a wanton. After she is seen bathing in a stream by four elders of the church, Susannah is ostracized. Sam returns home from hunting (and drinking) in the woods, having heard the gossip. Little Bat McLean has just confessed to Susannah that he has falsely admitted to the Elders that she had an inappropriate relationship with him after she was discovered bathing in a stream in the woods. Sam chases Little Bat off their property.

In the aria Sam laments the streak in human nature that lets such a thing happen like hurtful gossip, adding there is nothing they can do but weather the storm. "What's it all about?" asks Susannah. Sam is trying to comfort Susannah, but he is also saying that he is resolved that human nature is what it is. It is impossible to change people's nature, and even though "it must make the good Lord sad," this is the way that people are.

The highest pitch in the piece is high A above the staff, and although the G♯ and A are not sustained, the text must be clearly projected throughout the aria without vowel distortion. The melody and harmony are moving, and a key change brings new energy into the aria in the middle of the piece.

Piano/vocal score: p. 59 (Boosey & Hawkes)

No. 75

Voice: tenor

Aria Title: "Now signorini," The Contest
(Adolfo Pirelli)

Opera Title: *Sweeney Todd, The Demon Barber of Fleet Street*

Composer and Librettist: Stephen Sondheim (b. 1930), book by Hugh Wheeler (1912–1987)

Historical Style: 20th-century American (1979)

Range: B3 to C5

Fach: lyric

Aria Duration: 1:50

Tessitura: D♭3 to F4

Position: Act I, scene 4

Setting: 19th-century London, St. Dunstan's Place

> Aria plot notes from the *G. Schirmer American Aria Anthology: Tenor,* edited by Richard Walters (used by permission):
>
> The bill on Pirelli's painted wagon states: "Signor Adolfo Pirelli, Haircutter-Barber-Toothpuller to his Royal Majesty the King of Naples. Banish Baldness with Pirelli's Miracle Elixir." The hardened escaped prisoner and barber Benjamin Barker, now calling himself Sweeney Todd, has returned to London after many years in exile to avenge a personal grief. He calls Pirelli's elixir "piss," causing an uproar among those who have purchased the potion and who now want their money back. They demand Pirelli's presence, and he makes a grand entrance. Todd challenges the flamboyant Pirelli to a shaving contest, with a wager of five pounds. They each summon a volunteer and the contest begins, with the fastest and smoothest shave as the winner.

Marked agitato, the piece has Pirelli singing a cascade of wandering 8th notes in a broken-English dialect with many accidentals as he lathers and shaves a man, with a flourish. The accompaniment is staccato, with 8th-note chord on beats 1 and 4 of the measure. The range of the piece is challenging; it needs the notes around middle C as well as the sustained high C and must be sung with bravura.

Piano/vocal score: The composer adapted a new aria version of "The Contest" especially for the *G. Schirmer American Aria Anthology: Tenor* and wrote a new last line of lyric for it.

No. 76

Voice: tenor
Aria Title: "No more, false heart" (Valère)
Opera Title: *Tartuffe*
Composer and Librettist: Kirke Mechem
(b. 1925), based on the play by Molière (1664)
Historical Style: 20th-century English
(1980)
Range: D♯ to B♭ (B optional)

Fach: lyric
Aria Duration: 2:30
Tessitura: G♯3 to G♯4

Position: Act I

Setting: Paris, the 17th century; a well-furnished apartment in a house owned by the well-to-do Orgon

> Aria plot notes from the *G. Schirmer American Aria Anthology: Tenor,* edited by Richard Walters (used by permission):
>
> Molière's classic comedy deals with how Tartuffe, a religious hypocrite, finagles his way into an upper-middle-class Parisian home and nearly brings the family to ruin before the King intervenes. In this aria Valère has just learned that Mariane's father has decided that Mariane is to marry Tartuffe instead of him.

Marked allegro molto, risoluto, the piece has a strong beginning for the tenor. He sings, forte, to the G♯ at the top of the staff in strong, declamatory fashion. The tenor is also going to sing high, sustained A's and B's, and a diminuendo on F at the top of the staff. There are intervallic leaps and many accidentals. There is much repetition of text, but little repetition of music:

No more, false heart, shall I believe thy sighing. (*repeated*) Another's charms will soon these tears be drying. (*also repeated*) Away, apart, false heart, oh source of all my sorrow. Another's arms, another's charms, shall hold me. (*to a high B♭ sustained*)

Piano/vocal score: p. 152 (*G. Schirmer American Aria Anthology: Tenor*)

Notes by composer Kirke Mechem: The singer must heed both of the composer's directions: "risoluto" and "with exaggerated gestures." The aria is a spoof of the old-fashioned, melodramatic sentiments of outraged stage lovers. Think of the old silent films: such a character raises an arm pointing to heaven, pounds his chest, covers his eyes or forehead with one arm, wipes away a tear, pleads with outstretched arms. These gestures may begin infrequently and build toward such abundance that the tenor almost resembles a flagman sending semaphore signals. Nothing so energetic is required, but the tenor must do something to illustrate the absurdity of the words. They are pure parody, even travesty. So is the music, but because it is by no means easy, a balance must be struck between acting that is funny and singing that is effective.

No. 77

Voice: tenor
Aria Title: "Dei miei bollenti spiriti" (Alfredo)
Opera Title: *La traviata*
Composer: Giuseppe Verdi (1813–1901)
Historical Style: Italian Romantic (1852)
Range: E3 to A♭5

Fach: lyric
Librettist: Francesco Maria Piave (1810–1876), after Alexander Dumas fils's play *La dame aux camélias* (1852)
Aria Duration: 3:50
Tessitura: G3 to E♭4

Position: Act II, scene 1

Setting: Country house outside Paris, three months after Act I
    Alfredo has been with Violetta in their oasis outside the "evils" of Paris.

Traditionally Alfredo enters this scene in hunting clothes. All is good, Violetta shows signs of improved health, they are happy. However, his mood is belied by the orchestra in a repeated rhythmic accompaniment that gives a sense of underlying agitation, even though Alfredo is lyrically singing about his own youthful ardor that she calms with the smile of love. Although the aria must be lyrically sung, attention to text is very important.

> When she's away, there's no joy for me.
> Three months have flown since my Violetta has abandoned her Parisian life for me,
> Where every man was enslaved by her beauty.
> And now, content in these peaceful surroundings,
> I feel reborn and near to her, and by a breath of love regenerated.
> In its ecstasy (*high A♭*) I forget the past.
> She has tempered my youthful ardent spirit—tamed with the peaceful smile of love.
> Since the day she said, "I want to live faithful to you"
> I have forgotten the outside world, I live (*high A♭*), I live as if in heaven.

As the text repeats, Alfredo sings a fortissimo high A♭ ("io vivo/I live"), and then finishes pianissimo, dolcissimo, before the simple cadenza. Tenors will find the aria challenging because of where the piece lies in the *passaggio,* but many of the high notes are not sustained. The dynamics are extremely specific in the score and sometimes move between fortissimo and pianissimo in the space of two measures. The cabaletta ("o mio rimorso!/to my remorse!") that follows Annina's revelation to Alfredo that Violetta has been selling her belongings to provide money for them to live on is very difficult to sing. It has many repetitions and is often cut in productions of the opera.

Piano/vocal score: p. 70 (G. Schirmer)

No. 78

Voice: tenor

Aria Title: "Outside this house" (Anatol)

Opera Title: *Vanessa*

Composer: Samuel Barber (1910–1981)

Historical Style: 20th-century American (1958)

Range: D3 to A♭4

Fach: lyric

Librettist: Gian Carlo Menotti (b. 1911)

Aria Duration: 2:35

Tessitura: G3 to E4

Position: Act I, scene 2

Setting: A sunny winter morning in Vanessa's luxurious drawing room

Vanessa's lover, Anatol, left her 20 years before, and now his son has come back to her house. Vanessa, who has waited for Anatol's (the father) return while denying the passage of time, is convinced that they will spend their lives together. However, Erika, Vanessa's niece, and a young girl of 20, is the true object of the opportunistic young Anatol's lust. While he still flirts with Vanessa, he wants Erika to marry him.

Before singing this aria it is important to read the previous scene between Erika and Anatol. Anatol is sarcastic, verbally cruel, and abusive. At the same time he tries to tempt her to leave "this house" and see the world. The aria "Outside this house the world has changed" has rhythmic variety and energy as Anatol "presents his case" for her leaving the house and going into the exciting world. Anatol should imagine Erika's resistance and conflicts. After "Do you know Paris and Rome, Budapest, and Vienna," he should "see" the important stage direction included in the score, in which is "she rises and moves away from him, as if to escape him." This is the reason for the *con moto* section, as he tries to get her attention and "bring her back."

This aria uses varied dynamics for a kaleidoscope of vocal changes. The sung "Erika" at the end of the aria specifically demands a seductive crescendo/decrescendo of E♭ to high A♭ that diminuendos to pianissimo. This A♭ has an optional octave middle A♭, but if the tenor can sing it freely, the high note shows expression. The entire piece should be sung with confidence—something the character possesses in abundance.

Piano/vocal score: p. 104 (G. Schirmer)

No. 79

Voice: tenor
Aria Title: "New York Lights" (Rodolpho)
Opera Title: *A View from the Bridge*
Composer: William Bolcom (b. 1938)
Historical Style: 20th-century American
(1999)
Range: C♯3 to A♯5

Fach: lyric
Librettists: Arthur Miller (1915–2005) and
Arnold Weinstein (1927–2005), based on
Arthur Miller's play (1955, rev. 1957)
Aria Duration: 3:40
Tessitura: F♯3 to F♯4

Position: Act I

Setting: A close-knit immigrant neighborhood in Brooklyn, New York; 1950s

Rodolpho is an illegal immigrant from Sicily. Second-generation Italian-American Eddie Carbone and his wife, Beatrice, have taken him in. Rodolpho is the opposite of Eddie. Rodolpho is young, blond (and can't be trusted as a blond Sicilian), has a sense of humor, and is thrilled to be in America. Eddie is none of these things and calls Rodolpho a "hit-and-run guy." The ambitious Rodolpho falls in love with the Carbones' niece Catherine—to the despair of Eddie, who is desperate to stop the affair. After a drunken evening, Eddie betrays Rodolpho to the authorities.

The aria "New York Lights" is an opportunity for Rodolpho to reminisce about his home, Palermo. Ironically, he's only seen pictures of Milan and Rome; even so, they do not compare "to the New York lights." By the end of the piece, he reveals that since he was a boy he has been dreaming of nights in New York. "New York is always my dream!" The aria has no extended high notes and only one high A (a dotted 8th note that can be "broadened").

Piano/vocal score: p. 126 (Edward B. Marks and Bolcom Music)

Notes by composer William Bolcom: "New York Lights" is an amalgam of the Neapolitan canzona and American popular music (fitting Rodolpho's character and situation). Thus a young (or older) singer must combine the street lyricism of the canzona tradition with pearly-perfect American-style singing diction. Rodolpho mustn't sing the piece in a fake "wop" accent—Rodolpho has gone to the trouble of learning excellent English. I'd tell a singer, "Keep a beautiful lyrical line, get the words out, and keep it simple!"

No. 80

Voice: tenor
Aria Title: "Pourquoi me réveiller" (Werther)
Opera Title: *Werther*
Composer: Jules Massenet (1842–1912)
Historical Style: French Romantic (1892)
Range: F#3 to A#5

Fach: lyric
Librettists: Edouard Blau (1836–1906), Paul Milliet, and Georges Hartmann (1843–1900), after Johann Wolfgang von Goethe's novel *Die Leiden des jungen Werthers* (1774)
Aria Duration: 2:30
Tessitura: G3 to F#4

Position: Act III

Setting: The salon in Albert's house in Frankfurt, Germany, 1780. It is Christmas Eve, 5:00 P.M. Doors stage right and left open into the bedrooms of Albert and Charlotte. A small desk and a clavier are in the salon.

Charlotte, married to Albert, cannot stop thinking of Werther, a melancholy young poet of 23 who loves her. Charlotte's young sister, Sophie, interrupts her reverie: "Albert is away, your eyes are red. I am not blind. I know you have been weeping." Sophie tries to cheer Charlotte up. Sophie knows, however, that Charlotte is unhappy. After Sophie leaves her alone, Charlotte reflects on the fact that Werther has promised to visit on Christmas Eve. Charlotte prays to God for guidance. Upon finishing the prayer, Werther enters. They reminisce about when they listened to the same harpsichord and sang together. The poet observes the books and talks about old times of looking at them together. One book in particular, a translation of Ossian's verses, sparks Werther's aria.

Accompanied by the harp, Werther begins to softly sing, "Pourquoi me reveiller/Why do you awaken me, O breath of spring?" He crescendos to G above the staff on "Des orages et des tristesses/Of storms and sorrows" and, again, to a high sustained A sharp on "Pourquoi me reveiller/Why do you waken me." He follows softly with a rallentando phrase, "O breath of spring," on F# at the top of the staff. On the second verse, Werther begins softly, "Tomorrow into the valley, will come the traveler remembering my early glory." When he sings that the traveler "will in vain seek what became of his fame, and will discover only grief and misery," Werther repeats "pourquoi me reveiller" and again crescendos to the high A#. He finishes with the same text and melody on the F# at the top of the staff: "O souffle du printemps/O breath of spring."

The rapid contrasts of dynamics and articulation in this aria are consistent with the poet's moods. Control of the dynamic changes, even while the character almost seems emotionally out of control, is a challenge. The aria is not extremely high, but it goes through the *passaggio* frequently.

Piano/vocal score: p. 176 (Heugel)

No. 81

Voice: tenor
Aria Title: "Dies Bildnis ist bezaubernd schön" (Tamino)
Opera Title: *Die Zauberflöte*
Composer: Wolfgang Amadeus Mozart (1756–1791)
Historical Style: Singspiel (1791)
Range: F3 to A♭4

Fach: lyric
Librettist: Emanuel Schikaneder (1751–1812)
Aria Duration: 3:45
Tessitura: B♭4 to G4

Position: Act I

Setting: Legendary times in Egypt; a rocky landscape overgrown with trees here and there. Mountains are visible in the distance.

This larghetto, but lyric, aria comes early in the opera. The third lady has just told Tamino that they have saved him from the "monster," and the Queen has sent him a portrait of her daughter. Tamino is promised happiness and glory. Almost immediately upon looking at the portrait Tamino is hypnotized by her beauty. He sings, "Dies Bildnis ist bezaubernd schön/this portrait is bewitchingly beautiful, like none a human eye has ever seen!"

I feel it, how this divine image my heart with new emotion fills.
This something can I indeed not name, yet I feel it here like a fire burn.
Could this sensation be love?
Yes! This sensation can only be love.
Oh, if she I could find her, if she stood before me!
I would warmly and purely . . .
What would I do?

The aria takes the singer repeatedly through the *passaggio*. The phrases are not enormously long, but the aria keeps unfolding without repetition. After his initial indecision, "What would I do? (when I find her)," Tamino quickly makes up his mind: "Yes! I would hold her to me; she would always be mine!"

(Translation by Lea Frey)

Piano/vocal score: p. 25 (G. Schirmer)

> Notes by singer and voice professor George Shirley: The controlled spinning of long, lyrical lines is necessary to manifest the desired impact of this challenging air of wonder and awakening love. Tamino's amazement upon viewing the magical portrait of Pamina is characterized by the roller-coaster-like undulations of rising and falling intervals that reflect his ebbing and flowing emotions.
>
> Command of a limpid, flowing vocal line in the *passaggio* is again fundamental to mining the interpretative gold that inhabits this aria. Singing each phrase on the vowels of the text alone offers insights and pays dividends that can be applied to singing the words. Applying the *messa di voce* to the melodic line is time and effort well spent. One must master speaking the German text, gaining ownership of the proper articulation of the consonants and observing the rule pertaining to emphasis on initial vowels; this must be repeated until speaking the text—first conversationally, then in rhythm—is accomplished in a flowing, legato manner, and the tonal flow doesn't feel "fractured." At this point the singer is ready to sing the words to the melody.

No. 82

Voice: tenor
Aria Title: "Come un bel dì di maggio"
(Andrea Chénier)
Opera Title: *Andrea Chénier*
Composer: Umberto Giordano (1867–1948)
Historical Style: Verismo (1896)
Range: E3 to A♭4

Fach: spinto
Librettist: Luigi Illica (1857–1919)
Aria Duration: 2:45
Tessitura: F♯3 to G♭4

Position: Act IV

Setting: Courtyard of the St. Lazare Prison in Paris, late at night

Andrea Chénier is seated under a lantern that throws light on the prison yard. Chénier has been self-defiant in his Act III trial, but he is now sentenced to death. For saving Maddalena earlier in the opera he is wrongly accused of being a counter-revolutionary. He is writing agitatedly before his sentence is carried out. He reads out loud what he has written to Roucher, his friend.

The aria "Come un bel dì di maggio" is sweetly sung in a lilting 6/8 meter. It is Chénier's last poetic expression. He compares the last ray of the sun disappearing over the horizon at sunset to his life being extinguished. He is approaching his fate bravely, calmly, and as a poet—as he puts words to the feelings of those who will die with him. He calls the strophe of his poetry his "ultimate goddess," which inspires him. This is the most enthusiastic phrase of the aria, sung fortissimo on the G♭ and F at the top of the staff at the *passaggio*. After this aria, Maddalena comes to him in disguise to die alongside him.

Piano/vocal score: p. 221 (International)

No. 83

Voice: tenor
Aria Title: "Un dì all'azzurro spazio"
(Andrea Chénier)
Opera Title: *Andrea Chénier*
Composer: Umberto Giordano (1867–1948)
Historical Style: Verismo (1896)
Range: F3 to B♭5

Fach: spinto
Librettist: Luigi Illica (1857–1919)
Aria Duration: 4:45
Tessitura: G3 to F4

Position: Act I

Setting: A soirée at the home of the Countess de Coigny, during the French Revolution

The title character is Andrea Chénier, a poet. The libretto does not draw on historical fact but is based on ideas suggested by the real-life Chénier's poetic works. The Countess de Coigny is giving a soirée, at which her daughter Maddalena is interested in the ardent poet Chénier. It is observed that the poet is in a gloomy mood, and disrespectful to the hosts. He will not entertain the party. He is baited by Maddalena, who initiates a wager with her friends that she can "provoke a poem" from him. Maddalena provokes Chénier with ridicule to the point that the idealistic Chénier begins his creation with a narration that describes what the word *love* means to him.

First he sketches a poetic image of the blue sky and the golden sun. He was so overcome with beauty of his homeland that he wanted to pray, and so he goes into a church. There he meets an old, trembling man asking for bread who extends his hand. Chénier describes a miserable man shaking his fist at God. He turns to Maddalena:

You make my heart sad.
You look like an angel but scoff at the word "love."
Listen! You don't know love.
It is a divine gift.
The life and soul of the world is love!

These are not welcome words at a light social event, but they do fit the temper of the times (the French Revolution). Chénier is courageous to speak these passionate words. Now the narration pours out of him; he has been holding it back. There is scarcely time for a breath or time for someone to interrupt him. The music is set syllabically with very little sustaining of the notes. "Il firmamento/the heavens" are declaimed on a sustained G. The word "amor/love" is repeated three times and sustained. The singer must be passionate, argumentative, angry at times while also sustaining the notes and line of the music.

(Translation by Nico Castel)

Piano/vocal score: p. 50 (International)

No. 84

Voice: tenor
Aria Title: "È la solita storia del pastore," Lament (Federico)
Opera Title: *L'arlesiana*
Composer: Francesco Cilea (1866–1950)
Historical Style: Verismo (1897)
Range: E3 to A5 (B5)

Fach: spinto
Librettist: Leopoldo Marenco (1831–1899), after Alphonse Daudet's play *L'arlésienne* (1872)
Aria Duration: 4:20
Tessitura: A4 to F4

Position: Act II

Setting: The farm of Rosa Mamai in Provence, late 1800s, end of May. She has two sons: L'Innocente and Federico.

Federico is madly in love with a girl from Arles that his mother knows nothing about. Act II takes place on the banks of a body of water in the region of Camargue. In the background is the empty horizon. Federico has run away from home after finding out that his beloved from Arles (who never appears on stage) has been with the stable boy and betraying him. This he finds out before the wedding. Once he learns the truth, he is bitterly disillusioned. Wrestling with grief, Federico's torment is so great that he eventually kills himself—plunging from a high window to his death.

Federico's aria begins as he hears L'Innocente, his younger brother, talk in his sleep. His younger brother is a simpleton. Half asleep, L'Innocente speaks a line from a story told earlier about a goat. Federico sings softly on

A in the middle, "E la solita storia del pastore/It's the usual story of the shepherd." Federico moves closer, "the poor boy wanted to tell it, but fell asleep . . . there is oblivion in sleep, how I envy him!"

The beginning of the aria is atmospheric, moody, as the tenor sings lightly on repeated pitches. At the direction sostenuto he begins to sing melodically three pitches beginning at the lower end of the staff and then repeated sequentially at higher levels, still sung piano. "I only want to find peace," he sings as the line soars to a high, but still piano, A. "If only I could forget," he muses.

After two-measure rest, he crescendos to forte ("I still see her sweet visage before me") and then again to piano as he sings "il dolce sembiante!/her sweet face." After four measures he again climbs and crescendos as he sings, "But all struggles are in vain. She! How she always spoke to my heart." He cries out, "Leave me!" After the aria, Federico sees that the poor lad continues to sleep. Among the few recurring motifs in the opera is a descending figure of interlocking broken octaves associated with L'Innocente, which is skillfully woven into Federico's aria.

Piano/vocal score: p. 85 (Casa Musicale Sonzogno-Milan)

No. 85

Voice: tenor
Aria Title: "Ma se m'è forza perderti" (Riccardo)
Opera Title: *Un ballo in maschera*
Composer: Giuseppe Verdi (1813–1901)
Historical Style: Italian Romantic (1859)
Range: F♯3 to B♭5

Fach: spinto
Librettist: Antonio Somma (1809–1864), after Eugène Scribe's libretto *Gustave III* or *Le bal masqué* (1833)
Aria Duration: 5:15
Tessitura: G3 to G4

Position: Act III, scene 2

Setting: A private room in the Governor's house, Boston, late 17th century (or in the King's palace in Stockholm in the version set in 18th-century Sweden). It is handsomely furnished for writing and other official business.

To the rear are drapes, which later will open to reveal the ballroom for the last scene. The Governor is seated at his writing desk.

This scene takes place before the final scene (the masked ball) of the opera. Alone, Riccardo contemplates his misguided love for Amelia. He has fallen in love with the beautiful wife of Renato, his secretary and loyal friend. He decides to send Amelia and Renato to their homeland in an effort to rid his heart of the ill-gotten love. This story is told within the atmosphere of assassins conspiring to kill the Governor. In the end it is Renato himself who will murder Riccardo. Right before this scene, Renato is seen conspiring with the assassins, Tom and Sam.

Before the accompanied recitative begins, we hear a beautiful melody in the violins. During the recitative Riccardo is sure Renato and his wife will return to England. No farewells. The ocean will divide them, and the Governor's heart will have peace at last.

As Riccardo is about to sign the document that will send them away, he lets the pen fall onto the table. "Is it not my duty?" he exclaims. He signs the document and puts it inside his coat. The aria begins. He says that even if he is forced to lose her, his love will reach her "under whatever sky" she lives. He has a sense of foreboding and has a desire to see her again "as if it were the last hour of our love."

The recitative and aria alternate between forte and piano as Riccardo struggles with his feelings of duty, honor, and love. It is sometimes difficult to negotiate between the two dynamics, as the phrases lie in the *passaggio* and above the staff. The most difficult passage, perhaps, is when Riccardo sings "come se fosse l'ultima ora del nostro amor/as if it were the last hour of our love" to a deceptive cadence, and then repeats the text above the staff to a passing high B♭ (forte). Riccardo sings "l'ultima ora/last hour" one last time (piano) before ascending again above the staff (forte). As in all Verdi arias, articulation is extremely important, as is attention to the dynamics that describe Riccardo's conflicts. At the end of the aria, the Governor now receives a letter from an "unknown lady." The letter warns him that there will be an attempt on his life at the masked ball, but if he refrains from going, people will say that he is a coward.

Piano/vocal score: p. 216 (G. Schirmer)

No. 86

Voice: tenor

Aria Title: "La fleur que tu m'avais jetée" (Don José)

Opera Title: *Carmen*

Composer: Georges Bizet (1838–1875)

Historical Style: French Romantic (1863)

Range: E3 to B♭5

Fach: spinto

Librettists: Henri Meilhac (1831–1897) and Ludovic Halévy (1833–1908), after the novella by Prosper Mérimée (1845, rev. 1846)

Aria Duration: 3:45

Tessitura: A♭3 to F4

Position: Act II

Setting: A room at Lillas Pastia's Inn, late at night, Seville

While Carmen has been entertaining her fellow revelers at Lillas Pastia's inn, she meets (and flirts with) the matador Escamillo. But her flirting is interrupted by the news that Don José—who has been in prison for a month for letting the captured Carmen go in Act I—has been released from prison. The smugglers want Carmen to go with them to help them in their illicit deeds, but Carmen demurs: she is in love. They laugh and leave her alone. It is inevitable that Don José arrive. She dances for him, teases him. He hears the sound of the bugle calling him to the barracks, and she taunts him for his sense of duty. Their exchange is almost violent at this point (foreshadowing the conclusion of the opera).

At the beginning of the aria José is hurt, defensive, and shows her the flower that she has given him in Act I, and that he has kept in his prison cell to sustain him. Although the role needs power in many parts of the opera, this aria is extremely lyrical. There is much text, and the words are very important. There is no repetition. The aria describes José's obsession with Carmen. During his imprisonment, he cursed her, detested her, and asked why destiny put her on his path. Even so, his one desire and hope was to see Carmen again. When he sings, "et j'étais une chose à toi/and I was yours" there is an ascending line, rallantando, to the highest note of the aria, a high B♭. Sometimes it is sung full voice, but the entire phrase is much more effective as written, pianissimo, sung *voix mixte*. The last phrase, "Carmen, je t'aime!/Carmen, I love you," begins with José saying her name without accompaniment in the middle voice and continues to the "je t'aime!" still pianissimo with the orchestra echoing the opening haunting melody.

Piano/vocal score: p. 200 (G. Schirmer)

No. 87

Voice: tenor
Aria Title: "Chiudi il labbro" (Jacopo)
Opera Title: *I due Foscari*
Composer: Giuseppe Verdi (1813–1901)
Historical Style: Italian Romantic (1844)
Range: E♭3 to B♭5

Fach: spinto
Librettist: Francesco Maria Piave (1810–1876), after Lord Byron's historical tragedy *The Two Foscari* (1821)
Aria Duration: 4:15
Tessitura: A♭3 to A♭4

Position: Act I, scene 1

Setting: A hall in the Doge's Palace, Venice, 1457

Jacopo Foscari has returned from exile to face the Council of Ten. Even though Jacopo's father is the Doge of Venice, he is powerless to help him. An official in the Doge's palace has told Jacopo to sit and wait for the council's summons.

This is the cabaletta that follows "Dal più remoto esilio." After Jacopo completes his homesick reverie, the official returns to take him to the Council of Ten. Jacopo's father will be present, and Jacopo is terrified at the thought of meeting his father's gaze. But the official assures him that he may expect a fair sentence. "Liar, shut your mouth," says the defiant Jacopo, who then launches into the cabaletta to defend his innocence. "Listen to me," he commands. Dotted rhythms accent his defiance. Articulations are extremely specific and important. Ascending lines crescendo to A♭, and then, as the orchestra falls silent in two rubato phrases, the tenor climbs to a high B♭. This section is repeated, but this time is marked piano. Perhaps Jacopo is moving closer to the official, singing the repetition more directly, and more personally, to him.

> Hate only and hate atrocious in those souls is locked;
> Bloody, terrible war by them will be waged on me.
> But "You're a Foscari," a voice thunders in my heart,
> And your innocence shall give you strength to withstand their severity.

In quarter notes doubled by accented orchestra, Jacopo declares that he is innocent of the bloodshed and any crimes: "Ah l'innocenza ti dara/your innocence shall give you strength to withstand (*the war's*) severity." Then, head held high, he enters the Council's chambers.

(Translation by Nico Castel)

Piano/vocal score: p. 21 (Ricordi)

No. 88

Voice: tenor
Aria Title: "Dal più remoto esilio" (Jacopo)
Opera Title: *I due Foscari*
Composer: Giuseppe Verdi (1813–1901)
Historical Style: Italian Romantic (1844)
Range: F3 to A5

Fach: spinto
Librettist: Francesco Maria Piave (1810–1876), after Lord Byron's historical tragedy *The Two Foscari* (1821)
Aria Duration: 5:00
Tessitura: A♭3–F4

Position: Act I, scene 1

Setting: Venice, 1457; a hall in the Doge's Palace; a lagoon lit by the moon is seen through gothic arches. It is dark, and the scene is illuminated by two torches on the wall.

The scene is one of sinister gloom. In the orchestra a clarinet and bassoon help create the atmosphere; a muted men's chorus also contributes to the dark mood. Shadowy figures fill the hall. Jacopo Foscari, exiled and homesick, has been brought back to Venice to be interrogated. His elderly father is the Doge, but is powerless to intervene on his behalf. The all-powerful Council of Ten now controls his fate. An officer of the Council brings in Jacopo and tells him to await the Council's summons. The official leaves him alone. Jacopo drags himself to a window and looks at the moonlit Venice. "May I feel again the air not mixed with moans and sighs," he says in the recitative.

A solo flute paints a pastoral picture as Jacopo sings, "Breeze of my native land, may you fly to kiss the face on an innocent man." The adagio tempo means long lines for the tenor, sung through the *passaggio* at the top of the staff. This short section crescendos to a high A as he sings, "Queen of the waves (*Venice*), I salute you." Then, in three phrases of recitativo-like declamation: "Even though you (*Venice*) have been cruel, I am faithful." Then, once again, a soft, lyric expression, in 6/8 meter now: "From the most remote exile my thoughts were always of you, Venice." These are classic bel canto lines (orchestra in short chordal accompaniment), and the ornaments are heartfelt, not merely decorative. Articulations are clearly marked. There are two cadences ("grief almost disappeared for me when I thought of Venice"), and between the last two phrases there are two descending chromatic lines in the orchestra.

(Translation by Nico Castel)

Piano/vocal score: p. 16 (Ricordi)

No. 89

Voice: tenor

Aria Title: "Ch'ella mi creda libero e lontano" (Dick Johnson)

Opera Title: *La fanciulla del West*

Composer: Giacomo Puccini (1858–1924)

Historical Style: Italian Romantic (1910)

Range: E♭3 to B♭5

Fach: spinto

Librettists: Guelfo Civinini (1873–1954) and Carlo Zangarini (1874–1843), based on David Belasco's play *The Girl of the Golden West* (1905)

Aria Duration: 2:15

Tessitura: G♭3 to G♭4

Position: Act III

Setting: California, the foot of the mountains, a mining camp at the time of the 1849–50 Gold Rush

Dick Johnson is actually Ramerrez, a "bandit from birth." He falls in love with Minnie, who has no idea of his true identity. When he is identified and shot by men in the camp, she shelters him. In the third act, set in a nearby forest, "Johnson" has been caught and is about to be strung up on a tree by the men. When asked for his last words, he asks of the men that after they kill him by hanging that Minnie not be told how he has been killed (like a common bandit).

Let her think me free and far away, leading a new decent life!
She'll wait for my return and the days will drag on and on, and I'll not come back.

At the end of the request, he speaks directly to her vision: "Minnie, only flower of my life. Minnie, you who have loved me so much." The first phrase is sung very softly, but then he cries out her name. The aria is brief, yet it shows a long legato line in the middle voice. Control is very important. The high notes (G♭'s and a B♭) should not "stick out" of the shaped phrase. The highest sustained note is Johnson's crying out to Minnie. His cry is heard, and Minnie gallops into the scene and pleads for his release. He is saved.

Piano/vocal score: p. 304 (Ricordi)

No. 90

Voice: tenor

Aria Title: "Amor ti vieta" (Count Loris Ipanoff)

Opera Title: *Fedora*

Composer: Umberto Giordano (1867–1948)

Historical Style: Verismo (1898)

Range: A4 to A5

Fach: spinto

Librettist: Arturo Colautti (1851–1913), after the drama by Victorien Sardou (1882)

Aria Duration: 1:30

Tessitura: B4 to G4

Position: Act II

Setting: A party at Fedora's house, Paris, France, late 19th century

Countess Fedora Romazoff has found out that Count Loris Ipanoff of St. Petersburg has killed her fiancé, and she swears to avenge his death. As the first step of capturing Loris, she goes to Paris and attempts to get him to fall in love with her. They are in a salon in Fedora's house. Shortly after the act begins in a conversational manner with the guests in the salon, Loris meets Fedora, and she spars with him. He is entranced with her and sings this heartfelt aria, "amor ti vieta/love bars you."

> Love itself bars you from loving
> Your light hand that repels me, still looks for the stroke of my hand:
> You eyes exclaim: "I love you," even when your lips say: "I will not love you!"

The vocal line is strong and sweeping, with strong rhythmic definition in its expression. The Count is confident, even arrogant, as he sings. The aria cannot be sung too heavily; it begins around the *passaggio* and then climbs to the high A above the staff on "T'amo!/I love you!" The aria does not need to be sung too strongly (even though it is a passionate expression), as the accompaniment does not double the vocal line.

Piano/vocal score: p. 89 (Casa Musicale Sonzogno)

No. 91

Voice: tenor
Aria Title: "O tu che in seno agli angeli"
(Don Alvaro)
Opera Title: *La forza del destino*
Composer: Giuseppe Verdi (1813–1901)
Historical Style: Italian Romantic (1862)
Range: Db3 to Bb5

Fach: spinto
Librettist: Francesco Maria Piave (1810–
1876), based on Angel de Saavedra, Duke of
Rivas's drama *Don Alvaro, o la fuerza del
sino* (1835)
Aria Duration: 6:10
Tessitura: Ab3 to F4

Position: Act III

Setting: Italy, near the town of Velletri, mid-18th century; War of the Austrian Succession (Spain, with the help of Naples, drove the Austrians out of much of Southern Italy); a pitch-dark forest

At the beginning of the act is heard offstage voices engaged in a game of cards. Then, with a plaintive clarinet solo, we are in a world of dreams. Don Alvaro is in the uniform of a Spanish captain in the Royal Grenadiers. He is of Inca blood from Peru and has darker skin. His recitative is marked with sadness, but also with strength. "Life is hell to the unfortunate. In vain I long for death. Seville! Leonora!"

Instead of going directly into the aria he recounts (in 26 measures of allegro moderato) the attempt of Alvaro's father in Peru to make himself King, his failure and imprisonment. When he finally sings the Romanza "O tu che in seno agli angeli/Oh, you who to the bosom of the angels" it is a prayer to the soul of Leonora to be his guardian angel. The rising 6ths in the melody mirror the spirit of the prayer, which "rises lovely, untouched by mortal calamity/salisti bella incolume dalla mortal jattura." The long legato line contrasts meaningfully when the tenor sings "Ahi misero, chiedo anelando, ahi, misero, la morte d'incontrar/who without a name, exiled and the prey of cruel fate, seeks to meet death" on 16th-note values. He pleads to the vision of Leonora for "pity on his suffering/pietà del mio penar." It is sung softly on high Bb (on an unstressed syllable) and Ab that finally crescendos to forte. Specific double-dotted rhythms, accents, and articulations common to Verdi's style are to be observed.

Piano/vocal score: p. 173 (Ricordi)

No. 92

Voice: tenor
Aria Title: "Durch die Wälder" (Max)
Opera Title: *Der Freischütz*
Composer: Carl Maria von Weber (1786–1826)
Historical Style: German Romantic (1821)
Range: (C3) D3 to A5

Fach: spinto
Librettist: Johann Friedrich Kind (1768–1843), after Johann August Apel and Friedrich Laun's *Gespensterbuch* (1811)
Aria Duration: 6:25
Tessitura: F3 to F4

Position: Act I

Setting: In front of an inn in the Bohemian forest

Max, a forester, has lost a shooting competition at the beginning of the opera. He is completely discouraged and is taunted by the peasant chorus, and only the arrival of the head forester, Cuno, prevents a fight. Caspar, another forester, mockingly suggests that Max should call on the dark powers for assistance. Cuno rebukes this suggestion; however, he warns Max that if he fails in the shooting contest, he will not be allowed to marry his daughter, Agathe. Alone, Max ponders his options, while Samiel, the Black Huntsman, observes him.

In the recitative Max feels darkness in his spirit. The first section talks of former times: he was filled with joy; every bird was easy prey for him; he was a master marksman. Most importantly (he repeats five times up to F and G at the top of the staff), Agathe greeted him with a smile. Samiel appears from behind the trees—he not visible to Max—as Max asks, "What directs me now?"

In the andante con moto (G major), Max thinks of Agathe and tries to have hope: "All in vain, no voice replies." The aria (allegro con fuoco) has two beats per measure, as Max fights against depression—a power that closes round him. "Will no ray of light illumine the darkness?" he asks, fortissimo, sustained on high G and F. "Lives there no God?" he asks, climbing to a high sustained A. He fights, singing forte with accents at the high A♭ and G, but ends in despair. He is primed for a visit from Caspar and his evil spirits. The aria is heavily orchestrated, with trumpets, horns, woodwinds, and kettledrums joining the strings.

Piano/vocal score: p. 38 (G. Schirmer)

No. 93

Voice: tenor

Aria Title: "Amore o grillo" (Pinkerton)

Opera Title: *Madama Butterfly*

Composer: Giacomo Puccini (1858–1924)

Historical Style: Verismo (1904)

Range: F3 to B♭5

Fach: spinto

Librettists: Giuseppe Giacosa (1847–1906) and Luigi Illica (1857–1919), after the play by David Belasco, which was based on a story by John Luther Long (1898)

Aria Duration: 1:05

Tessitura: B♭4 to F4

Position: Act I

Setting: Nagasaki, Japan, 19th century; the terrace and garden of a house leased by Lieutenant B. F. Pinkerton

Before the wedding party enters. Pinkerton (Lieutenant in the U.S. Navy and about to marry Butterfly) is alone, sharing a drink with Sharpless, United States Consul at Nagasaki. Although this is a brief excerpt from the opera, it shows ranges of dynamics while displaying capability of power as well.

Love or whim, I couldn't say.
Certainly she attracted me with her ingenuous arts.
Slight as delicate blown glass in stature,
In bearing she seems like a figure from a screen.
But from its shiny lacquer background how, with sudden motion, she breaks loose.
Like a little butterfly, she flutters and comes to rest with such quiet gracefulness,
That a frenzy to pursue her seizes me, even though I may crush her wings.

The climax of the aria is high B♭ on the word "furor/frenzy," as Pinkerton passionately decides "I must pursue her." Sharpless asks, "Are you completely mad?" Pinkerton answers with passion that he is "completely infatuated." Foreshadowing the end of the opera, Pinkerton recognizes that she "is a butterfly fluttering, coming to rest with such silent grace. I must pursue her—even though I damage her."

Piano/vocal score: p. 35 (G. Schirmer)

Notes by conductor and conducting professor David Effron: Pinkerton is a cad—but he can also be sincere and genuine in this aria.

He is young, wears a uniform, is in an exotic land with a beautiful young woman, and sings tenor! Pinkerton believes everything he says, and this aria must be sung with heartfelt meaning.

No. 94

Voice: tenor
Aria Title: "Donna non vidi mai" (Des Grieux)
Opera Title: *Manon Lescaut*
Composer: Giacomo Puccini (1858–1924)
Historical Style: Verismo (1893)
Range: E3 to B♭5

Fach: spinto
Librettists: Ruggero Leoncavallo (1857–1919), Marco Praga, Domenico Oliva, Luigi Illica (1857–1919), and Giuseppe Giacosa (1847–1906) (with contributions by Giulio Ricordi and the composer), based on the Abbé Antoine-François Prévost's novel *L'histoire du chevalier des Grieux et de Manon Lescaut* (1731)
Aria Duration: 1:55
Tessitura: B♭4 to F4

Position: Act I

Setting: A square in 18th-century Amiens, France, outside an inn

In the Puccini version of the Prévost novel, Des Grieux appears at the beginning of the opera. He interrupts Edmondo and his companions by mocking love before joining his friends in praise of carefree pleasure. He sees the young Manon with her brother and learns that she must go to join a convent the following day. Alone with Manon, Des Grieux persuades her to meet him again later.

Left alone, he muses over her beauty and his awakening love for her in the aria: "I have never seen a woman as this one! To tell her: I love you, my soul awakens to a new life." His musings turn dramatic only momentarily when he sings, "Sweet thoughts, do not cease!" with an accented F, G, A (sung on 8th notes). Another fully sung line at the end of the aria is his memory of how she told him her name (sung forte beginning on A♭): "How these fragrant words wander around in my mind, and come to caress my innermost being. Oh, sweet thoughts." He ends the aria with a sustained B♭: "Deh! Non cessar!/Ah! Do not cease!" The legato vocal line with long phrases that shift between pianissimo and forte show both sides of the character—musing and passion—in the one piece.

Piano/vocal score: p. 47 (International)

No. 95

Voice: tenor
Aria Title: "I'm not a boy, she says" (Mitch)
Opera Title: *A Streetcar Named Desire*
Composer: André Previn (b. 1929)
Historical Style: 20th-century American (1998)
Range: F3 to G♭4

Fach: spinto
Librettist: Philip Littell, based on the play by Tennessee Williams (1947)
Aria Duration: 2:35
Tessitura: F3 to D4

Position: Act II, scene 2

Setting: A bedroom in Stanley and Stella's apartment in the French Quarter of New Orleans during the restless years following World War II; about 2:00 A.M.

> Aria plot notes from the *G. Schirmer American Aria Anthology: Tenor,* edited by Richard Walters (used by permission):
> Stanley's poker buddy Mitch has been courting Blanche DuBois, Stanley's eccentric sister-in-law. Late at night they return from a date. Mitch tells Blanche that he talked to his ill and aged mother about her: "She won't live too long. She wants to see me settled before . . . " He then launches into the aria, quoting his mother's words and sentiments.

It is a "musing" aria, filled with a great number of accidentals and challenging intervals, including the tritone. Mitch ardently asserts, "You know when it's the right thing" and moves with increasing momentum and energy toward his decision: "and you do it. You just do it. That is all there is to love, to true love."

His own fragmented thoughts intervene, "But when . . . but . . . sometimes," but are soon followed by the soaring phrase: "When you lose the one you love, your one true love, what do you do? You still believe in love. No matter who you are." After a thoughtful two measures, he reiterates: "No matter what you've been through. You still need to love." The only extended higher tone in the piece is F at the top of the staff for two beats.

Piano/vocal score: p. 171 (*G. Schirmer American Aria Anthology: Tenor*)

No. 96

Voice: tenor
Aria Title: "E lucevan le stelle" (Cavaradossi)
Opera Title: *Tosca*
Composer: Giacomo Puccini (1858–1924)
Historical Style: Verismo (1900)
Range: F♯3 to A5

Fach: spinto
Librettists: Giuseppe Giacosa (1847–1906) and Luigi Illica (1857–1919), based on Victorien Sardou's play *La Tosca* (1887)
Aria Duration: 2:45
Tessitura: F♯3 to F♯4

Position: Act III

Setting: Cavaradossi is imprisoned in the Castel Sant'Angelo on the roof. It is a starry night. In the distance are seen the Vatican and St. Peter's Basilica.

Cavaradossi has used his ring to bribe the guard to take a letter to Tosca, so he sits down to write the letter. The stars at night (a melody played by a mournful clarinet) remind him of sweet memories of another night in which "she came and fell into my arms." He reminisces of her "Sweet kisses, languid caresses." But he realizes that his dream of love is gone: "He dies in despair, but never has loved life this much."

As Cavaradossi haltingly writes, each phrase is separated by the melody played by the orchestra (a Puccini device). He joins in the melody with the pianissimo phrase "Oh! dolce baci/sweet kisses!" The following phrases, sung strongly to a G and A above the staff, are difficult to sing because of the dramatic despair displayed and because the melody is doubled by the full strings of the orchestra.

Cavaradossi is different from some of the youthful heroes of opera. The two mature lovers of *Tosca* are hardly the young innocents of *La bohème*. Cavaradossi knows what he is getting into, whether it is harboring a political enemy, loving a woman, or facing his ultimate fate.

Piano/vocal score: p. 265 (G. Schirmer)

No. 97

Voice: tenor
Aria Title: "Recondita armonia" (Cavaradossi)
Opera Title: *Tosca*
Composer: Giacomo Puccini (1858–1924)
Historical Style: Verismo (1900)
Range: F3 to B♭5

Fach: spinto
Librettists: Giuseppe Giacosa (1847–1906) and Luigi Illica (1857–1919), based on Victorien Sardou's play *La Tosca* (1887)
Aria Duration: 2:45
Tessitura: A4 to F4

Position: Act I

Setting: The church of Sant'Andrea Della Valle. At right, the Attavanti Chapel; a dais on the left: on it, a large picture on an easel covered by a piece of cloth. Painter's tools lie about, also a basket. Rome, June 1800. (Historical note: there was no Pope in power in the Vatican at this time.)

Mario Cavaradossi is painting a Madonna in a church chapel. Cavaradossi is idealistic and has an eye for beauty and for drama. His Madonna that he is painting in the chapel is modeled on a woman who prays there frequently. He starts to paint, interrupting his work often to scrutinize his work. He takes out of his pocket a medallion, and his eyes begin to wander from the miniature in the medallion to the painting. As Cavaradossi looks at the painting he muses (while the aria begins pianissimo) upon the differences between the "unknown beauty, framed by fair hair, possessor of blue eyes," and his beloved Tosca: "dark eyes, and his passionate lover is a brunette."

The aria (6/8 meter, più lento) begins at the top of the staff as he sings lyrically, then rises with great passion to high G (quarter note) on the -u-vowel. While Cavaradossi is singing passionately, the Sacristan mutters under his breath about the painter's secular interests—which are blasphemous to the church. The painter, inspired, sings up to high A, but still within the vocal line (without sustaining the pitch) as he sings, "And you, unknown beauty, crowned with golden hair . . . you have blue eyes," he observes. "Tosca's are dark. Art, in its mysterious way blends all kinds of beauty together." At the climax of the aria, Cavaradossi sings, "But as I paint the other, I only think of you, Tosca (*singing the high Bb, allargando*), it's you!"

(Translation by Mark Harris)

Piano/vocal score: p. 16 (G. Schirmer)

No. 98

Voice: tenor
Aria Title: "Ah sì, ben mio; coll'essere" (Manrico)
Opera Title: *Il trovatore*
Composer: Giuseppe Verdi (1813–1901)
Historical Style: Italian Romantic (1853)
Range: E3 to G4

Fach: spinto
Librettists: Salvatore Cammarano (1801–1852) and Leone Emanuele Bardare (1820–1874), after Antonio García Gutiérrez's play *El trovador* (1836)
Aria Duration: 2:55
Tessitura: G3 to G4

Position: Act III (The Gypsy's Song), scene 2

Setting: A room or hall adjoining the chapel at Castellor, 1409

Manrico and Leonara are about to be married. The aria "Ah, si, ben mio" is marked cantabile con espressivo. The aria quickly crescendos to a high Ab: "my soul will be fearless, my *arm* will be stronger." Manrico concludes, bittersweetly, that if it is his destiny that he will fall in battle (note the importance of the word *destiny* in this opera), then in his last moments all thoughts will fly to Leonora, and death will mean only that he will wait for her in heaven. There are four more musical climaxes, all on Ab, with a cadenza at the conclusion of the aria.

Before singing the aria, look at the dialogue between Manrico and Leonora that precedes it. Many of Leonora's phrases are questions. She needs comforting and answers at this point. His aria in response to her tentative state of mind is sensitive, but shows a confident character. The cabaletta that follows the primo tempo is "Di quella pira."

Piano/vocal score: p.163 (G. Schirmer)

No. 99

Voice: tenor
Aria Title: "Di quella pira" (Manrico)
Opera Title: *Il trovatore*
Composer: Giuseppe Verdi (1813–1901)
Historical Style: Italian Romantic (1853)
Range: E3 to Ab4 (C5)

Fach: spinto
Librettists: Salvatore Cammarano (1801–1852) and Leone Emanuele Bardare (1820–1874), after Antonio García Gutiérrez's play *El trovador* (1836)
Aria Duration: 3:15
Tessitura: G3 to G4

Position: Act III (The Gypsy's Song), scene 2

Setting: A room or hall adjoining the chapel at Castellor, 1409

Before singing the cabaletta "Di quella pira," take a look at the dialogue between Manrico and Leonora and the text of the cavatina "Ah sì, ben mio; coll'essere." Manrico and Leonora are about to be married, and she needs comforting and answers. In the cavatina Manrico tries to provide that comfort and those answers. If the cabaletta is sung out of context, look at the text that immediately precedes it. Leonora is calmed, and they sing of their joy together. Then Ruiz enters and announces that the gypsy Azuscena is going to be put to death at the stake.

A trembling and furious Manrico tells Leonora that the gypsy is his mother, and he must fly to her aid. He calls his comrades to arms to save her. He calls out to the "cowards" to put out the fire, or he will shortly do it with their own blood. Naturally, the cabaletta is sung forte at the top of the range with many accents. However, Verdi gives the tenor some vocal relief when singing "era già figlio prima d'amarti, Non può frenarmi il tuo martir/I was your son before I began to love you, your torments won't stop me." This passage is marked piano and is written in the middle range.

Leonora has a line before Manrico repeats "Di quella pira." The male chorus sings "All'armi!/To arms!" punctuating Manrico's battle cry and anguish. The highest tone is only A♭ and is within a connected phrase with the men doubling in the first tenor. Manrico will sometimes sing a high C at the end of the cabaletta, which is not written in the score, but can be thrilling with the men's chorus singing in support.

Piano/vocal score: p. 170 (G. Schirmer)

No. 100

Voice: tenor
Aria Title: "Inutiles regrets" (Enée)
Opera Title: *Les Troyens*
Composer: Hector Berlioz (1803–1869)
Historical Style: French Romantic (1863)
Range: E3 to B♭5 (C5)

Fach: spinto
Librettist: Libretto by the composer, based on books 1, 2, and 4 of the *Aeneid* by Virgil (c. 19 B.C.)
Aria Duration: 6:10
Tessitura: F3 to A♭4

Position: Act V, scene 1

Setting: Carthage on the north coast of Africa, soon after the fall of Troy

The piece begins allegro as Enée (Aeneas) sings, "Inutiles regrets . . . je dois quitter Carthage!/Useless regrets . . . I must leave Carthage!" The recitative is accompanied by a galloping figure in the orchestra. Enée's text is epiclike in its power of description in this monologue before the aria. "Dido knows," he says. He can't forget how her fair face turned deadly pale in terror and amazement (sung in a long phrase after disjunctive, shorter bursts). He told her of the greatness of his sacred mission (to found Rome), his son's future, and the destiny of the Trojans: "The heroic death (*arpeggio up to G♭ above the staff*) promised by the fates." But she was not moved ("Nothing moved her. I could not break her silence"), and so he fled from the terrible power of her look.

The recitative has much chromaticism, and a great variety of rhythmic figures. The language and inflection, of course, are of supreme importance. G above the staff is the highest tone, but the phrases are sustained near the *passaggio.* With the text "She would not say a word, but her eyes stared and blazed darkly," the tenor has the opportunity to sing piano in the middle register.

The aria begins (andante) as Enée talks about the moment for the last farewell. He arpeggiates with a crescendo up to high A♭: "How to bear the dreadful sight of her indignant grief?" The agitato section describes his desire to "go down and perish in the depths of the sea if I should leave Carthage without seeing her again." Many of his expressions in this section are in the form of questions: "Without seeing her? Am I a coward? To spurn the sacred laws of hospitality?" But he also answers: "No, beloved Queen." He repeats "beloved queen" on a high A♭. When Enée decides that he will see Dido once more, his rhythms become more vigorous, and his vocal lines ascend. "For the last time press your trembling hands, wash your knees with my burning tears, though the despair of it should break me utterly." He repeats this phrase, while rising to the high B♭ for the last musical phrase.

Piano/vocal score: p. 258 (Choudens)

No. 101

Voice: tenor
Aria Title: "Am stillen Herd" (Walther)
Opera Title: *Die Meistersinger von Nürnberg*
Composer and Librettist: Richard Wagner
(1813–1883), after German history
Historical Style: German Romantic (1862)
Range: D3 to A5

Fach: dramatic
Aria Duration: 4:00
Tessitura: F♯3 to F♯4

Position: Act I, scene 2

Setting: A makeshift arena in Nuremberg, mid-16th century

Walther von Stolzing, a young Franconian knight who has sold his estate with the help of the goldsmith Pogner, has made his home in Nuremburg, and he has fallen in love with Pogner's daughter, Eva. Pogner promises

Eva's hand in marriage to the master singer that wins the singing competition. Walther has no choice but to join the master singers' guild and to enter the competition. The masters ask Walther what kind of training he has had. The masters have strict rules about composition. He tells them his educational background, which isn't very substantial. The named references he gives are dead, and the rest of his learning is from life and from the depths of the forest. The reaction from the masters is skeptical.

The aria "Am stillen Herd" begins in the low range and is sung piano. It has a gentle, sensitive feeling; it is also mysterious, with the repetition of a quarter–8th note rocking rhythm. Walther sings a second verse ("wann dann die Flur/when then the meadow") after comments by Hans Sachs and Beckmesser. This time the melody expands at the top to G above the staff ("da lernt ich auch/there I learned singing"). After more comments and criticisms from the master singers, Walter sings a forte section that shows more range. The section, which begins "was Rosses Schritt beim Waffenritt/ the steed's step on the ride to war," continues the quarter-8th-note rhythmic pattern, but with more rhythmic variety added (duplets), and the line continues to ascend to high F♯, G, and finally a passing high A. Walther has a lot at stake in this excerpt. He has just met Eva in the church, and the masters are scrutinizing him; his replies will determine his future with Eva.

Piano/vocal score: p. 126 (G. Schirmer)

No. 102

Voice: tenor
Aria Title: "Be not afeard" (Caliban)
Opera Title: *The Tempest*
Composer: Lee Hoiby (b. 1926)
Historical Style: 20th-century American (1986)
Range: E♭3 to A5

Fach: dramatic
Librettist: Mark Shulgasser (b. 1947), after the play by William Shakespeare (1611)
Aria Duration: 3:15
Tessitura: F3 to F4

Position: Act II, scene 2

Setting: Prospero's island, location and time unknown

Aria plot notes from the *G. Schirmer American Aria Anthology: Tenor,* edited by Richard Walters (used by permission):

A violent storm, created by the master sorcerer Prospero, the rightful but exiled Duke of Milan, has created a violent storm that has caused the wreck of a ship carrying his deceitful brother and others. The survivors make their way to the island, but do not immediately find one another. The island is home to strange beings, including the half-human Caliban, described as "a feckled welp, hag born," who serves Prospero due to an enchanted spell. He comes upon Trinculo, a court jester, who is amazed at the sight of Caliban. A drunk Stephano, a court butler, stumbles upon the two of them. Caliban, whom they call "monster," tries his first taste of wine. Caliban is so delighted with its effects that he pledges to serve Stephano and Trinculo as gods. The three become quite intoxicated.

In a comic scene, Ariel, an invisible spirit of the island and loyal to Prospero, sets the three characters against each another. Ariel plays a tune on a tabor and pipe, causing Stephano and Trinculo to be afraid at this music coming from no apparent source. Caliban calms them with a description of the strange music of the island: "Be not afeard, the isle is full of noises."

Sounds and sweet airs, that give delight, and hurt not.
Sometimes a thousand twangling instruments will hum about mine ears, and sometimes voices,
If I then had wak'd after long sleep, will make me sleep again.

An offstage chorus, which sounds like the wind, accompanies the aria. Caliban has a sustained high G and A above the staff. Quarter rests punctuate many of the phrases, and the intervals are difficult.

Piano/vocal score: p. 198 (*G. Schirmer American Aria Anthology: Tenor*)

Part IV

Baritone and Bass Arias

No. 1

Voice: baritone
Aria Title: "Tickling a trout, poaching a hare" (Sid)
Opera Title: *Albert Herring*
Composer: Benjamin Britten (1913–1976)
Historical Style: 20th-century English (1947)
Range: A3 to G♯4

Fach: lyric
Librettist: Eric Crozier (1914–1994), after Guy de Maupassant's short story "Le rosier de Madame Husson" (1888)
Aria Duration: 1:25
Tessitura: E3 to E4

Position: Act I, scene 2

Setting: Mrs. Herring's greengrocery, Loxford, East Suffolk, England, a night in late April, 1900

Act I scene 2 is our introduction to Sid, the butcher's shop hand. He is physical, loud, and confident and will use obscenities, even in front of children. In other words, he is everything that Albert is not. Sid also has a playful side that we often see with his girlfriend Nancy from the bakery.

Disgusted by Albert's boring character, Sid recites the wonders of getting away from your parents and spending time just having fun. Chiefmost among these pleasures is the pleasure of meeting a girl. Sid has a strong, virile entrance, *con slacio*, on C♯ in the upper middle voice. The piece begins with the section marked più vivo, piano:

Tickling a trout, poaching a hare, fighting wild geese (*3/4 meter*) is pretty good sport for a chap to enjoy. Living without a regular share of pleasures like these is hard to support for your kind of a boy. But courting a girl is the King of sports in a class of its own (*pianissimo, leggiero*), where there aren't any rules so long as she's caught and you catch her alone.

Girls mean Spring six days a week and twice on Sundays, The whole year round . . . the winter through . . . Girls mean . . . games of . . . hide and seek . . . on summer evenings, when someone's bound to fall for you (*sung accompanied by accents on a high E*). Girls mean: prowling round in meek and wintry . . . weather . . . whispering, . . . whispering, . . . whispering . . . I love you!

Although Sid would like to show Albert "the ropes, and give him some advice "man to man," he also teases Albert in this piece. And although crisp diction and rhythm are always important in Britten's operas, Sid's character is less refined and is resplendent with accents to show his confidence and virility. The piece needs a strong D and E at the top, with passing 16th-note high F#'s, but not sustained. The piece lies in the upper middle of the voice, although it also calls for a low A half note (marked pianissimo).

Piano/vocal score: p. 115 (Boosey & Hawkes)

No. 2

Voice: baritone
Aria Title: "Dearest Amelia" (Husband)
Opera Title: *Amelia Goes to the Ball* (*Amelia al ballo*)
Composer and Librettist: Gian Carlo Menotti (b. 1911)
Historical Style: 20th-century American/ Italian (1937)
Range: B♭3 to F4

Fach: lyric
Aria Duration: 1:45
Tessitura: C3 to C4

Position: One-act opera

Setting: A "grand city" in Europe; an upper-class apartment; a balcony upstage. In the background the city can be seen, bathed in the moonlight.

Amelia is a "shapely young lady with red hair." She wants to go to the ball. At this point in the one-act opera, her husband has confronted her; he has evidence that Amelia is seeing someone else. In fact, he has found a letter, and it is signed "honey bunny." After the initial confrontation, the husband proceeds to read the letter. The aria is written in E♭ major in 3/4 meter, marked piano in the opening:

Dearest Amelia, let me behold you radiant with moonlight, let me enfold you,
Meet me at midnight just as I told you.
Where darkness hovers let us recapture deep in the shadows love's silent rapture.

(*This next line commences on high F.*)

Night will conceal us unhappy lovers.

(*The following line repeats the first melody, but develops.*)

Hasten, O moonlight, where love confesses.

Languid caresses sunlight defies me.

(*He sings climactic, passionate phrases at the top of the range.*)

Oh night have pity, As love's accomplice, give me those kisses that day denies me.

The aria in its most lyric passages lies in the upper middle range of middle C and D. In the shape of the opening melody, the low B♭ and C are needed.

Although the husband is rightfully angry and shocked by the letter, he is also astounded and surprised by the letter's passionate poetic language and can be crushed not only because of Amelia's betrayal—but also by the mystery lover's ability to romantically woo his own wife through beautiful prose the husband is incapable of expressing.

Piano/vocal score: p. 40 (G. Ricordi)

No. 3

Voice: baritone
Aria Title: "Lieben, Hassen, Hoffen, Zagen" (Harlequin)
Opera Title: *Ariadne auf Naxos*
Composer: Richard Strauss (1864–1949)
Historical Style: 20th-century German Romantic (1916)
Range: C3 to F4

Fach: lyric
Librettist: Hugo von Hofmannsthal (1874–1929)
Aria Duration: 1:30
Tessitura: E3 to D4

Position: From the Opera "proper" section after the Prologue

Setting: On stage during an operatic performance of *Ariadne auf Naxos,* an opera seria, in the mansion of a wealthy Viennese businessman, 18th century; mouth of a cave in mythological times

A commedia dell'arte troupe has come to a rich patron's house in Vienna to entertain the guests. An opera seria company also arrives. However, because the patron is running out of time for entertainment with an imminent display of fireworks scheduled, the two companies must put on their pieces at the same and thus overlap and interact.

In the opera seria company's production, Ariadne's despair is great because she has been abandoned on a remote island by her lover, Theseus. Ariadne welcomes the idea of death. Harlequin (from the commedia dell'arte troupe) tries to cheer her up, saying that she should give life another chance, since life's joys can really be surprising.

> *Harlequin (from the wings):* I am afraid a great sorrow has unhinged her mind.
> *Zerbinetta:* Let us try to cheer her up with some music!
> *Scaramuccio, Truffaldino (from the wings):* Quite assuredly, she is mad.
> *Ariadne (to herself, as if she had heard the last words in her dream):* Mad, but wise, yes!
> I know what is good, when one can keep it far from one's poor heart.

The accompaniment for the aria is light, marked staccato. Harlequin sings, "Love and hatred, hope and fear, every joy (*a high sustained F on "Lust/joy"*) and every pain, all this can a heart endure once and many times again." (Accents help to define the text—"hassen/hate"—as well as dynamic markings: pianissimo for "Zagen/fear." This next section is marked "starker/stronger.")

"But to feel no joy nor sadness, even pain itself being dead, that is fatal to your heart, this you must not be for me! You must lift yourself out of the darkness, were it but to new refreshment! You must live (*he sings a D to high F for a quarter-note value*), for life is lovely. Live once again, this one time."

The rhythms are playful, often off the beat. Text is very important, as is the inflection of the text. A nice "bit" is for the Harlequin to give a "look" to the pianist (for an audition) at the final dissonant chord, a sound that the commedia dell'arte actor disapproves of. The "look" can be: "Can't you help me in this task, trying to cheer up Ariadne?!" before the accompanist "agrees" to resolve the chord.

Piano/vocal score: p. 114 (Boosey & Hawkes)

No. 4

Voice: baritone
Aria Title: "Largo al factotum" (Figaro)
Opera Title: *Il barbiere di Siviglia*
Composer: Gioacchino Rossini (1792–1868)
Historical Style: Bel canto (1816)
Range: D3 to G4

Fach: lyric
Librettist: Cesare Sterbini (1784–1831), after Pierre-Augustin Caron de Beaumarchais's play *Le barbier de Séville* (1775) and Giuseppe Petrosellini's libretto for Giovanni Paisiello (1782)
Aria Duration: 4:00
Tessitura: G3 to E4

Position: Act I, scene 1

Setting: In front of Dr. Bartolo's house in Seville, 18th century; morning

Figaro rushes onto the stage and introduces himself as a man of superior talents that make him a superb doctor, barber, matchmaker, etc. He is a man of many trades and is in great demand. It is possible that he has come here to make his first delivery of the morning to the servants of Doctor Bartolo.

The aria is marked allegro vivace. Figaro is an "everyman," the new emerging middle class of France. (The popular newspaper *Le Figaro* in Paris represents this working middle class.) The singer needs to look for specific articulation markings (staccato, grace notes, accents, to energize the opening).

Translation by Martha Gerhart from the *G. Schirmer Opera Anthology: Arias for Baritone,* edited by Robert L. Larsen (used by permission):

Tra la la la la, tra la la la la . . . [*entrance*]
Make way for the factotum of the city! Quickly to your shops, because it's already daybreak!
[*legato*] Ah, what a beautiful life: what beautiful pleasure for a barber of quality!
Ah, well done, Figaro—very well done! Most lucky, in truth!
[*This is written in a high tessitura: to the high E and F.*]
Well done!
[*In the new section there are more staccato markings, and the text is set syllabically à la "patter song" style.*]
Ready to do anything, night and day he's always out and about.
A better feast for a barber—a life more noble—no, it is not to be had.

[*A new section describes his tools-of-the-trade.*]
Razors and combs, lancets and scissors—at my command everything is here.
[*This next section is freely sung, unaccompanied, between the measures of orchestra playing, to set off the text.*]
There are benefits beyond the job itself with the little lady . . . tra la la la—
With the cavalier . . . tra la la la.
Ah, what a beautiful life: what beautiful pleasure for a barber of quality.

The text is repeated here, marked legato. The short, fragmented expressions will grow to longer phrases, with a variety of articulation markings in the syllabically set delivery; this is for fun, playful, with Figaro pretending that everyone is knocking down his door for his services.

Translation by Martha Gerhart from the *G. Schirmer Opera Anthology: Arias for Baritone,* edited by Robert L. Larsen (used by permission):

Everyone calls me, everyone wants me—
Ladies, lads, old men and maidens: . . .
Quick, the shave . . . the bleeding here . . . quick, the love note!
Hey, Figaro! Mercy, what frenzy! Mercy, what a crowd!
[*Figaro sings high E and F here, lending more intensity to the text in the high range.*]
One at a time, for heaven's sake!
Figaro! I'm here. Hey, Figaro! I'm here, Figaro there; Figaro up, Figaro down!
I'm fast . . . fast as can be—quick as lightning; I am the factotum of the city!
[*This last section is sung very fast, marked piano with a variety of articulations and building to the cadence, singing to high G before the final middle C.*]
Ah, well done, Figaro—very well done!
Good fortune will not fail you!

Piano/vocal score: p. 31 (G. Schirmer)

No. 5

Voice: baritone
Aria Title: "Look, through the port comes the moonshine astray" (Billy Budd)
Opera Title: *Billy Budd*
Composer: Benjamin Britten (1913–1976)
Historical Style: 20th-century English (1951)
Range: C3 to E4

Fach: lyric
Librettists: E. M. Forster (1879–1970) and Eric Crozier (1914–1994), adapted from Herman Melville's story *Billy Budd, Foretopman* (1891)
Aria Duration: 6:00
Tessitura: E3 to C4

Position: Act II, scene 4

Setting: *H.M.S. Indomitable*, 1797; main deck and quarterdeck

Billy Budd is a tragic figure, based on the character in the Herman Melville novel. Billy is an able-bodied sailor who has one major flaw—a stammer that comes and goes. He is assigned to the foretop, and he is overjoyed to be able to work high above the deck.

The master-at-arms, Claggart, is suspicious and jealous of Billy from the beginning. Confronted by Claggart and surprised by accusations of mutiny, Billy is unable to speak and strikes Claggart, killing him without such intent. Toward the end of the opera, in a bay of the gun decks, Billy lies in irons before dawn, thinking about his impending execution and his watery grave ("Look, through the port comes the moonshine astray"). He is alone and it is quiet.

The vocal line is lyric, and at the end of each repeated phrase is the sound of a flourish played by the flute. Is this representing Billy's memories of freedom, when he was out on deck, feeling "free as a bird?" What will his death mean? Will he see a friendly face before he is executed? He is finally at peace with his death, equating his execution at sea with sleep.

Piano/vocal score: p. 310 (Boosey & Hawkes)

No. 6

Voice: baritone
Aria Title: "Va pur, va pur, va seco"
(Mercury)
Opera Title: *La Calisto*
Composer: Francesco Cavalli (1602–1676)
Historical Style: Italian Baroque (1651)
Range: D3 to E4

Fach: lyric
Librettist: Giovanni Faustini (1615–1651)
Aria Duration: 1:45
Tessitura: E3 to D4

Position: Act I

Setting: A parched forest, Pelsgia, Peloponnesus

Calisto has gone off with the god Giove, who she thinks is her mistress Diana. Watching the deception, Mercury comments that trickery is the best way to win a woman.

Go away! Echo will make the sound of kisses throughout the forest. Away!
If your youth and prayers do not find the tears of the ungrateful mistress, then hear, lovers!
Practice every trick, because a cheating lover's the one who will enjoy her.
(*Tempo 1*) The carnal sensuality of the joys Cupid can provide
Are more enjoyed when flavored with deception, I can assure you,
Because the cheating lover's the one who will enjoy her.

This piece has a very simple melodic line that moves with momentum. The text and inflection are very important. The 3/4 meter has a dancelike feeling. Although the piece lies in the middle of the staff, an easy high E and F are needed.

Piano/vocal score: p. 45 (Faber Music)

No. 7

Voice: baritone
Aria Title: "Dear boy" (Dr. Pangloss)
Opera Title: *Candide*
Composer: Leonard Bernstein (1918–1990)
Historical Style: 20th-century American (1956)
Range: B3 to F#4

Fach: lyric
Librettist: Lillian Hellman (1905–1984) (rev. versions by Hugh Wheeler), based on the novel by Voltaire (1756); lyrics by Richard Wilbur; additional lyrics by John Latouche, Dorothy Parker, Hellman, Bernstein, and (in revised versions) Stephen Sondheim
Aria Duration: 4:10
Tessitura: E3 to D4

Position: Act I

Setting: The baron's castle, 18th century

Candide is the illegitimate nephew of a German baron. He grows up in the baron's castle under the tutelage of the scholar/philosopher Pangloss, who teaches him that this world is the best of all possible worlds. Candide falls in love with the baron's young daughter, Cunegonde. The baron catches them kissing and kicks Candide out of his home. Pangloss is an exaggerated parody of Enlightenment philosophers.

Pangloss tells Candide of syphilis and how he caught it: through the powers of love. The beginning is marked allegro con spirito, all'ungarese, forte. Verse 1:

Dear boy, you will not hear me speak with sorrow or with rancor
Of what has shriveled up my cheek and blasted it with canker;
'Twas Love, great Love, that did the deed, through Nature's gentle laws,
And how should ill effects proceed from so divine a cause? Dear boy: . . .

The next section is marked andantino, pianissimo, dolce:

Sweet honey comes from bees that sting, as you are well aware; To one adept in reasoning, whatever pains disease may bring (*mezza voce, to high E♭ quarter note*) are but the tangy seasoning to Love's delicious fare.

Marked ppp, the falsetto voice is permissible on the high sustained E♭: "Dear boy . . . "

The piece is mostly set in the middle voice, with only a passing low G♯ and A. Also is needed a high E♭, sung falsetto. Diction, dynamics, articulations, and style are important for a strong performance.

Piano/vocal score: p. 58 (Boosey & Hawkes)

No. 8

Voice: baritone
Aria Title: "Come un'ape ne'giorni d'aprile," Cavatina (Dandini)
Opera Title: *La Cenerentola*
Composer: Gioacchino Rossini (1792–1868)
Historical Style: Bel canto (1817)
Range: B♭3 to F4

Fach: lyric
Librettist: Jacopo Ferretti (1784–1852), after Charles Perrault's story *Cendrillon* (1697), Charles-Guillaume Étienne's libretto *Cendrillon* (1810), and Francesco Fiorini's libretto *Agatina* for Stefano Pavesi (1814)
Aria Duration: 5:25
Tessitura: D3 to F4

Position: Act I, scene 1

Setting: The "mansion" of Don Magnifico; a shabby old room in the house; to one side is a fireplace and a small table with a mirror, as well as some chairs

Dandini, a valet, is disguised as his master, Prince Ramiro, to help him investigate the marital possibilities at Don Magnifico's house. He sings that, although he has hopped like a bee from "flower to flower," he cannot find a woman who is special enough to be his wife. Meanwhile, he makes side remarks to Prince Ramiro (who is disguised as a courtier) about how well he is doing. The aria is composed in 12/8 meter:

"As a bee in the days of April goes flying lightly and playfully." The vocal line begins at low C and goes up to middle C at "d'aprile/of April" with an intervallic leap up to high F, then back to middle C. "It darts to the lily, then springs to the rose, seeking a sweet flower for itself."

The singer repeats the first melody, at first lightly embellished and becoming more florid as the aria continues: "Among the fair maids I rove and look them over; I have seen already so many and then some; But I can't find a mind, or a face, a tidbit delicious to suit me."

This piece is not demanding as far as the high range is concerned. The importance here is upon style and character, which is flamboyant. Dandini paints in broad strokes. As the aria continues he becomes more confident in his disguise, and thus the added decorative touches.

Piano/vocal score: p. 74 (Ricordi)

No. 9

Voice: baritone	**Fach:** lyric (dramatic)
Aria Title: "Scintille, diamant" (Dappertutto)	**Librettists:** Jules Barbier (1825–1901) and
Opera Title: *Les contes d'Hoffmann*	Michel Carré (1819–1872), based on their
Composer: Jacques Offenbach (1819–1880)	play (1851), based on tales by E. T. A. Hoff-
Historical Style: French Romantic (1881)	mann
Range: B3 to G♯4/A3 to F♯4	**Aria Duration:** 3:40
	Tessitura: B3 to E4/A3 to D4

Position: Act II

Setting: Venice, 19th century; a lavishly decorated palace overlooking the Grand Canal

Dappertutto (one of the "four villains") has been watching Hoffmann wait for Giulietta, who is one of the loves of his life. The villain produces a giant diamond, with which, he says, he will persuade Giulietta to capture Hoffmann's soul for him. She has only to look into his magic mirror, and their souls stay with their reflections.

Dappertutto hears Hoffmann say, "If the devil allows me to love her, I consent to be damned by him!" Dappertutto says, "Go! To begin my assault on you, Hoffmann, Giulietta's eyes are an unerring weapon! It was necessary that Schlemil succumbed . . . by my faith as devil and as captain you will do as Schlemil did. I wish that Giulietta bewitch him, bewitch him today."

Aria:

Sparkle, diamond! Mirror where is trapped the lark.
Fascinate, attract her! Both lark and woman come,
At the sight of this conquering lure,
The former on its wings and the latter from her heart.
The one there parts with his life and the other there parts with her
soul.
Lovely diamond, attract her!

Giulietta enters and comes toward Dappertutto as if fascinated by the
diamond he holds out to her.

The aria has a sustained, seductive line from the beginning in the low
range, and later climbing to the higher notes. It has a beautiful melody. It
can be set in the higher baritone key—with the top note F♯ sustained—or
one step lower for the deeper voice who may be singing all four villains.

Piano/vocal score: p. 136 (G. Schirmer)

No. 10

Voice: baritone
Aria Title: "Donne mie la fate a tanti," No.
26 (Guglielmo)
Opera Title: *Così fan tutte*
Composer: Wolfgang Amadeus Mozart
(1756–1791)
Historical Style: Classical (1790)
Range: B3 to E4

Fach: lyric
Librettist: Lorenzo da Ponte (1749–1838)
Aria Duration: 3:30
Tessitura: D3 to D4

Position: Act II, scene 2

Setting: The garden of Fiordiligi and Dorabella near the seashore, Naples,
18th century

Aria plot notes from the *G. Schirmer Opera Anthology: Arias for Baritone,* edited by Robert L. Larsen (used by permission):

The young soldiers Ferrando and Guglielmo have made a wager with their friend, the [cynical] aging bachelor Don Alfonso, that their girl-friends will remain faithful to them despite any temptations. Disguised as Albanians as part of the wager, they pursue the ladies.

Ferrando is pleased that Fiordiligi has remained "pure as a dove" and has not given in to his advances. Guglielmo, having succeeded in wooing his friend's fiancée, comments on the unfaithfulness of women. He declares that women who treat all men in such a bad way deserve to have their lovers complain about them.

The aria is marked allegretto:

Aria translation by Martha Gerhart from the *G. Schirmer Opera Anthology: Arias for Baritone,* edited by Robert L. Larsen (used by permission):

Dear ladies, you deceive so many men that, to tell you the truth, if your lovers complain I begin to sympathize with them. I am fond of the fair sex. You know it, everyone knows it. Every day I prove it to you, I give you proofs of friendship; but this deceiving of so many men mortifies me, in truth.

A thousand times my weapon I've drawn to save your honor . . . a thousand times I've defended you with my mouth and even more, with my heart; it's an annoying little vice.

You're lovely, you're pleasant, many treasures heaven has bestowed upon you, and graces surround you from head to toe; but you deceive so many and so many, that it is unbelievable.

That, if the lovers protest, they surely have a very good reason.

The text is set syllabically and delivered in a straightforward manner—consistent with Guglielmo's blunt personality. Many of the phrases begin at the higher level, usually on D. As the "rant" continues, Guglielmo must find ways to sing so that the aria is not sung with too much bluster, because it will wear on the singer (and the audience). The baritone must add for variety some other emotions to color the voice and diminish some of the constant syllabic coarseness.

Try the varied emotions of sarcasm, inspiration, awe, self-righteousness, for example, to balance the anger.

Piano/vocal score: p. 267 (G. Schirmer)

Notes by singer and voice professor Richard Stilwell: I advocate certain principles when singing Mozart. "Donne mie" is filled with repetitive 8th notes throughout. To keep the run of even 8th's interesting, one must find certain words to accent or "underline," and crescendo (for the most part) to the end of the phrase, as in "ogni giorno ve lo mostro, ve lo mostro, ve lo mostro, vi dò segno d'amistà/each day I show it and always take your part." I am also a stickler on articulation, which helps sustain interest. On words such as "m'avvilisce/discourages me," sing triple "v's." The same on "mille volte/a thousand times" and "è un vizietto seccator/is pernicious and a bore": lots of double consonants. The "siete vaghe/you're attractive" line is a complete change of attitude and should be sung molto legato, reverting back to the more staccato only on "ma, ma, ma . . . " And again with "che se gridano gli amanti/and if your lovers complain," make the slow crescendo to the forte of "gran perché/good reason." This aria should never sound blustery. Success with Mozart comes in singing through the notes, in particular the shorter note values. Connecting words to make meaningful phrases should be the goal.

No. 11

Voice: baritone
Aria Title: "Non siate ritrosi," No. 15 (Guglielmo)
Opera Title: *Così fan tutte*
Composer: Wolfgang Amadeus Mozart (1756–1791)
Historical Style: Classical (1790)
Range: D3 to E4

Fach: lyric
Librettist: Lorenzo da Ponte (1749–1838)
Aria Duration: 1:45
Tessitura: D3 to D4

Position: Act I

Setting: The living room of Dorabella and Fiordiligi's house, Naples, 18th century

After Fiordiligi asks the soldiers disguised as Albanians to leave, Guglielmo (a soldier) sings this aria describing the young men's many virtues, including their big muscles and their large moustaches. The aria (which directly follows Fiordiligi's protestations in her "opera seria" aria "Come scoglio") is presented in an exaggerated style that is playful and on the edge of bursting out in laughter by Guglielmo and Ferrando.

Don't be shy, pretty eyes. Send two loving, flashing glances in our direction. Love us, make us happy, and we in turn will make you very happy. Look, touch, observe everything; we're two dear madmen, we're strong and well built, and as everyone can see, be it merit, be it chance, we have lovely feet, lovely eyes, a fine nose, and these moustaches can be called triumphs of manhood, fancy feathers of love.

The piece is confident, broadly sung, straightforward and simple, as befits the personality of Guglielmo. The main melody is built on a D major arpeggio from the lower note to the upper octave. The piece can be especially funny when the "brave" Guglielmo uses Ferrando as a model: "we have lovely feet, eyes, nose . . . " It is sung playfully, not seriously, and Guglielmo dissolves in laughter by the end.

Piano/vocal score: p. 124 (Schirmer)

Notes by singer and voice professor Richard Stilwell: "Non siate" should be imbued with fun and frivolity and yet still have those clean leaps between notes necessary to impart the proper style. A cadenza is effective on the final "il tutto osservate." Innovative staging can make this short aria work.

No. 12

Voice: baritone
Aria Title: "Carlo, ch'è sol il nostro amore,"
Romanza (Rodrigo)
Opera Title: *Don Carlo* (Italian version)
Composer: Giuseppe Verdi (1813–1901)
Librettists: François Joseph Méry (1798–
1865) and Camille du Locle (1832–1903),
based on Johann Christoph Friedrich von
Schiller's play *Don Carlos, Infant von
Spanien* (1787) and on Eugène Cormon's
play *Philippe II, roi d'Espagne* (1846) for the
original five-act French version. The revised
Italian four-act version was adapted by
Antonio Ghislanzoni.
Historical Style: Italian Romantic (1867)
Range: C♯3 to F♯4

Fach: lyric
Aria Duration: 3:30
Tessitura: D♯3 to D4

Position: Act I

Setting: The gates of the cloisters of Saint-Just Monastery, Madrid, 1559. Outside the monastery a fountain, some grassy banks, groups of orange trees and pines are seen. The blue mountains of Estremadura are visible in the background.

Rodrigo tells Elizabeth of the emotional pain Carlos has been through recently. Carlos, who was in love with Elizabeth when she was forced to marry Carlos's father for political reasons, has been in misery since the marriage. Rodrigo says that Carlos's spirits would be greatly improved if he could see her again. Rodrigo is a stable, noble man of principle—while Carlo was historically weak and epileptic. Rodrigo is also a loyal friend to Carlo, demonstrated many times in the opera.

The aria is marked cantabile, piano.

Carlo, who has all of our love, lives in grief in this land, and no one knows how much grief withers the flower of his noble heart. He who moans in grief can find hope only in you! May he find the peace and the strength; may it be granted him that he see you again; he shall be saved if he is allowed to see you again.

This piece has some decorative but subtle embellishments. It is mainly sung piano, but crescendos at "dato gli sia che vi riveda, . . . se tornera, salvo sara/may it be granted him that he see you again," as the line extends up to a high F♯ ("ri-ve-da") for a quarter-note value.

Following the text above, Eboli remarks: "One day when I was standing close to Elizabeth I saw Carlo trembling. Could he be in love with me? Why does he hide it from me?" Elizabeth: "The pain in me is getting worse. To see him again is to die!"

Rodrigo (singing the second verse):

Ah! Carlo always found the heart of the King, his father, closed; yet I don't know in truth which of them is more worthy of being loved. Only one loving word from you to him can banish the grief from his heart. And he can be saved once he returns here.

The aria shows the legato line of the voice and needs flexibility for the simple embellishments. The piece demands a free F♯ at the top, not sustained, but part of the shape of the vocal line. Many markings need to be observed, including dynamics and articulation.

Piano/vocal score: p. 107 (Ricordi), p. 53 (G. Schirmer)

No. 13

Voice: baritone
Aria Title: "Per me giunto . . . Io morrò, ma lieto in core" (Rodrigo)
Opera Title: *Don Carlo* (Italian version)
Composer: Giuseppe Verdi (1813–1901)
Historical Style: Italian Romantic (1867)
Range: E3 to F♯4

Fach: lyric
Librettists: François Joseph Méry (1798–1865) and Camille du Locle (1832–1903), based on Johann Christoph Friedrich von Schiller's play *Don Carlos, Infant von Spanien* (1787) and on Eugène Cormon's play *Phillipe II, roi d'Espagne* (1846) for the original five-act French version. The revised Italian four-act version was adapted by Antonio Ghislanzoni.
Aria Duration: 8:30
Tessitura: F3 to F♯4

Position: Act IV, scene 2

Setting: The prison cell of Don Carlos in Madrid, 1559

Rodrigo visits his friend Carlos in prison to tell him of his imminent release. While he is in the prison arranging the release, he is shot in the back by henchmen of the Inquisition.

Rodrigo lies dying, but he does not fear death, for his death will save the life of Carlos and Spain. He has been the idealist, willing to stand up to King Philip II to articulate his views, and Rodrigo has earned the King's respect and friendship.

I shall die, but happy in my heart, that I could thus keep for Spain a savior! Ah! Do not forget me! Give your hand to me . . . Ah! Save Flanders! Carlos, farewell . . . ah!

Rodrigo sings this beautiful melody with his last dying breath in the high-middle range. Although sung pianissimo, it has urgency to it, for Rodrigo does not have very much time, and Don Carlo is filled with guilt that his friend is dying. Rodrigo must convince Carlo in a very short time that he dies for a principle, and that Carlo must make sure that Rodrigo does not die in vain, thus the repeat of the melody. This "energy of purpose" propels Rodrigo to the high G♭ three times before expiring.

Note: "Io morrò" can also be paired with "per me giunto," which Rodrigo sings to Carlo in the cell before he is shot. Their conversation has the same urgency because Rodrigo knows that he is a marked man: "My last

·day has come. No, we shall not see each other again. May God reunite us in heaven, He who rewards His faithful. In your eyes the tears I see; weeping thus, why? No, take heart, for he who will die for you will breathe his last in happiness." As Rodrigo breathes his last gasp, a reminiscence of his "Friendship Duet" with Carlo in Act I is quoted by the orchestra, piano.

The singer needs a high F sung piano and within the legato line observe all articulations and dynamics to discover its serious purpose in the context of the scene.

Piano/vocal score: p. 303 (Ricordi)

No. 14

Voice: baritone
Aria Title: "Deh vieni alla finestra," No. 16, Canzonetta (Don Giovanni)
Opera Title: *Don Giovanni*
Composer: Wolfgang Amadeus Mozart (1756–1791)
Historical Style: Classical (1787)
Range: D3 to E4

Fach: lyric (dramatic)
Librettist: Lorenzo da Ponte (1749–1838), after Giovanni Bertati and Giuseppe Gazzinga's opera *Don Giovanni Tenorio, o sia Il convitato di pietra* (1787)
Aria Duration: 2:10
Tessitura: F3 to D4

Position: Act II, scene 1

Setting: Seville, 17th century; the front of an inn where Donna Elvira is staying; night

After Leporello has led Donna Elvira away, Don Giovanni serenades her chambermaid.

Verse 1 (marked allegretto, not too slow—or dramatically heavy):

> Aria translation by Martha Gerhart from the *G. Schirmer Opera Anthology: Arias for Bass*, edited by Robert L. Larsen (used by permission):
>
> Pray, come to the window, oh my treasure. Pray, come console my weeping.
> If you refuse to grant me some solace, before your eyes I want to die.

> [Verse 2:]
>   You whose mouth is more sweet than honey—
>   You who bear sugar in your heart of hearts—
>   Do not, my delight, be cruel with me.
>   At least let yourself be seen, my beautiful love.

Don Giovanni, accompanying himself lightly, sings a beautiful, lyric melody that needs legato singing to the D and E at the top of the staff without strain. The Don intends to seduce a maidservant of Donna Elvira's. He sings beneath her window. The Don doubtless has sung the piece many times before.

The first verse is sung softly, tenderly, and asks for pity to "console my weeping." The second verse is sung more urgently with more determination, for there is no response after verse 1. Don Giovanni is an impatient man, even while singing such a compelling melody.

Piano/vocal score: p. 174 (G. Schirmer)

> Notes by singer Gino Quilico: This is one of my favorite roles. The role can be approached in many ways. The Don must be confident, secure, most definitely arrogant. His body language is extremely important, especially his posture, which I make a conscious effort to engage in the role. When I saw a dancer in the classic Don Juan ballet role, I learned about the power of Don Giovanni's carriage. "Deh vieni" should be sung in a sexy way, but without crooning with the voice.

No. 15

Voice: baritone
Aria Title: "Fin ch'han dal vino," No. 11
(Don Giovanni)
Opera Title: *Don Giovanni*
Composer: Wolfgang Amadeus Mozart
(1756–1791)
Historical Style: Classical (1787)
Range: D3 to E4

Fach: lyric (dramatic)
Librettist: Lorenzo da Ponte (1749–1838),
after Giovanni Bertati and Giuseppe
Gazzinga's opera *Don Giovanni Tenorio,
o sia Il convitato di pietra* (1787)
Aria Duration: 1:15
Tessitura: F3 to D4

Position: Act I, scene 4

Setting: Near Seville, 17th century; the garden of Don Giovanni's palace

As Don Giovanni arrives at his palace with the peasants awaiting the wedding party of Masetto and Zerlina inside, he declares that there shall be an incredible party with much wine and many women. He is a hunted man, and he is excited by the danger, though not afraid of the consequences.

The piece is marked presto, 2/4 meter; the introduction is marked forte, but the voice entrance is marked piano.

Aria translation by Martha Gerhart from the *G. Schirmer Opera Anthology: Arias for Baritone,* edited by Robert L. Larsen (used by permission):

Until their heads are hot from the wine; have a grand party prepared. If you find some girl in the piazza, try to bring her with you too. Let the dancing be without any order; you will make some dance the minuet, some the follia, some the allemande. And meanwhile I, in the other corner, want to flirt with this girl and that one. Ah, tomorrow morning you should augment my catalogue by about ten.

The aria is urgently sung, almost frenzied, but with Don Giovanni's confidence and nobility. The text is repeated at a higher range and a level of delivery that is more intense, culminating with sustained high E♭. With the repetitions of high E♭ and D, the singer must keep the line and not strain for the higher pitches. There are constant intervallic leaps up of the 7th (F to E♭): "Senza alcun ordine la danza sia, chi'l minuetto, chi la follia, chi l'alemanna farai ballar/Without any order; you will make some dance the minuet, some the follia, some the allemande."

Piano/vocal score: p. 100 (G. Schirmer)

> Notes by singer Gino Quilico: I approach this aria like a fighter, light on the toes. To quote Muhammad Ali, "Float like a butterfly, sting like a bee!" Although the singer has no room to breathe and it is sung urgently, you must not appear to tire and the aria must be sung with ease.

No. 16

Voice: baritone
Aria Title: "Ho capito, signor, si" (Masetto)
Opera Title: *Don Giovanni*
Composer: Wolfgang Amadeus Mozart
(1756–1791)
Historical Style: Classical (1787)
Range: C3 to C4

Fach: lyric
Librettist: Lorenzo da Ponte (1749–1838),
after Giovanni Bertati and Giuseppe
Gazzinga's opera *Don Giovanni Tenorio,
o sia Il convitato di pietra* (1787)
Aria Duration: 1:25
Tessitura: C3 to C4

Position: Act I

Setting: A village next to Don Giovanni's palace. The scene opens as peasant men and women are celebrating Masetto and Zerlina's wedding with dancing and music.

After Don Giovanni meets the wedding celebration, he invites them to come to his house—all of them, except Zerlina (whom he wants to remain with him). Masetto knows that he cannot oppose a nobleman, but he is worried about leaving Zerlina alone with Don Giovanni and capitulates to him sarcastically as he is being dragged away by Giovanni's servant Leporello under the Don's orders to get Masetto out of the way.

I understand, yes sir! (*sarcastically*) I bow my head and I go; since it pleases you like that, further objections I won't make, no. Cavalier you are indeed, to doubt I cannot in faith; I can tell by the kindness that you wish to have for me. (*to Zerlina, aside*) You little rogue, you little rascal, you were always my downfall. (*to Leporello, who is trying to get him away*) I'm coming! (*back to Zerlina*) You stay! It's the very upright thing to do! Let our cavalier make a "cavalieress" out of you too.

Masetto is dragged off by Leporello, followed by all the peasants. Giovanni and Zerlina remain alone.

This piece sits low in the baritone voice, so a strong "attitude" is necessary, including sarcasm and snarling. The highest note in the aria is middle C. The piece also requires momentum and concentrated focus shifts. There is much repetition for Masetto to get his message out before he is dragged away.

Piano/vocal score: p. 58 (G. Schirmer)

No. 17

Voice: baritone
Aria Title: "Metà di voi quà vadano,"
No. 17 (Don Giovanni)
Opera Title: *Don Giovanni*
Composer: Wolfgang Amadeus Mozart
(1756–1791)
Historical Style: Classical (1787)
Range: C3 to E4

Fach: lyric (dramatic)
Librettist: Lorenzo da Ponte (1749–1838),
after Giovanni Bertati and Giuseppe
Gazzinga's opera *Don Giovanni Tenorio,
o sia Il convitato di pietra* (1787)
Aria Duration: 2:45
Tessitura: F3 to D4

Position: Act II

Setting: Seville, the 17th century; the front of an inn

Masetto and his peasant friends meet up with Don Giovanni, who is disguised as Leporello. They are looking to capture and punish Don Giovanni for seducing Zerlina. He offers to help them find the Don and suggests that he and Masetto should search offstage right, and the rest of the peasants should go off in the other direction so that the Don (disguised) will be alone with Masetto. Don Giovanni enjoys the game as he fools the peasants and Masetto. His playfulness shows through the lively rhythms as he orders the peasants around the stage and even puts his arm around Masetto's shoulders in mock familiarity. Much of the text is set syllabically to the music. There is one strong high E quarter note, as the Don desires to grab their attention.

The aria is marked andante con moto:

Half of you go here, and the others go there, and quietly, very quietly look for him. He isn't far from here. If a man and a girl are strolling by a piazza, if under a window you hear someone making love, strike then—my master it will be. On his head he has a hat with white plumes. And on his back a big cloak and he has a sword at his side. (*To the peasants:*) Go, make haste! (*To Masetto:*) You alone will come with me. We must do the rest, and soon you will see what that is.

The peasants leave in opposite directions, leaving Masetto and Giovanni alone, whereupon the Don proceeds to give the peasant a sound thrashing.

Piano/vocal score: p. 177 (G. Schirmer)

> Notes by singer Gino Quilico: I begin the aria singing with the heavier voice of bass-baritone Leporello, since the Don is disguised as the servant, then go to his own voice. I return to Leporello's darker voice in the recitative that follows the aria.

No. 18

Voice: baritone
Aria Title: "Bella siccome un angelo,"
No. 2, Romanza (Dr. Malatesta)
Opera Title: *Don Pasquale*
Composer: Gaetano Donizetti (1797–1848)
Historical Style: Bel canto (1843)
Range: A♭2 to F4

Fach: lyric
Librettists: Gaetano Donizetti and Giacomo Ruffini (1807–1881), after the libretto by Angelo Anelli for *Ser Marc'Antonio* by Pavesi (1810)
Aria Duration: 3:20
Tessitura: D♭3 to D♭4

Position: Act I

Setting: A room in Don Pasquale's house, Rome, early 19th century

For a long time, Don Pasquale has been looking for a young woman to marry. He has asked his friend Doctor Malatesta to find a suitable spouse for him. Malatesta describes his fictitious sister as the perfect bride.

The opening is marked larghetto cantabile, piano. The accompaniment mimics the sound of the "fluttering of the heart" described by three sets of 16th-note chords lightly played in each measure.

Aria translation by Martha Gerhart from the *G. Schirmer Opera Anthology: Arias for Baritone,* edited by Robert L. Larsen (used by permission):

Beautiful as an angel on a pilgrimage to earth,
Fresh as the lily that opens upon morning,
Eyes that speak and laugh, [*marked accelerando e crescendo*]
A glance that conquers hearts. [*The end of the phrase has a rallentando, and a fermata on middle C.*]
Hair that transcends ebony, an enchanting smile. [*dolce*]

[Verse 2:]

An innocent, ingenuous soul that disregards itself,
Incomparable modesty, goodness that makes you fall in love.
[*Here the melody is propelled after a double dotted rhythm up to a cadenza ending at the high F before continuing the melody.*]
Merciful to the poor, gentle, sweet, affectionate . . .
Heaven made her be born in order to make a heart happy.

This is a fine lyric piece for the upper-middle voice of the baritone. There are no notes above E except for a passing 32nd note in the suggested cadenzas in the piece. Observe the dotted rhythms and the marked accents. We do not know a lot about Dr. Malatesta's background, but in this aria at the beginning of the opera it is clear that he is trying to convince Pasquale to "take the bait." He is also enjoying the game, no doubt, and becomes more confident as you can imagine that Pasquale becomes more interested. The first verse describes her physical characteristics, while the second verse describes more her inner qualities.

Piano/vocal score: p. 12 (Ricordi)

Notes by singer Gino Quilico: This aria calls for a clean, lyrical, legato sound. The role is more elusive to pin down, as Dr. Malatesta is a chameleon-like character. We don't know a lot about him. There is something magical in his personality, allowing him to bring many colors to the aria. This is true "bel canto" for the baritone voice.

No. 19

Voice: baritone
Aria Title: "Questo amor, vergogna mia"
(Frank)
Opera Title: *Edgar*
Composer: Giacomo Puccini (1858–1924)
Historical Style: Verismo (1889)
Range: D3 to F4

Fach: lyric
Librettist: Ferdinando Fontana (1850–1919), based on Alfred de Musset's verse drama *La coupe et les lèvres* (1832)
Aria Duration: 3:00
Tessitura: F3 to E4

Position: Act I

Setting: The main public square of a Flemish village at dawn, April 1302

> Aria plot notes from the *G. Schirmer Opera Anthology: Arias for Baritone,* edited by Robert L. Larsen (used by permission):
> In medieval Flanders, Frank and Fidelia's father has brought up a black girl, Tigrana, abandoned as a baby by gypsies. Frank is in love with the beautiful Tigrana who, like Fidelia, is attracted to Edgar. Once more Tigrana has spitefully denounced Frank, but when she leaves, her spell continues to enslave him.

Frank has grown up with her and loves her very much, but she does not return the love (she loves Edgar), and, in fact, she feels it is wrongful since they are almost like brother and sister.

The beginning is marked andante lento, piano; this lyric melody is set in the upper middle of the baritone's range, and it unfolds upward as the passion increases.

> Aria translation by Martha Gerhart from the *G. Schirmer Opera Anthology: Arias for Baritone,* edited by Robert L. Larsen (used by permission):
>
> This love—my shame—I should want to break off, to forget; but of a terrible enchantment my feelings are slaves. Thousands of times I swore to heaven to flee from her, and I came back to her! [*This phrase of text is repeated with a fermata on high F on "giurai/I swore" on the -i- vowel.*]
>
> She laughs about my weeping, and I—wretched, with my heart broken, humble myself at her feet. She laughs about my weeping; she makes fun of my disdain. [*This text is repeated with the opening melodic material.*] And I, wretched, with my heart broken, humble myself at her feet. And only her I dream about, I desire!
>
> Ah, misfortune! I love her—love her! [*repeated "Ah! sventura!/misfortune!"*]

The high F is sung on the unaccented last syllable, with the F repeated while singing "L'amo!/love her" with his realization that whatever the reason he should break off the relationship, he loves her.

In this aria the legato vocal line is of utmost importance, as is vocal control, since some of the higher pitches are unaccented, so they should not be stressed. There is frequent rubato at the end of phrases, as if the singer is hoping to linger in thought and emotion for a second longer. Many of the lines begin piano and unfold. Observe the importance of the dotted rhythms and the gentle grace note embellishments.

Piano/vocal score: p. 28 (Ricordi)

No. 20

Voice: baritone
Aria Title: "Come paride vezzoso," Cavatina (Belcore)
Opera Title: *L'elisir d'amore*
Composer: Gaetano Donizetti (1797–1848)
Historical Style: Bel canto (1832)
Range: B♭3 to E4

Fach: lyric
Librettist: Felice Romani (1788–1865), after Eugène Scribe's libretto for Daniel-François Auber's *Le philtre* (1831)
Aria Duration: 3:00
Tessitura: C3 to D4

Position: Act I, scene 1

Setting: Outside a small Italian town on the grounds of Adina's property; the 19th century, early afternoon

> Aria and plot notes from the *G. Schirmer Opera Anthology: Arias for Baritone,* edited by Robert L. Larsen (used by permission):
> Sergeant Belcore marches with his men onto Adina's estate. Then, with swaggering bravado, he presents her with a bouquet of flowers in token of his love.

The Sergeant is everything that Nemorino is not: confident, proud, straightforward, and a baritone. Even Belcore's end-of-phrase cadenzas are deliberate and confident. Watch the double-dotted rhythm at the beginning of the line. This aria needs strong vocal control, as some of the lines ("poiche in prefio del mio dono ne riporto il tuo bel corsince/in reward for my gift I carry away your beautiful heart," for example) begin in the higher range, and the singer should not have to reach for the E to start the phrase.

> Aria translation by Martha Gerhart from the *G. Schirmer Opera Anthology: Arias for Baritone,* edited by Robert L. Larsen (used by permission):
>
> As gracious Paris offered the apple to the most beautiful woman,
> My delightful peasant girl, I offer you these flowers.
> But I am more proud, more happy than he,
> Since in reward for my gift I carry away your beautiful heart.
> I see clearly in that little face that I'm winding my way into your breast.
> That's nothing surprising, I'm gallant, and I'm a Sergeant.

[The opening melody that was heard earlier is now sung with this new text, sung piano:]

There is not a beautiful woman who resists the sight of a military crest
[*More embellishments are sung here.*]
Even the Mother of Love yields to Mars, the God of War.

Although Belcore is presenting flowers to Adina, he is looking over all of the girls, showing off, and Adina is well aware of this.

Piano/vocal score: p. 26 (Ricordi)

No. 21

Voice: baritone
Aria Title: "Kogda bi zhizn domashnim krugom" (Eugene Onegin)
Opera Title: *Eugene Onegin*
Composer: Pyotr Ilyich Tchaikovsky (1840–1893)
Historical Style: Russian Romantic (1879)
Range: D3 to F4

Fach: lyric (dramatic)
Librettists: The composer and Konstantin Shilovsky (1849–1893), based on Aleksandr Pushkin's verse novel *Eugene Onegin* (1831)
Aria Duration: 4:13
Tessitura: F3 to E♭4

Position: Act I, scene 3

Setting: The gardens on Madame Larina's estate, St. Petersburg, Russia, late 1700s; thick lilac and acacia bushes, neglected flower beds and an old wooden bench; servant girls singing as they work in the background

Tatiana has written Onegin a letter in which she declares her love for him. Onegin, however, doesn't want Tatiana. Although he does not make fun of her love, he does tell the truth: that he loves her only in a brotherly way. He asks her to find another man who would return her love. She collapses onto a bench before he begins.

The aria is marked andante non troppo in 3/2 meter.

If I had wished to pass my life within the confines of the family
circle,
And a kindly fate had decreed for me the role of husband and father,
Then, most like, I would not choose any other bride than you.
But I was not made for wedded bliss, it is foreign to my soul,
Your perfections are vain, I am quite unworthy of them.
Believe me, I give you my word, marriage would be a torment for us.
No matter how much I loved you, habit would kill that love.
Judge what a thorny bed of roses Hymen would prepare for us,
And, perhaps, to be endured at length! One cannot return to dreams
and youth
(*The next section is marked più mosso; forte; with more emotion; the line as-
cends to high F and E natural within the phrase, which are the highest notes
in the piece.*)
I cannot renew my soul! I love you with a brother's love, a brother's
love,
Or, perhaps, more than that! Listen to me without getting angry,
More than once will a girl exchange one passing fancy for another.

The first section is lyric, gentle, and tender. Although we feel for Tatiana
and her pain, Onegin is not misleading her here. He is telling her straightforward truths about himself, though he will live to regret it.

Piano/vocal score: p. 117 (Richard Schauer–London)

No. 22

Voice: baritone
Aria Title: "Uzhel ta samaja Tatiana"
(Eugene Onegin)
Opera Title: *Eugene Onegin*
Composer: Pyotr Ilyich Tchaikovsky (1840–
1893)
Historical Style: Russian Romantic (1879)
Range: F3 to G♭4

Fach: lyric (dramatic)
Librettists: The composer and Konstantin
Shilovsky (1849–1893), based on Aleksandr
Pushkin's verse novel *Eugene Onegin* (1831)
Aria Duration: 3:07
Tessitura: F3 to D4

Position: Act III, scene 1

Setting: A fancy ballroom in a house in St. Petersburg, Russia, late 1700s

After years in hiding and exile after the duel in which he killed his friend Lensky, Onegin attends a ball in St. Petersburg. He sees Tatiana once more, but, to his surprise, she is happily married to Prince Gremin. Remembering how he rejected her love in the past, he realizes the true extent of his feelings for her. He expresses the deep love for her that he has found inside himself and the sorrow that he feels because he has lost her.

Tatiana leaves on Gremin's arm, returning the greetings of the guests. Onegin follows her with his eyes. Onegin's aria is marked allegro moderato: "Can this really be the same Tatiana to whom, tête-à-tête, in the depths of a distant countryside, I, in a fine moral outburst, once read a lecture on principles?"

The next section is marked allegro moderato, and is more animated. "The same girl, whom in her humble station I disdained? Was this really her, so poised, so self-possessed?" (accelerando) "But what's the matter with me? I must be dreaming!" (allegro giusto) "What is stirring in the depths of my cold and slothful heart? Vexation, vanity or, once again, that preoccupation of youth—love?" These phrases build to a sustained high F.

The next section is marked allegro moderato: "Alas, there's no doubt, I'm in love, in love like a boy, a passionate youth!" There is a pause, then the melody is continued, poco animando. "Let me perish, but first let me summon, in dazzling hope the magic poison of desire, Intoxicate myself with dreams! Everywhere I look I see that beloved, desired image. Wherever I look, I see her!" he sings, to a high G♭ that is sustained by a fermata.

The aria begins, in a party setting, with Onegin beginning his narration in a musing tone, then becoming more animated and passionate. The accompaniment, with its rising and falling 16th-note patterns, is both turbulent and passionately felt.

Piano/vocal score: p. 215 (Richard Schauer–London)

No. 23

Voice: baritone
Aria Title: "E sogno? O realtà" (Ford)
Opera Title: *Falstaff*
Composer: Giuseppe Verdi (1813–1901)
Historical Style: Italian Romantic (1893)
Range: B♭3 to G4

Fach: lyric (dramatic)
Librettist: Arrigo Boito (1842–1918), after William Shakespeare's comedy *The Merry Wives of Windsor* (1600–1601) and incorporating material from his histories *Henry IV,* Parts I and II (1597–1598)
Aria Duration: 3:55
Tessitura: C3 to E♭4

Position: Act II, scene 1

Setting: The inside of the Garter Inn, Windsor, England, early 15th century during the reign of Henry IV. Inside the inn the table bears the remains of a meal, numerous bottles, a glass, inkwell, a pen, paper, and a lighted candle.

Falstaff is comfortably seated in his armchair, drinking his sack (a white Spanish wine). Mr. Ford, a wealthy man, has been alerted to Falstaff's plan to seduce his wife. Ford dresses in disguise and offers Falstaff money to help seduce his own wife (Falstaff doesn't know this, obviously, because Ford is in disguise) to set the trap. When Falstaff tells him that he has already "made the acquaintance" of the lady and leaves him there to dress and "make himself beautiful" for the assignation, Ford becomes furious and horrified at the prospect of becoming cuckolded as he imagines his wife, Alice, willingly giving in to Falstaff's advances.

The beginning of the monologue is marked un poco più moderato; the orchestral accompaniment is extremely descriptive dramatically of the emotions and thoughts Ford is struggling with.

"Is it a dream? Or reality?" Ford begins piano an ascending line that in three measures crescendos to a high G♭. "Two enormous branches are growing over my head," he sings, sotto voce. "Is it a dream?" This is marked allegro agitato, also reflected in the rapid 16th notes heard in the orchestra. "Master Ford! Are you asleep? Wake up! Get up! Rouse yourself! Your wife is straying and compromising your honor, your house, and your bed!" as he builds to a sustained high F. "The time is set, plotted the deceit; you're mocked and tricked!" he expansively sings, to E♭. "And then they'll say that a jealous husband is a senseless man!" (a tempo, agitato) "Already behind my back I'm being branded with infamous names that pass by, whistling. Contempt is murmuring."

He now sings another expansive vocal line and crescendos to high E♭. "Oh marriage: Hell! Woman!" The excitement takes him to sing a high F. "Demon! Let simpletons have faith in their wives!" Each of the phrases to follow is delineated by two measures of orchestral commentary. "I would entrust my beer to a German, all my table to a gluttonous Dutchman, my bottle of brandy to a Turk, and not . . . " (he sings a sustained high F) "my wife to herself. Oh, foul fate! That ugly word to my heart comes back!" He shouts—a high G♭ pickup to the lower G♭. "The horns! Ox! Billy goat! The spindles crooked, ah! The horns!" The orchestra crescendos here to "ma/ but," as he sings on the sustained high G♭. "But you won't escape me! No! filthy man! Guilty man! Damned epicurean! First I pair them, then I catch them!" His temperature is building, he is choking, as he violently spews out the words. "I am bursting!"

Ford marshals his forces for his decision, which is sung as an octave from low E♭ to a sustained high E♭. "I shall avenge the insult!" This final line has the baritone beginning low and piano, going up the scale nobly to the high G, then finishing the line on the sustained E♭ on the unaccented vowel as the orchestra swells underneath him before Falstaff enters, dressed for the meeting with Ford's wife. "May jealousy be forever praised in the depths of my heart!"

This aria is aptly called "Ford's monologue" because it contains much text and many changes of focus and musical direction, both recitative-like and melodic. The jealous man wants to sing it blustery and angrily, but Ford has reasons to sing some phrases reflectively. He is both thinking aloud and aware that Falstaff is not far away and could come in at any moment.

Piano/vocal score: p. 177 (G. Schirmer)

No. 24

Voice: baritone
Aria Title: "Avant de quitter ces lieux,"
No. 4, Cavatina (Valentin)
Opera Title: *Faust*
Composer: Charles Gounod (1818–1893)
Historical Style: French Romantic (1859)
Range: C3 to G4

Fach: lyric (dramatic)
Librettists: Jules Barbier (1825–1901) and
Michel Carré (1865–1945), after Part I of
Johann Wolfgang von Goethe's play *Faust*
(1808)
Aria Duration: 4:20
Tessitura: E♭3 to E♭4

Position: Act II, scene 2

Setting: A celebration in a public square in a German city, 16th century

Valentin, a soldier and the brother of Marguerite, has been called off to war. He is not worried about going to battle because of the sacred medallion that he has been given. The youth Siebel has promised to protect Marguerite, with whom he is in love, while her brother Valentin is away. Valentin thanks him and then reflects on the sadness of leaving home and family. He asks God to take care of Marguerite while he fights. He declares that he shall fight valiantly for his country, and if he dies, he prays that he will be allowed to watch over his sister from heaven.

The opening is marked moderato. His first phrases show the upper middle of the baritone voice as he holds up the medallion. He sings a high F in passing and must negotiate many accidentals in tune:

Aria translation by Martha Gerhart from the *G. Schirmer Opera Anthology: Arias for Baritone,* edited by Robert L. Larsen (used by permission): "Oh sacred medallion, which comes to me from my sister—on the day of the battle in order to avert death, remain there upon my heart!"

The next section is marked andante; it is necessary to sing an even vocal line from the top to bottom of the range. It takes a resonant lower C and a strong high E♭ and E through the *passaggio* of the voice:

Aria translation by Martha Gerhart from the *G. Schirmer Opera Anthology: Arias for Baritone,* edited by Robert L. Larsen (used by permission): "Before leaving this place, native soil of my ancestors, to you, Lord and King of the heavens, I entrust my sister. Deign, from all danger, to protect her always—this sister so dear, Deign to protect her from all danger."

The next section moves (but not too fast). It is marked più animato and has the characteristic of a military march–like accompaniment. In this section Valentin must sing a full high G♭ at the top of an arpeggio that needs to be in place vocally, and sung without strain:

> Aria translation by Martha Gerhart from the *G. Schirmer Opera Anthology: Arias for Baritone*, edited by Robert L. Larsen (used by permission): "Freed from a sad thought, I shall go to seek glory in the midst of the enemies. The best, the bravest in the heat of the combat, I shall fight for my country. And if God summons me to Him, I shall watch over you faithfully, oh Marguerite!"

Here is now the recapitulation of the melody and text "Avant de quitter ces lieux":

> Aria translation by Martha Gerhart from the *G. Schirmer Opera Anthology: Arias for Baritone*, edited by Robert L. Larsen (used by permission): "Before leaving this place, native soil of my ancestors, to you, Lord and King of the heavens, I entrust my sister." [He has a high sustained entrance—G♭—at the beginning of the final vocal line.] "Oh King of the heavens, cast forth your eyes—Protect Marguerite, King of the heavens!"

This aria captures the character of Valentin: noble, idealistic, and protective of his sister.

Piano/vocal score: p. 56 (G. Schirmer)

No. 25

Voice: baritone
Aria Title: "Con un' vezzo all'Italiana,"
No. 14 (Roberto)
Opera Title: *La finta giardiniera*
Composer: Wolfgang Amadeus Mozart
(1756–1791)
Historical Style: Classical (1775)
Range: E3 to E4

Fach: lyric
Librettist: Raniero de Calzabigi (1714–
1795), revised by Marco Coltellini
Aria Duration: 3:05
Tessitura: E3 to E4

Position: Act II

Setting: The country estate of the Mayor Anchise at Lagonero near Milan, a hall in the mayor's house, mid-18th century

Roberto (Nardo) is the servant of Violante (Sadrina) and is in love with Serpetta. Serpetta says that, if Roberto will sing her a love song, she will love him. He sings her this multilingual aria, which includes phrases of love in Italian, French, and English to try to impress her. She is not impressed though, and he becomes frustrated.

Nardo (Roberto) tries to do everything she asks, and she orders him around unmercifully. She wants him to execute the "French" bow, which consists of dragging the foot from front to rear while the upper body bends forward.

The aria is marked andantino grazioso at the beginning; the melody begins on high E, and the E is sung often; there are trills in the aria for effect.

"I'll tell you with Italian charm that your sweet face has enflamed my heart and my breast" (there is a ritardando, fermata; the melody is then repeated) "and constantly makes me languish for you." Serpetta indicates to him that she doesn't like his affected manner. "You don't like it, it's no good? Well, let's try the French way." (The meter changes from 3/4 to 2/4, marked piano, the style is affected and mannered.) "Ah, madam, here I am. This is no good either? Come, let's see . . . a bit the English way." (adagio) "Ah, my love, say yes."

Serpetta reacts as above. Marked allegretto, the melody is repeated. "Cursed indifference, she makes me lose my patience; here is no use the French way, she doesn't understand the English way, she doesn't like the Italian way. Oh, what mood, what a strange woman, I am lost in truth." He exits.

Piano/vocal score: p. 79 (Breitkopf)

No. 26

Voice: baritone

Aria Title: "J'ai pu frapper," No. 13 (Hamlet)

Opera Title: *Hamlet*

Composer: Ambroise Thomas (1811–1896)

Historical Style: French Romantic (1868)

Range: C♯3 to D♯4

Fach: lyric (dramatic)

Librettists: Michel Carré (1819–1872) and Jules Barbier (1825–1901), after the tragedy by William Shakespeare (1601)

Aria Duration: 2:52

Tessitura: F♯3 to C♯4

Position: Act III, scene 1

Setting: Elsinore Castle, Denmark, 16th century. At the end of a room in the Queen's apartments are two full-length portraits, one of the old King and one of the new King; there is a lamp on the table and a prayer stool. Hamlet is seated on a couch.

The King of Denmark (father of Hamlet) has died under mysterious circumstances. Rumor has it that he was murdered by his brother, Claudius, who has assumed the crown and married Gertrude, his brother's widow, herself conceivably implicated in the murder.

At the beginning of Act III Hamlet sings the famous monologue "To be or not to be" in his attempt to decide whether being dead or alive is better. The beginning of the aria is marked forte, with double-dotted rhythms for dramatic intensity; many of these phrases are sung on one pitch for emphasis of text; then the pitch levels are changed.

Hamlet: "I could have killed that villain (*Claudius, the King*), and I did not do it. What is it then that I am waiting for? Do I have any doubts about his guilt? No! Why delay any longer and let time slip by? (*andante, unaccompanied*) Alas! What has become of you now, oh my father?"

(The next section is marked adagio and is unaccompanied): "To be or not to be! . . . (*forte*) Oh mystery! To die! (*piano*) To sleep! . . . Ah! If I were allowed, in order to go find you, to break the bond that binds me to this earth! But then? . . . What is that land unknown from where not one traveler has yet returned? To dream, perchance?"

This monologue underlines the text, as the accompaniment punctuates the vocal phrases, commenting on the words and emotions that are described in the text.

"But who then dares to follow me here? The King! It is God who delivers him to me!" (The King enters.)

Piano/vocal score: p. 187 (Heugel)

No. 27

Voice: baritone
Aria Title: "O vin dissipe la tristesse,"
No. 10, Chanson bacique (Hamlet)
Opera Title: *Hamlet*
Composer: Ambroise Thomas (1811–1896)
Historical Style: French Romantic (1868)
Range: C#3 to G4

Fach: lyric (dramatic)
Librettists: Michel Carré (1819–1872) and
Jules Barbier (1825–1901), after the tragedy
by William Shakespeare (1601)
Aria Duration: 3:20
Tessitura: F3 to F4

Position: Act II, scene 1

Setting: Gardens of Elsinore Castle, Denmark, 16th century, late afternoon/
early evening

The King of Denmark (father of Hamlet) has died under mysterious
circumstances. Rumor has it that he was murdered by his brother, Claudius,
who has assumed the crown and married Gertrude, his brother's widow,
herself conceivably implicated in the murder.

Hamlet meets with a troupe of actors that will perform a play for the
court. With them, he sings a drinking song in which he calls for wine and
laughter to dispel his sadness after the death of his father. He is ready to
launch his plot to implicate King Claudius in the death.

The beginning of this drinking song is marked andante con moto, forte:

Aria translation by Martha Gerhart from the *G. Schirmer Opera Anthology:
Arias for Baritone*, edited by Robert L. Larsen (used by permission):

Oh, wine, dispel the sadness that weighs on my heart!
Give me the illusions of intoxication and the mocking laughter!
[*The next phrases are marked risoluto e marcato, written in the higher range
for strongest effect.*]
Oh, enchanting liqueur, pour intoxication and oblivion into my
heart! Sweet liqueur!
[*un poco animato, pianissimo*]
Life is gloomy; the years are short. Of our happy days God knows
the number.
Each man, alas, bears here on earth his heavy chain—
Cruel duties, lasting afflictions of the human soul! [*piano, poco
ritardando*]

Away from us, dark forebodings! The wisest ones are the fools! Ah!—

[*Hamlet sings a cadenza to high G. Here is a recapitulation of beginning melody and text, again in the key of B♭ major.*]

Wine dispels the sadness that weighs upon my heart! Pour intoxication upon us! [*He sings a high sustained F to conclude.*]

An easy high F is important in successful performance of this aria, as is the articulation of text, ease and command of delivery, and awareness of articulation markings and accents. Hamlet has an energy that indicates readiness to take his revenge upon Claudius.

Piano/vocal score: p. 131 (Heugel)

No. 28

Voice: baritone
Aria Title: "Spectre infernal!" No. 5, Invocation (Hamlet)
Opera Title: *Hamlet*
Composer: Ambroise Thomas (1811–1896)
Historical Style: French Romantic (1868)
Range: C♯3 to C♯4

Fach: lyric (dramatic)
Librettists: Michel Carré (1865–1945) and Jules Barbier (1825–1901), after the tragedy by William Shakespeare (1601)
Aria Duration: 3:33
Tessitura: C♯3 to C♯4

Position: Act I, scene 2

Setting: Elsinore castle, Denmark; it is night on the ramparts of the castle, and the moon is partially hidden by black clouds

The King of Denmark (father of Hamlet) has died under mysterious circumstances. Rumor has it that he was murdered by his brother, Claudius, who has assumed the crown and married Gertrude, his brother's widow, herself conceivably implicated in the murder.

Hamlet, Prince of Denmark, has heard a report of the ghost of his father appearing on the battlements of the castle. At midnight he goes to the battlements and invokes the spirit of his father, hoping that the ghost will appear to him.

> (*The ghost appears*)
> *Hamlet:* Angels of heaven, defend us!
> *Mercellus, Horatio:* God! I feel my knees give way!
> *Hamlet (addressing the ghost with terror, in a stifled voice):* Ghost of hell! Venerated image! Oh my father! Oh my King!
> Answer, alas, to my tearful voice. Speak to me! (*The text is repeated.*)
> *Marcellus, Horatio:* My heart is frozen with fear!
> *Hamlet:* Why, answer me out of the cold earth, into which I saw you going down, lifeless.
> Why have you risen, oh mystery, the crown upon your brow and all in armor?
> (*The ghost signals Horatio and Marcellus to leave.*)

Hamlet's terror is reflected by broken fragmented phrases in halting speech. The diction and inflection are of greatest importance. There are no sustained high pitches, but Hamlet enters on a high F♯ in one phrase.

Piano/vocal score: p. 72 (Heugel)

No. 29

Voice: baritone
Aria Title: "Ho un gran peso" (Taddeo)
Opera Title: *L'italiana in Algeri*
Composer: Gioacchino Rossini (1792–1868)
Historical Style: Bel canto (1813)
Range: C♯3 to E4

Fach: lyric (bass-baritone)
Librettist: Angelo Anelli (1761–1820)
Aria Duration: 2:30
Tessitura: E3 to D4

Position: Act II, scene 1

Setting: A small hall in the palace of the Bey of Algiers, early 19th century. The room is between the apartments of the Bey and those of his wife, Elvira; in between there is a sofa.

Taddeo is described as "a bumbling suitor of Isabella." The Bey of Algiers tells Taddeo that he will make him the Grand Kaimakan of Algiers. Taddeo said that the role of Kaimakan does not quite fit him. When the Bey becomes angry, Taddeo tries to reassure him, saying that he would rather be Kaimakan than dead. The Moors dress Taddeo in Turkish fashion, with a large turban, a saber, and a Turkish garment.

The aria is marked allegro, fortissimo, and the text is syllabically set. Taddeo is afraid, scattered, confused; in the accompaniment there is a constant stream of four groups of 16th notes in the treble. D is the highest note in this section, and articulation markings should be observed. The phrases also call for vocal control, because the upper D's at the ends of the phrases are unaccented.

This turban weighs on my head, Taddeo sings, and this costume is uncomfortable. And if you'll pardon my frankness I really don't want to be a Kaimakan, and I thank your Lordship for the honor he does me.
(He's fuming! . . . Woe is me! . . . What angry glances!)
(*These phrases are repeated.*)
(*To Mustafa:*) Have mercy on me . . . listen to me . . .
(*Aside:*) He makes me shudder. I must think matters over.
If I refuse, the stake will be ready; and if I accept? . . .
It will be my duty (to be a chaperone).
Ah! Taddeo, what a dilemma is this! But that stake? . . . what shall I do?
Kaimakan, my lord, I will remain. (*He makes an intervallic leap up to unaccented high E.*)
I've no wish to displease you.
Chorus: Viva the grand Kaimakan!
Taddeo: So much bowing! . . . such honors. (*to high E and F♯*)
A thousand thanks, gentlemen, do not trouble yourselves.
I'll do all that I can, and now, my lord, I'll go present myself
To my worthy niece with this Turkish costume (saddle pack) on my back.
(*A sustained D-fermata is sung before continuing.*)
Ah, Taddeo, How much better it would have been
If you had gone to the bottom of the sea.

He sings up to D, E, and back to the A and B for the long cadence, then exits.

Piano/vocal score: p. 217 (G. Schirmer)

No. 30

Voice: baritone

Aria Title: "Hai già vinta la causa . . . Vedro mentr'io sospiro," No. 17 (Count Almaviva)

Opera Title: *Le nozze di Figaro*

Composer: Wolfgang Amadeus Mozart (1756–1791)

Historical Style: Classical (1786)

Range: A3 to F♯4

Fach: lyric (dramatic)

Librettist: Lorenzo da Ponte (1749–1838), after Pierre-Augustin Caron de Beaumarchais's play *La folle journée, ou Le mariage de Figaro* (1784)

Aria Duration: 4:35

Tessitura: C3 to D4

Position: Act III

Setting: Count Almaviva's castle, about three leagues from Seville, evening

Count Almaviva, the lord of the castle, believes Susanna will be meeting him in his gardens on the night of her marriage to Figaro. He thought he might be able to prevent the marriage through legal means, since Figaro owes money to Marcellina. However, we have just found out that Figaro is the long-lost son of Marcellina and Bartolo. The Count overhears the two lovers talking confidently about winning the case and becomes incensed.

> Aria translation by Martha Gerhart from the *G. Schirmer Opera Anthology: Arias for Baritone,* edited by Robert L. Larsen (used by permission):
>
> [*Recitative*] You have already won the case! What do I hear! Into what trap did I fall? Traitors! I want to punish you badly; the verdict will be as I please. But if he should pay the old pretender? Pay her! In what way? And then there's Antonio, who to the insignificant Figaro refuses to give a niece in marriage. Cultivating the pride of this fool, everything is useful for a deception; the die is cast.

Each line of the recitative is given space by the composer to allow the Count to think through, consider, and scheme. It alternates between bluster ("Perfidi!/traitors") and a thoughtful strategy. Each line has a different focus, accompaniment, and tempo marking.

The aria is marked allegro maestoso:

> Aria translation by Martha Gerhart from the *G. Schirmer Opera Anthology: Arias for Baritone,* edited by Robert L. Larsen (used by permission):

> Shall I see one of my servants happy, while I languish? And must he possess a treasure, which I desire in vain? Shall I see the one who aroused in me a desire which she, then, doesn't have for me, united by the hand of love to a miserable creature? Shall I see that he will possess a treasure I desire? Shall I see that?

The singer will observe that the Count has many questions in the first section of this aria, becoming decisive (again) after the fermata rest, beginning with allegro assai and the following text:

> Aria translation by Martha Gerhart from the *G. Schirmer Opera Anthology: Arias for Baritone*, edited by Robert L. Larsen (used by permission) "Ah, no, I don't wish you this satisfaction of being left in peace. You were not born, audacious one, to give me torment and, furthermore, to laugh at my unhappiness. Already the lone hope of my vindications comforts this soul and makes me rejoice" [which is musically indicated by ornate vocal passages.]

The challenge for the end of this aria is the 8th-note triplet figures, which are sung quickly (but not too fast—the Count is never out of control), and the final F♯, which is not a high note for the baritone, but can be if the recitative and first part of the aria are delivered in too much of a blustery, heavy, and serious sung delivery. As "the lone hope of my vindications" causes the Count to rejoice with the difficult passage of the 8th-note triplet patterns, the singer should almost laugh as he rejoices to "lighten and energize" this passage that carries momentum forward to the high F♯. The more the singer braces and sets for this one high note, the more strained it will appear. It is better if it can be "thrown off."

Piano/vocal score: p. 291 (G. Schirmer)

> Notes by director Thor Steingraber: In Act III of *Figaro*, the audience witnesses the gradual unraveling of the Count's presumed control and authority. It never occurred to him that he couldn't have everything he wanted and less so that a servant could, in any way, usurp him. Clearly the Count holds Susanna in the highest esteem—whether it's just lust or something more complex and heartfelt must be decided by the character's interpreter. Regardless, everyone knows what it feels like to be rejected, and furthermore to feel conspired against. Even if the Count's intentions are less

than honorable, the actor/singer must approach "Hai già vinta la causa" with empathy for this character and a willingness to express something more complex than the vitriol apparent in the text. I once asked a singer at an audition to rethink the character and start the recitative and aria again, this time making these assumptions: that the Count is generally a likable guy who is just having a particularly bad day, and that his anger comes in many varieties, some that might even render him sympathetic to the audience. I asked the singer if he could retain a twinkle in his eye as he sang the aria. The result was a rendition of the piece that was more compelling dramatically and more varied musically, with a new array of possibilities in tone and dynamics. One must remember that for the Count, the fun is the chase. At this moment the chase isn't going well, but it's still just a chase. This is how a singer can continue to find the character he portrays as likable and interesting, an essential aspect of creating one.

No. 31

Voice: baritone
Aria Title: "When the air sings of summer,"
Bob's Bedroom Aria (Bob)
Opera Title: *The Old Maid and the Thief*
Composer and Librettist: Gian Carlo
Menotti (b. 1911)
Historical Style: 20th-century American
(1939)
Range: A3 to F4

Fach: lyric
Aria Duration: 5:10
Tessitura: D3 to D4

Position: Scene 8

Setting: A small New England town, 1939; "Bob's bedroom" in Miss Todd's house

Bob has come to the door looking for a handout. Miss Todd, her maid Laetitia, and a neighbor, Miss Pinkerton, not used to having a man in the house to take care of, gladly take in the poor man, and they are clearly attracted to him. He enjoys the daily care, including meals brought to his room—and sleeping for as long as he wants—in a real bed with a roof over his head. But he is itching to leave. Why?

He sings a beautiful melody, marked mezzo piano, andante calmo, senza trascinare in 5/4 meter. The melody—and tonality—wanders during the piece (just like Bob). There is an unsettled feeling in the aria, with a great variety of articulation and meter change. The singer needs an easy high D and Eb. At the climax of the piece he attacks an exclaimed, "Ah!" on the high F, sustained, before the beginning melody returns. The aria shows many emotions, including contentment contrasted with restlessness and a poetic nature that possesses vision. The piece has a beautiful conclusion, ending on the high, sustained D with a lovely chord progression to conclude the piece.

Piano/vocal score: p. 103 (G. Ricordi)

No. 32

Voice: baritone
Aria Title: "L'orage s'est calmé" (Zurga)
Opera Title: *Les pêcheurs de perles*
Composer: Georges Bizet (1838–1875)
Historical Style: French Romantic (1863)
Range: C3 to F#4

Fach: lyric
Librettists: Eugène Cormon (1810–1903) and Michel Carré 1865–1945
Aria Duration: 5:20
Tessitura: A4 to D4

Position: Act III, scene 1

Setting: Ceylon; it is night and the storm has abated; a lamp burns on a little bamboo table inside an Indian hut. Zurga is alone and sitting on a mat, absorbed in his thoughts; after a while he gets up, lifts the hanging that covers the exit, and looks outside.

Zurga, alone in his tent, regrets his rage against his old friend, Nadir, and recalls Leila's radiant beauty. He has found Nadir and Leila together. As he is the elected chief of the village and, blind with jealousy, wants vengeance, Zurga condemns them to death.

The storm has calmed down . . . already the winds are silent,
Like them, wrath is appeased.
(*He lets the hanging fall.*)
I alone call in vain for calm and sleep.
Fever devours me, and my oppressed soul has only one thought.
Ah, Nadir must die at the rising of the sun!
Oh, Nadir, tender friend of my young age, Oh Nadir!
When unto death I delivered you, alas, by what blind rage,
By what blind and mad rage my heart was torn?
No! It is impossible! I had a horrible dream!
No, you were not able to betray your faith, and the culprit, alas, am I.
Oh, remorse! Regrets! Ah, what have I done?
O, Leila, radiant beauty! Forgive my blind rage!
For pity's sake forgive the transports of a heart angered!
Despite myself remorse oppresses me!
I am ashamed of my cruelty!

This is a beautiful piece for the lyric baritone. It is emotionally moving, and the singer has the obstacles necessary for dramatic tension: the love of Leila and the friendship of Nadir. The aria shows much in the way of vocal legato and sensitive, intimate delivery, as well as strength of voice and range.

Piano/vocal score: p. 154 (Choudens)

No. 33

Voice: baritone
Aria Title: "Ah! Per sempre io ti perdei . . . Bel sogno beato" (Riccardo)
Opera Title: *I puritani*
Composer: Vincenzo Bellini (1801–1835)
Historical Style: Bel canto (1835)
Range: A♭2 to E♭4

Fach: lyric
Librettist: Count Carlo Pepoli (1796–1881), after Jacques-Arsène Ancelot and Joseph-Xavier Boniface's play *Têtes Rondes et Cavaliers* (1833)
Aria Duration: 5:00
Tessitura: E♭3 to E♭4

Position: Act I, scene 1

Setting: Outside a fortress near Plymouth, England, held by Sir Gualtiero Valton; the 17th century (during the English Civil War), daybreak

---

Aria plot notes from the *G. Schirmer Opera Anthology: Arias for Baritone,* edited by Robert L. Larsen (used by permission):

As the opera begins, it is the day of Elvira Valton's wedding to Lord Arturo Talbo. On the ramparts of a Puritan fortress near Plymouth, Sir Riccardo Forth confides to Sir Bruno Robertson that he is despondent over the fact that he is not the bridegroom.

He has lost Elvira to Arturo.

Recitative (marked allegro maestoso):

Aria translation by Martha Gerhart from the *G. Schirmer Opera Anthology: Arias for Baritone,* edited by Robert L. Larsen (used by permission):

Now wherever will I flee? Wherever will I hide my terrible sufferings?
How those songs resound in my soul as bitter weeping!
[*andante affettuoso; piano*]
Oh, Elvira, oh my gentle desired one, I have lost you forever!
Without hope and love, what is left for me now in this life?
[*Marked larghetto sostenuto, there is a four-measure introduction before the aria proper begins, marked pianissimo in a 9/8 {lilting} meter.*]
Ah, I have lost you forever, flower of love, oh my hope.
Ah, the life that is left to me will be full of sorrow!
As I wandered for years and years in the power of destiny,
I defied misfortune and sufferings in the hope [*con abbandono, pianissimo*] of your love.

Strong E♭'s are necessary at the top, some sustained, but all are within the vocal line. There are 32nd-note embellishments to negotiate, energized dotted rhythms, and many accents, all contributing to define the energy of the vocal line.

Piano/vocal score: p. 28 (Ricordi)

No. 34

Voice: baritone

Aria Title: "Mab, la reine des mensonges"
(Mercutio)

Opera Title: *Roméo et Juliette*

Composer: Charles Gounod (1818–1893)

Historical Style: French Romantic (1867)

Range: D♯3 to F♯4

Fach: lyric

Librettists: Jules Barbier (1825–1901) and
Michel Carré (1822–1872), after the tragedy
by William Shakespeare (1596)

Aria Duration: 2:15

Tessitura: E3 to E4

Position: Act I

Setting: Verona, Italy, 14th century; a masked ball in the Capulets' residence, evening

---

Aria translation by Martha Gerhart and plot notes from the *G. Schirmer Opera Anthology: Arias for Baritone,* edited by Robert L. Larsen (used by permission):

Romeo, Mercutio, and their Montague friends have come in disguise to a ball in the rival house of the Capulets. Mercutio thinks they should remove their masks and create havoc with their enemies, but Romeo says that he wanted to come only because of a disturbing dream he has had. Mercutio paraphrases the famous Shakespearean text concerning Queen Mab, who is responsible for wondrous dreams and illusions in the minds of men.

The aria begins allegro, in 6/8 meter, pianissimo:

Mab, the queen of illusions, presides over dreams.
Lighter than the fickle wind, through space,
Through the night, she passes, she slips away!
Her chariot, which the swift mite draws through the limpid ether,
Was made from a hollow hazelnut by an earthworm, the wheelwright!
The harness, delicate lace, was carved from the wing
Of some green grasshopper by her coachman, the gnat!
A cricket's bone serves as handle for his whip,
Whose white lash is fashioned from a ray of light shed by Phoebus
While assembling his court.
Every night, in that carriage, Mab visits, along her way,

The husband who dreams of widowerhood and the suitor who dreams of love!

At her approach, the coquette dreams of finery and of dressing up,
The courtier shows servile deference, the poet rhymes his verses!
To the miser in his dingy quarters she opens numberless treasures,
And freedom smiles in the darkness at the prisoner fettered with chains.

The soldier dreams of ambushes, of battles, and of thrusts;
She pours him bumpers of wine with which his laurels are celebrated.
And you, whom a sigh startles when you are resting on your bed,
Oh maiden—she grazes your mouth and makes you dream of kisses!
Mab, the queen of illusions, presides over dreams.
Lighter than the fickle wind, through space,
Through the night, she passes, she slips away!

Much of the piece is through composed as Mercutio tells the story. It is narrated at the beginning quietly (marked piano), but as he becomes more excited the singer ascends by half steps in the upper part of the range. An easy E is important to be able to articulate the French without strain. The accompaniment largely is light and transparent. There are very few places to rest, and the presentation of the story has a breathless quality, an excitement.

Piano/vocal score: p. 36 (Choudens)

No. 35

Voice: baritone

Aria Title: "O du, mein holder Abendstern" (Wolfram von Eschenbach)

Opera Title: *Tannhäuser*

Composer and Librettist: Richard Wagner (1813–1883), after medieval German history and legends

Historical Style: German Romantic (1845)

Range: B♭3 to E4

Fach: lyric (dramatic)

Aria Duration: 3:15

Tessitura: G3 to C4

Position: Act III

Setting: The Wartburg Valley in Germany; an autumn evening during the early 13th century

Aria plot notes from the *G. Schirmer Opera Anthology: Arias for Baritone*, edited by Robert L. Larsen (used by permission):

The erring Tannhäuser has been away on a pilgrimage to Rome for many months to seek salvation for his sins. Elisabeth, who loves him, has waited patiently but now longs to leave this life and seek heavenly peace. She thanks Wolfram, whom she knows loves her, for his friendship and climbs to the Wartburg to die. Wolfram remains to strum his harp and pray for the blessings of the evening star on Elisabeth, his unrequited love.

Recitative: the recitative begins darkly, in the low-middle range, needing a low B♭. Also needed is clear diction, correct rhythm, and a long vocal line on each breath.

Aria translation by Martha Gerhart from the *G. Schirmer Opera Anthology: Arias for Baritone*, edited by Robert L. Larsen (used by permission):

Like foreboding of death, dusk veils the land; It covers the valley with dark residue.
The soul, which aspires to lofty heights, is made uneasy in the face of its flight, through darkness and horror.
[*A tremolo is now heard in the accompaniment as the singer begins to sing*

> *pianissimo in his upper range. The line climbs to D and E♭, repeatedly back to the D.]*
> There you shine, oh loveliest of stars; You send forth your gentle light from afar.
> Your dear ray parts the gloomy dusk; and, kindheartedly, you point the way out of the valley.

The aria is written in 6/8 meter, and there are four measures of introduction as the poet is inspired to sing this aria.

Aria translation by Martha Gerhart from the *G. Schirmer Opera Anthology: Arias for Baritone*, edited by Robert L. Larsen (used by permission)

Oh you, my lovely evening star, I have always greeted you so gladly. From the heart which she never betrayed greet her, when she passes by you—
when she hovers over the valley of earth to become, yonder, a blessed angel.

The vocal line is lyrical, floating up to a high D and E. Also important are chromatic steps, carefully marked articulations and dynamics, and momentum. Although the range demands are not extreme and the aria is lyrical, intensity and focus are important. It is a dramatic piece, and the poet who sings it has his heart broken by Elizabeth.

Piano/vocal score: p. 342 (Breitkopf & Härtel)

Notes by singer and master teacher Håkan Hagegård: "O du, mein holder Abendstern" is not so good for an audition because it does not appear to be short and it does not show enough vocal impressiveness. But it shows musicality and that the singer is more than an "opera singer." It helps to play the flute introduction before the aria. That sets the environment so it will catch the listener early. Make a crescendo at "und freundlich"; decrescendo to "aus dem Tal."

Make sure that you practice with a metronome so you do not slow down in the second part of the bar in the aria. Finally—do not sing it as if you like your own voice, but that you love the evening star!

No. 36

Voice: baritone

Aria Title: "Mein Sehnen, mein Wähnen," Pierrot's Tanzlied (Fritz)

Opera Title: *Die tote Stadt*

Composer: Erich Wolfgang Korngold (1897–1957)

Historical Style: 20th-century German (1920)

Range: C3 to Gb4

Fach: lyric

Librettist: Paul Schott (pseudonym of Erich and Julius Korngold [1860–1945]), after Georges Rodenbach's novel *Bruges-la-morte* (1892)

Aria Duration: 4:15

Tessitura: Gb3 to Eb4

Position: Act II

Setting: A quay outside Marietta's house, near a convent, Bruges, late 19th century

After Marietta has made a toast with the rest of her troupe, she asks Fritz to sing a song. He sings a yearning dance song that looks into his past.

Marietta: And now music! A song that's not too gay and not too sad— A song that makes you dance and sway, dream sweetly. Pierrot, get up! You will be fine. You're German, from the Rhine!

Fritz (enters a capella, with a lyric, passionate delivery):

My yearning, my dreaming, (*subito a tempo*) returns to the past, The days of parties, dancing, never to last. We danced by the Rhine in moonlight. Two heavenly blue eyes looking (*he sings a high F, marked piano*) deep into mine. Pleading, they said: stay, don't go away, For your happiness (*high Gb is sung, piano*) is here in your homeland. (*as the beginning*) My yearning, dreaming, returns to the past.

The next section is marked sehr weich und gefangvoll—calling for movement in the phrase "The magic of distant lands sets my heart aglow. The magic of distant lands lured me, I played Pierrot." This text is set to quarter note values at the high Gb to F. "I Followed my wondrous goddess, learned to love with tears and kisses," he sings. "Joy and pain, hope and strife, that's the life of a comedian," he continues.

Fritz then repeats music and text from beginning: "My yearning, dreaming, returns to the past, the past, the past . . . " (he sinks to Marietta's feet).

This is not an easy aria to sing well. Much of it is delivered as if sung like a German Lied: intimately, delicately, with strong attention to the poetry and the German consonants. It is also challenging to sing high and softly in regards to intonation and being careful not to "croon" too much, because it is easier to manage vocally—but it will not convey the sufficient passion necessary for a powerful performance.

Piano/vocal score: p. 110 (Schott)

No. 37

Voice: baritone
Aria Title: "Der Vogelfänger bin ich ja," No. 2 (Papageno)
Opera Title: *Die Zauberflöte*
Composer: Wolfgang Amadeus Mozart (1756–1791)
Historical Style: Singspiel (1791)
Range: D3 to E4

Fach: lyric
Librettist: Emanuel Schikaneder (1751–1812)
Aria Duration: 2:20
Tessitura: E3 to D4

Position: Act I

Setting: A magical forest with a rocky landscape where Papageno catches birds for the Queen of the Night, mythological times

Papageno introduces himself to the audience and Prince Tamino, who is hiding and observing the bird-catcher. Papageno says that he could probably catch women like he catches birds. The piece is strophic in three verses, for the "Jederman/everyman" Papageno. The vocal line needs an even quality in the octave skips between the low and high D, and the melody needs to touch on the high E without straining. The vocal line is articulated by separating the notes for the sake of text clarification, while alternately connecting some of the 16th notes. The orchestra clearly models this articulation in the introduction. Although the aria is strophic, the variety is in the text. Papageno is proud and happy in verse 1. He lacks nothing. In verse 2 he does want something, which leads to a sweeter and more personal purpose in verse 3, so that the delivery and color is quite different between the three verses.

> I am the bird-catcher, always jolly: yippie hippety hop!
> As bird-catcher I'm well-known by young and old in the whole land
> I know how to handle the bait, and how to work the panpipes!
> Therefore I can be happy and jolly, for all the birds are truly mine.

The first text is repeated here before the text that follows:

> I'd like a net for girls; I'd capture them for myself by the dozens!
> Then I'd shut them up with me, and all the girls would be mine.
> If all the girls were mine, then I'd exchange them for fine sugar.
> The one who was my favorite—to her I'd gladly hand over the sugar.
> And if she kissed me sweetly then, she'd be my wife, and I her husband.
> She'd sleep by my side; I'd rock her to sleep like a child.

Piano/vocal score: p. 22 (G. Schirmer)

No. 38

Voice: baritone
Aria Title: "Ein Mädchen oder Weibchen" (Papageno)
Opera Title: *Die Zauberflöte*
Composer: Wolfgang Amadeus Mozart (1756–1791)
Historical Style: Singspiel (1791)
Range: B3 to D4

Fach: lyric
Librettist: Emanuel Schikaneder (1751–1812)
Aria Duration: 3:45
Tessitura: F3 to C4

Position: Act II, scene 5

Setting: Mythological times, a hall in a temple in Egypt
  After drinking a glass of wine which magically appears, Papageno (the

bird-catcher) sings (accompanied by magic bells). What he really wants in life is a wife.

The aria is in strophic form (for the "common man" Papageno) in two sections for each verse, marked andante and allegro: "A sweetheart or a little wife Papageno wants for himself. Oh, such a soft little dove would be bliss for me." The next section is marked allegro. "Then I'd enjoy drinking and eating; then I'd rank myself with princes, be happy as a philosopher of life (*sustained-fermata D at the top of the line*), and be as if in Elysium."

"A sweetheart or a little wife Papageno wants for himself. Oh, such a soft little dove would be bliss for me!" Papageno repeats the text of verse 1, marked andante.

(Allegro) "Alas, so I can't be pleasing to one among all the charming girls? May just one help me out of my need (*a sustained-fermata D at the top of the line*), or else I'll surely die of a broken heart. If no one will grant me love, then the flame must consume me; but if a womanly mouth should kiss me, then I'll be well again." Once again, a sustained-fermata D at the top of the line is written.

As in his first song, Papageno has a variety of articulations in the vocal phrase, with some of the phrase marked legato—while in the midst of a vigorous dotted rhythmic figure. Once again, this is modeled by the orchestra in the introduction and in the intervals where the magic bells play. However, the differences between the two pieces should be strongly delineated. Before "Ein Mädchen" begins he is magically delivered a glass of wine. He is surprised to have it, and he feels its excitement and warmth inside, while he also feels confused and frustrated about the opera's turn of events. Life is not as simple as it was when he sang "Der Vogelfänger" at the beginning of the opera.

This is a good piece for a young baritone—for articulating the German text, singing a lyric melody with purpose and meaning to differentiate between verses, and energizing the rhythms without sacrifice of line or tone.

Piano/vocal score: p. 118 (G. Schirmer)

No. 39

Voice: baritone
Aria Title: "Zazà, piccolo zingara" (Cascart)
Opera Title: *Zazà*
Composer and Librettist: Ruggero Leon-cavallo (1857–1919), after the play by Charles Simon and Pierre Berton (1898)
Historical Style: Verismo (1900)
Range: F3 to A♭4

Fach: lyric
Aria Duration: 1:50
Tessitura: A♭3 to F4

Position: Act II

Setting: Outside Paris, c. 1900; the receiving room in Zazà's house

Aria plot notes from the *G. Schirmer Opera Anthology: Arias for Baritone,* edited by Robert L. Larsen (used by permission):

Zazà is a concert hall singer in love with Dufresne, one of her many admirers. Unbeknownst to Zazà, Dufresne is married. Cascart, an old friend and former lover, comes to visit. With typical charm he suggests that there may be another woman in Dufresne's life, and that Zazà must return to her calling.

The aria is marked andantino affettuoso, con affettuoso semplicita in 6/8 meter:

Aria translation by Martha Gerhart from the *G. Schirmer Opera Anthology: Arias for Baritone,* edited by Robert L. Larsen (used by permission):

Zazà, little gypsy, slave of a foolish love, you have not reached the end of your grief yet!
[*dolce, piano*] How good that it should fall upon your face as tears . . .
[*Cascart sings a high G♭, con accento, forte.*]
Before your solitary and humble pilgrimage begins again!
You believed him to be free; now hope is dead.
[*The next section is marked ritardando, with accents, a high F entrance as the phrase begins.*]
Now it's you who are the free one! [*piano, sung on middle C*]
And remember your obligation . . . your obligation!
[*The next phrase, crescendo molto, ascends to high F and E♭.*]

> Ah, the charm of the dreamed-of-idyll disappeared all of a sudden!
> [*The final phrase begins on high G♭ with accents for the climactic phrases of the piece.*]
> A little angel's hand has made you come back!
> [*A strong, passionate final phrase, sung to high E♭, ending on the tonic {D♭}.*]

Piano/vocal score: p. 154 (Casa Musicale Sonzogno)

No. 40

Voice: baritone
Aria Title: "Eterna la memoria" (Gusmano)
Opera Title: *Alzira*
Composer: Giuseppe Verdi (1813–1901)
Historical Style: Italian Romantic (1845)
Aria Duration: 2:40
Range: D♭3 to F4

Fach: dramatic
Librettist: Salvatore Cammarano (1801–1852), based on Voltaire's play *Alzire* (1736)
Tessitura: D♭3 to F4

Position: Act I (A Life for a Life)

Setting: The main square of Lima, Peru, mid-16th century

Alvaro is ceremoniously resigning as Governor of Peru. He presents his son Gusmano to the crowd as his successor, and Gusmano's first act is to declare peace with the Incas.

After ordering Ataliba, a tribal head and his prisoner, to offer up his allegiance to Spain, Gusmano also implies that it might be nice if he could have Alzira, Ataliba's daughter. After Ataliba warns him that it may not be the best idea because Alzira loves someone else, Gusmano sings of how he is able to conquer entire nations, but he cannot claim victory of one woman's love. He has never feared a mortal foe; but against a ghost, an eternal memory, he is powerless. "I fully understand," he says.

The aria is marked andante sostenuto, cantabile, written in 3/4 meter.

She is burdened by the eternal memory of a mad love! (*con forza*) From the kingdom of the dead (*ascending to high F*) a ghost competes with me for her.

The man whom I vanquished while he was alive, I now must fear after he has died. (*There is chromatic subtlety in the vocal line here.*) A thousand battles I have won, vanquish I cannot vanquish a heart! (*He repeats the E♭ at the top for emphasis, then to the high F doubled by the orchestra, followed by the cadenza.*)

There are many various markings of articulation and double-dotted, energized rhythmic values.

Piano/vocal score: p. 58 (Ricordi)

No. 41

Voice: baritone
Aria Title: "Quanto un mortal può chiedere," cabaletta after "Eterna la memoria" (Gusmano)
Opera Title: *Alzira*
Composer: Giuseppe Verdi (1813–1901)
Historical Style: Italian Romantic (1845)
Range: E3 to F4

Fach: dramatic
Librettist: Salvatore Cammarano (1801–1852), based on Voltaire's play *Alzire* (1736)
Aria Duration: 1:45
Tessitura: E3 to E4

Position: Act I, scene 1

Setting: The main square of Lima, Peru, mid-16th century

After ordering Ataliba, a tribal head and his prisoner, to offer up his allegiance to Spain, Gusmano also implies that it might be nice if he could have Alzira, Ataliba's daughter. Ataliba tells him that it might not be a good idea because Alzira loves another, but Gusmano does not care. He orders Ataliba to make her love him and then sings that if he cannot have Alzira, his great success in war will have no value in his life.

The cabaletta is preceded by the following text:

Alvaro: Persist and you'll win! Love gives rise to love.
Ataliba: One must grant Alzira a period of delay for her suffering.
Gusmano: I feel an ardor that doesn't tolerate any delay.

Ataliba, make her give in to my wishes . . . You're her father . . .
You were a King . . . command . . . exhort her . . . beg her.
Ataliba: I'm going . . . trust in me.

The piece is marked allegro con brio; the accompaniment begins pianissimo: "All that a mortal can ask for, a benign heaven offered me . . . With glory it covered me, it placed a world at my feet." The first phrase goes up to D, and the second phrase up to E in accented half notes. The next section is written in E minor: "But my soul isn't satisfied with all that, because it longs for another love." Now the aria returns to the rhythms and shape of the beginning of the cabaletta with the "ah" sung on the E held by a fermata. "Ah, without the heart of Alzira the world means little to me!" This section is filled with grace notes, accents, and 8th-note triplets. The chorus sings seven measures ("May your desired Alzira grant her love to you") as the cabaletta is repeated.

(Translation by Nico Castel)

Piano/vocal score: p. 64 (Ricordi)

No. 42

Voice: baritone
Aria Title: "Compiacente a' colloqui del cicisbeo . . . Son sessant'anni" (Charles Gérard)
Opera Title: *Andrea Chénier*
Composer: Umberto Giordano (1867–1948)
Historical Style: Verismo (1896)
Range: C3 to F♯4

Fach: dramatic
Librettist: Luigi Illica (1857–1919), based on the life of André Chénier
Aria Duration: 4:10
Tessitura: E3 to E4

Position: Act I

Setting: The ballroom in the Coigny chateau; a winter afternoon in the year 1789. Under the orders of an imperious majordomo, lackeys, servants, and valets are dashing about putting the finishing touches to the furnishings and appointments of the splendid hall. In servant's livery, Charles Gérard is helping his aged father bring in a heavy blue sofa.

Gérard, along with his fellow servants, have been setting up for a party. Observing his father, an older crippled man struggling with cumbersome furniture, Gérard decries the class system that keeps them in virtual slavery. He denounces the gilded house and hypocritical aristocrats that condemn him to the life he is living. When the setting up of the party is completed, all leave except Gérard, who remains to smooth the fringes and fluff the pillows.

He is thoughtful, and conversational at the beginning of the piece:

Obliging to the conversations of the dandy . . . You are the sofa that obligingly has witnessed the conversations of dandies offering their hands to matrons! Here the red-heel (*name applied to aristocracy*) to beauty-mark sighing spoke: Orythia . . . (*from Greek mythology*) oh, Chloris (*shepherdess*). Oh, Nike (*personification of victory, winged and flying at great speed*) powdered, old hags overly made-up, I want you, and, moreover, for this alone, maybe I love you! This is the custom of the times. (*derisive laughter*)

There is a seven-measure interlude as his father enters carrying a duster, brings it into the room, and exits. Gérard, much moved, watches his father go.

It's been sixty years, old man, that you have served! To your haughty, arrogant masters you have poured forth loyalty, sweat, the strength of your sinews, your soul, your mind . . . And as if your life weren't enough to render endless the terrible suffering, you have given existence to your sons . . . you have sired menials!

Aria: I hate you, gilded house! The image you are is of a world powdered and vain! (*Sung on C♯ to sustained high E; the setting of the text is syllabic and delivered with anger.*) Prissy dandies in silks and in laces, hasten to sing your joyful gavottes and minuets. Your fate is settled. Race that is elegant and guilty, I, the son of servants (*Gérard sings a high F♯*) and myself a servant, hereby judge you. I shout to you: The hour of your death is here! (*The phrase ends on a high sustained F♯.*)

The last two pages are sung with text set syllabically predominantly on middle C and D.

Piano/vocal score: p. 3 (Ricordi)

No. 43

Voice: baritone

Aria Title: "Nemico della patria" (Charles Gérard)

Opera Title: *Andrea Chénier*

Composer: Umberto Giordano (1867–1948)

Historical Style: Verismo (1896)

Range: C#3 to F#4

Fach: dramatic

Librettist: Luigi Illica (1857–1919), based on the life of André Chénier

Aria Duration: 4:30

Tessitura: E3 to D4

Position: Act III

Setting: The Revolutionary Tribunal in Paris, 1789, where many men and women are hastily judged or misjudged; the proceedings are cruel and heartless.

Chénier has been arrested, and Gérard, a servant, asks the sinister Incredibile if Maddalena (the Countess's daughter) has surfaced. Incredibile responds no, but with Chénier in prison it will not be happening now. Gérard prepares to write the indictment against Chénier as an "Enemy of His Country." He begins, but stops as he realizes his discontent with the Revolution and all that it means. He puts down the pen.

Enemy of this country? It's the same old fable that the people blissfully drink up. Born in Constantinople? A foreigner? He studied at Saint-Cyr? A soldier! A traitor? An accomplice? He's a poet? A subverter of hearts and of customs!

This first section is in the style of accompanied recitative, with fragmented phrases and words and many thoughts and varied focuses. There are now seven measures of orchestral interlude as his pen slips from his fingers. He stares fixedly, and his eyes fill with tears. He rises and walks slowly about. This is marked con tristezza/sadly, piano.

One day it was a joy for me to walk unaffected among hate and revenge. Pure innocent and strong! A giant, I thought myself! I am always a servant . . . I have changed masters! (*violently*) A servant obedient with violent passions! Ah, worse yet! I kill and tremble, and while I kill I weep! (*The vocal line climbs to the high E and D#.*) I, of the redemptress (*French Revolution*) a son, was the first to hear its cry throughout the world united with my own cry. Have I now lost faith in that destiny I dreamt of? (*He pauses and as old memories come back to him, he is overcome with sorrow.*) How my path shown with glory! To awaken the awareness in people's hearts! To assuage the tears of the downtrodden and suffering people! (*The aria here is heroically sung, animando, with energetic dotted rhythms to the high D♯ and E culminating in the sustained high F♯ at the word "bacio/kiss."*)

To make the world a Pantheon (*the Utopian shrine*) to change men into gods and in one single kiss and embrace to love all of mankind!

Piano/vocal score: p. 163 (Casa Musicale Sonzogno di Piero Ostali–Milan)

No. 44

Voice: baritone
Aria Title: "Dagl'immortali vertici" (Ezio)
Opera Title: *Attila*
Composer: Giuseppe Verdi (1813–1901)
Historical Style: Italian Romantic (1846)
Range: E♭3 to F4

Fach: dramatic
Librettist: Temistocle Solera (1815–1878), with alterations by Francesco Maria Piave (1810–1876), after Zacharias Werner's tragedy *Attila, König der Hunnen* (1808)
Aria Duration: 2:25
Tessitura: E3 to D4

Position: Act II, scene 1

Setting: Ezio's camp, 5th century; in the distance can be seen the City of the Seven Hills (Rome)

Ezio, a Roman general, is an ambitious figure in the opera. In the Prologue he has proposed a secret pact by which he and Attila, King of the Huns, would divide Italy between them. The Eastern ruler, he points out, is old and feeble, and the Roman ruler a young boy. Why should they not agree to share the spoils? Attila rejects Ezio's offer, calls him a traitor, and prepares to march on Rome.

After being commanded by the young Emperor Valentinian to return to Rome because the Huns were withdrawing, Ezio declares that he shall not be controlled by a mere boy and calls the spirits of his ancestors to return Rome back to its former greatness.

Recitative (reading the letter from the boy Emperor): Truce there is with
the Huns. To Rome Ezio soon will return . . . by order of Valentinian,
Ezio is to return to Rome.
He commands! . . . a boy wearing a crown is commanding me to
be recalled?
Unless you, Valentinian, are afraid of my troops more so than
Attila's . . .
A brave and veteran gray-haired warrior always will have to submit
before a faint-hearted puny slave?
I will go then . . . but as it befits the hero, whose supreme might can
lift (*he sings a sustained high G*) the homeland from its present straits!

The aria is marked andante. The opening structure is two measure
phrases beginning in the upper middle of the voice, and the shape of each
phrase is up to the third and then the fifth above the tonic (Eb) There is a
gently arpeggiated accompaniment.

"From the immortal, beautiful peaks of former glory, may the spirits of
our ancestors rise around us only for one instant! From there the conquering eagle took off in flight throughout the world . . . Who can recognize
Rome now as the corpse it is?" The phrases are repeated, building to an
ascension to high F ("cadavere/corpse"), completed by a cadenza. The dynamics are carefully marked between fortissimo and pianissimo.

(Translation by Nico Castel)

Piano/vocal score: p. 116 (Belwin Mills)

No. 45

Voice: baritone
Aria Title: "E'gettata la mia sorte,"
cabaletta after "Dagl'immortali vertici" (Ezio)
Opera Title: *Attila*
Composer: Giuseppe Verdi (1813–1901)
Historical Style: Italian Romantic (1846)
Range: F3 to F4

Fach: dramatic
Librettist: Temistocle Solera (1815–1878),
with alterations by Francesco Maria Piave
(1810–1876), after Zacharias Werner's
tragedy *Attila, König der Hunnen* (1808)
Aria Duration: 2:30
Tessitura: Bb3 to F4

Position: Act II, scene 1

Setting: Ezio's camp, 5th century; in the distance can be seen the City of the Seven Hills (Rome)

Ezio, a Roman general, is an ambitious figure in the opera. In the Prologue he has proposed a secret pact by which he and Attila, King of the Huns, would divide Italy between them. The Eastern ruler, he points out, is old and feeble, and the Roman ruler a young boy. Why should they not agree to share the spoils? Attila rejects Ezio's offer, calls him a traitor, and prepares to march on Rome.

After being commanded by the young Emperor Valentinian to return to Rome because the Huns were withdrawing, Ezio declares that he shall not be controlled by a mere boy and calls the spirits of his ancestors to return Rome back to its former greatness.

Foresto, a knight of Aquileia (city-port on the Adriatic coast which was decimated by Attila and the Huns), is in love with Odabella, daughter of the lord of Aquileia, and she is in love with him. Foresto is in disguise and now appears as an attending slave to speak with Ezio.

Foresto proposes here that Attila be assassinated. Foresto suggests a trap with the Roman army in waiting while he signals with fire on a hill that the time is right. The Huns will be surprised, and Italy will be defended.

The traditional cabaletta rhythm is heard in the accompaniment—for momentum. The first two phrases ascend to high F: "ogni guerra/every war; da forte/hero; Romano/Roman."

My lot is cast, I'm ready for every war. If I fall, I'll fall as a hero, and my name will remain. I won't see my beloved country decay slowly and reduced to pieces . . . over the last Roman all Italy will weep.

The cabaletta is repeated. At the stretto to close the cabaletta the marking is più animato, as the notes lie high and continue to build and repeat. Momentum is important. It is further energized through double-dotted rhythms and well-placed accents. A high F is sustained in the last phrase ("piangerà/will weep").

(Translation by Nico Castel)

Piano/vocal score: p. 122 (Belwin Mills)

Note: Sherrill Milnes in his first album of recorded arias took the high octave B♭ on the last note.

No. 46

Voice: baritone
Aria Title: "Votre toast, je peux vous le render" (Escamillo)
Opera Title: *Carmen*
Composer: Georges Bizet (1838–1875)
Historical Style: French Romantic (1875)
Range: B♭3 to F4

Fach: dramatic
Librettists: Henri Meilhac (1831–1897) and Ludovic Halévy (1834–1908), after the novella by Prosper Mérimée (1845, rev. 1846)
Aria Duration: 5:10
Tessitura: C3 to C4

Position: Act II

Setting: Outside Seville, Spain, 1820s; Lillas Pastia's Inn; late night

Carmen and her gypsy friends, Frasquita and Mercedes, entertain officers in Lillas Pastia's tavern. Zuniga tells Carmen that José has been released after a month in prison; she is delighted. A late night festive torchlight procession accompanies Escamillo, the famous bullfighter, to the tavern. He enters with his entourage he is toasted by the crowd. The great bullfighter sings of his adventures in the bullring, intent on impressing Carmen and her friends.

The beginning of the aria is marked allegro moderato, beginning with energy on middle C and descending at the end of the line to the low B♭, low for the baritone voice.

Aria translation by Martha Gerhart from the *G. Schirmer Opera Anthology: Arias for Baritone*, edited by Robert L. Larsen (used by permission):

"I can reciprocate your toast, gentlemen, for with soldiers, yes," [now he sings up to the D♭ and E♭ above middle C] "bullfighters can agree: For pleasure, they have fights! The arena is full; it's a holiday! The arena is full from top to bottom. The spectators, losing their heads, heckle each other boisterously!" [to sustained high F at the end of the phrase] "Insults, screams, and commotion pushed to the point of frenzy! For it's the celebration of courage! It's the celebration of people of spirit. Let's go—on guard!" [The challenge takes the singer to high E and then to middle C for the "Ah!" which connects to the well-known refrain, marked piano.] "Toreador, on guard! And do keep in mind—yes, keep in mind, while fighting, that a dark eye is watching you [*sustained high E*] and that love awaits you!"

[The second verse describes the personal drama of a bullfighter,

---

while the first verse sets the atmosphere.] "All of a sudden the people are silent. Ah, what's happening! No more screaming—this is the moment! The bull rears, bounding out of the pen! He rears, he enters, he strikes! A horse rolls over, dragging along a picador. 'Ah, well done, bull,' roars the crowd! The bull goes, comes, and strikes again!"

"Shaking his *banderillas*, full of rage, he runs! The arena is strewn with blood! People are running away; they are leaping over the railings! It's your turn now! Let's go—on guard! Ah!"

The refrain is followed by a five-measure ending (tag) of the text "l'amour t'attend!/love awaits you," which cadences on a final high F, marked fortissimo.

Piano/vocal score: p. 133 (G. Schirmer)

Notes by singer Gino Quilico: This aria is difficult to sing: too low for a baritone, too high for a bass. Make sure you have the low notes and the high notes requisite for a strong performance, then forget the music—the notes, the voice. Become the star matador. This piece needs character and charisma, especially when sung on stage.

No. 47

Voice: baritone
Aria Title: "Il cavallo scalpita" (Alfio)
Opera Title: *Cavalleria rusticana*
Composer: Pietro Mascagni (1863–1945)
Historical Style: Verismo (1890)
Range: D#3 to F#4

Fach: dramatic
Librettists: Giovanni Targioni-Tozzetti (1863–1934) and Guido Menasci (1867–1925), after the play by Giovanni Verga (1883)
Aria Duration: 2:55
Tessitura: E♭3 to E♭4

Position: One-act opera

Setting: A beautiful Easter Sunday in the main square of a Sicilian village, late 1800s. One sees the façade of the church to one side and Mama Lucia's tavern to the other.

Some time before Turiddu went off to serve in the army, he had an affair with Lola. While he was away, Lola married the carter Alfio. On his return Turiddu seduced Santuzza, who is now pregnant by him and has been excommunicated because of her condition. She loves him sincerely, but to her chagrin Lola could not endure seeing him with another and has resumed her affair with the inconstant Turiddu.

Alfio enters at the beginning of the opera, after the villagers comment on the season. "The orange trees perfume the air . . . The men are tired and must rest from their rustic labors . . . the serene virgin rejoices in the savior." The sound of the horses' hooves, the jingling of harness bells, and the cracking of a whip are heard. Alfio enters on his cart accompanied by some men.

Alfio, a village teamster, sings that, though the world is full of troubles, it doesn't bother him for he has a wonderful wife and a lusty life. The horse paws the ground, the harness bells jingle, he cracks the whip. "Hey there!" (sung on a sustained E♭) "Let blow the icy wind, let fall the water or let it snow, to me what does it matter?" He repeats the opening text at a higher pitch level to a high sustained F at "Ehi la!/Hey there!" Men: "Oh what a jolly occupation to be a carter, to go from here to there!" The second verse includes interjections by the chorus offstage. Alfio: "Lola awaits me at home, who loves and consoles me, who is loyalty itself. The horse, let it paw the ground, the harness bells let them jingle, it's Easter and I am here!"

Piano/vocal score: p. 29 (G. Schirmer)

> Notes by conductor and conducting professor David Effron: "Il cavallo scalpita" is one of the most underestimated difficult entrances in opera. First of all, the baritone must show his acting ability and define the character of Alfio in a simple melody with no lyricism and at the same time catch the tempo from the conductor while running on stage. As soon as things seem to be set, Mascagni gives us a slower rendition of the melody but with off beats in the orchestra which have no relationship to the baritone's line (now sung lyrically). This juxtaposition of singer and orchestra has been the demise of many experienced singers. The fast part returns, and here again the baritone must rely on the conductor to get back to the original tempo. All in all a full evening's work in about two minutes.

No. 48

Voice: baritone
Aria Title: "Minnie, dalla mia casa son partito" (Jack Rance)
Opera Title: *La fanciulla del West*
Composer: Giacomo Puccini (1858–1924)
Historical Style: Verismo (1910)
Range: C#3 to F#4

Fach: dramatic
Librettists: Guelfo Civinini (1873–1954) and Carlo Zangarini (1874–1943), after David Belasco's play *The Girl of the Golden West* (1905)
Aria Duration: 2:16
Tessitura: E3 to D#4

Position: Act I

Setting: 1840s California, inside a saloon

Aria plot notes from the *G. Schirmer Opera Anthology: Arias for Baritone,* edited by Robert L. Larsen (used by permission):

Minnie is the owner of the Polka saloon at the foot of the Cloudy Mountain, California. The miners are gathered there, and when she enters, the atmosphere is charged with the love she inspires in them. Jack Rance, the sheriff, sings openly of his passion for Minnie.

The aria is marked andante sostenuto in 4/8 meter; the beginning lies low for the baritone:

Aria translation by Martha Gerhart from the *G. Schirmer Opera Anthology: Arias for Baritone,* edited by Robert L. Larsen (used by permission):

Minnie, I left my home, which is beyond the mountains, Across another ocean.
Not a single regret, Minnie, followed me.
[*The meter changes to 2/8.*]
Not a single regret could I leave there!
No one ever loved me; I haven't loved anyone.
[*He now ascends to the upper middle voice.*]
Nothing whatever gave me pleasure!
I hold enclosed in my breast a gambler's heart—bitter, poisoned—
Which laughs at love and at fate.
[*He sings a repetition of the opening melody.*]
I set out on the road attracted only by the fascination of gold

---

> [*The next phrases are marked movendo un poco.*]
> This is the only thing which has not deceived me.
> [*The aria is now marked rallentando, largamente; the vocal line extends up to high E, then to sustained fermata on high F, ending on E.*]
> Now, for a kiss of yours, I'll throw away a fortune!

The text is set to the music syllabically, with complex rhythms, many changes of dynamics; a strong lower range (C♯) is necessary; inflections for meaning are very important. At the same time, the vocal line must be connected.

Piano/vocal score: p. 86 (Ricordi)

No. 49

Voice: baritone
Aria Title: "Morir! Tremenda cosa! . . . Urna fatale del mio destino" (Don Carlo)
Opera Title: *La forza del destino*
Composer: Giuseppe Verdi (1813–1901)
Historical Style: Italian Romantic (1862)
Range: B2 to F4

Fach: dramatic
Librettist: Francesco Maria Piave (1810–1876), based on Angel de Saavedra, Duke of Rivas's drama *Don Alvaro, o la fuerza del sino* (1835)
Aria Duration: 4:15
Tessitura: E3 to C4

Position: Act III, scene 1

Setting: A military camp near Velletri, south of Rome, 18th century; the battle is over; night

Don Carlo di Vargas is the brother of Leonora and is the son of the Marquis of Calatrava. Alvaro, a half-caste South American Prince in love with Leonora, and Carlo have concealed their true identities from each other. Alvaro has been wounded and is undergoing surgery. Alvaro has been entrusted with Carlo's papers and is debating searching them for proof of his true identity. The surgeon enters and tells him that Alvaro shall live. Carlo proclaims great joy and imagines finding Alvaro and Leonora together and dispatching them both to hell with one blow from his sword.

The surgeon and the orderlies carry the wounded Alvaro into another room.

To die! . . . terrible thing! . . . so intrepid, so brave. And yet he must die! What a strange man. (*allegro*) He shuddered at the name of Calatrava! To him known is perhaps my dishonor? Heaven! What a flash! . . . If he were the seducer? . . . He, in my hand . . . and alive! If I were wrong?..This key will tell me.

(*He opens the case in great agitation and removes from it a sealed envelope.*)

Here are the papers! (*He is about to open the package.*) What am I trying to do? (*He stops.*) And the oath that I swore? And this life of mine, that I owe to his valor? Also I saved him! What if he were that accursed Indian who sullied my blood? (*with determination*) The seal—let it be broken. (*He begins to do so.*) No one here can see me . . . (*He stops himself.*) No? Maybe no one can see me . . . but I can certainly see myself.

He throws down the envelope and walks away in horror. The aria is marked andante sostenuto, cantabile, piano.

Fatal urn of my destiny, Go, away with you! You tempt me in vain. I came here to cleanse my honor, and I won't stain it with a new shame. An oath is sacred to a man of honor; those papers, may they keep their mystery . . . perish the evil thought which to the unworthy deed spurred me.

The aria is marked dolce, and it must move because of the lightly embellished phrases that rise up to the high D and E, followed by a passing F♯ in a florid passage.

Piano/vocal score: p. 203 (Ricordi)

No. 50

Voice: baritone
Aria Title: "Ah, pescator, affonda l'esca,"
Barcarolle (Barnaba)
Opera Title: *La Gioconda*
Composer: Amilcare Ponchielli (1834–1886)
Historical Style: Italian Romantic (1876)
Range: C3 to F4

Fach: dramatic
Librettist: Arrigo Boito (1842–1918) (under
the pseudonym Tobia Gorrio), based on
Victor Hugo's play *Angélo, tyran de Padoue*
(1835)
Aria Duration: 3:25
Tessitura: E♭3 to E♭4

Position: Act II

Setting: The deck of Enzo's ship, at anchor near a deserted island, near Venice, 17th century

Barnaba, a spy for the Inquisition, is disguised as a fisherman and appears in a small boat alongside the ship of Enzo Grimaldo, a nobleman of Genoa. He completes his masquerade by singing a merry fisherman's ballad along with Enzo's crew. However, his cheerfulness is merely a guise to measure the strength of Enzo's men.

The aria is marked allegretto con spirito, con brio, in 6/8 meter.

Ah! Fisherman, cast the bait; may the waves be true to you. The sea and the sky promise you a happy evening and good fishing. Go, tranquil lullaby, through the blue vastness. Ah, a placid siren will fall into the net! (*A subito piano and staccato in a conspiring tone is marked here.*) Watch with your lightning, cunning glances; and in the darkness count your dead. Yes, from this deserted and dark island your fortune should rise now.

Be on guard, and divert the quick suspicion, and laugh and be on the alert, and sing and keep watch! (*The melody is now recapitulated.*) Ah, serene Venus shines in a heaven of voluptuousness; a luminous siren will fall into the net. The siren will fall into the net—yes, she will fall!

The aria has should be sung with a legato vocal line, but also a vitality in its 6/8 "swing." The aria needs an E♭ and passing F on top, and the vocal line frequently begins on the high E♭ with an accent, or on the middle C 8th-note pick-up to the E♭.

Piano/vocal score: p. 133 (Ricordi)

No. 51

Voice: baritone

Aria Title: "Franco son io" (Giacomo)

Opera Title: *Giovanna d'Arco*

Composer: Giuseppe Verdi (1813–1901)

Historical Style: Italian Romantic (1845)

Range: B3 to F4

Fach: dramatic

Librettist: Temistocle Solera (1815–1878), in part after Johann Christoph Friedrich von Schiller's tragedy *Die Jungfrau von Orleans* (1801)

Aria Duration: 3:20

Tessitura: G3 to F4

Position: Act I, scene 1

Setting: a rocky area close to the city of Rheims, 1429. There are scattered groups of English soldiers, women weeping over their dead, and others tending the wounded

The English are in retreat and are about to pull out of France altogether when Giacomo, a shepherd, approaches them. He offers to hand over his daughter to them, for she was the one who rallied the French to victory. He does love his country, but he cannot help but fight against the French King whom he believes has brought dishonor upon them all.

The beginning is marked andante sostenuto; piano; grandioso declamato.

French I am but in my heart comes first homeland, honor; I swore that if someone attacks France, to avenge the attack or die. (*dolce*) Now Carlo has burdened with shame my hair which is already white . . . I ask to let me fight together with you against Carlo, that base Frenchman.

E memoria/It's the memory of a daughter who betrayed her father. I know that original sin leads us along a path of thorns. I also know that a brighter and dear land will be revealed to the wretched of this world. Ah, the father's tear, let it be shed upon the vile mud! The flesh is weak, but the soul is greater than any pain.

The aria is filled with accents and double-dotted rhythms, and it is followed by a cabaletta. The baritone will need to sing a legato line, but with accents. At the end of some phrases a florid decorative flourish is necessary. The high tone needed is a sustained F, and it is sung frequently at different dynamic levels.

Piano/vocal score: p. 91 (Ricordi)

No. 52

Voice: baritone
Aria Title: "Presti omai l'egizia terra," No. 1 (Cesare)
Opera Title: *Giulio Cesare*
Composer: George Frideric Handel (1685–1759)
Historical Style: Italian Baroque (1724)
Range: D3 to D4

Fach: dramatic (bass)
Librettist: Nicola Francesco Haym (1678–1729), after Giacomo Francesco Bussani's *Giulio Cesare in Egitto* set by Antonio Sartorio (1677) and a 1685 version of the same libretto
Aria Duration: 1:55
Tessitura: D3 to D4

Position: Act I, scene 1

Setting: Egyptian landscape: over a bridge crossing a branch of the Nile come Cesare (Caesar) and Curio and supporters, hailed by the Egyptian populace.

Cesare enters the scene triumphantly. He is in Egypt to defeat or to make terms with his old rival Pompeius (Pompey). Egypt is ruled jointly by Cleopatra and her brother, Ptolemaeus (Ptolemy), each of them claiming sole right to the crown.

After the chorus "Hail, Caesar," he sings a vigorous and triumphant aria, marked allegro. "Now may Egypt claim its own: may it be the triumphant victor. Lend homage to the Egyptian land" ("le sue palme/her palms" is repeated here in a melisma of upward sequences to the top of the staff). The opening text is now repeated with growing embellishments and sequences of 8th- and 16th-note combinations. The highest pitch in the piece is D, and the singer can finish on the high (D) octave.

The aria needs strength and nobility; it is deliberate in its purpose, but also requires flexibility in the melismatic passages.

Piano/vocal score: p. 2 (International)

No. 53

Voice: baritone

Aria Title: "Sois immobile," part of No. 18 (William Tell)

Opera Title: *Guillaume Tell*

Composer: Gioacchino Rossini (1792–1868)

Historical Style: French Romantic (1829)

Range: C3 to F4

Fach: dramatic

Librettists: Etienne de Jouy (1764–1846) and Hippolyte-Louis-Florent Bis (1789–1855), after Johann Christoph Friedrich von Schiller's play *Wilhelm Tell* (1804)

Aria Duration: 2:35

Tessitura: F3 to D♯/E♭4

Position: Act III, scene 2

Setting: Swiss mountains, the main square of Altdorf; Gesler's castle is seen in the background. To one side a dais has been erected for the Governor; the square is embellished by various trees such as apple, lime, etc. A pole has been set up in the middle on which Gesler's hat has been placed; all are required to make an obeisance to it.

When William Tell, a Swiss patriot, refuses to genuflect at the symbol of the Austrian government, Gesler picks out Tell's son Jemmy and orders Tell to shoot an apple off Jemmy's head or Jemmy will be killed. Before shooting, however, Tell warns Jemmy to stay completely still and to think of his mother.

Recitative: Jemmy: "Courage, my father!" Tell: "At his voice my hand lets fall my weapons. My eyes are clouded by dangerous tears. My son, let me kiss you for the last time." (At a sign from Gesler, Jemmy runs to his father's side.)

Stay motionless and toward the ground. Kneel down and pray to God. (*The boy kneels.*)
It is He alone, my child, can save my life, all of our lives and our country, through you.
Stay kneeling but look up into the sky.
As it threatens that head so dear to me, the arrow steel point may cause you to flinch.
Look up to the sky, Jemmy, and concentrate on your mother; don't make the slightest movement.
She awaits us, the two of us!

Piano/vocal score: p. 328 (Kalmus)

Notes from singer and voice professor Timothy Noble: The important element in performing this aria is the legato of the vocal line. The aria is marked sostenuto, and with the delicate orchestral accompaniment, the voice is exposed. Too much too soon is something the singer must watch out for, with the climactic F#'s to sing.

Tell sings this in an intimate manner. Although many people are on the stage, it is really Tell speaking with his son. His son does not really understand that his own life is in danger—he is too young. At one point Tell almost has to shake the boy so that he will realize the gravity of the situation.

No. 54

Voice: baritone
Aria Title: "Ach, wir armen, armen Leute" (Peter)
Opera Title: *Hänsel und Gretel*
Composer: Engelbert Humperdinck (1854–1921)
Historical Style: German Romantic (1893)
Range: E3 to E4

Fach: dramatic
Librettist: Adelheid Wette (1858–1916), after a story by the Brothers Grimm
Aria Duration: 6:25
Tessitura: G3 to E4

Position: Act I

Setting: Germany, 19th century; a poor mountain cottage

Returning from town after having celebrated a successful day selling his brooms, Peter ambles back to his country cottage and his family, singing all the way home. The beginning is marked gemächlich, pianissimo): "Tralalala, tralalala!" (sung on a high E).

Hey mother—here I am!
Tralalala, tralalala! I bring happiness and glory!
Ah, we poor, poor people—every day just like today: in the purse a big hole,
And in the stomach even a bigger one, tralalala, tralalala!

Hunger is the best cook!

Yes, you rich people may feast; we who have nothing to eat

Nibble, alas, the whole week long—seven days on one bone!

Tralalala, tralalala! Hunger is the best cook!

Ah, we enjoy being content, for happiness is of many different kinds!

But true it is, nonetheless—poverty is a heavy yoke!

Tralalala, tralalala! Hunger is the best cook!

Yes, indeed, hunger does cook well, so far as it does the commanding;

But what good is the commander if the seasoning is missing in the pot?

Tralalala, tralalala!

Kümmel is my favorite liqueur!

The baritone will need to sing many E's in this aria in a "thrown off" and carefree, not forced manner. The music is filled with vigorous rhythms, reflecting a successful day selling his brooms. There are ritardandos in a number of the cadences. Good diction is necessary in all verses, since the orchestration is rather heavy and active. The orchestration for the last verse is especially active.

Piano/vocal score: p. 42 (G. Schirmer)

No. 55

Voice: baritone
Aria Title: "Qui donc commande"
(Henry VIII)
Opera Title: *Henry VIII*
Composer: Camille Saint-Saëns (1835–1921)
Historical Style: French Romantic (1883)
Range: D3 to F♯4

Fach: dramatic
Librettists: Léonce Détroyat (1829–1898)
and Armand Silvestre (1837–1901)
Aria Duration: 3:13
Tessitura: F♯3 to D4

Position: Act I

Setting: A room in the palace of Henry VIII (1491–1547), England
    The opera libretto concentrates on Henry VIII's renunciation of Rome,

his rejection of Catherine of Aragon, and his marriage to Anne Boleyn. Henry's political ambitions and defiance of Rome with the jealousy of two Queens and their confrontations are exciting. The role of Henry ranges from tenderness and suspicion to defiance and menace. Henry was a man of enormous appetites and strength of will. He was also not without musical talent, having composed a number of songs that are very fine.

The first act takes place in the royal palace, where Don Gomez (tenor), the Spanish Ambassador, is introduced and reveals his love for Anne Boleyn, to whom he has written a letter containing love passages. This letter has come into the possession of Queen Catherine. The Dukes of Norfolk and Surrey warn him to be careful, since the King himself has shown interest in Anne. Making no secret of his passion for her, he is seeking a divorce from Catherine in order to make Anne his Queen. When the King enters, he sings the following aria in the presence of Surrey.

The beginning of the aria is marked pianissimo:

How can one command when he loves?
And which empire remains with the heart?
(*Henry muses, in the middle voice; he repeats the text.*)
(*Larghetto, 3/4 meter*) Where love puts its victorious foot
Ah! It is supreme torture: She will, and then she will not.
She seeks me, then avoids me. The memory of Marguerite, my
desires superfluous.
(*sung in fragmented phrases, more agitated, più marcato*)
Ah! It is supreme torture: To hope and fear at the same time.
And to live in exile of oneself. Having caprices for laws.
Ah! It is supreme torture.
(*The opening, musing melody is repeated, larghetto, pianissimo.*)
How can one command when he loves? And which empire remains
with the heart,
Where love puts its victorious foot? How can one command when he
loves?

The King forcefully informs the Queen that he has a new maid of honor for her, who is Anne Boleyn. The King creates a new title for Anne: Marchioness of Pembroke. The Queen is compelled to accept the new maid. The baritone will need to enunciate clearly to the high E. The singer will need to sing a high F♯, but only a quarter note and then a dotted half note in duration.

Piano/vocal score: p. 43 (Durand)

No. 56

Voice: baritone

Aria Title: "Vision fugitive" (Hérode)

Opera Title: *Hérodiade*

Composer: Jules Massenet (1842–1912)

Historical Style: French Romantic (1881)

Range: C3 to G♭4

Fach: dramatic

Librettists: Paul Milliet (1858–?) and Henri Gremont (Georges Hartmann) (1843–1900), after the story *Hérodias* by Gustave Flaubert (1877)

Aria Duration: 3:05

Tessitura: F3 to E4

Position: Act II, scene 1

Setting: Hérode's apartment, Jerusalem, during the reign of King Herod Antipas (30 A.D.)

As he reclines on his couch Hérode is brought a potion which is reputed to conjure up the vision of the one loved most. He drinks and sees a vision of the ravishingly beautiful Salomé. Hérode sings of his passionate desire for Salomé, whom he does not know is actually his wife's daughter. The markings at the beginning are allegro appassionato, forte.

> This potion could give me such a dream! I should be able to see her again . . . to gaze on her beauty! (*andante*)
> Divine voluptuousness promised to my sight! Hope too brief, (*piano*)
> Which comes to lull my heart (*the forte vocal phrase ascends to high F*) and trouble my mind . . .
> Ah, don't slip away, (*piano, molto ritardando*) sweet illusion!

The aria is marked andante and is composed in 9/8 meter, piano:

> Vision fleeting and always pursued—mysterious angel, who takes possession of my whole life . . .
> Ah, it's you whom I want to see, oh my love, oh my hope!
> (*piano-dolce, without ritartando*) Fleeting vision, it's you
> (*The singer will need a high, sustained F with a crescendo to a forte-accented cadence.*)
> Who takes possession of my whole life, to press you in my arms!
> To feel your heart beat (*dolce*) with a loving ardor! Then to die entwined in a shared ecstasy.
> (*Here is written a fermata on a high E, marked piano.*)
> For those joys, for that passion.
> Ah, without remorse and without complaint I would give my soul for

you, my love, my hope!

Yes! It's you, my love! (*on a high, sustained G♭*) You, my only love, my hope!

At the end of the piece there occurs a recollection of the "vision fugitive" melody, marked pianissimo; then there is a passionately sung sustained high F, G♭, with accents and rhythmic vitality. This piece is a study of contrasts between the singer possessed by a hypnotic spell and an "in the moment" active awareness.

Piano/vocal score: p. 172 (G. Hartmann)

No. 57

Voice: baritone
Aria Title: "My friends, you do me too much honor" (Frederick Douglass)
Opera Title: *John Brown*
Composer and Librettist: Kirke Mechem (b. 1925)
Historical Style: 20th-century American (1989)
Range: B3 to D4

Fach: dramatic
Aria Duration: 3:40
Tessitura: B3 to B4

Position: Act II

Setting: The plains of Kansas, May 1856

> Aria plot notes from the *G. Schirmer American Aria Anthology: Baritone/Bass*, edited by Richard Walters (used by permission):
>
> The opera concerns abolitionist John Brown (1800–1859), an activist who was executed for his attempts to end slavery by violence amid a complex prewar political situation. In the aftermath of the 1854 Kansas-Nebraska Act passed by Congress, which dictated that the question of slavery in those territories was to be decided by their resi-

dents in elections, Kansas became a bloody political battleground for North and South. At a gathering of sympathizers John Brown introduces former slave Frederick Douglass (1818–1895) as "slavery's greatest enemy." Douglass, one of the foremost civil rights activists and a brilliant speaker, addresses the crowd.

This piece calls for a rich middle voice. Dynamics are varied and specifically marked. The range is not challenging, reaching only to a passing D above middle C. "Music is my greatest joy . . . The songs of the slave are the sorrows of his heart," he continues, and then repeats for emphasis to the crowd. "He is relieved by them as an aching heart is relieved by tears," he expressively sings.

Piano/vocal score: p. 118 (*G. Schirmer American Aria Anthology: Baritone/Bass*)

> Notes by composer Kirke Mechem: Douglass was an admirer and close friend of John Brown for years. After Brown's execution, Douglass declared, "John Brown will need no defender . . . until the lives of tyrants and murderers shall become more precious in the sight of men than justice and liberty." In this aria Douglass poignantly corrects the myth that the singing of slaves was proof that they were happy. The composer has adapted the words from Douglass's autobiography.

No. 58

Voice: baritone
Aria Title: "O lieto augurio," Arioso (Macbeth)
Opera Title: *Macbeth*
Composer: Giuseppe Verdi (1813–1901)
Historical Style: Italian Romantic (1847)
Range: E♭3 to F4

Fach: dramatic
Librettist: Francesco Maria Piave (1810–1876) with additions by Andrea Maffei (1798–1885), after the tragedy by William Shakespeare (1605)
Aria Duration: 1:30
Tessitura: G3 to E♭4

Position: Act III

Setting: Scotland, Medieval times; a dark cave with a boiling cauldron in the center

The witches surround Macbeth. Lightning and storms accompany apparitions to follow. A child appears, wearing a crown. Told by this ghost that he will not be conquered until "great Birnam Wood" come to "high Dunsinane hill," Macbeth rejoices in this arioso, for he does not believe that such a thing is possible.

The aria is marked allegro in cut time. He repeats in each phrase the ascent to high Eb, sustained, with double-dotted rhythms. The text is repeated, climaxing at the high sustained F, then descending with accents:

Oh, happy wishes!
For magic power no wood ever moved itself.
(*To the witches*) And now tell me: will the sons of Banquo ever ascend my throne?
I want to know it, or my sword will descend on you!

Macbeth, delirious with excitement, sings allegro with momentum to the highest notes of the range, with energized rhythms and accents.

Piano/vocal score: p. 230 (G. Schirmer)

No. 59

Voice: baritone
Aria Title: "La sua lampada vitale," Cavatina (Francesco)
Opera Title: *I masnadieri*
Composer: Giuseppe Verdi (1813–1901)
Historical Style: Italian Romantic (1847)
Range: C3 to F4

Fach: dramatic
Librettist: Andrea Maffei (1798–1885), after Johann Christoph Friedrich von Schiller's tragedy *Die Räuber* (1781)
Aria Duration: 2:15
Tessitura: F3 to Db4

Position: Act I, scene 2

Setting: A room in the castle of Count Moor; Germany, early 18th century
Francesco, son of Massimiliano, Count of Moor, congratulates himself on

his villainy. He rails at his subordinate position as a second son. We learn that he has intercepted the letter in which Carlo had asked his father for forgiveness for his waywardness and has substituted one forged by himself. Francesco contemplates his father's frailty and plans to "help" nature along in killing him. He can thus become master of the Count's property. He orders the family servant Arminio (whom he believes he can trust) to go to Massimiliano in disguise and announce that Carlo has died in battle outside Prague. Francesco is confident that this news will hasten his father's death.

After some reflection Francesco sings a recitative that is spewed out with venom. Some of the phrases are fragmented. Many dotted and double-dotted rhythms augment the character's intensity and inner anger, rising to the high E♭: "Old man! I plucked from you that hated first born of yours! The whining letter that he wrote you—I destroyed it. You read instead one of my letters, in which I painted Carlo in such dear colors . . . At last I have punished my brother for nature's misdeed, which made me a lesser man than he by virtue of being second born. Now on my father—punish it I must . . . Rights! Conscience! Such eminent scarecrows fit for feeble little foolish men." He addresses himself here: "Dare, Francesco! Get rid of the old man . . . He's alive barely, that worn out pile of bones: one puff of wind . . . and he is dead."

The aria is marked andante sostenuto in 3/4 meter; the piece begins piano; double-dotted rhythms and accents continue to underline Francesco's anger. He crescendos ("se va lenta, la natura, guiro al cielo, guiro al ciel! /I will speed it along, I swear to heaven!") up to the sustained high F, double dotted, as the orchestra cuts off and allows the voice to cadence forcefully.

"The lamp of his life burns low, it's true, but it's lasting too long. If nature moves slowly, I will speed it along, I swear by heaven!" Marked piano, the accompaniment is constant, with repeated 16th notes. "Brain of mine, find a dagger that will pierce the human heart, without being able to reveal the hand" (this is sung to the high F, energized by a double-dotted rhythm) "that grasped and wielded it." The text is repeated to the final cadence.

(Translation by Nico Castel)

Piano/vocal score: p. 24 (Belwin Mills)

No. 60

Voice: baritone
Aria Title: "Jehosophat!" (Marcus Schouler)
Opera Title: *McTeague*
Composer: William Bolcom (b. 1938)
Historical Style: 20th-century American (1992)
Range: A3 to F4

Fach: dramatic
Librettists: Arnold Weinstein and Robert Altman, based on the novel by Frank Norris (1870–1902)
Aria Duration: 1:30
Tessitura: C♯3 to E4

Position: Act II, scene 5

Setting: The desert outside a Nevada ghost town, c. 1900

> Aria plot notes from the *G. Schirmer American Aria Anthology: Baritone/ Bass,* edited by Richard Walters (used by permission):
>
> Greed is the undoing of McTeague, his wife, and her cousin Schouler in this verismo tale. Schouler and McTeague were once great pals, but had a violent falling out over a woman and money. Schouler has followed a demented cleaning woman's advice and traveled from San Francisco to a ghost town in Nevada in search of promised gold, which is not there. Schouler encounters a sheriff and posse and recognizes McTeague on a "wanted" poster—he has killed his wife. Schouler is quickly made deputy and goes off into the desert alone to find McTeague, singing of his determination to get even.

Piano/vocal score: p. 231 (*G. Schirmer American Aria Anthology: Baritone/Bass*)

Notes by composer William Bolcom: This aria was written for Tim Nolen, who is an acting singer. It is a character piece, to be sung with greater force than tonal beauty and absolute rhythmic strictness.

No. 61

Voice: baritone
Aria Title: "Si può?" Prologue (Tonio)
Opera Title: *I Pagliacci*
Composer and Librettist: Ruggero Leon-
cavallo (1857–1919), based on a legal case
his father heard as a judge
Historical Style: Verismo (1892)
Range: B3 to F4

Fach: dramatic
Aria Duration: 5:25
Tessitura: C3 to E♭4

Position: Prologue

Setting: In front of the curtain before the action begins

Tonio steps out in front of the curtain in the middle of the overture to explain why the composer wrote the opera as he did. He then says that the story the audience is viewing is not only a play, but a real story with actors who have real feelings. He promises that the entertainment offered will be filled with powerful human emotions.

Aria translation by Martha Gerhart from the *G. Schirmer Opera Anthology: Arias for Baritone,* edited by Robert L. Larsen (used by permission):

"May I? Ladies, Gentlemen! Excuse me if I present myself all alone. I am the prologue." [The beginning is marked andantino sostenuto and legato.]

"Since the author puts the ancient (*commedia dell'arte*) characters on the stage again he wishes, in part, to recapture [*to a high E*] the old traditions, and again he sends me to you.

But not to tell you, as before: The tears that we shed are feigned! Do not be alarmed at our sufferings and our torments! [*molto meno, with many accidentals in the vocal line*] No! The author has tried, rather, to paint for you a slice of life. [*pausa, deciso*] He has for his sole maxim that the artist is a man and that he must write for men. And he was inspired by the truth. [*ritardando*] A nest of memories sang in the depth of his soul one day, and he wrote with real tears, and the sobs beat time for him! [*This section is in 9/8 meter, animando a poco a poco, to 3/4 meter.*] And so, you will see loving the way human beings love each

---

other; you will see the sad fruits of hatred. You will hear cries of grief, screams of rage, and cynical laughter!

[*Andante cantabile*] And you: consider our souls, rather than our shabby actor's garb, because we are men of flesh and blood and because we, just like you, breathe the air of this forsaken world! [*Optional: the upper octave leading the vocal line up to a high F-fermata. This last section is marked più lento, quasi recitato.*]

I've told you the concept . . . now listen to how it is developed. Let's go. Begin!" [*optional high G*]

This is one of the great arias from the Italian repertoire. The baritone has the opportunity to show everything in the voice: range, power, sensitivity, legato contrasted with declamatory phrases in which the text is set syllabically, and many dynamic contrasts that help to introduce this complex, tortured character.

Piano/vocal score: p. 6 (G. Schirmer)

Notes by conductor and conducting professor David Effron: This piece is difficult because the singer is all alone in front of the curtain—no set, no action—basically a concert in costume. A note for conductors: Tempi in this aria should be extremely flexible. Whatever helps the baritone to sing well is the correct tempo. I have done this aria incredibly slowly and quite quickly: it works if you can line the right tempo up with whoever is singing. This aria also gives the baritone a giant opportunity to experiment with lots of colors and emotions.

No. 62

Voice: baritone
Aria Title: "Voilà donc la terrible cité"
(Athanaël)
Opera Title: *Thaïs*
Composer: Jules Massenet (1842–1912)
Historical Style: French Romantic (1894)
Range: B3 to F4

Fach: dramatic
Librettist: Louis Gallet (1835–1898), after
the novel by Anatole France (1890)
Aria Duration: 3:30
Tessitura: F♯3 to C♯4

Position: Act I, scene 2

Setting: Alexandria, Egypt, late 4th century A.D.; the home of Nicias

Aria plot notes from the *G. Schirmer Opera Anthology: Arias for Baritone*,
edited by Robert L. Larsen (used by permission):

Athanaël, a young Cenobite monk, has come to visit a friend of his
youth, the wealthy Nicias, at his home in Alexandria. He pauses on the
terrace and looks out over the city of his birth, convinced that it has
fallen on evil days.

The piece is marked allegro maestoso avec ampleur in 9/8 meter. The first
section of the aria has a flowing figure of a repeated "flourish" of 16th
notes on beats one and two of each measure. The vocal line lies in the
upper-middle of the baritone's range of C♯, D♯, and E.

Aria translation by Martha Gerhart from the *G. Schirmer Opera Anthology:
Arias for Baritone*, edited by Robert L. Larsen (used by permission):

Behold the terrible city, Alexandria, where I was born in sin—
The sparkling air where I breathed the hideous scent of lust!
There is the voluptuous sea where I listened to the golden-eyed siren
sing!
Yes, there is my cradle according to the flesh.
Alexandria! Oh my homeland! My cradle, my homeland!
[*The next section is marked un peu plus agité; there are more accents in the
melody, ascending to high sustained F.*]
From your love I turned away my heart. For your opulence I
hate you!

For your knowledge and your beauty, I hate you!
And now I curse you as a temple haunted by impure spirits!

[The aria modulates back to the key of E major and is marked piano. There is a crescendo to the end of the piece.] "Come, angels of heaven, breaths from God! Scent, with the flapping of your wings, the tainted air which is going to surround me. Come, angels o heaven, breaths from God!"

The last word "Venez!/come!" is sung on high E as it crescendos from C♯ ("Venez! Soufflés de Dieu! Anges du ciel/Come! Breaths from God! Angels from heaven!") to the last "Venez!"

Piano/vocal score: p. 30 (Heugel)

No. 63

Voice: baritone
Aria Title: "Di Provenza il mar" (Giorgio Germont)
Opera Title: *La traviata*
Composer: Giuseppe Verdi (1813–1901)
Historical Style: Italian Romantic (1853)
Range: D♭3 to G♭4

Fach: dramatic
Librettist: Francesco Maria Piave (1810–1876), after Alexandre Dumas fils's play *La dame aux camélias* (1852)
Aria Duration: 4:35
Tessitura: F3 to F4

Position: Act II, scene 1

Setting: A country house near Paris, 1850

Aria plot notes from the *G. Schirmer Opera Anthology: Arias for Baritone*, edited by Robert L. Larsen (used by permission):
    Having discovered that his son Alfredo is living with the courtesan Violetta Valéry on a country estate near Paris, Giorgio Germont comes to convince the woman to leave his son to save the family's name. She

responds to his entreaties and pens a note to her lover, telling him that she is returning to her life in Paris. After she leaves, Alfredo returns, reads the note, and is heartbroken. His father attempts to console him, but his intent is to take Alfredo away from Violetta.

The aria is marked andante più tosto mosso/not too slow:

Aria translation by Martha Gerhart from the *G. Schirmer Opera Anthology: Arias for Baritone,* edited by Robert L. Larsen (used by permission):

Who erased the sea, the soil of Provence from your heart?
What destiny stole you away from your native, resplendent sun?
Oh, do remember in your sorrow that joy glowed in you there and that there alone peace
Can still shine upon you. God has guided me!
[*Verse 2:*]
Ah, you don't know how much your old father has suffered!
With you far away, his home became full of misery.
But if in the end I find you again, if hope didn't fail me, if the voice of honor didn't become completely silenced in you, God has heard me!

A case can be made to describe Giorgio Germont as a simple provincial man and not the urbane nobleman. In those days it was common for an allowance to be given to the son to go to live in Paris, and Germont is not in approval with his son's choices. He does sing this aria in a simple strophic form, and the accompaniment sounds like it emanates from a hurdy-gurdy when heard alone. It is clear that Papa Germont wants something from his son, but does not get the desired reaction by the end of the first verse. Germont must sing verse 2 more urgently, even though it is marked piano. He is appealing for sympathy from his son, but by the end of the verse it is possible that Germont is more frustrated with Alfredo's unresponsiveness, and Germont can sing the final cadenza ("ma—se alfin it trovo ancor/ but—if in the end I find you again"), beginning on the sudden high F♯, with some anger.

This piece has very carefully marked articulation and dynamics, for Germont's motives are extremely calculated, and he seems to always want to be in control.

Piano/vocal score: p. 109 (G. Schirmer)

Notes by singer and voice professor Sherrill Milnes: Germont is often the first Verdi role for a future Verdi baritone. Therefore the youngest member of the cast portraying the oldest member of the cast often sings it. He cannot be too active and must control his muscularity. He is not stooped over or feeble, but feels the weight of his family responsibilities on his shoulders. When Germont sings "Piangi/Weep" to Violetta in the duet preceding "Di Provenza," he means it! Germont is considered the "bad guy," but he is defending the honor of his daughter and her impending marriage. From this point of view he is doing what he must. He should be a sympathetic character, but greatly frustrated by the free and immoral life of his son, Alfredo, living in sin with someone whom Germont considers a prostitute. He must find a way to make him leave Violetta and return home to Provence. Germont has many dramatic choices in the aria as far as the inflections of the text. These choices determine the singer's effectiveness. I know that Germont is sorry to do what he must, but the family honor is his priority.

No. 64

Voice: baritone
Aria Title: "Il balen del suo sorriso" (Count di Luna)
Opera Title: *Il trovatore*
Composer: Giuseppe Verdi (1813–1901)
Historical Style: Italian Romantic (1853)
Range: A3 to G4

Fach: dramatic
Librettists: Salvatore Cammarano (1801–1852) and Leone Emanuele Bardare (1820–1874), after the play *El trovador* by Antonio García Gutiérrez (1836)
Aria Duration: 3:40
Tessitura: F3 to F4

Position: Act II (The Gypsy), scene 2

Setting: A convent near Castellor, Spain, 1409. It is night; there are trees at the back of the inner courtyard. Count di Luna, Ferrando, and some followers come in cautiously, wrapped in their cloaks.

The Count di Luna, a young nobleman, is about to send his men to kidnap his love Leonora from the convent she is planning on entering. The Count sings of how his life is meaningless if he cannot have her.

Most of the following vocal phrases are unaccompanied. The text flows, is hushed, and is urgently declaimed:

> *Count:* All is deserted: nor in the air yet resounds the usual hymn. I have come in time!
> *Ferrando:* A bold errand, master, you are undertaking.
> *Count:* Bold, and what a furious love and provoked pride have de-manded of me. My rival killed, every obstacle to my desires seemed to have fallen. Now Leonora prepares a new and more powerful (*rival*): The altar of God . . . Ah no! She must not belong to another. Leonora! (*He ascends to a sustained high F.*) Leonora is mine!

The aria is marked largo, cantabile, and piano:

> The flash of her smile outshines a star's ray.
> (*The beginning of the phrase is repeated, then unfolds to be sung, dolcissimo, to high E and F.*)
> The splendor of her fair face instills new courage in me.
> Ah! The love, the love that enflames me.
> Let it speak to her in my favor.
> (*Once again the same melodic "motive" is heard at the beginning of the phrase, then the line ascends and crescendos at the top of the range through the passaggio.*)
> Let the sun of one of her glances dispel the tempest in my heart.

A cadenza is written in the Schirmer edition. It is noble and deliberate. (Translation by Nico Castel)

Piano/vocal score: p. 88 (G. Schirmer)

> Notes by singer and voice professor Sherrill Milnes: First of all, the singer should not attempt to sing this aria unless he has a solid high G. This applies to any real baritone aria. One must know how to "turn over" into top voice before undertaking study of the piece. The Count begins the aria almost a capella, in that the only orchestral support is a clarinet and soft strings underneath. This line should be sung lovingly, caressingly. The beginning of the aria softens the character and humanizes him. Yes, the Count is the vil-lain in the opera, as most baritones are, but *he* does not think so. He is sincere about his love for Leonora. The singer must sing lyri-

cally through the *passaggio,* and then later as the brass doubles the melody must sing powerfully at "Ah, l'amor, l'amore ond'ardo/the love, the love that inflames me." Something needs to be saved for the cadenza, which really requires another high G. The aria is a killer.

No. 65

Voice: bass
Aria Title: "Ves' tabor spit," Cavatina (Aleko)
Opera Title: *Aleko*
Composer: Sergey Rakhmaninov (1873–1943)
Historical Style: Russian Nationalist (1892)
Range: B♭2 to F4

Fach: bass-baritone
Librettist: Vladimir Nemirovich-Danchenko, after Aleksandr Pushkin's poem *Tsygany* (1824)
Aria Duration: 4:50
Tessitura: C3 to C4

Position: One-act opera

Setting: A gypsy encampment, 1892; evening, the moon is high in the sky
   An old gypsy is the father of Zemfira, and at a campfire he reminisces about his youth. He was happy, but his wife left him for someone else. Aleko, husband of Zemfira, reacts violently to the story and is surprised the old man did not take revenge. If it had happened to him he would have put the rival to death. Aleko's reaction has frightened Zemfira, but she often invokes the right to freedom, resulting in suffering at the hands of her temperamental husband. All fall asleep, and Zemfira, who has fallen in love with a young gypsy, tells him she promises to meet with him when the moon rises. She then goes to her tent to rock her baby and wait. She sings a song about an old husband who kills his wife in a fit of jealousy, and Aleko overhears the song. Zemfira admits the song was about him. Alone, Aleko then sings of the loss of his wife's love.
   The recitative-like setting is marked piano at the beginning, moderato.
   "The camp is asleep. The moon shines in its midnight splendor. Why does my heart suffer? What is this pain that gnaws at me? (*allegro non troppo*)

Without care or regret I lead a nomad's life. Having scorned the chains of society, I am free. I have lived without recognizing the power of fate. But God! How passion took hold of my soul and then tortured it!"

The next section is pianissimo and freely sung: "Zemfira! How she loved me once!" A new tempo marked meno mosso con anima, more of a lyric expression, with movement follows: "With tenderness she spent long hours in the silence of the desert. How well she knew how to change my gloomy thoughts with a gentle kiss! I remember how she would whisper to me with breathless passion," he sings, with a broadened, passionate vocal line: "I love you! I am in your power! I am yours, Aleko, forever! The next section is marked con moto, with increasing number of accidentals: "I forgot everything, hearing her words, and—mad with love . . . " he strongly sings to the high E♭. "I kissed her bewitching eyes, her black-as-night hair, and her lips. And she, passionately huddled up against me and looked into my eyes . . . and now?" he pauses, and then, with the realization, he wrenchingly reveals, "My Zemfira is unfaithful! My Zemfira has become cold!" The sustained middle C is held over into the orchestra's passionate entrance of the melody.

With this last realization, Aleko sings of his raw anguish in pain while sustaining the middle C, and the orchestra swells with a beautiful, poignant, full palate of Romantic chords with melody. The pianist must play many notes with passionate feeling. The baritone will need a strong high E♭, with only the F in passing. As it becomes more passionate, the voice lies at the middle C level.

Piano/vocal score: p. 61 (Gutheil)

No. 66

Voice: bass
Aria Title: "Warm as the autumn light" (Horace Tabor)
Opera Title: *The Ballad of Baby Doe*
Composer: Douglas Moore (1893–1969)
Historical Style: 20th-century American (1956)
Range: B3 to E4

Fach: bass-baritone
Librettist: John Latouche (1914–1956), based on the life of Elizabeth "Baby Doe" Tabor, 1854–1935
Aria Duration: 4:10
Tessitura: E3 to C♯4

Position: Act I

Setting: Leadville, Colorado, 1880; late evening outside Tabor's hotel, where Baby Doe is also staying

The silver king, Horace Tabor, has stayed in the street below the apartment he shares with his wife after a concert at the opera house to smoke a cigar. He hears Baby Doe, a recent arrival from Central City, accompanying herself at the piano in the lobby of the Clarendon Hotel and is deeply moved. Horace is about 50 years old and has started from scratch, never reluctant to work hard physically before finally striking it rich. He is now involved in local politics and has aspirations for higher office. His wife, Augusta, is extremely practical and continues to badger him to not be too reckless in business. Augusta is a rather plain woman, who does not wear makeup or expensive clothes, even though they can afford them.

This aria is sung after he hears Baby Doe's "Willow Song," which is attractive and youthful. She knows that he is a powerful man who almost owns the town and has larger political aspirations. She compliments him on his appearance, and makes him feel young and passionate again.

The aria is lyrically sung and melodic. It is set in the baritone's upper-middle voice, with sustained B, C♯, and at the climactic phrase, high E.

The aria immediately shows the audience the affect Baby Doe's singing has had on Tabor. It takes him back to his youth, and he recalls episodes of that time, referring to Augusta as "a girl I knew back in Vermont" and the first time he saw the mountains. He connects the important events in his life to that very night hearing her singing "that feeling of wonder of longing and pain," which brings him back to a brief recapitulation of the opening melody with a text that is personal: "Deep in your lovely eyes all of enchantment lies and tenderly beckons"—this is sung with no punctuation or pause, because he doesn't want this feeling to stop. He sings out "Baby Doe" to the high E, and then sings softly, almost as if he remembers that Augusta is just upstairs, "Dearest Baby Doe." This is a poignant moment, tender, and sung as if he is in awe of a rediscovery of a part of himself he thought buried and lost.

Piano/vocal score: p. 44 (Chappell Music)

No. 67

Voice: bass
Aria Title: "I've got a ram, Goliath" (Daniel
Webster)
Opera Title: *The Devil and Daniel Webster*
Composer: Douglas Moore (1893–1969)
Historical Style: 20th-century American
(1939)
Range: B♭3 to G♭4

Fach: bass-baritone
Librettist: Stephen Vincent Benét (1898–
1943)
Aria Duration: 2:12
Tessitura: E♭3 to E♭4

Position: One-act opera

Setting: The home of Jabez Stone in Cross Corners, New Hampshire, 1840s
All has been going well for Jabez and Mary Stone of New Hampshire.
The now wealthy Jabez was once poor and sold his soul to the devil, who
comes in the person of a sinister Boston lawyer to collect his due. Also on
hand is the famous historical statesman Daniel Webster to challenge the
lawyer on his own ground. A trial is arranged, with a showdown inevitable
between Webster and the Devil.

Mary Stone: Oh, Mr. Webster, can you save him? Can you?
Webster: I shall do my best, madam. That's all you can ever say, till
you've seen what the jury looks like.
Mary: But even you, Mr. Webster—oh, I know you're Secretary of
State—I know you're a great man, but its different fighting the devil!
Webster: Have you ever seen my farm at Marshfield, madam?
Mary: No, sir
Webster: Well—it's a pretty place, if I do say myself.

The aria is marked allegro marziale, piano.

I've got a ram, Goliath. He was raised on Marshfield grain.
He's got horns like a morning glory vine And he butts like a railroad
train.
I've got a ram, Goliath, named for the Philistine.
And I wrestle him every Tuesday night with these two hands of
mine.
(*poco mosso*) I've got a bull, King Stephen, a bull with a roving eye.
When he stamps his foot, the stars come out and the lightening
blinks in the sky.

I've got a bull, King Stephen, with a kick like a cannon ball.

But he acts like a sucking turtle dove when I go into his stall.

I'm not an idle boaster. Let this be said of me.

(*marziale*) I was born in old New Hampshire and always fought for the free.

They know about Daniel Webster wherever the eagle flies,

And they know he stands for the union.

(*The vocal line ascends to high Eb and remains in the upper middle voice.*)

And he doesn't stand for lies—Ask at the workmen's cottage, ask at the farmer's gate!

They know about Daniel Webster, as only neighbors can

And he'll fight ten thousand devils to save a New Hampshire man!

The aria has a strong finish to end on the high, sustained Eb, after singing a high Gb in the middle of the phrase.

The text is set syllabically to the music and displays specific rhythmic definition and variety that characterizes Webster's confidence and determination. The piece does not have melodic repetition as much as rhythmic repetition.

Piano/vocal score: p. 49 (Boosey & Hawkes)

No. 68

Voice: bass
Aria Title: "Ella giammai m'amò" (Filippo)
Opera Title: *Don Carlo* (Italian version)
Composer: Giuseppe Verdi (1813–1901)
Historical Style: Italian Romantic (1882)
Range: G2 to E4

Fach: bass-baritone
Librettists: François Joseph Méry (1798–1865) and Camille du Locle (1832–1903), based on Johann Christoph Friedrich von Schiller's play *Don Carlos, Infant von Spanien* (1787) and on Eugène Cormon's play *Philippe II, roi d'Espagne* (1846) for the original five-act French version. The revised Italian four-act version was adapted by Antonio Ghislanzoni.
Aria Duration: 9:00
Tessitura: D3 to D4

Position: Act IV, scene 1

Setting: Madrid, 1559, the private chambers of Filippo (King Philip II)

Filippo's famous soliloquy is expressed at dawn after brooding on his situation through the night. He is seated at his desk, candles flickering after burning all night. The achingly lonely sound of the cello is heard in the lengthy orchestral introduction. His wife, Elizabeth, has never loved him, and the King will always remain an isolated lonely leader.

> She never loved me! No, her heart is closed to me, she does not love me.
> I can see her, looking with sadness in her face at my white hair the day she arrived from France.
> No (*the phrase culminates with the high, sustained E on the word "amor/love"*) she does not have love for me!
> (*He "awakes" from his reverie in this recitative-like section:*)
> Where am I? . . . Those candles near their end . . .
> Dawn whitens my balcony! Already breaks the day!
> I see my days passing slowly!
> Oh God! Sleep has vanished from my dropping eyes!

The aria that now begins is sustained, but attention must be paid to the rhythmic values:

> I shall sleep alone in my royal mantle, when I arrive at the evening of my days.
> I shall sleep alone under the black vault, there in the tomb of the Escurial. (*the royal mausoleum where Spanish kings are buried in the monastery*)
> (*The next section is more dramatically expressed, energized by stronger singing at the top of the staff.*)
> If the crown royal to me gave the power of reading in the hearts what God can alone see! . . .
> If the Prince is asleep, the traitor is awake watching.
> The King loses his crown, his consort, and his honor!
> (*Repeated from the beginning.*)
> She never loved me! No, her heart is closed to me, she does not love me.

Piano/vocal score: p. 194 (G. Schirmer)

No. 69

Voice: bass
Aria Title: "Infelice! E tuo credevi" (Don
Ruy Gomez de Silva)
Opera Title: *Ernani*
Composer: Giuseppe Verdi (1813–1901)
Historical Style: Italian Romantic (1844)
Range: G♭2 to F4

Fach: bass-baritone
Librettist: Francesco Maria Piave (1810–
1876), after Victor Hugo's play *Hernani*
(1830)
Aria Duration: 3:15
Tessitura: E♭3 to B♭3

Position: Act I

Setting: Spain, c. 1519; Elvira's apartment, the castle of Don Ruy Gomez de Silva, grandee of Spain

Elvira is pledged to marry Silva, an elderly gentleman. She is, however, in love with the bandit chief Ernani, who is the disguised John of Aragon. King Don Carlo also loves Elvira. He has observed the entrance signal to the apartment and imitates it. After entering he is repulsed after trying to take her away by force. He is then stopped by Ernani. Silva enters and is horrified to find two men in Elvira's chambers.

The beginning is allegro, strongly declaimed, all sung in the upper middle voice—to show strong intensity, but no tones are written above the middle C.

"Whatever do I see! In the most sacred chamber of my dwelling, near, her, who is to be the bride of a Silva, I discover two seducers? Enter, you there, my faithful cavaliers. May each be witness to he dishonor, to the shame that is being brought to his lord."

The aria is marked andante; Silva sings energized dotted rhythms to show his intense anger, but he also connects the vocal line over the chordal accompaniment off the beat, giving music a "heartbeat" and momentum. Tuning is also important, as there are many accidentals written.

Aria:

Unhappy man, you believed such a beautiful lily of yours to be chaste?
Among the snows of your hair falls, instead, dishonor.

This next section builds to a crescendo up to a sustained high E♭. Watch for carefully marked articulation marks. There is a traditional cadenza at the end of the aria. The cabaletta follows:

Ah, why has aged preserved a youthful heart in my breast?
The years should at least have turned my heart to ice.

His notes lie high and continue to build and repeat. Momentum of the vocal line is important, as it must not drag and lose its direction. It is further energized through double-dotted rhythms and well-placed accents. A high F is sustained in the last phrase ("piangerà/will weep").

Piano/vocal score: p. 73 (Kalmus)

No. 70

Voice: bass
Aria Title: "Hat man nicht auch Gold beineben" (Rocco)
Opera Title: *Fidelio*
Composer: Ludwig van Beethoven (1770–1827)
Historical Style: German Romantic (1805)
Range: B♭3 to D4

Fach: bass-baritone
Librettist: Joseph von Sonnleithner (1766–1835), with revisions by Stephan von Breuning (1774–1827) and Georg Friedrich Treitschke (1776–1842), after Jean-Nicholas Bouilly's French libretto *Léonore, ou L'amour conjugal* (1789)
Aria Duration: 2:20
Tessitura: F3 to D4

Position: Act I, scene 1

Setting: Seville, 18th century; by the prison gatehouse

Rocco, the jail keeper and father of Marzelline, is pleased that his daughter is spending time with the new clever helper he has hired, Fidelio (who is really Leonora, a noblewoman of Seville in disguise, trying to make contact with her political prisoner-husband Florestan). Rocco warns the "couple" that money is just as important as love—with this aria, which has two verses:

If you don't have gold close by, you cannot be completely happy;
Your life plods on unhappily, many griefs arise.
(*New melodic material is sung for the second part of the piece.*)

But when it rings and rolls in your pockets, then you hold your fate captive.

And might and love obtain the gold for you.

And silence your boldest desires. Your luck serves like a serf for pay,

It is a beautiful thing, Gold. (*The text repeats for emphasis.*)

(*2nd verse:*)

When nothing with nothing is combined, the sum is and stays small;

Who at the table only finds love, will after dinner be hungry.

Therefore fate smiles upon us mercifully and friendly,

And blesses and guides our aspiration;

The loved one in your arms, in your purse the gold,

So you would like to live through many years.

Your luck serves like a serf for pay,

It is a mighty thing, Gold!

Keep in mind that Rocco is addressing his daughter and Fidelio.

There are two simple verses, for Rocco is a simple man. Much of this aria is sung tongue-in-cheek and can be expressed playfully, with a wink. The diction is very important, and the singer will need to sing a D at the top of the staff a number of times.

Piano/vocal score: p. 31 (Boosey & Hawkes)

No. 71

Voice: bass

Aria Title: "Schweig'! Schweig'! damit dich niemand warnt," No. 5 (Caspar)

Opera Title: *Der Freischütz*

Composer: Carl Maria von Weber (1786–1826)

Historical Style: German Romantic (1821)

Range: F#2 to E4

Fach: bass-baritone

Librettist: Friedrich Kind (1768–1843), after Johann August Apel and Friedrich Laun's *Gespensterbuch* (1811)

Aria Duration: 3:00

Tessitura: D3 to D4

Position: Act I

Setting: The Bohemian forest shortly after the end of the Thirty Years War; a clearing before an inn in the forest

Max, one of the greatest marksmen in the country, has lost his skill before he is to compete for the prize of the position of chief forester and the hand of Agathe, whom he loves. Caspar, who is controlled by the evil Black Huntsman, has just persuaded Max to meet him at the Wolf's Glen at midnight to forge magic bullets, so Max will win the contest. Caspar gloats that Samiel will have Max in his place.

The opera opens with the toast to Kilian, who is the marksman of the moment. Max despairs, and Caspar is there to tease and to sing a drinking song before he brings Max into his net.

Caspar is alone; he begins, pianissimo:

Keep silent—so that no one may warn you! (*fortissimo, allegro*)
Hell has snared you in its net! Nothing can save you from the deep abyss,
From the deep abyss nothing can save you!
Surround him, you spirits winged with darkness!
Already he lies in your chains, gnashing his teeth!
Triumph, triumph, triumph. Revenge is assured!

The aria needs a strong declamatory voice on the high-middle C♯, D, and up to sustained E for the baritone, but the piece also calls for a strong resonant quality in the low voice in the low A and passing low F♯. Also, there are rapid sections, as if Caspar is conjuring up a strong wind with his voice. These 8th-note diatonic scales go all the way down to low F♯ up to the high E to extend to almost a two-octave range. With repeated phrases and text, the singer—who is singing full at the top of the voice—must not strain, oversing, or become blustery in his delivery. Try varied emotions for the repetitions that do not all say "evil anger" sung by the villain.

Piano/vocal score: p. 53 (Roycroft)

No. 72

Voice: bass
Aria Title: "Pour les couvents c'est fini"
(Marcel)
Opera Title: *Les Huguenots*
Composer: Giacomo Meyerbeer (1791–1864)
Historical Style: French Romantic (1836)
Range: F2 to E4

Fach: bass-baritone
Librettists: Eugène Scribe (1791–1861) and Emile Deschamps (1791–1871), based on historical events
Aria Duration: 3:35
Tessitura: C3 to D4

Position: Act I

Setting: France, 1572; a banquet hall in the castle of Comte de Nevers

Marcel is the old servant of the young Huguenot nobleman Raoul de Nangis, who has just received a commission in the Lancers. The host, the Comte de Nevers, has included Raoul in a social evening with his Catholic friends. Marcel, a fanatical Huguenot, is outspoken in his contempt for them, to the embarrassment of Raoul. When they good-naturedly ask him to sing, he chooses the battle song of the Protestants, which is a denunciation of papists, bigots, and women.

The recitative is largely unaccompanied, and declamatory, as fits the text.

Gladly I will sing: An old Huguenot air against the servants of the
pope and the abominable sex. You know it well.
It's our song of battle—the one from La Rochelle.
It was then to the noise of the drums, of the cymbals,
Accompanied by the bang, bang, boom of the bullets.

The aria is marked allegretto in 3/8 meter. Characteristic of the piece are low rhythmic staccato octaves in the bass, and a high flute is heard in the treble of the accompaniment. The voice sings a legato line with dotted rhythms up and down the scale to a low, sustained G.

I sang: bang, bang. For the convents it's over; the monks are felled.
War to every blessed hypocrite; war to papists.
We'll deliver their temples of hell to the blaze of swords;
(*At each vocal entrance there are the pitches of repeated high E♭ and D.*)
Let's knock them down, besiege them, Strike them, run them
through—bang, bang, boom.

(At this text there is a sustained phrase that ascends to high E.)
Let them cry, let them die; But mercy—never, no, never!

A repetition of the opening melody follows:

Never will my arm tremble at the moans of women.
Woe to those Dalilas who lose their souls;
We'll break up their infernal charms at the cutting of the sword.
Those fair demons—pursue them, round them up, strike them . . .
Bang, bang, boom.

Now there is a repetition of the text and melody to the end of the aria: "Let them cry, let them die: but mercy, no, never," he sings, with the voice rising to a molto crescendo in the last phrase, to fortissimo accents on the word "jamais/never" for the emphatic conclusion.

Piano/vocal score: p. 56 (Bendit Ainé)

No. 73

Voice: bass
Aria Title: "Kennst du das Land?" (Friedrich Bhaer)
Opera Title: *Little Women*
Composer and Librettist: Mark Adamo (b. 1962), after the novel by Louisa May Alcott (1869)
Historical Style: 20th-century American (1998)
Range: A♯3 to F♯4

Fach: bass-baritone
Aria Duration: 3:45
Tessitura: C♯3 to D♯4

Position: Act II, scene 2

Setting: The U.S. Civil War era; a boarding house in New York City where Jo March resides
    The adventures of the New England March sisters, going through the

privations of the Civil War, are the backdrop against which sister Jo resists moving into adulthood. Jo March, a successful young writer of sensational cheap fiction, has struck out on her own and lives in Manhattan. Professor Friedrich Bhaer is a German teacher who lives at the same boarding house. At 39 he is quite a few years older than Jo, but they strike up a warm friendship. They are debating the merits of opera after attending a performance. Jo loves the melodrama, but Bhaer will have none of it. They bond in conversation about art, love, and relationships. Jo asks him, "Well, if the opera isn't, and my stories aren't, what's 'proper' art?" Bhaer responds with Goethe's "Kennst du das Land" (Do you know the land?). When Jo asks for a translation, it becomes a declaration of his feelings for her.

This piece is challenging for the young singer, because it calls for a resonant rich depth in the lower tones and an easy piano legato at the top of the range—and a *messa di voce* at the high F (fermata). Otherwise, the piece is tremendously rewarding to sing and accessible to the ear.

Piano/vocal score: p. 281 (G. Schirmer)

> Notes by composer Mark Adamo: Trying to raise Jo's artistic expectations of herself, Bhaer first recites, in German, Goethe's *Mignon's Song* simply as an example of ambitious lyric art: it's only when Jo presses him for a translation that he reveals, in English, that Mignon's longing for love matches Bhaer's for Jo.

No. 74

Voice: bass
Aria Title: "Lost in the Stars" (Stephen)
Opera Title: *Lost in the Stars*
Composer: Kurt Weill (1900–1950)
Historical Style: 20th-century American (1949)
Range: A♭2 to F4

Fach: bass-baritone
Librettist: Maxwell Anderson (1888–1959), based on Alan Paton's novel *Cry the Beloved Country* (1848)
Aria Duration: 2:48
Tessitura: B3 to C4

Position: Act I, scene 12

Setting: A small village in South Africa, Stephen's Shantytown lodging, 1949
The following lines precede Stephen's song:

Alex: Uncle Stephen—who will not come home?
Stephen: My son Absalom.
Alex: But Uncle Stephen, you are an *umfundisi,* and you can ask God
to help you, and he will surely help you.
Stephen: I don't know, Alex.

The beginning of the song is marked piano:

Before Lord God made the sea and the land, He held all the stars in
the palm of his hand,
And they ran through his fingers like grains of sand, And one little
star fell alone.
(*The melody repeats here with minor variation.*)
Then the Lord God hunted through the wide night air for the little
dark star on the wind down there.
And he stated and promised he'd take special care so it wouldn't get
lost again.
(*The middle section is marked poco più mosso and has forward momentum.*)
Now, a man don't mind if the stars grow dim and the clouds blow
over and darken him,
So long as the Lord God's watching over them, keeping track how it
all goes on.
(*Tempo 1 is marked for a repetition of the first melody.*)
But I've been walking through the night and the day
Till my eyes get weary and my head turns gray,
(*forte*) And sometimes it seems maybe God's gone away,
Forgetting the promise that we heard him say,
And we're lost out here in the stars, little stars, big stars, blowing
though the night.
(*chorus enters*)
And we're lost out here in the stars, little stars, big stars, blowing
though the night
And we're lost out here in the stars.

The song needs a solid low A♭, and the tessitura is low; the climactic
phrases rise only to C and a passing D at the top. The melody is moving,
inspiring, and needs to be sung legato in long phrases.

Piano/vocal score: p. 102 (Chappell)

No. 75

Voice: bass
Aria Title: "Dalle stanze ove Lucia"
(Raimondo)
Opera Title: *Lucia di Lammermoor*
Composer: Gaetano Donizetti (1797–1848)
Historical Style: Bel canto (1835)
Range: A♯3 to E4

Fach: bass-baritone
Librettist: Salvatore Cammarano (1801–1852), after Sir Walter Scott's novel *The Bride of Lammermoor* (1819)
Aria Duration: 2:15
Tessitura: D♯3 to B4

Position: Act III, scene 2

Setting: Scotland, c. 1700; a great hall in Lammermoor Castle

Lucia Ashton's tutor, Raimondo Bidebent, interrupts the wedding celebration in honor of the marriage between Lord Arturo Bucklaw to Lucia. In a grave tone he tells the wedding guests that when he heard a groan of anguish he rushed to a room to find Lucia, over the body of her husband, with a knife in her hand.

The beginning (allegro vivace) is unaccompanied. The vocal line begins on a high D with double-dotted rhythms: "Stop that joy. Cease, cease . . . a cruel event! Ah!"

The next section (larghetto) has repeated rhythms in the accompaniment. There are also strong dotted rhythms in the vocal line and short fragmented phrases, lending an almost breathless quality to the text. Accents are added that help get the assembled guests' attention, and the accents are on commonly unaccented syllables.

From the rooms where Lucia had withdrawn with her husband a
cry, a cry emerged.
As of a man near death! I ran quickly to within those walls . . .
Ah, terrible disaster! Arturo was lying on the floor silent, cold,
bloody!
And Lucia was clasping the blade that was used for the murder!
(*There is a return to tempo 1; the intensity of the melody builds with double-dotted rhythms, accents, and triplet figures for momentum.*)
She stared at me.
"My husband, where is he?" she said; and on her pale face a smile
flashed!
Unhappy one—her mind was gone—ah!

(The next section [maestoso] is in 2/4 meter; there is a full 17-measure orchestral interlude.)

Ah, may that hand, impure with blood, not call the revenge of heaven upon us!

The text is important, building in intensity to high E. The singer should also be aware of articulations, dynamics, and tempo markings that reflect the emotional intensity of the dramatic situation.

Piano/vocal score: p. 180 (G. Schirmer)

No. 76

Voice: bass
Aria Title: "Als Büblein klein" (Falstaff)
Opera Title: *Die lustigen Weiber von Windsor*
Composer: Otto Nicolai (1810–1849)
Historical Style: German Romantic (1849)
Range: E2 to E4

Fach: bass-baritone
Librettist: Salomon Hermann von Mosenthal (1821–1877), after the comedy by William Shakespeare (1600–1601)
Aria Duration: 4:06
Tessitura: B3 to B4

Position: Act II, scene 1

Setting: The country village of Windsor, England, c. 1600; the Garter Inn

Aria plot notes from the *G. Schirmer Opera Anthology: Arias for Bass,* edited by Robert L. Larsen (used by permission):

Sir John Falstaff sits with his cronies at the Garter Inn drinking sack [a white Spanish wine] and trying to dry out from his dunking in the river Thames, thrown from a laundry basket. The text is a parody of the clown's final song from Shakespeare's play *Twelfth Night.*

The aria is marked andante comodo in 4/8 and 3/8 meter in the key of E major. At the beginning the piece is lightly sung with staccato in the accompaniment as Falstaff draws them all into his story in the tavern.

Aria translation by Martha Gerhart from the *G. Schirmer Opera Anthology: Arias for Bass,* edited by Robert L. Larsen (used by permission):
> When a tiny little boy at my mother's breast—heigh-ho in the rain and the wind—
> Then sparkling wine was already my pleasure, for the rain, it rained every day!

The word "komm/come" is accented, forte; then the meter alternates back and forth between 4/8 and 3/8; the marking is piano with subito forte and accents.

Aria translation by Martha Gerhart from the *G. Schirmer Opera Anthology: Arias for Bass,* edited by Robert L. Larsen (used by permission):

> Come here, tawny Jane—pass me the jug, fill my flask!
> Quench my parched throat. Drinking is no disgrace; Bacchus drank too, of course!
> Now on your mark! [*spoken*] Ready, get set! Open your throats wide! One, two, and three!
> [*Verse 2:*]
> And when I outwore my childhood shoes—heigh-ho in the rain and the wind—
> Then the girls locked themselves in from me, for the rain, it rained every day!
> And if the pocket is empty, and the bottle becomes empty, out come the dice!
> Good fortune is a stubborn guest; the one who grabs it by the neck—
> leads it home—yes!

The final phrases of each verse are unaccompanied up to the high E to the words "eins, zwei, drei/one, two, three" as Falstaff readies himself for the draught.

Telling the story, it has the form and feeling of a drinking song, with very little of the more subtle wit found in the *Henry IV* Shakespearian character of Falstaff. This Falstaff is very comic, full of himself and his liquor. I have seen a singer sing this piece in audition using his tie to wipe his mouth between verses to comic effect.

Piano/vocal score: p. 111 (Peters)

No. 77

Voice: bass
Aria Title: "What what is it?" (Daniel Webster)
Opera Title: *The Mother of Us All*
Composer: Virgil Thomson (1896–1989)
Historical Style: 20th-century American (1947)
Range: G2 to E4

Fach: bass-baritone
Librettist: Gertrude Stein (1874–1946)
Aria Duration: 2:05
Tessitura: B3 to B4

Position: Act II, scene 2

Setting: 19th-century America; the drawing room of Susan B. Anthony

Daniel Webster enters and tells Susan B. Anthony that she is far too impatient and lacks a broader vision. Suffrage for women need not be hastened. It is only a step along the road of progress to America's glory. He reproaches Susan for fixating on unimportant details like women's suffrage.

The beginning is marked alla marcia, forte. Great rhythmic and dynamic variety is characteristic of this aria, and there are a number of key changes.

"When mine eyes" in the text is repeated four times in the piece, with the word "eyes" held four beats each time. "I hear that you say that the word male . . . should (*spoken*) not be written into the constitution of the United States of America" is underlined by the spoken delivery. The last section of the piece is back in the key of A major, with percussive accompaniment, like a snare drum, underneath. It builds from piano at the beginning of the section to a crescendo, accelerando, to conclude on a sustained high E, fortissimo.

> That so long that the gorgeous ensign of the republic,
> Still full high advanced, its arms and trophies streaming in their original luster
> Not a stripe erased or polluted not a single star obscured.

Piano/vocal score: p. 125 (Music Press)

No. 78

Voice: bass
Aria Title: "Aprite un po' quegl'occhi"
(Figaro)
Opera Title: *Le nozze di Figaro*
Composer: Wolfgang Amadeus Mozart
(1756–1791)
Historical Style: Classical (1786)
Range: B♭3 to E♭4

Fach: bass-baritone
Librettist: Lorenzo da Ponte (1749–1838),
after Pierre-Augustin Caron de Beaumarchais's play *La folle journée, ou Le mariage
de Figaro* (1784)
Aria Duration: 2:35
Tessitura: E♭3 to E♭4

Position: Act IV

Setting: Outside Seville, Spain; 17th century; Count Almaviva's garden;
night

> Aria plot notes from the *G. Schirmer Opera Anthology: Arias for Bass,* ed-
> ited by Robert L. Larsen (used by permission):
>
> On the night of their wedding, Figaro believes that Susanna is de-
> ceiving him with the Count. Furious, Figaro denounces all of woman-
> kind.

Figaro's speech as written in the Beaumarchais play is highly charged po-
litically. Figaro calls the Count's position "an accident of birth." The Da
Ponte monologue is all Italian jealousy, which manifests itself in the aria
through highly charged triplet figures, which ascend to the E♭, repeated on
"no, no, no, no!" at the end of both sections of the aria. The accompaniment in the recitative is varied and responsive. Figaro is increasingly agitated.

> Aria translation by Martha Gerhart from the *G. Schirmer Opera An-
> thology: Arias for Bass,* edited by Robert L. Larsen (used by permission):
>
> Everything is ready; the hour must be near. I hear people . . . it's
> she! It's no one.
> The night is dark, and I'm just beginning to practice the idiotic
> profession of husband.
> Ungrateful girl! At the moment of my ceremony he was enjoying
> reading;
> and, seeing him I laughed at myself without knowing it.

Oh, Susanna, how much pain you caused me!
With that ingenuous face, with those innocent eyes,
who would ever have believed it? Ah, how trusting in a woman is
always folly.

The aria is marked andante, and should not be sung too fast or the eventual triplet figures will be too rushed. The accompaniment at the beginning of the aria is based on pulsating 8th notes, off the beat.

Aria:

Aria translation by Martha Gerhart from the *G. Schirmer Opera Anthology: Arias for Bass,* edited by Robert L. Larsen (used by permission):

Open those eyes a bit, rash and foolish men. Look at these women; see what they are!
Deceived by your senses, you call these women goddesses, to whom weak reason offers incense.
They are witches who charm in order to make us suffer, sirens who sing in order to make us drown,
owls that allure in order to pull out our feathers, comets that shine in order to blind us.
They are thorny roses; they are grateful foxes. They are tame she-bears, malicious doves,
Mistresses of deception, friends of suffering who fabricate, lie.
They don't feel love; they don't feel pity—no.
I'm not saying the rest; every man already knows it.

Figaro sings many dotted rhythms and repeated patterns of 8th-note triplet figures, but the singer needs to keep the vocal line legato. Not only is Figaro angry and blustery—wanting revenge—but he is also hurt and self-pitying.

Piano/vocal score: p.403 (G. Schirmer)

No. 79

Voice: bass
Aria Title: "Non più andrai" (Figaro)
Opera Title: *Le nozze di Figaro*
Composer: Wolfgang Amadeus Mozart
(1756–1791)
Historical Style: Classical (1786)
Range: C3 to E4

Fach: bass-baritone
Librettist: Lorenzo da Ponte (1749–1838),
after Pierre-Augustin Caron de Beaumarchais's play *La folle journée, ou Le mariage
de Figaro* (1784)
Aria Duration: 3:30
Tessitura: C3 to C4

Position: Act I, finale

Setting: Outside Seville, Spain; 17th century; the unfurnished apartment of Figaro and Susanna in Count Almaviva's castle; morning

> Aria plot notes from the *G. Schirmer Opera Anthology: Arias for Bass*, edited by Robert L. Larsen (used by permission):
> Count Almaviva, annoyed by the antics of the court page Cherubino [who keeps showing up where he should not], has consigned the boy to military duty to get him out of the way. Susanna looks on as Figaro describes for him the joys and sorrows of a soldier's life.

The aria is marked vivace. The piece is playfully sung, using dotted rhythms, much repetition, and opportunity to deliver the text using many different emotions and colors as he addresses the young Cherubino: playful, stern, condescending, sarcasm, and charm, to name a few. The arpeggiated melodic shape is written to sound like the bugle calling the soldier to duty—Cherubino, in this case, in the key of C major. An easy high E is extremely important—vocal production that is not too "covered" or "spread-wide open." The repetitions of middle C's must not be sung too blustery, for it tires the voice.

> Aria translation by Martha Gerhart a from the *G. Schirmer Opera Anthology: Arias for Bass*, edited by Robert L. Larsen (used by permission):
>
> You won't be flitting around anymore like a big amorous butterfly night and day
> disturbing the repose of beautiful women, little Narcissus, little Adonis of love.
> [*Here Figaro comes up with new melodic material, connected and legato.*]

You'll no longer have these pretty feathers, that light and gallant hat, that head of hair, that sparkling air, that bright red womanish color! You'll no longer have those feathers, that hat, that head of hair, that sparkling personality!

Among soldiers, by Jove!

[*This is a new section musically, where the text is especially important.*]

Big moustache, tight tunic, gun on your shoulder, saber at your side,

Neck straight, face forward, a big helmet or a big turban, much honor,

little cash.

And instead of the fandango, a march through the mud . . .

over mountains, through glens, in the snows and the hot suns,

to the accompaniment of trombones, of bombards, of cannons that fire the cannonballs,

amidst all the thunder, whistle in your ears.

Cherubino, to victory—to military glory!

Piano/vocal score: p. 116 (G. Schirmer)

No. 80

Voice: bass
Aria Title: "Se vuol ballare" (Figaro)
Opera Title: *Le nozze di Figaro*
Composer: Wolfgang Amadeus Mozart (1756–1791)
Historical Style: Classical (1786)
Range: C3 to F4

Fach: bass-baritone
Librettist: Lorenzo da Ponte (1749–1838), after Pierre-Augustin Caron de Beaumarchais's play *La folle journée, ou Le mariage de Figaro* (1784)
Aria Duration: 2:35
Tessitura: C3 to C4

Position: Act I

Setting: Outside Seville, Spain; 17th century; the unfurnished apartment of Figaro and Susanna in Count Almaviva's castle; morning

Aria translation by Martha Gerhart and plot notes from the *G. Schirmer Opera Anthology: Arias for Bass,* edited by Robert L. Larsen (used by permission):

Figaro, valet to Count Almaviva, has just discovered from Susanna that the trip to London that the Count plans to take with Figaro and his bride to be—Susanna—is probably designed so that the Count can lavish his attentions on Susanna. Left alone, Figaro muses that he has a few ideas of his own especially desined for his employer. "Bravo, lord master!" he declaims. "Now I begin to understand the mystery, and to see clearly your whole plan; to London, really? You as minister, I as courier, and Susanna . . . secret ambassadress. That will not be—Figaro says so!"

The first section of the aria is in 3/4 meter to sarcastically mimic the dance of the Count's station:

Aria translation by Martha Gerhart from the *G. Schirmer Opera Anthology: Arias for Bass,* edited by Robert L. Larsen (used by permission):

If you want to dance, little Count, I'll play the guitar for you, yes.
If you want to come to my school, I'll teach you the caper, yes.
I'll learn, but quietly; [*piano*]
I'll be able to discover every secret better while playing the part.
[*fermata rest*]
[*The tempo marking is now presto, in two beats per measure.*]
Defending my cunning, using my craftiness, stinging here, joking there,
I'll turn all your plots upside down. [*The text is repeated.*]
[*The piece returns to tempo 1, in recapitulation of music and text.*]
If you want to dance, little Count, I'll play the guitar for you, yes.
If you want to come to my school, I'll show you the ropes, yes.

This aria needs varied mercurial emotions (playfulness, sarcasm, confidence, and defensiveness). It also requires a high F on the -i-vowel, and an easy high E that is strong and projected.

Piano/vocal score: p. 38 (G. Schirmer)

No. 81

Voice: bass
Aria Title: "The same, old room" (Horace
Giddens)
Opera Title: *Regina*
Composer and Librettist: Marc Blitzstein
(1905–1964), based on Lillian Hellman's
play *The Little Foxes* (1939)
Historical Style: 20th-century American
(1949)
Range: A3 to E4

Fach: bass-baritone
Aria Duration: 1:20
Tessitura: B3 to D4

Position: Act II, scene 1

Setting: Bowden, Alabama, 1900; the living room of the Giddens' house;
evening

The opera is about how greed destroys a Southern American family.
Horace is the unwilling source of money that will fund the business venture put together by his wife Regina and her two brothers, Ben and Oscar.
Horace has advanced heart disease and has been in treatment for several
months at Johns Hopkins in Baltimore. The scheming Regina, needing
Horace's signature and capital, sends their daughter Alexandra to bring him
home. Horace and Alexandra are late in arriving from the trip. Upon entering the house, the weak and frail Horace first encounters the friendly
and welcome presence of Addie, his longtime African-American servant.
Here is the text of the musical lines that precede Horace's aria:

> *Horace:* How are you, Addie? How have you been?
> *Addie (spoken):* All right, Mr. Horace. Mighty worried about you.
> *Horace (sung):* Well, here we are at last. I'm glad to be home, glad to
> be sitting down.
> How are the others? Have I asked that before? I guess I'm quite
> tired. How is Cal? It's been so long since I've seen friends, only
> doctors.
> *Addie (spoken):* Them fancy doctors give you help?
> *Horace (sung):* They did their best. Well, here we are home.
> (*The aria is marked con moto, poco più mosso.*)
> The same old room—I had forgotten, and yet here it was all this
> time.

It's funny. The same old stairs—I had forgotten. (*tempo 1*) What a strange unfamiliar room to come back to.

Alexandra (spoken): I'll better call Mama.

Horace (sung): Not yet, Zan. No, please dear. Don't call anyone right a way. Just let me stay here for a while.

(*He sings in quarter-notes values at the bottom of the staff.*)

Alexandra (spoken, holding up a bottle of medicine): Oh, Papa, you feel bad again.

Horace (spoken): No, I'm all right, darling, (*sung at the bottom of the staff*) just tired.

This piece has many enharmonic tones, giving it a jazz-inflected sound. The meter changes throughout. The aria is set very low, and the top note sung is middle C.

Piano/vocal score: p. 100 (Chappell)

No. 82

Voice: bass
Aria Title: "Di due figli vivea" (Ferrando)
Opera Title: *Il trovatore*
Composer: Giuseppe Verdi (1813–1901)
Historical Style: Italian Romantic (1853)
Range: B3 to E4

Fach: bass-baritone
Librettists: Salvatore Cammarano and Leone Emanuele Bardare (1820–1874), after the play *El trovador* by Antonio García Gutiérrez (1836)
Aria Duration: 3:55
Tessitura: B3 to E4

Position: Act I, scene 1

Setting: Northern Spain, 15th century; the hall of the Aliaferia Palace; to one side, a door leading to the apartments of the Count di Luna. Ferrando and many retainers of the Count are lying near the door: some armed men pace to and fro at the rear; they are sleepily guarding the apartments.

The captain, Ferrando, explains that the Count, who spends the night keeping a vigil below his lady's balcony, has a rival in a troubadour whose serenading can be heard each night in the palace gardens. He goes on to tell the soldiers the story of the kidnapping of the Count's infant brother long ago and how, although the child was presumed to have died at the hands of his abductor, his father nevertheless believed till his death that he was still alive.

The narrative at the beginning of the opera commences mysteriously, marked piano, with specifically marked articulation. The men want to hear the true story of Garcia, the Count's infant brother, so that they will stay awake. The Captain is drawing the men in with his story. Most of this section is sung between C♯4 and D4 in the middle of the voice. "Whom did the nurse see beside the child?" he asks. The next section has a rhythm that grabs one's attention, sung with energized rhythm, but is marked pianissimo. The voice line repeats phrases at higher and higher levels, with crescendo: "The nurse was pierced with horror and let out a scream: the servants rushed into the room and drove out the old hag who had dared to enter" he sings—up to high E, and repeats the B to E interval of the 4th on continuous 8th notes. The men are struck with horror, and Ferrando continues with another verse: "The sorceress was pursued and taken and condemned to the stake. But she left a cursed daughter to be the instrument of horrible vengeance! This fiend caused a hideous crime. The child disappeared, and among the spent embers of the very place where the witch was brought to be burned were found—alas!—the half charred bones of a child, still smoldering."

The text is set syllabically in this aria, including the high E in passing on the -i- and -u- vowels without vocal strain.

Piano/vocal score: p. 4 (G. Schirmer)

No. 83

Voice: bass
Aria Title: "You rascal, you! I never knew
you had a soul!" (Doctor)
Opera Title: *Vanessa*
Composer: Samuel Barber (1910–1981)
Historical Style: 20th-century American
(1958)
Range: A3 to F♯4

Fach: bass-baritone
Librettist: Gian Carlo Menotti (b. 1911)
Aria Duration: 3:50
Tessitura: C3 to C4

Position: Act II

Setting: A northern county, c. 1905; Vanessa's country house, the entrance
hall with the ballroom beyond; New Year's Eve

At a party at which he will announce the engagement of Anatol to
Vanessa, the old family doctor shows the effects of too much champagne.
As the old Doctor has become tipsy, he sings many of these phrases in fragments, with a playful, active orchestra. Just as the Doctor is shifting his
balance, the meter shifts rapidly between 2/4 and 3/4. Although he is tipsy,
the rhythms need to be sung as written, for then the result is the percep-
tion of tipsiness.

You rascal, you! (*he sings piano*) I never knew you had a soul. What an
evening! What women, what champagne. (*sustaining a high E with a glissando to low C♯*) What am I doing with two glasses? (*spoken*) I must have
been carrying one to some charming lady. (*sung*) Who was she? . . . Oh,
well . . . (*He descends to the low A.*)

(*After a 10-measure orchestral interlude, he freely sings:*) I should never have
been a doctor, Nicholas; a gentleman, a poet, that's what I am. (*The next
phrases are marked piano, slower.*) A naked body, what is it to a doctor? We
see them every day. (*The line moves ahead with increasing gusto, still marked
piano.*) But under a chandelier, with the right music, the right perfume, a
naked arm, a shoulder . . . Oh God . . . (*at the sustained fermata high D*)

(*fortissimo*) I lose my mind!

The Doctor sustains a high F♯ on the word "mind" over 12 lively, and almost raucous, measures in the orchestra.

Piano/vocal score: p. 136 (G. Schirmer)

Notes by singer and voice professor Giorgio Tozzi, who created the role of the Doctor. This piece was added to the opera by the composer for Mr. Tozzi: Personality is very important in this piece. The composer has described the Doctor's "condition" in the accompaniment very actively, and the singer should be aware of this. Look also to the words of the piece as the Doctor loses his inhibitions. Under the influence, he is seduced—as are a number of the characters in the opera. He should never have been a doctor, he says. A poet is what he is.

No. 84

Voice: bass
Aria Title: "La callunia" (Don Basilio)
Opera Title: *Il barbiere di Siviglia*
Composer: Gioacchino Rossini (1792–1868)
Historical Style: Bel canto (1816)
Range: B3 to E4/C♯3 to F♯4

Fach: lyric
Librettist: Cesare Sterbini (1784–1831), after Pierre-Augustin Caron de Beaumarchais's play *Le barbier de Séville* (1775) and Giuseppe Petrosellini's libretto for Giovanni Paisiello (1782)
Aria Duration: 4:20
Tessitura: E3 to C4/F♯3 to D4

Position: Act I, scene 2

Setting: Seville, Spain, 17th century, a room inside Dr. Bartolo's house

Aria plot notes from the *G. Schirmer Opera Anthology: Arias for Bass,* edited by Robert L. Larsen (used by permission):

Don Basilio, gossip and music teacher, tells Don Bartolo that Count Almaviva has been seen lurking in the neighborhood and that he believes him to be Bartolo's rival for the hand of Rosina. Basilio is sure that the situation can be handled by spreading suspicion and slander about the young man.

Don Basilio is Rosina's music teacher. He is often played long in limb, neck, arm, and hands—as one could imagine the mannered affectations of a dilettante musician.

Originally composed in the key of D major, it is often today sung in the key of C major, and the aria is readily available in this key. Set in the key of D major, the singer must crescendo and go up the scale to a high F♯ (fermata) two times, whereas in the key of C the high pitch is E.

Basilio begins the aria very intimately, conspiratorially, even the intervals up to D in the first phrases—as if he has a secret. Diction is important, and he can linger on the s- of "simulante/hissing" for effect.

Aria translation by Martha Gerhart from the *G. Schirmer Opera Anthology: Arias for Bass*, edited by Robert L. Larsen (used by permission):

Slander is a little wind, a very gentle little breeze,
which, imperceptibly and subtly, lightly, delicately begins to whisper.
Softly, along the ground, hissing under its breath it goes gliding along,
it goes buzzing along; it slips deftly into people's ears and stuns and inflates their heads and brains.
Coming out of the mouth the hubbub starts to grow; it gathers force little by little;
now it flies hither and yonder; it seems like thunder, the storm that whistles and rumbles
in the bosom of the forest and makes you freeze with horror.
In the end it overflows and bursts, spreads, doubles, and produces an explosion like a cannon shot,
[*Here Basilio sings sustained higher pitches of middle C and D.*]
an earthquake, a thunderstorm—a general turmoil that makes the air resound.
And the miserable slandered one—humiliated, trampled on—
under the public scourge by good fortune goes off to die.

This aria gives the singer opportunity to develop comic characterization in the voice, articulation contrasts between staccato and legato, and the ability to produce the large sound as the voice moves up through the *passaggio* as the singer stays in character. The singer must be careful not to sing too heavy and blustery in the characterization. Beautiful, connected singing is still possible—for remember that Basilio is the music teacher!

Piano/vocal score: p. 88 (Boosey & Hawkes)

No. 85

Voice: bass
Aria Title: "Vecchia zimarra" (Colline)
Opera Title: *La bohème*
Composer: Giacomo Puccini (1858–1924)
Historical Style: Verismo (1896)
Range: C♯3 to E♭4

Fach: lyric
Librettists: Giuseppe Giacosa (1847–1906) and Luigi Illica (1857–1919), based on Henry Mürger's novel *Scènes de la vie de bohème* (1845–9) and his play (with Théodore Barrière) *La vie de bohème* (1849)
Aria Duration: 1:30
Tessitura: C♯3 to C♯4

Position: Act IV

Setting: Paris, c. 1830s; the unheated apartment of the "bohemian" artists Rodolfo and Marcello

The aria is marked allegretto mosso e triste; it should not be sung too slow:

Aria translation by Martha Gerhart from the *G. Schirmer Opera Anthology: Arias for Bass,* edited by Robert L. Larsen (used by permission):

Shabby old overcoat, listen—I remain on the ground while you now ascend to the sacred mountain.
[*A pun—in Italian, "mountain of mercy" is the name for a pawnshop*]
Receive my thanks. You never bowed your worn back to the rich and the powerful.
[*This phrase is sung on the high E♭, marked piano.*]
Through your pockets, as if in tranquil dens, philosophers and poets have passed.
Now that happy days have fled, I say farewell to you, my faithful friend—farewell, farewell.

Musetta has left with Marcello to sell her earrings for medicine for Mimì, but it is most likely too late. Yes, Colline is also about to sell his well-worn old coat for the same reason, to make Mimì more comfortable in her last hours—but as he empties his pockets of his little novellas, it occurs to him that for all of them their "bohemian" student life is coming to an end, and this aria represents this realization. The last scene demonstrates to the philosopher Colline that they are not immortal. They must value their relationships, for life is not endless. From now on, life will have a new meaning.

Piano/vocal score: p. 273 (G. Schirmer)

No. 86

Voice: bass
Aria Title: "Madamina! Il catalogo è questo" (Leporello)
Opera Title: *Don Giovanni*
Composer: Wolfgang Amadeus Mozart (1756–1791)
Historical Style: Classical (1787)
Range: A3 to E4

Fach: buffo
Librettist: Lorenzo da Ponte (1749–1838), after Giovanni Bertati and Giuseppe Gazzinga's opera *Don Giovanni Tenorio, o sia Il convitato di pietra* (1787)
Aria Duration: 5:10
Tessitura: D3 to D4

Position: Act I, scene 2

Setting: Outside Seville, Spain, 17th century; a desolate street at dawn
Don Giovanni and his servant Leporello unexpectedly run into a woman, Donna Elvira, who recognizes the Don as he approaches to look her over. She recognizes him as someone who made promises to her in the past and has discarded her. Before she can corner Don Giovanni, he gives her the slip—leaving her with his servant Leporello (once more) to explain the Don's behavior.
The aria begins allegro:

Aria translation by Martha Gerhart from the *G. Schirmer Opera Anthology: Arias for Bass*, edited by Robert L. Larsen (used by permission):

My little lady, this is the catalogue of the beautiful women whom my master has loved;
it's a list that I've made myself—look, read with me!

In Italy 640, in Germany 231; 100 in France, 91 in Turkey—but, in Spain are already 1,003!

[*The next section is marked legato.*]

Among these there are country girls, chambermaids, city girls;

There are countesses, baronesses, marquises, princesses;

and there are women of every rank, of every shape, of every age.

To the blond he has the habit of extolling her kindness—

to the brunette, her constancy, to the fair one, her sweetness.

In winter he wants the plump one; in summer, he wants the skinny one

and the tall, stately one. The tiny one is always charming;

the old ones he conquers for the pleasure of putting them on the list.

His predominant passion is the young beginner.

He takes no offense, be she rich, be she ugly, be she beautiful;

as long as she wears a skirt, you know what he does.

Leporello sings very rapidly in the opening in patter-style delivery. He has given this speech many times. He is most likely irritated that he has to do it again, and especially after the murder of the Commendatore, at which time the Don has made humorous quips as the Commendatore died. At the opening of the opera, Leporello was already fed up attending to the Don's every wish. It is also possible that in the legato section Leporello is playing the Don. Leporello can also imagine in the aria that Elvira is wanting to grab the book to see if her name is in it, and with that discovery wanting to destroy it. This aria shows the singer's ability to enunciate text with understanding, project a character with attitude, and show a legato delivery as he can imagine the Don would sing. Leporello also needs a strong, projected, free high E to that he will be able to sing on the -o- vowel.

Piano/vocal score: p. 46 (Boosey & Hawkes)

No. 87

Voice: bass
Aria Title: "Lyubvi vse vozrastï pokornï"
(Prince Gremin)
Opera Title: *Eugene Onegin*
Composer: Pyotr Ilyich Tchaikovsky (1840–1893)
Historical Style: Russian Romantic (1879)
Range: G♭2 to E♭4

Fach: bass
Librettists: The composer and Konstantin Shilovsky (1849–1893), based on Aleksandr Pushkin's verse novel *Eugene Onegin* (1831)
Aria Duration: 5:30
Tessitura: E♭3 to E♭4

Position: Act III scene 1

Setting: Russia, 19th century; the St. Petersburg home of a wealthy and middle-aged retired general Prince Gremin; a fashionable ball is in progress.

It is three years since the duel between Onegin and Lensky. Tatiana is now married to Prince Gremin and at first does not recognize her former love, Onegin. A remorseful Onegin is now only 26 years old. Prince Gremin sings the praises of his wife, telling Onegin how much her love has meant to him as the only ennobling element of his life.

The beginning of the aria is marked andante sostenuto composed in 2/4 meter

All ages are to love submissive, its impulses are beneficial to blossoming youth,
Barely having seen the world.
And to those hardened by fate, the gray-headed warrior!
Onegin, I will not conceal, madly I love Tatiana!
Drearily my life flowed, she appeared and gave,
Like a sun's ray in foul weather,
Life to me, and youth, yes, youth and happiness!
Amidst the sly, the faint hearted, the mad and spoiled children,
The scoundrels and the absurd, and the dull,
The obtuse, the quick to judge;
Amidst the religious coquettes, amidst the voluntary slaves,
Amidst the frigid verdicts of cruel-hearted vanity,
Amidst the annoying emptiness of calculations, thoughts and conversations,
She shines, like a star in the gloom of night, in the clear sky,

And appears to me always in the aureole of an angel,
Radiant in the aureole of an angel!
All ages are to love submissive, its impulses are beneficial to blossom-
ing youth,
Barely having seen the world, and to those hardened by fate, the
gray-headed warrior.
Onegin, I will not conceal, madly I love Tatiana!
Drearily my life flowed, she appeared and gave,
Like sun's rays in foul weather life to me, and youth, yes,
Youth and happiness, life and youth and happiness!

The melody is legato and sweeping. At times it is passionate, and becomes more so as the aria unfolds. The aria ends on the low E.

Piano/vocal score: p. 207 (Richard Schauer)

No. 88

Voice: bass

Aria Title: "Vous qui faites l'endormie,"
Serenade (Mephistopheles)

Opera Title: *Faust*

Composer: Charles Gounod (1818–1893)

Historical Style: French Romantic (1859)

Range: G2 to G4

Fach: dramatic

Librettists: Jules Barbier (1825–1901) and
Michel Carré (1822–1872), after Part I of
Johann Wolfgang von Goethe's play *Faust*
(1808)

Aria Duration: 2:35

Tessitura: D3 to D4

Position: Act III, scene 3

Setting: A town in Germany, 16th century; the street outside Marguerite's
home

At the beginning of the scene the soldiers pour into the square, returning
from war. Among the soldiers is Valentin, the brother of Marguerite. Faust,
accompanied by Mephistopheles, returns to Marguerite's house to see once
more the girl he has dishonored and who carries his child. The devil throws
back his cloak, strums his mandolin, and sings a diabolical parody of a

lover's serenade, complete with legato embellishments. The aria is sung legato and seductively, but the intervals are awkward and unsettling, with an unusual shape of the vocal line. Such is the charm of the devil—that he can sing a charming and seductive melody punctuated at the end of each verse by a cackling laugh.

The beginning of the aria is in the key of G minor and is in 3/4 meter, marked allegretto.

Aria translation by Martha Gerhart from the *G. Schirmer Opera Anthology: Arias for Bass,* edited by Robert L. Larsen (used by permission):

You who are pretending to be asleep,
don't you hear, oh Catherine, my love, my voice and my steps?
Thus does your suitor call you, and your heart gives in to him.
Ah! Ah! Ah! Ah!
[*The piece moves into the key of G major, but with chromatic "wandering."*]
Don't open your door, my beautiful one,
without the ring on your finger!
[*Verse 2:*]
Catherine, whom I adore, why refuse to the lover who implores you
so sweet a kiss?
Thus does your suitor beseech you, and your heart gives in to him.
Ah! Ah! Ah! Ah!
Don't grant a kiss, my love, without the ring on your finger!
Ah! Ah! Ah! Ah! Ah! Ah! Ah! Ah!
[*Three octaves are sung on "Ah!" from high G to the low G at the bottom of the bass staff.*]

Piano/vocal score: p. 227 (G. Schirmer)

No. 89

Voice: bass
Aria Title: "Sì! Morir ella de'!" (Alvise)
Opera Title: *La Gioconda*
Composer: Amilcare Ponchielli (1834–1886)
Historical Style: Italian Romantic (1876)
Range: G2 to F4

Fach: dramatic
Librettist: Arrigo Boito (1842–1918) (under the pseudonym Tobia Gorrio), based on Victor Hugo's play *Angélo, tyran de Padoue* (1835)
Aria Duration: 5:04
Tessitura: C3 to C4

Position: Act III, scene 1

Setting: Venice, 17th century; Palace of the Duke, known as the House of Gold

Duke Alvise finds that his wife, Laura, was once engaged to Enzo Grimaldo, and she still loves him. Their relationship is exposed by Barnaba, an evil man who is in love with La Gioconda, and of course she is also in love with Enzo. So Barnaba therefore has an opportunity to dispose of Enzo by letting Alvise know of his wife's affection for Enzo. He is a mysterious figure with a complex past. He has been outlawed in Venice and is there in disguise.

In scene 1 of Act III, the Duke is planning festivities and a revenge on his wife, Laura. He has everything planned out. He will summon his wife, draw a curtain to reveal a bier ready to receive her body, and will hand her a vial of poison with instructions that it must be drunk as he leaves her alone.

> Yes! Die she must! Shall infamy be written on my name with impunity?
> Who betrays me can hope for no pity! . . .
> If yesterday on that fatal island this hand of mine did not seize her, expiation will be no less terrible!
> (*The opening has a violent energy that pushes the line forward.*)
> (*In thought*) A dagger should have pierced her breast. Today . . . it will not be steel . . . but poison!" (*pointing to the adjoining rooms*)
> (*This next section is wildly rhythmic and energized.*)
> There let the party keep on its whirling dances. Here with a groan of agony let the festivities be mixed!
> (*The new section is dark, set in the lower-middle voice, then rises in a de-*

clamatory fashion for the final phrases, which gain momentum and "swirl upward.")

Shades of my forefathers do not blush yet!

Death revenges everything—even betrayed honor!

Tremble in your dances and songs! . . . It is a faithless wife who dies!

Piano/vocal score: p. 207 (Ricordi)

No. 90

Voice: bass

Aria Title: "Si la rigueur" (Cardinal Brogni)

Opera Title: *La Juive*

Composer: Jacques-François-Fromental Halévy (1799–1862)

Historical Style: French Romantic (1835)

Range: E2 to C4

Fach: bass

Librettist: Eugène Scribe (1791–1861)

Aria Duration: 3:30

Tessitura: C3 to A4

Position: Act I

Setting: Constance, Switzerland; 1414; a village square; on one side is the door of the church; on the other the house and workshop of Éléazar, a Jewish goldsmith. It is a Christian feast day.

The congregation pours out of the church after a great "Hosanna!" is heard, and the crowd listens as the town provost proclaims the news of the public holiday. However, in Éléazar's shop work continues, and this causes friction. "Why should the Jews bow to the Christian laws?" Éléazar asks. At that moment Cardinal Brogni passes by and inquires as to the reason for the noise. He recognizes Éléazar, whom he spared from death in the past when Éléazar was condemned to death in Rome for usury. The Cardinal banished Éléazar from Rome. Cardinal Brogni is duty-bound by the holy laws, and this will prove to condemn him at the end of the opera. Brogni prays that enlightenment may come to the Jewish unbelievers.

"If I offended you, forgive me!" He sings, before beginning the aria:

If harshness and vengeance make them hate Thy holy law, let forgiveness, let clemency, my God, Gather them on this day towards Thee!

The aria shows the low/middle voice to best advantage in the bass voice. The aria is basically a lyric expression from C an octave above to middle C, with no tones higher than middle C. The singer needs a free low F, and the ability to move the phrases, so that they do not sound to be too pompous and lugubrious in the low bass range with the triplet figures. The text and melody is repeated, for Éléazar is angry and bitter about the past, and stands up in anger against the Cardinal, who is trying to placate him.

Piano/vocal score: p. 55 (Choudens)

No. 91

Voice: bass
Aria Title: "Come dal ciel precipita" (Banquo)
Opera Title: *Macbeth*
Composer: Giuseppe Verdi (1813–1912)
Historical Style: Italian Romantic (1847)
Range: A3 to E4

Fach: bass
Librettist: Francesco Maria Piave (1810–1876) with additions by Andrea Maffei (1798–1885), after the tragedy by William Shakespeare (1605)
Aria Duration: 3:00
Tessitura: B3 to E4

Position: Act II, scene 2

Setting: Scotland, Medieval times; a park near Macbeth's castle, late at night

Uneasily aware that assassins are in wait to attack him and his young son, Banquo, one of Macbeth's generals, enters a park near the castle at night. At the conclusion of the aria Banquo is murdered, but his son escapes.

The recitative is marked adagio, pianissimo:

> Aria translation by Martha Gerhart from the *G. Schirmer Opera Anthology: Arias for Bass*, edited by Robert L. Larsen (used by permission): "Watch your step, oh my son! Let us leave this darkness. I feel rising in my breast a strange feeling full of ill omen and of suspicion."

The last phrase is unaccompanied and is sung in the low range. This passage is eerily reminiscent of the one before Banquo discovers the murdered Duncan in Act I.

The aria begins, marked adagio, mezzo forte: the first vocal phrases rise to D at the top of the range, accented, sung fortissimo:

> Aria translation by Martha Gerhart from the *G. Schirmer Opera Anthology: Arias for Bass*, edited by Robert L. Larsen (used by permission):
>
> How the shadows fall from the sky ever more dark!
> On such a night they slew Duncan, my lord.
> A thousand troubled images prophesy misfortune to me
> and encumber my thoughts with apparitions and terror.

This text repeats, leading the singer to the high, sustained E at the end of the piece.

The beginning of the piece is marked pianissimo, as Banquo does not want to be heard. But as the aria comes to the end he has accepted his fate and wants to meet his death head on like a warrior (not like Duncan, who was murdered in his bed), and he most wants to protect his young son.

Piano/vocal score: p. 123 (Ricordi)

> Notes by singer and voice professor Giorgio Tozzi: Listen to the music! Feel the music—the harmonic language is an audible language that the singer needs to hear, and that language creates the urgency and emotion needed to perform this piece.

No. 92

Voice: bass
Aria Title: "Épouse quelque brave fille"
(Des Grieux)
Opera Title: *Manon*
Composer: Jules Massenet (1848–1912)
Historical Style: French Romantic (1884)
Range: C3 to F4

Fach: bass
Librettists: Henri Meilhac (1831–1897) and
Philippe Gille (1831–1901), based on the
Abbé Antoine-François Prévost's novel *L'his-
toire du chevalier des Grieux et de Manon
Lescaut* (1731)
Aria Duration: 2:50
Tessitura: C3 to C4

Position: Act III, scene 2

Setting: Church of Saint-Sulpice, 18th century; a reception room in the church

The old Count des Grieux comes to visit his son to try to persuade him to leave the church, marry some respectable young lady, and settle down. But the young abbé resolutely refuses, for he has resolved to forget Manon in the religious life, and the worldly old count leaves his son with an ironical farewell.

The beginning is marked moderato, forte.

> What lofty words those are!
> What path have you followed, then, and what do you know about this life
> To think that it ends with this?
> Marry some fine girl worthy of us, worthy of you;
> Become a family father neither worse nor better than I: heaven wishes no more.
> Your duty is there—do you understand?
> Your duty is there!

The next section is un poco animando, quasi declamando.

> Virtue, which is ostentatious is already no longer virtue!
> (*The text is repeated.*)
> Become a family father neither worse nor better than I;
> (*The Count has a high F 8th note.*)
> Heaven wishes no more. (*forte*) Your duty is there!
> (*piano*) It is your duty!

During the recitative the father can see that his blustery approach has disturbed his son. He begins the aria piano, with a rational argument intended to sway him from staying in the church. The father has to fight his impulse to be forceful (forte) as he sings up to a sustained, high E♭ and is also aware of the setting where they speak (the church).

Piano/vocal score: p. 254 (G. Schirmer)

No. 93

Voice: bass
Aria Title: "Un ignoto, tre lune or saranno" (Massimiliano)
Opera Title: *I masnadieri*
Composer: Giuseppe Verdi (1813–1901)
Historical Style: Italian Romantic (1847)
Range: B♭3 to E♭4

Fach: bass
Librettist: Andrea Maffei (1798–1885), after Johann Christoph Friedrich von Schiller's tragedy *Die Räuber* (1781)
Aria Duration: 2:45
Tessitura: E♭3 to C4

Position: Act III, scene 2

Setting: Germany, the beginning of the 18th century; a forest. In the center rises the ruins of an ancient tower; night.

The aged Count Massimilano Moor has two sons: Carlo and Francesco. Carlo is estranged from his father and has left home to go to a university, while Francesco remains at home where he schemes against his older brother.

In act III, scene 2, Carlo has turned to life as a bandit. He had longed to return home, but had received a letter purportedly from his father rejecting him—but this letter is really forged by Francesco. Massimiliano, thought to have died from grief after reading a false report of Carlo's death, is in hiding from his evil son Francesco in a tower outside Prague. Carlo comes upon his father, but neither of the men recognize each other at first. Reunited finally, an exhausted, hungry, and vindictive Massimiliano tells his story:

The aria begins piano, mysterious: "An unknown—it will be three moons ago now—told me that my Carlo had been killed. I fainted, overcome by sudden grief, and my swoon was thought to be death. Reviving, I found myself enclosed within four boards: I moved about, I cried for help. The shroud was raised . . . Francesco was by my side." (The narrative becomes quite dramatic in its declamation here with the voice on middle C; thick chords are played in 16th-note rhythms by the orchestra.

"'What,' he exclaimed, 'have you revived?' The coffin was closed again and brought here and the lid not lifted again." (He now has two measures of interlude to catch his breath and regain his composure. The next phrase begins legato with energized rhythms within as the phrase finishes with a crescendo building to high D for the bass with some of his last strength.) "'Throw that casket down there; he has lived too long!' cried my son."

Now is heard a new melodic section, legato, but still vigorous with rhythmic energy, crescendoing in ascent to high E♭, with accents to the final cadence on the tonic, low E♭.

"Entreaties and lamentations were in vain, I was hurled into this horrible den. And it was my inhuman son himself who locked the dungeon doors." He faints. There are sudden changes in dynamics and articulation.

This aria is not demanding as far as range is concerned, but has the Verdian characteristics that are fun to sing, including dramatic, declamatory lines, and some beautiful sections where legato is called for.

(Translation by Nico Castel)

Piano/vocal score: p. 160 (Ricordi)

No. 94

Voice: bass
Aria Title: "De son coeur j'ai calmé la fièvre," Berceuse (Lothario)
Opera Title: *Mignon*
Composer: Ambroise Thomas (1811–1896)
Historical Style: French Romantic (1866)
Range: A3 to D4

Fach: bass
Librettists: Michel Carré (1819–1872) and Jules Barbier (1825–1901), after Johann Wolgang von Goethe's novel *Wilhelm Meisters Lehrjahre* (1796)
Aria Duration: 3:20
Tessitura: E3 to D4

Position: Act III

Setting: Italy, late 18th century; a gallery in the Cipriani Palace adorned with statues; a window with a wide view of the country; at back, a closed door; a door at either side

Lothario is an Italian nobleman who, crazed by the loss of his child and the death of her mother, is wandering about the earth as a minstrel seeking the daughter who, he is convinced, is still alive, even though many years have passed since she was carried away by gypsies.

Desperately ill, Mignon has been taken by Wilhelm to Italy to his ancestral palace. This is the land which had haunted her memory from childhood, but for which she has no name. It is where she wished to live, in which to die. Lothario is on a path to mental recovery after meeting Mignon and bringing her to Italy. Lothario prays for her recovery as a barcarolle is heard from the lake below.

(Entering from door stage right)

I have calmed the fever in her heart!
A sweet and contented smile parted her lips on hearing my voice;
sleep has closed her eyes.
Poor child! May God protect and defend you!
Sleep in peace—sleep, poor child!
On her brow, spreading his wings, and on her behalf, leaving the heavens,
A good angel watches over her!
Sleep has closed her eyes.
Poor child! May God protect and defend you!
Sleep in peace! Sleep, poor child!

The piece is sung piano, as befits a lullaby. The voice touches the high D and sometimes sustains it for a quarter beat, and at other times begins the phrase on the high D. This aria needs an even support and clear articulation of the text and specific rhythms, while maintaining the integrity of an even vocal line.

Piano/vocal score: p. 286 (G. Schirmer)

No. 95

Voice: bass

Aria Title: "Tu sul labbro" (Zachariah)

Opera Title: *Nabucco*

Composer: Giuseppe Verdi (1813–1901)

Historical Style: Italian Romantic (1842)

Range: G2 to E4

Fach: bass

Librettist: Temistocle Solera (1815–1878)

Aria Duration: 2:50

Tessitura: D3 to B4

Position: Act II (The Blasphemy)

Setting: Babylon in the reign of Nebuchadnezzar. The royal apartments, a room in the palace; at the back a communicating door giving access to other apartments. Right, a door leading to a gallery; left, another door leading to the royal apartments. It is evening; a lamp is burning.

Zachariah, High Priest of the Hebrews, enters, followed by a Levite carrying the Tables of the Law. The orchestral introduction is 17 measures, featuring the plaintive sound of the solo cello. The beginning of the sung recitative is unaccompanied with orchestral punctuation.

> Come, stand beside me, the holy law set before me.
> God this day commands me, in wondrous revelation.
> He bids His servant to show an unbeliever the holy light of truth, for Israel's glory.

The aria (andante) again begins unaccompanied, marked sotto voce with gentle accents:

> Through Thy servants Thou proclaimest Thy commandments, oh Lord God almighty!
> On this day, with voice of thunder, to Assyria Thou hast spoken!
> (*New melodic material is introduced.*)
> And with hymns, with hymns of praise unto Thee, Jehovah
> Every temple shall resound o'er the shattered gods of the heathen.
> Thou Jehovah, shalt arise again.
> And with hymns of praise and glory every temple shall resound.

Zacharia goes into Fenena's apartment followed by the Levite.

A legato vocal line is important in this aria, as is attention to rhythm and dynamics, for forceful, energized delivery. At "Thou Jehovah, shalt arise again" the singer requires a high, sustained E as well as a G at the bottom of the staff.

Piano/vocal score: p. 170 (Ricordi)

> Notes by singer and voice professor Giorgio Tozzi: Zachariah prays in order to prepare himself to convert Fenena, Nabucco's daughter, to Judaism. It is an intimate, prayerful—marked by the introduction to the piece of the solo cello. The aria is also filled with expressive fervor.

No. 96

Voice: bass
Aria Title: "Il lacerato spirito" (Fiesco)
Opera Title: *Simon Boccanegra*
Composer: Giuseppe Verdi (1813–1901)
Historical Style: Italian Romantic (1857)
Range: F#2 to D4

Fach: dramatic
Librettist: Francesco Maria Piave (1810–1876)
Aria Duration: 4:45
Tessitura: D3 to B4

Position: Prologue

Setting: Genoa, 1339; the public square; night

Jacopo Fiesco is a nobleman and the grandfather of Amelia (daughter of Simon Boccanegra). In a clandestine meeting, politicians who represent the democratic faction approach Simon Boccanegra to discuss his becoming the new Doge—head of state. He chooses not to run, but they change his mind. Simon has had a clandestine love affair with Maria, who is the daughter of Fiesco, a nobleman. Should Boccanegra be elected Doge, he would have the rank of a Prince, and Fiesco could not deny his consent. Boccanegra agrees, and the political conspirators summon a group of voters around them. They argue against Fiesco—who would be the political rival of Boccanegra—by saying that he keeps a beautiful woman locked up as a prisoner in his palace. In reality the woman he has locked up is his daughter, Maria, the beloved of Simon, and she has just died.

In the aria, sung outside near the church of San Lorenzo, Fiesco speaks of his sorrow as the offstage chorus sings a Miserere.

Aria translation by Martha Gerhart from the *G. Schirmer Opera Anthology: Arias for Bass,* edited by Robert L. Larsen (used by permission):

To you my last farewell, proud palace, cold sepulcher of my angel!
I was worth nothing in protecting her. Oh cursed man! Oh vile seducer!
And you, Virgin—you let her be robbed of her virginal crown?
[*Recoiling, as Fiesco has a recitative-like sudden recanting of his sacrilegious words*]
Ah, what have I said? I'm raving!
Ah, forgive me!" [*slowly, sustained, the "perdona/pardon" to cadence to low A*]
Aria:
The broken spirit of the sad father
was reserved for the agony of infamy and of sorrow.
[*cantabile; in the key of F♯ major—an abrupt change for the accompanist— six sharps*]
Heaven mercifully bestowed upon her the wreath of martyrs.
Returned to the radiance of the angels, pray, Maria, for me.

The last phrase is an unaccompanied chord outline from C♯ down to a low, sustained F♯: "Prega Maria per me/Pray, Maria for me."

The opening (in B minor) is angry and self-pitying without becoming strident. The double-dotted rhythms are helpful in this expression. The aria shows the lower range of the singer, with only the D's in the recitative above the staff. It is somber, but each line must be focused and pointed.

Piano/vocal score: p. 22 (Ricordi)

No. 97

Voice: bass
Aria Title: "Vi ravviso" (Count Rodolfo)
Opera Title: *La sonnambula*
Composer: Vincenzo Bellini (1801–1835)
Historical Style: Bel canto (1831)
Range: C3 to E♭4

Fach: bass
Librettist: Felice Romani (1788–1865), after Eugène Scribe's ballet-pantomine *Sonnambule* (1827)
Aria Duration: 2:10
Tessitura: E♭3 to D♭4

Position: Act I, scene 1

Setting: A Swiss mountain village, 19th century; the village square outside Lisa's inn

Count Rodolfo, lord of the manor, who disappeared from his Swiss mountain village as a child, returns in an officer's uniform and asks directions from the villagers to the manor. They tell him that it is three miles beyond the village and that he should rest in the inn for the night. As he looks around at the mill, the fountain, and the fields, a flood of pleasant memories overtakes him.

The beginning of the piece is marked andante. The recitative is initially unaccompanied with only 8th-note chords punctuating the pauses: "The mill . . . the fountain . . . the woods . . . and the farmhouse nearby!"

The next section (andante cantabile) has chordal arpeggios in the treble. The melody is characteristic of true bel canto: simple, heartfelt embellishments; at the ends of some lines the unaccented syllables rise but should not be emphasized.

I see you once again, oh pleasant surroundings in which I so peacefully
Spent the happy and serene days of my early youth!
Dear surroundings, I've found you, but those days I find no more!
(*Now it is marked allegro in 6/8 meter, characterized by fragmented phrases; the last phrases of the section are unaccompanied.*)
But among you, if I'm not mistaken, some celebration is taking place?
And the bride—it is she? She's refined, very charming. Let me look
at you! Oh, the lovely face!

In the introduction to the new section (allegro moderato) is heard a four-measure preview of the melody; the dotted rhythm at the beginning of each phrase is reminiscent of the "vi ravviso/I see you once again" melody.

You don't know how sweetly you touch my heart with those beautiful eyes,
what an adorable beauty you recall to my thoughts.
That one was—ah, as you are—In the morning of her years—yes!

The final section (più mosso) is a stretta that picks up momentum to the end, with repeated high E♭ and D.

Aria translation by Nico Castel

Piano/vocal score: p. 57 (Ricordi)

Notes by singer and master teacher Kevin Langan: "Vi ravviso" gives the bass a chance to show off seamless legato phrasing, as well as dynamic variance, all in the mid-19th-century bel canto style of singing. It is a good piece to study for the young bass singer who is blessed with a steady, even sound, and it makes for a ideal companion piece to complement the Mozart bass repertoire. It also helps the young bass prepare for the more mature Verdi arias, which are a logical progression to study after he has mastered the Bellini style of this work. The character, Count Rodolfo, reminisces of his youthful experiences and how much he realizes he cherishes those memories. The music is very mellow, the text flowing from the singer like a cool breeze through one's hair. The singer can learn a lot about bel canto phrasing in this work: where to stress, and where not to, all according to the Italian text, as well as when to bring up the dynamic and when to soften, again all according to the text. It offers the traditional cadenza after the cavatina as well, which can be adjusted to show off the individual singer's ability. This aria is for the bass singer who wants to show off the high style of finesse singing, an art not commonly found among bass opera singers of today. Most basses want to show off how big their voice is, or how loud they can sing, or how high or low they can sing. While this may be impressive to some fans of vocal artistry, I find I am more impressed by the singer who can "control" his voice, finesse his sound, display his ability to vary his vocal colors as well as dynamic variety.

No. 98

Voice: bass
Aria Title: "Everyday at church" (Orgon)
Opera Title: *Tartuffe*
Composer and Librettist: Kirke Mechem
(b. 1925), based on the play by Molière
(1664)
Historical Style: 20th-century American
(1980)
Range: G#2 to D4

Fach: bass
Aria Duration: 3:45
Tessitura: C#3 to D♭4

Position: Act I

Setting: Paris, 17th century; the house of Orgon, a wealthy aristocrat

> Aria plot note from the *G. Schirmer American Aria Anthology: Baritone/
> Bass*, edited by Richard Walters (used by permission):
> Molière's classic comedy is about how Tartuffe, a religious hypocrite,
> finagles his way into a wealthy, middle-class Parisian home and nearly
> brings the family to ruin before the King intervenes. At this point in
> the plot Orgon, the master of the house, has returned home. Dorine,
> the maid, tries to tell him that his wife has been ill. But he is not in-
> terested in such news. He asks about Tartuffe. He is alone on the stage
> as he sings this aria until, near the end, Elmire, his wife, joins him. He
> does not notice her and continues his unabated praise of Tartuffe:
> "Tartuffe was kneeling across from me in prayer. His fervor caught
> the attention of those present. When I rose to leave, he'd run before
> me to give me the holy water. He was destitute and refused alms, while
> if he had something, he would share it with the poor. Such loving care
> deserved more. I brought him here to live, and he finally found peace."

The aria is sustained, and deliberately sung, requiring a high D♭ and D,
forte as well as one passage sung piano, also on the D. Some glissandi are
written as vocal characteristic gestures.

Piano/vocal score: p. 219 (*G. Schirmer American Aria Anthology: Baritone/Bass*)

Comments by composer Kirke Mechem: The opera is based on the
famous play by Molière. The playwright and *opera buffa* both had

their roots in *commedia dell'arte,* an Italian form of popular comedy developed during the 16th and 17th centuries, characterized by the use of stock characters and familiar plots.

In some respects Orgon is the typical stubborn buffo bass of comic opera, but in Molière's hands stock characters always took on added dimensions. Orgon's stubbornness relates to his refusal to see the true nature of Tartuffe, a con man posing as a pious guru. Everyone else in the family—with the exception of Orgon's equally blind mother—sees through the scoundrel whom Orgon is trying to force his daughter to marry. Orgon is a man in midlife crisis, losing control of his family and searching for easy answers. Tartuffe manipulates him shamelessly. Orgon invites him to live with him and his family, which Tartuffe—"sacrificing himself"—agrees to do and soon has Orgon eating out of his hand. In this aria we learn how Orgon first met "that holy man." The music is a parody of operatic religiosity, but the singer should sing it with all the sincere devotion that Orgon feels.

No. 99

Voice: bass
Aria Title: "O tu Palermo" (Procida)
Opera Title: *I vespri siciliani* (Italian version)
Composer: Giuseppe Verdi (1813–1901)
Historical Style: Italian Romantic (1855)
Range: F2 to Eb4

Fach: bass
Librettists: Eugène Scribe (1791–1861) and Charles Duveyrier (1803–1866), after their libretto for Donizetti's opera *Le duc d'Albe* (1839), based on historical events
Aria Duration: 4:25
Tessitura: Db3 to Db4

Position: Act II

Setting: A valley outside the Sicilian city of Palermo, 1282

Aria plot note from the *G. Schirmer Opera Anthology: Arias for Bass,* edited by Robert L. Larsen (used by permission):

> Giovanni da Procida is a Sicilian doctor who, until his banishment, was the leader of the patriots in Sicily opposing French domination. He has secretly returned to stir up the resistance movement and wanders in a valley outside the city of Palermo, extolling his beloved native land.

The recitative begins unaccompanied, with a sustained chord underneath the vocal line in the fourth measure. The marking is dolcissimo.

> Aria translation by Martha Gerhart from the *G. Schirmer Opera Anthology: Arias for Bass,* edited by Robert L. Larsen (used by permission):
>
> Oh fatherland, oh dear fatherland, at last I see you!
> The exile greets you after such a long absence . . .
> Full of love, I kiss your flowering soil;
> I bring my vow to you with my arms and my heart!

The aria has a four-measure introduction, giving the singer an opportunity to survey the land from which he was exiled. The chordal outline in the accompaniment is characteristic of the bel canto style. The music (cantabile) displays a variety of rhythm and articulation, which are important elements of the aria. The vocal line is very connected, legato, and the piece is sung simply and heartfelt.

> Aria translation by Martha Gerhart from the *G. Schirmer Opera Anthology: Arias for Bass,* edited by Robert L. Larsen (used by permission):
>
> Oh you, Palermo, adored ground, Light of love so dear to me—ah,
> [*The "ah" comes from an emotional reaction to what is felt and is not vocalized.*]
> Raise your brow, so much abused; recapture your former splendor!
> I called to foreign nations for help—I roved through castles and cities;
> But, indifferent to my impassioned plea, all said:
> Sicilians, where is your courage of old?
> Come, rise to victory, to honor!
> Ah, return to your former noble splendor!

He finishes with a traditional cadenza from low F below the staff up to the high E♭.

Procida has been exiled and sings of his love of the land as he looks at the beauty of his country. At the same time, he is calling his countrymen to action. The aria calls for warm, legato singing in the middle voice, as well as strongly sung accents, double-dotted rhythms, and a forte sustained middle C and high E♭.

Piano/vocal score: p. 84 (Ricordi)

Index A
Arias Listed Alphabetically

Aria Title	Opera Title	Lang.	Fach	No.	Historical Style
Abscheulicher! Wo eilst du hin? . . . Komm, Hoffnung	*Fidelio*	Ger.	dramatic	99	German Romantic
Acerba voluttà	*Adriana Lecouvreur*	It.	lyric	19	Verismo
Ach, ich fühl's	*Die Zauber-flöte*	Ger.	lyric	58	Singspiel
Ach, ich liebte	*Die Entfüh-rung aus dem Serail*	Ger.	dramatic coloratura	65	Singspiel
Ach, so fromm (M'apparì tutt'amor)	*Martha*	Ger./It.	lyric	57	German Romantic
Ach, wir armen, armen Leute	*Hänsel und Gretel*	Ger.	dramatic baritone	54	German Romantic
Adieu, forêts	*The Maid of Orleans*	Fr.	lyric	35	Russian Romantic
Adieu, Mignon!	*Mignon*	Fr.	lyric	58	French Romantic
Adieu, notre petite table	*Manon*	Fr.	lyric	44	French Romantic
Ah, come il cor di giubilo	*L'italiana in Algeri*	It.	leggiero	14	Bel canto
Ah! Fuyez douce image	*Manon*	Fr.	lyric	55	French Romantic
Ah, je ris de me voir (Jewel Song)	*Faust*	Fr.	full lyric (coloratura)	76	French Romantic
Ah, la paterna mano	*Macbeth*	It.	lyric	54	Italian Romantic
Ah, lève-toi, soleil!	*Roméo et Juliette*	Fr.	lyric	70	French Romantic
Ah lo veggio quell'anima bella	*Così fan tutte*	It.	lyric	33	Classical
Ah, mes amis . . . Pour mon âme	*La fille du régiment*	Fr.	lyric	42	Bel canto
Ah, Michele, don't you know?	*The Saint of Bleecker Street*	Eng.	dramatic	82	20th-century American
Ah! Mon fils, sois béni	*Le prophète*	Fr.	dramatic	77	French Romantic
Ah, my darling, we could grow together like a single vine	*The Bartered Bride*	Eng.	lyric	33	Czech Nationalist
Ah! Per sempre io ti perdei . . . Bel sogno beato	*I puritani*	It.	lyric baritone	33	Bel canto

Aria Title	Opera Title	Lang.	Fach	No.	Historical Style
Ah, pescator, affonda l'esca	*La Gioconda*	It.	dramatic baritone	50	Italian Romantic
Ah, se fosse intorno al trono	*La clemenza di Tito*	It.	lyric	30	Classical
Ah sì, ben mio; coll'essere	*Il trovatore*	It.	spinto	98	Italian Romantic
Ah, sweet Jesus, spare me this agony	*The Saint of Bleecker Street*	Eng.	lyric	51	20th-century America
Ain't it a pretty night?	*Susannah*	Eng.	lyric	53	20th-century American
Al suon del tamburo	*La forza del destino*	It.	lyric	29	Italian Romantic
Albert the Good!/ Heaven helps those who help themselves!	*Albert Herring*	Eng.	leggiero	1	20th-century English
All that gold!	*Amahl and the Night Visitors*	Eng.	dramatic	55	20th-century American
Allor che i forti corrono	*Attila*	It.	dramatic coloratura	59	Italian Romantic
Als Büblein klein	*Die lustigen Weiber von Windsor*	Ger.	bass-baritone	76	German Romantic
Always through the changing	*The Ballad of Baby Doe*	Eng.	lyric	29	20th-century American
Am stillen Herd	*Die Meister-singer von Nürnberg*	Ger.	dramatic	101	German Romantic
Amici, in ogni evento . . . Pensa alla patria	*L'italiana in Algeri*	It.	lyric coloratura	8	Bel canto
Amor ti vieta	*Fedora*	It.	spinto	90	Italian Romantic
Amore o grillo	*Madama Butterfly*	It.	spinto	93	Verismo
Amour! Viens aider ma faiblesse!	*Samson et Dalila*	Fr.	dramatic	83	French Romantic
Anch'io dischiuso un giorno	*Nabucco*	It.	dramatic coloratura	69	Italian Romantic
And where is the one who will mourn me	*Down in the Valley*	Eng.	lyric	36	20th-century American
Aprite un po' quegl'occhi	*Le nozze di Figaro*	It.	bass-baritone	78	Classical
Augusta! How can you turn away?	*The Ballad of Baby Doe*	Eng.	dramatic	56	20th-century American
Avancez! Reculez!	*Cendrillon*	Fr.	contralto	88	French Romantic
Avant de quitter ces lieux	*Faust*	Fr.	lyric baritone (dramatic)	24	French Romantic
Ave Maria	*Otello*	It.	full lyric	83	Italian Romantic
Batti, batti	*Don Giovanni*	It.	soubrette	17	Classical
Be not afeard	*The Tempest*	Eng.	dramatic	102	20th-century American

Aria Title	Opera Title	Lang.	Fach	No.	Historical Style
Bel raggio lusinghier	*Semiramide*	It.	lyric coloratura	15	Bel canto
Bella siccome un angelo	*Don Pasquale*	It.	lyric baritone	18	Bel canto
The Black Swan	*The Medium*	Eng.	lyric	46	20th-century American
Blow ye the trumpet	*John Brown*	Eng.	lyric	31	20th-century American
Cara sposa	*Rinaldo*	It.	lyric coloratura	13	Italian Baroque
Carlo, ch'è sol il nostro amore	*Don Carlo*	It.	lyric baritone	12	Italian Romantic
Caro nome	*Rigoletto*	It.	lyric (coloratura)	49	Italian Romantic
Casta diva	*Norma*	It.	dramatic	103	Bel canto
Chacun le sait	*La fille du régiment*	Fr.	lyric coloratura	6	Bel canto
Che farò senza Euridice?	*Orfeo ed Euridice*	It.	lyric	42	Italian Baroque
Che gelida manina	*La bohème*	It.	lyric	28	Verismo
Che non avrebbe il misero	*Attila*	It.	lyric	22	Italian Romantic
Ch'ella mi creda libero e lontano	*La fanciulla del West*	It.	spinto	89	Verismo
Chi il bel sogno di Doretta	*La rondine*	It.	lyric	50	Verismo
Chiudi il labbro	*I due Foscari*	It.	spinto	87	Italian Romantic
Come dal ciel precipita	*Macbeth*	It.	bass	91	Italian Romantic
Com'è gentil la notte	*Don Pasquale*	It.	lyric	35	Bel canto
Come paride vezzoso	*L'elisir d'amore*	It.	lyric baritone	20	Bel canto
Come scoglio	*Così fan tutte*	It.	dramatic coloratura	62	Classical
Come un bel dì di maggio	*Andrea Chénier*	It.	spinto	82	Verismo
Come un'ape ne'giorni d'aprile	*La Cenerentola*	It.	lyric baritone	8	Bel canto
Compiacente a' colloqui del cicisbeo . . . Son sessant'anni	*Andrea Chénier*	It.	dramatic baritone	42	Verismo
Con un' vezzo all'Italiana	*La finta giardiniera*	It.	lyric baritone	25	Classical
Condotta ell'era in ceppi	*Il trovatore*	It.	dramatic	86	Italian Romantic
Connais-tu le pays?	*Mignon*	Fr.	lyric	38	French Romantic
Cruda sorte	*L'italiana in Algeri*	It.	lyric coloratura	9	Bel canto
Dagl'immortali vertici	*Attila*	It.	dramatic baritone	44	Italian Romantic
Dal labbro il canto	*Falstaff*	It.	leggiero	13	Italian Romantic

Aria Title	Opera Title	Lang.	Fach	No.	Historical Style
Dal più remoto esilio	*I due Foscari*	It.	spinto	88	Italian Romantic
Dalla sua pace	*Don Giovanni*	It.	leggiero	8	Classical
Dalle stanze ove Lucia	*Lucia di Lammermoor*	It.	bass-baritone	75	Bel canto
De son coeur j'ai calmé la fièvre (Berceuse)	*Mignon*	Fr.	bass	94	French Romantic
Dear boy	*Candide*	Eng.	lyric baritone	7	20th-century American
Dearest Amelia	*Amelia Goes to the Ball/ Amelia al ballo*	Eng.	lyric baritone	2	20th-century American/ Italian
Dearest Mama	*The Ballad of Baby Doe*	Eng.	lyric	30	20th-century American
Deh per questo istante solo	*La clemenza di Tito*	It.	lyric coloratura	6	Classical
Deh vieni alla finestra	*Don Giovanni*	It.	lyric baritone (dramatic)	14	Classical
Dei miei bollenti spiriti	*La traviata*	It.	lyric	77	Italian Romantic
Dein ist mein ganzes Herz	*Das Land des Lächelns*	Ger.	lyric	51	Viennese Operetta
Del più sublime soglio	*La clemenza di Tito*	It.	lyric	31	Classical
Della crudel Isotta	*L'elisir d'amore*	It.	soubrette	19	Bel canto
Der Hölle Rache kocht in meinem Herzen	*Die Zauber-flöte*	Ger.	dramatic coloratura	72	Singspiel
Der kleine Taumann heiss' ich	*Hänsel und Gretel*	Ger.	lyric (soubrette)	41	German Romantic
Der Vogelfänger bin ich ja	*Die Zauberflöte*	Ger.	lyric baritone	37	Singspiel
Di due figli vivea	*Il trovatore*	It.	bass-baritone	82	Italian Romantic
Di Provenza il mar	*La traviata*	It.	dramatic baritone	63	Italian Romantic
Di quella pira	*Il trovatore*	It.	spinto	99	Italian Romantic
Di te mi rido	*Alcina*	It.	lyric coloratura	1	Italian Baroque
Dich such' ich Bild!	*Die tote Stadt*	Ger.	spinto	92	20th-century German
Dich teure Halle	*Tannhäuser*	Ger.	dramatic	104	German Romantic
Dies Bildnis ist bezaubernd schön	*Die Zauberflöte*	Ger.	lyric	81	Singspiel
Do I not draw tears from your eyes?	*Too Many Sopranos*	Eng.	contralto	98	20th-century American
Do not utter a word	*Vanessa*	Eng.	spinto	94	20th-century American
Do you wish we had wed?	*Regina*	Eng.	lyric	44	20th-century American

Aria Title	Opera Title	Lang.	Fach	No.	Historical Style
Donde lieta	*La bohème*	It.	lyric	34	Verismo
Donna non vidi mai	*Manon Lescaut*	It.	spinto	94	Verismo
Donne mie la fate a tanti	*Così fan tutte*	It.	lyric baritone	10	Classical
Donnez, donnez	*Le prophète*	Fr.	dramatic	78	French Romantic
Dry those eyes	*The Tempest*	Eng.	lyric	50	English Baroque
Du bist der Lenz	*Die Walküre*	Ger.	dramatic	106	German Romantic
Durch die Wälder	*Der Freischütz*	Ger.	spinto	92	German Romantic
Èla solita storia del pastore	*L'arlesiana*	It.	spinto	84	Verismo
E lucevan le stelle	*Tosca*	It.	spinto	96	Verismo
E sogno? O realtà?	*Falstaff*	It.	lyric baritone (dramatic)	23	Italian Romantic
E Susanna non vien! . . . Dove sono	*Le nozze di Figaro*	It.	full lyric	81	Classical
Ebben! Ne andrò lontana	*La Wally*	It.	spinto	95	Verismo
Ecco ridente in cielo	*Il barbiere di Siviglia*	It.	leggiero	4	Bel canto
Eccomi in lieta vesta . . . Oh! Quante volte, Oh! Quante	*I Capuletti e i Montecchi*	It.	lyric coloratura	3	Bel canto
E'gettata la mia sorte	*Attila*	It.	dramatic baritone	45	Italian Romantic
Ein Mädchen oder Weibchen	*Die Zauber-flöte*	Ger.	lyric baritone	38	Singspiel
Ella giammai m'amò	*Don Carlo*	It.	bass-baritone	68	Italian Romantic
Ella mi fu rapita . . . Parmi veder le lagrime	*Rigoletto*	It.	lyric	65	Italian Romantic
Elle a fui, la tourterelle	*Les contes d'Hoffmann*	Fr.	lyric	38	French Romantic
En fermant les yeux (Le Rêve)	*Manon*	Fr.	lyric	56	French Romantic
En vain pour éviter (Card Aria)	*Carmen*	Fr.	dramatic	60	French Romantic
Entweihte Götter!	*Lohengrin*	Ger.	dramatic	73	German Romantic
Épouse quelque brave fille	*Manon*	Fr.	bass	92	French Romantic
Ernani, Ernani involami	*Ernani*	It.	dramatic coloratura	66	Italian Romantic
Es gibt ein Reich	*Ariadne auf Naxos*	Ger.	dramatic	98	20th-century German
Es lebt' eine Vilja, ein Waldmägdelein (Vilja's Lied)	*Die lustige Witwe*	Ger.	lyric (full lyric)	43	Viennese Operetta
Eterna la memoria	*Alzira*	It.	dramatic baritone	40	Italian Romantic

Aria Title	Opera Title	Lang.	Fach	No.	Historical Style
Everyday at church	*Tartuffe*	Eng.	bass	98	20th-century American
Fair Robin I love	*Tartuffe*	Eng.	soubrette (lyric coloratura)	25	20th-century American
Faites-lui mes aveux	*Faust*	Fr.	lyric	27	French Romantic
Fantaisie aux divins mensonges	*Lakmé*	Fr.	leggiero	15	French Romantic
Fin ch'han dal vino	*Don Giovanni*	It.	lyric baritone (dramatic)	15	Classical
Firenze è come un albero fiorito	*Gianni Schicchi*	It.	lyric	45	20th-century Italian
Franco son io	*Giovanna d'Arco*	It.	dramatic baritone	51	Italian Romantic
Frisch zum Kampfe!	*Die Entführung aus dem Serail*	Ger.	lyric	38	Singspiel
Gerechter Gott	*Rienzi*	Ger.	lyric (dramatic)	45	German Romantic
Già di pietà mi spoglio	*Mitridate, re di Ponto*	It.	leggiero	17	Classical
Giunse alfin il momento . . . Deh vieni, non tardar	*Le nozze di Figaro*	It.	soubrette	24	Classical
Give him this orchid	*The Rape of Lucretia*	Eng.	dramatic	80	20th-century English
Glück, das mir verblieb (Marietta's Lied)	*Die tote Stadt*	Ger.	spinto	93	20th-century German
God o' mercy	*Billy Budd*	Eng.	lyric	24	20th-century English
Hai già vinta la causa . . . Vendro mentr'io sospiro	*Le nozze di Figaro*	It.	lyric baritone (dramatic)	30	Classical
Hat man nicht auch Gold beineben	*Fidelio*	Ger.	bass-baritone	70	German Romantic
Have you seen her, Samantha?	*The Ballad of Baby Doe*	Eng.	dramatic	57	20th-century American
Hello, hello? Oh, Margaret, it's you	*The Telephone*	Eng.	lyric	55	20th-century American
Here I stand . . . Since it is not by merit	*The Rake's Progress*	Eng.	lyric	61	20th-century English
Ho capito, signor, si	*Don Giovanni*	It.	lyric baritone	16	Classical
Ho un gran peso	*L'italiana in Algeri*	It.	lyric baritone (bass-baritone)	29	Bel canto
Hold on a moment, dear	*Tartuffe*	Eng.	lyric	49	20th-century American
Horch, die Lerche singt im Hain!	*Die lustigen Weiber von Windsor*	Ger.	lyric	53	German Romantic

Aria Title	Opera Title	Lang.	Fach	No.	Historical Style
I accept their verdict	*Billy Budd*	Eng.	lyric	25	20th-century English
I am an old man	*Billy Budd*	Eng.	lyric	26	20th-century English
I do not judge you, John	*The Crucible*	Eng.	dramatic	65	20th-century American
I know a bank where the wild thyme grows	*A Midsummer Night's Dream*	Eng.	contralto	97	20th-century English
I know that you all hate me	*The Saint of Bleecker Street*	Eng.	lyric	71	20th-century American
I shall find for you (Lullaby)	*The Consul*	Eng.	contralto	90	20th-century American
I thought I heard a distant bird	*Gallantry*	Eng.	lyric	43	20th-century American
I want magic!	*A Streetcar Named Desire*	Eng.	full lyric	85	20th-century American
Ich habe keine gute Nächte	*Elektra*	Ger.	dramatic	68	20th-century German
Ich lade gern mir Gäste ein	*Die Fleder-maus*	Ger.	lyric	28	Viennese Operetta
Il balen del suo sorriso	*Il trovatore*	It.	dramatic baritone	64	Italian Romantic
Il cavallo scalpita	*Cavalleria rusticana*	It.	dramatic baritone	47	Verismo
Il dolce suono mi colpì di sua voce (Mad Scene)	*Lucia di Lammermoor*	It.	dramatic coloratura	67	Bel canto
Il est doux, il est bon	*Hérodiade*	Fr.	full lyric	78	French Romantic
Il était une fois à la cour d'Eisenach	*Les contes d'Hoffmann*	Fr.	lyric	32	French Romantic
Il lacerato spirito	*Simon Boccanegra*	It.	bass (dramatic)	96	Italian Romantic
Il mio tesoro	*Don Giovanni*	It.	leggiero	9	Classical
Il segreto per esser felici	*Lucrezia Borgia*	It.	contralto	95	Bel canto
Il vecchiotto cerca moglie	*Il barbiere di Siviglia*	It.	lyric	21	Bel canto
Illustratevi, o cieli	*Il ritorno di Ulisse in patria*	It.	lyric	46	Italian Baroque
I'm not a boy, she says	*A Streetcar Named Desire*	Eng.	spinto	95	20th-century American
In quelle trine morbide	*Manon Lescaut*	It.	spinto	89	Verismo
In questa reggia	*Turandot*	It.	dramatic	105	20th-century Italian
In si barbara	*Semiramide*	It.	lyric coloratura	16	Bel canto
In uomini, in soldati	*Così fan tutte*	It.	soubrette	15	Classical
Infelice! E tuo credevi	*Ernani*	It.	bass-baritone	69	Italian Romantic
Inkslinger's Song	*Paul Bunyan*	Eng.	lyric	59	20th-century English

Aria Title	Opera Title	Lang.	Fach	No.	Historical Style
Inutiles regrets	*Les Troyens*	Fr.	spinto	100	French Romantic
Io seguo sol fiero	*Partenope*	It.	lyric coloratura	11	Italian Baroque
It must be so	*Candide*	Eng.	lyric	29	20th-century American
It's about the way people is made	*Susannah*	Eng.	lyric	74	20th-century American
I've dined so well (Tipsy Waltz)	*La Périchole*	Eng.	lyric	43	French Romantic
I've got a ram, Goliath	*The Devil and Daniel Webster*	Eng.	bass-baritone	67	20th-century American
Ja nye sposobna k grusti tomnoy	*Eugene Onegin*	Russ.	contralto	92	Russian Romantic
J'ai pu frapper	*Hamlet*	Fr.	lyric baritone (dramatic)	26	French Romantic
Je crois entendre encore	*Les pêcheurs de perles*	Fr.	lyric	60	French Romantic
Je dis que rien ne m'épouvante	*Carmen*	Fr.	lyric	37	French Romantic
Je suis Titania	*Mignon*	Fr.	lyric coloratura	11	French Romantic
Je veux vivre dans ce rêve	*Roméo et Juliette*	Fr.	lyric coloratura	14	French Romantic
Jehosophat!	*McTeague*	Eng.	dramatic baritone	60	20th-century American
Kennst du das Land?	*Little Women*	Ger.	bass-baritone	73	20th-century American
Kiss me not goodbye	*The Mighty Casey*	Eng.	lyric (soprano)	37	20th-century American
Klänge der Heimat (Czàrdàs)	*Die Fledermaus*	Ger.	full lyric	77	Viennese Operetta
Kogda bi zhizn domashnim krugom	*Eugene Onegin*	Russ.	lyric baritone (dramatic)	21	Russian Romantic
Kuda, kuda, kuda, vy udalilis	*Eugene Onegin*	Russ.	lyric	39	Russian Romantic
La callunia	*Il barbiere di Siviglia*	It.	bass (lyric)	84	Bel canto
La donna è mobile	*Rigoletto*	It.	lyric	66	Italian Romantic
La fleur que tu m'avais jetée	*Carmen*	Fr.	spinto	86	French Romantic
La luce langue	*Macbeth*	It.	dramatic	74	Italian Romantic
La sua lampada vitale	*I masnadieri*	It.	dramatic baritone	59	Italian Romantic
L'amour est un oiseau (Habañera)	*Carmen*	Fr.	dramatic	61	French Romantic
L'angue offeso	*Giulio Cesare*	It.	lyric	46	Italian Baroque
Languir per una bella	*L'italiana in Algeri*	It.	lyric	49	Bel canto

Aria Title	Opera Title	Lang.	Fach	No.	Historical Style
Largo al factotum	*Il barbiere di Siviglia*	It.	lyric baritone	4	Bel canto
Les oiseaux dans la charmille	*Les contes d'Hoffmann*	Fr.	lyric coloratura	4	French Romantic
Les tringles des sistres tintaient	*Carmen*	Fr.	dramatic	62	French Romantic
Lieben, Hassen, Hoffen, Zagen	*Ariadne auf Naxos*	Ger.	lyric baritone	3	20th-century German
Light of my soul	*The Song of Majnun*	Eng.	lyric	72	20th-century American
Lo vidi e 'l primo palpito	*Luisa Miller*	It.	full lyric	79	Italian Romantic
Lonely House	*Street Scene*	Eng.	lyric	73	20th-century American
Look, through the port comes the moon-shine astray	*Billy Budd*	Eng.	lyric baritone	5	20th-century English
L'orage s'est calmé	*Les pêcheurs de perles*	Fr.	lyric baritone	32	French Romantic
Lorsqu'on a plus de vingt quartiers	*Cendrillon*	Fr.	contralto	89	French Romantic
Lost in the Stars	*Lost in the Stars*	Eng.	bass-baritone	74	20th-century American
Love, too frequently betrayed	*The Rake's Progress*	Eng.	lyric	62	20th-century English
Lyubvi vse vozrastï pokornï	*Eugene Onegin*	Russ.	bass	87	Russian Romantic
Ma quando tornerai	*Alcina*	It.	lyric	26	Italian Baroque
Ma se m'è forza perderti	*Un ballo in maschera*	It.	spinto	85	Italian Romantic
Mab, la reine des mensonges	*Roméo et Juliette*	Fr.	lyric baritone	34	French Romantic
Madame Pompous's Audition	*Too Many Sopranos*	Eng.	full lyric (spinto)	86	20th-century American
Madamina! Il catalogo è questo	*Don Giovanni*	It.	bass (buffo)	86	Classical
Me voici dans son boudoir	*Mignon*	Fr.	lyric	39	French Romantic
Mein Herr Marquis	*Die Fleder-maus*	Ger.	soubrette	23	Viennese Operetta
Mein Sehnen, mein Wähnen (Pierrot's Tanzlied)	*Die tote Stadt*	Ger.	lyric baritone	36	20th-century German
Mercè, dilette amiche	*I vespri siciliani*	It.	dramatic coloratura	71	Italian Romantic
Metà di voi quà vadano	*Don Giovanni*	It.	lyric baritone (dramatic)	17	Classical
Mi chiamano Mimì	*La bohème*	It.	lyric	35	Verismo
Mia madre aveva una povera ancella (Willow Song)	*Otello*	It.	full lyric	84	Italian Romantic
Minnie, dalla mia casa son partito	*La fanciulla del West*	It.	dramatic baritone	48	Verismo

Aria Title	Opera Title	Lang.	Fach	No.	Historical Style
O du, mein holder Abendstern	*Tannhäuser*	Ger.	lyric baritone (dramatic)	35	German Romantic
O lieto augurio	*Macbeth*	It.	dramatic baritone	58	Italian Romantic
O mio babbino caro	*Gianni Schicchi*	It.	lyric	40	20th-century Italian
O mio Fernando	*La favorita*	It.	dramatic	69	Bel canto
O paradis sorti de l'onde	*L'Africaine*	Fr.	lyric	21	Italian Romantic
O patria mia	*Aida*	It.	dramatic	96	Italian Romantic
O tu che in seno agli angeli	*La forza del destino*	It.	spinto	91	Italian Romantic
O tu Palermo	*I vespri siciliani*	It.	bass	99	Italian Romantic
O vin dissipe la tristesse	*Hamlet*	Fr.	lyric baritone (dramatic)	27	French Romantic
O wär' ich schon mit dir vereint	*Fidelio*	Ger.	lyric (soubrette)	39	German Romantic
O wie ängstlich	*Die Entführung aus dem Serail*	Ger.	leggiero	12	Singspiel
O zittre nicht . . . Zum Leiden bin ich auserkoren	*Die Zauberflöte*	Ger.	dramatic coloratura	73	Singspiel
Oh, don't you see that lonesome dove?	*Down in the Valley*	Eng.	lyric (soprano)	26	20th-century American
Oh! Nel fuggente nuvolo	*Attila*	It.	dramatic coloratura	60	Italian Romantic
Oh, patria! Dolce, e ingrate patria! . . . tu que accendi questo core	*Tancredi*	It.	lyric coloratura	18	Bel canto
Oh, the lion may roar (Aria of the Worm)	*The Ghosts of Versailles*	Eng.	lyric	44	20th-century American
Oh, what a lovely ballroom this is!	*The Consul*	Eng.	leggiero	6	20th-century American
Ombra mai fu	*Serse (Xerxes)*	It.	lyric	48	Italian Baroque
Où va la jeune Hindoue (Bell Song)	*Lakmé*	Fr.	lyric coloratura	10	French Romantic
Outside this house	*Vanessa*	Eng.	lyric	78	20th-century American
Pace, pace mio Dio!	*La forza del destino*	It.	spinto	88	Italian Romantic
Parto, parto	*La clemenza di Tito*	It.	lyric coloratura	7	Classical
Per lui che adoro	*L'italiana in Algeri*	It.	lyric coloratura	10	Bel canto
Per me giunto . . . Io morrò, ma lieto in core	*Don Carlo*	It.	lyric baritone	13	Italian Romantic

Aria Title	Opera Title	Lang.	Fach	No.	Historical Style
Per pietà	*Così fan tutte*	It.	dramatic coloratura	63	Classical
Per questa fiamma indomita	*Anna Bolena*	It.	lyric coloratura	4	Bel canto
Piangerò la sorte mia	*Giulio Cesare*	It.	lyric coloratura	7	Italian Baroque
Porgi amor	*Le nozze di Figaro*	It.	full lyric	82	Classical
Possente amor mi chiama	*Rigoletto*	It.	lyric	67	Italian Romantic
Pour les couvents c'est fini	*Les Huguenots*	Fr.	bass-baritone	72	French Romantic
Pourquoi me réveiller	*Werther*	Fr.	lyric	80	French Romantic
Prendi; prendi, per me sei libero	*L'elisir d'amore*	It.	soubrette	20	Bel canto
Près des remparts de Séville (Seguidilla)	*Carmen*	Fr.	dramatic	63	French Romantic
Presti omai l'egizia terra	*Giulio Cesare*	It.	dramatic baritone (bass)	52	Italian Baroque
Printemps qui commence	*Samson et Dalila*	Fr.	dramatic	85	French Romantic
Priva son d'ogni conforto	*Giulio Cesare*	It.	contralto	94	Italian Baroque
Qual fiamma avea nel guardo!	*I Pagliacci*	It.	lyric	48	Verismo
Quando le sere al placido	*Luisa Miller*	It.	leggiero	16	Italian Romantic
Quando m'en vo' (Musetta's Waltz)	*La bohème*	It.	lyric	36	Verismo
Quanto è bella	*L'elisir d'amore*	It.	leggiero	10	Bel canto
Quanto un mortal può chiedere	*Alzira*	It.	dramatic baritone	41	Italian Romantic
Que fais-tu, blanche tourterelle	*Roméo et Juliette*	Fr.	lyric	47	French Romantic
Quel guardo il cavaliere . . . So anch'io la virtù magica	*Don Pasquale*	It.	lyric coloratura	5	Bel canto
Quel mesto gemito	*Semiramide*	It.	lyric coloratura	17	Bel canto
Quel ribelle e quell'ingrato	*Mitridate, re di Ponto*	It.	leggiero	18	Classical
Quel volto mi piace	*Partenope*	It.	lyric coloratura	12	Italian Baroque
Questa o quella	*Rigoletto*	It.	lyric	68	Italian Romantic
Questo amor, vergogna mia	*Edgar*	It.	lyric baritone	19	Verismo
Qui donc commande	*Henry VIII*	Fr.	dramatic baritone	55	French Romantic
Qui la voce . . . Vien, diletto	*I puritani*	It.	lyric coloratura	13	Italian Romantic

Aria Title	Opera Title	Lang.	Fach	No.	Historical Style
Rachel, quand du Seigneur	*La Juive*	Fr.	lyric	50	Italian Romantic
Re dell'abisso, affrettati (Invocation Aria)	*Un ballo in maschera*	It.	dramatic	58	Italian Romantic
Recondita armonia	*Tosca*	It.	spinto	97	Verismo
Regnava nel silenzio	*Lucia di Lammermoor*	It.	dramatic coloratura	68	Bel canto
Ritorna vincitor!	*Aida*	It.	dramatic	97	Italian Romantic
Rosa del ciel	*L'Orfeo*	It.	leggiero	20	Italian Baroque
Ruskai pogibnu (Letter Scene)	*Eugene Onegin*	Russ.	full lyric	75	Russian Romantic
Salut! Demeure chaste et pure	*Faust*	Fr.	lyric	40	French Romantic
Saper vorreste	*Un ballo in maschera*	It.	lyric coloratura	1	Italian Romantic
Scherza infida	*Ariodante*	It.	leggiero	3	Italian Baroque
Schweig'! Schweig'! damit dich niemand warnt	*Der Freischütz*	Ger.	bass-baritone	71	German Romantic
Scintille, diamant	*Les contes d'Hoffmann*	Fr.	lyric baritone (dramatic)	9	French Romantic
Scorned! Abused! Neglected!	*The Rake's Progress*	Eng.	dramatic	79	20th-century English
Se di lauri	*Mitridate, re di Ponto*	It.	leggiero	19	Classical
Se vuol ballare	*Le nozze di Figaro*	It.	bass-baritone	80	Classical
Senza mamma	*Suor Angelica*	It.	spinto	90	Verismo
Sgombra è la sacra selva . . . Deh! Proteggimi, O Dio!	*Norma*	It.	dramatic	76	Bel canto
Si la rigueur	*La Juive*	Fr.	bass	90	French Romantic
Sì! Morir ella de'!	*La Gioconda*	It.	bass (dramatic)	89	Italian Romantic
Si può?	*I Pagliacci*	It.	dramatic baritone	61	Verismo
Sì, ritrovarla io giuro	*La Cenerentola*	It.	leggiero	5	Bel canto
Signore, ascolta	*Turandot*	It.	lyric	56	20th-century Italian
The Silver Aria	*The Ballad of Baby Doe*	Eng.	lyric	31	20th-century American
Skuchno Marine, akh kak skuchno-to!	*Boris Godunov*	Russ.	dramatic	59	Russian Nationalist
Smanie implacabili	*Così fan tutte*	It.	lyric	23	Classical
Sois immobile	*Guillaume Tell*	Fr.	dramatic baritone	53	French Romantic
Sombre forêt	*Guillaume Tell*	Fr.	lyric coloratura (dramatic)	9	French Romantic

Aria Title	Opera Title	Lang.	Fach	No.	Historical Style
Someday I'm sure to marry you	*The Sojourner and Mollie Sinclair*	Eng.	lyric	52	20th-century American
Son pochi fiori	*L'amico Fritz*	It.	lyric	28	Verismo
Soon now my dearest	*The Bartered Bride*	Eng.	lyric	23	Czech Nationalist
Spectre infernal!	*Hamlet*	Fr.	lyric baritone (dramatic)	28	French Romantic
Spirto gentil	*La favorita*	It.	lyric	41	Bel canto
Stà nell'Ircana pietrosa tana	*Alcina*	It.	lyric coloratura	2	Italian Baroque
Steal me, sweet thief	*The Old Maid and the Thief*	Eng.	lyric	47	20th-century American
Stella del marinar	*La Gioconda*	It.	dramatic	70	Italian Romantic
Stranger and darker	*The Ice Break*	Eng.	dramatic	71	20th-century English
Stride la vampa	*Il trovatore*	It.	dramatic	87	Italian Romantic
Suicidio!	*La Gioconda*	It.	dramatic	100	Italian Romantic
Sul fil d'un soffio etesio	*Falstaff*	It.	soubrette	22	Italian Romantic
Svegliatevi nel core	*Giulio Cesare*	It.	lyric	47	Italian Baroque
Tacea la notte	*Il trovatore*	It.	full lyric	87	Italian Romantic
Tandis qu'il sommeille	*La Juive*	Fr.	lyric	42	French Romantic
Tarquinius does not wait	*The Rape of Lucretia*	Eng.	lyric	64	20th-century English
Temer? Perchè?	*Andrea Chénier*	It.	lyric	20	Verismo
The same, old room	*Regina*	Eng.	bass-baritone	81	20th-century American
The trees on the mountain are cold and bare	*Susannah*	Eng.	lyric	54	20th-century American
Things change, Jo	*Little Women*	Eng.	lyric	32	20th-century American
This is my box	*Amahl and the Night Visitors*	Eng.	leggiero	2	20th-century American
Tickling a trout, poaching a hare	*Albert Herring*	Eng.	lyric baritone	1	20th-century English
To this we've come (Paper Aria)	*The Consul*	Eng.	full lyric	74	20th-century American
Tombe degl' avi miei . . . Fra poco a me ricovero	*Lucia di Lammermoor*	It.	lyric	52	Bel canto
Tradito, schernito	*Così fan tutte*	It.	lyric	34	Classical
Tu che di gel sei cinta	*Turandot*	It.	lyric	57	20th-century Italian

Aria Title	Opera Title	Lang.	Fach	No.	Historical Style
Tu punischimi, o signore . . . a brani, a brani o perfido	*Luisa Miller*	It.	full lyric	80	Italian Romantic
Tu sul labbro	*Nabucco*	It.	bass	95	Italian Romantic
Un dì, all'azzurro spazio	*Andrea Chénier*	It.	spinto	83	Verismo
Un ignoto, tre lune or saranno	*I masnadieri*	It.	bass	93	Italian Romantic
Una donna a quindici anni	*Così fan tutte*	It.	soubrette	16	Classical
Una furtiva lagrima	*L'elisir d'amore*	It.	leggiero	11	Bel canto
Una macchia è qui tuttora!	*Macbeth*	It.	dramatic (mezzo-soprano)	101	Italian Romantic
Una voce poco fa	*Il barbiere di Siviglia*	It.	lyric	22	Bel canto
Un'aura amorosa	*Così fan tutte*	It.	leggiero	7	Classical
Uzhel ta samaja Tatiana	*Eugene Onegin*	Russ.	lyric baritone (dramatic)	22	Russian Romantic
Va! Laisse couler mes larmes	*Werther*	Fr.	lyric	52	French Romantic
Va pur, va pur, va seco	*La Calisto*	It.	lyric baritone	6	Italian Baroque
V'adoro, pupille	*Giulio Cesare*	It.	lyric coloratura	8	Italian Baroque
Vainement, ma bien-aimée	*Le roi d'Ys*	Fr.	lyric	69	French Romantic
Vary the song, o London, change	*The Rake's Progress*	Eng.	lyric	63	20th-century English
Vecchia zimarra	*La bohème*	It.	bass (lyric)	85	Verismo
Vedrai carino	*Don Giovanni*	It.	soubrette	18	Classical
Venti, turbini, prestate	*Rinaldo*	It.	lyric coloratura	14	Italian Baroque
Verdi prati e selve amene	*Alcina*	It.	lyric coloratura	3	Italian Baroque
Ves' tabor spit	*Aleko*	Russ.	bass-baritone	65	Russian Romantic
Vi ravviso	*La sonnambula*	It.	bass	97	Bel canto
Vieni! T'affretta . . . Or tutti, sorgete	*Macbeth*	It.	dramatic (mezzo-soprano)	102	Italian Romantic
Vision fugitive	*Hérodiade*	Fr.	dramatic baritone	56	French Romantic
Vissi d'arte	*Tosca*	It.	spinto	91	Verismo
Voce di donna o d'angelo	*La Gioconda*	It.	contralto	93	Italian Romantic
Voi che sapete	*Le nozze di Figaro*	It.	lyric	41	Classical
Voi lo sapete, o mamma	*Cavalleria rusticana*	It.	dramatic	64	Verismo

Aria Title	Opera Title	Lang.	Fach	No.	Historical Style
Voilà donc la terrible cité	*Thaïs*	Fr.	dramatic baritone	62	French Romantic
Volta la terrea	*Un ballo in maschera*	It.	lyric coloratura	2	Italian Romantic
Votre toast, je peux vous le render	*Carmen*	Fr.	dramatic baritone	46	French Romantic
Vous qui faites l'endormie	*Faust*	Fr.	bass (dramatic)	88	French Romantic
Warm as the autumn light	*The Ballad of Baby Doe*	Eng.	bass-baritone	66	20th-century American
We cannot retrace our steps	*The Mother of Us All*	Eng.	dramatic	75	20th-century American
We committed his body to the deep	*Billy Budd*	Eng.	lyric	27	20th-century English
Welche Wonne, welche Lust	*Die Entfüh-rung aus dem Serail*	Ger.	soubrette	21	Singspiel
Wenn der Freude Tränen fliessen	*Die Entfüh-rung aus dem Serail*	Ger.	lyric	37	Singspiel
Werther, Werther (Letter Aria)	*Werther*	Fr.	lyric	53	French Romantic
We've always known each other	*The Wings of the Dove*	Eng.	lyric	54	20th-century American
What am I forbidden?	*Lizzie Borden*	Eng.	lyric (dramatic)	33	20th-century American
What what is it?	*The Mother of Us All*	Eng.	bass-baritone	77	20th-century American
When I am laid in earth	*Dido and Aeneas*	Eng.	contralto	91	English Baroque
When the air sings of summer	*The Old Maid and the Thief*	Eng.	lyric baritone	31	20th-century American
While I waste these precious hours	*Amelia Goes to the Ball/ Amelia al ballo*	Eng.	lyric	27	20th-century American/ Italian
Wie du warst!	*Der Rosen-kavalier*	Ger.	dramatic	81	20th-century German
Willow Song	*The Ballad of Baby Doe*	Eng.	lyric	32	20th-century American
Wo in Bergen du dich birgst	*Die Walküre*	Ger.	contralto	99	German Romantic
Yes! I am she!	*Madame Mao*	Eng.	lyric (dramatic)	34	20th-century American
You rascal, you! I never knew you had a soul!	*Vanessa*	Eng.	bass-baritone	83	20th-century American
Zazà, piccolo zingara	*Zazà*	It.	lyric baritone	39	Verismo

Index B
Arias by Opera

Opera Title	Aria Title	Lang.	Fach	No.	Historical Style
Adriana Lecouvreur	Acerba voluttà	It.	lyric	19	Verismo
L'Africaine	O paradis sorti de l'onde	Fr.	lyric	21	Italian Romantic
Aida	O patria mia	It.	dramatic	96	Italian Romantic
Aida	Ritorna vincitor!	It.	dramatic	97	Italian Romantic
Albert Herring	Albert the Good!/ Heaven helps those who help themselves!	Eng.	leggiero	1	20th-century English
Albert Herring	Tickling a trout, poaching a hare	Eng.	lyric baritone	1	20th-century English
Alcina	Di te mi rido	It.	lyric coloratura	1	Italian Baroque
Alcina	Ma quando tornerai	It.	lyric	26	Italian Baroque
Alcina	Stà nell'Ircana pietrosa tana	It.	lyric coloratura	2	Italian Baroque
Alcina	Verdi prati e selve amene	It.	lyric coloratura	3	Italian Baroque
Aleko	Ves' tabor spit	Russ.	bass-baritone	65	Russian Romantic
Alzira	Eterna la memoria	It.	dramatic baritone	40	Italian Romantic
Alzira	Quanto un mortal può chiedere	It.	dramatic baritone	41	Italian Romantic
Amahl and the Night Visitors	All that gold!	Eng.	dramatic	55	20th-century American
Amahl and the Night Visitors	This is my box	Eng.	leggiero	2	20th-century American
Amelia Goes to the Ball/ Amelia al ballo	Dearest Amelia	Eng.	lyric baritone	2	20th-century American/ Italian
Amelia Goes to the Ball/ Amelia al ballo	While I waste these precious hours	Eng.	lyric	27	20th-century American/ Italian
L'amico Fritz	Son pochi fiori	It.	lyric	28	Verismo
Andrea Chénier	Come un bel dì di maggio	It.	spinto	82	Verismo
Andrea Chénier	Compiacente a' colloqui del cicisbeo . . . Son sessant'anni	It.	dramatic baritone	42	Verismo
Andrea Chénier	Nemico della patria	It.	dramatic baritone	43	Verismo
Andrea Chénier	Temer? Perchè?	It.	lyric	20	Verismo

Opera Title	Aria Title	Lang.	Fach	No.	Historical Style
Andrea Chénier	Un dì, all'azzurro spazio	It.	spinto	83	Verismo
Anna Bolena	Per questa fiamma indomita	It.	lyric coloratura	4	Bel canto
Ariadne auf Naxos	Es gibt ein Reich	Ger.	dramatic	98	20th-century German
Ariadne auf Naxos	Lieben, Hassen, Hoffen, Zagen	Ger.	lyric baritone	3	20th-century German
Ariodante	Scherza infida	It.	leggiero	3	Italian Baroque
L'arlesiana	È la solita storia del pastore	It.	spinto	84	Verismo
Attila	Allor che i forti corrono	It.	dramatic coloratura	59	Italian Romantic
Attila	Che non avrebbe il misero	It.	lyric	22	Italian Romantic
Attila	Dagl'immortali vertici	It.	dramatic baritone	44	Italian Romantic
Attila	E'gettata la mia sorte	It.	dramatic baritone	45	Italian Romantic
Attila	Oh! Nel fuggente nuvolo	It.	dramatic coloratura	60	Italian Romantic
The Ballad of Baby Doe	Always through the changing	Eng.	lyric	29	20th-century American
The Ballad of Baby Doe	Augusta! How can you turn away?	Eng.	dramatic	56	20th-century American
The Ballad of Baby Doe	Dearest Mama	Eng.	lyric	30	20th-century American
The Ballad of Baby Doe	Have you seen her, Samantha?	Eng.	dramatic	57	20th-century American
The Ballad of Baby Doe	The Silver Aria	Eng.	lyric	31	20th-century American
The Ballad of Baby Doe	Warm as the autumn light	Eng.	bass-baritone	66	20th-century American
The Ballad of Baby Doe	Willow Song	Eng.	lyric	32	20th-century American
Un ballo in maschera	Ma se m'è forza perderti	It.	spinto	85	Italian Romantic
Un ballo in maschera	Re dell'abisso, affrettati (Invocation Aria)	It.	dramatic	58	Italian Romantic
Un ballo in maschera	Saper vorreste	It.	lyric coloratura	1	Italian Romantic
Un ballo in maschera	Volta la terrea	It.	lyric coloratura	2	Italian Romantic
Il barbiere di Siviglia	Ecco ridente in cielo	It.	leggiero	4	Bel canto
Il barbiere di Siviglia	Il vecchiotto cerca moglie	It.	lyric	21	Bel canto
Il barbiere di Siviglia	La callunia	It.	bass (lyric)	84	Bel canto
Il barbiere di Siviglia	Largo al factotum	It.	lyric baritone	4	Bel canto
Il barbiere di Siviglia	Una voce poco fa	It.	lyric	22	Bel canto

Opera Title	Aria Title	Lang.	Fach	No.	Historical Style
The Bartered Bride	Ah, my darling, we could grow together like a single vine	Eng.	lyric	33	Czech Nationalist
The Bartered Bride	Soon now my dearest	Eng.	lyric	23	Czech Nationalist
Billy Budd	God o' mercy	Eng.	lyric	24	20th-century English
Billy Budd	I accept their verdict	Eng.	lyric	25	20th-century English
Billy Budd	I am an old man	Eng.	lyric	26	20th-century English
Billy Budd	Look, through the port comes the moonshine astray	Eng.	lyric baritone	5	20th-century English
Billy Budd	We committed his body to the deep	Eng.	lyric	27	20th-century English
La bohème	Che gelida manina	It.	lyric	28	Verismo
La bohème	Donde lieta	It.	lyric	34	Verismo
La bohème	Mi chiamano Mimì	It.	lyric	35	Verismo
La bohème	Quando m'en vo' (Musetta's Waltz)	It.	lyric	36	Verismo
La bohème	Vecchia zimarra	It.	bass (lyric)	85	Verismo
Boris Godunov	Skuchno Marine, akh kak skuchno-to!	Russ.	dramatic	59	Russian Nationalist
La Calisto	Va pur, va pur, va seco	It.	lyric baritone	6	Italian Baroque
Candide	Dear boy	Eng.	lyric baritone	7	20th-century American
Candide	It must be so	Eng.	lyric	29	20th-century American
I Capuletti e i Montecchi	Eccomi in lieta vesta . . . Oh! Quante volte, Oh! Quante	It.	lyric coloratura	3	Bel canto
Carmen	En vain pour éviter (Card Aria)	Fr.	dramatic	60	French Romantic
Carmen	Je dis que rien ne m'épouvante	Fr.	lyric	37	French Romantic
Carmen	La fleur que tu m'avais jetée	Fr.	spinto	86	French Romantic
Carmen	L'amour est un oiseau (Habañera)	Fr.	dramatic	61	French Romantic
Carmen	Les tringles des sistres tintaient	Fr.	dramatic	62	French Romantic
Carmen	Près des remparts de Séville (Seguidilla)	Fr.	dramatic	63	French Romantic
Carmen	Votre toast, je peux vous le render	Fr.	dramatic baritone	46	French Romantic
Cavalleria rusticana	Il cavallo scalpita	It.	dramatic baritone	47	Verismo

Opera Title	Aria Title	Lang.	Fach	No.	Historical Style
Cavalleria rusticana	Voi lo sapete, o mamma	It.	dramatic	64	Verismo
Cendrillon	Avancez! Reculez!	Fr.	contralto	88	French Romantic
Cendrillon	Lorsqu'on a plus de vingt quartiers	Fr.	contralto	89	French Romantic
La Cenerentola	Come un'ape ne'giorni d'aprile	It.	lyric baritone	8	Bel canto
La Cenerentola	Non più mesta	It.	lyric coloratura	5	Bel canto
La Cenerentola	Sì, ritrovarla io giuro	It.	leggiero	5	Bel canto
La clemenza di Tito	Ah, se fosse intorno al trono	It.	lyric	30	Classical
La clemenza di Tito	Deh per questo istante solo	It.	lyric coloratura	6	Classical
La clemenza di Tito	Del più sublime soglio	It.	lyric	31	Classical
La clemenza di Tito	Non più di fiori	It.	dramatic coloratura	61	Classical
La clemenza di Tito	Parto, parto	It.	lyric coloratura	7	Classical
The Consul	I shall find for you (Lullaby)	Eng.	contralto	90	20th-century American
The Consul	Oh, what a lovely ballroom this is!	Eng.	leggiero	6	20th-century American
The Consul	To this we've come (Paper Aria)	Eng.	full lyric	74	20th-century American
Les contes d'Hoffmann	Elle a fui, la tourterelle	Fr.	lyric	38	French Romantic
Les contes d'Hoffmann	Il était une fois à la cour d'Eisenach	Fr.	lyric	32	French Romantic
Les contes d'Hoffmann	Les oiseaux dans la charmille	Fr.	lyric coloratura	4	French Romantic
Les contes d'Hoffmann	Scintille, diamant	Fr.	lyric baritone (dramatic)	9	French Romantic
Così fan tutte	Ah lo veggio quell'anima bella	It.	lyric	33	Classical
Così fan tutte	Come scoglio	It.	dramatic coloratura	62	Classical
Così fan tutte	Donne mie la fate a tanti	It.	lyric baritone	10	Classical
Così fan tutte	In uomini, in soldati	It.	soubrette	15	Classical
Così fan tutte	Non siate ritrosi	It.	lyric baritone	11	Classical
Così fan tutte	Per pietà	It.	dramatic coloratura	63	Classical
Così fan tutte	Smanie implacabili	It.	lyric	23	Classical
Così fan tutte	Tradito, schernito	It.	lyric	34	Classical
Così fan tutte	Una donna a quindici anni	It.	soubrette	16	Classical
Così fan tutte	Un'aura amorosa	It.	leggiero	7	Classical
The Crucible	I do not judge you, John	Eng.	dramatic	65	20th-century American

Opera Title	Aria Title	Lang.	Fach	No.	Historical Style
The Devil and Daniel Webster	I've got a ram, Goliath	Eng.	bass-baritone	67	20th-century American
The Devil and Daniel Webster	Now may there be a blessing	Eng.	lyric	24	20th-century American
Dido and Aeneas	When I am laid in earth	Eng.	contralto	91	English Baroque
Don Carlo	Carlo, ch'è sol il nostro amore	It.	lyric baritone	12	Italian Romantic
Don Carlo	Ella giammai m'amò	It.	bass-baritone	68	Italian Romantic
Don Carlo	Nel giardin del bello (Veil Song)	It.	dramatic	66	Italian Romantic
Don Carlo	O don fatale!	It.	dramatic	67	Italian Romantic
Don Carlo	Per me giuntò . . . Io morrò, ma lieto in core	It.	lyric baritone	13	Italian Romantic
Don Giovanni	Batti, batti	It.	soubrette	17	Classical
Don Giovanni	Dalla sua pace	It.	leggiero	8	Classical
Don Giovanni	Deh vieni alla finestra	It.	lyric baritone (dramatic)	14	Classical
Don Giovanni	Fin ch'han dal vino	It.	lyric baritone (dramatic)	15	Classical
Don Giovanni	Ho capito, signor, si	It.	lyric baritone	16	Classical
Don Giovanni	Il mio tesoro	It.	leggiero	9	Classical
Don Giovanni	Madamina! Il catalogo è questo	It.	bass (buffo)	86	Classical
Don Giovanni	Metà di voi quà vadano	It.	lyric baritone (dramatic)	17	Classical
Don Giovanni	Non mi dir	It.	dramatic coloratura	64	Classical
Don Giovanni	Vedrai carino	It.	soubrette	18	Classical
Don Pasquale	Bella siccome un angelo	It.	lyric baritone	18	Bel canto
Don Pasquale	Com'è gentil la notte	It.	lyric	35	Bel canto
Don Pasquale	Quel guardo il cavaliere . . . So anch'io la virtù magica	It.	lyric coloratura	5	Bel canto
Don Quichotte	Ne pensons qu'au plaisir d'aimer	Fr.	lyric	25	French Romantic
Down in the Valley	And where is the one who will mourn me	Eng.	lyric	36	20th-century American
Down in the Valley	Oh, don't you see that lonesome dove?	Eng.	lyric (soprano)	26	20th-century American
I due Foscari	Chiudi il labbro	It.	spinto	87	Italian Romantic
I due Foscari	Dal più remoto esilio	It.	spinto	88	Italian Romantic
Edgar	Questo amor, vergogna mia	It.	lyric baritone	19	Verismo

Opera Title	Aria Title	Lang.	Fach	No.	Historical Style
Elektra	Ich habe keine gute Nächte	Ger.	dramatic	68	20th-century German
L'elisir d'amore	Come paride vezzoso	It.	lyric baritone	20	Bel canto
L'elisir d'amore	Della crudel Isotta	It.	soubrette	19	Bel canto
L'elisir d'amore	Prendi; prendi, per me sei libero	It.	soubrette	20	Bel canto
L'elisir d'amore	Quanto è bella	It.	leggiero	10	Bel canto
L'elisir d'amore	Una furtiva lagrima	It.	leggiero	11	Bel canto
Die Entführung aus dem Serail	Ach, ich liebte	Ger.	dramatic coloratura	65	Singspiel
Die Entführung aus dem Serail	Frisch zum Kampfe!	Ger.	lyric	38	Singspiel
Die Entführung aus dem Serail	O wie ängstlich	Ger.	leggiero	12	Singspiel
Die Entführung aus dem Serail	Welche Wonne, welche Lust	Ger.	soubrette	21	Singspiel
Die Entführung aus dem Serail	Wenn der Freude Tränen fliessen	Ger.	lyric	37	Singspiel
Ernani	Ernani, Ernani involami	It.	dramatic coloratura	66	Italian Romantic
Ernani	Infelice! E tuo credevi	It.	bass-baritone	69	Italian Romantic
Eugene Onegin	Ja nye sposobna k grusti tomnoy	Russ.	contralto	92	Russian Romantic
Eugene Onegin	Kogda bi zhizn domashnim krugom	Russ.	lyric baritone (dramatic)	21	Russian Romantic
Eugene Onegin	Kuda, kuda, kuda, vy udalilis	Russ.	lyric	39	Russian Romantic
Eugene Onegin	Lyubvi vse vozrastï pokornï	Russ.	bass	87	Russian Romantic
Eugene Onegin	Ruskai pogibnu (Letter Scene)	Russ.	full lyric	75	Russian Romantic
Eugene Onegin	Uzhel ta samaja Tatiana	Russ.	lyric baritone (dramatic)	22	Russian Romantic
Falstaff	Dal labbro il canto	It.	leggiero	13	Italian Romantic
Falstaff	E sogno? O realtà?	It.	lyric baritone (dramatic)	23	Italian Romantic
Falstaff	Sul fil d'un soffio etesio	It.	soubrette	22	Italian Romantic
La fanciulla del West	Ch'ella mi creda libero e lontano	It.	spinto	89	Verismo
La fanciulla del West	Minnie, dalla mia casa son partito	It.	dramatic baritone	48	Verismo
Faust	Ah, je ris de me voir (Jewel Song)	Fr.	full lyric (coloratura)	76	French Romantic
Faust	Avant de quitter ces lieux	Fr.	lyric baritone (dramatic)	24	French Romantic
Faust	Faites-lui mes aveux	Fr.	lyric	27	French Romantic
Faust	Salut! Demeure chaste et pure	Fr.	lyric	40	French Romantic

Opera Title	Aria Title	Lang.	Fach	No.	Historical Style
Faust	Vous qui faites l'endormie	Fr.	bass (dramatic)	88	French Romantic
La favorita	O mio Fernando	It.	dramatic	69	Bel canto
La favorita	Spirto gentil	It.	lyric	41	Bel canto
Fedora	Amor ti vieta	It.	spinto	90	Italian Romantic
Fidelio	Abscheulicher! Wo eilst du hin? . . . Komm, Hoffnung	Ger.	dramatic	99	German Romantic
Fidelio	Hat man nicht auch Gold beineben	Ger.	bass-baritone	70	German Romantic
Fidelio	O wär' ich schon mit dir vereint	Ger.	lyric (soubrette)	39	German Romantic
La fille du régiment	Ah, mes amis . . . Pour mon âme	Fr.	lyric	42	Bel canto
La fille du régiment	Chacun le sait	Fr.	lyric coloratura	6	Bel canto
La finta giardiniera	Con un' vezzo all'Italiana	It.	lyric baritone	25	Classical
Die Fledermaus	Ich lade gern mir Gäste ein	Ger.	lyric	28	Viennese Operetta
Die Fledermaus	Klänge der Heimat (Czàrdàs)	Ger.	full lyric	77	Viennese Operetta
Die Fledermaus	Mein Herr Marquis	Ger.	soubrette	23	Viennese Operetta
La forza del destino	Al suon del tamburo	It.	lyric	29	Italian Romantic
La forza del destino	Morir! Tremenda cosa! . . . Urna fatale del mio destino	It.	dramatic baritone	49	Italian Romantic
La forza del destino	O tu che in seno agli angeli	It.	spinto	91	Italian Romantic
La forza del destino	Pace, pace mio Dio!	It.	spinto	88	Italian Romantic
Der Freischütz	Durch die Wälder	Ger.	spinto	92	German Romantic
Der Freischütz	Schweig'! Schweig'! damit dich niemand warnt	Ger.	bass-baritone	71	German Romantic
Gallantry	I thought I heard a distant bird	Eng.	lyric	43	20th-century American
The Ghosts of Versailles	Oh, the lion may roar (Aria of the Worm)	Eng.	lyric	44	20th-century American
Gianni Schicchi	Firenze è come un albero fiorito	It.	lyric	45	20th-century Italian
Gianni Schicchi	O mio babbino caro	It.	lyric	40	20th-century Italian
La Gioconda	Ah, pescator, affonda l'esca	It.	dramatic baritone	50	Italian Romantic
La Gioconda	Sì! Morir ella de'!	It.	bass (dramatic)	89	Italian Romantic

Opera Title	Aria Title	Lang.	Fach	No.	Historical Style
La Gioconda	Stella del marinar	It.	dramatic	70	Italian Romantic
La Gioconda	Suicidio!	It.	dramatic	100	Italian Romantic
La Gioconda	Voce di donna o d'angelo	It.	contralto	93	Italian Romantic
Giovanna d'Arco	Franco son io	It.	dramatic baritone	51	Italian Romantic
Giulio Cesare	L'angue offeso	It.	lyric	46	Italian Baroque
Giulio Cesare	Piangerò la sorte mia	It.	lyric coloratura	7	Italian Baroque
Giulio Cesare	Presti omai l'egizia terra	It.	dramatic baritone (bass)	52	Italian Baroque
Giulio Cesare	Priva son d'ogni conforto	It.	contralto	94	Italian Baroque
Giulio Cesare	Svegliatevi nel core	It.	lyric	47	Italian Baroque
Giulio Cesare	V'adoro, pupille	It.	lyric coloratura	8	Italian Baroque
Guillaume Tell	Ne m'abandonne point . . . Asile héréditaire	Fr.	lyric	48	French Romantic
Guillaume Tell	Sois immobile	Fr.	dramatic baritone	53	French Romantic
Guillaume Tell	Sombre forêt	Fr.	lyric coloratura (dramatic)	9	French Romantic
Hamlet	J'ai pu frapper	Fr.	lyric baritone (dramatic)	26	French Romantic
Hamlet	O vin dissipe la tristesse	Fr.	lyric baritone (dramatic)	27	French Romantic
Hamlet	Spectre infernal!	Fr.	lyric baritone (dramatic)	28	French Romantic
Hänsel und Gretel	Ach, wir armen, armen Leute	Ger.	dramatic baritone	54	German Romantic
Hänsel und Gretel	Der kleine Taumann heiss' ich	Ger.	lyric (soubrette)	41	German Romantic
Henry VIII	Qui donc commande	Fr.	dramatic baritone	55	French Romantic
Hérodiade	Il est doux, il est bon	Fr.	full lyric	78	French Romantic
Hérodiade	Vision fugitive	Fr.	dramatic baritone	56	French Romantic
Les Huguenots	Nobles seigneurs, salut!	Fr.	lyric	30	French Romantic
Les Huguenots	Pour les couvents c'est fini	Fr.	bass-baritone	72	French Romantic
The Ice Break	Stranger and darker	Eng.	dramatic	71	20th-century English
L'italiana in Algeri	Ah, come il cor di giubilo	It.	leggiero	14	Bel canto

Opera Title	Aria Title	Lang.	Fach	No.	Historical Style
L'italiana in Algeri	Amici, in ogni evento . . . Pensa alla patria	It.	lyric coloratura	8	Bel canto
L'italiana in Algeri	Cruda sorte	It.	lyric coloratura	9	Bel canto
L'italiana in Algeri	Ho un gran peso	It.	lyric baritone (bass-baritone)	29	Bel canto
L'italiana in Algeri	Languir per una bella	It.	lyric	49	Bel canto
L'italiana in Algeri	Per lui che adoro	It.	lyric coloratura	10	Bel canto
John Brown	Blow ye the trumpet	Eng.	lyric	31	20th-century American
John Brown	My friends, you do me too much honor	Eng.	dramatic baritone	57	20th-century American
La juive	Rachel, quand du Seigneur	Fr.	lyric	50	Italian Romantic
La Juive	Si la rigueur	Fr.	bass	90	French Romantic
La Juive	Tandis qu'il sommeille	Fr.	lyric	42	French Romantic
The Knot Garden	Now I am no more afraid	Eng.	dramatic	72	20th-century English
Lakmé	Fantaisie aux divins mensonges	Fr.	leggiero	15	French Romantic
Lakmé	Où va la jeune Hindoue (Bell Song)	Fr.	lyric coloratura	10	French Romantic
Das Land des Lächelns	Dein ist mein ganzes Herz	Ger.	lyric	51	Viennese Operetta
Little Women	Kennst du das Land?	Ger.	bass-baritone	73	20th-century American
Little Women	Things change, Jo	Eng.	lyric	32	20th-century American
Lizzie Borden	What am I forbidden?	Eng.	lyric (dramatic)	33	20th-century American
Lohengrin	Entweihte Götter!	Ger.	dramatic	73	German Romantic
Lost in the Stars	Lost in the Stars	Eng.	bass-baritone	74	20th-century American
Lucia di Lammermoor	Dalle stanze ove Lucia	It.	bass-baritone	75	Bel canto
Lucia di Lammermoor	Il dolce suono mi colpì di sua voce (Mad Scene)	It.	dramatic coloratura	67	Bel canto
Lucia di Lammermoor	Regnava nel silenzio	It.	dramatic coloratura	68	Bel canto
Lucia di Lammermoor	Tombe degl' avi miei . . . Fra poco a me ricovero	It.	lyric	52	Bel canto
Lucrezia Borgia	Il segreto per esser felici	It.	contralto	95	Bel canto

Opera Title	Aria Title	Lang.	Fach	No.	Historical Style
Martha	Nimmermehr wird mein Herze sich grämen	Ger.	lyric	36	German Romantic
I masnadieri	La sua lampada vitale	It.	dramatic baritone	59	Italian Romantic
I masnadieri	Un ignoto, tre lune or saranno	It.	bass	93	Italian Romantic
McTeague	Jehosophat!	Eng.	dramatic baritone	60	20th-century American
The Medium	The Black Swan	Eng.	lyric	46	20th-century American
The Medium	Monica's Waltz	Eng.	lyric	45	20th-century American
Die Meistersinger von Nürnberg	Am stillen Herd	Ger.	dramatic	101	German Romantic
A Midsummer Night's Dream	I know a bank where the wild thyme grows	Eng.	contralto	97	20th-century English
The Mighty Casey	Kiss me not good-bye	Eng.	lyric (soprano)	37	20th-century American
Mignon	Adieu, Mignon!	Fr.	lyric	58	French Romantic
Mignon	Connais-tu le pays?	Fr.	lyric	38	French Romantic
Mignon	De son coeur j'ai calmé la fièvre (Berceuse)	Fr.	bass	94	French Romantic
Mignon	Je suis Titania	Fr.	lyric coloratura	11	French Romantic
Mignon	Me voici dans son boudoir	Fr.	lyric	39	French Romantic
Mitridate, re di Ponto	Già di pietà mi spoglio	It.	leggiero	17	Classical
Mitridate, re di Ponto	Nel sen mi palpita	It.	lyric coloratura	12	Classical
Mitridate, re di Ponto	Quel ribelle e quell'ingrato	It.	leggiero	18	Classical
Mitridate, re di Ponto	Se di lauri	It.	leggiero	19	Classical
The Mother of Us All	We cannot retrace our steps	Eng.	dramatic	75	20th-century American
The Mother of Us All	What what is it?	Eng.	bass-baritone	77	20th-century American
Nabucco	Anch'io dischiuso un giorno	It.	dramatic coloratura	69	Italian Romantic
Nabucco	Tu sul labbro	It.	bass	95	Italian Romantic
Norma	Casta diva	It.	dramatic	103	Bel canto
Norma	Sgombra è la sacra selva . . . Deh! Proteggimi, O Dio!	It.	dramatic	76	Bel canto
Le nozze di Figaro	Aprite un po' quegl'occhi	It.	bass-baritone	78	Classical

Opera Title	Aria Title	Lang.	Fach	No.	Historical Style
Le nozze di Figaro	E Susanna non vien! . . . Dove sono	It.	full lyric	81	Classical
Le nozze di Figaro	Giunse alfin il momento . . . Deh vieni, non tardar	It.	soubrette	24	Classical
Le nozze di Figaro	Hai già vinta la causa . . . Vendro mentr'io sospiro	It.	lyric baritone (dramatic)	30	Classical
Le nozze di Figaro	Non più andrai	It.	bass-baritone	79	Classical
Le nozze di Figaro	Non so più cosa son, cosa faccio	It.	lyric	40	Classical
Le nozze di Figaro	Porgi amor	It.	full lyric	82	Classical
Le nozze di Figaro	Se vuol ballare	It.	bass-baritone	80	Classical
Le nozze di Figaro	Voi che sapete	It.	lyric	41	Classical
The Old Maid and the Thief	Steal me, sweet thief	Eng.	lyric	47	20th-century American
The Old Maid and the Thief	When the air sings of summer	Eng.	lyric baritone	31	20th-century American
L'Orfeo	Rosa del ciel	It.	leggiero	20	Italian Baroque
Orfeo ed Euridice	Che farò senza Euridice?	It.	lyric	42	Italian Baroque
Otello	Ave Maria	It.	full lyric	83	Italian Romantic
Otello	Mia madre aveva una povera ancella (Willow Song)	It.	full lyric	84	Italian Romantic
I Pagliacci	Qual fiamma avea nel guardo!	It.	lyric	48	Verismo
I Pagliacci	Si può?	It.	dramatic baritone	61	Verismo
Partenope	Io seguo sol fiero	It.	lyric coloratura	11	Italian Baroque
Partenope	Quel volto mi piace	It.	lyric coloratura	12	Italian Baroque
Paul Bunyan	Inkslinger's Song	Eng.	lyric	59	20th-century English
Les pêcheurs de perles	Je crois entendre encore	Fr.	lyric	60	French Romantic
Les pêcheurs de perles	L'orage s'est calmé	Fr.	lyric baritone	32	French Romantic
La Périchole	I've dined so well (Tipsy Waltz)	Eng.	lyric	43	French Romantic
Le prophète	Ah! Mon fils, sois béni	Fr.	dramatic	77	French Romantic
Le prophète	Donnez, donnez	Fr.	dramatic	78	French Romantic
I puritani	Ah! per sempre io ti perdei . . . Bel sogno beato	It.	lyric baritone	33	Bel canto

Opera Title	Aria Title	Lang.	Fach	No.	Historical Style
I puritani	Qui la voce . . . Vien, diletto	It.	lyric coloratura	13	Italian Romantic
The Rake's Progress	Here I stand . . . Since it is not by merit	Eng.	lyric	61	20th-century English
The Rake's Progress	Love, too frequently betrayed	Eng.	lyric	62	20th-century English
The Rake's Progress	No word from Tom . . . I go to him	Eng.	dramatic coloratura	70	20th-century English
The Rake's Progress	Scorned! Abused! Neglected!	Eng.	dramatic	79	20th-century English
The Rake's Progress	Vary the song, o London, change	Eng.	lyric	63	20th-century English
The Rape of Lucretia	Give him this orchid	Eng.	dramatic	80	20th-century English
The Rape of Lucretia	Tarquinius does not wait	Eng.	lyric	64	20th-century English
Regina	Do you wish we had wed?	Eng.	lyric	44	20th-century American
Regina	The same, old room	Eng.	bass-baritone	81	20th-century American
Rienzi	Gerechter Gott	Ger.	lyric (dramatic)	45	German Romantic
Rigoletto	Caro nome	It.	lyric (coloratura)	49	Italian Romantic
Rigoletto	Ella mi fu rapita . . . Parmi veder le lagrime	It.	lyric	65	Italian Romantic
Rigoletto	La donna è mobile	It.	lyric	66	Italian Romantic
Rigoletto	Possente amor mi chiama	It.	lyric	67	Italian Romantic
Rigoletto	Questa o quella	It.	lyric	68	Italian Romantic
Rinaldo	Cara sposa	It.	lyric coloratura	13	Italian Baroque
Rinaldo	Venti, turbini, prestate	It.	lyric coloratura	14	Italian Baroque
Il ritorno di Ulisse in patria	Illustratevi, o cieli	It.	lyric	46	Italian Baroque
Le roi d'Ys	Vainement, ma bien-aimée	Fr.	lyric	69	French Romantic
Roméo et Juliette	Ah, lève-toi, soleil!	Fr.	lyric	70	French Romantic
Roméo et Juliette	Je veux vivre dans ce rêve	Fr.	lyric coloratura	14	French Romantic
Roméo et Juliette	Mab, la reine des mensonges	Fr.	lyric baritone	34	French Romantic
Roméo et Juliette	Que fais-tu, blanche tourterelle	Fr.	lyric	47	French Romantic
La rondine	Chi il bel sogno di Doretta	It.	lyric	50	Verismo
Der Rosenkavalier	Wie du warst!	Ger.	dramatic	81	20th-century German

Opera Title	Aria Title	Lang.	Fach	No.	Historical Style
The Saint of Bleecker Street	Ah, Michele, don't you know?	Eng.	dramatic	82	20th-century American
The Saint of Bleecker Street	Ah, sweet Jesus, spare me this agony	Eng.	lyric	51	20th-century America
The Saint of Bleecker Street	I know that you all hate me	Eng.	lyric	71	20th-century American
Samson et Dalila	Amour! Viens aider ma faiblesse!	Fr.	dramatic	83	French Romantic
Samson et Dalila	Mon coeur s'ouvre à ta voix	Fr.	dramatic	84	French Romantic
Samson et Dalila	Printemps qui commence	Fr.	dramatic	85	French Romantic
Semiramide	Bel raggio lusinghier	It.	lyric coloratura	15	Bel canto
Semiramide	In sì barbara	It.	lyric coloratura	16	Bel canto
Semiramide	Quel mesto gemito	It.	lyric coloratura	17	Bel canto
Serse (Xerxes)	Ombra mai fu	It.	lyric	48	Italian Baroque
Simon Boccanegra	Il lacerato spirito	It.	bass (dramatic)	96	Italian Romantic
The Sojourner and Mollie Sinclair	Someday I'm sure to marry you	Eng.	lyric	52	20th-century American
The Song of Majnun	Light of my soul	Eng.	lyric	72	20th-century American
La sonnambula	Vi ravviso	It.	bass	97	Bel canto
Street Scene	Lonely House	Eng.	lyric	73	20th-century American
A Streetcar Named Desire	I want magic!	Eng.	full lyric	85	20th-century American
A Streetcar Named Desire	I'm not a boy, she says	Eng.	spinto	95	20th-century American
Suor Angelica	Senza mamma	It.	spinto	90	Verismo
Susannah	Ain't it a pretty night?	Eng.	lyric	53	20th-century American
Susannah	It's about the way people is made	Eng.	lyric	74	20th-century American
Susannah	The trees on the mountain are cold and bare	Eng.	lyric	54	20th-century American
Sweeney Todd	Now signorini (The Contest)	Eng.	lyric	75	20th-century American
Tancredi	Oh, patria! Dolce, e ingrate patria! . . . tu que accendi questo core	It.	lyric coloratura	18	Bel canto
Tannhäuser	Dich teure Halle	Ger.	dramatic	104	German Romantic
Tannhäuser	O du, mein holder Abendstern	Ger.	lyric baritone (dramatic)	35	German Romantic
Tartuffe	Everyday at church	Eng.	bass	98	20th-century American

Opera Title	Aria Title	Lang.	Fach	No.	Historical Style
Tartuffe	Fair Robin I love	Eng.	soubrette (lyric coloratura)	25	20th-century American
Tartuffe	Hold on a moment, dear	Eng.	lyric	49	20th-century American
Tartuffe	No more, false heart	Eng.	lyric	76	20th-century American
The Telephone	Hello, hello? Oh, Margaret, it's you	Eng.	lyric	55	20th-century American
The Tempest	Be not afeard	Eng.	dramatic	102	20th-century American
The Tempest	Dry those eyes	Eng.	lyric	50	English Baroque
Thaïs	Voilà donc la terrible cité	Fr.	dramatic baritone	62	French Romantic
Too Many Sopranos	Do I not draw tears from your eyes?	Eng.	contralto	98	20th-century American
Too Many Sopranos	Madame Pompous's Audition	Eng.	full lyric (spinto)	86	20th-century American
Tosca	E lucevan le stelle	It.	spinto	96	Verismo
Tosca	Recondita armonia	It.	spinto	97	Verismo
Tosca	Vissi d'arte	It.	spinto	91	Verismo
Die tote Stadt	Dich such' ich Bild!	Ger.	spinto	92	20th-century German
Die tote Stadt	Glück, das mir verblieb (Marietta's Lied)	Ger.	spinto	93	20th-century German
Die tote Stadt	Mein Sehnen, mein Wähnen (Pierrot's Tanzlied)	Ger.	lyric baritone	36	20th-century German
La traviata	Dei miei bollenti spiriti	It.	lyric	77	Italian Romantic
La traviata	Di Provenza il mar	It.	dramatic baritone	63	Italian Romantic
Il trovatore	Ah sì, ben mio; coll'essere	It.	spinto	98	Italian Romantic
Il trovatore	Condotta ell'era in ceppi	It.	dramatic	86	Italian Romantic
Il trovatore	Di due figli vivea	It.	bass-baritone	82	Italian Romantic
Il trovatore	Di quella pira	It.	spinto	99	Italian Romantic
Il trovatore	Il balen del suo sorriso	It.	dramatic baritone	64	Italian Romantic
Il trovatore	Stride la vampa	It.	dramatic	87	Italian Romantic
Il trovatore	Tacea la notte	It.	full lyric	87	Italian Romantic
Les Troyens	Inutiles regrets	Fr.	spinto	100	French Romantic
Turandot	In questa reggia	It.	dramatic	105	20th-century Italian
Turandot	Signore, ascolta	It.	lyric	56	20th-century Italian

Opera Title	Aria Title	Lang.	Fach	No.	Historical Style
Turandot	Tu che di gel sei cinta	It.	lyric	57	20th-century Italian
Vanessa	Do not utter a word	Eng.	spinto	94	20th-century American
Vanessa	Must the winter come so soon?	Eng.	lyric	51	20th-century American
Vanessa	Outside this house	Eng.	lyric	78	20th-century American
Vanessa	You rascal, you! I never knew you had a soul!	Eng.	bass-baritone	83	20th-century American
I vespri siciliani	Mercè, dilette amiche	It.	dramatic coloratura	71	Italian Romantic
I vespri siciliani	O tu Palermo	It.	bass	99	Italian Romantic
A View from the Bridge	New York Lights	Eng.	lyric	79	20th-century American
Die Walküre	Du bist der Lenz	Ger.	dramatic	106	German Romantic
Die Walküre	Wo in Bergen du dich birgst	Ger.	contralto	99	German Romantic
La Wally	Ebben! Ne andrò lontana	It.	spinto	95	Verismo
Werther	Pourquoi me réveiller	Fr.	lyric	80	French Romantic
Werther	Va! Laisse couler mes larmes	Fr.	lyric	52	French Romantic
Werther	Werther, Werther (Letter Aria)	Fr.	lyric	53	French Romantic
The Wings of the Dove	We've always known each other	Eng.	lyric	54	20th-century American
Die Zauberflöte	Ach, ich fühl's	Ger.	lyric	58	Singspiel
Die Zauberflöte	Der Hölle Rache kocht in meinem Herzen	Ger.	dramatic coloratura	72	Singspiel
Die Zauberflöte	Der Vogelfänger bin ich ja	Ger.	lyric baritone	37	Singspiel
Die Zauberflöte	Dies Bildnis ist bezaubernd schön	Ger.	lyric	81	Singspiel
Die Zauberflöte	Ein Mädchen oder Weibchen	Ger.	lyric baritone	38	Singspiel
Die Zauberflöte	O zittre nicht . . . Zum Leiden bin ich auserkoren	Ger.	dramatic coloratura	73	Singspiel
Zazà	Zazà, piccolo zingara	It.	lyric baritone	39	Verismo

Index C
Arias by Language

Aria Title	Opera Title	Fach	No.	Historical Style
Give him this orchid	*The Rape of Lucretia*	dramatic	80	20th-century English
God o' mercy	*Billy Budd*	lyric	24	20th-century English
Have you seen her, Samantha?	*The Ballad of Baby Doe*	dramatic	57	20th-century American
Hello, hello? Oh, Margaret, it's you	*The Telephone*	lyric	55	20th-century American
Here I stand . . . Since it is not by merit	*The Rake's Progress*	lyric	61	20th-century English
Hold on a moment, dear	*Tartuffe*	lyric	49	20th-century American
I accept their verdict	*Billy Budd*	lyric	25	20th-century English
I am an old man	*Billy Budd*	lyric	26	20th-century English
I do not judge you, John	*The Crucible*	dramatic	65	20th-century American
I know a bank where the wild thyme grows	*A Midsummer Night's Dream*	contralto	97	20th-century English
I know that you all hate me	*The Saint of Bleecker Street*	lyric	71	20th-century American
I shall find for you (Lullaby)	*The Consul*	contralto	90	20th-century American
I thought I heard a distant bird	*Gallantry*	lyric	43	20th-century American
I want magic!	*A Streetcar Named Desire*	full lyric	85	20th-century American
I'm not a boy, she says	*A Streetcar Named Desire*	spinto	95	20th-century American
Inkslinger's Song	*Paul Bunyan*	lyric	59	20th-century English
It must be so	*Candide*	lyric	29	20th-century American
It's about the way people is made	*Susannah*	lyric	74	20th-century American
I've dined so well (Tipsy Waltz)	*La Périchole*	lyric	43	French Romantic
I've got a ram, Goliath	*The Devil and Daniel Webster*	bass-baritone	67	20th-century American
Jehosophat!	*McTeague*	dramatic baritone	60	20th-century American
Kiss me not goodbye	*The Mighty Casey*	lyric (soprano)	37	20th-century American
Light of my soul	*The Song of Majnun*	lyric	72	20th-century American
Lonely House	*Street Scene*	lyric	73	20th-century American
Look, through the port comes the moonshine astray	*Billy Budd*	lyric baritone	5	20th-century English
Lost in the Stars	*Lost in the Stars*	bass-baritone	74	20th-century American
Love, too frequently betrayed	*The Rake's Progress*	lyric	62	20th-century English

Aria Title	Opera Title	Fach	No.	Historical Style
Madame Pompous's Audition	*Too Many Sopranos*	full lyric (spinto)	86	20th-century American
Monica's Waltz	*The Medium*	lyric	45	20th-century American
Must the winter come so soon?	*Vanessa*	lyric	51	20th-century American
My friends, you do me too much honor	*John Brown*	dramatic baritone	57	20th-century American
New York Lights	*A View from the Bridge*	lyric	79	20th-century American
No more, false heart	*Tartuffe*	lyric	76	20th-century American
No word from Tom . . . I go to him	*The Rake's Progress*	dramatic coloratura	70	20th-century English
Now I am no more afraid	*The Knot Garden*	dramatic	72	20th-century English
Now may there be a blessing	*The Devil and Daniel Webster*	lyric	24	20th-century American
Now signorini (The Contest)	*Sweeney Todd*	lyric	75	20th-century American
Oh, don't you see that lonesome dove?	*Down in the Valley*	lyric (soprano)	26	20th-century American
Oh, the lion may roar (Aria of the Worm)	*The Ghosts of Versailles*	lyric	44	20th-century American
Oh, what a lovely ballroom this is!	*The Consul*	leggiero	6	20th-century American
Outside this house	*Vanessa*	lyric	78	20th-century American
Scorned! Abused! Neglected!	*The Rake's Progress*	dramatic	79	20th-century English
The Silver Aria	*The Ballad of Baby Doe*	lyric	31	20th-century American
Someday I'm sure to marry you	*The Sojourner and Mollie Sinclair*	lyric	52	20th-century American
Soon now my dearest	*The Bartered Bride*	lyric	23	Czech Nationalist
Steal me, sweet thief	*The Old Maid and the Thief*	lyric	47	20th-century American
Stranger and darker	*The Ice Break*	dramatic	71	20th-century English
Tarquinius does not wait	*The Rape of Lucretia*	lyric	64	20th-century English
The same, old room	*Regina*	bass-baritone	81	20th-century American
The trees on the mountain are cold and bare	*Susannah*	lyric	54	20th-century American
Things change, Jo	*Little Women*	lyric	32	20th-century American
This is my box	*Amahl and the Night Visitors*	leggiero	2	20th-century American
Tickling a trout, poaching a hare	*Albert Herring*	lyric baritone	1	20th-century English

Aria Title	Opera Title	Fach	No.	Historical Style
To this we've come (Paper Aria)	*The Consul*	full lyric	74	20th-century American
Vary the song, o London, change	*The Rake's Progress*	lyric	63	20th-century English
Warm as the autumn light	*The Ballad of Baby Doe*	bass-baritone	66	20th-century American
We cannot retrace our steps	*The Mother of Us All*	dramatic	75	20th-century American
We committed his body to the deep	*Billy Budd*	lyric	27	20th-century English
We've always known each other	*The Wings of the Dove*	lyric	54	20th-century American
What am I forbidden?	*Lizzie Borden*	lyric (dramatic)	33	20th-century American
What what is it?	*The Mother of Us All*	bass-baritone	77	20th-century American
When I am laid in earth	*Dido and Aeneas*	contralto	91	English Baroque
When the air sings of summer	*The Old Maid and the Thief*	lyric baritone	31	20th-century American
While I waste these precious hours	*Amelia Goes to the Ball/Amelia al ballo*	lyric	27	20th-century American/ Italian
Willow Song	*The Ballad of Baby Doe*	lyric	32	20th-century American
Yes! I am she!	*Madame Mao*	lyric (dramatic)	34	20th-century American
You rascal, you! I never knew you had a soul!	*Vanessa*	bass-baritone	83	20th-century American

French

Aria Title	Opera Title	Fach	No.	Historical Style
Adieu, forêts	*The Maid of Orleans*	lyric	35	Russian Romantic
Adieu, Mignon!	*Mignon*	lyric	58	French Romantic
Adieu, notre petite table	*Manon*	lyric	44	French Romantic
Ah! Fuyez douce image	*Manon*	lyric	55	French Romantic
Ah, je ris de me voir (Jewel Song)	*Faust*	full lyric (coloratura)	76	French Romantic
Ah, lève-toi, soleil!	*Roméo et Juliette*	lyric	70	French Romantic
Ah, mes amis . . . Pour mon âme	*La fille du régiment*	lyric	42	Bel canto
Ah! Mon fils, sois béni	*Le prophète*	dramatic	77	French Romantic
Amour! Viens aider ma faiblesse!	*Samson et Dalila*	dramatic	83	French Romantic
Avancez! Reculez!	*Cendrillon*	contralto	88	French Romantic

Aria Title	Opera Title	Fach	No.	Historical Style
Avant de quitter ces lieux	*Faust*	lyric baritone (dramatic)	24	French Romantic
Chacun le sait	*La fille du régiment*	lyric coloratura	6	Bel canto
Connais-tu le pays?	*Mignon*	lyric	38	French Romantic
De son coeur j'ai calm la fièvre (Berceuse)	*Mignon*	bass	94	French Romantic
Donnez, donnez	*Le prophète*	dramatic	78	French Romantic
Elle a fui, la tourterelle	*Les contes d'Hoffmann*	lyric	38	French Romantic
En fermant les yeux (Le Rêve)	*Manon*	lyric	56	French Romantic
En vain pour éviter (Card Aria)	*Carmen*	dramatic	60	French Romantic
Épouse quelque brave fille	*Manon*	bass	92	French Romantic
Faites-lui mes aveux	*Faust*	lyric	27	French Romantic
Fantaisie aux divins mensonges	*Lakmé*	leggiero	15	French Romantic
Il est doux, il est bon	*Hérodiade*	full lyric	78	French Romantic
Il était une fois à la cour d'Eisenach	*Les contes d'Hoffmann*	lyric	32	French Romantic
Inutiles regrets	*Les Troyens*	spinto	100	French Romantic
J'ai pu frapper	*Hamlet*	lyric baritone (dramatic)	26	French Romantic
Je crois entendre encore	*Les pêcheurs de perles*	lyric	60	French Romantic
Je dis que rien ne m'épouvante	*Carmen*	lyric	37	French Romantic
Je suis Titania	*Mignon*	lyric coloratura	11	French Romantic
Je veux vivre dans ce rêve	*Roméo et Juliette*	lyric coloratura	14	French Romantic
La fleur que tu m'avais jetée	*Carmen*	spinto	86	French Romantic
L'amour est un oiseau (Habañera)	*Carmen*	dramatic	61	French Romantic
Les oiseaux dans la charmille	*Les contes d'Hoffmann*	lyric coloratura	4	French Romantic
Les tringles des sistres tintaient	*Carmen*	dramatic	62	French Romantic
L'orage s'est calmé	*Les pêcheurs de perles*	lyric baritone	32	French Romantic
Lorsqu'on a plus de vingt quartiers	*Cendrillon*	contralto	89	French Romantic
Mab, la reine des mensonges	*Roméo et Juliette*	lyric baritone	34	French Romantic
Me voici dans son boudoir	*Mignon*	lyric	39	French Romantic

Aria Title	Opera Title	Fach	No.	Historical Style
Mon coeur s'ouvre à ta voix	*Samson et Dalila*	dramatic	84	French Romantic
Ne m'abandonne point . . . Asile héréditaire	*Guillaume Tell*	lyric	48	French Romantic
Ne pensons qu'au plaisir d'aimer	*Don Quichotte*	lyric	25	French Romantic
Nobles seigneurs, salut!	*Les Huguenots*	lyric	30	French Romantic
O paradis sorti de l'onde	*L'Africaine*	lyric	21	Italian Romantic
O vin dissipe la tristesse	*Hamlet*	lyric baritone (dramatic)	27	French Romantic
Où va la jeune Hindoue (Bell Song)	*Lakmé*	lyric coloratura	10	French Romantic
Pour les couvents c'est fini	*Les Huguenots*	bass-baritone	72	French Romantic
Pourquoi me réveiller	*Werther*	lyric	80	French Romantic
Près des remparts de Séville (Seguidilla)	*Carmen*	dramatic	63	French Romantic
Printemps qui commence	*Samson et Dalila*	dramatic	85	French Romantic
Que fais-tu, blanche tourterelle	*Roméo et Juliette*	lyric	47	French Romantic
Qui donc commande	*Henry VIII*	dramatic baritone	55	French Romantic
Rachel, quand du Seigneur	*La Juive*	lyric	50	Italian Romantic
Salut! Demeure chaste et pure	*Faust*	lyric	40	French Romantic
Scintille, diamant	*Les contes d'Hoffmann*	lyric baritone (dramatic)	9	French Romantic
Si la rigueur	*La Juive*	bass	90	French Romantic
Sois immobile	*Guillaume Tell*	dramatic baritone	53	French Romantic
Sombre forêt	*Guillaume Tell*	lyric coloratura (dramatic)	9	French Romantic
Spectre infernal!	*Hamlet*	lyric baritone (dramatic)	28	French Romantic
Tandis qu'il sommeille	*La Juive*	lyric	42	French Romantic
Va! Laisse couler mes larmes	*Werther*	lyric	52	French Romantic
Vainement, ma bien-aimée	*Le roi d'Ys*	lyric	69	French Romantic
Vision fugitive	*Hérodiade*	dramatic baritone	56	French Romantic
Voilà donc la terrible cité	*Thaïs*	dramatic baritone	62	French Romantic
Votre toast, je peux vous le render	*Carmen*	dramatic baritone	46	French Romantic
Vous qui faites l'endormie	*Faust*	bass (dramatic)	88	French Romantic

German

Aria Title	Opera Title	Fach	No.	Historical Style
Werther, Werther (Letter Aria)	*Werther*	lyric	53	French Romantic
Abscheulicher! Wo eilst du him? . . . Komm, Hoffnung	*Fidelio*	dramatic	99	German Romantic
Ach, ich fühl's	*Die Zauberflöte*	lyric	58	Singspiel
Ach, ich liebte	*Die Entführung aus dem Serail*	dramatic coloratura	65	Singspiel
Ach, so fromm (M'apparì tutt'amor)	*Martha*	lyric	57	German Romantic
Ach, wir armen, armen Leute	*Hänsel und Gretel*	dramatic baritone	54	German Romantic
Als Büblein klein	*Die lustigen Weiber von Windsor*	bass-baritone	76	German Romantic
Am stillen Herd	*Die Meistersinger von Nürnberg*	dramatic	101	German Romantic
Dein ist mein ganzes Herz	*Das Land des Lächelns*	lyric	51	Viennese Operetta
Der Hölle Rache kocht in meinem Herzen	*Die Zauberflöte*	dramatic coloratura	72	Singspiel
Der kleine Taumann heiss' ich	*Hänsel und Gretel*	lyric (soubrette)	41	German Romantic
Der Vogelfänger bin ich ja	*Die Zauberflöte*	lyric baritone	37	Singspiel
Dich such' ich Bild!	*Die tote Stadt*	spinto	92	20th-century German
Dich teure Halle	*Tannhäuser*	dramatic	104	German Romantic
Dies Bildnis ist bezaubernd schön	*Die Zauberflöte*	lyric	81	Singspiel
Du bist der Lenz	*Die Walküre*	dramatic	106	German Romantic
Durch die Wälder	*Der Freischütz*	spinto	92	German Romantic
Ein Mädchen oder Weibchen	*Die Zauberflöte*	lyric baritone	38	Singspiel
Entweihte Götter!	*Lohengrin*	dramatic	73	German Romantic
Es gibt ein Reich	*Ariadne auf Naxos*	dramatic	98	20th-century German
Es lebt' eine Vilja, ein Waldmägdelein (Vilja's Lied)	*Die lustige Witwe*	lyric (full lyric)	43	Viennese Operetta
Frisch zum Kampfe!	*Die Entführung aus dem Serail*	lyric	38	Singspiel
Gerechter Gott	*Rienzi*	lyric (dramatic)	45	German Romantic
Glück, das mir verblieb (Marietta's Lied)	*Die tote Stadt*	spinto	93	20th-century German
Hat man nicht auch Gold beineben	*Fidelio*	bass-baritone	70	German Romantic

Aria Title	Opera Title	Fach	No.	Historical Style
Horch, die Lerche singt im Hain!	*Die lustigen Weiber von Windsor*	lyric	53	German Romantic
Ich habe keine gute Nächte	*Elektra*	dramatic	68	20th-century German
Ich lade gern mir Gäste ein	*Die Fledermaus*	lyric	28	Viennese Operetta
Kennst du das Land?	*Little Women*	bass-baritone	73	20th-century American
Klänge der Heimat (Czàrdàs)	*Die Fledermaus*	full lyric	77	Viennese Operetta
Lieben, Hassen, Hoffen, Zagen	*Ariadne auf Naxos*	lyric baritone	3	20th-century German
Mein Herr Marquis	*Die Fledermaus*	soubrette	23	Viennese Operetta
Mein Sehnen, mein Wähnen (Pierrot's Tanzlied)	*Die tote Stadt*	lyric baritone	36	20th-century German
Nimmermehr wird mein Herze sich grämen	*Martha*	lyric	36	German Romantic
O du, mein holder Abendstern	*Tannhäuser*	lyric baritone (dramatic)	35	German Romantic
O wär' ich schon mit dir vereint	*Fidelio*	lyric (soubrette)	39	German Romantic
O wie ängstlich	*Die Entführung aus dem Serail*	leggiero	12	Singspiel
O zittre nicht . . . Zum Leiden bin ich auserkoren	*Die Zauberflöte*	dramatic coloratura	73	Singspiel
Schweig'! Schweig'! damit dich niemand warnt	*Der Freischütz*	bass-baritone	71	German Romantic
Welche Wonne, welche Lust	*Die Entführung aus dem Serail*	soubrette	21	Singspiel
Wenn der Freude Tränen fliessen	*Die Entführung aus dem Serail*	lyric	37	Singspiel
Wie du warst!	*Der Rosenkavalier*	dramatic	81	20th-century German
Wo in Bergen du dich birgst	*Die Walküre*	contralto	99	German Romantic

Italian

Aria Title	Opera Title	Fach	No.	Historical Style
Acerba voluttà	*Adriana Lecouvreur*	lyric	19	Verismo
Ah sì, ben mio; coll'essere	*Il trovatore*	spinto	98	Italian Romantic
Ah, come il cor di giubilo	*L'italiana in Algeri*	leggiero	14	Bel canto
Ah, la paterna mano	*Macbeth*	lyric	54	Italian Romantic
Ah lo veggio quell'anima bella	*Così fan tutte*	lyric	33	Classical

Aria Title	Opera Title	Fach	No.	Historical Style
Ah! per sempre io ti perdei . . . Bel sogno beato	*I puritani*	lyric baritone	33	Bel canto
Ah, pescator, affonda l'esca	*La Gioconda*	dramatic baritone	50	Italian Romantic
Ah, se fosse intorno al trono	*La clemenza di Tito*	lyric	30	Classical
Al suon del tamburo	*La forza del destino*	lyric	29	Italian Romantic
Allor che i forti corrono	*Attila*	dramatic coloratura	59	Italian Romantic
Amici, in ogni evento . . . Pensa alla patria	*L'italiana in Algeri*	lyric coloratura	8	Bel canto
Amor ti vieta	*Fedora*	spinto	90	Italian Romantic
Amore o grillo	*Madama Butterfly*	spinto	93	Verismo
Anch'io dischiuso un giorno	*Nabucco*	dramatic coloratura	69	Italian Romantic
Aprite un po' quegl'occhi	*Le nozze di Figaro*	bass-baritone	78	Classical
Ave Maria	*Otello*	full lyric	83	Italian Romantic
Batti, batti	*Don Giovanni*	soubrette	17	Classical
Bel raggio lusinghier	*Semiramide*	lyric coloratura	15	Bel canto
Bella siccome un angelo	*Don Pasquale*	lyric baritone	18	Bel canto
Cara sposa	*Rinaldo*	lyric coloratura	13	Italian Baroque
Carlo, ch'è sol il nostro amore	*Don Carlo*	lyric baritone	12	Italian Romantic
Caro nome	*Rigoletto*	lyric (coloratura)	49	Italian Romantic
Casta diva	*Norma*	dramatic	103	Bel canto
Che farò senza Euridice?	*Orfeo ed Euridice*	lyric	42	Italian Baroque
Che gelida manina	*La bohème*	lyric	28	Verismo
Che non avrebbe il misero	*Attila*	lyric	22	Italian Romantic
Ch'ella mi creda libero e lontano	*La fanciulla del West*	spinto	89	Verismo
Chi il bel sogno di Doretta	*La rondine*	lyric	50	Verismo
Chiudi il labbro	*I due Foscari*	spinto	87	Italian Romantic
Come dal ciel precipita	*Macbeth*	bass	91	Italian Romantic
Com'è gentil la notte	*Don Pasquale*	lyric	35	Bel canto
Come paride vezzoso	*L'elisir d'amore*	lyric baritone	20	Bel canto
Come scoglio	*Così fan tutte*	dramatic coloratura	62	Classical
Come un bel dì di maggio	*Andrea Chénier*	spinto	82	Verismo
Come un'ape ne'giorni d'aprile	*La Cenerentola*	lyric baritone	8	Bel canto

Aria Title	Opera Title	Fach	No.	Historical Style
Compiacente a' colloqui del cicisbeo . . . Son sessant'anni	*Andrea Chénier*	dramatic baritone	42	Verismo
Con un' vezzo all'Italiana	*La finta giardiniera*	lyric baritone	25	Classical
Condotta ell'era in ceppi	*Il trovatore*	dramatic	86	Italian Romantic
Cruda sorte	*L'italiana in Algeri*	lyric coloratura	9	Bel canto
Dagl'immortali vertici	*Attila*	dramatic baritone	44	Italian Romantic
Dal labbro il canto	*Falstaff*	leggiero	13	Italian Romantic
Dal più remoto esilio	*I due Foscari*	spinto	88	Italian Romantic
Dalla sua pace	*Don Giovanni*	leggiero	8	Classical
Dalle stanze ove Lucia	*Lucia di Lammermoor*	bass-baritone	75	Bel canto
Dei miei bollenti spiriti	*La traviata*	lyric	77	Italian Romantic
Deh per questo istante solo	*La clemenza di Tito*	lyric coloratura	6	Classical
Deh vieni alla finestra	*Don Giovanni*	lyric baritone (dramatic)	14	Classical
Del più sublime soglio	*La clemenza di Tito*	lyric	31	Classical
Della crudel Isotta	*L'elisir d'amore*	soubrette	19	Bel canto
Di due figli vivea	*Il trovatore*	bass-baritone	82	Italian Romantic
Di Provenza il mar	*La traviata*	dramatic baritone	63	Italian Romantic
Di quella pira	*Il trovatore*	spinto	99	Italian Romantic
Di te mi rido	*Alcina*	lyric coloratura	1	Italian Baroque
Donde lieta	*La bohème*	lyric	34	Verismo
Donna non vidi mai	*Manon Lescaut*	spinto	94	Verismo
Donne mie la fate a tanti	*Così fan tutte*	lyric baritone	10	Classical
È la solita storia del pastore	*L'arlesiana*	spinto	84	Verismo
E lucevan le stelle	*Tosca*	spinto	96	Verismo
E sogno? O realtà?	*Falstaff*	lyric baritone (dramatic)	23	Italian Romantic
E Susanna non vien! . . . Dove sono	*Le nozze di Figaro*	full lyric	81	Classical
Ebben! Ne andrò lontana	*La Wally*	spinto	95	Verismo
Ecco ridente in cielo	*Il barbiere di Siviglia*	leggiero	4	Bel canto
Eccomi in lieta vesta . . . Oh! Quante volte, Oh! Quante	*I Capuleti e i Montecchi*	lyric coloratura	3	Bel canto
E'gettata la mia sorte	*Attila*	dramatic baritone	45	Italian Romantic
Ella giammai m'amò	*Don Carlo*	bass-baritone	68	Italian Romantic

Aria Title	Opera Title	Fach	No.	Historical Style
Ella mi fu rapita . . . Parmi veder le lagrime	*Rigoletto*	lyric	65	Italian Romantic
Ernani, Ernani involami	*Ernani*	dramatic coloratura	66	Italian Romantic
Eterna la memoria	*Alzira*	dramatic baritone	40	Italian Romantic
Fin ch'han dal vino	*Don Giovanni*	lyric baritone (dramatic)	15	Classical
Firenze è come un albero fiorito	*Gianni Schicchi*	lyric	45	20th-century Italian
Franco son io	*Giovanna d'Arco*	dramatic baritone	51	Italian Romantic
Già di pietà mi spoglio	*Mitridate, re di Ponto*	leggiero	17	Classical
Giunse alfin il momento . . . Deh vieni, non tardar	*Le nozze di Figaro*	soubrette	24	Classical
Hai già vinta la causa . . . Vendro mentr'io sospiro	*Le nozze di Figaro*	lyric baritone (dramatic)	30	Classical
Ho capito, signor, si	*Don Giovanni*	lyric baritone	16	Classical
Ho un gran peso	*L'italiana in Algeri*	lyric baritone (bass-baritone)	29	Bel canto
Il balen del suo sorriso	*Il trovatore*	dramatic baritone	64	Italian Romantic
Il cavallo scalpita	*Cavalleria rusticana*	dramatic baritone	47	Verismo
Il dolce suono mi colpì di sua voce (Mad Scene)	*Lucia di Lammermoor*	dramatic coloratura	67	Bel canto
Il lacerato spirito	*Simon Boccanegra*	bass (dramatic)	96	Italian Romantic
Il mio tesoro	*Don Giovanni*	leggiero	9	Classical
Il segreto per esser felici	*Lucrezia Borgia*	contralto	95	Bel canto
Il vecchiotto cerca moglie	*Il barbiere di Siviglia*	lyric	21	Bel canto
Illustratevi, o cieli	*Il ritorno di Ulisse in patria*	lyric	46	Italian Baroque
In quelle trine morbide	*Manon Lescaut*	spinto	89	Verismo
In questa reggia	*Turandot*	dramatic	105	20th-century Italian
In si barbara	*Semiramide*	lyric coloratura	16	Bel canto
In uomini, in soldati	*Così fan tutte*	soubrette	15	Classical
Infelice! E tuo credevi	*Ernani*	bass-baritone	69	Italian Romantic
Io seguo sol fiero	*Partenope*	lyric coloratura	11	Italian Baroque
La callunia	*Il barbiere di Siviglia*	bass (lyric)	84	Bel canto
La donna è mobile	*Rigoletto*	lyric	66	Italian Romantic
La luce langue	*Macbeth*	dramatic	74	Italian Romantic
La sua lampada vitale	*I masnadieri*	dramatic baritone	59	Italian Romantic
L'angue offeso	*Giulio Cesare*	lyric	46	Italian Baroque

Aria Title	Opera Title	Fach	No.	Historical Style
Languir per una bella	*L'italiana in Algeri*	lyric	49	Bel canto
Largo al factotum	*Il barbiere di Siviglia*	lyric baritone	4	Bel canto
Lo vidi e 'l primo palpito	*Luisa Miller*	full lyric	79	Italian Romantic
Ma quando tornerai	*Alcina*	lyric	26	Italian Baroque
Ma se m'è forza perderti	*Un ballo in maschera*	spinto	85	Italian Romantic
Madamina! Il catalogo è questo	*Don Giovanni*	bass (buffo)	86	Classical
Mercè, dilette amiche	*I vespri siciliani*	dramatic coloratura	71	Italian Romantic
Metà di voi quà vadano	*Don Giovanni*	lyric baritone (dramatic)	17	Classical
Mi chiamano Mimì	*La bohème*	lyric	35	Verismo
Mia madre aveva una povera ancella (Willow Song)	*Otello*	full lyric	84	Italian Romantic
Minnie, dalla mia casa son partito	*La fanciulla del West*	dramatic baritone	48	Verismo
Morir! Tremenda cosa! . . . Urna fatale del mio destino	*La forza del destino*	dramatic baritone	49	Italian Romantic
Nel giardin del bello (Veil Song)	*Don Carlo*	dramatic	66	Italian Romantic
Nel sen mi palpita	*Mitridate, re di Ponto*	lyric coloratura	12	Classical
Nella fatal di Rimini	*Lucrezia Borgia*	contralto	96	Bel canto
Nemico della patria	*Andrea Chénier*	dramatic baritone	43	Verismo
Non mi dir	*Don Giovanni*	dramatic coloratura	64	Classical
Non più andrai	*Le nozze di Figaro*	bass-baritone	79	Classical
Non più di fiori	*La clemenza di Tito*	dramatic coloratura	61	Classical
Non più mesta	*La Cenerentola*	lyric coloratura	5	Bel canto
Non siate ritrosi	*Così fan tutte*	lyric baritone	11	Classical
Non so più cosa son, cosa faccio	*Le nozze di Figaro*	lyric	40	Classical
O don fatale!	*Don Carlo*	dramatic	67	Italian Romantic
O lieto augurio	*Macbeth*	dramatic baritone	58	Italian Romantic
O mio babbino caro	*Gianni Schicchi*	lyric	40	20th-century Italian
O mio Fernando	*La favorita*	dramatic	69	Bel canto
O patria mia	*Aida*	dramatic	96	Italian Romantic
O tu che in seno agli angeli	*La forza del destino*	spinto	91	Italian Romantic
O tu Palermo	*I vespri siciliani*	bass	99	Italian Romantic

Aria Title	Opera Title	Fach	No.	Historical Style
Oh! Nel fuggente nuvolo	*Attila*	dramatic coloratura	60	Italian Romantic
Oh, patria! Dolce, e ingrate patria! . . . tu que accendi questo core	*Tancredi*	lyric coloratura	18	Bel canto
Ombra mai fu	*Serse (Xerxes)*	lyric	48	Italian Baroque
Pace, pace mio Dio!	*La forza del destino*	spinto	88	Italian Romantic
Parto, parto	*La clemenza di Tito*	lyric coloratura	7	Classical
Per lui che adoro	*L'italiana in Algeri*	lyric coloratura	10	Bel canto
Per me giunto . . . Io morrò, ma lieto in core	*Don Carlo*	lyric baritone	13	Italian Romantic
Per pietà	*Così fan tutte*	dramatic coloratura	63	Classical
Per questa fiamma indomita	*Anna Bolena*	lyric coloratura	4	Bel canto
Piangerò la sorte mia	*Giulio Cesare*	lyric coloratura	7	Italian Baroque
Porgi amor	*Le nozze di Figaro*	full lyric	82	Classical
Possente amor mi chiama	*Rigoletto*	lyric	67	Italian Romantic
Prendi; prendi, per me sei libero	*L'elisir d'amore*	soubrette	20	Bel canto
Presti omai l'egizia terra	*Giulio Cesare*	dramatic baritone (bass)	52	Italian Baroque
Priva son d'ogni conforto	*Giulio Cesare*	contralto	94	Italian Baroque
Qual fiamma avea nel guardo!	*I Pagliacci*	lyric	48	Verismo
Quando le sere al placido	*Luisa Miller*	leggiero	16	Italian Romantic
Quando m'en vo' (Musetta's Waltz)	*La bohème*	lyric	36	Verismo
Quanto è bella	*L'elisir d'amore*	leggiero	10	Bel canto
Quanto un mortal può chiedere	*Alzira*	dramatic baritone	41	Italian Romantic
Quel guardo il cavaliere . . . So anch'io la virtù magica	*Don Pasquale*	lyric coloratura	5	Bel canto
Quel mesto gemito	*Semiramide*	lyric coloratura	17	Bel canto
Quel ribelle e quell'ingrato	*Mitridate, re di Ponto*	leggiero	18	Classical
Quel volto mi piace	*Partenope*	lyric coloratura	12	Italian Baroque
Questa o quella	*Rigoletto*	lyric	68	Italian Romantic
Questo amor, vergogna mia	*Edgar*	lyric baritone	19	Verismo
Qui la voce . . . Vien, diletto	*I puritani*	lyric coloratura	13	Italian Romantic

Aria Title	Opera Title	Fach	No.	Historical Style
Re dell'abisso, affrettati (Invocation Aria)	*Un ballo in maschera*	dramatic	58	Italian Romantic
Recondita armonia	*Tosca*	spinto	97	Verismo
Regnava nel silenzio	*Lucia di Lammermoor*	dramatic coloratura	68	Bel canto
Ritorna vincitor!	*Aida*	dramatic	97	Italian Romantic
Rosa del ciel	*L'Orfeo*	leggiero	20	Italian Baroque
Saper vorreste	*Un ballo in maschera*	lyric coloratura	1	Italian Romantic
Scherza infida	*Ariodante*	leggiero	3	Italian Baroque
Se di lauri	*Mitridate, re di Ponto*	leggiero	19	Classical
Se vuol ballare	*Le nozze di Figaro*	bass-baritone	80	Classical
Senza mamma	*Suor Angelica*	spinto	90	Verismo
Sgombra è la sacra selva . . . Deh! Proteggimi, O Dio!	*Norma*	dramatic	76	Bel canto
Si può?	*I Pagliacci*	dramatic baritone	61	Verismo
Sì! Morir ella de'!	*La Gioconda*	bass (dramatic)	89	Italian Romantic
Sì, ritrovarla io giuro	*La Cenerentola*	leggiero	5	Bel canto
Signore, ascolta	*Turandot*	lyric	56	20th-century Italian
Smanie implacabili	*Così fan tutte*	lyric	23	Classical
Son pochi fiori	*L'amico Fritz*	lyric	28	Verismo
Spirto gentil	*La favorita*	lyric	41	Bel canto
Stà nell'Ircana pietrosa tana	*Alcina*	lyric coloratura	2	Italian Baroque
Stella del marinar	*La Gioconda*	dramatic	70	Italian Romantic
Stride la vampa	*Il trovatore*	dramatic	87	Italian Romantic
Suicidio!	*La Gioconda*	dramatic	100	Italian Romantic
Sul fil d'un soffio etesio	*Falstaff*	soubrette	22	Italian Romantic
Svegliatevi nel core	*Giulio Cesare*	lyric	47	Italian Baroque
Tacea la notte	*Il trovatore*	full lyric	87	Italian Romantic
Temer? Perchè?	*Andrea Chénier*	lyric	20	Verismo
Tombe degl' avi miei . . . Fra poco a me ricovero	*Lucia di Lammermoor*	lyric	52	Bel canto
Tradito, schernito	*Così fan tutte*	lyric	34	Classical
Tu che di gel sei cinta	*Turandot*	lyric	57	20th-century Italian
Tu punischimi, o signore . . . a brani, a brani o perfido	*Luisa Miller*	full lyric	80	Italian Romantic

Aria Title	Opera Title	Fach	No.	Historical Style
Tu sul labbro	*Nabucco*	bass	95	Italian Romantic
Un dì, all'azzurro spazio	*Andrea Chénier*	spinto	83	Verismo
Un ignoto, tre lune or saranno	*I masnadieri*	bass	93	Italian Romantic
Una donna a quindici anni	*Così fan tutte*	soubrette	16	Classical
Una furtiva lagrima	*L'elisir d'amore*	leggiero	11	Bel canto
Una macchia è qui tuttora!	*Macbeth*	dramatic (mezzo-soprano)	101	Italian Romantic
Una voce poco fa	*Il barbiere di Siviglia*	lyric	22	Bel canto
Un'aura amorosa	*Così fan tutte*	leggiero	7	Classical
Va pur, va pur, va seco	*La Calisto*	lyric baritone	6	Italian Baroque
V'adoro, pupille	*Giulio Cesare*	lyric coloratura	8	Italian Baroque
Vecchia zimarra	*La bohème*	bass (lyric)	85	Verismo
Vedrai carino	*Don Giovanni*	soubrette	18	Classical
Venti, turbini, prestate	*Rinaldo*	lyric coloratura	14	Italian Baroque
Verdi prati e selve amene	*Alcina*	lyric coloratura	3	Italian Baroque
Vi ravviso	*La sonnambula*	bass	97	Bel canto
Vieni! T'affretta . . . Or tutti, sorgete	*Macbeth*	dramatic (mezzo-soprano)	102	Italian Romantic
Vissi d'arte	*Tosca*	spinto	91	Verismo
Voce di donna o d'angelo	*La Gioconda*	contralto	93	Italian Romantic
Voi lo sapete, o mamma	*Cavalleria rusticana*	dramatic	64	Verismo
Voi che sapete	*Le nozze di Figaro*	lyric	41	Classical
Volta la terrea	*Un ballo in maschera*	lyric coloratura	2	Italian Romantic
Zazà, piccolo zingara	*Zazà*	lyric baritone	39	Verismo

Russian

Aria Title	Opera Title	Fach	No.	Historical Style
Ja nye sposobna k grusti tomnoy	*Eugene Onegin*	contralto	92	Russian Romantic
Kogda bi zhizn domashnim krugom	*Eugene Onegin*	lyric baritone (dramatic)	21	Russian Romantic
Kuda, kuda, kuda, vy udalilis	*Eugene Onegin*	lyric	39	Russian Romantic
Lyubvi vse vozrastï pokornï	*Eugene Onegin*	bass	87	Russian Romantic
Ruskai pogibnu (Letter Scene)	*Eugene Onegin*	full lyric	75	Russian Romantic

Aria Title	Opera Title	Fach	No.	Historical Style
Skuchno Marine, akh kak skuchno-to!	*Boris Godunov*	dramatic	59	Russian Nationalist
Uzhel ta samaja Tatiana	*Eugene Onegin*	lyric baritone (dramatic)	22	Russian Romantic
Ves' tabor spit	*Aleko*	bass-baritone	65	Russian Romantic

Index D
Arias by Historical Period

Historical Period	Aria Title	Opera Title	Lang.	Fach	No.
17th century (English Baroque)	Dry those eyes	*The Tempest*	Eng.	lyric	50
17th century (English Baroque)	When I am laid in earth	*Dido and Aeneas*	Eng.	contralto	91
17th century (Italian Baroque)	Illustratevi, o cieli	*Il ritorno di Ulisse in patria*	It.	lyric	46
17th century (Italian Baroque)	Rosa del ciel	*L'Orfeo*	It.	leggiero	20
17th century (Italian Baroque)	Va pur, va pur, va seco	*La Calisto*	It.	lyric baritone	6
18th century (Italian Baroque)	Cara sposa	*Rinaldo*	It.	lyric coloratura	13
18th century (Italian Baroque)	Di te mi rido	*Alcina*	It.	lyric coloratura	1
18th century (Italian Baroque)	Io seguo sol fiero	*Partenope*	It.	lyric coloratura	11
18th century (Italian Baroque)	L'angue offeso	*Giulio Cesare*	It.	lyric	46
18th century (Italian Baroque)	Ma quando tornerai	*Alcina*	It.	lyric	26
18th century (Italian Baroque)	Ombra mai fu	*Serse (Xerxes)*	It.	lyric	48
18th century (Italian Baroque)	Piangerò la sorte mia	*Giulio Cesare*	It.	lyric coloratura	7
18th century (Italian Baroque)	Presti omai l'egizia terra	*Giulio Cesare*	It.	dramatic baritone (bass)	52
18th century (Italian Baroque)	Priva son d'ogni conforto	*Giulio Cesare*	It.	contralto	94
18th century (Italian Baroque)	Quel volto mi piace	*Partenope*	It.	lyric coloratura	12
18th century (Italian Baroque)	Scherza infida	*Ariodante*	It.	leggiero	3
18th century (Italian Baroque)	Stà nell'Ircana pietrosa tana	*Alcina*	It.	lyric coloratura	2
18th century (Italian Baroque)	Svegliatevi nel core	*Giulio Cesare*	It.	lyric	47
18th century (Italian Baroque)	V'adoro, pupille	*Giulio Cesare*	It.	lyric coloratura	8
18th century (Italian Baroque)	Venti, turbini, prestate	*Rinaldo*	It.	lyric coloratura	14
18th century (Italian Baroque)	Verdi prati e selve amene	*Alcina*	It.	lyric coloratura	3
18th century (Classical)	Ah lo veggio quell'anima bella	*Così fan tutte*	It.	lyric	33

Historical Period	Aria Title	Opera Title	Lang.	Fach	No.
18th century (Classical)	Ah, se fosse intorno al trono	*La clemenza di Tito*	It.	lyric	30
18th century (Classical)	Aprite un po' quegl'occhi	*Le nozze di Figaro*	It.	bass-baritone	78
18th century (Classical)	Batti, batti	*Don Giovanni*	It.	soubrette	17
18th century (Classical	Che farò senza Euridice?	*Orfeo ed Euridice*	It.	lyric	42
18th century (Classical)	Come scoglio	*Così fan tutte*	It.	dramatic coloratura	62
18th century (Classical)	Con un' vezzo all'Italiana	*La finta giardiniera*	It.	lyric baritone	25
18th century (Classical)	Dalla sua pace	*Don Giovanni*	It.	leggiero	8
18th century (Classical)	Deh per questo istante solo	*La clemenza di Tito*	It.	lyric coloratura	6
18th century (Classical)	Deh vieni alla finestra	*Don Giovanni*	It.	lyric baritone (dramatic)	14
18th century (Classical)	Del più sublime soglio	*La clemenza di Tito*	It.	lyric	31
18th century (Classical)	Donne mie la fate a tanti	*Così fan tutte*	It.	lyric baritone	10
18th century (Classical)	E Susanna non vien! . . . Dove sono	*Le nozze di Figaro*	It.	full lyric	81
18th century (Classical)	Fin ch'han dal vino	*Don Giovanni*	It.	lyric baritone (dramatic)	15
18th century (Classical)	Già di pietà mi spoglio	*Mitridate, re di Ponto*	It.	leggiero	17
18th century (Classical)	Giunse alfin il momento . . . Deh vieni, non tardar	*Le nozze di Figaro*	It.	soubrette	24
18th century (Classical)	Hai già vinta la causa . . . Vendro mentr'io sospiro	*Le nozze di Figaro*	It.	lyric baritone (dramatic)	30
18th century (Classical)	Ho capito, signor, si	*Don Giovanni*	It.	lyric baritone	16
18th century (Classical)	Il mio tesoro	*Don Giovanni*	It.	leggiero	9
18th century (Classical)	In uomini, in soldati	*Così fan tutte*	It.	soubrette	15
18th century (Classical)	Madamina! Il catalogo è questo	*Don Giovanni*	It.	bass (buffo)	86
18th century (Classical)	Metà di voi quà vadano	*Don Giovanni*	It.	lyric baritone (dramatic)	17
18th century (Classical)	Nel sen mi palpita	*Mitridate, re di Ponto*	It.	lyric coloratura	12
18th century (Classical)	Non mi dir	*Don Giovanni*	It.	dramatic coloratura	64
18th century (Classical)	Non più andrai	*Le nozze di Figaro*	It.	bass-baritone	79

Historical Period	Aria Title	Opera Title	Lang.	Fach	No.
18th century (Classical)	Non più di fiori	*La clemenza di Tito*	It.	dramatic coloratura	61
18th century (Classical)	Non siate ritrosi	*Così fan tutte*	It.	lyric baritone	11
18th century (Classical)	Non so più cosa son, cosa faccio	*Le nozze di Figaro*	It.	lyric	40
18th century (Classical)	Parto, parto	*La clemenza di Tito*	It.	lyric coloratura	7
18th century (Classical)	Per pietà	*Così fan tutte*	It.	dramatic coloratura	63
18th century (Classical)	Porgi amor	*Le nozze di Figaro*	It.	full lyric	82
18th century (Classical)	Quel ribelle e quell'ingrato	*Mitridate, re di Ponto*	It.	leggiero	18
18th century (Classical)	Se di lauri	*Mitridate, re di Ponto*	It.	leggiero	19
18th century (Classical)	Se vuol ballare	*Le nozze di Figaro*	It.	bass-baritone	80
18th century (Classical)	Smanie implaca-bili	*Così fan tutte*	It.	lyric	23
18th century (Classical)	Tradito, schernito	*Così fan tutte*	It.	lyric	34
18th century (Classical)	Una donna a quindici anni	*Così fan tutte*	It.	soubrette	16
18th century (Classical)	Un'aura amorosa	*Così fan tutte*	It.	leggiero	7
18th century (Classical)	Vedrai carino	*Don Giovanni*	It.	soubrette	18
18th century (Classical)	Voi che sapete	*Le nozze di Figaro*	It.	lyric	41
18th century (Singspiel)	Ach, ich fühl's	*Die Zauber-flöte*	Ger.	lyric	58
18th century (Singspiel)	Ach, ich liebte	*Die Entfüh-rung aus dem Serail*	Ger.	dramatic coloratura	65
18th century (Singspiel)	Der Hölle Rache kocht in meinem Herzen	*Die Zauber-flöte*	Ger.	dramatic coloratura	72
18th century (Singspiel)	Der Vogelfänger bin ich ja	*Die Zauber-flöte*	Ger.	lyric baritone	37
18th century (Singspiel)	Dies Bildnis ist bezaubernd schön	*Die Zauber-flöte*	Ger.	lyric	81
18th century (Singspiel)	Ein Mädchen oder Weibchen	*Die Zauber-flöte*	Ger.	lyric baritone	38
18th century (Singspiel)	Frisch zum Kampfe!	*Die Entföh-rung aus dem Serail*	Ger.	lyric	38
18th century (Singspiel)	O wie ängstlich	*Die Entföh-rung aus dem Serail*	Ger.	leggiero	12
18th century (Singspiel)	O zittre nicht . . . Zum Leiden bin ich auserkoren	*Die Zauber-flöte*	Ger.	dramatic coloratura	73

Historical Period	Aria Title	Opera Title	Lang.	Fach	No.
18th century (Singspiel)	Welche Wonne, welche Lust	*Die Entführung aus dem Serail*	Ger.	soubrette	21
18th century (Singspiel)	Wenn der Freude Tränen fliessen	*Die Entführung aus dem Serail*	Ger.	lyric	37
19th century (Bel canto)	Ah, come il cor di giubilo	*L'italiana in Algeri*	It.	leggiero	14
19th century (Bel canto)	Ah, mes amis . . . Pour mon âme	*La fille du régiment*	Fr.	lyric	42
19th century (Bel canto)	Ah! Per sempre io ti perdei . . . Bel sogno beato	*I puritani*	It.	lyric baritone	33
19th century (Bel canto)	Amici, in ogni evento . . . Pensa alla patria	*L'italiana in Algeri*	It.	lyric coloratura	8
19th century (Bel canto)	Bel raggio lusinghier	*Semiramide*	It.	lyric coloratura	15
19th century (Bel canto)	Bella siccome un angelo	*Don Pasquale*	It.	lyric baritone	18
19th century (Bel canto)	Casta diva	*Norma*	It.	dramatic	103
19th century (Bel canto)	Chacun le sait	*La fille du régiment*	Fr.	lyric coloratura	6
19th century (Bel canto)	Com'è gentil la notte	*Don Pasquale*	It.	lyric	35
19th century (Bel canto)	Come paride vezzoso	*L'elisir d'amore*	It.	lyric baritone	20
19th century (Bel canto)	Come un'ape ne'giorni d'aprile	*La Cenerentola*	It.	lyric baritone	8
19th century (Bel canto)	Cruda sorte	*L'italiana in Algeri*	It.	lyric coloratura	9
19th century (Bel canto)	Dalle stanze ove Lucia	*Lucia di Lammermoor*	It.	bass-baritone	75
19th century (Bel canto)	Della crudel Isotta	*L'elisir d'amore*	It.	soubrette	19
19th century (Bel canto)	Ecco ridente in cielo	*Il barbiere di Siviglia*	It.	leggiero	4
19th century (Bel canto)	Eccomi in lieta vesta . . . Oh! Quante volte, Oh! Quante	*I Capuletti e i Montecchi*	It.	lyric coloratura	3
19th century (Bel canto)	Ho un gran peso	*L'italiana in Algeri*	It.	lyric baritone (bass-baritone)	29
19th century (Bel canto)	Il dolce suono mi colpì di sua voce (Mad Scene)	*Lucia di Lammermoor*	It.	dramatic coloratura	67
19th century (Bel canto)	Il segreto per esser felici	*Lucrezia Borgia*	It.	contralto	95
19th century (Bel canto)	Il vecchiotto cerca moglie	*Il barbiere di Siviglia*	It.	lyric	21
19th century (Bel canto)	In si barbara	*Semiramide*	It.	lyric coloratura	16
19th century (Bel canto)	La callunia	*Il barbiere di Siviglia*	It.	bass (lyric)	84

Historical Period	Aria Title	Opera Title	Lang.	Fach	No.
19th century (Bel canto)	Languir per una bella	*L'italiana in Algeri*	It.	lyric	49
19th century (Bel canto)	Largo al factotum	*Il barbiere di Siviglia*	It.	lyric baritone	4
19th century (Bel canto)	Nella fatal di Rimini	*Lucrezia Borgia*	It.	contralto	96
19th century (Bel canto)	Non più mesta	*La Cenerentola*	It.	lyric coloratura	5
19th century (Bel canto)	O mio Fernando	*La favorita*	It.	dramatic	69
19th century (Bel canto)	Oh, patria! Dolce, e ingrate patria! . . . tu que accendi questo core	*Tancredi*	It.	lyric coloratura	18
19th century (Bel canto)	Per lui che adoro	*L'italiana in Algeri*	It.	lyric coloratura	10
19th century (Bel canto)	Per questa fiamma indomita	*Anna Bolena*	It.	lyric coloratura	4
19th century (Bel canto)	Prendi; prendi, per me sei libero	*L'elisir d'amore*	It.	soubrette	20
19th century (Bel canto)	Quanto è bella	*L'elisir d'amore*	It.	leggiero	10
19th century (Bel canto)	Quel guardo il cavaliere . . . So anch'io la virtù magica	*Don Pasquale*	It.	lyric coloratura	5
19th century (Bel canto)	Quel mesto gemito	*Semiramide*	It.	lyric coloratura	17
19th century (Bel canto)	Regnava nel silenzio	*Lucia di Lammermoor*	It.	dramatic coloratura	68
19th century (Bel canto)	Sgombra è la sacra selva . . . Deh! Proteggimi, O Dio!	*Norma*	It.	dramatic	76
19th century (Bel canto)	Sì, ritrovarla io giuro	*La Cenerentola*	It.	leggiero	5
19th century (Bel canto)	Spirto gentil	*La favorita*	It.	lyric	41
19th century (Bel canto)	Tombe degl' avi miei . . . Fra poco a me ricovero	*Lucia di Lammermoor*	It.	lyric	52
19th century (Bel canto)	Una furtiva lagrima	*L'elisir d'amore*	It.	leggiero	11
19th century (Bel canto)	Una voce poco fa	*Il barbiere di Siviglia*	It.	lyric	22
19th century (Bel canto)	Vi ravviso	*La sonnambula*	It.	bass	97
19th century (Czech Nationalist)	Ah, my darling, we could grow together like a single vine	*The Bartered Bride*	Eng.	lyric	33
19th century (Czech Nationalist)	Soon now my dearest	*The Bartered Bride*	Eng.	lyric	23
19th century (French Romantic)	Adieu, Mignon!	*Mignon*	Fr.	lyric	58

Historical Period	Aria Title	Opera Title	Lang.	Fach	No.
19th century (French Romantic)	Adieu, notre petite table	*Manon*	Fr.	lyric	44
19th century (French Romantic)	Ah! Fuyez douce image	*Manon*	Fr.	lyric	55
19th century (French Romantic)	Ah, je ris de me voir (Jewel Song)	*Faust*	Fr.	full lyric (coloratura)	76
19th century (French Romantic)	Ah, lève-toi, soleil!	*Roméo et Juliette*	Fr.	lyric	70
19th century (French Romantic)	Ah! Mon fils, sois béni	*Le prophète*	Fr.	dramatic	77
19th century (French Romantic)	Amour! Viens aider ma faiblesse!	*Samson et Dalila*	Fr.	dramatic	83
19th century (French Romantic)	Avancez! Reculez!	*Cendrillon*	Fr.	contralto	88
19th century (French Romantic)	Avant de quitter ces lieux	*Faust*	Fr.	lyric baritone (dramatic)	24
19th century (French Romantic)	Connais-tu le pays?	*Mignon*	Fr.	lyric	38
19th century (French Romantic)	De son coeur j'ai calmé la fièvre (Berceuse)	*Mignon*	Fr.	bass	94
19th century (French Romantic)	Donnez, donnez	*Le prophète*	Fr.	dramatic	78
19th century (French Romantic)	Elle a fui, la tourterelle	*Les contes d'Hoffmann*	Fr.	lyric	38
19th century (French Romantic)	En fermant les yeux (Le Rêve)	*Manon*	Fr.	lyric	56
19th century (French Romantic)	En vain pour éviter (Card Aria)	*Carmen*	Fr.	dramatic	60
19th century (French Romantic)	Épouse quelque brave fille	*Manon*	Fr.	bass	92
19th century (French Romantic)	Faites-lui mes aveux	*Faust*	Fr.	lyric	27
19th century (French Romantic)	Fantaisie aux divins mensonges	*Lakmé*	Fr.	leggiero	15
19th century (French Romantic)	Il est doux, il est bon	*Hérodiade*	Fr.	full lyric	78
19th century (French Romantic)	Il était une fois à la cour d'Eisenach	*Les contes d'Hoffmann*	Fr.	lyric	32
19th century (French Romantic)	Inutiles regrets	*Les Troyens*	Fr.	spinto	100
19th century (French Romantic)	I've dined so well (Tipsy Waltz)	*La Périchole*	Eng.	lyric	43
19th century (French Romantic)	J'ai pu frapper	*Hamlet*	Fr.	lyric baritone (dramatic)	26
19th century (French Romantic)	Je crois entendre encore	*Les pêcheurs de perles*	Fr.	lyric	60
19th century (French Romantic)	Je dis que rien ne m'épouvante	*Carmen*	Fr.	lyric	37
19th century (French Romantic)	Je suis Titania	*Mignon*	Fr.	lyric coloratura	11

Historical Period	Aria Title	Opera Title	Lang.	Fach	No.
19th century (French Romantic)	Je veux vivre dans ce rêve	*Roméo et Juliette*	Fr.	lyric coloratura	14
19th century (French Romantic)	La fleur que tu m'avais jetée	*Carmen*	Fr.	spinto	86
19th century (French Romantic)	L'amour est un oiseau (Habañera)	*Carmen*	Fr.	dramatic	61
19th century (French Romantic)	Les oiseaux dans la charmille	*Les contes d'Hoffmann*	Fr.	lyric coloratura	4
19th century (French Romantic)	Les tringles des sistres tintaient	*Carmen*	Fr.	dramatic	62
19th century (French Romantic)	L'orage s'est calmé	*Les pêcheurs de perles*	Fr.	lyric baritone	32
19th century (French Romantic)	Lorsqu'on a plus de vingt quartiers	*Cendrillon*	Fr.	contralto	89
19th century (French Romantic)	Mab, la reine des mensonges	*Roméo et Juliette*	Fr.	lyric baritone	34
19th century (French Romantic)	Me voici dans son boudoir	*Mignon*	Fr.	lyric	39
19th century (French Romantic)	Mon coeur s'ouvre à ta voix	*Samson et Dalila*	Fr.	dramatic	84
19th century (French Romantic)	Ne m'abandonne point . . . Asile héréditaire	*Guillaume Tell*	Fr.	lyric	48
19th century (French Romantic)	Nobles seigneurs, salut!	*Les Huguenots*	Fr.	lyric	30
19th century (French Romantic)	O vin dissipe la tristesse	*Hamlet*	Fr.	lyric baritone (dramatic)	27
19th century (French Romantic)	Où va la jeune Hindoue (Bell Song)	*Lakmé*	Fr.	lyric coloratura	10
19th century (French Romantic)	Pour les couvents c'est fini	*Les Huguenots*	Fr.	bass-baritone	72
19th century (French Romantic)	Pourquoi me réveiller	*Werther*	Fr.	lyric	80
19th century (French Romantic)	Près des remparts de Séville (Seguidilla)	*Carmen*	Fr.	dramatic	63
19th century (French Romantic)	Printemps qui commence	*Samson et Dalila*	Fr.	dramatic	85
19th century (French Romantic)	Que fais-tu, blanche tourterelle	*Roméo et Juliette*	Fr.	lyric	47
19th century (French Romantic)	Qui donc commande	*Henry VIII*	Fr.	dramatic baritone	55
19th century (French Romantic)	Salut! Demeure chaste et pure	*Faust*	Fr.	lyric	40
19th century (French Romantic)	Scintille, diamant	*Les contes d'Hoffmann*	Fr.	lyric baritone (dramatic)	9
19th century (French Romantic)	Si la rigueur	*La Juive*	Fr.	bass	90
19th century (French Romantic)	Sois immobile	*Guillaume Tell*	Fr.	dramatic baritone	53

Historical Period	Aria Title	Opera Title	Lang.	Fach	No.
19th century (French Romantic)	Sombre forêt	*Guillaume Tell*	Fr.	lyric coloratura (dramatic)	9
19th century (French Romantic)	Spectre infernal!	*Hamlet*	Fr.	lyric baritone (dramatic)	28
19th century (French Romantic)	Tandis qu'il sommeille	*La Juive*	Fr.	lyric	42
19th century (French Romantic)	Va! Laisse couler mes larmes	*Werther*	Fr.	lyric	52
19th century (French Romantic)	Vainement, ma bien-aimée	*Le roi d'Ys*	Fr.	lyric	69
19th century (French Romantic)	Vision fugitive	*Hérodiade*	Fr.	dramatic baritone	56
19th century (French Romantic)	Voilà donc la terrible cité	*Thaïs*	Fr.	dramatic baritone	62
19th century (French Romantic)	Votre toast, je peux vous le render	*Carmen*	Fr.	dramatic baritone	46
19th century (French Romantic)	Vous qui faites l'endormie	*Faust*	Fr.	bass (dramatic)	88
19th century (French Romantic)	Werther, Werther (Letter Aria)	*Werther*	Fr.	lyric	53
19th century (German Romantic)	Abscheulicher! Wo eilst du hin? . . . Komm, Hoffnung	*Fidelio*	Ger.	dramatic	99
19th century (German Romantic)	Ach, so fromm (M'apparì tutt'amor)	*Martha*	Ger./ It.	lyric	57
19th century (German Romantic)	Ach, wir armen, armen Leute	*Hänsel und Gretel*	Ger.	dramatic baritone	54
19th century (German Romantic)	Als Büblein klein	*Die lustigen Weiber von Windsor*	Ger.	bass-baritone	76
19th century (German Romantic)	Am stillen Herd	*Die Meister-singer von Nürnberg*	Ger.	dramatic	101
19th century (German Romantic)	Der kleine Tau-mann heiss' ich	*Hänsel und Gretel*	Ger.	lyric (soubrette)	41
19th century (German Romantic)	Dich teure Halle	*Tannhäuser*	Ger.	dramatic	104
19th century (German Romantic)	Du bist der Lenz	*Die Walküre*	Ger.	dramatic	106
19th century (German Romantic)	Durch die Wälder	*Der Freischütz*	Ger.	spinto	92
19th century (German Romantic)	Entweihte Götter!	*Lohengrin*	Ger.	dramatic	73
19th century (German Romantic)	Gerechter Gott	*Rienzi*	Ger.	lyric (dramatic)	45
19th century (German Romantic)	Hat man nicht auch Gold beine-ben	*Fidelio*	Ger.	bass-baritone	70
19th century (German Romantic)	Horch, die Lerche singt im Hain!	*Die lustigen Weiber von Windsor*	Ger.	lyric	53

Historical Period	Aria Title	Opera Title	Lang.	Fach	No.
19th century (German Romantic)	Nimmermehr wird mein Herze sich grämen	*Martha*	Ger.	lyric	36
19th century (German Romantic)	O du, mein holder Abend-stern	*Tannhäuser*	Ger.	lyric baritone (dramatic)	35
19th century (German Romantic)	O wär' ich schon mit dir vereint	*Fidelio*	Ger.	lyric (soubrette)	39
19th century (German Romantic)	Schweig'! Schweig'! damit dich niemand warnt	*Der Freischütz*	Ger.	bass-baritone	71
19th century (German Romantic)	Wo in Bergen du dich birgst	*Die Walküre*	Ger.	contralto	99
19th century (Italian Romantic)	Ah, la paterna mano	*Macbeth*	It.	lyric	54
19th century (Italian Romantic)	Ah, pescator, affonda l'esca	*La Gioconda*	It.	dramatic baritone	50
19th century (Italian Romantic)	Ah sì, ben mio; coll'essere	*Il trovatore*	It.	spinto	98
19th century (Italian Romantic)	Al suon del tamburo	*La forza del destino*	It.	lyric	29
19th century (Italian Romantic)	Allor che i forti corrono	*Attila*	It.	dramatic coloratura	59
19th century (Italian Romantic)	Amor ti vieta	*Fedora*	It.	spinto	90
19th century (Italian Romantic)	Anch'io dischiuso un giorno	*Nabucco*	It.	dramatic coloratura	69
19th century (Italian Romantic)	Ave Maria	*Otello*	It.	full lyric	83
19th century (Italian Romantic)	Carlo, ch'è sol il nostro amore	*Don Carlo*	It.	lyric baritone	12
19th century (Italian Romantic)	Caro nome	*Rigoletto*	It.	lyric (coloratura)	49
19th century (Italian Romantic)	Che non avrebbe il misero	*Attila*	It.	lyric	22
19th century (Italian Romantic)	Chiudi il labbro	*I due Foscari*	It.	spinto	87
19th century (Italian Romantic)	Come dal ciel precipita	*Macbeth*	It.	bass	91
19th century (Italian Romantic)	Condotta ell'era in ceppi	*Il trovatore*	It.	dramatic	86
19th century (Italian Romantic)	Dagl'immortali vertici	*Attila*	It.	dramatic baritone	44
19th century (Italian Romantic)	Dal labbro il canto	*Falstaff*	It.	leggiero	13
19th century (Italian Romantic)	Dal più remoto esilio	*I due Foscari*	It.	spinto	88
19th century (Italian Romantic)	Dei miei bollenti spiriti	*La traviata*	It.	lyric	77
19th century (Italian Romantic)	Di due figli vivea	*Il trovatore*	It.	bass-baritone	82
19th century (Italian Romantic)	Di Provenza il mar	*La traviata*	It.	dramatic baritone	63
19th century (Italian Romantic)	Di quella pira	*Il trovatore*	It.	spinto	99

Historical Period	Aria Title	Opera Title	Lang.	Fach	No.
19th century (Italian Romantic)	E sogno? O realtà?	*Falstaff*	It.	lyric baritone (dramatic)	23
19th century (Italian Romantic)	E'gettata la mia sorte	*Attila*	It.	dramatic baritone	45
19th century (Italian Romantic)	Ella giammai m'amò	*Don Carlo*	It.	bass-baritone	68
19th century (Italian Romantic)	Ella mi fu rapita . . . Parmi veder le lagrime	*Rigoletto*	It.	lyric	65
19th century (Italian Romantic)	Ernani, Ernani involami	*Ernani*	It.	dramatic coloratura	66
19th century (Italian Romantic)	Eterna la memoria	*Alzira*	It.	dramatic baritone	40
19th century (Italian Romantic)	Franco son io	*Giovanna d'Arco*	It.	dramatic baritone	51
19th century (Italian Romantic)	Il balen del suo sorriso	*Il trovatore*	It.	dramatic baritone	64
19th century (Italian Romantic)	Il lacerato spirito	*Simon Boccanegra*	It.	bass (dramatic)	96
19th century (Italian Romantic)	Infelice! E tuo credevi	*Ernani*	It.	bass-baritone	69
19th century (Italian Romantic)	La donna è mobile	*Rigoletto*	It.	lyric	66
19th century (Italian Romantic)	La luce langue	*Macbeth*	It.	dramatic	74
19th century (Italian Romantic)	La sua lampada vitale	*I masnadieri*	It.	dramatic baritone	59
19th century (Italian Romantic)	Lo vidi e 'l primo palpito	*Luisa Miller*	It.	full lyric	79
19th century (Italian Romantic)	Ma se m'è forza perderti	*Un ballo in maschera*	It.	spinto	85
19th century (Italian Romantic)	Mercè, dilette amiche	*I vespri siciliani*	It.	dramatic coloratura	71
19th century (Italian Romantic)	Mia madre aveva una povera ancella (Willow Song)	*Otello*	It.	full lyric	84
19th century (Italian Romantic)	Morir! Tremenda cosa! . . . Urna fatale del mio destino	*La forza del destino*	It.	dramatic baritone	49
19th century (Italian Romantic)	Nel giardin del bello (Veil Song)	*Don Carlo*	It.	dramatic	66
19th century (Italian Romantic)	O don fatale!	*Don Carlo*	It.	dramatic	67
19th century (Italian Romantic)	O lieto augurio	*Macbeth*	It.	dramatic baritone	58
19th century (Italian Romantic)	O paradis sorti de l'onde	*L'Africaine*	Fr.	lyric	21
19th century (Italian Romantic)	O patria mia	*Aida*	It.	dramatic	96
19th century (Italian Romantic)	O tu che in seno agli angeli	*La forza del destino*	It.	spinto	91
19th century (Italian Romantic)	O tu Palermo	*I vespri siciliani*	It.	bass	99

Historical Period	Aria Title	Opera Title	Lang.	Fach	No.
19th century (Italian Romantic)	Oh! Nel fuggente nuvolo	*Attila*	It.	dramatic coloratura	60
19th century (Italian Romantic)	Pace, pace mio Dio!	*La forza del destino*	It.	spinto	88
19th century (Italian Romantic)	Per me giunto . . . Io morrò, ma lieto in core	*Don Carlo*	It.	lyric baritone	13
19th century (Italian Romantic)	Possente amor mi chiama	*Rigoletto*	It.	lyric	67
19th century (Italian Romantic)	Quando le sere al placido	*Luisa Miller*	It.	leggiero	16
19th century (Italian Romantic)	Quanto un mor-tal può chiedere	*Alzira*	It.	dramatic baritone	41
19th century (Italian Romantic)	Questa o quella	*Rigoletto*	It.	lyric	68
19th century (Italian Romantic)	Qui la voce . . . Vien, diletto	*I puritani*	It.	lyric coloratura	13
19th century (Italian Romantic)	Rachel, quand du Seigneur	*La Juive*	Fr.	lyric	50
19th century (Italian Romantic)	Re dell'abisso, affrettati (Invocation Aria)	*Un ballo in maschera*	It.	dramatic	58
19th century (Italian Romantic)	Ritorna vincitor!	*Aida*	It.	dramatic	97
19th century (Italian Romantic)	Saper vorreste	*Un ballo in maschera*	It.	lyric coloratura	1
19th century (Italian Romantic)	Sì! Morir ella de'!	*La Gioconda*	It.	bass (dramatic)	89
19th century (Italian Romantic)	Stella del marinar	*La Gioconda*	It.	dramatic	70
19th century (Italian Romantic)	Stride la vampa	*Il trovatore*	It.	dramatic	87
19th century (Italian Romantic)	Suicidio!	*La Gioconda*	It.	dramatic	100
19th century (Italian Romantic)	Sul fil d'un soffio etesio	*Falstaff*	It.	soubrette	22
19th century (Italian Romantic)	Tacea la notte	*Il trovatore*	It.	full lyric	87
19th century (Italian Romantic)	Tu punischimi, o signore . . . a brani, a brani o perfido	*Luisa Miller*	It.	full lyric	80
19th century (Italian Romantic)	Tu sul labbro	*Nabucco*	It.	bass	95
19th century (Italian Romantic)	Un ignoto, tre lune or saranno	*I masnadieri*	It.	bass	93
19th century (Italian Romantic)	Una macchia è qui tuttora!	*Macbeth*	It.	dramatic (mezzo-soprano)	101
19th century (Italian Romantic)	Vieni! T'affretta . . . Or tutti, sorgete	*Macbeth*	It.	dramatic (mezzo-soprano)	102
19th century (Italian Romantic)	Voce di donna o d'angelo	*La Gioconda*	It.	contralto	93
19th century (Italian Romantic)	Volta la terrea	*Un ballo in maschera*	It.	lyric coloratura	2

Historical Period	Aria Title	Opera Title	Lang.	Fach	No.
19th century (Russian Nationalist)	Skuchno Marine, akh kak skuchno-to!	*Boris Godunov*	Russ.	dramatic	59
19th century (Russian Romantic)	Adieu, forêts	*The Maid of Orleans*	Fr.	lyric	35
19th century (Russian Romantic)	Ja nye sposobna k grusti tomnoy	*Eugene Onegin*	Russ.	contralto	92
19th century (Russian Romantic)	Kogda bi zhizn domashnim krugom	*Eugene Onegin*	Russ.	lyric baritone (dramatic)	21
19th century (Russian Romantic)	Kuda, kuda, kuda, vy udalilis	*Eugene Onegin*	Russ.	lyric	39
19th century (Russian Romantic)	Lyubvi vse vozrastï pokornï	*Eugene Onegin*	Russ.	bass	87
19th century (Russian Romantic)	Ruskai pogibnu (Letter Scene)	*Eugene Onegin*	Russ.	full lyric	75
19th century (Russian Romantic)	Uzhel ta samaja Tatiana	*Eugene Onegin*	Russ.	lyric baritone (dramatic)	22
19th century (Russian Romantic)	Ves' tabor spit	*Aleko*	Russ.	bass-baritone	65
19th century (Verismo)	Che gelida manina	*La bohème*	It.	lyric	28
19th century (Verismo)	Come un bel dì di maggio	*Andrea Chénier*	It.	spinto	82
19th century (Verismo)	Compiacente a' colloqui del cicisbeo . . . Son sessant'anni	*Andrea Chénier*	It.	dramatic baritone	42
19th century (Verismo)	Donde lieta	*La bohème*	It.	lyric	34
19th century (Verismo)	Donna non vidi mai	*Manon Lescaut*	It.	spinto	94
19th century (Verismo)	É la solita storia del pastore	*L'arlesiana*	It.	spinto	84
19th century (Verismo)	Ebben! Ne andrò lontana	*La Wally*	It.	spinto	95
19th century (Verismo)	Il cavallo scalpita	*Cavalleria rusticana*	It.	dramatic baritone	47
19th century (Verismo)	In quelle trine morbide	*Manon Lescaut*	It.	spinto	89
19th century (Verismo)	Mi chiamano Mimì	*La bohème*	It.	lyric	35
19th century (Verismo)	Nemico della patria	*Andrea Chénier*	It.	dramatic baritone	43
19th century (Verismo)	Qual fiamma avea nel guardo!	*I Pagliacci*	It.	lyric	48
19th century (Verismo)	Quando m'en vo' (Musetta's Waltz)	*La bohème*	It.	lyric	36
19th century (Verismo)	Questo amor, vergogna mia	*Edgar*	It.	lyric baritone	19
19th century (Verismo)	Si può?	*I Pagliacci*	It.	dramatic baritone	61
19th century (Verismo)	Son pochi fiori	*L'amico Fritz*	It.	lyric	28

Historical Period	Aria Title	Opera Title	Lang.	Fach	No.
19th century (Verismo)	Temer? Perchè?	*Andrea Chénier*	It.	lyric	20
19th century (Verismo)	Un dì, all'azzurro spazio	*Andrea Chénier*	It.	spinto	83
19th century (Verismo)	Vecchia zimarra	*La bohème*	It.	bass (lyric)	85
19th century (Verismo)	Voi lo sapete, o mamma	*Cavalleria rusticana*	It.	dramatic	64
19th century (Viennese Operetta)	Ich lade gern mir Gäste ein	*Die Fleder-maus*	Ger.	lyric	28
19th century (Viennese Operetta)	Klänge der Heimat (Czàrdàs)	*Die Fleder-maus*	Ger.	full lyric	77
19th century (Viennese Operetta)	Mein Herr Marquis	*Die Fleder-maus*	Ger.	soubrette	23
20th century (American)	Ah, Michele, don't you know?	*The Saint of Bleecker Street*	Eng.	dramatic	82
20th century (American)	Ah, sweet Jesus, spare me this agony	*The Saint of Bleecker Street*	Eng.	lyric	51
20th century (American)	Ain't it a pretty night?	*Susannah*	Eng.	lyric	53
20th century (American)	All that gold!	*Amahl and the Night Visitors*	Eng.	dramatic	55
20th century (American)	Always through the changing	*The Ballad of Baby Doe*	Eng.	lyric	29
20th century (American)	And where is the one who will mourn me	*Down in the Valley*	Eng.	lyric	36
20th century (American)	Augusta! How can you turn away?	*The Ballad of Baby Doe*	Eng.	dramatic	56
20th century (American)	Be not afeard	*The Tempest*	Eng.	dramatic	102
20th century (American)	The Black Swan	*The Medium*	Eng.	lyric	46
20th century (American)	Blow ye the trumpet	*John Brown*	Eng.	lyric	31
20th century (American)	Dear boy	*Candide*	Eng.	lyric baritone	7
20th century (American/Italian)	Dearest Amelia	*Amelia Goes to the Ball/ Amelia al ballo*	Eng.	lyric baritone	2
20th century (American)	Dearest Mama	*The Ballad of Baby Doe*	Eng.	lyric	30
20th century (American)	Do I not draw tears from your eyes?	*Too Many Sopranos*	Eng.	contralto	98
20th century (American)	Do not utter a word	*Vanessa*	Eng.	spinto	94

Historical Period	Aria Title	Opera Title	Lang.	Fach	No.
20th century (American)	Do you wish we had wed?	*Regina*	Eng.	lyric	44
20th century (American)	Everyday at church	*Tartuffe*	Eng.	bass	98
20th century (American)	Fair Robin I love	*Tartuffe*	Eng.	soubrette (lyric coloratura)	25
20th century (American)	Have you seen her, Samantha?	*The Ballad of Baby Doe*	Eng.	dramatic	57
20th century (American)	Hello, hello? Oh, Margaret, it's you	*The Telephone*	Eng.	lyric	55
20th century (American)	Hold on a moment, dear	*Tartuffe*	Eng.	lyric	49
20th century (American)	I do not judge you, John	*The Crucible*	Eng.	dramatic	65
20th century (American)	I know that you all hate me	*The Saint of Bleecker Street*	Eng.	lyric	71
20th century (American)	I shall find for you (Lullaby)	*The Consul*	Eng.	contralto	90
20th century (American)	I thought I heard a distant bird	*Gallantry*	Eng.	lyric	43
20th century (American)	I want magic!	*A Streetcar Named Desire*	Eng.	full lyric	85
20th century (American)	I'm not a boy, she says	*A Streetcar Named Desire*	Eng.	spinto	95
20th century (American)	It must be so	*Candide*	Eng.	lyric	29
20th century (American)	It's about the way people is made	*Susannah*	Eng.	lyric	74
20th century (American)	I've got a ram, Goliath	*The Devil and Daniel Webster*	Eng.	bass-baritone	67
20th century (American)	Jehosophat!	*McTeague*	Eng.	dramatic baritone	60
20th century (American)	Kennst du das Land?	*Little Women*	Ger.	bass-baritone	73
20th century (American)	Kiss me not goodbye	*The Mighty Casey*	Eng.	lyric (soprano)	37
20th century (American)	Light of my soul	*The Song of Majnun*	Eng.	lyric	72
20th century (American)	Lonely House	*Street Scene*	Eng.	lyric	73
20th century (American)	Lost in the Stars	*Lost in the Stars*	Eng.	bass-baritone	74
20th century (American)	Madame Pompous's Audition	*Too Many Sopranos*	Eng.	full lyric (spinto)	86
20th century (American)	Monica's Waltz	*The Medium*	Eng.	lyric	45
20th century (American)	Must the winter come so soon?	*Vanessa*	Eng.	lyric	51
20th century (American)	My friends, you do me too much honor	*John Brown*	Eng.	dramatic baritone	57

Historical Period	Aria Title	Opera Title	Lang.	Fach	No.
20th century (American)	New York Lights	*A View from the Bridge*	Eng.	lyric	79
20th century (American)	No more, false heart	*Tartuffe*	Eng.	lyric	76
20th century (American)	Now may there be a blessing	*The Devil and Daniel Webster*	Eng.	lyric	24
20th century (American)	Now signorini (The Contest)	*Sweeney Todd*	Eng.	lyric	75
20th century (American)	Oh, don't you see that lonesome dove?	*Down in the Valley*	Eng.	lyric (soprano)	26
20th century (American)	Oh, the lion may roar (Aria of the Worm)	*The Ghosts of Versailles*	Eng.	lyric	44
20th century (American)	Oh, what a lovely ballroom this is!	*The Consul*	Eng.	leggiero	6
20th century (American)	Outside this house	*Vanessa*	Eng.	lyric	78
20th century (American)	The Silver Aria	*The Ballad of Baby Doe*	Eng.	lyric	31
20th century (American)	Someday I'm sure to marry you	*The Sojourner and Mollie Sinclair*	Eng.	lyric	52
20th century (American)	Steal me, sweet thief	*The Old Maid and the Thief*	Eng.	lyric	47
20th century (American)	The same, old room	*Regina*	Eng.	bass-baritone	81
20th century (American)	The trees on the mountain are cold and bare	*Susannah*	Eng.	lyric	54
20th century (American)	Things change, Jo	*Little Women*	Eng.	lyric	32
20th century (American)	This is my box	*Amahl and the Night Visitors*	Eng.	leggiero	2
20th century (American)	To this we've come (Paper Aria)	*The Consul*	Eng.	full lyric	74
20th century (American)	Warm as the autumn light	*The Ballad of Baby Doe*	Eng.	bass-baritone	66
20th century (American)	We cannot re-trace our steps	*The Mother of Us All*	Eng.	dramatic	75
20th century (American)	We've always known each other	*The Wings of the Dove*	Eng.	lyric	54
20th century (American)	What am I forbidden?	*Lizzie Borden*	Eng.	lyric (dramatic)	33
20th century (American)	What what is it?	*The Mother of Us All*	Eng.	bass-baritone	77
20th century (American)	When the air sings of summer	*The Old Maid and the Thief*	Eng.	lyric baritone	31
20th century (American/Italian)	While I waste these precious hours	*Amelia Goes to the Ball/ Amelia al ballo*	Eng.	lyric	27

Historical Period	Aria Title	Opera Title	Lang.	Fach	No.
20th century (American)	Willow Song	*The Ballad of Baby Doe*	Eng.	lyric	32
20th century (American)	Yes! I am she!	*Madame Mao*	Eng.	lyric (dramatic)	34
20th century (American)	You rascal, you! I never knew you had a soul!	*Vanessa*	Eng.	bass-baritone	83
20th century (English)	Albert the Good!/Heaven helps those who help themselves!	*Albert Herring*	Eng.	leggiero	1
20th century (English)	Give him this orchid	*The Rape of Lucretia*	Eng.	dramatic	80
20th century (English)	God o' mercy	*Billy Budd*	Eng.	lyric	24
20th century (English)	Here I stand . . . Since it is not by merit	*The Rake's Progress*	Eng.	lyric	61
20th century (English)	I accept their verdict	*Billy Budd*	Eng.	lyric	25
20th century (English)	I am an old man	*Billy Budd*	Eng.	lyric	26
20th century (English)	I know a bank where the wild thyme grows	*A Midsummer Night's Dream*	Eng.	contralto	97
20th century (English)	Inkslinger's Song	*Paul Bunyan*	Eng.	lyric	59
20th century (English)	Look, through the port comes the moonshine astray	*Billy Budd*	Eng.	lyric baritone	5
20th century (English)	Love, too fre-quently betrayed	*The Rake's Progress*	Eng.	lyric	62
20th century (English)	No word from Tom . . . I go to him	*The Rake's Progress*	Eng.	dramatic coloratura	70
20th century (English)	Now I am no more afraid	*The Knot Garden*	Eng.	dramatic	72
20th century (English)	Scorned! Abused! Neglected!	*The Rake's Progress*	Eng.	dramatic	79
20th century (English)	Stranger and darker	*The Ice Break*	Eng.	dramatic	71
20th century (English)	Tarquinius does not wait	*The Rape of Lucretia*	Eng.	lyric	64
20th century (English)	Tickling a trout, poaching a hare	*Albert Herring*	Eng.	lyric baritone	1
20th century (English)	Vary the song, o London, change	*The Rake's Progress*	Eng.	lyric	63
20th century (English)	We committed his body to the deep	*Billy Budd*	Eng.	lyric	27
20th century (French Romantic)	Ne pensons qu'au plaisir d'aimer	*Don Quichotte*	Fr.	lyric	25
20th century (German)	Dich such' ich Bild!	*Die tote Stadt*	Ger.	spinto	92

Historical Period	Aria Title	Opera Title	Lang.	Fach	No.
20th century (German)	Es gibt ein Reich	*Ariadne auf Naxos*	Ger.	dramatic	98
20th century (German)	Glück, das mir verblieb (Marietta's Lied)	*Die tote Stadt*	Ger.	spinto	93
20th century (German)	Ich habe keine gute Nächte	*Elektra*	Ger.	dramatic	68
20th century (German)	Lieben, Hassen, Hoffen, Zagen	*Ariadne auf Naxos*	Ger.	lyric baritone	3
20th century (German)	Mein Sehnen, mein Wähnen (Pierrot's Tanzlied)	*Die tote Stadt*	Ger.	lyric baritone	36
20th century (German)	Wie du warst!	*Der Rosenkavalier*	Ger.	dramatic	81
20th century (Italian)	Firenze è come un albero fiorito	*Gianni Schicchi*	It.	lyric	45
20th century (Italian)	In questa reggia	*Turandot*	It.	dramatic	105
20th century (Italian)	O mio babbino caro	*Gianni Schicchi*	It.	lyric	40
20th century (Italian)	Signore, ascolta	*Turandot*	It.	lyric	56
20th century (Italian)	Tu che di gel sei cinta	*Turandot*	It.	lyric	57
20th century (Verismo)	Acerba voluttà	*Adriana Lecouvreur*	It.	lyric	19
20th century (Verismo)	Amore o grillo	*Madama Butterfly*	It.	spinto	93
20th century (Verismo)	Ch'ella mi creda libero e lontano	*La fanciulla del West*	It.	spinto	89
20th century (Verismo)	Chi il bel sogno di Doretta	*La rondine*	It.	lyric	50
20th century (Verismo)	E lucevan le stelle	*Tosca*	It.	spinto	96
20th century (Verismo)	Minnie, dalla mia casa son partito	*La fanciulla del West*	It.	dramatic baritone	48
20th century (Verismo)	Recondita armonia	*Tosca*	It.	spinto	97
20th century (Verismo)	Senza mamma	*Suor Angelica*	It.	spinto	90
20th century (Verismo)	Vissi d'arte	*Tosca*	It.	spinto	91
20th century (Verismo)	Zazà, piccolo zingara	*Zazà*	It.	lyric baritone	39
20th century (Viennese Operetta)	Dein ist mein ganzes Herz	*Das Land des Lächelns*	Ger.	lyric	51
20th century (Viennese Operetta)	Es lebt' eine Vilja, ein Waldmägdelein (Vilja's Lied)	*Die lustige Witwe*	Ger.	lyric (full lyric)	43

Mark Ross Clark is Director of Opera and Musical Theatre at the University of Louisiana–Monroe, and directs the Louisiana Lyric Opera. He is author of *Singing, Acting, and Movement in Opera* (Indiana University Press, 2002).

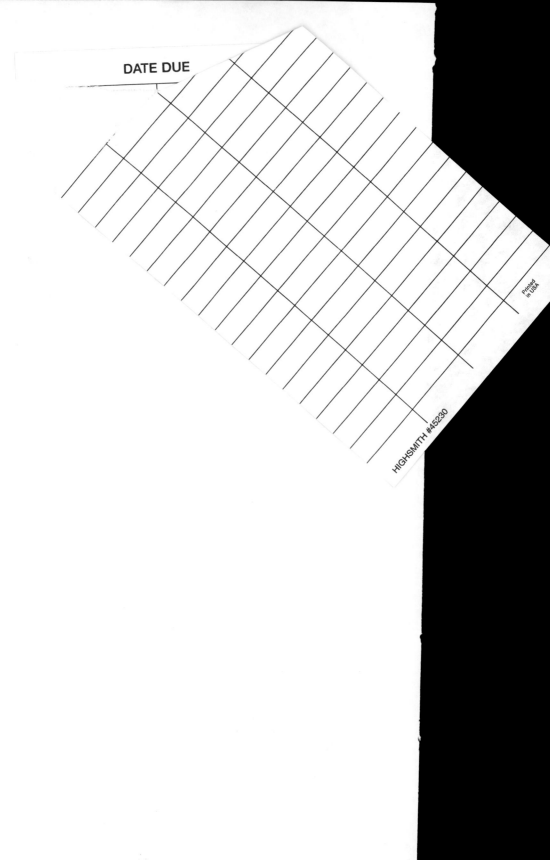

DATE DUE

HIGHSMITH #45230

Printed
in USA